NUDGE AND THE LAW

Behavioural sciences help refine our understanding of human decision-making. Their insights are immensely relevant for policy-making since public intervention works much better when it targets real people rather than imaginary beings assumed to be perfectly rational. Increasingly, governments around the world are keen to rely on those insights for reshaping public interventions in a wide range of policy areas such as energy, health, financial services and data protection. When policy-making meets behavioural sciences, effective and low-cost regulations can emerge in the form of default rules, smart disclosure and simplification requirements. While behaviourally-informed intervention has a huge potential for policy-making, it also attracts legitimacy and practicability concerns. Nudge and the Law takes a European perspective on those issues and explores the legal implications of the emergent phenomenon of behavioural regulation by focusing on the challenges and opportunities it may offer to EU policy-making and beyond.

Modern Studies in European Law
Recent titles in this series:

EU Environmental Law, Governance and Decision-Making
Maria Lee

Shaping the Single European Market in the Field of Foreign Direct Investment
Philip Strik

Nationalism and Private Law in Europe
Guido Comparato

EU Asylum Procedures and the Right to an Effective Remedy
Marcelle Reneman

The EU Accession to the ECHR
Edited by Vasiliki Kosta, Nikos Skoutaris and Vassilis P Tzevelekos

The European Court of Justice and External Relations: Constitutional Challenges
Edited by Marise Cremona and Anne Thies

A Critique of Codification
Leone Niglia

Protecting Vulnerable Groups: The European Human Rights Framework
Edited by Francesca Ippolito and Sara Iglesias Sanchez

EU International Relations Law Second Edition
Panos Koutrakos

Fundamental Rights in the EU: A Matter for Two Courts
Edited by Sonia Morano-Foadi and Lucy Vickers

What Form of Government for the European Union and the Eurozone?
Federico Fabbrini, Ernst Hirsch Ballin and Han Somsen

The UK and European Human Rights: A Strained Relationship?
Edited by Katja S Ziegler, Elizabeth Wicks and Loveday Hodson

The European Union in International Organisations and Global Governance:
Recent Developments
Edited by Christine Kaddous

**For the complete list of titles in this series, see
'Modern Studies in European Law' link at
www.hartpub.co.uk/books/series.asp**

Nudge and the Law

A European Perspective

Edited by
Alberto Alemanno
and
Anne-Lise Sibony

·HART·
PUBLISHING
OXFORD AND PORTLAND, OREGON
2017

Hart Publishing
An imprint of Bloomsbury Publishing Plc

Hart Publishing Ltd
Kemp House
Chawley Park
Cumnor Hill
Oxford OX2 9PH
UK

Bloomsbury Publishing Plc
50 Bedford Square
London
WC1B 3DP
UK

www.hartpub.co.uk
www.bloomsbury.com

Published in North America (US and Canada) by
Hart Publishing
c/o International Specialized Book Services
920 NE 58th Avenue, Suite 300
Portland, OR 97213-3786
USA

www.isbs.com

HART PUBLISHING, the Hart/Stag logo, BLOOMSBURY and the
Diana logo are trademarks of Bloomsbury Publishing Plc

First published in hardback, 2015
Paperback edition, 2017

© The Editors and Contributors severally 2015

The Editors and Contributors have asserted their right under the Copyright, Designs and Patents
Act 1988 to be identified as the Authors of this work.

All rights reserved. No part of this publication may be reproduced or transmitted in any form or by
any means, electronic or mechanical, including photocopying, recording, or any information
storage or retrieval system, without prior permission in writing from the publishers.

While every care has been taken to ensure the accuracy of this work, no responsibility for loss or
damage occasioned to any person acting or refraining from action as a result of any statement in
it can be accepted by the authors, editors or publishers.

All UK Government legislation and other public sector information used in the work is Crown
Copyright ©. All House of Lords and House of Commons information used in the work is
Parliamentary Copyright ©. This information is reused under the terms of the Open Government
Licence v3.0 (http://www.nationalarchives. gov.uk/doc/open-government-licence/version/3)
except where otherwise stated.

All Eur-lex material used in the work is © European Union,
http://eur-lex.europa.eu/, 1998–2017.

British Library Cataloguing-in-Publication Data
A catalogue record for this book is available from the British Library.

ISBN: PB: 978-1-50991-835-5
HB: 978-1-84946-732-2

Typeset by Compuscript Ltd, Shannon
Printed and bound in Great Britain by
Lightning Source UK Ltd

To find out more about our authors and books visit www.hartpublishing.co.uk. Here you will
find extracts, author information, details of forthcoming events and the option to sign up for our
newsletters.

Foreword

The Ethics of Nudging

CASS R SUNSTEIN

I. THE CENTRAL ARGUMENT

This book offers an exceptionally impressive, and wide-ranging, set of essays on behaviourally informed approaches to law and regulation in Europe, with particular reference to nudges. In Europe as elsewhere, an important question is drawing increasing attention: what are the ethical limits on nudges? This question is in the background of many of the chapters, and sometimes it emerges in the foreground (chapter 4 by Van Aaken, chapter 13 by Feldman and Lobel, chapter 14 by Alemanno and Sibony). It is on this question that I would like to focus in this Foreword. In free societies, respectful of human dignity and dedicated to the idea of self-government, the issue is a pressing one.

My central argument is that at least if they are taken in general or in the abstract, the leading ethical objections lack a great deal of force, and for two different reasons. *First*, both nudges and choice architecture are inevitable, and it is therefore pointless to wish them away. *Second*, many nudges, and many forms of choice architecture, are defensible and even required on ethical grounds, whether we care about welfare, autonomy, dignity, self-government, fair distribution, or some other value.

Nonetheless, it is true that all government action, including nudges, should face a burden of justification (and sometimes a heavy burden). If the government requires disclosure of information, or establishes particular default rules, it must explain and defend itself. The fact that people retain freedom of choice, and are ultimately permitted to go their own way, does not give public officials a kind of license to do whatever they want. If we value democratic self-government, we will be inclined to support nudges and choice architecture that can claim a democratic pedigree and that promote democratic goals. Any democracy has a form of choice architecture that helps define and constitute its own aspirations to self-government.

Of course no one should approve of nudges or choice architecture in the abstract or as such. Some nudges, and some forms of choice architecture, do indeed run into convincing ethical objections. Suppose, for example, that a nation establishes a default rule stating that unless voters explicitly indicate otherwise, they will be presumed to support the incumbent leader in the election. Or suppose that a nation establishes a default rule to the effect that unless citizens indicate otherwise, their estates will revert to the nation's most powerful political party upon their death. There is ample reason to question a default rule of this kind even if citizens are authorised to opt out.

A central question is whether nudges and choice architecture promote welfare or autonomy and dignity. Another question is whether they are consistent with democratic norms. Some nudges have illicit ends, and they are objectionable for that reason.

II. CONCEPTS AND DEFINITIONS

A. In General

Nudges are interventions that steer people in particular directions but that also allow them to go their own way.[1] A reminder is a nudge; so is a warning. A GPS nudges; a default rule nudges. To qualify as a nudge, an intervention must not impose significant material incentives.[2] A subsidy is not a nudge; a tax is not a nudge; a fine or a jail sentence is not a nudge. To count as such, a nudge must fully preserve freedom of choice. If an intervention imposes significant material costs on choosers, it might of course be justified, but it is not a nudge. Some nudges work because they inform people; other nudges work because they make certain choice easier; still other nudges work because of the power of inertia and procrastination.

Attention is a scarce resource. When applications (for loans, for educational opportunities, for refinancing mortgages, for training, for financial benefits of any kind) are complex and difficult, people may not apply; a great deal of money might be lost as a result.[3] This point has implications for regulatory design. It suggests that the private sector may help or hurt people by focusing their attention in certain ways. The same is true for the public sector, whether or not it seeks to do so. A regulation might be written or applied in a way that makes certain features of a situation especially salient.

For the future, we could imagine nudges that are designed to improve anti-poverty programmes; environmental programmes; energy programmes;[4] retirement and social security programmes; anti-obesity programmes; educational programmes; health care programmes; and programmes to increase organ donation.[5]

---

[1] See R Thaler and CR Sunstein, *Nudge* (New Haven, CT, Yale University Press, 2008).
[2] On some of the complexities here, see CR Sunstein, *Why Nudge?* (New Haven, CT, Yale University Press, 2014).
[3] See B Keys et al, 'Failure to Refinance' (2014), available at www.nber.org/papers/w20401.
[4] ibid.
[5] For an interesting empirical result, see J Kessler and A Roth, 'Don't Take "No" For An Answer: An Experiment With Actual Organ Donor Registrations' (2014), available at www.nber.org/papers/w20378 (finding that required active choosing has a smaller effect, in terms of getting people to sign up for organ donation, than prompted choice).

We could also imagine forms of choice architecture that are designed to combat race and sex discrimination, to help disabled people, and to promote economic growth. A great deal of future work needs to be devoted to choice architecture in these and related domains.

There is no question that certain nudges, and certain kinds of choice architecture, can raise serious ethical problems. Consider, for example, a government that used nudges to promote discrimination on the basis of race, sex, or religion. Any fascist government might well (and almost certainly does) nudge. Terrorists nudge. Even truthful information (eg about crime rates) might fan the flames of violence and prejudice. (If people learn that crime is widespread, they might be more likely to engage in crime, because it is the social norm). Groups or nations that are committed to violence often enlist nudges in their cause. Even if nudges do not have illicit ends, it is possible to wonder whether those who enlist them are treating people with respect.

Consider in this light a tale from the novelist David Foster Wallace:

> There are these two young fish swimming along and they happen to meet an older fish swimming the other way, who nods at them and says 'Morning, boys. How's the water?' And the two young fish swim on for a bit, and then eventually one of them looks over at the other and goes 'What the hell is water?'[6]

This is a tale about choice architecture. Such architecture is inevitable, whether or not we see it. It is the equivalent of water. Weather is itself a form of choice architecture, because it influences what people decide. Human beings cannot live without some kind of weather. Nature nudges. The common law is a regulatory system, and it will nudge, even if it allows people to have a great deal of flexibility.

Nor can the state and the legal system avoid nudging. Any government, even one that is or purports to be firmly committed to laissez-faire, has to establish a set of prohibitions and permissions, including a set of default entitlements, establishing who has what before bargaining begins. Recall that the rules of contract (as well as property and tort) provide a form of choice architecture for social ordering. It is true that choice architecture can maintain freedom of choice; it is also true that choice architects can at least aspire to neutrality. But choice architecture itself is inevitable, which means that it is pointless to object to it on ethical groups.

B. Nudging System 1

In behavioural science, it has become standard to distinguish between two families of cognitive operations: System 1, which is fast, automatic, and intuitive, and System 2, which is slow, calculative, and deliberative.[7] System 2 can and does err, but System 1 is distinctly associated with identifiable behavioural biases. To be sure,

---

[6] Available at moreintelligentlife.com/story/david-foster-wallace-in-his-own-words.
[7] See D Kahneman, *Thinking, Fast and Slow* (New York, NY, Farrar, Strauss and Giroux, 2011).

there is, in some circles, intense controversy about the appropriate evaluation of the automatic system and about the extent to which it should be associated with error. Perhaps our intuitions usually work well in the situations in which we ordinarily find ourselves. But there is no question that our intuitions often misfire, and that a good nudge could provide a great deal of help.

Some nudges, imposed by law and regulatory agencies, attempt to strengthen the hand of System 2 by improving the role of deliberation and people's considered judgements—as, for example, through disclosure of relevant information, debiasing, and the use of precommitment strategies. Other nudges are designed to appeal to, or to activate, System 1—as in the cases of graphic warnings. Some nudges do not appeal to System 1, but work because of its operation—as, for example, where default rules have large effects because of the power of inertia.

A nudge might be justified on the ground that it helps counteract a behavioural bias, and (as we shall see) some people object to such efforts, especially if they seem to target or to exploit System 1. But (and this is an important point) a behavioural bias is *not* a necessary justification for a nudge, and nudges need not target or exploit System 1 in any way, as emphasised by several authors in this volume (Alemanno and Sibony in chapter 14). Disclosure of information can be helpful even in the absence of any bias. A default rule simplifies life and might therefore be desirable whether or not a behavioural bias is involved. A GPS is useful even for people who do not suffer from any such bias.

As the GPS example suggests, many nudges have the goal of *increasing navigability*—of making it easier for people to get to their preferred destination. Such nudges stem from an understanding that life can be simple or hard to navigate, and a goal of helpful choice architecture is desirable as a way of promoting simple navigation. To date, there has been far too little attention to the close relationship between navigability and (good) nudges. Insofar as the goal is to promote navigability, the ethical objections are greatly weakened and might well dissipate. In this regard, Alemanno and Sibony in their concluding chapter offer some helpful reflections on how to assess the autonomy objection to nudges. They argue, plausibly in my view, that many behavioural interventions are neutral with respect to autonomy because they affect behaviour in instances where, in all likelihood, no deliberation would have taken place.

C. 'As Judged by Themselves'

When third parties are not at risk, and when the welfare of choosers is all that is involved, the objective of nudging is to 'influence choices in a way that will make choosers better off, *as judged by themselves*'.[8] In many cases, that standard is straightforward to apply. If a GPS steers people toward a destination that is not

---

[8] Thaler and Sunstein (n 1) 5.

their own, it is not working well. And if it offers them a longer and less convenient route, it will not make choosers better off by their own lights.

Many nudges can be understood in precisely the same terms; consider a reminder, a warning, or disclosure of relevant information. To enlist the 'as judged by themselves' standard, we would have to take each nudge on its own, and sometimes the standard will raise hard normative and empirical issues. But the standard will often provide sufficient guidance, and even when it does not, it is the place to start.

III. ILLICIT REASONS AND TRANSPARENCY

It must be acknowledged that nudges can be introduced for illicit reasons. Indeed many of the most powerful objections to nudges, and to changes in choice architecture, are based on a judgement that the underlying motivations are illicit. With these points, there is no objection to nudges as such; the objection is to the grounds for the particular nudges.

For example, an imaginable default rule might skew the democratic process by saying that voters are presumed to vote for the incumbent politician, unless they specify otherwise. Such a rule would violate principles of neutrality that are implicit in democratic norms; it would be unacceptable for that reason. Alternatively, a warning might try to frighten people about the supposedly nefarious plans of members of a minority group. Social norms might be used to encourage people to buy unhealthy products. In extreme cases, private or public institutions might try to nudge people toward violence.

Nudges should be transparent and subject to public scrutiny, certainly if public officials are responsible for it. At a minimum, this proposition means that when such officials institute some kind of reform, they should not hide it from the public. If officials alter a default rule so as to promote clean energy or conservation, they should disclose what they are doing. Self-government itself requires public scrutiny of nudges. Such scrutiny is an important ex ante safeguard against harmful nudges; it is also an important ex post corrective. Transparency and public scrutiny can reduce the likelihood of welfare-reducing choice architecture. Nations should also treat their citizens with respect, and public scrutiny shows a measure of respect at the same time that it reduces the risk that nudges will intrude on either autonomy or dignity.

IV. THE PROBLEM OF PATERNALISM

Choice architecture may or may not be paternalistic. But it is true that nudges can be seen as a form of 'libertarian paternalism' insofar as they attempt to use choice architecture to steer choosers in directions that will promote their welfare (again, as judged by choosers themselves).

Recall that this is a distinctive form of paternalism in the sense that it is: (a) soft; and (b) means-oriented. It is soft insofar as it avoids coercion or material incentives, and thus fully maintains freedom of choice. It is means-oriented insofar as it does not attempt to question or alter people's ends. Like a GPS, it respects those ends (subject to the various complexities discussed above). To those who object to paternalism, the most serious concerns arise in the face of coercion (where freedom of choice is blocked) and when social planners, or choice architects, do not respect people's ends. To this extent, nudges aspire to avoid some of the standard ethical objections to paternalism.

Nonetheless, we might object to paternalism as such, although, as pointed out by Alemanno and Sibony in chapter 14, this objection tends to be offered less often and less vigorously in Europe than in the US. Perhaps people are the best judges not only of their ends, but also of the best means to achieve those ends, given their own tastes and values. (People might reject the route suggested by the GPS on the ground that they prefer the scenic alternative; the GPS might not easily capture or serve their ends). Moreover, the distinction between means and ends is not always simple and straightforward. One question is the level of abstraction at which we describe people's ends. If we describe people's ends at a level of great specificity—eating that brownie, having that cigarette, texting while driving—then people's means effectively *are* their ends. The brownie is exactly what they want; it is not a means to anything at all (except the experience of eating it).

If, by contrast, we describe people's ends at a level of high abstraction—'having a good life'—then nearly everything is a means to those ends. But if we do that, then we will not be capturing people's actual concerns; we will be disregarding what matters to them. These points do raise some problems for those who favour a solely means-oriented form of paternalism. They must be careful to ensure that they are not describing people's ends at a sufficiently high level of abstraction as to misconceive what people care about.

But insofar as a GPS is a guiding analogy, it is not easy to see nudges as objectionably paternalistic. Many nudges are entirely focused on helping people to identify the best means for achieving their preferred ends. Consider cases in which people are *mistaken about facts* (with respect to the characteristics of, say, a consumer product or an investment). If a nudge informs them, then it is respecting their ends. Or suppose that certain product characteristics are in some sense shrouded, and the nudge helps people to see them for what they are. Or suppose that people suffer from a behavioural bias—perhaps because they use the availability heuristic, perhaps because of unrealistic optimism. A nudge that corrects their mistake can help them to achieve their ends.

Let us bracket the most difficult issues and acknowledge that some forms of choice architecture count as paternalistic. Is that a problem? One reason for regulators and other policymakers to reject paternalism involves welfare. Perhaps people are the best judges of what will promote their interests, and perhaps outsiders will blunder (as John Stuart Mill believed).[9]

---

[9] John Stuart Mill, *On Liberty* (first published 1859, Kathy Casey (ed), 2002).

In fact it is possible that welfarists should ultimately embrace coercive paternalism, at least in the face of such biases.[10] When paternalism would improve welfare, welfarists should support paternalism. For welfarists, paternalism should be evaluated on a case-by-case basis—unless there is some systematic, or rule-welfarist, reason to support a principle or presumption against paternalism.

Perhaps there is good reason for such a presumption, rooted in a judgement that choosers are likely to have better information than choice architects. But in some cases, that judgement is incorrect, because choosers lack knowledge of facts. Information-providing nudges are a natural corrective. In some cases, a good default rule—say, automatic enrollment in pension programmes—is hard to reject on welfarist grounds. To be sure, active choosing might be better, but that conclusion is not obvious. Welfarists might well be inclined to favour choice-preserving approaches, on the theory that individuals usually well know what best fits their circumstances, but the fact that a default rule has a paternalistic dimension should not be decisive against it.

Another reason to reject paternalism involves autonomy and the idea of respect for persons. Stephen Darwell writes that the

> objectionable character of paternalism of this sort is not that those who seek to benefit us against our wishes are likely to be wrong about what really benefits us ... It is, rather, primarily a failure of respect, a failure to recognize the authority that persons have to demand, within certain limits, that they be allowed to make their own choices for themselves.[11]

This brings us to the next objection.

V. NUDGES AND AUTONOMY

Do nudges intrude on autonomy? Autonomy requires informed choices, and many nudges are specifically designed to ensure that choices are informed. In the face of a behavioural bias, or some kind of systematic mistake (by the actor's own reflective lights), it is hardly clear that a nudge infringes on autonomy, rightly understood. When they help correct some kind of bias, nudges might well promote people's autonomy. We might identify autonomy with people's reflective judgements, and many nudges operate in the interest of autonomy, so understood. (In chapter 14, Alemanno and Sibony offer relevant discussion).

Indeed, it is important to recognise that autonomy does not require choices everywhere; it does not justify an insistence on active choosing in all contexts. There is a close relationship between time-management and autonomy. People should be allowed to devote their attention to the questions that, in their view, deserve that attention. If people have to make choices everywhere, their autonomy is reduced, if only because they cannot focus on those activities that seem to them most worthy of their attention.

---

[10] See S Conly, *Against Autonomy* (Cambridge, Cambridge University Press, 2012).
[11] See S Darwell, 'The Value of Autonomy and the Autonomy of the Will' (2006) 116 *Ethics* 263, 269.

It is nonetheless true that on grounds of autonomy (as well as welfare) the best choice architecture often calls for active choosing. Even though they preserve freedom of choice, default rules might intrude on autonomy, certainly if they do not track people's likely choices. The problem is that because of the force of inertia, people might not reject harmful defaults. If so, there is arguably an intrusion on their autonomy, because they will end up with outcomes that they did not specifically select.

Whether the interest in autonomy calls for active choosing, as opposed to reliance on a default rule, depends on the circumstances. Along some dimensions, default rules are actually superior to active choosing on autonomy grounds. If people choose not to choose, or if they would make that choice if asked, it is an insult to their autonomy to force them to choose.[12] And if people would like to choose, a default rule does not deprive them of that choice; they can reject the default. Even in the face of inertia, many people will do so.

Preservation of freedom of choice is not sufficient, but it goes some distance toward ensuring that people's autonomy is respected. So does a requirement that any paternalistic nudges focus on people's own ends and otherwise have legitimate goals. But with respect to autonomy, a continuing problem lies in the possibility of manipulation; I will turn to that problem below.

VI. DIGNITY

The idea of 'dignity' is complex and contested. We might begin by suggesting that the antonym of coercion is freedom; the antonym of dignity is humiliation. Some nudges might seem to compromise dignity and respect for persons. Imaginable nudges could indeed undermine dignity. Unjust societies, including communist and fascist societies, produce a large number of dignity-destroying nudges.

There are, of course, large questions about the place of dignity in ethics and about the appropriate specification of the basic idea. On one view, dignity is properly part of an assessment of welfare. If people feel humiliated, or feel that they have been treated disrespectfully, they suffer a welfare loss. That loss might be extremely serious. In any assessment of welfare consequences, such a loss must be considered. It might turn out to be exceedingly important—and to argue against particular nudges. Under the German Constitution, of course, dignity is highlighted, and under the familiar proportionality test in the legal framework of the European Union, dignity might well play a significant role.

A good welfarist should also acknowledge that an offence to dignity is qualitatively distinct; in its nature, it is a different kind of loss from the loss of (say) money, or an opportunity to visit a beach. But on the welfarist view, a dignity loss is just one kind of loss, to be weighed against the other goods that are at stake. Suppose, for purposes of argument, that a graphic and highly emotional

---

[12] See CR Sunstein, 'Choosing Not to Choose' (2014) 64 *Duke Law Journal* 1.

appeal, triggering strong emotions (System 1) in order to discourage people from smoking, is plausibly seen as an offence to dignity—as a way of treating smokers disrespectfully (and perhaps infantilising them). Some smokers might so regard such an appeal and object for that reason. A welfarist might be willing to support the emotional appeal, notwithstanding the relevant loss, if it saves a significant number of lives.

On another view, an insult to dignity is not merely part of a welfarist calculus. Such an insult does not depend on people's subjective feelings, and it is a grave act, perhaps especially if it comes from government. An insult to dignity should not be permitted unless (perhaps) it has an overwhelmingly strong justification. If we endorse this view, it is especially important to ask whether nudges offend human dignity.

To return to my general plea: the force of the objection depends on the particular nudge. A GPS insults no one's dignity. Disclosure of factual information can hardly be seen as an offence to dignity—certainly if the information is useful and not based on a false and demeaning belief that people need it.

But we can easily imagine nudges that would offend one or another conception of dignity. Consider a public health campaign, directed at the prevention of obesity, that stigmatised and humiliated people who are overweight, by portraying them in a demeaning light.[13] Or consider, as a somewhat more difficult case, an anti-smoking campaign that did the same for smokers. Here again, the fact that nudges preserve freedom of choice, and do not require anyone to do anything, should not be taken as a kind of license to do anything at all. It is possible to imagine public education campaigns that offend dignity, though admittedly the more familiar real-world campaigns do not have anything approaching that vice. Here as well, there is no objection to the relevant nudges in the abstract, but there is an objection to imaginable nudging.

VII. MANIPULATION

To deal with this objection, we need to say something about the complex idea of 'manipulation'. It should be clear that an action does not count as manipulative merely because it is an effort to alter people's behaviour. If you warn a driver that he is about to get into a crash, you are not engaged in manipulation. The same is true if you remind someone that a bill is due. A calorie label and an energy efficiency label are not ordinarily counted as forms of manipulation.

An action can be counted as *manipulative if it attempts to influence people subconsciously or unconsciously, in a way that does not respect or that undermines their capacity for conscious choice*. Consider some variations on this idea. On Wilkinson's account, manipulation 'is a kind of influence that bypasses or subverts the target's

---

[13] I am grateful to Gertrude Lubbe-Wolff for this example.

rational capacities'.[14] Wilkinson urges that manipulation 'subverts and insults a person's autonomous decision making', in a way that treats its objects as 'tools and fools'.[15] He thinks that 'manipulation is intentionally and successfully influencing someone using methods that pervert choice'.[16]

Some nudges could plausibly be counted as manipulative. Suppose that public officials try to persuade people to engage in certain behaviour with the help of relative risk information: 'If you do not do X, your chances of death from heart disease will triple!' Suppose that for the relevant population, the chance of death from heart disease is very small—say, one in 50,000—and that people are far more influenced by the idea of 'tripling the risk' than they would be if they learned that they could increase a 1/50,000 risk to a 3/50,000 risk. On one view, the choice of the relative risk frame does not respect people's decision-making capacities—and it appeals directly to System 1.

But we have to be careful here, because a plausible understanding of manipulation might sweep up and perhaps condemn a great deal of conduct that is generally seen as unobjectionable, and reasonably so. It would be fussy, and too stringent, to condemn all such conduct, even if the word 'manipulation' is reasonably applied to it.

Recall that many nudges are educative, and that many of them do not enlist or exploit System 1, or attempt in any way to 'outmanoeuver' people. But consider some testing cases, where the charge is not self-evidently misplaced.

(a) Choice architects might choose a graphic health warning, on the theory that an emotional, even visceral presentation might have significant effects.
(b) They might be aware that a statement that a product is '90 percent fat-free' has a different impact from a statement that a product is '10 percent fat', and they might choose the frame that has the desired effect.
(c) They might make a strategic decision about how to present social norms, knowing that the right presentation—for example, emphasising behaviour within the local community—could have a large impact on people's behaviour.
(d) They might decide to list options—in a cafeteria or on a form—so as to make it more likely that people will make certain choices.

It is an understatement to say that none of these cases involves the most egregious forms of manipulation. There is no lying and no deceit. But is there an effort to subvert or to insult people's decision-making powers? It is not absurd to say that in at least some of these cases, the answer is yes.

I have said that government should be transparent about what it is doing. It should not hide its actions or its reasons for those actions. Does transparency

---

[14] T Wilkinson, 'Nudging and Manipulation' (2013) *Political Studies* 61, 314.
[15] ibid 345.
[16] ibid.

rebut the charge of manipulation? Probably not. If government engages in egregious forms of manipulation, transparency is not a defence. A genuine insult to autonomy and dignity, in the form of a subversion of people's decision-making capacities, does not become acceptable merely because people are allowed to know about it.

We could even imagine cases where full democratic control, alongside a high degree of transparency, is plainly insufficient to rebut that charge. Imagine that a democratic government adopted, freely and openly, a programme of subliminal advertising—designed, let us say, for purposes of promoting public health (say, reducing smoking) rather than for illicit purposes. The programme would be objectionable on the ground that it would be unacceptably manipulative, even if it was adopted openly and would produce good consequences.

Perhaps a graphic health warning could be counted as manipulative if it is designed to target people's emotions, rather than to inform them of facts. But what if the warning is explained, in public, on exactly that ground? What if a warning is introduced and justified as effective, because it appeals to people's emotions, and thus saves lives? What if it is welcomed by the relevant population—say, smokers—for exactly that reason? Similar questions might be asked about strategic uses of framing effects, social norms, and order effects. TM Wilkinson convincingly argues that it is too crude to say that manipulation infringes upon autonomy, because 'manipulation could be consented to. If it were consented to, in the right kind of way, then the manipulation would at least be consistent with autonomy and might count as enhancing it'.[17]

We could understand consent as suggesting support from System 2, which might welcome a little manipulation (or possibly a lot) as a way of cabining the adverse effects of System 1 (recall present bias). To be sure, there are dangers in authorising public officials to pursue this line of argument. But in certain contexts, the argument is more than plausible. Imagine, for example, a public education campaign that is designed to reduce the risks associated with texting while driving, or an effort to combat the use of drugs or to convince people to stay in school. Many such campaigns are vivid and have an emotional component; they can be understood as efforts to combat self-control problems and to focus people on the long term.

It is appropriate to conclude that even with full transparency, at least some degree of manipulation may be involved whenever a choice architect is targeting emotions or seeking a formulation that will be effective because of how it interacts with people's intuitive or automatic thinking (System 1). It should be acknowledged that some (certainly not all) nudges can be considered as manipulative within an ordinary understanding of that term. But when nudges fall within the periphery of the concept, when they have legitimate purposes, when they would be effective, and when they do not diverge from the kinds of influences that are common and unobjectionable in ordinary life, the burden of justification can often be met.

---

[17] ibid.

VIII. LEARNING

Choice-making is a muscle, and the ability to choose can be strengthened through exercise. If nudges would make the muscle atrophy, we would have an argument against them. We could imagine an ethical objection that would contend that some nudges do not allow people to build up their own capacities, and might even undermine their incentive to do so. Here too, it is necessary to investigate the particulars—the kinds of nudges and choice architecture that are involved.

Active choosing and prompted choice hardly impede learning. Nor do information and reminders. On the contrary, they promote learning. Here the evidence is compelling: nudges of this kind exercise the choice-making muscle, rather than the opposite.

With respect to learning, a potential problem comes from default rules. It is possible to say that active choosing is far better than defaults, simply because choosing may promote learning. Consider, for example, the question whether employers should ask employees to make active choices about their retirement plans, or whether they should instead default people into plans that fit their situations. The potential for learning might well count in favour of active choosing. If people are defaulted into certain outcomes, they do not add to their stock of knowledge, and that may be a significant lost opportunity.

The argument for learning depends on the setting. (For most people, it is not important to become experts in the numerous decisions that lead to default settings in cell phones, and hence the use of such settings is not objectionable). The same point holds in many other contexts in which institutions rely on defaults rather than active choosing. To know whether choice architects should opt for active choosing, it is necessary to explore whether the context is one in which it is valuable, all things considered, for choosers to acquire a stock of knowledge.

IX. BIASED OFFICIALS

Choice architects, including judges and regulators, are emphatically human, and fully subject to behavioural biases; they are often unreliable. The growing field of *behavioural public choice* draws on this point to offer an account of official error. It is reasonable to object to some nudges, and to some efforts to intervene in existing choice architecture, on the ground that the choice architects might blunder. They might lack important information (the knowledge problem). They might be biased, perhaps because their own parochial interests are at stake (the public choice problem). They might themselves display behavioural biases—suffering, for example, from present bias, optimistic bias, or probability neglect. In a democratic society, public officials are responsive to public opinion, and if the public is mistaken, officials might be mistaken as well, as might be experts who advise officials (chapter five by Oren Perez).

This objection does identify an important cautionary note. One reason for nudges, as opposed to mandates and bans, is that choice architects may err. No one should deny that proposition, which argues in favour of choice-preserving approaches. If choice architects blunder, at least it can be said that people are entitled to go their own way. And if we emphasise the risk of official error, we might want to avoid public officials to avoid nudges and choice architecture as well.

The initial response to this objection should be familiar: a certain degree of nudging, from the public sector, cannot be avoided, and there is no use in wishing it away. Nonetheless, choice architects who work for government might decide that it is best to rely on free markets, and to trust in invisible hand mechanisms. If so, they would select (or accept) choice architecture that reflects those mechanisms.

To be sure, free markets have many virtues. But in some cases, disclosure, warnings, and reminders can do far more good than harm. As we have seen, active choosing is sometimes inferior to default rules, someone has to decide in favour of one or another, and in some cases, that someone is inevitably the government. In addition, it is possible to train regulatory policymakers, including those who use nudges, and (an important point) to foster a culture of regulatory humility (chapter six by Dunlop and Radaelli), which fits well with choice-preserving approaches. It is true that distrust of public officials will argue against nudging, at least where it is avoidable, but if it is dogmatic and generalised, such distrust will likely produce serious losses in terms of both welfare and freedom.

X. CONCLUSION

It is pointless to object to nudges and choice architecture as such. Even the most minimal government must nudge, and must create choice architecture of many different kinds. A modest regulatory state will influence people's decisions even if it seeks not to do so. Consider the effects of default rules, of the sort that are pervasive in the law of property, contract, and tort.

The modern regulatory state imposes numerous mandates and bans, and some of them are properly characterised as paternalistic. Consider the requirement that people obtain prescriptions before using certain medicines, or fuel economy and energy efficiency rules, or occupational safety and health law; all these, and many others, have paternalistic features. Paternalistic mandates and bans are subject to obvious ethical concerns, many of them identical to those explored here. Because nudges preserve freedom of choice, those concerns are weakened.

Nonetheless, any changes in choice architecture, including those that preserve freedom, can run into serious and even convincing ethical objections—most obviously, where the underlying goals are illicit. But where the goals are legitimate, nudges are less likely to run afoul of ethical constraints, not least because and when they promote informed choices (as in the case of reminders). Transparency and public scrutiny are important safeguards, especially when public officials are responsible for nudges and choice architecture. Nothing should be hidden or covert.

Nonetheless, some imaginable nudges are objectionable, even when legitimate goals are involved, even when freedom of choice is preserved, and even in the face of full transparency. Most important, some nudges can be counted as forms of manipulation, raising objections from the standpoint of both autonomy and dignity.

That is a strong point against them. Even when nudges target System 1, it might well strain the concept of manipulation to categorise them as such (consider a graphic warning). The concept of manipulation has a core and a periphery; some nudges fit within the core, others within the periphery, and others outside of both.

Many nudges, and many changes in choice architecture, are not merely permissible on ethical grounds; they are actually required. On grounds of welfare, the point should be straightforward; much nudging promises to increase social welfare. But the point holds for autonomy, dignity, and self-government as well.

The history of freedom-respecting nations is full of changes in choice architecture that have permitted them to move further in the direction of their highest ideals. It should go without saying that those ideals have yet to be fully realised. In moving closer to them, new nudges, and new forms of choice architecture, will prove indispensable.

Contents

Foreword by Cass R Sunstein..v
Figures...xxi
Tables..xxiii
Contributors...xxv

1. The Emergence of Behavioural Policy-Making:
   A European Perspective..1
   Anne-Lise Sibony and Alberto Alemanno

   Part I: Integrating Behavioural Sciences into EU Law-Making

2. Behavioural Sciences in Practice: Lessons for EU Rulemakers.......29
   Fabiana Di Porto and Nicoletta Rangone

3. Nudging and Evidence-Based Policy in Europe:
   Problems of Normative Legitimacy and Effectiveness....................61
   Muireann Quigley and Elen Stokes

4. Judge the Nudge: In Search of the Legal Limits of
   Paternalistic Nudging in the EU...83
   Anne van Aaken

   Part II: De-Biasing Through EU Law and Beyond

5. Can Experts be Trusted and what can be done about it?
   Insights from the Biases and Heuristics Literature 115
   Oren Perez

6. Overcoming Illusions of Control: How to Nudge and
   Teach Regulatory Humility...139
   Claire A Dunlop and Claudio M Radaelli

   Part III: The Impact of Behavioural Sciences on EU Policies

7. Behavioural Sciences and EU Data Protection Law:
   Challenges and Opportunities 161
   Eoin Carolan and Alessandro Spina

8. Behavioural Sciences and the Regulation of Privacy
   on the Internet 179
   Frederik Zuiderveen Borgesius

9. EU Consumer Protection and Behavioural Sciences:
   Revolution or Reform? 209
   Anne-Lise Sibony and Geneviève Helleringer

10. What can EU Health Law Learn from Behavioural Sciences?
    The Case of EU Lifestyle Regulation..235
    Alberto Alemanno

11. Conduct of Business Rules in EU Financial Services
    Regulation: Behavioural Rules Devoid of Behavioural Analysis?...............255
    Pieter Van Cleynenbreugel

Part IV: Problems with Behaviourally Informed Regulation

12. Making Sense of Nudge-Scepticism: Three Challenges to
    EU Law's Learning from Behavioural Sciences 279
    Péter Cserne

13. Behavioural Trade-Offs: Beyond the Land of Nudges Spans
    the World of Law and Psychology..301
    Yuval Feldman and Orly Lobel

14. Epilogue: The Legitimacy and Practicability of EU
    Behavioural Policy-Making..325
    Alberto Alemanno and Anne-Lise Sibony

Index 349

Figures

Figure 1: Nudging v empowerment (Ch 2)

Figure 2: An example of smart information nudging (Ch 2)

Figure 3: An imaginary restyling of refrigerators' label (Ch 2)

Figure 4: IPCC view of the relationship between evidence, agreement and confidence (Ch 5)

Figure 5: Surgical safety checklist (Ch5)

Figure 6: Aviation safety checklists (Ch 5)(B-32 checklist, 1943)

Tables

Table 1: Cognitive evidence (Ch 2)
Table 2: The de-biasing landscape (Ch 5)
Table 3: MINDSPACE biases and policymakers (Ch 6)

Contributors

Alberto Alemanno
Jean Monnet Professor of EU Law and Risk Regulation, HEC Paris
Global Clinical Professor, New York University School of Law

Anne van Aaken
Professor of Law, University of St Gallen

Eoin Carolan
Senior Lecturer, University College Dublin

Péter Cserne
Senior Lecturer, University of Hull

Claire A Dunlop
Senior Lecturer, University of Exeter

Yuval Feldman
Professor of Law, Bar-Ilan University

Geneviève Helleringer
Associate law professor at Essec Business School Paris-Singapore and Fellow of the Institute of European and Comparative Law, Oxford University

Orly Lobel
Don Weckstein Professor of Labor and Employment Law, University of San Diego School of Law

Fabiana Di Porto
Professor of Law, University of Salento

Murieann Quigley
Professor of Law, Innovation and Society, Newcastle University

Claudio M Radaelli
Jean Monnet Professor in European Public Policy, University of Exeter

Nicoletta Rangone
Professor of Law, LUMSA University of Rome

Anne-Lise Sibony
Professor of EU Law, Catholic University of Louvain

Alessandro Spina
Data Protection Officer, European Medicines Agency

Elen Stokes
Senior Lecturer, Cardiff University

Cass R Sunstein
Robert Walmsley University Professor, Harvard Law School

Pieter Van Cleynenbreugel
Assistant Professor, Leiden University

Frederik Zuiderveen Borgesius
Researcher at Institute for Information Law, University of Amsterdam

1

The Emergence of Behavioural Policy-Making: A European Perspective

ANNE-LISE SIBONY AND ALBERTO ALEMANNO

NUDGE AND THE LAW explores the legal implications of the emergent phenomenon of behaviourally informed intervention. It focuses on the challenges and opportunities it may offer to the policy-making of the European Union (hereinafter, EU). This dual focus on law and on Europe characterises our endeavour. Like many readers around the globe, we discovered with appetite and excitement the books that initially brought the basics of behavioural sciences to a wider audience.[1] Several books later, while the new accessibility of behavioural insights has inspired both theoretical and applied work on behavioural economics and policy-making, relatively little attention has been given to the legal dimension.[2] This is what this book focuses on.

For any degree of precision to be achieved, legal implications of a phenomenon need to be studied within a legal system—or several if a comparative approach is chosen. In this regard, our focus is on the European Union, both because, as EU legal scholars, this was something we could do and, more importantly, because the European dimension has to date been largely absent from the conversation on behaviourally-inspired policy-making.

Part I of this chapter sets the scene for the volume by providing a legal perspective on nudging and, more broadly, on behaviourally-informed intervention.

---

[1] RH Thaler and CR Sunstein, *Nudge: Improving Decisions about Health, Wealth, and Happiness* (New Haven, Yale University Press, 2008); D Ariely, *Predictably Irrational: The Hidden Forces that Shape Our Decisions* (New York, Harper Collins, 2008); S Levitt and S Dubner, *Freakonomics: A Rogue Economist Explores the Hidden Side of Everything* (New York, William Morrow, 2005); D Kahneman, *Thinking Fast and Slow* (New York, Farrar, Straus and Giroux, 2011); MH Bazerman and AE Tenbrunsel, *Blind Spots: Why We Fail to Do What's Right and What to Do about It* (Princeton, Princeton University Press, 2011).

[2] To mention only books: E Shafir (ed), *The Behavioral Foundations of Public Policy* (Princeton, Princeton University Press, 2012); R Jones, J Pykett and M Whitehead, *Changing Behaviours—On the Rise of the Psychological State* (Cheltenham, Edward Elgar, 2013): as an emerging approach to behavioural government; A Oliver, *Behavioural Public Policy* (Cambridge, Cambridge University Press, 2013); and, from a literary perspective, D Brooks, *The Social Animal* (New York, Random House, 2011).

It explores if, when and how behavioural insights can be accommodated in the legal system. Part II defines the scope of our editorial project and explains why it makes sense to adopt a singularly European perspective. Part III sets out the methodology chosen in editing this volume and outlines the content of the book.

I. NUDGE AND THE LAW

A. The Universal Appeal of Behaviourally Informed Intervention

Following the successful publication of several of books popularising the major findings of behavioural sciences, the observation that people make imperfect decisions has become mainstream and, today, almost a truism.[3] The general public but also, in several countries, policymakers have become increasingly aware of key insights from behavioural sciences. A behavioural approach can provide new explanations for the many limits of conventional policy-making that is based on neoclassical assumptions of rationality. As such, it is set to reveal that many premises policymakers and courts have taken for granted over time cannot survive the test of empirical scrutiny. The potential of behavioural teachings to help improve policy design appears intuitive and explains increasing interest in policy circles.[4]

The global appeal of behaviourally informed intervention has largely to do with its being presented as 'nudging', that is designing 'any aspect of the choice architecture that alters people's behaviour in a predictable way without forbidding any options or significantly changing their economic incentives'.[5] First of all, nudging is presented as a cheap and smart alternative to expensive traditional regulatory measures.[6] Indeed, the fact that behaviourally savvy intervention does not always require legislation is sometimes presented as one of its attractive features for governments.[7] Even when it is not used as an alternative to but in combination with traditional legal tools, such as fines, behaviourally informed intervention can still represent a cheap alternative, not to law, but to costly enforcement mechanisms.[8] This is due to the fact that leveraging behavioural traits ensures a higher rate of

---

[3] For a critical, yet minority, view denying the inherent shortcomings of human cognitive function, see G Gigerenzer, *Risk Savvy: How to Make Good Decisions* (New York, Penguin Group, 2014).

[4] See, eg P Lunn, *Regulatory Policy and Behavioural Economics* (Paris, OECD, 2014). In November 2014, the UK Behavioural Insights Team successfully raised awareness about behavioural insights at the World Economic Forum by setting up a new initiative under the lead of David Halpern and Eldar Shafir.

[5] Thaler and Sunstein (n 1) 6.

[6] CR Sunstein, 'Empirically Informed Regulation' (2011) 78 *University of Chicago Law Review* 1349; K Yeung, 'Nudge as a Fudge' (2012) 75 *MLR* 122.

[7] T Marteau et al, 'Judging Nudging: Can Nudging Improve Population Health?' (2011) 342 *British Medical Journal* d228, cited in P Rainford and J Tinkler, *Designing for Nudge Effects: How Behaviour Management can Ease Public Sector Problems* (2011) available at: eprints.lse.ac.uk/37810/.

[8] A Alemanno and A Spina, 'Nudging Legally: On the Checks and Balances of Behavioural Regulation' (2014) 12 *International Journal of Constitutional Law* 2.

voluntary compliance.⁹ Second, nudging promises to be choice-preserving, by always enabling the addressee to opt out of the preferred policy option.¹⁰ Third, in specific areas, regulation needs to become behaviourally informed not to 'nudge' citizens but to offer a 'counter-nudging' force against the exploitative use of behavioural insights by market actors. As illustrated in chapter seven by Alessandro Spina and Eoin Carolan, businesses, in particular the new actors of the digital economy, are using behaviourally informed strategies to steer consumer choices.¹¹ The perceived manipulative character of some marketing practices prompts calls for regulation, but such intervention can only aptly address citizens' concerns if it is based on a sound understanding of how behaviour is influenced.¹²

B. Behavioural Insights in a Nutshell

The central findings of behavioural research that are of interest to policy-making may be summarised in four statements:¹³ i) humans display a tendency to inertia and procrastination; ii) they are very sensitive to how information is presented (framing); iii) as well as to social influences; and iv) humans do not handle probabilities very well.

Inertia refers to the natural propensity of humans to accept their environment (including, eg their current mobile phone plan) as a given rather than take affirmative choices to change it, even when it would be in their best interest to do so and even when it could be done fairly easily. In other words, small hurdles matter a lot.

---

⁹ eg an experiment conducted in the UK showed that our sensitivity to being addressed by our own name (a behavioural trait that seems to be almost universally shared) could be leveraged to save collection costs of court fines. An experiment compared the effectiveness of reminders sent by mail and by text messages, as well as several variations in the text of the reminder. Text messages proved more effective than letters and messages containing the name of the addressee worked best. The conclusion was that, if scaled on a national basis, texting personalised reminders would increase revenues from fines by £30 million and save the cost of 150,000 bailiff interventions annually (L Haynes et al, 'Test, Learn, Adapt: Developing Public Policy with Randomised Controlled Trials' (Cabinet Office and Behavioural Insights Team, 2012) 10 available at: www.gov.uk/government/uploads/system/uploads/attachment_data/file/62529/TLA-1906126.pdf).

¹⁰ This claim is found, eg in C Jolls and CR Sunstein, 'Debiasing through Law' (2006) 35 *Journal of Legal Studies* 199, 202. This 'pre-commitment to regulatory tools that preserve choice', has been pinpointed as its major weakness by R Bubb and R Pildes, 'How Behavioral Economics Trims Its Sails and Why' (2014) 127 *Harvard Law Review*. Baldwin, for his part, points out that not all nudges do in fact preserve meaningful choices. 'Nudges of the third degree', which he defines as those that shape decisions and preferences in a manner that is 'resistant to unpacking' (by System 2), do not in fact, leave a realistic possibility to resist to the nudge. R Baldwin, 'From Regulation to Behaviour Change: Giving Nudge the Third Degree' (2014) 77 *MLR* 831, 836.

¹¹ For an insightful perspective on 'digital nudging', see R Calo, 'Digital Market Manipulation' (2014) 82(4) *George Washington Law Review* 995–1051 and, in this volume, ch 8 on 'Behavioural Sciences and the Regulation of Privacy on the Internet' by FZ Borgesius.

¹² See ch 7 by A Spina and E Carolan and ch 8 by FZ Borgesius.

¹³ CR Sunstein, 'Empirically Informed Regulation' (2011) 78 *University of Chicago Law Review* 1349.

One consequence is that people strongly tend to stick to the default option, which, in some cases, is set by law[14] or otherwise regulated.

The term 'framing effects' captures the fact that choices do not depend solely on the content and properties of the options subjects face but also, crucially, of the way in which they are framed.[15] For instance, test subjects are more likely to opt for surgery if told that the 'survival' rate is 90 per cent, than if they are informed that the mortality rate is 10 per cent.

'Social influence' expresses how our preferences are not only context-dependent but also shaped by the behaviour of others. This trait not only makes us prefer a full over an empty restaurant, it can also be leveraged in the legal sphere. For example, reminders for late tax payers may be drafted in such a way as to appeal to a social norm by indicating the proportion of taxpayers in a similar situation in the same locality who have already paid their taxes.[16]

Meanwhile, probability neglect refers to our tendency to completely disregard probabilities when making a decision under conditions of uncertainty. This tendency has obvious impact, for example, on financial choices people make and, consequently, is relevant for consumer protection in the area of financial services.[17]

What these insights collectively suggest is that cognitive and attentional limitations, the social environment and prevailing social norms matter for individual choices.[18] They are not only relevant to understand behaviour, which is the perspective of science, but also to regulate behaviour, which is the perspective of law.[19] If we

---

[14] An example is organ donation. Where the law provides that consent is presumed (is the default), the proportion of donors in the population is much higher than where people have to sign up to a donors register. For a discussion, see ch 3 by M Quigley and E Stokes. Legal defaults are not always sticky: LE Willis, 'When Nudges Fail: Slippery Defaults' (2013) 80 *University of Chicago Law Review* 1115.

[15] A Tversky and D Kahneman, 'The Framing of Decisions and the Psychology of Choice' (1981) 211 *Science* 453.

[16] An experiment run in the UK has shown that such a move achieves savings in collection costs: Behavioural Insights Team, 'Annual Update' (2010–11) 15–16, www.gov.uk/government/uploads/system/uploads/attachment_data/file/60537/Behaviour-Change-Insight-Team-Annual-Update_acc.pdf.

[17] The Financial Conduct Authority in the UK has been investigating how to use behavioural insights. See K Erta et al, 'Applying Behavioural Economics at the Financial Conduct Authority' Financial Conduct Authority (UK) (2013) 1 Occasional Paper, www.fca.org.uk/static/documents/occasional-papers/occasional-paper-1.pdf. For an analysis of EU Financial Services regulation, see in this volume ch 11 by P Van Cleynenbreugel, 'Conduct of Business Rules in EU Financial Services Regulation: Behavioural Rules Devoid of Behavioural Analysis?'.

[18] CR Sunstein, 'Nudges.gov: Behavioural Economics and Regulation' in E Zamir and D Teichman (eds), *Oxford Handbook of Behavioural Economics and the Law* (Oxford, Oxford University Press, 2014); CR Sunstein, 'Empirically Informed Regulation' (2011) 78 *University of Chicago Law Review* 1349.

[19] For a US perspective see, eg M Vandebergh, A Carrico and L Schultz, 'Regulation in the Behavioral Era' (2011) 95 *Minnesota Law Review* 715. For an EU approach, see E Ciriolo, 'Behavioral Economics at the European Commission: Past, Present and Future' [2011] *Oxera Agenda* 1; A Alemanno et al, 'Nudging Healthy Lifestyles—Informing Regulatory Governance with Behavioural Research' (2012) 3 *European Journal of Risk Regulation* 3. For an OECD perspective, 'Consumer Policy Toolkit' available at www.oecd.org/sti/consumer/consumerpolicytoolkit.htm. For a contract law perspective, see O Bar-Gill, *Seduction by Contract, Law Economics, and Psychology in Consumer Markets* (Oxford, Oxford University Press, 2012); for a public health law perspective, A Alemanno, 'Informing the

want to regulate the behaviour of humans who populate the real world rather than the behaviour of econs who inhabit econland, it makes sense to take into consideration how the former are known to operate. It is a matter of effectiveness: if the law operates on an inaccurate model for the behaviour it seeks to regulate (eg investment choices), it is likely to miss its target.[20] For example, rather than making it mandatory for firms to provide all the information theoretically needed to enable rational and informed choice, it seems preferable to make sure that consumers receive meaningful information: less information but presented in a way that is easier to process, so that it is less likely that they ignore it altogether.[21] In the constant search for increased effectiveness, lawmakers have every reason to be allured by behavioural science.[22] To go from promises to practice, it is necessary to take a look at the behavioural toolbox, but because legal tools are made of words, some clarifications about the language we use to speak about nudging and related endeavours should come first.

C. Labelling: Do You Speak Nudgese?

Due to its popularising intent and resulting appeal, 'nudge' is by far the most frequent term used to refer to behaviourally inspired intervention. Despite its dominating effect on the behavioural discourse, the concept presents two significant shortcomings. First, its normative identity is far from clear—as recognised by its creators themselves.[23] Second, it fails to capture the entire reality of behavioural action. In any event, empirically informed intervention, even though it is indifferently referred to as nudging, behaviourally informed regulation or evidence-based policy-making, consists essentially in the application of behavioural insights to policy-making.[24] However, different names carry different meanings and several concepts lie behind this semantic variety.[25]

Non-Communicable Diseases Agenda with Behavioural Insights' in A Alemanno and A Garde (eds), *Regulating Lifestyles—Europe, Alcohol, Tobacco and Unhealthy Diets* (Cambridge, Cambridge University Press, 2015). For an international law perspective, T Broude, 'Behavioral International Law' (2013) 12–13 Hebrew University of Jerusalem International Law Forum Research Paper, available at ssrn.com/abstract=2320375.

[20] A Tor, 'The Methodology of the Behavioral Analysis of Law' (2008) 4 *Haifa Law Review* 237, 241.
[21] For a discussion of information requirement in the context of EU consumer law, see O Bar-Gill and O Ben-Shahar, 'Regulatory Techniques in Consumer Protection: A Critique of European Consumer Contract Law' (2013) 50 *CML Rev* 109. More generally, see O Ben Shahar and CE Schneider, *More than You Wanted to Know: The Failure of Mandated Disclosure* (Princeton, Princeton University Press, 2014) and, for a more scholarly version of the argument, O Ben Shahar and CE Schneider, 'The Failure of Mandated Disclosure' (2010) 159 *University of Pennsylvania Law Review* 647.
[22] We borrow this apt characterisation from Robin Feldman, who writes more generally about the 'allure of science': R Feldman, *The Role of Science in Law* (Oxford, Oxford University Press, 2009) 3.
[23] The same co-promoter of 'nudge' thinking seems to have recently recognised this point. See, CR Sunstein, 'It's for your Own Good', Book Review of Sarah Conly's *Against Autonomy*, The New York Review of Books, April 2013.
[24] CR Sunstein, 'Empirically Informed Regulation' (2011) 78 *University of Chicago law Review* 1349.
[25] For a valuable effort at unpacking the various concepts embedded in the notion of nudging, see R Baldwin (n 10).

Labelling is also a highly contextual exercise. Often, when a discussion is imported from the US to Europe, the US terminology travels along. Yet, as is well known in the study of transplants, the way in which an institution or a discourse takes shape is context-dependant.[26] This also applies to labels for behaviourally informed government action as well as to academic labels applied to the study of such action. US names may or may not fit European realities.

i. Labelling Matters

Despite the limited scholarship triggered by the behavioural turn of regulation, EU scholars seem particularly interested in questions of characterisation revolving around behavioural government action. Thus, their publications engage with definitional issues aimed at characterising the precise boundaries of behavioural action and its relationship with the nudge movement.[27]

From a European perspective, this interest in characterisation and definitional issues seems surprising because—unlike in the US—these labelling questions do not carry legal consequences. In the US, deciding whether graphic visual warnings on cigarettes must be considered mere 'information' (telling consumers about the adverse effects stemming from tobacco) or a 'nudge' (aimed at changing behaviour) determines their legality.[28] The warnings are valid if they qualify as 'notice', by virtue of a carve-out to the usual scrutiny to which coerced speech is subject under the First Amendment, but they become invalid if they qualify as a nudge.[29] This bifurcated approach has been severely criticised[30] in light of recent research showing that emotional communication does not bypass the cognitive system.[31] Simply because communication is non-verbal does not imply that the adressee will be unable to make a reasoned decision. While in Europe, there is also a sentiment that bypassing the cognitive system of citizens poses a problem, there is no reason to think that this US legal development could be replicated in Europe. In the EU

---

[26] A Watson, *Legal Transplants* (Edinburgh, Scottish Academic Press, 1974). In the context of management practices: GS Drori, MA Höllerer and P Walgenbach (eds), *Global Themes and Local Variations in Organization and Management: Perspectives on Glocalization* (London, Routledge, 2013).

[27] See, eg L Bovens, 'The Ethics of Nudge' in T Grüne-Yanoff and SO Hansson (eds), *Preference Change: Approaches from Philosophy, Economics and Psychology* (New York, Springer, 2008) 207; and R Jones, J Pykett and M Whitehead, *Changing Behaviours—On the Rise of the Psychological State* (Cheltenham, Edward Elgar, 2013) 163 et seq.

[28] See, eg EP Goodman, 'Visual Gut Punch: Persuasion, Emotion and the Constitutional Meaning of Graphic Disclosure' (2014) 99 *Cornell Law Review*; R Calo, 'Code, Nudge or Notice?' (2013) 2013-04 University of Washington Research Paper, available at papers.ssrn.com/sol3/papers.cfm?abstract_id=2217013.

[29] *RJ Reynolds Tobacco Co v FDA*, 696 F 3d 1205, 1221–22 (DC Circuit 2012).

[30] Goodman (n 28). See also R Tushnet, 'More than a Feeling: Emotion and the First Amendment' (2014) 127 *Harvard Law Review* 2392.

[31] For a perspective on contemporary theory of emotions see, eg GL Clore and M Tamir, 'Affects as Embodied Information' (2007) 13(1) *Psychology Inquiry* 37. For a philosophical enquiry into the nature of emotions, see M Nussbaum, *Upheavals of Thought: The Intelligence of Emotions* (Cambridge, Cambridge University Press, 2003) (who argues that emotions are built on 'cognitive appraisal or evaluations').

legal order, it is not clear to what extent characterisation of behaviourally inspired public action may engender divergent legal consequences.[32]

ii. Labels for Government Action

As mentioned, 'nudging' is the most widely used label for government action, but it is slightly misleading because it describes only one form of behaviourally informed public action. Nudge presents two defining features: first, the authority preserves free choice by not preventing the selection of presumably suboptimal options, and, second, behavioural insights are used to alter the choice architecture so as to make preferred decisions more likely.[33] Acting as 'choice architects', policymakers organise the context, process and environment in which individuals make decisions.[34] Nudge is therefore presented as a distinctive, alternative way, characterised as being minimally burdensome, low-cost and choice-preserving, to help promote regulatory goals.[35]

However, neither this notion nor the legal instruments best suited to implement governmental nudges have received much attention in the legal community. Thus, for instance, it is not clear whether a nudge may be embedded into the law. Equally, it is ambiguous whether the mere provision of information or incentives can qualify as nudges[36] (in principle, according to the original definition the former should but the latter should not).[37] It is even less clear whether the growing interest in nudging may trigger the enactment of more regulation[38] or whether it should rather be construed as the continuation of a deregulatory agenda.[39] Because of its uncertain contours and because it cuts across many different legal categories, 'nudge' is not a notion that lends itself easily to integration in the language of the law or legal scholarship.[40]

---

[32] A Alemanno and A Spina, 'On the Checks and Balances of Behavioural Regulation' (2014) 12 *International Journal of Constitutional Law* 429.

[33] Thaler and Sunstein, *Nudge* (n 1); Ariely, *Predictably Irrational* (n 1). CR Sunstein, *Simpler, The Future of Government* (New York, Simon & Schuster, 2013) 39. See also, eg J Baron, *Thinking and Deciding* (Cambridge, Cambridge University Press, 2007).

[34] ibid.

[35] Thaler and Sunstein, *Nudge* (n 1).

[36] For an introduction to the debate about what qualifies as a nudge, see L Bovens (n 27) 207.

[37] Sunstein, *Simpler* (n 33) 39.

[38] CR Sunstein, 'Nudges.gov' (n 18) 9.

[39] About his time as the head of the Office of Informationa and Regulatory Affairs (OIRA), Sunstein writes 'We were not only focussed on issuing smart regulation. We were focused on deregulation too', Sunstein, *Simpler* (n 33) 8. Similarly, in the UK, the Behavioural Insights Unit was set up by David Cameron as a step in the pursuit of a deregulation agenda. See David Halpern (head of Nudge Unit): 'We try to avoid legislation and ordering' *The Guardian*, 5 February 2013, theguardian.com/society/2013/feb/05/david-halpern-government-nudge-unit.

[40] The same co-promoter of 'nudge' thinking seems to have recently recognised this point. See, CR Sunstein, 'It's for Your Own Good', Book Review of Sarah Conly's *Against Autonomy*, *The New York Review of Books*, April 2013.

In addition, even if it could be legally defined, nudging is—as previously illustrated—only one of several possible approaches available to incorporate behavioural insights into policy-making. Yet, current language use seems to have selected this word as the most appealing shorthand for behaviourally informed rulemaking.[41] In light of this fact, we chose to use 'nudge' in the title of this volume, although we note that this cannot (and should not) subsume the broader phenomenon of use of behavioural sciences in law.

iii. Labels for Academic Endeavours

From a descriptive point of view, 'law and psychology' would probably be the most accurate name for the study of whether law should incorporate findings from cognitive and social psychology and how it could do so.[42] The reason why this label has not prevailed in the US seems to be twofold. First, it was already taken. To those for whom the phrase 'law and psychology' is familiar, it is associated with studies focussing mainly on psychology of judges, jurors, witnesses, and criminals.[43] The legal implications of psychological traits that play out in the decisions of citizens, consumers, investors or corporate board members are not part of the field. This argument has much less weight in continental Europe than in the US or the UK, because most continental legal scholars are not aware of law and psychology studies. The time lag between the EU and in the US is the more weighty reason to not go for the label 'law and psychology' as it would not do a service to the incipient European research on law and decision-making research (to use a hopefully neutral label) to give it a name that US scholars would almost certainly misunderstand.

The second reason why 'law and psychology' has not picked up in the US as a general label for interdisciplinary legal scholarship relying on psychological insights is that there was a powerful incentive to call the new field another name. 'Behavioural law and economics'[44] had the advantage that it clearly presented the scholarly innovation as a competitive entry on the market dominated by law and

---

[41] Baldwin (n 10), makes the same statement although he seems to also object to widespread usage.

[42] For a thorough discussion in the US context, see J Rachlinski, 'New Law and Psychology' (2000) 85 *Cornell Law Review* 739.

[43] A relatively broad description of the field found on the Stanford Law School website lists 'Conflict resolution and negotiation; judgment and decision-making capacity; prejudice and stereotyping; criminal responsibility; competency; assessment of evidence, including the reliability of eyewitnesses, and lie detection; hedonics; developmental psychology and educational policy; addiction and drug policy' (www.law.stanford.edu/degrees/joint-degrees/law-and-psychology).

[44] See, eg C Jolls et al, 'A Behavioural Approach to Law and Economics' (1998) 50 *Stanford Law Review* 1471; C Jolls, 'Governing America: The Emergence of Behavioural Law and Economics' Max Weber Lecture Series, 2010/3; R Bubb and R Pildes, 'How Behavioral Economics Trims Its Sails and Why' (2014) 127 *Harvard Law Review* 1593. In the EU context: H Luth, *Behavioural Economics in Consumer Policy: The Economic Analysis of Standard Terms in Consumer Contracts Revisited* (Antwerpen, Intersentia, 2010); M Lissowska, 'Overview of Behavioural Economics Elements in the OECD Consumer Policy Toolkit' (2011) 34 *Journal of Consumer Policy* 393; P Lunn (n 4).

economics. The publicity was worth the irony. It is indeed a little ironic that, after having embraced the rationality hypothesis for about five decades as a matter of disciplinary identity, economics should appear as the discipline that brings behavioural wisdom to the study of law. As Daniel Kahneman writes, 'Labels matter, and the mislabelling of applied behavioural sciences as behavioural economics has consequences'.[45] The consequences Kahneman points to are, first, that 'important contributions of psychology to public policy are not recognized as such' and, second, that this unfairness drives young psychologists away from applied research that could be useful to policy-making.[46]

From a legal scholar's perspective, this state of affairs is regrettable because it makes more sense to draw directly from empirical psychology studies rather than to take the detour via the selection of psychological insights labelled behavioural economics. It amounts to using a filter that was designed to retain what psychology could offer to a discussion internal to the discipline of economics, when there is no reason to believe that this filter is suited to legal needs.

'Behavioural analysis of law'[47] has the advantage of avoiding the unwelcome, US-centric reference to economics and is, for this reason alone, preferable. Yet, it suffers from a different inaccuracy. It is not the law that is analysed with the tools of behavioural sciences. Rather it is human behaviour (ie facts, not law) that is scrutinised in light of behavioural concepts (stemming from psychology). This imprecision is acceptable because the name works well in the US due to the analogy with the familiar 'economic analysis of law'. Again, the trade-off between accuracy and catchiness is different in Europe.

We prefer 'law and behavioural sciences' because it is ideologically neutral and descriptively accurate. It is fully compatible with the notion that the function of behavioural sciences may be to shed light on facts (rather than law), leaving it to legal analysis to decide whether and how this knowledge about facts could and should be incorporated. This name is also less charged with a US-shaped debate that neither fits the realities of EU scholarship nor predominant conceptions among practitioners and policymakers. Indeed, from a European perspective, the added value of the new approach is not that it is better than economic analysis of law *à la* Posner. The added value of the new field of studies at the intersection of law and psychology is, first and foremost, that it could help make laws more effective by reflecting empirical findings about human behaviour and promote regulatory goals while maintaining individual authority, ownership and control.

Another candidate name is 'law and emotions', which does not suffer from the same drawbacks as 'law and psychology' for transatlantic labelling purposes. Indeed, the phrase covers a very broad field of study of which behaviourally

---

[45] D Kahneman, Foreword to S Mullainathan and E Shafir, *Scarcity: Why Having Too Little Means So Much* (New York, Times Books, 2013) IX.
[46] ibid.
[47] A Tor (n 20), especially fn 13.

informed regulation would be a subset.[48] In our view, categorising the study of behaviourally informed regulation as a subtopic of law and emotions could bring the benefit of cross-fertilising the field with insights from reflections on a variety of enquiries into how law deals with emotions (and knowledge about them). Provided lawyers are not afraid of it,[49] it could thus provide a useful transatlantic umbrella label for the interdisciplinary study attempting to incorporate more wisdom about human behaviour into the law.

D. Translating Behavioural Insights into Policy-making

Nudging does not need law, at least not always. For example, nudging children to opt for the healthy choices at the canteen only takes an informed decision of the manager; no legal instrument comes into play. Likewise, no legal intervention is needed to make cities cleaner and induce citizens to use bins more often; green footprint stickers on the pavement may be all it takes to reduce the costs of garbage collection.[50] Similarly, handing out feedback cards on recycling habits of households is enough to induce citizens to recycle more.[51] More generally, designing or redesigning a choice architecture does not always require a permit.

Law meets nudging—or nudging meets the law, depending on which angle one takes—in two sets of circumstances. The first situation is when private entities such as companies, charities or other non-governmental entities nudge their consumers, employees or potential donors into desired behaviour (buying more, walking more, giving more). Most of this type of (private) nudging does not particularly call for regulation, but some of it might. For example, there is no reason to restrict the freedom of a company to design office space in such a way that employees get more exercise during their working day or to restrict the freedom of charities to use vivid narratives to catch donors' attention. There may, however, be reasons to restrict the freedom of companies when they use certain behaviourally informed marketing strategies to increase sales. For example, should a website that tracks users be allowed to display a higher price for an airplane ticket each time a consumer checks a certain route at certain dates? Relying in this manner on the psychology of scarcity appears intuitively unfair.[52] Similarly, the use of pre-ticked boxes to sell, for example, insurance services to purchasers of an airplane tickets

---

[48] For a survey, see TA Maroney, 'Law and Emotion: A Proposed Taxonomy of an Emerging Field' (2006) 30 *Law of Human Behaviour* 119. All fields of law where emotions are, could or should be relevant are potentially concerned by law and emotion studies (including civil matter such as trusts and estates, property and contract, divorce and child custody).

[49] K Abrams and H Keren, 'Who's Afraid of Law and the Emotions?' (1996) 94 *Minnesota Law Review* 1998.

[50] See, eg P Renfer and J Tinkler, 'Designing for Nudge Effect: How Behaviour Management Can Ease Public Sector' (2011) LSE Research Online.

[51] ibid.

[52] On the psychology of scarcity, see Mullainathan and Shafir, *Scarcity* (n 45).

may be considered an unfair exploitation of consumers' status quo bias.[53] While marketing is prevalent in a market economy, it is also common ground, at least in many jurisdictions, that it should be regulated.[54] In other words regulation of private nudging is the first point of contact between law and nudging. This is because 'counter-nudging' typically requires the intervention of the law.[55]

But nudging and the law meet in a second situation too. This occurs when public entities themselves, similarly to what private operators do, seek to nudge citizens into certain behaviour, such as agreeing to donate their organs. This typically requires legislation, regulation, or authorisation. While public nudging has attracted much attention (and criticism), both regulation of private nudging and public nudging itself constitute instances of behaviourally informed regulation and both should be considered when exploring the interplay of behavioural sciences and the law. As will be illustrated below in more detail, they both form part of public nudging and—as such—they can be distinguished from private nudging.

To further analyse the legal applications of behavioural insights, it is necessary to explore correspondence between the native categories used to describe nudges (with no particular attention to law) and legal categories. Thaler, Sunstein and others have invented tools—or simply, but powerfully, named them. What lawyers need to do is to analyse them in light of legal rules and principles in order to determine more precisely what legal uses of behavioural insights are possible within existing legal orders. Of course, another discussion needs to be conducted in parallel to assess the legitimacy of public nudging or, as the case may be, the legitimacy of public intervention to regulate private nudging. Legitimacy concerns are more frequently raised in the first case but may also arise in the second. In any event, it is only when they can be addressed that the enquiry into how to place behavioural tools in the legal toolbox will matter in practice.

i. Toolbox, Drawers and Tools

Lawyers are starting to familiarise themselves with tools that can bring behavioural insights to bear. These tools do not come with legal labels on them and legal

---

[53] Such is the assessment of the EU legislator: Directive 2011/83/EU on consumer rights [2011] OJ L304/64, art 22.

[54] See, eg O Bartlett and A Garde, 'Time to Seize the (Red) Bull by the Horns: The EU's Failure to Protect Children from Alcohol and Unhealthy Food Marketing' (2013) 38 *EL Rev* 498.

[55] Robert Baldwin uses the phrase 'counter nudging' in a different though not unrelated sense. Baldwin (n 10) 842. He calls counter-nudging the possible reaction of uncooperative regulated businesses who are compelled by regulation to nudge consumers in a certain way that runs contrary to corporate interests (eg when shops are mandated on pain of sanctions to check young consumer's ID before selling alcohol). The idea is essentially the same, namely the succession of action and reaction between businesses and government. In our acception, the starting point is the pre-regulatory state: absent any regulation, businesses nudge consumers unhindered. In this perspective, regulation of private nudging practices constitutes counter-nudging. Baldwin's starting point is a regulation compelling businesses to enforce a nudge. His 'counter nudging' amounts to creative compliance in the specific context of mandated nudging.

scholars are increasingly wondering whether and how these tools could fit in the existing regulatory toolbox(es). To this effect, several taxonomies aimed at clarifying the nature of behaviourally informed intervention have been proposed. They constitute different ways to organise the regulatory toolbox in drawers.

Jolls and Sunstein have initially described 'debiasing through law' as one of three possible responses to systematic errors of judgement, the two other being, respectively, doing nothing and what they call 'insulating strategies'. This last term refers to tools that seek to insulate outcomes from the choices that people make, for example by raising liability standards applicable to producers based on the notion that people systematically underestimate risks.[56] 'Debiasing' is distinguished from 'insulating strategies' in that it seeks to correct identified systematic errors rather than to adapt the rules to the persisting prevalence of errors in order to avoid their harmful consequences. While the aim of insulating strategies is to mitigate the consequences of errors, that of debiasing is to reduce the occurrence of errors. Another typology that aims at placing (public or private) behavioural interventions into a broader picture distinguishes tools that structure choice architecture from mandates and incentives.[57] Calo, for his part, distinguishes nudges both from codes (or architectures) and from notices, but admits that the categories overlap and suggests instead that the real distinction is between facilitation and friction, that is policy intervention that aims at making some behaviour either easier or more difficult.[58] Other typologies focus on a finer level of detail. In this vein, Baldwin distinguishes three degrees of nudges, depending on their impact on individual autonomy.[59] More detailed still, and with a practical outlook rather than theoretical ambition, Sunstein proposes a typology of 10 types of behavioural intervention.[60]

The production of taxonomies—a thriving line of business in academia—will probably go on for some time. This is all the more likely given that, besides first order categorisation issues (what drawers do we need to organise the toolbox?), there are also second order issues (do we need more than one toolbox?). For example, it is not entirely clear at this stage whether one should think of nudges (one particular kind of behaviourally informed regulatory tools) as belonging to the same or a different box from other legal tools.[61] In other words, if a behavioural scientist comes with her toolbox to play with a lawyer, spreads out her tools on the floor, how does the lawyer organise them in his own box? Can he do this satisfactorily without modifying the drawers his box comes with or does he need to build a new toolbox with drawers of a different shape? To make progress on these

---

[56] Jolls and Sunstein (n 10) 200.
[57] CR Sunstein and L Reisch, 'Redesigning Cockpits' (2014) 37 *Journal of Consumer Policy* 333.
[58] R Calo, 'Code, Nudge or Notice?' (2014) 99 *Iowa Law Review* 773 available at papers.ssrn.com/sol3/papers.cfm?abstract_id=2217013.
[59] Baldwin (n 10).
[60] CR Sunstein, 'Nudging: A Very Short Guide' (2014) 37 *Journal of Consumer Policy* 583.
[61] Baldwin (n 10) argues in favour of a separation of toolboxes because nudges rest on principles that, according to him, conflict which those that underpin classical instruments found in the regulatory toolbox (855 et seq).

questions, what is needed in our view is a tighter link between categories used to describe behavioural tools and legal categories, that is the categories on which legislation and adjudication operate.

ii. What the Law can do with Tools

To start with this multiple toolboxes problem, we will stick to a simple categorisation of behavioural tools proposed by Cass Sunstein, both as a scholar[62] and as a government official.[63] It comprises three types of tools: (a) smart disclosure requirements, (b) default rules, and (c) simplification. For each category of tools, we discuss possible correspondence with legal techniques (or drawers of the second box). It is possible that one kind of tool can be operationalised with more than one legal technique and, conversely, that several different behavioural tools will call for the same legal techniques to implement them (when law is needed at all to implement them in a given context).

a. Smart Disclosure Requirements

The confrontation between behavioural insights and existing rules on disclosure leads to a simple conclusion: disclosure requirements are both prevalent in legal systems and remarkably ineffective.[64] Behavioural research helps explain why and offers leads to design different disclosure requirements, based on an understanding of how people process and use information. A behaviourally informed disclosure requirement is 'smart' when its design ensures that disclosure is not merely technical but also meaningful,[65] useful,[66] and adequate in the given context, taking into account available processing capacities.[67] The potential impact of behavioural research for rules on disclosure is colossal. Its importance for EU law cannot be exaggerated since EU regulations contain a vast number of disclosure requirements that are not behaviourally informed.[68] Yet, from the point of view of legal technique, the incorporation of behavioural wisdom into information requirements

---

[62] Sunstein (n 13).
[63] Executive Order 13563, 'Improving Regulation and Regulatory Review'.
[64] Bar-Gill and Ben-Shahar (n 21); Ben Shahar and Schneider (n 21); Calo (n 58); A Fung, M Graham, and D Weil, *Full Disclosure: The Perils and Promise of Transparency* (Cambridge, Cambridge University Press, 2007) 5–6.
[65] A number of gigabytes in a mobile internet plan, eg does not mean much to most consumers. In contrast, a number of kilometres per litre of fuel is a meaningful way to describe a car's fuel consumption (more meaningful than litres per kilometre).
[66] Information about the size of a handbag (preferably a picture that allows someone to visualise the bag and compare it to body size rather than exact measurements) is useful to consumer shopping online. Information about jurisdiction on the sales contract is not useful to the consumer, first of all because it is very unlikely that she will sue the seller, whatever mishaps may occur in the transaction and second because, at least if she is domiciled in an EU country, the courts of her country of residence will have jurisdiction (art 18 of Regulation 1215/2012 on jurisdiction and the recognition and enforcement of judgments in civil and commercial matters (recast) [2012] OJ L351/1).
[67] Terms and conditions running to dozens of pages do not correspond to the level of attention a consumer can reasonably be expected to deploy before buying a song online.
[68] See ch 9 by AL Sibony and G Helleringer.

would not require a major change. It is the content of mandated disclosure that needs to change, not the technique itself.[69] Indeed, this change is underway. Several examples of smarter disclosure requirements can be found in EU legislation in the area of tobacco,[70] food labelling[71], and financial products.[72] The radical version of the behavioural critique of disclosure requirements would lead to repeal many of them and to revamp others in order for the information to be tailored to the needs of intermediaries rather than consumers.[73] While this would be a major overhaul affecting a vast number of legislative and regulatory acts in the EU—just like in the US—the legal techniques involved would not be new in any way. Behavioural suggestions translate as either repeal of existing regulation or changes in the content of mandates, two courses of action for which the existing legal toolbox suffices.

b. Default Rules

Defaults are a tool of choice in the behavioural toolbox. By operationalising the power of inertia and procrastination, they induce individuals towards a predetermined choice. Defaults, as such, are not foreign to lawyers; they have long existed across various fields of law. For example, when administrative law determines that, under the so-called 'positive silence rule', inertia of public authorities is presumptively considered indicative that the administration approves of a certain behaviour, it sets approval as a default.[74] Default rules have also been prevalent

---

[69] This less than revolutionary nature of smart disclosure requirement is what makes Ben-Shahar and Schneider sceptical of their potential to truly improve consumer protection (n 21).

[70] Art 10 of Directive 2014/40/EU of the European Parliament and of the Council of 3 April 2014 on the approximation of the laws, regulations and administrative provisions of the Member States concerning the manufacture, presentation and sale of tobacco and related products [2014] OJ L127/1 requires the display of a combined warning (graphic and pictorial) occupying 65% of the two main surfaces of the pack.

[71] Recital 41 of Regulation (EU) 1169/2011 of the European Parliament and of the Council of 25 October 2011 on the provision of food information to consumers [2011] OJ L304/18, says that 'to appeal to the average consumer and to serve the informative purpose for which it is introduced, and given the current level of knowledge on the subject of nutrition, the nutrition information provided should be simple and easily understood'. This translates into a requirement—foreseen in Arts 9 and 13—to provide a set of major information, such as the name of the food, the net quantity and the nutritional content, in the principle field of vision, ie that which is most likely to be seen at first glance by the consumer at the time of purchase and that enables the consumer to immediately identify a product in terms of its character or nature and, if applicable, its brand name.

[72] See, eg Commission Regulation 583/2010 of 1 July 2010 implementing Directive 2009/65/EC of the European Parliament and of the Council as regards key investor information and conditions which must be met when providing key investor information or the prospectus in a durable medium other than paper or by means of a website [2010] OJ L176/1, which requires that the provision of the most relevant information for aspiring investors be disclosed in accessible terms (rather than merely imposing the disclosure of all relevant information (as a prospectus would do).

[73] Ben-Shahar and Schneider (2014) (n 21), envisage advice by intermediaries as a substitute rather than a complement to mandated disclosure (190). We take a less radical view on this issue.

[74] Several countries recognise some forms of 'silence equals consent'. However, it must be said that the reason of the creation of this *fictio juris* has probably more to do with the recognised failure of public authorities to respect the time limits laid down in the relevant procedures than with a reasoned endorsement of the findings of behavioural sciences.

in contract law, procedural law and private international law. Rules determining which court has jurisdiction over a contract when parties have not specified it are a case in point.

Given their huge potential for affecting outcomes, default rules, may complement or provide an alternative to more traditional regulatory options such as restrictions or bans.[75] A classic example of the use of default in policy-making is when legislation provides that, unless a person explicitly objects, her consent to donate her organs will be presumed.

What the behavioural perspective brings to the existing use of defaults in the legal system is a degree of awareness and deliberation about the power and weakness of defaults. The power of defaults is the first message of behavioural sciences and has been hailed in *Nudge*. More recently however, behavioural analysis has drawn attention to the weaknesses of defaults in two types of situations. First, when the target group is too diverse and the domain is familiar, mandating active choices (ie requiring individuals to express their choice) might be a more sensible option than default rules.[76] Second, when powerful corporate actors have incentives to nudge consumers to opt out of the default set by law, these defaults become slippery.[77] For example if the mandated default option for bank account is 'no overdraft', banks will make sure that consumers opt out of the default by including an appropriate form in the stack consumers have to sign when they open an account. In such settings, mandating informed consent may not be of much help in practice.[78]

EU law has recently drawn on some but not all of these ideas and warnings. For example, it was with full knowledge of the behavioural evidence on the power of defaults that the European Commission introduced a prohibition of pre-ticked boxes on e-commerce websites.[79] The more complex message about slippery defaults, and the ensuing invitation to take behavioural wisdom into account also at the stage of anticipating corporate strategies in reaction to legal defaults,[80] is yet to be accepted. This is not surprising since we are still in the early days of regulating defaults in the field of consumer protection.

Like rules on disclosures, the legal rules pertaining to defaults are not of a special nature. They consist in legal presumptions (of administrative approval), rules

---

[75] See, eg E Johnson et al, 'Framing, Probability Distortions, and Insurance Decisions' (1993) 7(1) *Journal of Risk and Uncertainty* 35.

[76] G Carroll et al, 'Optimal Defaults and Active Decisions' (2005) NBER Working Paper; CR Sunstein, 'Impersonal Default Rules vs Active Choices vs Personalized Default Rules: A Triptych' available at ssrn.com/abstract=2171343. 'Forced choice' constitutes another alternative technique. G Liebig and J Rommel, 'Active and Forced Choice for Overcoming Status Quo Bias: A Field Experiment on the Adoption of "No junk mail" Stickers in Berlin, Germany' (2014) 37 *Journal of Consumer Policy* 427.

[77] Willis (n 14).

[78] Ben-Shahar and Schneider (n 21) 192.

[79] Art 22 CDR (n 53). DG Sanco presented this provision in the Directive as a product of its investigations on the teachings of behavioural sciences. See ec.europa.eu/consumers/consumer_evidence/behavioural_research/index_en.html.

[80] What Baldwin (n 10) calls counter-nudging strategies.

that lawyers themselves call default rules (eg in private international law), prohibitions (addressed to corporations about defaults they may or may not set), and mandates addressed to administrations or corporations (to prompt active choice). More rarely, the law on defaults takes the form of a delegation: for example, the new Belgian rules on class actions do not express a legislative choice between opt-in and opt-out; they provide that the court will decide on a case-by-case basis under what rule the class should be constituted.[81] Even in this example, however, the legal technique is not original at all: the legislator empowers the court to decide on an issue, which happens to be related to defaults.

c. Simplification

Simplification is a third category of behaviourally savvy intervention. Indeed 'simplify' it is a general behavioural mantra. As Thaler and Sunstein put it, if you want people to do something, make it simple.[82] Simplification carries the potential to promote regulatory goals, by easing participation and providing clearer messages to targeted groups about what they are expected to do.[83] The implementation of simplification measures typically requires a careful observation and direct questioning and understanding of the behaviour of the relevant actors. Simplification is often operationalised through design-driven solutions.[84]

From a legal standpoint, simplification typically involves low-level legal instruments, such as administrative guidance documents requiring forms to be shortened and some information made more salient, official letters to be written in plain language, and red tape cut. Reductions of compliance costs and administrative costs can also be achieved by promoting exchange between administrations in order to avoid duplicating administrative burden for regulatees. In the EU context, this strategy is often implemented by a requirement addressed to Member States to interconnect administrative authorities in order to facilitate compliance with national rules for businesses and professionals based in other Member States.[85]

On a cursory view, based on a simple and purpose-oriented categorisation of policy use of behavioural insights, it appears that there is not always a clear

---

[81] Art XVII. 43. § 2, 3° Economic Code (in force since 1 September 2014) inserted by Law of 28 March 2014, *Moniteur Belge*, 29 April 2014, C-2014/11217, 35204.

[82] Thaler and Sunstein (n 1).

[83] See, eg S Mullainathan, WJ Congdon and JR Kling, *Policy and Choice: Public Finance through the Lens of Behavioral Economics* (Washington DC, Brookings Institution Press, 2011).

[84] The work performed by Katrin Brems Olsen at the Danish Business Authority is particularly pioneering in this regard. See, 'The Vision of the Danish Design Committee 2020' available at danishbusinessauthority.dk/file/301679/vision-danish-design-2020.pdf.

[85] See, eg Directive 2006/123/EC of the European Parliament and of the Council of 12 December 2006 on services in the internal market [2006] OJ L376/36. Art 6 provides for the setting up of points of single contact, whose function is to simplify compliance for businesses: ec.europa.eu/internal_market/eu-go/index_en.htm. More generally, the Internal Market Information System (IMI) enables national administrative bodies to obtain information in their own language from their counterpart from other Member States on a variety of regulatory issues such as recognition of diplomas: ec.europa.eu/internal_market/imi-net/index_en.htm.

correspondence between types of behavioural intervention and legal techniques and little need for novel legal categories. Smart disclosures can be implemented by command and control regulation whose content is smarter than is still often the case. From a technical legal standpoint, what matters is whether disclosure is mandated or not. A behavioural perspective contributes to more effective streamlining of what information must be disclosed and draws attention to the importance of regulating how it must be disclosed but none of this calls for novel legal tools. Smart disclosure can fit into the mandates drawer. Behavioural insights about defaults may have more than one legal translation, essentially substantive rules setting a default—as in the case of organ donation—and procedural rules determining who is to set a default and how.[86] Again, behavioural insights give food for thought about the content of rules and do not call for new types of legal instruments. Simplification corresponds in the legal sphere to an array of administrative practices, which may be regulated by more or less formalised guidance (from guidelines internal to an administration to an EU Directive setting up a network of administrations), but again no novel regulatory technique. Law is and remains low tech[87] and genuine policy innovations such as behaviourally informed public intervention do not translate in a reconstruction of the legal toolbox. This does not mean that the law already does a good job from a behavioural standpoint, only that it is largely by choosing and using existing legal tools differently that the law can do a better job. A caveat concerns techniques for making defaults stick where they can be expected to be vulnerable to corporate strategies. As previously observed, existing legal techniques, at least as currently used, seem ill suited to tackle that problem effectively and legal creativity would be very desirable in this regard.

iii. Regulatory Contexts

In addition to a classification of tools, it is useful to distinguish between regulatory contexts. While we do not purport to have a complete typology of relevant attributes of regulatory contexts, we would like to highlight two dimensions that deserve further attention.[88]

---

[86] An example is the new Belgian Law on Class Actions. The system it institutes for constituting a class is neither opt-in nor opt-out. Rather, the statute provides that it is for the court to determine on a case-by-case basis whether the class will be constituted on an opt-in or opt-out basis. Art XVII. 43. § 2, 3° Economic Code (in force since 1 September 2014) inserted by Law of 28 March 2014, *Moniteur Belge*, 29 April 2014, C-2014/11217, 35204.
[87] AL Sibony, 'Can EU Consumer Law Benefit from Behavioural Insights? An Analysis of the Unfair Practices Directive' in K Mathis (ed), *European Perspectives on Behavioural Law and Economics* (Heidelberg, Springer, 2015) para 5.1.6.
[88] A third important dimension, that we do not explore here, is individual differences in the population targeted by regulation. Heterogeneity with regard to one bias may not be a problem when law only seeks to debias those that do suffer from a bias (Jolls and Sunstein (n 10) 229), but that is not the case of all behaviourally informed regulation. For an early discussion of distributive concerns with debiasing measures, see C Camerer et al, 'Regulation for Conservatives: Behavioral Economics and the Case for "Asymmetric Paternalism"' (2003) 151 *University of Pennsylvania Law Review* 1211, 1211–12. On individual differences, see further A Tor, 'Understanding Behavioral Antitrust' (2014) 92 *Texas Law Review* 573, 608 et seq; A Tor, 'Law for a Behaviorally-Complex World' unpublished manuscript.

The first is the policy impetus behind a policy. In this regard, it is useful to distinguish between two perspectives already mentioned above: the first is that of a public authority which seeks to steer behaviour in the public interest, taking into account one or more existing bias(es) (eg default enrolment for organ donation takes into account inertia bias). We call this pure public nudging. The second perspective is where public authorities react to exploitation of biases by market forces by regulating private nudging. We call this 'counter-nudging'. Pure public nudging is characterised by the intention to either help people correct errors they may be subject to (this is the perspective of debiasing through law) regardless of their exploitative use by market forces or to alter their preferences. The public authority is the initiator and the architect of nudges and citizens are nudged. While pure public nudging never happens in a vacuum and there is always a context to the decisions people make, the perspective is nevertheless somewhat different where public intervention primarily aims at countering active corporate strategies to nudge consumers. In the latter case, the context of decisions has been engeneered to serve business interests and public authorities step in to regulate the corporate activity of context shaping. In such situations, public intervention does not only seek to correct a bias that (some) people may have; it seeks to counter active corporate exploitation of such biases. In the behavioural law jargon, which builds on the terminology of law and economics, counter-nudging is said to be justified by the existence of a 'behavioural market failure',[89] a 'fourth type of market failure'.[90] A case in point is the prohibition of pre-ticked boxes previously mentioned.[91] In this example, the commonly-used commercial strategy of pre-ticking boxes is designed to leverage inertia bias. Legislation prohibiting pre-ticked boxes directly aims at avoiding this form of exploitation of inertia bias and constitutes an example of counter-nudging.

The distinction between pure public nudging and counter-nudging, while possibly not absolute, seems helpful on two counts. First, when discussing legitimacy concerns about behavioural public intervention, it makes sense to reserve a different treatment to 'pure' government influence on people on the one hand and to government regulation of private influence on the other. These two strands of nudging may resort to the same regulatory techniques, but, from a normative point of view, should not be held to the same standard of scrutiny. One reason is because they are supported by different justifications and, consequently, raise different objections. Where consumers are confronted with avoidable framing effect, such as those abusively used by market operators to boost sales, it is possible to make a case for intervention not only on welfare grounds (people are better off

---

[89] O Bar-Gill, *Seduction by Contract, Law Economics, and Psychology in Consumer Markets* (Oxford, Oxford University Press, 2012).
[90] M Bennet et al, *What Behavioural Economics Means for Competition Policy* (UK Office of Fair Trading, March 2010) 2. The first three types of market failures, which classically justify public intervention, are: information asymetry, externalities and public goods. However, there are richer classifications of market failures (including market power, missing markets, incomplete markets and inequalities).
[91] See n 53.

drinking less soda) but also in the name of autonomy. Autonomy is about letting people choose in a meaningful manner. In our view, taking choice seriously is not only about formal freedom of choice between options whose features, number and complexity are designed by private operators in their commercial interest. Streamlining choice can help make choice more mindful and more meaningful. As is now well known, too much choice makes people unhappy.[92] We do not deny that a certain idea of welfare comes into play at the stage of deciding how to streamline individual choices. Our point is that there is another dimension to the discussion, one that could appeal to those who promote choice as a value.[93] Where, by contrast, public intervention does not seek to compensate for some private influence on choice, the rationale is only to enhance welfare. There will of course be disagreements about the legitimacy of behavioural intervention depending on value jugdements and the weight attributed respectively to autonomy and to welfare. Our point is only to say that disagreements can be usefully articulated using the distinction between pure public nudging and regulation of private nudging. In our view, pure public nudging, which can only be justified on welfare arguments and not on choice arguments, should be subject to a stricter scrutiny than counter-nudging.[94]

Second, pure public nudging and counter-nudging may well call for different uses of behavioural insights in law-making. While pure public nudging can be implemented through administrative practices and does not always require legislation, regulation of private nudging, even when behaviourally informed, tends to take the form of classic command and control rules. This suggests that consideration of behavioural insights in policy-making and, in particular, rule design may take different forms according to the regulatory context but also to the regulatory intent. It is the aim pursued by the action—attempting to neutralise a bias or countering its exploitative use by the market—that determines the legal treatment of the behaviourally inspired intervention. Another dimension of regulatory context that calls further exploration is the position of possibly biased actors in the regulatory process. These actors include in particular experts—who play a key role in EU regulation[95]—policymakers themselves,[96] and may also involve judges.[97]

---

[92] B Schwarz, *The Paradox of Choice: Why More is Less* (New York, Harper Perennial, 2004).
[93] In a different context (that of global antitrust), see NW Averitt and RH Lande, 'Using the "Consumer Choice" Approach to Antitrust Law' (2007) 74 *Antitrust Law Journal* 175; RH Lande, 'Consumer Choice as the Best Way to Recenter the Mission of Competition Law' in Academic Society for Competition Law, *Common Ground for International Competition Law* (Edward Elgar, 2010); P Nihoul, 'Freedom of Choice: The Emergence of a Powerful Concept in European Competition Law' (2012) 3 *Revue Concurrences* 55.
[94] On this issue (not this distinction), see in this volume ch 4 by A van Aaken, 'Judge the Nudge: In Search of the Legal Limits of Paternalistic Nudging in the EU'.
[95] See in this volume ch 5 by O Perez, 'Can Experts be Trusted and what Can be Done About It? Insights from the Biases and Heuristics Literature'.
[96] See in this volume ch 6 'Overcoming Illusions of Control: How to Nudge and Teach Regulatory Humility' by CA Dunlop and C Radaelli.
[97] To our knowledge, no study has been conducted with EU judges or national judges in the context of applying EU Law. However, research conducted in the US almost surely would prove relevant as the

II. A EUROPEAN PERSPECTIVE

To date, most scholarly discussions about behaviourally informed intervention are either set in either a US or a UK context or framed in general terms, so that they have global relevance. The European Union (EU) is scarcely mentioned at all.[98] In fact, Europe is doubly absent from the emerging behavioural regulation scene: both as a regulatory power and as a subject of study for law and behavioural studies. As a (mass) producer of regulation, the EU is as yet making scarce use of behavioural insights. Besides a few isolated initiatives displaying some behavioural consideration (eg revised Tobacco Products Directive,[99] Consumer Information Regulation,[100] behavioural advertising,[101] guidance on the Unfair Commercial Practices Directive,[102] occasional behavioural remedies in competition law,[103] and

---

core insights are linked to psychology and not to law. See, eg JJ Rachlinski, 'How Judges Make Decisions' in RWM Giard (ed), *Judicial Decision Marking in Civil Law: Determinants, Dynamics and Delusions* (The Hague, Eleven International Publishing, 2012) 87; JJ Rachlinski, AJ Wistrich and C Guthrie, 'Probability, Probable Cause, and the Hindsight Bias' (2011) 8 *Journal of Empirical Legal Studies* 72.

[98] When Europe is mentioned, this reference generally boils down to a tribute to the UK's pioneering experience with the Behavioural Insights Team. For a cursory mention of European energy labels, see Sunstein and Reisch (n 57) and M Vandebergh, A Carrico and L Schultz, 'Regulation in the Behavioral Era' (2011) 95 *Minnesota Law Review* 715. For an exploration in the specific EU context and on a core issue of EU law, see JU Franck and K Purnhagen, 'Homo Economicus, Behavioural Sciences, and Economic Regulation: On the Concept of Man in Internal Market Regulation and its Normative Basis' in K Mathis (ed), *Law and Economics in Europe: Foundations and Applications* (Dordrecht, Springer, 2014) 329.

[99] In particular Art 9 of Directive 2014/40/EU of the European Parliament and of the Council of 3 April 2014 on the approximation of the laws, regulations and administrative provisions of the Member States concerning the manufacture, presentation and sale of tobacco and related products [2014] OJ L127/1, requires each unit pack and outside packaging of tobacco products to carry general warnings covering 50% of the lateral surfaces (rendered fully visible and salient by a black frame). Moreover, Art10 requires the display of a combined warning (graphic and pictorial) occupying 65% of the two main surfaces of the pack. See A Alemanno, 'Nudging Smokers: The Behavioural Turn of Tobacco Risk Regulation' (2012) *European Journal of Risk Regulation* 32; A Alemanno, 'Out of Sight Out of Mind: Towards a New European Tobacco Products Directive' (2012) 18 *Columbia Journal of European Law* 197.

[100] While falling short of requiring a 'front of the pack' display, the EU Food Information Regulation also requires that the information be legible and presented per 100ml or per 100g. See Regulation 1169/2011 on the provision of food information to consumers [2011] OJ L304/18.

[101] See Comprehensive Standard for Online Behavioural Advertising (OBA), ec.europa.eu/justice/news/consulting_public/0006/contributions/organisations/epc_annex2a_en.pdf.

[102] Commission Staff Working Document, 'Guidance on the Implementation/Application of Directive 2005/29/EC on Unfair Commercial Practices' SEC (2009) 1666, ec.europa.eu/justice/consumer-marketing/files/ucpd_report_en.pdf, 32.

[103] In the *Microsoft* (browser) case, the Commission imposed a choice prompt: users would see a pop up screen that prompted them to choose a browser from among 12 different programmes. The order in which the browsers appeared was randomised. Commission Decision of 16 December 2009, *Microsoft* (tying) (Case COMP/C-3/39.530). The browser choice screen can be seen at: www.browserchoice.eu/BrowserChoice/browserchoice_en.htm. A similar arrangement is currently at the centre of the negotiations between the EU Commission and Google in the framework of investigation. See EU Commission Press Release, 'Antitrust: EU Commission obtains from Google comparable display of specialised rival search engines' Brussels, 4 February 2014, available at europa.eu/rapid/press-release_IP-14-116_en.htm.

consumer rights),[104] the EU has not yet shown a general commitment to integrate behavioural research into policy-making. Given the potential of this regulatory approach to attain effective, low-cost and choice-preserving policies, such a stance seems inadequate, especially when measured against the EU's commitment to smart and evidence-based regulation.[105]

Europe is not only absent as an actor and a producer of behaviourally informed rules. It is also not yet an object of study for law and behavioural sciences scholars, most of whom are based in the United States or in Israel. Clearly, it does not suffice that EU law is accessible in 23 languages, including English, to draw the interest of non-European scholars into how behavioural insights could be used in the specific EU legal context. In order to explore the European dimension and find out whether there are any meaningful differences with other legal contexts, it is necessary to draw more European legal scholars to this field of study and pave the way for a new EU-specific research agenda. There are several reasons why the endeavour is worthy of interest.

A. Comparisons

Some questions, for example 'how much do we value individual choice?' can be posed in similar terms in various jurisdictions. Answers may vary, notably because of differences in political history, thus making comparisons interesting. This alone would justify taking a closer look at Europe, without assuming that US scholarship is entirely relevant or could mechanically be extended to the other side of the Atlantic. In this regard, it is our hope that some contributions in this volume will provide new examples to feed existing discussions—such as the one on the legitimacy of public nudging.

Another instance of variance between the two sides of the Atlantic pertains to the use of the market failure language. While it is almost native English legalese in the US, this is not the case in all European languages and legal cultures. Importing that language to Europe does not seem like a good idea because findings about the behavioural traits of humans are very different from what economists call market failure. Characteristics of human decision-making exist irrespective of markets and can be at work in a variety of non-market contexts relevant to the law.[106] Where participants in a discussion immediately associate 'market failure' with 'justification for intervention', it can make rhetorical sense to connect behavioural insights to the notion of market failures despite the unduly restrictive character

---

[104] In particular art 22 of Directive 2011/83/EU on consumer rights [2011] OJ L304/64, which prohibits the use of pre-ticked boxes on e-commerce websites.
[105] See European Commission, 'Communication on Smart Regulation in the EU' COM (2010) 543 final; for a related and more recent policy espousal, see European Commission, 'Communication on Regulatory Fitness' COM (2012) 746 final.
[106] See in this volume ch 2 by F Di Porto and N Rangone, 'Behavioural Sciences in Practice: Lessons for EU Rulemakers'.

of such language. In Europe, the limited usefulness of such a connection allows scholars to avoid a conceptual confusion.

B. Different Academic Landscapes

Other questions need to be framed differently in Europe and elsewhere, so that it is not the answers, but the questions themselves that can be a meaningful object of comparison. A case in point is the perception of behavioural insights by lawyers. In the US, law and economics has formed part of mainstream legal scholarship for several decades. Not so in Europe.[107] Standard law and economics is still greeted with the sort of scepticism expressed by US legal scholars in the 1980s.[108] As a result, behavioural studies, even if they do take hold in European legal scholarship, will not occupy the same space, simply because that space will not be designed in the same landscape. In the US, the study of interactions between law and behavioural insights was quickly—and understandably, though somewhat ironically—termed 'law and behavioural economics'.[109]

The behavioural turn was—and remains—novel and exciting for lawyers because they had integrated the tale of *homo oeconomicus* as part of a standard scholarly discourse. Empirical findings establishing that this familiar figure was probably not a very helpful proxy for modelling human behaviour called for a revision of an entire body of scholarship. In academia, this justifies excitement. In Europe, legal academia has, by and large, displayed a strong resistance to economic analysis of law, not necessarily through opposition, but through polite marginalisation.[110]

---

[107] E MacKaay, *Law and Economics for Civil Law Systems* (Cheltenham, Edward Elgar, 2013). For an elaboration on EU/US differences in this regard, see K Purnhagen, 'Never the Twain Shall Meet? A Critical Perspective on Cultural Limits between Internal Continental Dogmatism and Consequential US-Style Law and Economics Theory' in K Mathis (ed), *Law and Economics in Europe—Foundations and Applications* (Dordrecht, Springer, 2014) 3.

[108] T Ulen, 'European and American Perspectives on Behavioral Law and Economics' in K Mathis (ed), *European Perspectives on Behavioural Law and Economics, Economic Analysis of Law in European Legal Scholarship*, vol 2 (Zurich, Springer, 2015) 5, fn 4, recalling that, when he first began presenting papers to law faculties in the early 1980s and would begin his presentation by saying that he would be assuming rational choice by decisionmakers, someone would usually ask some version of the question: 'Who are these rational decisionmakers you're talking about?'.

[109] Section I. C. iii. above.

[110] French legal scholarship may be taken as an example. In the relatively few books published to date in France on Economic analysis of law (less than 12 titles, 2 of which are translations of US books), the focus is usually on establishing the legitimacy and the usefulness of the economic approach both in general and in a particular field specifically. French scholars who write in the field in French almost never take it for granted that their readers will know the basic tenets of economic analysis. This is a reasonable assumption since it is rarely taught in law schools. See, eg B Deffains, *L'analyse économique du droit dans les pays de droit civil* (Paris, Éditions Cujas, 2002) (the first edited volume in economic analysis of law in France); G Maître, *La responsabilité civile à l'épreuve de l'analyse économique du droit* (Paris, LGDJ, 2005) (first French PhD in law dealing with civil liability in light of economic analysis). To date, the only textbook of economic analysis of law in French is the work of two authors from Quebec, E Mackaay and S Rousseau, *Analyse économique du droit* (Paris/Montréal, Dalloz-Sirey/Éditions Thémis, 2008). A more advanced textbook, B Deffains and E Langeais, *Analyse économique du droit: Principes, méthodes* (Brussels, De Boeck, 2009), is clearly addressed to economics rather than to law students.

Although the situation is not uniform across countries and despite the fact that a number of European publications, research programmes and university chairs in law and economics could be named, it is nevertheless largely the case that doctrinal approaches dominate the legal academic scene in Europe. This means that behavioural insights are exciting for a significantly smaller proportion of lawyers than in the US. And for those for whom they actually are exciting, their overall impact is epistemically less dramatic. Where lawyers work with an implicit representation of human action based on common sense and intuition, empirical studies showing that humans do not behave like econs will still gather interest. Yet this is more as something any educated person will enjoy bringing to a dinner conversation than as the seeds of a major shift in how law is made and studied.[111]

An additional reason why the selection from behavioural insights that could enrich the regulator toolbox may be different in Europe is because there is no expectation that lessons from psychology should take a detour via law and economics—and its characteristic filtering devices—before reaching the policy-making sphere. The selection of policy-relevant teachings from psychology will be different if it is performed by lawyers with little or no economic background or simply less allegiance to the economic way of framing policy questions. For example, in Europe, far fewer legal scholars than in the US would spontaneously embrace the notion that the ultimate goal of policy-making must consist in 'maximising welfare'. Similarly, they would not assume that people have well defined preferences over a well-defined and very broad set of both product characteristics and social issues. This bears directly on the discussion of whether or not behaviourally informed regulation 'manipulates' choices. Indeed, can choice really be 'distorted' if it has not been clearly formed in the first place? Why would it be acceptable for marketing to shape preferences but not for public intervention? With regards to these two questions, individual opinions vary and are usually affirmed. Despite large individual variations, it is our perception that the intuitive baseline of the average European lawyer is more intervention-friendly than that of her US counterpart and that this may help explain why the debate about behaviourally informed regulation will take a distinct shape in Europe.

The sum of these considerations underpins our endeavour to provide the incipient nudge debate with a European perspective.

---

[111] Ulen (n 108) explains how law is more open than economics to behavioural innovations (5). Our point is related but distinct: we anticipate that behavioural law will be perceived by legal scholars as less innovative in Europe than in the US because their baseline representation of human behaviour is common sense rather than economic rationality. This does not detract from Ulen's point that innovation in legal academia matters less in Europe than in the US because competition between law schools is much milder. Both point to the prediction that, although there are no epistemological obstacles to the penetration of behavioural insights into the sphere of law, behavioural legal studies may be slow to pick up in Europe because incentives are weak (scholars who engage in the pursuit of behavioural studies will be perceived as only moderately innovative and their degree of innovativeness affects their career prospects only moderately).

24 Anne-Lise Sibony and Alberto Alemanno

III. STRUCTURE AND CONTENT OF THE VOLUME

This volume has been structured by taking as a point of departure the current nudging debate, which mainly comprises two strands of enquiry: when is it legitimate for states to use psychology to inform policy? (the legitimacy debate) and, to the extent that it is legitimate, how can behavioural insights in practice be incorporated into the decision-making processes? (the practicability debate). Against this backdrop we brought together scholars who could analyse what behavioural insights might bring to EU law, both at a horizontal level and at a sectoral level. The following chapters endeavour to present the results of their research in a manner that is accessible both to EU law specialists who are not yet familiar with behavioural sciences and to behavioural lawyers who are not specialists in EU law.

Part I focuses on the major challenges brought about by the progressive integration of behavioural sciences into the law by discussing in particular the issues of legitimacy and practicability. In chapter two, Fabiana Di Porto and Nicoletta Rangone offer general lessons to EU policymakers on how to make use of behavioural insights. Chapter three, by Murieann Quigley and Elen Stokes address the challenges of evidence-based policy both from a normative and and from an efficiency standpoint. In chapter four, Anne van Aacken offers a critical perspective on behaviourally informed intervention. She does so by focusing on the inability of such intervention to satisfy the proportionality requirement, which under EU law applies in a variety of contexts to both EU and national measures.

Part II discusses the potential of behavioural sciences, once integrated in the policy process, to debias not only the citizens but also the experts and the policymakers themselves. No less than ordinary people, policymakers as well as experts rely on heuristics and, as a result, are subject to predictable biases.[112] Experts play a very important role in many areas of EU policies and chapter five presents the 'debiasing projects' in relation to them. Oren Perez draws on the available literature and experiments to invite a reflection on whether experts can be trusted and what the EU should do about it. In chapter six, Claire Dunlop and Claudio Radaelli take a behavioural look at regulatory impact assessment, the dominant analytical tool guiding EU policy-making. After providing an insightful analysis on the EU system of impact assessment, they warn about the illusion of control that can bias policymakers.

In Part III, our contributors predict the impact that behavioural sciences may have on specific EU policies: data protection (chapter seven by Eoin Carolan and Alessandro Spina and chapter eight by Frederik Borgesius), consumer protection (chapter nine by Geneviève Helleringer and Anne-Lise Sibony), health law (chapter ten by Alberto Alemanno), financial law (chapter eleven by Pieter Van Cleynenbreugel). We asked our contributors to, first, assess whether there was a place for behavioural insights in their field of study. Second, in the affirmative, to identify the most important reasons why behavioural sciences are relevant to their field

---

[112] Jolls and Sunstein (n 10) 233.

of law. We finally asked them to consider at what stages of policy-making, or the implementation of rules, behavioural insights should be brought to bear. While it has not always been possible to answer these questions with the same degree of detail, the chapters in this part provide some useful elements for comparing the use of behavioural insights in EU regulations across policy areas.

Part IV provides a critical perspective on behavioural informed regulation, by identifying its major flaws, and formulating a few recommendations on how to overcome them. In chapter twelve, Péter Cserne addresses the growing scepticism surrounding the nudge discourse and discusses three major limits that may lessen what EU Law can learn from behavioural sciences. Last but note least, in chapter thirteen, Yuval Feldman and Orly Lobel alert us to the existence of behavioural trade-offs: frequently, more than one behavioural insight may be relevant to a single policy decision. Therefore, to avoid falling into the trap of oversimplification when relying on behavioural insights, dealing with the resulting trade-offs appears as a necessity.

The chapters in this volume are far from speaking with one voice. Their authors are neither unanimously nudge enthusiasts nor nudge sceptics. What unites them is a common interest in understanding more about the legal and policy implications stemming from the emergence of behaviourally informed policy-making. Their reflections identify many challenges that need to be addressed to allow policymakers, administrative authorities and courts in Europe to knowledgeably and responsibly use behavioural insights. In so doing, the sum of the individual chapters collectively reinforces our claim that the study of law and behavioural sciences could have a bright future in Europe. It is by relying on those contributions that the final chapter strives to map out the future research agenda of the emerging behavioural informed policy-making in Europe and beyond.

Part I

Integrating Behavioural Sciences into EU Law-Making

2
Behavioural Sciences in Practice: Lessons for EU Rulemakers

FABIANA DI PORTO AND NICOLETTA RANGONE[*]

I. INTRODUCTION

INSIGHTS FROM COGNITIVE sciences may become a turning point for rule-making theory and practice.[1] By showing how people actually make choices, cognitive sciences enable the formulation of rules that may better address the public interest that they intend to pursue. Therefore, cognitive sciences may contribute to rulemaking by reducing the risk of regulatory failure induced by a lack of consideration of behavioural limitations.[2]

According to this approach, this chapter suggests that in regulatory discourse it is preferable to refer to 'cognitive and behavioural limitations' instead of cognitive errors, and to 'unresponsive behaviours' instead of irrationality and bounded rationality. 'Unresponsive behaviours' indicate behaviours that are 'unresponsive' to traditional regulatory interventions, in the sense that they differ from what regulators expect.[3] These behaviours may be due to 'cognitive and behavioural

---

[*] This chapter has been conceived and structured in common. However, sections II, III, III.A, IV.B, and V.A were written by Nicoletta Rangone, and sections III.B, IV.A, IV.C, and V.B were written by Fabiana Di Porto. Both authors drafted section I.

[1] Rule-making as employed here is to be understood as referring to sources of law approved at political level, as well as administrative provisions adopted by public administrations through discretionary or technical powers and self-regulation, whenever it is delegated by public powers. What interests us here (what is of interest here) is the regulatory 'content', meaning the ability of rules to directly affect regulatees' activity, production, or organisation. Therefore, rule-making includes both legislation-making and (secondary, implementing) regulation-making.

[2] Although we support the idea that behavioural limitations may give rise to some market failures, we do not agree with R Bubb and RH Pildes, 'How Behavioural Economics Trims Its Sails and Why' (2014) 127 *Harvard Law Review* 1603, in qualifying behavioural limitations themselves as a new category of market failure justifying alone regulatory intervention (see also below in text at section II, C).

[3] ibid. Somehow departing from mainstream behavioural economics, we contend that reactions to rules are difficult to predict and identify even when rulemakers are aware of cognitive and behavioural limitations, because of complexity (several different psychological mechanisms can be at work, not all biases and heuristics are equally spread among the population, etc).

limitations', which in turn are not due to irrationality, in the sense that they are part of the normal behaviour of real people, as determined by brain activity and conditioned by heuristics and biases, personal attitudes, emotional and social contexts, culture, morals, institutional environment, and the interactions among them.

This is why insights from cognitive sciences are so relevant for rulemakers. Our contention is that incorporating insights from cognitive sciences into rulemaking should imply that the context of human learning and individual decision-making should be investigated in order to assess the need for a regulatory intervention in the first place.

Moreover, cognitive insights should be taken into account when designing a regulatory response in a particular context. This may require revisiting traditional regulatory tools (to make rulemakers more aware of possible unresponsive behaviours), as well as creating new strategies, that are therefore named 'cognitive-based'. The latter include two typologies: 'nudging' and 'empowerment'. Although both are based on similar cognitive insights, we contend that while 'nudging' is meant to 'exploit' individual emotional responses, 'empowerment' is aimed at enhancing people's capacity to manage and overcome their emotional responses, in order to adopt deliberately conscious decisions.

Moreover, in order to assess future compliance, it is essential to know what reactions any newly introduced regulation will probably trigger in the real world. And this is all the more true in times of economic distress, when regulators can no longer afford regulatory failure, either economically or socially.

The chapter is organised as follows. First (section II), it establishes how the regulatory process should change in order to allow evidence from cognitive sciences to emerge and then use it. Second (section III), it discusses the impact of cognitive sciences on the regulatory toolkit and sets out the emergence of two regulatory strategies that incorporate cognitive insights, namely 'nudging' and 'empowerment'. Sections IV and V describe in greater detail the characteristics of such strategies by providing typologies and examples. Strengths and weaknesses of both strategies are the core focus of section IV; while we conclude (at section V) by providing some guidelines to rulemakers as far as the choice among different regulatory options is concerned.

II. COGNITIVE-BASED APPROACH TO THE REGULATORY PROCESS

Cognitive findings about unresponsive behaviours constitute a turning point for rulemaking. As a result, the latter is expected to change in order to let cognitive and behavioural limitations emerge, to use findings about them to avoid regulatory failures and, more generally, to adopt more effective regulations. A cognitive-based approach to regulation imposes a radical change in the rulemaking process and consequently an increase in costs and time. Therefore, these changes should be justified (and necessary) only where there is a 'behavioural element' to a regulated area,[4] and where such an element is relevant (eg considering the number of people involved or the magnitude of consequences of their limited cognitive capacity). A behavioural element can be said to exist, and cognitive findings are crucial, in two cases: first, whenever the main objective of regulation is a change of individual behaviour (such as food or energy consumption practices, household-waste recycling, transport habits, etc); second, anytime people's behavioural response might hinder the effectiveness of a given regulation (eg information disclosure mandates in stock market regulations are often implemented through long prospectuses that individual investors hardly process or understand).

That said, for the regulatory process to improve, an effort should be made to incorporate cognitive insights into almost all of its phases. Elaborating on the Organisation for Economic Cooperation and Development's (OECD) guidance[5] and on the life-cycle doctrine on policy-making and rulemaking,[6] we suggest the following comprehensive phases for rulemaking: definition of the problem; analysis of the baseline;[7] identification of the objectives; definition of alternative and feasible policy options; evaluation of potential impacts of different policy options (eventually assessed through an RIA); collection of information; reason giving; enforcement; and maintenance (monitoring and revision or abrogation) of the adopted regulation. In the following, we discuss those phases where we deem it useful for regulators to incorporate cognitive findings in the rulemaking process.

A. Problem Definition

At the earliest stage, the 'definition of the problem' phase is where cognitive insights are crucial. In this phase regulators might want to question whether an existing regulation (the baseline, eg regulation mandating banks to assess customers' risk profiles before investing in securities) did not attain its goals and have led to unresponsive behaviours (eg low income low risk investors keep authorising banks to invest in risky activities), because of regulatees' cognitive and behavioural limitations. In an unregulated area, where there is no baseline, rule-makers might still take advantage of knowing to what extent individuals' cognitive and behavioural limitations affect a given social problem, before deciding whether to intervene or not.

---

[4] See also R van Bavel et al, *Applying Behavioural Sciences to EU Policy-Making*, JRC Scientific and Policy Reports (Luxembourg, Publications Office of the European Union, 2013) 6.

[5] See OECD, *Reference Checklist for Regulatory Decision-Making* (Paris, 1995); OECD, *Guiding Principles for Regulatory Quality and Performance* (Paris, 2005); OECD, *Recommendation of the Council on Regulatory Policy and Governance* (Paris, 2012).

[6] M Howlett and M Ramesh, *Studying Public Policy: Policy Cycles and Policy Subsystems* (Oxford, Oxford University Press, 1995); A La Spina and G Majone, *Lo Stato regolatore* (Bologna, Il Mulino, 2000) 103.

[7] Meaning how the defined problem is likely to develop in the future if no new regulation is adopted.

B. Analysis of the Baseline

Then, when 'analysing the baseline' in regulated areas, the socio-cultural-emotional context of the target population should also be considered. Here, a cognitive-based approach (such as behavioural or neuroscience experiments) would be of special help to clarify how to draft a new regulation (if at all necessary). Where a regulation already exists, such an approach could be useful to understand what went wrong, so as to segment the target population and tease out the groups that were unresponsive to the regulatory intervention. This analysis should be preceded by a literature review on end-users' habits, needs and feelings, characteristics (eg whether they are firms or individuals, expert or naïf, etc) and the social context, a preliminary phase which might help to understand the target population and contribute to the better design of a cognitive experiment.

C. Objectives

The 'identification of the objectives' that regulators want to attain is a step that should remain their prerogative. By this, we mean that the public interest regulation grasps should never coincide with the aim of preventing or avoiding unresponsive behaviours themselves; or, put in other words, the very presence of such limitations should not per se constitute a market failure justifying regulatory intervention. It follows that only if limitations are so widespread in the target population, that they can cause regulation to fail achieving its goals, can rulemakers give room to cognitive and behavioural considerations.

D. Policy Options

The 'definition of alternative and feasible policy options', that is the phase where rulemakers identify possible strategies to tackle the problem (including the option not to intervene), might also benefit from a cognitive approach. These options might consist of traditional regulatory tools (such as command and control, disclosure, 'public tutoring' and incentive regulation),[8] which might be 'revisited' to include consideration for cognitive and behavioural limitations. However, these options might also include two new strategies, which bear a 'cognitive DNA' (as will be discussed later, section III).

---

[8] On this point, see further F Di Porto and N Rangone, 'Cognitive-Based Regulation: New Challenges for Regulators?' (2013) 20 *federalismi.it* 6.

E. Evaluation of Potential Impacts

In a smart regulatory process, the impacts of different policy options should always be considered and assessed in a specific regulatory impact assessment (RIA), or analysed without it (see below at F). Indeed, targeting RIA precisely to evaluate in advance the potential impacts of rules, knowledge about cognitive and decisional processes of regulatees should improve rulemakers' knowledge.

Moreover, the comparison between different policy options and the doing nothing option[9] might be useful in order to avoid any over-estimation of the costs of unresponsive behaviours[10] and the resulting need to correct them through regulation (which, according to some critics, could end up justifying over-regulation).[11] Such a comparison might also avoid any under-estimation of the costs of a cognitive-based regulation in terms, for instance, of individual liberty limitation.[12] However, in order to fulfil this role, RIA should evolve both in terms of information gathering and of evaluating the impacts of rules. Indeed, when based on a cost-benefit analysis, RIA tends to assume that end-users are rational self-interested maximisers. Otherwise, an analysis should be used, which assesses end-users' biases or unexpected behaviours in terms of probability and effects. The result of such an assessment could help rulemakers decide whether or not to deal with biases through regulation, and to identify a 'minimum threshold' which justifies regulatory intervention.[13] This threshold of course does not correspond to the simple presence of the risk of unresponsive behaviours, but to those risks that regulators had considered as unacceptable.[14]

---

[9] See ch 6, CA Dunlop and CM Radaelli, 'Overcoming Illusions of Control: How to Nudge and Teach Regulatory Humility', in this volume.

[10] According to JD Wright and DH Ginsburg, 'Behavioral Law and Economics: Its Origins, Fatal Flaws, and Implications for Liberty' (2012) 106 *Northwestern University Law Review* 1033, 1041, behavioural law and economics scholars would have failed to consider that regulation has its own costs, that might overcome the benefit produced in a reduction in the rate of errors. In the authors' view, these scholars tend to overestimate the social costs of errors and therefore are urged to intervene through regulation by the mere identification of systematic decision errors. Moreover, such scholars would tend to ignore the social benefit of errors, meaning the knowledge derived from experience, which in the long run could generate a reduction in errors.

[11] On Obama's 're-regulation' of the financial sector following the crisis, see eg A Ferguson, 'Nudge Nudge, Wink Wink. Behavioral Economics—The Governing Theory of Obama's Nanny State' 105 *The Weekly Standard*, 19 April 2010.

[12] Wright and Ginsburg, 'Behavioral Law and Economics' (n 10) 1041.

[13] H Pildes and CR Sunstein, 'Reinventing the Regulatory State' (1995) 62 *University of Chicago Law Review* 43.

[14] Although evidence shows that most minors are affected by conformism that encourages them to start smoking, regulators should not intervene on this ground, but rather only if their goal is to reduce smoking among the youngest. On the difficulties to find the relevant threshold, see CR Sunstein, 'The Real World of Cost-Benefit: Thirty-Six Questions (and Almost as Many Answers)' (2013) 13 Harvard Public Law Working Paper 2; for discussion on the right selection of biases to assess, see R Baldwin, M Cave and M Lodge, *Understanding Regulation. Theory, Strategy, and Practice*, 2nd edn (Oxford, Oxford University Press, 2012) 283ff.

A comparison between the status quo and a cognitive-based rule should always be performed in rulemaking, even when RIA is not used. Indeed, using a randomly assigned control group (RCT) might partially compensate for the lack of RIA.[15] RCT is intended to measure the effectiveness of a given regulatory option by testing it on a 'treatment group' of the target population. Its results are then compared with what happened to a control group, which has not been treated (corresponding to the 'doing-nothing option' in RIA jargon).[16]

F. Collection of Information

One of the most important challenges for cognitive-based rulemaking is to enrich the way information is collected. Where there is a 'behavioural element' to a regulated area, the information gathering might start through a literature review on emotional reactions to a given issue, on social norms, or other environmental elements which might shape individual decision-making. This step could help in the design of more effective consultations (through surveys, notices and comments, panels, semi-structured interviews, and focus groups). Indeed, stakeholders' consultations should be organised in such a way as to pinpoint potential unresponsive behaviours and (where necessary) carried out with the help of behavioural science experts. For instance, in order to evaluate the role of inertia and procrastination in the low switching rate in energy retail markets,[17] those consulted could be consumers and not suppliers. For example, the former should be asked about their knowledge of their own consumption rates and related costs; if they have ever switched providers in other markets (if they have saved money, and if they have then checked the continuing benefit of this choice); if they are aware of alternative offers and how they heard of them, etc.

If literature reviews and consultations do not provide sound information about the risks of unresponsiveness, a cognitive experiment (with or without a randomised control trial),[18] could be conducted in order to gain a better understanding of how people act, think or feel. A number of different types of experiments might be used. The most commonly used in rulemaking are behavioural experiments

---

[15] While RIA, as known, compares the foreseen effects of all feasible policy alternatives, RCT is used to assess the potential effectiveness of one regulatory intervention at a time. Therefore, RCT may be less complete and provide limited empirical evidence than RIA; however, it may still help to improve the empirical robustness of an impact assessment whenever RIA is not performed for any reasons.

[16] L Haynes et al, *Test, Learn, Adapt: Developing Public Policies with Randomised Control Trials*, Cabinet Office Behavioural Insights Team (2012). See also van Bavel et al, *Applying Behavioural Sciences* (n 4) 14ff.

[17] OFGEM (Office of Gas and Electricity Markets), *What Can Behavioural Economics Say about GB Energy Consumers?* (21 March 2011).

[18] Haynes et al (n 16) 4; M Abramowicz, I Ayres, and Y Listokin, 'Randomizing Law' (2011) 159 *University of Pennsylvania Law Review* 929.

(laboratory or online), where the behaviour of two groups of people are compared, only one of which being exposed to a given regulatory option. Otherwise, the behaviour of the same group of people might be measured at two points in time, before and after being exposed to such an intervention. As far as neuroscience experiments are concerned, brain imaging methods (eg magnetic resonance imagining or eye-tracking) could also be used in rulemaking.[19]

G. Reason Giving

Where cognitive-based experiments have been performed to inform the regulatory process, regulations should give reasons for why they took into account (or not) the results of experiments that were conducted. For instance, this should include the type of experiment and choice made during the experiment (sample, number of 'treatments',[20] reasons why an RCT has been used or not). All of this information and the gathered scientific evidence might also be mentioned in a non-technical summary, in order to be thoroughly accessible. However, this information and behavioural studies are not *the final decision* and they are only intended to enrich evidence for a more effective final decision,[21] while regulators should justify any inconsistency with such evidence.

H. Maintenance

Finally, the monitoring and ex post evaluation of regulation should enable rulemakers to check if a given cognitive-based rule was really justified, and if it was the result of a good balance between the aim either to overcome or deal with end-users' limited cognitive capacity, and individuals' freedom.

So far, we have discussed how the rulemaking process should change in order to include evidence of cognitive and behavioural limitations and of unresponsive behaviours. The section has shown that most phases of this process would benefit a lot from considering behavioural evidence, with the notable exception of the regulatory objectives, the definition of which should only barely be affected. Now we move on to consider how cognitive insights impact on the regulatory strategies. Once regulation is the selected mode of policy intervention, we claim

---

[19] On the contribution that neuroscientific insights might provide to public policies in the context of consumer and health protection, see Centre d'Analyse Stratégique, *Improving Public Health Prevention with Behavioural, Cognitive and Neuroscience* (supervised by O Oullier and S Sauneron) (Paris, 2010).
[20] Meaning the regulatory options that are tested throughout the experiment.
[21] On the issue of generalisation of findings of a non-representative sample, see van Bavel et al, *Applying Behavioural Sciences* (n 4) 19.

that cognitive-based strategies should also be included in the regulatory toolkit as viable alternatives.

III. COGNITIVE-BASED STRATEGIES

The bursting onto the scene of cognitive sciences has contributed to the emergence of new regulatory strategies, that we suggest to name 'cognitive-based', provided that consideration is given to biases and heuristics, emotional and socio-cultural contexts, and neuroscientific insights into behaviour.

A caveat. So far and in the following pages, we have dealt and will only deal with 'regulatory' cognitive-based strategies. This means that we only analyse tools aimed at modifying individuals' behaviour which have been introduced by rules (irrespective of the source, which can be the law, governmental decisions or administrative regulation), thus excluding other public policies, such as choice architecture, that are not introduced through rules.

This rather recent form of regulatory action, includes 'nudging' and 'empowerment'. Although they have some features in common, for example neither is based on financial incentives,[22] both are said to leave freedom of choice untouched and not to be too expensive; nevertheless, we suggest that they should be distinguished. On the one hand, only cognitive-based regulatory strategies, which are meant to exploit, often in an undisclosed manner, the emotional responses of individuals should count as 'true' nudging.[23] On the other hand, empowerment tools are aimed at enhancing people's capacity to manage emotional responses and to adopt deliberately conscious decisions.[24] Therefore, nudge strategies are bias-preserving, while empowerment tools are truly de-biasing techniques.

The difference between nudging and empowerment might be clearer considering the two pictures below (Figure 1). An example of a nudge towards more physical activity (and ultimately, better health) could be a rule which obliges builders to make stairs in public buildings more attractive, over the escalators or elevators, for instance by transforming them into a piano keyboard which plays when stepped on (left picture in Figure 1).[25]

---

[22] See also L Bovens, 'Real Nudge' (2012) 1 *European Journal of Risk Regulation* 43.

[23] In the same vein is L Bovens' qualification of nudge (as opposed, in his work, to social advertisement) where 'some pattern of irrationality is being exploited'. This is why this tool typically works better in the dark: L Bovens, 'The Ethics of Nudge' in T Grune-Yanoff and SO Hansson (eds), *Preference Change: Approaches from Philosophy, Economics and Psychology* (Berlin and New York, Springer, 2008) 207. See also below (section VI, A).

[24] See also ch 13, Y Feldman and O Lobel, 'Behavioural Trade-offs: Beyond the Land of Nudges Spans the World of Law and Psychology', in this volume.

[25] The experiment shown in the picture was performed, among others, in Odenplan metro station in Stockholm in 2009: see www.thefuntheory.com/piano-staircase.

Behavioural Sciences in Practice 37

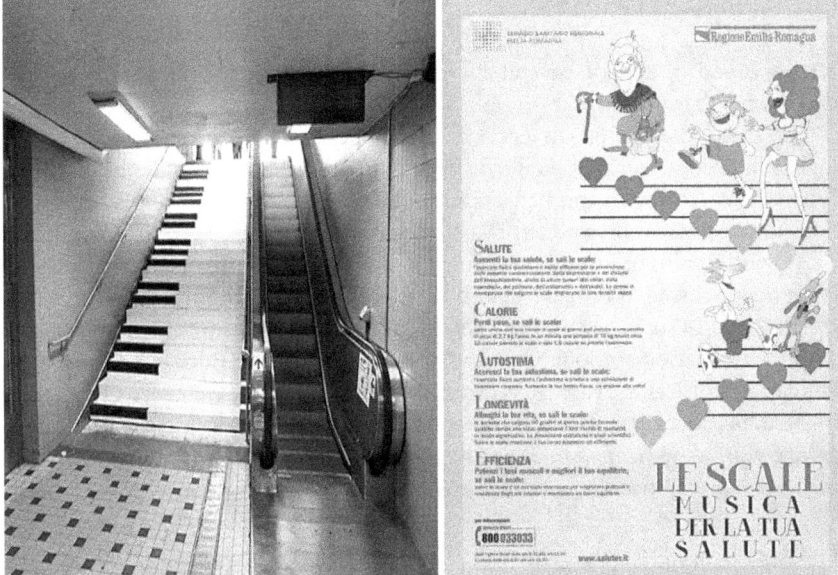

Figure 1: *Nudging v empowerment*

Differently from the piano staircase, the picture on the right-hand side shows a poster providing a quite similar message: 'Stairs. Music for your health'. Therefore, both tools are aimed at achieving the same goal that is, let more people use stairs instead of lifts.[26] However, the poster (an example of empowerment) simplifies medical information about healthy activities and, unlike the former nudge, requires people to read and to engage in an effort of self-education to overcome laziness, procrastination and inertia.

We now move onto examining the characters of each of the two strategies.

A. Nudging

Below, nudge strategies are classified in three main categories and exemplified through implementation in different fields.

i. Default Rules

'A default rule ... specifies the outcome in a given situation if people make no choice at all'.[27] Where opt-out is simple and essentially costless, this strategy can

---

[26] The second figure shows a (Ministry of Health-sponsored) poster displayed at the bottom of stairs and escalators of all Italian hospitals in the Emilia Romagna Region.

[27] Office of Information and Regulatory Affairs (OIRA), *Disclosure and Simplification as Regulatory Tools* (18 June 2010) 9.

have a significant effect on behaviour[28] and can make regulation effective in many regulated areas (such as health care, consumer protection, the availability of human organs,[29] energy use and environmental protection,[30] mortgages, savings, and many other topics).[31]

The great potential effectiveness of this tool is threefold. First, defaults exploit inertia in order to nudge people to choose something considered better for them. Secondly, it creates an implicit endorsement over a given choice, which people tend to consider to be selected because helpful or appropriate.[32] Thirdly, where the potential gains or losses of making a choice are unclear, accepting the default is often the preferred option, because it costs nothing in time and effort.[33]

Therefore, in some contexts the default rule can promote automatic compliance with the regulation,[34] though not always, nor in every situation. In order to make regulation more effective, it is not sufficient to consider the existence of inertia or to introduce an easy and costless opt-out system: cognitive response is not universal and should be verified in a specific relevant market and in relation to different individual preferences.[35]

ii. Smart Information Nudging

Using knowledge about framing and salience, rulemakers can draft smart information nudge strategies. In such schemes, data is provided in a 'relational' way, as it includes comparisons and unspoken assessments in order to orientate behaviours by leveraging the emotional spheres of end-users (ie the 'tell people what others are doing' strategy). For instance, in many North American cities, energy saving has significantly increased by sending out personalised statements about energy use, rating people on their energy use compared with that of neighbours in 100 homes of similar size where the same heating fuel was used, and also compared with the 20 neighbours who were especially energy efficient (see Figure 2).[36]

---

[28] For an application in retirement savings plans, see S Benartzi and R Thaler, 'Save More Tomorrow: Using Behavioral Economics to Increase Employee Saving' (2004) 112 *Journal of Political Economy* S164.

[29] EJ Johnson and D Goldstein, 'Do Default Save Lives?' (2003) 302 *Science* 1338.

[30] D Pichert and KV Katsikopoulos, 'Green Defaults: Information Presentation and Pro-Environmental Behavior' (2008) 28 *Journal of Environmental Psychology* 63.

[31] CR Sunstein, 'Impersonal Default Rules vs Active Choices vs Personalized Default Rules: A Triptych' (2012) 17 Regulatory Policy Program Working Paper 11.

[32] OIRA, *Disclosure* (n 27) 9.

[33] Sunstein, 'Impersonal Default Rules' (n 31).

[34] CR Sunstein, 'Empirically Informed Regulation' (2011) 78 *University of Chicago Law Review* 1349, 1398.

[35] Moreover, on this ground, differentiated default rules (ie based on different abilities to opt-out, eventually grouped by geographical areas or people's past choices) might be taken into consideration by rulemakers (see Sunstein, 'Impersonal Default Rules' (n 31)).

[36] Tax collection provides a similar example. An experiment performed in the UK involving 100,000 taxpayers with overdue bills, half of whom received letters where the request for payment was accompanied by other messages, the most effective of which turned out to be that the recipient who had not yet paid was in the minority ('Lessons from Behavioural Economics Can Boost Tax Compliance', *The Economist*, 24 May 2014).

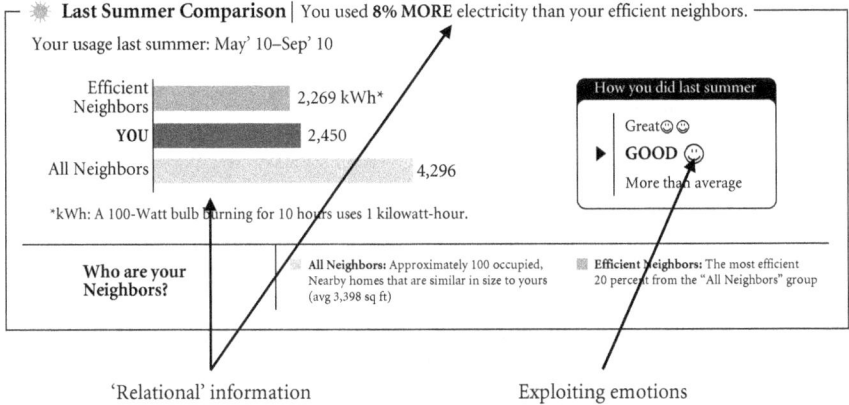

Figure 2: An example of smart information nudging
Source: Opower, City of Pasadena 2014.

Here, social influence (or the perceived behaviour of peers) is used to push householders to consume less energy (making people envious of their neighbours' energy consumption rates),[37] as it has been proven that perception of the norm in the pertinent community can affect human behaviour more than traditional regulation.[38] This tool is not intended just to over-simplify information given to consumers (as with empowerment, on which see below section III.B.i); rather, the data provided is limited to what can be used to influence behaviour. In the energy bill example, only the information about peers (ie the social proof) represents a nudge, because it is empirically demonstrated that this piece of information (and not other) can modify one's habits by exploiting his/her conformism. Moreover, by the use of coloured columns in Figure 2 to compare one's energy consumption with that of others, data is not only simplified and standardised, so as to let consumers understand what their consumption rates are (as in empowerment), but also framed to be salient and eye-catching in order to reinforce the 'do what others are doing' effect. Many are the examples of this kind showing that nudging—unlike empowerment—relies on one bias (conformism in the energy letter example)[39] to 'offset' other biases (eg procrastination or inertia).[40]

The main benefit of this strategy is that it requires nearly no effort in terms of enforcement, while usually ensuring high rates of compliance.[41] However, special attention must be given to designing such nudge strategies, as they might produce

---

[37] L Kaufman, 'Utilities Turn Their Customers Green, With Envy', *The New York Times*, 31 January 2012.
[38] RB Cialdini, *Influence. Science and Practice*, 5th edn (Boston, Pearson, 2008) 109.
[39] PW Schultz et al, 'The Constructive, Destructive and Reconstructive Power of Social Norms' (2007) 18 *Psychological Science* 429.
[40] R Korobkin, 'Libertarian Welfarism' (2009) 97 *California Law Review* 1676 and AE Carlson, 'Recycling Norms' (2001) 89 *California Law Review* 1231.
[41] Sunstein, 'Empirically Informed Regulation' (n 34) 1349.

a 'boomerang effect', in terms of undesirable reactions of people who have already adopted the desired behaviour above the average (eg people who save energy above the average might start to 'let their use creep up above the average').[42] Behavioural insights show that this effect can be neutralised by adding a message indicating social approval or disapproval (eg through a positive or negative emoticon, as in the right side of Figure 2).[43]

Another possible 'boomerang effect' in designing a nudge is to highlight the behaviour regulators want to prevent or limit. For instance, the attempt to mobilise action against a problem (tax evasion) may suggest drafting a message which depicts it as regrettably frequent and in so doing regulators end up communicating that 'many people *are* doing this'. In other words, the behaviour, which is to be curtailed is in fact being highlighted inducing salience and imitation.[44]

iii. Exploiting/Neutralising Emotional Responses

Another nudge strategy seeks to influence end-users' choices by exploiting their emotional responses (sometimes by neutralising them, as in the 'plain package' example explained below) in order to achieve effects on individual behaviour.

The Framework Convention on Tobacco Control (FCTC) suggests a standardisation of tobacco product packaging (the so-called plain or generic packaging) with the only remaining possibility being to print brand and product names (displayed in a standard colour and font style), the quantity of the product, health warnings and other mandatory information.[45] This nudge towards lower consumption works by neutralising tobacco's appeal through a standardisation of the appearance of all cigarette boxes.[46] At the same time, the cigarette box surface can be used in another way to nudge, that is, by exploiting emotional responses through the use of macabre images of sick people[47] (as experimented in Australia since 2012).

---

[42] S Rahim, 'Finding the "Weapons" of Persuasion to Save Energy', *The New York Times*, 21 June 2010.
[43] Schultz et al, 'The Constructive, Destructive' (n 39) 429ff.
[44] RB Cialdini, 'Crafting Normative Messages to Protect the Environment' (2003) 12 *Current Direction in Psycological Science* 105.
[45] World Health Organization (WHO), *Guidelines for Implementation of Article 11 of the Framework Convention on Tobacco Control, Packaging and Labeling of Tobacco Products* (November 2008) pnt 46. In Europe, see DG SANCO's Impact Assessment, *Assessing the Impacts of Revising the Tobacco Products Directive (No 2001/37/EC)* (September 2010). For comments, see A Alemanno and E Bonadio, 'Do You Mind My Smoking? Plain Packaging of Cigarettes under TRIPS Agreement' (2011) 10 *John Marshall Review of Intellectual Property Law* 451.
[46] On the drawbacks of using nudging in anti-tobacco policies, see A Alemanno, 'Nudging Smokers. The Behavioural Turn of Tobacco Risk Regulation' (2012) 3 *European Journal of Risk Regulation* 32.
[47] According to R Baldwin, 'From Regulation to Behaviour Change: Giving Nudge the Third Degree' (2014) *MLR* (forthcoming) 6, this nudge makes 'use of the level of emotional power' to manipulate regulatees' actions by substituting their preferences with those of the regulator.

While plain package is a nudge that *neutralises* the emotional response attached to a brand[48] (it is a social norm to buy cigarettes because their branded boxes are perceived as 'cool' or 'sophisticated'),[49] pictorial warnings are nudges that *exploit* fear and emotional responses to induce healthy behaviours.[50]

B. Empowerment

Empowerment[51] uses rules to tackle cognitive limitations in an aim to prevent or help individuals overcoming biases, so as to allow them to take considerate decisions. It does so by framing information in a standardised[52] or super-simplified way (subsections i and ii), or by using targeted education (subsection iii), or by simplifying individuals' choice itself (subsection iv), or by helping end-users to override their emotional responses (subsection v).[53]

Empowerment tools are to be included among cognitive-based strategies in that they are based on empirical evidence of substantial and diffused cognitive and behavioural limitations that have led traditional regulation to fail. For instance, in healthcare, 'informed consent' has been replaced by 'patient empowerment', based

---

[48] On the importance of brands and the emotional responses attached to them, see SM McClure et al, 'Neural Correlates of Behavioral Preference for Culturally Familiar Drinks' (2004) 44 *Neuron* 379, and N Dawar and PM Parker, 'Marketing Universals: Consumers' Use of Brand Name, Price, Physical Appearance and Retailer Reputation as Signals of Product Quality' (1995) 58 *Journal of Marketing* 81.

[49] In Bovens' words ('Real Nudge' (n 22) 44) 'social norm enforcement through conformity' is a nudge that exploits 'the common psychological disposition to conform to social norms'.

[50] In this we dissent from Bovens (ibid, 43) who sees 'scare tactics' as 'nannying intervention' and not as nudging.

[51] J Geller et al, 'A National Survey of Consumer Empowerment at the State Level' (1998) 49 *Psychiatric Services* 498; M Nardo et al, *The Consumer Empowerment Index. A Measure of Skills, Awareness and Engagement of European Consumers*, JRC Scientific and Technical Reports, no EUR 24791 EN (11 June 2011).

[52] Empowerment tools based on information differ from traditional disclosure mandates in that they are based on evidence about cognitive and behavioural limitations (as discussed further in the text). Therefore, standardisation is an empowerment tool anytime its introduction is preceded by an analysis of individuals' decisional capabilities, and these insights are used in order to tease the 'really informative' piece of information to be standardised. This happened, eg in the Commission, 'Report on Consumer Decision-Making in Retail Investment Services: A Behavioural Economics Perspective' (November 2010) (ec.europa.eu/consumers/strategy/docs/final_report_en.pdf). Of course, this does not say much about the ability of standardisation to empower investors or consumers to take the most deliberately conscious decisions.

[53] Empowerment, as we define it, can be largely assimilated to 'second degree nudge' identified by R Baldwin, 'From Regulation to Behaviour Change: Giving Nudge the Third Degree' (n 47). Feldman and Lobel, 'Behavioral Tradeoffs' (n 24) would probably include empowerment in tools aimed at 'shifting decision-making from System 2 to System 1', ie in encouraging deliberation to correct intuitive decisions. We prefer not to refer to the simplistic vision of a 'System 1 vs System 2' way of functioning of our brain, provided that the latter has been recently challenged by cognitive psychologists and neuroscientists providing a more complex model, where partitions are more than just two and a set of interactions is possible, shaping our decision-making and behavioural processes. See SM Kosslyn and GW Miller, *Top Brain, Bottom Brain: Surprising Insights into How You Think* (New York, Simon & Schuster, 2013).

on the inability of the former to attain better self-selected health choices;[54] in some newly liberalised markets, codes of commercial conduct and their disclosure obligations failed to increase consumers' activism;[55] complexity in long-lasting financial relationships has made clear the failure of many of the existing disclosure mandates;[56] energy efficient purchasing behaviour is still far from being reached, despite the many information campaigns run by the state.[57]

Empowerment rests on the idea that individuals depart from considered choices because they are not aware, informed, or educated enough to act reasonably. Biases leading to misjudgements can be overcome and regulation (based on empirical evidence) be used in order to select what information should be provided (and how it should be presented), as well as how education to raise awareness and, possibly, reasonable action should be structured.

The theory on which empowerment strategies rest is therefore still attached to the accounts of rational choice, which *do* accept violations of, or deviations from conventional rationality, and assume that decisionmakers *can learn to overcome and correct* such deviations, by giving them the right opportunities, information and data.[58] Because empowerment tools are aimed at overcoming cognitive and behavioural limitations,[59] they, rather than nudging tools, can be understood as 'true' *de-biasing techniques*,[60] as opposed to nudge strategies that exploit biases.[61]

---

[54] On this issue, see subsection iii below.

[55] See, eg OFGEM, *The Retail Market Review—Implementation of Simpler Tariff Choices and Clearer Information* (27 August 2013) discussing the poor performance of existing disclosure regulation; and OFGEM, *What Can Behavioural Economics Say about GB Energy Consumers?* (n 17) analysing biases affecting UK energy consumers' behaviour, and how regulation should deal with them.

[56] See Commission, 'Report on Consumer Decision-Making in Retail Investment Services' (n 52).

[57] See, eg UK Behavioural Insights Team, *Behaviour Change and Energy Use* (6 July 2011) 19, discussing how, in relation to energy consumption, 'providing people with information does not necessarily encourage them to change their behaviour'; and endorsing the 'drawing on insights from behavioural economics and psychology' to 'convey information to consumers in ways that enable them to save energy and money'.

[58] A Tversky and D Kahneman, 'The Framing of Decisions and the Psychology of Choice' (1981) 211 *Science* 453.

[59] They are aimed at correcting what O Amir and O Lobel in, 'Stumble, Predict, Nudge: How Behavioral Economics Informs Law and Policy' (2008) 108 *Columbia Law Review* 2098, 2110 call 'Type 1 biases' (ie 'biases caused by intuitive/reflexive reactions').

[60] Recalling, though diverging from, C Jolls and CR Sunstein, 'Debiasing through Law' (2006) 35 *Journal of Legal Studies* 199.

[61] According to Amir and Lobel, 'Stumble, Predict, Nudge' (n 59), 'correction [of Type 1 biases], in fact, may rely simply on asking people to think carefully or allowing them time to do so … By contrast, biases that are caused by controlled processes generated through System 2 ("Type 2 biases") may not be as easy to correct … In the latter cases, it might be simpler to consider "rebiasing choices", i.e., manipulating outcomes without eliminating (but rather using) the source of the bias, if a more appropriate direction is agreed upon'.

i. Simplification of Information

Empirical studies have shown that reducing and standardising information[62] on, for example, financial products[63] and energy bills[64] (though there may be more examples) have a greater effect on the choices of investors and consumers[65] than an increased amount of information, given that attention is a scarce resource and information overload might consume it.[66] Thus, the easiest and most popular way to facilitate people's choices is through the *simplification of information to be given to individuals*.[67] The latter is to be understood primarily as a quantitative reduction of the amount of information given, but also as a smart (ie cognitive-based) selection of the 'really informative' data to be provided (ie the data that would effectively lead to a change in regulatees' behaviour). Indeed, not all information is relevant to help make good decisions: selecting the right information to be given to consumers could increase their ability to overcome cognitive and behavioural limitations.

For instance, compelling utilities to inform consumers about how much they have been spending over time (not just in the current month), or about better deals made available by their provider (including how much consumers may save by switching to the proposed tariff),[68] could be a good strategy to overcome consumers' inertia and attain, for instance, higher switching rates. Adding personalised communications and tips in monthly energy reports, that is telling consumers how much they could save if some suggested behaviours (eg using energy-saving light bulbs, installing timers for air-con, etc) were adopted, as did the Guantanamo Bay Housing Department's energy report,[69] is another way to induce virtuous behaviour. Lastly, in order to ease consumer switching, regulators should make sure to mandate provision not only of 'product attribute information' (eg the characteristics of a cell phone), but also of 'product

---

[62] See OIRA, *Disclosure* (n 27).

[63] EC Commission, 'Consumer Decision-Making in Retail Investment Services' (n 52).

[64] EC Commission Working Group, 'Report on Transparency in EU Retail Energy Markets' (13–14 November 2012).

[65] On lack of evidence of such effect O Ben-Shahar and CE Schneider, 'The Futility of Cost Benefit Analysis in Financial Disclosure Regulation' (2014) 14-008 University of Michigan Law School, Law and Economics Research Paper Series. Working Paper 2.

[66] 'A wealth of information creates a poverty of attention and a need to allocate that attention efficiently among the overabundance of information sources that might consume it': HA Simon, 'Designing Organizations for an Information-Rich World' in M Greenberger (ed), *Computers, Communication, and the Public Interest* (Baltimore, Johns Hopkins Press, 1971) 40.

[67] See F Marotta-Wurgler, 'Will Increased Disclosure Help? Evaluating the Recommendations of the ALI's "Principles of the Law of Software Contracts"' (2011) 78 *University of Chicago Law Review* 165; CR Sunstein, 'Humanizing Cost-Benefit Analysis' (2011) 1 *European Journal of Risk Regulation* 3.

[68] OFGEM, *The Retail Market Review—Implementation of Simpler Tariff Choices and Clearer Information* (n 55) 28.

[69] See the Naval Station of Guantanamo Bay's Energy Report (media.miamiherald.com/smedia/2011/12/10/17/22/IOUof.So.56.pdf).

use information' (ie what use that particular consumer made of a cell phone or phone service).[70]

A variation of this strategy is the simplification of information *asked of consumers* (make it easy).[71] For instance, if the target population is extensively affected by inertia, the switching from one supplier to another could be made simpler by using forms which have been pre-filled[72] by the traditional supplier and that contain information about the consumers and the use they make of a service. By mandating the circulation of such information, regulators are ultimately simplifying consumers' choice (see below subsection iv).

ii. Framing of Information

Inducing a desired behaviour may depend not only on the selection of the right items of data or the reduction of the information provided, but also, and especially, on *how* it is presented (framed). Unlike simplification, framing of information refers to the *format* in which the informative content is given.

The framing of acts, contingencies, or outcomes might change regulatees' perception of the desirability of an option[73] and thus influence their choice (known as 'framing effect' bias).[74] Framing information can be a powerful de-biasing empowerment technique.[75]

Empirical evidence suggests that consumers are not necessarily able to assess compound interest, or that they are likely to underestimate the overall costs of their loans[76] and mortgages.[77] This may be due to 'the practice of acting on the most readily available frame',[78] which can lead disclosure regulation to fail.[79]

In the context of household appliance labelling, for instance, it has been proven that 'relative information' (like scales) is more motivating, better understood and more effective in facilitating choice about energy efficient products, than is information presented in technical or statistical formats.[80] Thus, facing regulatees

---

[70] O Bar-Gill, *Seduction by Contract* (Oxford, Oxford University Press, 2012) 13, and O Bar-Gill and O Board, 'Product-Use Information and the Limits of Voluntary Disclosure' (2012) 14 *American Law and Economics Review* 235.

[71] UK Behavioural Insights Team, *Applying Behavioural Insights to Reduce Fraud, Error and Debt* (2012) 8. See also International SCM Network, *International Standard Costs Model Manual* (August 2004).

[72] ibid, 4.

[73] Tversky and Kahneman, 'The Framing' (n 58) 458.

[74] For discussion of 'inattention' see P Lunn, *Regulatory Policy and Behavioural Economics* (Paris, OECD, 2014) 47.

[75] EC Commission Working Group, 'Report on Transparency in EU Retail Energy Markets' (n 64) 18.

[76] See A Lusardi, 'Americans' Financial Capability' Report Prepared for the Financial Crisis Inquiry Commission (26 February 2010).

[77] Bar-Gill, *Seduction by Contract* (n 70) 22.

[78] Tversky and Kahneman, 'The Framing' (n 58) 458.

[79] See Australian Government, *Influencing Consumer Behaviour: Improving Regulatory Design* (18 December 2012).

[80] Ipsos MORI, London Economics and AEA, *Research on EU Product Labelling Options and Consumer Understanding*, delivered for the European Commission (October 2012) 68. See Sunstein,

affected by inertia or over-discounting of future energy costs, in other words consumers who will hardly ever invest in energy efficiency today to make savings on their bill tomorrow, regulators might frame the design of labels for household appliances accordingly, for example, by replacing technical data (kWh consumed per year) with more eye-catching and 'relative' information (ie equating the absolute amount of kWh consumed per year to a meaningful amount of Euro spent per year). Figure 3 below shows an imaginary restyling of refrigerator labels as harmonised by the Energy Labelling Directive (2010/30/EU).[81]

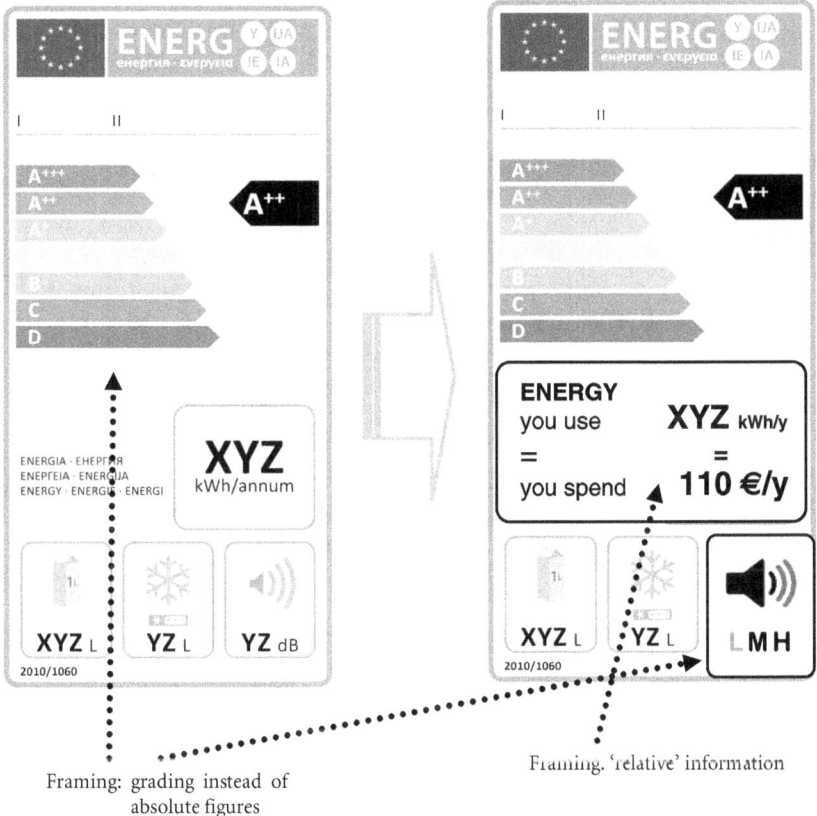

Figure 3: An imaginary restyling of refrigerators' label

'Empirically Informed Regulation' (n 37) 1354; RE Nisbett et al, 'Popular Induction: Information Is Not Necessarily Informative' in D Kahneman, P Slovic, and A Tversky (eds), *Judgment under Uncertainty: Heuristics and Biases* (Cambridge, Cambridge University Press, 1982) 112.

[81] Directive 2010/30/EU of the European Parliament and of the Council of 19 May 2010 on the indication by labelling and standard product information of the consumption of energy and other resources by energy-related products [2010] OJ L153/1.

Other framing effects have been observed in the context of anti-tobacco and the energy efficiency labelling regulations, suggesting that EU and national regulators should emphasise successful stories (inspiring ex-smokers) or potential losses (deriving from not moving from a B to an A-rated product), as they appear to be more motivating (in quitting smoking or buying efficient appliances) than reporting negative data (X per cent of lung cancer related deaths) or gains (to be made from shifting from B to A-rated products).[82]

iii. Targeted Education

In the area of health care, traditional information disclosure has proven insufficient to change one's habits, especially if the patient is affected by *unrealistic optimism* when assessing adverse outcomes associated with risky activities (such as smoking). These findings explain the shift from an 'informed consent' strategy, characterised by mere information disclosure about disease and foreseen treatment,[83] to 'patient empowerment' strategies.[84] Under such a scheme, the care-giver could be required by regulation to undertake education activities (communication, dialogue and decision aids), to provide information (leaflets, videos, group presentations, etc) but also to teach self-management and problem-solving skills to patients so as to help them understand their illness, make informed choices about their health and affect lasting changes in their lives.[85]

The real efficacy of targeted education, however, is far from having been ascertained and no agreement exists as far as its ability to overcome cognitive limitations.[86] For example, in retail financial investment decisions, some contend that it could worsen the incidence of some biases, like overconfidence.[87] Also, as highlighted above, targeted education may negatively affect the efficacy of other strategies, such as default rules (eg in the realm of organ donation).[88]

---

[82] For the EU-wide campaign 'Ex-Smokers are Unstoppable' (2011–13), see EC Commission's Staff Working Document, 'Report on Consumer Policy (July 2010–December 2011)' COM (2012) 225 final, 22 March 2012, 14. See also the UK Department for Environment, Food and Rural Affairs (Defra), *Behavioural Economics in Defra: Applying Theory to Policy* (July 2013) 9.

[83] D Doumont and I Aujoulat, *L'empowerment et l'éducation du patient* (Louvain, UCL–RESO, dossier technique, 18 August 2002).

[84] I Aujoulat, W d'Hoore and A Deccache, 'Patient Empowerment in Theory and Practice: Polysemy or Cacophony?' (2007) 66 *Patient Education and Counseling* 13. See also I Holmström and M Röing, 'The Relation between Patient-Centeredness and Patient Empowerment: A Discussion on Concepts' (2010) 79 *Patient Education and Counselling* 167; C Feste and RM Anderson, 'Empowerment: From Philosophy to Practice' (1995) 26 *Patient Education and Counselling* 139.

[85] Holmström and Röing, ibid, 170.

[86] See J Garcia and GL Cohen, 'A Social Psychological Approach to Educational Intervention' in E Shafir (ed), *The Behavioural Foundations of Public Policy* (Princeton NJ, Princeton University Press, 2012) 329.

[87] See, eg LE Wills, 'Against Consumer Financial Literacy Education' (2008) 94 *Iowa Law Review* 12.

[88] Wright and Ginsburg, 'Behavioural Law and Economics' (n 10) 1048 underline how the framing effect might be reduced if the addressee is made aware of what he or she is doing through targeted education. For further comments on this issue, see below at section V.B.

iv. Simplifying Choices

Other empowerment tools aim at facilitating people's choices by making comparison among products or services easier.[89] 'Pro-choice' web applications (making use of RECAP[90] schemes) are frequently employed in the area of utilities, securities, bank, and insurance services,[91] where choices are particularly complex and contractual relationships often long-lasting. The adoption of such applications could be required of the private sector by public authorities, or run directly by the latter, to ensure truly independent comparisons.[92] By allowing consumers to save search costs and by providing them with easy comparisons of existing commercial offers, these tools may prove effective in overcoming inertia and status quo biases, thus increasing the consumers' ability to make good choices. In order for such tools to reach their goal, information provided should be complete (although super-simplified and framed according to the gathered cognitive insights), relevant and comprehensible.

Recently, 'open data' initiatives have been undertaken in the US (MyData),[93] the UK (Midata)[94] and at European level[95] mandating public administrations and the private sector to disclose data (eg in utilities) in machine-readable format so that private and, we suggest, also the public sector develop applications that may help consumers to make comparisons. This strategy might help consumers overcome their cognitive limitations when facing complex choices in domains such as health, education, energy and personal finance. However, in order to be effective they should ensure the widest transparency and independence (eg through the adoption of codes of conduct) when provided by private intermediaries.[96]

---

[89] G Dworkin, *The Theory and Practice of Autonomy* (Cambridge, Cambridge University Press, 1988) 48ff.

[90] Acronym for Record, Evaluate, and Compare Alternative Prices, put forward by CR Sunstein and RH Thaler, *Nudge: Improving Decisions about Health, Wealth, and Happiness* (New Haven, Yale University Press, CT, 2008) ch 5; see also RH Thaler and W Tucker, 'Smarter Information, Smarter Consumers' (2013) 3 *Harvard Business Review* 7.

[91] On Price and Quality Comparison Websites (PQCWs) see Commission, 'Report on the Application of Directive 2005/29 (Unfair Commercial Practices Directive)' COM (2013) 139 final, 14 March 2013, para 3.4.2. On the benefits of RECAP see RH Thaler, CR Sunstein and JP Balz, 'Choice Architecture' in E Shafir (ed), *The Behavioural Foundations of Public Policy* (Princeton, Princeton University Press, 2013) 435.

[92] For price comparison web applications accessible on the regulator's portal in Italy, see Istituto per la Competitività (I-Com), *Rapporto sui consumatori* (Rome, April 2014) 103ff.

[93] For details on 'data.gov' see: Executive Office of the President National Science and Technology Council, *Smart Disclosure and Consumer Decision Making: Report of the Task Force on Smart Disclosure* (30 May 2013).

[94] See Midata Government response to 2012 consultation, of 19 November 2012 and US National Science and Technology Council, Task Force on Smart Disclosure, 7. See also the Executive Order, 'Making Open and Machine Readable the New Default for Government Information' (9 May 2013).

[95] See Commission Communication, 'Towards a Thriving Data-driven Economy' COM (2014) 442 final, 2 July 2014, and the accompanying 'Report on the Implementation of the Communication "Unleashing the Potential of Cloud Computing in Europe"' SWD(2014) 214 final, 2 July 2014.

[96] See Commission, 'Report on the Application of Directive No 2005/29' (n 91) 23, underlying that 'the information provided to consumers through information intermediaries, such as [Price Comparison Websites, or] PCWs, is frequently partial and sometimes misleading and incorrect, especially in relation to the price, whether the retailer has paid to have its product listed, the criteria for ranking the offers, or delivery costs'.

Once the deal has been made, and is hopefully a good one, consumers may still be unable to use the service in a way that is consistent with their interest, because, for example, of their inability to discount future gains or losses, or due to optimistic forecasts on their consumption. So for instance, if consumers are mainly unable to stop using their mobile phone over their flat rates, despite wishing to do so (*optimistic bias*), telephone companies may be compelled to send personalised texts warning that a consumption threshold is about to be overcome, or to stop the connection if the threshold is overcome.

v. Overcoming Emotional Responses

Another operational empowerment strategy is represented by *cooling off* or 'timing of choice' rules.[97] These are intended to help people make considered choices and overcome emotional responses, based on a waiting period being imposed by the regulator before a final decision (eg to buy) is made.[98] A *cooling off* rule, eventually supported by empowerment through simplification of requested information, could be a good strategy to help those who, having misjudged commercial offers, changed their provider and ended up paying more.[99] However, as with other empowerment tools analysed so far, evidence of the efficacy of cooling off rules is still controversial. Some contend that there is hardly any statistical data indicating how many consumers actually make use of their withdrawal right.[100] Also, even though a cooling off period allows deliberation, it does not necessarily, as such, prompt it.

IV. STRENGTHS AND WEAKNESSES OF COGNITIVE-BASED REGULATORY TOOLS

A. A General Overview

Cognitive-based strategies have strong points as well as weaknesses. Despite being expensive to design (ie experiments are time and resource consuming), they

---

[97] Here we dissent from those authors who classify the cooling off rule among nudging tools (see, eg Korobkin, 'Libertarian Welfarism' (n 43) 1664.

[98] See Directive 2011/83/EU of the European Parliament and of the Council of 25 October 2011 on consumer rights, amending Council Directive 93/13/EEC and Directive 1999/44/EC of the European Parliament and of the Council and repealing Council Directive 85/577/EEC and Directive 97/7/EC of the European Parliament and of the Council [2011] OJ L304/64 (Consumer Rights Directive).

[99] C Wilson and C Waddams Price, 'Do Consumers Switch for the Best Supplier?' (2010) 62 *Oxford Economic Papers* 657.

[100] See EM Tscherner, 'Consumer Contract Law and Behavioural Sciences' (Nudging in Europe: What can EU Law Learn from Behavioural Sciences? conference, University of Liège, 12 December 2013).

should allow savings as far as enforcement is concerned.[101] Furthermore, they are innovative approaches worth considering in areas where traditional regulatory tools have not satisfactorily addressed regulatory needs.

Cognitive-based tools can be used in combination with traditional regulation, eventually helping increase the overall compliance with it, and thus leading to greater adhesion to public decisions.[102] For instance, compliance with obligations on product information, as set forth in the Unfair Commercial Practices Directive,[103] could be increased if product comparison websites (an example of empowerment) were introduced by the regulator to discourage cheating by the industry.

Also, such tools can help advance competition. Indeed, while increasing market transparency and reducing information asymmetry, they foster competition among service providers, either because they make choice easier (empowerment)[104] or because they strengthen the disciplining effect on competition of, for example, opt-out nudging default rules for class actions.

At the same time, they are not without limitations. For instance, the debate around nudging has highlighted the risk of limiting and, in the worst case, manipulating regulatees' choices. Therefore, a general criticism concerns transparency. The latter regards mainly nudging, as empowerment is a fully transparent tool, and keeps autonomy intact. Nudge strategies are less identifiable than empowerment and than those connected to 'traditional' paternalism.[105] For this reason, nudging is usually a strategy where end-users have neither participated nor shared.[106] However, as we have argued above (section II), critical points referring to transparency might (at least partially) be settled in an open and transparent rulemaking process. Decisionmakers should make an effort towards greater transparency and participation,[107] for instance, by explaining the expected effects of a default option

---

[101] See Korobkin, 'Libertarian Welfarism' (n 40) 1684, discussing greater enforcement costs associated with command and control as compared to libertarian tools in the context of strategies to induce increased recycling behaviours.

[102] Sunstein, 'Empirically Informed Regulation' (n 34) 1351.

[103] Directive 2005/29/EC of the European Parliament and of the Council of 11 May 2005, concerning unfair business-to-consumer commercial practices in the internal market and amending Council Directive 84/450/EEC, Directives 97/7/EC, 98/27/EC and 2002/65/EC of the European Parliament and of the Council and Regulation (EC) No 2006/2004 of the European Parliament and of the Council [2005] L 149/22.

[104] For instance, by strengthening individuals' ability to exploit market possibilities, empowerment serves by rebalancing the demand vis-à-vis the supply side.

[105] Bubb and Pildes, 'How Behavioural Economics Trims Its Sails and Why' (n 2) 1605.

[106] A Alemanno and A Spina, 'Nudging Legally. On the Checks and Balances of Behavioural Regulation' (2013) 6 NYU School of Law—Jean Monnet Working Papers; Feldman and Lobel, 'Behavioral Tradeoffs' (n 26). On expressive law theory, see R Cooter, 'Expressive Law and Economics' (June 1998) 27 Journal of Legal Studies 585 and CR Sunstein, 'On the Expressive Function of the Law' (1996) 144 *University of Pennsylvania Law Review* 2021, 2045.

[107] As suggested by Feldman and Lobel, 'Behavioral Tradeoffs' (n 26), participation in deliberative processes might increase not only adhesion but also the sustainability overtime of a given cognitive-based regulation. However, because nudge strategies work better in the dark, extensive awareness could hardly be their main characteristic.

during the consultation process,[108] or through a well-designed justification of the final decision. However, it cannot be forgotten that 'the more actual token interference we demand, the less effective these [nudging] techniques are'.[109]

Empowerment tools might be less prone to criticism of manipulation than of nudging, in that they tend to preserve individual choice by easing it. Indeed, they do not frame the environment choice in an attempt to *exploit* biases; rather, they are meant to help individuals *overcome* their emotional responses and automatic choices without directly favouring any given behaviour. Moreover, empowerment might also be less exposed to criticism of paternalism than nudging, because it assumes, as argued above (at section III.B), that cognitive and behavioural limitations can be overcome, thus positioning itself in line with the liberal 'consumer sovereignty' paradigm.

Another critical point concerns the ability of cognitive-based tools to promote the public interest. Because we support the idea that such strategies could be used where cognitive and behavioural limitations are detected within a target population, which requires the definition of a threshold of intervention, one might contend that by using nudging and empowerment regulators end up fostering the welfare of a limited group (ie those affected by a bias), and not that of everyone. However, although we recognise the difficulties of identifying the target group and of setting a threshold for intervention, we contend that by using cognitive-based regulation that targets *also* those that are affected by some cognitive limitations (ie the target population *and* the others), a greater protection of the overall public interest may result. For instance, if empowerment pro-choice tools are used that help people affected by inertia to become proactive in the market, the resulting effect might be an increase in competition, which is, in the end, the final public interest such a regulation is intended to pursue.

Of course, the identification of the public interest may be difficult when there is a high degree of uncertainty about public goals (eg regarding which new energy technologies or renewable energy sources are to be incentivised), and impossible when there is a wide variety of needs to be satisfied.[110]

Other criticisms pertain to costs. Cognitive-based tools can be more expensive (eg than command and control strategies) to design because they may require repeated experiments to be conducted and prior identification of groups in the relevant market that suffer from specific biases to be made.

Furthermore, cognitive-based regulation being still relatively recent, its effects and outcomes are far from being fully assessed.[111] Moreover, the efficacy of

---

[108] P John et al, *Nudge, Nudge, Think, Think: Using Experiments to Change Civic behavior* (London, Bloomsbury Academic, 2011).
[109] Bovens, 'The Ethics of Nudge' (n 23) ch 10.
[110] Korobkin, 'Libertarian Welfarism' (n 40) 1665ff.
[111] For an assessment of information about peers, see J Alm, KM Bloomquist and M McKee, 'When You Know Your Neighbor Pays Taxes: Information, Peer Effects, and Tax Compliance' (2013) 22 Appalachian State University—Department of Economics, Working Papers.

cognitive-based tools utterly depends on whether the same mental mechanisms will occur everywhere in the relevant market and for all in the targeted group.[112] Therefore, maintenance overtime of both nudging and empowerment regulations, especially those based on framing, is urged. Due to the continuous changing of individual preferences, cognitive-based strategies might require constant maintenance to check whether they are still consistent with the cognitive and behavioural limitations on which basis they were adopted. For instance, pictorial warnings and shocking images on cigarette packages—as has been suggested—should be changed on a regular basis in order to avoid inurement.[113]

B. Drawbacks Specific to Nudging

Other critical points relate to single nudge tools.

Default rule is usually considered the most effective and least expensive (for regulators); however, whether effective or not, it is also the most controversial of the nudge strategies. The most widespread and well-founded criticisms concern its libertarian nature, and are basically connected to the ease of opting-out (ie for default rules to overcome inertia in a libertarian way, opting-out must be easy). Opting-out risks being overturned if it proves to be problematic, for any reason (eg because it incurs costs—time or monetary—or if the opt-out possibility is not clear).[114] Moreover, default rule might act as command and control for many regulatees.[115] Lastly, policy defaults may not be as effective in increasing welfare as many have hoped, in at least two respects. First, defaults ... are not always sticky and can even be slippery. Second, those who opt-out are not consistently the ones who are better off outside of the default.[116]

As regards 'smart information' and 'exploiting/neutralising the emotional response' to nudge strategies, a risk might exist that they prove insufficiently effective because the adoption of a new or different behaviour (eg a new consumption model) could take years in order to bear fruit. In general, it is also difficult to measure the level of efficacy of these two strategies, due to the fact that they are not usually the only regulatory strategy employed. For instance, even if plain packaging is adopted for cigarettes, health-relevant information must always be available;[117] in addition, the advertising ban and the prohibition of sales to minors

---

[112] UK Behavioural Insights Team, *Applying Behavioural Insights to Reduce* (n 71) 17.
[113] Centre d'Analyse Stratégique, *Improving Public Health Prevention with Behavioural, Cognitive and Neuroscience* (n 19) 87.
[114] On the feasibility of opting-out R Baldwin, 'The New Scholarship: Celebrating the "I" in Ideas' (2012) 5 LSE Law, Society and Economy Working Papers 12; see also Baldwin, Cave and Lodge, *Understanding Regulation* (n 14) 123ff.
[115] Bubb and Pildes, 'How Behavioural Economics Trims Its Sails and Why' (n 2) 1619.
[116] LE Willis, 'When Nudges Fail: Slippery Defaults' (2013) 80 *University of Chicago Law Review* 1155, 1159. See also ch 7, E Carolan and A Spina, 'Behavioural Sciences and EU Data Protection Law: Challenges and Opportunities in this volume.
[117] Alemanno, 'Nudging Smokers. The Behavioural Turn of Tobacco Risk Regulation' (n 46).

must remain in force. There are other nudge tools used along with the plain packaging (such as the shock images of diseases caused by smoking printed on plain packages in Australia) which could counterbalance the potential efficacy of the former.[118] Indeed, the optimism bias and availability heuristics might lead us not to consider the possibility that these events could concern us.

C. Drawbacks Specific to Empowerment

Despite the many advantages highlighted above, some empowerment strategies are subject to limitations.

Empowerment can be time and resource-demanding. For instance, in healthcare it may require patients and physicians to engage in continuous relations and training activities to improve patients' medical literacy and healthcare experience. Although the public health system could avoid part of these costs by encouraging 'big data-inspired' initiatives (eg requiring information on illnesses and treatments to be exchanged among patients and doctors on web platforms),[119] nonetheless, some public oversight or funding may still be needed to avoid the risk of shifting the responsibility of healthier choices or the burden of costs solely onto individuals and the private sector.

Another weak point is the risk of *aversion to be empowered*. Sometimes patients do not wish to take an active role in decisions about their healthcare; and the same may happen with utilities or consumers of financial services, whose willingness to engage in costly self-education activities may be very feeble compared to the potential gains.[120]

Tools based on the 'big data' philosophy (such as RECAP or the requirement to release personal information) can increase one's ability to make good choices (eg comparing and selecting the best mortgages, insurance, healthcare, or telecom services; or applying to certain public programmes such as grants or funding projects); however, they may nonetheless disadvantage vulnerable people, such as the elderly, who are less 'internet literate'.[121] A first trade-off regulators might face is between information completeness and simplicity (ie between being fully or better informed). Furthermore, a trade-off might also arise between simplicity and

---

[118] The dissuasive effect of plain packaging could be overcome by the concomitant use of shocking images. The latter may induce a denial reaction ('lung cancer would not happen to me'), making smokers persist. For further details on this boomerang effect see Centre d'Analyse Stratégique, *Improving Public Health Prevention with Behavioural, Cognitive and Neuroscience* (n 19).

[119] Like in the CureTogether.com platform, created in 2008 (and acquired by 23andMe in 2012) as a platform to allow patients to share information about their health symptoms and treatments so that users could see what treatments worked for people with similar symptoms, comorbidities, or demographic parameters: B Prainsack, 'The Powers of Participatory Medicine' (2014) 12 *PLOS Biology* 1.

[120] B Carlin, S Gervais and G Manso, 'Libertarian Paternalism, Information Production and Financial Decision Making' (2013) 26 *Review of Financial Studies* 2205.

[121] See Lunn, *Regulatory Policy and Behavioural Economics* (n 74) 43.

accessibility of information (where access to big-data/my data applications is not available to many).[122]

Further, in order to be correctly processed, meaningful and useful in helping to make the right choice, smart information should always be kept updated, and be as accurate and reusable as possible. This raises the question of who, between the information uploader or the processing institution (be it public or private), should bear the costs. Another question is whether the platform owner or the readily accessible information processor should be allowed to make profits out of individuals' voluntarily uploaded data.[123]

Moreover, empowerment through framing or simplification may fail if regulators, for instance, highlight the wrong piece of information thus obfuscating the one that is more motivating to help people make reasonable choices.

Finally, too much targeting may endanger the efficacy of empowerment as, for instance, consumers may decide to invest less and less in self-education, ending up being disempowered. Also, empowerment through information simplification may limit product differentiation, which is based on consumers' accumulation of knowledge about the products, as well as technological innovation.[124]

V. LESSON DRAWING FOR RULEMAKERS

A. Regulatory Strategies in Relation to Unresponsive Behaviours

This chapter has demonstrated that cognitive and behavioural limitations offer crucial information to rulemakers on the reactions of end-users, thus enabling the reduction of the risk of unresponsive behaviours (which can cause regulation to fail). Anytime there is a relevant 'behavioural element' to a regulation, incorporating cognitive insights requires a re-thinking of the regulatory process, the development of new regulatory tools, and the use of more differentiated rules.

In order for the regulatory process to become cognitive-based, consultations should be made more apt to gather information about individuals' cognitive and behavioural limitations. Experiments, combined with surveys and a review of cognitive sciences literature, could be the right answer. The justification of regulation should therefore be enriched not only by mentioning the cognitive-based studies performed and their results, but also by justifying the main methodological choices.

---

[122] O Bar-Gill, *Seduction by Contract* (n 70).
[123] This point has received much attention in the '23andMe/CureTogether.com saga'. See B Prainsack, '23andMe's "Designer Baby" Patent: When Corporate Governance and Open Science Collide' (2013) *Genomes Unzipped*.
[124] See X Gabaix et al, *La protection du consommateur: rationalité limitée et régulation*, Conseil d'Analyse Economique (Paris, La documentation française, 2012) 9.

The output of a cognitive-based regulatory process, besides providing stronger evidence as to when and why a regulation is not needed (eg because free markets provide significant protection against such cognitive and behavioural limitations), could be: the enrichment of traditional tools (such as command and control, incentive-based, and disclosure regulation), and the emergence of new regulatory tools (such as empowerment and nudging).

Table 1 below summarises what we mean by grafting cognitive evidence into a traditional strategy and how to design cognitive-based empowerment and nudge tools, as well as their weaknesses and strengths.

As far as the choice of the most suitable strategy is concerned, one should bear in mind that the very presence of cognitive or behavioural limitations, even if recurrent in given relevant markets and in various groups of the target population, does not (and we think that should not) per se justify the recourse to regulation (as an alternative to the free market and individual liberty). In addition, it should be clear that a cognitive-based approach to regulation does not justify any automatic connection between evidence of a given reaction of end-users (possibly due to a bias) and a specific regulatory tool. Nor should it justify the preference for one tool among the many in the toolkit.[125]

Our contention is that many if not most regulatory tools could benefit from adopting a cognitive-based approach to the rulemaking process. So, while nudging and empowerment have a cognitive built-in element, more traditional regulatory strategies are not necessarily attentive to cognitive and behavioural limitations. However, we contend that applying a cognitive-based approach to the latter might help to reduce some of their weak points. For instance, in order to address conflicts of interest affecting a financial advisor, a prohibition on negotiating (command and control) might prove more effective than a smart disclosure duty if it is established (through experiments) that a substantial portion of the target population in the relevant market is affected by overconfidence, and lack of any financial education.

Our claim is that the selection of a regulatory strategy must be made on a case-by-case basis: possibly following experiments, regulatory intervention should regard the specific relevant market and the relevant goals (public interests) to be pursued.

B. How to Choose among Different Regulatory Options?

More specific findings of the chapter are now summarised so as to provide some indications that might prove useful for regulators.

---

[125] As argued also by Bubb and Pildes, 'How Behavioural Economics Trims Its Sails and Why' (n 2) 1638 'a full comparison of advantage and disadvantages of different regulatory instruments' is needed.

Table 1: Traditional and cognitive-based regulatory tools

STRATEGY	REGULATORY TOOL	CHARACTERS	PROS	CONS
		IN RELATION TO COGNITIVE AND BEHAVIOURAL LIMITATIONS		
Command and Control	Bans, duties, standards (eg seat belts)	Intended to avoid risk of unresponsive behaviours; General rules that apply to everyone (irrespective of biases, emotional or social context)	Low cost design (except for standards that are very costly to define) and implementation; Can help reducing creative compliance	Paternalism; Risk of biases by the rulemaker; Over-regulation and excessive limitations on those not affected by unresponsive behaviours
Disclosure regulation	Ex ante information disclosure duties (eg informed consent); Ex post (control of) prohibitions of false information; misleading advertising, unfair commercial practices	Neutral with regard to individual preferences and cognitive context	Preserves autonomy	Does not ensure effective comprehension; Can exacerbate information asymmetry (information overload)
Public tutoring*	Ex officio powers by public bodies to co-enforce individual rights; Class actions, collective redress;	Aims at avoiding risk of unresponsive behaviours; Assumes weakness of regulatees (disregarding cognitive context)	Strengthens deterrent effect of private enforcement; Does not limit private autonomy	Heavily paternalistic (complements individual autonomy with public intervention); Lacks delegation;

(continued)

* Public tutoring occurs when the public powers are made responsible for supporting or easing the exercise of private rights, no matter whether individuals are effectively in need of protection or if they are actually affected by some cognitive or behavioural limitations.

Table 1: *(Continued)*

STRATEGY	REGULATORY TOOL	CHARACTERS	PROS	CONS
		IN RELATION TO COGNITIVE AND BEHAVIOURAL LIMITATIONS		
	Simplification of litigation (Alternative Dispute Resolutions)			Stuck to notional (average) consumer
Incentive Regulation	Economic incentives; Differentiated tax regimes; Subsidies (eg benefits for energy savers; higher taxes for polluters)	Assumes rationality of regulatees; General rules that apply to everyone (disregarding cognitive context)	Preserves autonomy; Easy to enforce	Can be costly to define; Disregards importance of motivations other than the economic one
Empowerment	Simplification of information and smart disclosure; Framing; Simplification of choice tools (eg price comparison apps); Targeted education; Overcoming emotional responses (eg cooling-off rules)	Aims at avoiding or overcoming unresponsive behaviours (truly de-biasing techniques); Emphasis on education, information simplification, overcoming emotional responses	Preserves autonomy; Reduces information asymmetry; Strengthens demand vis-à-vis the supply; Can promote competition; Can increase compliance with the law and participation in public programs Can save enforcement costs	Can be costly to design; Possible aversion to be empowered; Efficacy not assessed yet
Nudging	Default rules; Smart information nudge; Exploiting emotional responses	Is not aimed at avoiding or overcoming unresponsive behaviours; Exploits bias, emotional and social context	Libertarian (paternalism) approach Potentially successful in changing behaviours where other tools fail Can save enforcement costs	Can be costly to design; Risk of manipulation; Lack of transparency; Low coercion, but still limits autonomy Efficacy not assessed yet

Sometimes a single regulatory strategy may have limited efficacy and a *combination of different strategies* could be suggested to regulators. Such a solution may, of course, combine either various cognitive-based regulations or both the latter and traditional regulation. For instance, default rules may be coupled with rules mandating a certain framing of information (an example of empowerment) regarding opt-out, in order to increase its ease and thus reduce the risk of excessive paternalism.

Similarly, nudges which tend to 'exploit or neutralise' emotional responses could be matched (as is often the case) with other—traditional—regulations. For instance, if the public interest to be protected is of particular importance, such as health, strategies like plain packaging and pictorial warnings may be coupled with a general obligation on tobacco producers to provide basic information about health effects, or with ban of sales to minors.

Sometimes tools belonging to different strategies may be used 'incrementally' to raise the effectiveness of regulatory intervention gradually. So, for instance, default rules can operate to complement regulatory requirements in order to increase compliance.[126] Also, 'smart information nudging' could increase the efficacy of both traditional disclosure regulation and information simplification empowerment. As is known, traditional disclosure tends to increase the amount of data provided, causing an adverse reaction of real people to complex information (information overload), who, consequently, will go in the opposite direction of the desired behaviour (eg people will hold on to risky investments, or they will not save energy). If it is proven that the effect of having too much information is equal to not being informed (about financial risks and potential savings), then some empowerment tools, such as framing or targeted education, could be justified to strengthen the efficacy of traditional regulation based on information.

Even the 'simplification of choice' tool could be more effective (eg to prompt switching provider) if coupled with 'targeted education'. However, if a feedback of ineffectiveness of regulation persists (eg low switching rates in a newly liberalised market), regulators could consider overcoming inertia by using 'smart or relational information nudging'. In other words, they could exploit one social norm (eg emulation within a group) and emphasise positive models in the community (eg those who switched are better off) so as to create new habits. Of course, since the efficacy of such nudging tools utterly depends on whether the same mental mechanism will occur everywhere in the relevant market and for everyone in the targeted group, targeting education might help cope with specificities of different social contexts.

However, a regulatory mix of strategies might not always be the best solution, because undesirable effects may arise that reduce (instead of reinforcing) the overall efficacy of the combined strategies. For instance, where the organ donation

---

[126] Sunstein, 'Empirically Informed Regulation' (n 34) 1398–99.

default option (an example of nudging) is combined with targeted education (an empowerment tool), the latter might 'caus[e] people to consider the decision more carefully and perhaps to consult their families, a reactive effect may [thus] emerge and the donation rate may not increase to the desired level'.[127] Therefore, regulators should also take into consideration possible boomerang effects associated with the use of a mix of strategies.

Once a cognitive-based regulatory answer proves to be justified, we claim that in selecting the best one, a crucial question is whether rules may help individuals to adopt deliberately conscious decisions (if empowerment is used) or to choose what is best for them (in case nudging is employed). We argue that to establish the efficacy of rules in inducing the desired behaviour, regulators should engage in the difficult task of establishing whether cognitive and behavioural limitations (and the resulting unresponsiveness of behaviours) *can be overcome or not*, in the first place. We claim that a yes–no answer to the problem of establishing whether biases can be overcome through empowerment rules is not given.

Yet, only a cognitive-based regulatory process, which is informed—where necessary—by cognitive experiments, could help to detect this.[128] Where evidence is gathered in the rulemaking process that cognitive and behavioural limitations can be avoided or overcome, we would suggest favouring empowerment regulation (aimed at increasing people's cognitive and behavioural capabilities), because it is more transparent than nudging and preserves regulatees' autonomy.

If, despite empowerment, biases and behavioural limitations persist, regulators might go for nudging (which exploits, often in an undisclosed manner, heuristics and biases while preserving regulatees' choice). In other words, we suggest that empowerment and nudging could be used sequentially to increase the chances that the pursued behaviour occurs. This could be done through experiments helping regulators to assess the effectiveness of empowerment rules in inducing deliberation and subsequent due course of action; and to further assess the feasibility of using nudging as a 'last resort' to help push people towards the desired behaviour. However, we should caution that nudging might not be the best option when the protected values are particularly sensitive, such as health, safety or the environment, and need a strengthened answer, in which circumstances more traditional regulations, such as command and control, might be preferable. Indeed, using nudging as a last resort strategy may be a source of serious consequences: if not effective, nudging strategies risk leaving the public interest they are intended to satisfy without adequate protection.

---

[127] Amir and Lobel, 'Stumble, Predict, Nudge' (n 59). See also Bovens, 'The Ethics of Nudge' (n 23) and John et al, *Nudge, Nudge, Think, Think* (n 108) 121–22.

[128] Correcting biases may rely simply on asking people to think carefully or allowing them time to do so: Amir and Lobel, 'Stumble, Predict, Nudge' (n 59).

To sum up, choosing the right regulatory tool should be the result of a omparison between all feasible regulatory options, which should include both traditional tools, eventually revisited in a cognitive vein, and the new ones, already cognitive-inspired, nudging and empowerment. Such a comparison should be based on empirical evidence of the possible effectiveness of all different options. In turn, gathering such empirical evidence might require the performance of experiments. Of the use of experiments, of their results and of the reason for taking the latter into account or not, traces should be found in the motivation of regulation.

3

Nudging and Evidence-Based Policy in Europe: Problems of Normative Legitimacy and Effectiveness

MUIREANN QUIGLEY AND ELEN STOKES[*]

I. INTRODUCTION: THE RISE OF THE 'NUDGE' REGULATORY STATE?

AS OTHER CONTRIBUTIONS to this book show, governments and policymakers have displayed a recent interest in, and uptake of, strategies, which draw on behavioural research to help to achieve a range of policy goals. While behavioural approaches have long been of interest to them, in the last few years attempts to apply the findings of behavioural research to law and policy have become much more *systematic*. In this respect, the United Kingdom's Behavioural Insights Team (BIT or the so-called 'Nudge Unit') has become the global poster child for the latest behavioural turn in policy and regulation. Until recently the Team was part of the Cabinet Office and was set up specifically to apply 'insights from academic research in behavioural economics and psychology to public policy and services'.[1] Amongst the initiatives trialled have been ones to encourage compliance with tax payments,[2] increase the uptake of employer pension schemes,[3] and to prompt those applying for a driving licence to sign up to the Organ Donation Register (ODR).[4] The perceived success of the schemes mentioned, along with the potential for further uses of behaviourally-informed regulation and policy,

---

[*] Muireann Quigley gratefully acknowledges the support provided by a Leverhulme Trust Research Fellowship in carrying out this research.

[1] See www.gov.uk/government/organisations/behavioural-insights-team. The Behavioural Insights Team spun out of Government in February 2014 see www.behaviouralinsights.co.uk/about-us.

[2] Behavioural Insights Team, 'Applying Behavioural Insights to Reduce Fraud, Error and Debt' (2012) 22–26. Available at www.behaviouralinsights.co.uk/sites/default/files/BIT_FraudErrorDebt_accessible.pdf.

[3] Behavioural Insights Team, 'EAST: Four Simple Ways to Apply Behavioural Insights' (2014) 11 www.behaviouralinsights.co.uk/sites/default/files/BIT%20Publication%20EAST_FA_WEB.pdf.

[4] Behavioural Insights Team, 'Applying Behavioural Insights to Organ Donation: Preliminary Results from a Randomised Controlled Trial' (2013) www.behaviouralinsights.co.uk/publications/applying-behavioural-insights-organ-donation.

has been influential abroad. In New South Wales, Australia the Department of Premier and Cabinet have set up their own behavioural insights team, with the UK team advising the Department for two years.[5] Additionally the UK successes have fuelled recent interest in utilising behavioural insights at European Union (EU) level.[6]

In the EU context the potential for the adoption of behaviourally-informed approaches to regulation coincides with the continuing drive to embrace Smart Regulation; that is, the Commission's own brand of Better Regulation.[7] A significant aspect of this is the promotion of evidence-based (or evidence-informed) policy, something which is promulgated on a wider policy basis as part of the Better Regulation agendas at national and European levels. To such ends, within the European Commission, DG SANCO (the Directorate General for Health and Consumers) has 'set up the Framework Contract for the Provision of Behavioural Studies, open to all Commission services. Its purpose is to facilitate the running of behavioural studies in support of EU policy-making'.[8] The Commission is also collaborating with the Joint Research Centre and has set up the Behavioural Studies for European Policies (BESTEP) to aid with this aim. Thus, the current policy landscape at EU level reveals three significant overlapping and interrelated agendas: better regulation, evidence-based policy, and the application of behavioural science to policy problems. This chapter examines some specific aspects and challenges at the intersection of these in the EU context. Despite the enthusiasm from some quarters regarding the integration of empirical work from the behavioural sciences into regulation and policy-making, there are largely unanswered questions about how (potentially) effective and appropriate (both ethically-speaking and in regulatory terms) behaviourally-informed strategies might be. Moreover, there are uncertainties about how (the success of) these ought to be evaluated.

In this chapter we are mindful of Lowenstein and Ubel's caution that behavioural economics 'is being asked to solve problems it wasn't meant to address'.[9] As such, we attempt to probe the grounds of this statement. There are two aspects in which we are interested here, and which the would-be EU nudger should bear in mind. The first relates to integrating the findings of behavioural science (which we sometimes refer to collectively as 'nudges' for the sake of brevity) into the policy-making process in general. In section II(A), using health and environmental policy

---

[5] See www.behaviouralinsights.co.uk/about-us.
[6] See, eg A Alemanno, 'Nudging Europe' *European Voice* (2012). Available at www.europeanvoice.com/article/imported/nudging-europe/74349.aspx.
[7] See European Commission, 'Communication on Smart Regulation in the EU' COM (2010) 543 final; for a related and more recent policy espousal see European Commission, 'Communication on Regulatory Fitness' COM (2012) 746 final.
[8] R van Bavel et al, 'Applying Behavioural Sciences to EU Policy-making' (2013) EUR 26033 EN, 8 ftp://ftp.jrc.es/pub/EURdoc/JRC83284.pdf.
[9] G Lowenstein and P Ubel, 'Economics Behaving Badly', *New York Times*, 14 July 2010, www.nytimes.com/2010/07/15/opinion/15loewenstein.html

as exemplars, we suggest that some regulatory problems lend themselves better to behavioural solutions than others. This much is unsurprising. It would be foolish to think that these represent the only appropriate or effective regulatory tools, and we do not make such a claim. As such, we should also bear in mind that not all techniques in the behavioural toolbox will be created equal. This means that the application of different behavioural techniques may be more or less appropriate or effective in different areas. This much is evident from the breadth of effects, techniques, and applications discussed in the contributions to this book. There is not space here to examine even a selection of these, so we restrict ourselves in section II(B) to making some general methodological observations, raising some issues with the predictive capabilities of behavioural science. Our consideration of methodological issues continues in section III where we examine how behavioural strategies might fit with the EU regulatory structure in general. We argue that some difficulties might be exacerbated by the distinct regulatory context within which the EU operates. The challenges in this respect are likely to be particularly acute because there is a large degree of heterogeneity amongst EU Member States (in socio-cultural and economic terms, as well as legislative and regulatory approaches).

II. POTENTIAL PROBLEMS WITH THE USE OF BEHAVIOURAL TOOLS

Behaviourally-informed policy is often presented as a *solution* to evidentially impoverished and behaviourally blinkered forms of traditional regulation. However, while nudge might seem to be a good bedfellow for better regulation and evidence-based policy in general terms, it is not without problems. The potential problems relating to both the better regulation and evidence-based policy approaches are brought into sharp focus by claims that some behaviourally-informed policies rest on firm(er) evidential foundations. Such claims can be problematic where it transpires that the evidence base is simply not strong enough; for example, the casual connections may be less clear-cut than expected and missing information may be overlooked.[10] Hence, certain policies or regulatory interventions may be exposed to the same criticisms made of more traditional regulatory attempts to change behaviour. We illustrate some of the actual and potential pitfalls using health and environmental examples, before outlining some general methodological challenges with behavioural approaches. Perhaps inevitably, we find that, given the relative novelty of particular interventions, there are still considerable gaps in our understanding of human behaviour and its practical implications.

---

[10] For discussion, see G Stoker, 'The Politics of Nudge: Dilemmas in Implementing Policies for Sustainable Consumption' in A Ulph and D Southerton (eds), *Sustainable Consumption: Multi-disciplinary Perspectives in Honour of Professor Sir Partha Dasgupta* (Oxford, Oxford University Press, forthcoming).

A. Some limitations: Two Exemplars

i. Health Nudges: On Organs and Calories

One of the early reports from the BIT focused on potential applications to health.[11] Possible applications which were outlined involved proposals for increasing the number of organs donated, improving diet, decreasing smoking and alcohol intake, and reducing prescription errors in the National Health Service (NHS).[12] In terms of implementation, the most significant example here is that of required choice with regards to organ donation. There has long been the option in the UK of signing up to the organ donation register when applying for a driving licence through the Driver and Vehicle Licensing Agency (DVLA). However, there is now a prompted choice system. The BIT conducted a randomised controlled trial (RCT) where they tested the effect of different messages on the numbers of people who would sign up to the Organ Donor Register (ODR). The prompt page appeared after individuals had applied for or renewed their vehicle tax disc or driving licence.[13] The team tested eight variants and found the 'reciprocity condition' was the most successful. The message displayed on this page said 'If you needed an organ transplant would you have one? If so please help others'.[14] This resulted in 1,203 extra people over and above the control group signing up to the ODR.[15] This seems promising yet it remains to be seen whether prompted choice will have a material impact.

One issue here is that, in assessing whether this intervention makes a difference, we need to decide what the goal is. This may seem obvious, but there is a tendency for initiatives to be claimed as policy victories based on debatable markers of success. An example of this in the UK is the target of a 50 per cent increase in organ donation figures that was set in the 2008 Organ Donation Taskforce Report.[16] This target was recently met. The UK has gone from having around 13 donations per

---

[11] Behavioural Insights Team, 'Applying Behavioural Insight to Health' (2010) available at www.gov.uk/government/uploads/system/uploads/attachment_data/file/60524/403936_BehaviouralInsight_acc.pdf.

[12] See Behavioural Insights Team, 'Behavioural Insights Team Annual Update' (2010–11). www.cabinetoffice.gov.uk/sites/default/files/resources/Behaviour-Change-Insight-Team-Annual-Update_acc.pdf and Cabinet Office Behavioural Insights Team, Behavioural Insights Team Annual Update 2011–12 www.gov.uk/government/uploads/system/uploads/attachment_data/file/83719/Behavioural-Insights-Team-Annual-Update-2011-12_0.pdf.

[13] Behavioural Insights Team, 'Applying Behavioural Insights to Organ Donation: Preliminary Results from a Randomised Controlled Trial' (2013) www.behaviouralinsights.co.uk/publications/applying-behavioural-insights-organ-donation.

[14] ibid, 6.

[15] ibid, 8.

[16] Organ Donation Taskforce, 'The Potential Impact of an Opt Out System for Organ Donation in the UK: An Independent Report from the Organ Donation Taskforce' (2008) www.odt.nhs.uk/pdf/the-potential-impact-of-an-opt-out-system-for-organ-donation-in-the-UK.pdf.

million population (pmp) pre-2008 to 19.1 pmp in 2012/13.[17] This is undoubtedly an achievement to be celebrated. However, this figure reflects the donations made not actual transplants carried out. A closer look at the figures reveals that there has in fact been a 30 per cent increase in solid organ transplants in the same time period.[18] While this is still good, we need to ask what the end goal is. We would suggest that the primary objective must be to increase the numbers of actual organs available for transplantation (although we might argue that the ultimate goal is for there to be an increase in the numbers of *successful* transplants). If this is correct then, even though prompted choice increases the numbers of people on the organ donor register,[19] this still needs to translate into actual organs. It may do, but there are a few interrelated issues which may hinder the realisation of this goal. First, a large proportion of donated organs come from those not on the ODR. In 2012, 38 per cent of those who donated had been on the register.[20] Sixty-two per cent of organs donated came from individuals who were not on the register. Therefore, while we might increase this proportion by eventually capturing more of the population on the register, it will not address barriers to donation for those not on it. Secondly, being on the register is simply evidence of willingness to donate at a particular point in time. When the time comes it might emerge that the deceased changed their mind before death. Thirdly, there may be objections to donations from family members despite the deceased being on the ODR. In practice this is likely to mean that a donation would not go ahead. There may also be other barriers to donation; for example, whether a person dies under conditions in which a donation can occur, or whether they die at a place and time in which the national organ retrieval teams can attend.

Our point here is not that great things have not already been achieved regarding organ donation (they have) nor that using prompted choice to nudge people into thinking about donation or making a decision is a bad thing (quite the opposite). Instead, it is an example of the need to be more circumspect about what behaviourally informed interventions have the potential to achieve *on their own*. It is, of course, correct that over time the number of drivers captured by the new prompted choice system will increase (as more people apply for or renew their driving licences and tax discs). However, this would still not solve the problems of translating the names on the ODR to actual/successful transplants. It is also

---

[17] NHS Blood and Transplant, Transplant, 'Organ Donation and Transplantation Activity Report' (2012/13) https://nhsbtmediaservices.blob.core.windows.net/organ-donation-assets/pdfs/activity_report_2012_13.pdf.

[18] From 3,235 (2007/08) to 4,212 (2012/13). There are many reasons for this disparity including an increase in the numbers of donations after circulatory death (as opposed to donations after brain death) and the increasing use of 'marginal' or extended criteria donors (those who are older, had blood pressures higher than normal, etc). This has implications for numbers of organs which can be transplanted as there are fewer DCD organs suitable for transplantation due to factors such as cold ischaemic time and the formation of micro-clots.

[19] 58% who signed up to the register in 2012/13 did so through the DVLA.

[20] NHS Blood and Transplant, Transplant, 'Organ Donation' (n 17).

the case that certain factors simply cannot be well controlled; for example, people will change their minds before death, will die in a manner which is not conducive to transplantation, and relatives will refuse to permit donations.[21] As such, to the extent that a behavioural prompt works, it is just one factor that needs to be taken into account. Infrastructural and other systems wide changes may be needed in order to facilitate *actual* increases in transplants. In the UK, at least, this is well recognised within organisations such as NHS Blood and Transplant, and something, which has been progressively addressed since the ODT Report.[22] Such factors, however, need to be borne in mind by those who believe that prompted choice or opt-out (and the behavioural findings behind them) is a *significant* part of the policy solution to the organ shortage problem. What then about other potential health applications?

The *potential* policies that have been mooted thus far fall firmly within the public health arena, where focus has been on traditional public health targets such as alcohol, smoking, diet, and exercise.[23] Here we are not going to examine whether these lifestyle factors ought to be considered to be within the proper ambit of government interference.[24] Although it is a contested area, we will assume for our purposes that, in so far as governments have a mandate and duties in respect of the health of citizens, factors such as these fall within their legitimate sphere of influence. Instead, we look at a recent example which illustrates the difficulty with applying behavioural insights in the real world: calorie labelling.

The 2010 BIT report on health advocated calorie labelling of menus at food outlets as a way to both empower citizens and aid them to make healthier (or at least more balanced) choices.[25] The idea that calorie labelling will affect food choice positively (ie that consumers will choose lower calorie foods) is an intuitive one. However, this may not necessarily be borne out in practice. To illustrate let us consider New York City where a law requiring that menu items be labelled was, somewhat controversially, implemented.[26] Here researchers looked at the before and after data following the introduction of the New York mandate. They

---

[21] Thank you to Alberto Alemanno for pointing out that the numbers of drivers captured by the new system will necessarily increase over time.

[22] Organ Donation Taskforce, 'The Potential Impact of an Opt-out System' (n 16). See also NHS Blood and Transplant, 'Taking Organ Transplantation to 2020: A Detailed Strategy',www.nhsbt.nhs.uk/to2020/resources/nhsbt_organ_donor_strategy_long.pdf, 9.

[23] See, eg HM Government, 'Healthy Lives, Healthy People: Our Strategy for Public Health in England' (The Stationary Office, 2010) www.gov.uk/government/publications/healthy-lives-healthy-people-our-strategy-for-public-health-in-england, and Behavioural Insights Team, 'Applying Behavioural Insight to Health' (n 11).

[24] See chapter 10 by A Alemanno in this volume.

[25] Behavioural Insights Team, 'Applying Behavioural Insight to Health' (n 11).

[26] Note that the law makes it compulsory for food service establishments with 15 or more outlets to display calories on their menus (New York City Health Code, s 81.50). As such, it is not a nudge for the businesses themselves. The so-called nudge is to the consumers whose behaviour may be altered by the display of the calorie information.

found that, although some people reported that the calorie count affected their choice of food, the information did not actually influence the number of calories purchased.[27] In fact another study suggests that the effect could be even worse if daily calorie targets are also provided; that is, calories consumed might rise.[28] The example of calorie labelling highlights two important points. First, that our intuitive predictions about effects on behaviour can be wrong. Relatedly, it shows the importance of having a solid evidence base before significant time and resources are expended on implementing a new policy. Before the labelling law was introduced in New York City there was little prior evidence of the effect of posting calorie counts on menus; and the evidence that was available was weak.[29] It may turn out that calorie labelling under certain circumstances does have the desired effect of reducing calorie consumption, but the evidence base for this is still being assembled. Despite what could be called a nudge policy failure, Lowenstein takes a positive view, noting that 'New York City's implementation of mandatory calorie labelling did the nation a service by providing an opportunity to test the actual effect of the policy'.[30] Perhaps not surprisingly the city had to defend two lawsuits from the food industry en route to its implementation.[31] Farley and colleagues take this as a lesson that we cannot trust that industry will take action voluntarily.[32] While this might be correct, it also demonstrates that we should avoid expensive policy 'experiments' where potential effectiveness has not been trialled and tested before widespread implementation. As we are about to see, this is a lesson which is also applicable in other areas where behavioural research could be used to inform policy initiatives.

ii. Environmental Nudges

The environment is perceived as another good candidate for nudge-style regulation. This is on the grounds that successful interventions to conserve habitats and natural resources require changes to human decisions and behaviour. The reason for targeting individuals is said to be that many of the most pressing environmental problems result directly or indirectly from people's everyday behaviours and that environmental protection requires buy-in from *all* stakeholders, not just governments and businesses.[33] According to the UK's Department for Environment, Food

---

[27] B Elbel et al, 'Calorie Labeling and Food Choices: A First Look at the Effects on Low-income People in New York City' [2009] *Health Affairs* w1110, w1117.

[28] JS Downs, G Loewenstein and J Wisdom, 'Strategies for Promoting Healthier Food Choices' (2009) 99 *American Economic Review* 159, 162.

[29] See G Lowenstein, 'Confronting Reality: Pitfalls of Calorie Posting' (2011) 93 *Journal of Clinical Nutrition* 679, 679 and Elbel et al, 'Calorie Labeling' (n 27) w1111.

[30] Lowenstein, ibid, 679.

[31] TA Farley et al, 'New York City's Fight over Calorie Labelling' (2009) *Health Affairs* w1098, w1103–06.

[32] ibid, w1107.

[33] K Akerlof and C Kennedy, *Nudging Towards a Healthy Natural Environment: How Behavioral Change Research Can Inform Conservation* (George Mason University Center for Climate Change Communication, 2013) 1.

and Rural Affairs (Defra), existing arrangements require more than a little tweaking: 'we will only succeed in making the changes we need if we adopt a new, comprehensive approach'.[34] To this end, Defra published a Framework for Pro-Environmental Behaviours that differentiates between various approaches to behavioural change that 'lead by *example*', or '*engage*', '*encourage*' or '*enable*' individuals and communities to achieve sustainability (hence the label the '4 Es' model').[35] Change, says Defra, will come 'in particular from moving towards more sustainable patterns of consumption, covering the purchase, use and disposal of goods and services'.[36] Defra's reports are among the many dealing with issues of lifestyle, attitudes, behaviours and the environment; others include: *I Will If You Will* (by the Sustainable Consumption Round Table); *Policies to Encourage Sustainable Consumption*,[37] and *Green Behaviour*[38] (both by the European Commission). The European Commission draws inspiration from models from the private sector where market research has long been undertaken. For instance, it cites Unilever's 5 levers for behavioural change[39] which are integrated into its marketing strategy to inspire consumers to adopt new sustainable products and ways of life. The levers are: (1) making it understood, (2) making it easy, (3) making it desirable, (4) making it rewarding, and (5) making it a habit. The European Commission relates this to the '4 A' principles of sustainable consumption: it must be *affordable* (not just a luxury), *available* (consumers have a 'right' to consume sustainably, says Unilever), and *attractive* to consumers, who must be made *aware* of how to consume sustainably.

One of the most striking features, betrayed by the titles of the reports, is the framing of environmental issues using language of individual behaviour and personal responsibility.[40] The United Nations Environment Programme (UNEP) adopts a similar tone, encouraging individuals to 'Kick the CO_2 habit'.[41] It is also interesting that many of the nudges deployed in this context aim to promote pro-environment behaviour through alternative patterns of consumption, essentially by 'shopping for sustainability'.[42] 'Green consumerism' is attractive because it

---

[34] Defra, *Changing Behaviour through Policy-Making*—Discussion Paper (Defra sou, 2005) para 3, http://web.archive.org/web/20100414195702/http://www.defra.gov.uk/sustainable/government/documents/change-behaviour-model.pdf.

[35] Defra, *A Framework for Pro-Environmental Behaviours* (Norwich, Office of Public Sector Information, 2008); see also HM Government, *Securing the Future: Delivering UK Sustainable Development Strategy* (Cm 6467, London, HMSO, 2005).

[36] Defra, *Pro-Environmental Behaviours,* ibid, 3.

[37] European Commission, *Policies to Encourage Sustainable Consumption*, Technical Report (2012–061).

[38] European Commission, *Science for Environment Policy—Future Brief: Green Behaviour* (October 2012) Issue 4.

[39] Unilever, 'Inspiring Sustainable Living: Expert Insights into Consumer Behaviour and Unilever's Five Levers for Change', www.unilever.com/Images/slp_5-Levels-for-Change_tcm13-387353_tcm224-409796.pdf.

[40] For excellent discussion, see E Shove, 'Beyond the ABC: Climate Change Policy and Theories of Social Change' (2010) 42 *Environment and Planning A* 1273–85.

[41] UNEP, 'Kick the Habit: The UN Guide to Climate Neutrality', www.grida.no/files/publications/kick-the-habit/kick_full_lr.pdf.

[42] Turn of phrase borrowed from G Seyfang, 'Shopping for Sustainability: Can Sustainable Consumption Promote Ecological Citizenship? (2005) 14(2) *Environmental Politics* 290.

offers the promise of an environmentally friendly solution without threatening the political or commercial status quo. Yet this approach raises two important issues.

First is the question of whether the types of interventions proposed will achieve high levels of success. An example is the use of smart meters to measure a household's energy consumption. In the UK there is an ambitious programme for the installation of smart meters to measure gas and electricity usage. Using powers afforded by the Energy Act 2008 (as amended 2011), the Government introduced new rules to establish a smart electricity grid and roll-out a smart meter implementation plan.[43] These goals formed part of the Coalition's programme for Government to fulfil a low carbon and eco-friendly economy.[44] As well as simple information provision regarding energy consumption, BIT suggests they be used for *comparative* energy consumption.[45] By comparing a household's energy use to that of their neighbours the hope would be to harness the power of social norms; that people would be influenced by the behaviour of others and reduce their usage. In support of this BIT cites a study from the US which showed that an intervention such as this led to lower energy consumption by some higher than average electricity users.[46] While this sounds promising the results of the study show that energy usage was lowered by only 1.4 to 3.3 per cent in those users.[47] As Lowenstein and Ubel note, this is 'modest relative to the hopes being pinned on it'.[48] Of course it is possible that, over time, bigger effects could take place (eg if there was widespread implementation and uptake as there might be following a new policy initiative), but the cumulative impacts would need to be properly followed up, monitored and evaluated. This would require some form of dedicated process. In the EU context this could be problematic, since the ex post evaluation of EU regulatory initiatives is currently neither regular nor routine.[49] But even if we can find behaviourally-informed interventions that do nudge people in a more substantive way, a number of unresolved issues still persist even when interventions are shown to be effective. These include questions of the kinds of behaviour change that are acceptable, who should be allowed to induce such change through nudging, and how they can be made accountable.[50]

The second issue raised by green consumerism relates to the 'who' question of nudging. The policy focus on the individualisation of responsibility for

---

[43] s 73.

[44] HM Government, *The Coalition: Our programme for Government* (London, HM Government, 2010) 16 www.gov.uk/government/uploads/system/uploads/attachment_data/file/78977/coalition_programme_for_government.pdf.

[45] Behavioural Insights Team, *Behaviour Change and Energy Use* (Crown Copyright, 2011) 19–21 www.behaviouralinsights.co.uk/sites/default/files/behaviour-change-and-energy-use.pdf.

[46] H Allcott, 'Social Norms and Energy Conservation' (2011) 95 *Journal of Public Economics* 1082.

[47] ibid, 1083.

[48] Lowenstein and Ubel, 'Economics Behaving Badly' (n 9).

[49] For discussion of the new emphasis on 'closing the policy cycle' and the challenges involved, see S Smismans, 'Policy Evaluation in the EU: The Challenges of Linking Ex Ante and Ex Post Appraisal' (2015) 6(1) *European Journal of Risk Regulation* 6.

[50] For further detail, see RE Ashcroft, 'Doing Good by Stealth: Comments on "Salvaging the Concept of Nudge"' (2013) 39 *Journal of Medical Ethics* 494.

environmental issues belies the role of institutions and other entities in the quest for sustainability.[51] Elizabeth Shove discusses the attitudes-behaviour-choice model (ABC)—which would undoubtedly encompass nudging—and remarks that

> the ABC is a political and not just a theoretical position in that it obscures the extent to which governments sustain unsustainable economic institutions and ways of life, and the extent to which they have a hand in structuring options and possibilities.[52]

In other words, the dispersal of responsibility that underpins such approaches to regulation fixes the policy spotlight on individuals, making institutional activities less visible or less obviously relevant.[53] Michael Maniates notes that 'when responsibility for environmental problems is individualised, there is little room to ponder institutions, the nature and exercise of political power, or ways of collectively changing the distribution of power and influence in society'.[54] Thus the role of private companies is often overlooked in debates about responsibility for global environmental harms, except to the extent that corporations generally are held to be socially responsible for the impacts of their decisions above and beyond their legal and policy obligations. Instead, the policy and literature rests on the assumption that decision-making responsibilities in certain (health, environmental) fields are best shifted onto and influenced at an individual level. This assumption may not be justified or universally shared.

The normative coupling of pro-environmental behaviour and consumption is equally open to criticism. Nudging consumers to reduce their environmental footprint by 'buying green' may, paradoxically, help to create a consumer-product growth industry.[55] The focus on consumption in reaching better environmental outcomes is not unique to behaviourally-informed interventions but is evident in several of the nudges showcased by policy in the area.[56] One of the assumptions underlying regulatory initiatives on green consumption is that increased environmental awareness on the part of consumers will exert pressure on manufacturers and retailers to take steps towards more sustainable production. It is not at all clear, however, that measures promoting green consumerism will result in any significant change at a broader, systemic level.[57] This criticism could of course be made of many types of policies seeking to regulate individual lifestyle and encourage

---

[51] Seyfang, 'Shopping for Sustainability' (n 42) 297.

[52] Shove, 'Beyond the ABC' (n 40) 1274.

[53] For a recent article which systematises the different forms of regulatory interventions existing within the EU and WHO lifestyle policies: A Alemanno and A Garde, 'The Emergence of an EU Lifestyle Policy: The Case of Alcohol, Tobacco and Unhealthy Diets' (2013) 50 *CML Rev* 1745.

[54] MF Maniates, 'Individualization: Plant a Tree, Buy a Bike, Save the World?' in T Princen, M Maniates and K Konca (eds), *Confronting Consumption* (London, MIT Press, 2002) 43, 45.

[55] Maniates, ibid.

[56] eg BIO Intelligence Service, *Policies to Encourage Sustainable Consumption*, Final Report Prepared for European Commission (DG ENV) (European Union Publications Office, Luxembourg, 2012) 13, which discusses policy tools for sustainable consumption including behavioural tools such as nudges.

[57] For discussion, see L Akenji, 'Consumer Scapegoatism and Limits to Green Consumerism' (2014) 63(15) *Journal of Cleaner Production* 13.

sustainable consumption, but, while the connection is often made in the context of nudging, it has yet to be fully scrutinised.

iii. Conclusion: Nudging in the Real World

What the discussion in these sections has indicated is that using behavioural science to inform public policy raises a range of questions which are yet to be answered adequately. These relate, not only to how nudges are implemented, but also to what sorts of behavioural changes are envisaged, as well as who is, and who is not, subject to these changes. Those seeking answers are not helped by the fact that, thus far, there have not been any large-scale initiatives on the ground. It might be that predicted challenges and problems can be averted once we move from theorising about potential applications to properly testing them. But even so, the real world is a complex and oftentimes unpredictable system. The challenges involved in moving from theory to practice are, therefore, not insubstantial. The examples regarding the display of calories on menus and electricity consumption monitoring demonstrate two important interrelated issues. First, our common sense intuitions about the effect of behavioural interventions may be wrong. The regulators' attempts to nudge us towards a particular outcome may have unforeseen consequences, which could possibly be very different from what they intended (such as an increase in daily calorific intake, or the creation of new markets in 'green' products discussed above). Secondly, it is clear that although theorising and experimental evidence from controlled settings might indicate the likely outcomes of these initiatives, these are not necessarily predictive of outcomes in real-world settings. There, therefore, needs to be a process by which these are tested and validated in practice.

Alemanno and Spina note that one of the key questions is 'how to turn the plentiful empirical findings about human behaviour into operational regulatory tools'.[58] In the next section we examine some general difficulties in doing this, before looking specifically at whether the randomised controlled trials of interventions can rescue nudge and bolster evidence-based policy.

B. Some Methodological Observations: On Evidence and Assumptions

In this section we suggest three main difficulties with the integration of behavioural insights into the regulatory process. First, the predictive capabilities of behavioural science are questionable, especially when applied to complex systems in the real world. Secondly, when we probe the aspirations of behavioural approaches to regulation we might not like what we find. Thirdly, the utility of such approaches may be limited to certain well-circumscribed types of policy problem.

---

[58] A Alemanno and A Spina, 'Nudging Legally: On the Checks and Balances of Behavioural Regulation' (2014) 12 *International Journal of Constitutional Law* 429.

i. Will this Policy Work Here?

As some of the examples in section A indicate, the predictive capabilities of behavioural science may not yet be coherent and generalisable, let alone easily applicable to real-world policy problems. The reason for this, for some such as Loevinger, is that the behavioural sciences have asked 'the wrong questions, and set ... the wrong tasks'.[59] This echoes Lowenstein and Ubel's concern mentioned in the introduction to this chapter. This, however, may be an overly harsh assessment. The problem seems to be not so much with the behavioural sciences writ large, but, the fact that while behaviour has long been the subject of laboratory tests, much less is known about how these translate into *policy* contexts. The UK's House of Lords' Science and Technology Committee noted in its 2011 report that 'there is a lack of applied research at a *population level* to support specific interventions to change the behaviour of large groups of people' (emphasis added).[60] While controlled experiments in laboratory like settings are a good starting point for forming hypotheses, more work needs to be done to test and ensure their applicability and generalisability, as well as their usefulness and effectiveness, in the real world. This is a particular issue when we consider that many proposed nudge-style policies would be rolled-out nationally or across the EU. Attempts by policymakers to apply the findings may cause problems if done in inappropriate ways; for example, without testing in the real world, or by not using large enough sample sizes or drawing unsound conclusions about how particular demographics will behave.[61] How then can regulators and policymakers exert their influence in an empirically robust manner?

One approach is to try to ensure that more of the right kind of research is done before the wholesale implementation of any policy. Currently gaining favour both within and outwith government (at national and EU level) is the potential to use RCTs of policy interventions. We have already seen an example of this, in section II above, regarding prompted choice and organ donation. RCTs, an import from medicine, are a way to try and test whether an intervention actually causes a particular outcome. In order to do this, subjects are randomly allocated to different groups; for example, control group (no intervention) versus intervention A versus intervention B. The groups are also matched for population characteristics in order to minimise the possibility that anything other than a change in intervention could be the *causal* explanation for the results obtained. For example, if we are testing an intervention to try and reduce youth re-offending, then adult re-offenders would not be used in the study. The BIT recently published a report which outlines a methodology which has RCTs as the lynchpin. It quite sensibly says that

---

[59] Such concerns have long been felt, see L Loevinger, 'Jurimetrics: Science and Prediction in the Field of Law' (1961) 46 *Minnesota Law Review* 255, as quoted in W Berns, 'Law and Behavioral Science' (1963) 28 *Law and Contemporary Problems* 185, 211.
[60] Science and Technology Select Committee, *Behaviour Change* (HL 2010–12, 179) para 8.2.
[61] Thank you to Alberto Alemanno for this point.

interventions need to be tested and that we ought to learn from the results of trials, before adapting the intervention based on the results. The key part of this type of study design is the presence of the *control* group. According to the BIT, 'Because we have a control group, we know that it is the intervention that achieves the effect and not some other factor (such as generally improving economic condition)'.[62] The potential to use RCTs has also gained support from academic commentators. Alemanno and Spina say 'experiments of new regulatory measures conducted in accordance with the scientific standards of RCTs could become a benchmark to assess the real impact of a proposed governmental intervention'.[63] They may well become such a benchmark, and anything which introduces more rigour into the policy-making and implementation process is to be welcomed. However, if we are to properly use this methodology in the policy arena, we should also be aware of some potential limitations.

One issue is that people (or subgroups of people) may respond differently to the same intervention. Take the calorie labelling example from earlier. A study by Downs and colleagues found that making it convenient to choose low-calorie sandwiches increased the chance that this option would be picked. However, when calorie information was also provided, self-reported dieters were 76 per cent *less likely* to choose this option.[64] Since RCTs are designed to equalise attributes and risks amongst subgroups in the different study arms, such subgroup variation could be missed if the potential differing responses are not built into the initial design of studies. While good study design and redesign can help to take account of this, it is unlikely that all such variation can be predicted, at least when a trial is run for the first time. Therefore, if en masse trials are conducted we might miss the fact that some subgroups derive no benefit from the test intervention, or worse that, for certain subgroups, there are dis-benefits. Although subgroup analysis could be conducted *post-hoc*, this would potentially not be as robust as building analysis of these groups into the initial study design. The reason for this is that *post-hoc* analyses run the risk of over-interpreting the data and attributing meaning to what is essentially random variation. This problem could be especially acute where the vested interests of politicians and policymakers are at stake. The lesson here is not that RCTs ought not to be carried out, but that more than one may be needed to gather the relevant information. If subgroup analysis of initial data suggests that there is some variation in response to an intervention, then further trials may be needed to test this.

Even if a RCT produces good robust results, what do these actually tell us? Well they *do not* necessarily prove that the policy under investigation will work everywhere. It may be neither generalisable nor transferable. A RCT is good evidence that some intervention worked somewhere, at some time, under certain

---

[62] L Haynes et al, 'Test, Learn, Adapt: Developing Public Policy with Randomised Controlled Trials' (Crown Copyright, 2012) 5.
[63] Alemanno and Spina, 'Nudging Legally' (n 58) 20–21.
[64] Downs et al, 'Healthier Food Choices' (n 28) 161.

conditions.[65] However, as Cartwright and Hardie point out, more needs to be done to move from '"this policy worked there" to "our proposed policy will work here"'.[66] If, for example, an intervention is tested in the UK (or indeed in just part of the UK), this is not evidence that the study findings are generalisable or transferable to other places or countries. We might have good reasons to believe that an intervention is transferable, but this should not always be assumed. There may be (infra)structural, cultural, legal, and other factors which are limiting in this respect; 'predicting policy outcomes is really betting that the policy can play the right causal role in your situation and that your situation will have the right support factors to allow it to do so'.[67]

As such, reproducibility is important. Policymakers in the clinical arena, such as the UK's National Institute for Health and Care Excellence (NICE), try to address this by conducting systematic reviews and meta-analyses of the evidence. Here good quality studies are chosen (based on predetermined search and quality criteria) and their results are combined. This is done in order to harness the power of numbers and see what results can be found across a number of similar studies. However, even doing this is no guarantee that the results are applicable in all settings.[68]

The Joint Research Centre at the European Commission seems aware of the limitations of RCTs. Its report notes that 'given the complexity of social systems, the result of a RCT is valid for a specific point in time, location and target group'.[69] This, however, may be problematic when trying to generalise and transfer findings from studies in one part of the EU to another. Specifically, time and resource constraints may mean that studies cannot be replicated across Member States. For this reason, other types of behavioural studies, including experiments, surveys, and qualitative research methods,[70] may have a role to play at national and EU level.[71] Another Joint Research Centre publication notes that 'studies can lead to results that are sufficiently robust for the EC without being replicated in each Member State (or in different broad geographical areas of the EU)'.[72] However, if we take the methodological challenges of generalisability and transferability seriously (as

---

[65] N Cartwright and J Hardie, *Evidence-Based Policy: A Practical Guide to Doing it Better* (Oxford, Oxford University Press, 2012) 122–34.

[66] ibid, 8.

[67] ibid, 9.

[68] Although about diagnostic studies see, eg Willis' recent work which demonstrates that metanalyses need to be tailored to the setting under consideration. BH Willis and CJ Hyde, 'Estimating a Test's Accuracy Using Tailored Meta-analysis: How Setting-specific Data May Aid Study Selection' (2014) 67 *Journal of Clinical Epidemiology* 538.

[69] van Bavel et al, 'Applying Behavioural Sciences to EU Policy-making' (n 8) 9.

[70] The pros and cons of these are set out in the JRC report. See van Bavel, ibid.

[71] N Rodríguez-Priego and R van Bavel, 'Good Behavioural Research for EU Policy-making' (2014) is.jrc.ec.europa.eu/pages/BE/documents/behavioural-workshop-report_en.pdf (accessed 10 October 2014).

[72] ibid, para 9.

we think we must—see section III below for further thoughts), then without further information it is not clear how the result would be 'sufficiently robust' given the lack of homogeneity between (and even within) Member States. We are not saying that RCTs ought not to be used for assessing the effectiveness of policy interventions, but our comments should be taken as a caution on how far the results from studies can be pushed.

ii. Problems of Principles?

Even if we were satisfied with the evidence-base for behaviourally-informed regulation, we might, nonetheless, question the assumptions behind it, as well as the aspirations driving it. It is not clear that the assumption of uniformly imperfect rationality associated with behavioural approaches to law and policy is any more tenable than that of uniformly perfect rationality found in more traditional types of analysis.[73] The new behavioural approach seeks to replace the 'perfect rationality' assumption underpinning law and economics inspired analysis with what Mitchell calls an assumption of 'equal incompetence'.[74] Proponents of the behavioural approach are united in their claim that everyone falls prey to biases and errors in their decision-making, and that these biases and errors lead to predictable irrational behaviour. Irrationality is what makes us human. Everyone displays foibles and fallibilities (or 'cognitive quirks') in exercising judgement. We are all, in this sense, 'incompetent'. This equality of incompetence argument is commonly used to prompt regulatory change and to explain the need for policies that would otherwise be viewed as unnecessary in a world of perfectly rational actors.[75] As Mitchell suggests, however, such an approach fails to account for the substantial empirical evidence that people are not equally irrational and that other factors or variables impinge on their behaviour. Having attacked *homo economicus* as empirically false, proponents of nudging are said now to seek to 'enshrine the very same fellow as the image of what people should want to be. Or, more precisely, what paternalists want people to be'.[76]

Yet the flipside of this argument is also weighty. If we accept that people are not equal as regards to their predisposition to a range of cognitive biases, then this is a problem for all regulatory efforts, not just those which purport to be behaviourally-based. While policies that utilise behavioural science can be criticised for treating the more rational actors as less competent than they are, policies

---

[73] For excellent discussion, see G Mitchell, 'Why Law and Economics' Perfect Rationality Should Not Be Traded for Behavioral Law and Economics' Equal Incompetence' (2002) 91 *Georgetown Law Journal* 67.
[74] Mitchell, ibid; also G Mitchell, 'Libertarian Paternalism is an Oxymoron' (2005) 99(3) *Northwestern University Law Review* 1245.
[75] We attribute this phrasing to Mitchell (n 73).
[76] TC Leonard, 'Book Review: Richard H Thaler, Cass R Sunstein, *Nudge: Improving Decisions About Health, Wealth, and Happiness*' (2008) 19(4) *Constitutional Political Economy* 356, 359.

that do not take its findings into account risk regarding some as *more* competent than they are. The crux of the problem appears to be the assumption, often apparent in the literature on behaviourally-informed regulation, that nudge policy can be extrapolated from single or a limited number of examples of nudge-style interventions. The issue here is the potential for over-extrapolation of the data (or at the very least political over-promising regarding the potential results). We have already seen a possible example of this in section II(A)(i) when we looked at organ donation policy. Here there has been a tendency to focus on the increase (or potential for increasing) the numbers of names on the ODR, when, as we discussed, this is not the end goal of organ donation. Such tendencies can represent over-extrapolation of the data, where downstream factors are not taken into account (eg family refusals or lack of suitability of organs) in predicting the effects of a policy. Since researchers themselves are often aware of the limitations of their studies and predictive capabilities, one might argue that this is not so much a problem of over-extrapolation, but over-promising on the part of politicians and policymakers. Either way there is a problem with the propensity of policymakers to exaggerate claims in favour of (or against) the increased reliance on behavioural evidence as a measure and/or mode of regulation (something we also saw earlier in relation to calorie labelling and smart meters).

Borrowing concepts from science and technology studies (STS), we may find particular patterns of argument or strategic 'repertoires' emerging.[77] Already, we can see that the policy coverage (in the UK, EU and many other jurisdictions besides) is largely positive about the potential contributions of behaviourally informed regulation. In STS, the phenomenon of 'promise-disappointment cycles' is a well-known way of describing situations where proponents make exaggerated claims about the benefits of a particular new initiative, only to discover later that the initiative failed fully to live up to expectations.[78] Adapted from the work of Latour and Woolgar is also the notion of the 'credibility cycle',[79] which may be relevant for any new policy entailing the mobilisation of resources. Policy strategies (eg nudging) accumulate credibility through claims about their potential rewards, in turn legitimating subsequent policy decisions to follow those courses of action. While it is probably too soon for any such patterns to be identified here, we should nevertheless be aware that nudge policy may follow similar cycles of hype and disappointment just as other policies can do.

---

[77] For discussion in the context of STS, see eg A Rip, 'Contextual Transformations in Contemporary Science' in *Keeping Science Straight: A Critical Look at the Assessment of Science and Technology* (Gothenburg, University of Gothenburg, 1988) 59–85.

[78] A Rip, 'In Praise of Speculation' in OECD, *Social Sciences for Knowledge and Decision Making* (Paris, OECD, 2000) ch 8. On the legal use of science generally, see also R Feldman, *The Role of Science in Law* (Oxford, Oxford University Press, 2009).

[79] Rip, 'Contextual Transformations' (n 78) 59–85. Rip bases the 'credibility cycle' on the work of B Latour and S Woolgar, *Laboratory Life: The Social Construction of Scientific Facts* (London, Sage, 1979).

III. THE EUROPEAN REGULATORY STATE? ON HARMONISATION AND HETEROGENEITY

Whereas previous sections have highlighted some of the practical and methodological implications of behavioural-informed regulation generally, in this section we explore how this form of regulatory intervention may fare in the EU context. Here we are predominantly interested in whether there are specific features of existing regulatory arrangements in the EU that would help or hinder nudge from flourishing. The discussion is necessarily speculative because, even though nudge-style regulation has been looked at favourably in EU policy circles, the EU has yet to incorporate behavioural research into its policy-making in a systematic and officially recognised way.[80] Our focus, then, is on how EU-level nudging might interact with existing regulatory approaches, should it be introduced more widely. Although some of the features discussed here are not necessarily EU-specific problems for nudge, they may become more pronounced in the EU context. For example, it may exacerbate a well-recognised tension between the EU's limited formal competences and its expanding list of policy activities.[81] Whereas the Treaty on the Functioning of the European Union (TFEU) permits the EU to act in the field of public health for example, it excludes the harmonisation of such laws.[82]

There is also a tension between the shaping of an effective and visible EU government on the one hand, and the 'behind the scenes' engineering of choice that is entailed in nudging on the other. In an effort generally to increase the visibility, and hence transparency, of EU regulatory activities, EU institutions have invested heavily in practices of impact assessment as the bedrock of its 'better regulation' and 'good governance' agendas. The idea of impact assessment has different specific connotations at different levels and in different contexts of EU regulation. However, in the most general terms it is about demonstrating the merits of particular regulatory initiatives before they are introduced. Impact assessments require policymakers to show how decisions are made between alternative policy options, how consultation exercises and socio-economic costs/benefits are brought to bear on those decisions, and how trade-offs across economic, social and environmental domains are resolved. The question is whether EU attempts to nudge individual behaviour would also be subject to these requirements (whether through stand-alone policies or 'softer' accompaniments to larger, more complex pieces of 'hard' legislation).

Not all policy initiatives in the EU need to be accompanied by an impact assessment. The Commission, the Parliament and the Council agree that impact assessment can improve the quality of EU law-making,[83] although the expectation is

---

[80] See chapter 1 by A Alemanno and AL Sibony in this volume.
[81] For discussion in the context of new governance, see G de Búrca, 'The Constitutional Challenge of New Governance in the European Union' (2003) 28(6) *EL Rev* 814.
[82] Art 168 TFEU.
[83] Interinstitutional Agreement on Better Law-making [2003] OJ C321/1, para 25.

that an impact assessment will only be undertaken for proposals likely to have far-reaching impacts or new policy implications.[84] The Commission's Guidelines on Impact Assessment indicate that, where a particular policy is under review, the choice of regulatory instrument (ie Regulation, Directive, Recommendation, Communication, self-regulation, co-regulation)[85] should be covered by an impact assessment. In most cases the 'operational detail' would not be included in the evaluation. The question is how nudge-inspired modes of action would be dealt with under such procedures. The fact that 'nudges' may consist of one of a range of different regulatory interventions—for example, incorporated into traditional legislative frameworks or as stand-alone initiatives—will itself produce inconsistency in whether and how they are impact assessed. Whereas those embedded in traditional legislation will be subject to an impact assessment (although it is unclear that the 'operational detail' of the nudge will be scrutinised), nudges in the narrower sense of a single, discrete action will escape such assessment. This latter point arises because the persistent framing of nudges as '*alternatives*' to regulation will take EU policy on some behaviourally-informed initiatives beyond the scope of formal impact assessment. Certainly, this is how nudging is framed by the current UK Government, where it is seen as a solution to what it perceives to be the heavy hand of EU regulation. They say that 'wherever possible, the Government will argue for alternatives to regulation at European level, drawing on behavioural science insights...wherever possible, seek to implement EU policy and legal obligations through the use of alternatives to regulation'.[86] If this view were taken at the EU level, it is possible that certain types of policy interventions—specifically those operating outside the remit of formal legislation—would escape formal, routine evaluation.

Even where nudge-style tools are subject to the rigours of impact assessment, close attention still needs to be paid to certain assumptions about the availability of data. As previously noted, EU impact assessment ordinarily focuses on the social, economic, and environmental impact of proposed and in situ schemes.[87] According to Alemanno, this now needs to be augmented by also including an assessment of the behavioural impact of different policy options. He argues that 'This would enable the Commission not only to foresee citizens' reaction to a given policy option, but also to design policies that actually take account of real-world behaviour'.[88] Indeed the Commission, in its proposed new Draft Guidelines on Impact Assessment, explicitly cites 'behavioural economics' and the related literature on how individuals make choices as important considerations in policy-making.[89]

---

[84] European Commission, 'Impact Assessment Guidelines' SEC(2009) 92, para 1.4.
[85] ibid, para 7.
[86] HM Government, 'Guiding Principles for EU Legislation', www.gov.uk/government/publications/guiding-principles-for-eu-legislation.
[87] J Wiener, 'Better Regulation in Europe' (2006) 59 *Current Legal Problems* 447, 468.
[88] Alemanno, 'Nudging Europe' (n 6).
[89] European Commission, '2014 Revision of the European Commission Impact Assessment Guidelines: Public Consultation Document', http://ec.europa.eu/smart-regulation/impact/docs/iag_pc_questionnaire_en.pdf.

However, the extent to which behavioural evidence is a useful ex ante predictor of good regulatory solutions rather depends on the availability and robustness of the data (as discussed in the previous section). Behavioural insights may hold more value in mid-term and ex post reflections on existing measures than in exercises of policy-making starting afresh, as Mullane and Sheffrin suggest. They maintain that 'It is typically easier to draw conclusions as to what behavioural tendencies caused policies to have certain outcomes than to demonstrate that these behavioural tendencies can be effectively used to create desired outcomes through their implementation in policy design'.[90] There is a growing focus in the EU on the interim and ex post evaluation of regulatory initiatives[91] and, as such, behavioural data have the potential to be extremely useful in improving regulatory performance.[92] To get the most from it, however, there needs to be an adequate supply of suitable evidence in order to allow evaluation to take place. As noted, in the early stages of policy development the data may be uncertain or unavailable.[93]

More problematic still is the current lack of coordination between the ex ante and ex post evaluation of EU initiatives. In order for the evaluation cycle to be complete ex post evaluation is used as a starting point and source of information for the ex ante assessment of new regulatory proposals. However, there is often a deep division between the two stages of evaluation, brought about by the fact ex post assessment is not always conducted, and when it is, it may be carried out by a different actor or organisation compared with the ex ante impact assessment.[94] While this lack of joined-up-thinking is a systematic weakness of EU policy evaluation generally, it suggests that behavioural data may be of only limited use unless (and until) a holistic approach to ex post/ex ante assessment is adopted. In other words, the utility of behavioural insights may be hampered by the policy procedures (ex post/ex ante evaluation) it inherits.

Finally, aside from potential problems of policy 'invisibility' and the lack of policy feedback loop (between ex ante and ex post evaluation), certain behaviourally-informed policies may exacerbate the tension between the goal of maintaining a degree of EU-wide uniformity and the issue of national and regional Member State diversities. Even if EU harmonisation does not necessarily mean the convergence of regulatory outcomes, EU law is predicated (where appropriate) on a certain degree of consistency between Member States. The same is true of governance. The Commission White Paper on Governance,[95] for instance, recognises the need

---

[90] M Mullane and S Sheffrin, 'White Paper: Regulatory Nudges in Practice' murphy.tulane.edu/files/events/Regulatory_Nudges_feb_24.pdf.
[91] See, eg, European Commission, 'Communication on Responding to Strategic Needs: Reinforcing the Use of Evaluation' SEC(2007)213.
[92] Indeed, behavioural evidence is already expected to play a role in evaluation, see European Commission, *Evaluating EU Activities: A Practical Guide for the Commission Services* (Luxembourg, European Communities, 2004) 87.
[93] Science and Technology Select Committee, *Behaviour Change* (n 60) paras 3.6–3.8.
[94] For detail, see Smismans 'Policy Evaluation in the EU' (n 49).
[95] European Commission, 'European Governance: A White Paper' COM (2001) 428 final.

for policy flexibility and adaptation (characteristics often associated with nudge-style regulation), but it also favours approaches that promote uniformity across the EU.[96] In this latter regard, some of the methodological difficulties are made more acute by the EU regulatory environment, where there is a large degree of heterogeneity between EU Member States (in socio-cultural and economic terms, as well as legislative and regulatory approaches). After all, the EU is characterised by its 'unity in diversity'—a motto applied (but later dropped from the text of the Treaties) during the negotiations of the Lisbon Treaty. This raises some unanswered questions: will there be a shared understanding of the concept of a nudge across different Member State jurisdictions? And will there be a shared understanding of the justifications for and limits of nudge strategies? Or does that even matter? It is problematic, according to Selinger and Whyte, *not* to recognise 'the diverse perceptions of meaning' (semantic variance)—brought about by differences in culture, identity and contexts—in the construction of a theory of choice architecture.[97] Semantic variance is an inescapable influence on the interpretation of not only nudges, but also any interaction with the choice environment. Heterogeneity, and the potential for divergence, means we must be alert to the possibility that the applicability of nudges may differ across European Member States. Shove warns that 'Discussions of *trans-national behaviour change* have yet to get underway—this is a field in which more research is needed' (emphasis added).[98] Thus, we find that while nudging raises issues that will be common to all jurisdictions (eg relating to practical problems, such as the lack of research into shared practices), it brings to the surface tensions that are specific to the use of such techniques for regulating Europe.

IV. CONCLUDING THOUGHTS

While behavioural perspectives illustrate the limitations of certain conceptions of human behaviour (such as those associated with utility-maximising *homo economicus*) they may fall short of generating a positive or normative theory of regulation. Part of the reason for this relates to difficulties with behavioural approaches generally. Problems here are partially methodological. We are lacking data from *well-designed* policy-relevant studies; that is, studies conducted in the real-world which can account for relevant confounding factors or subgroup behaviours. This may be overcome over time as more information about behaviour

---

[96] J Scott and DM Trubek, 'Mind the Gap: Law and New Approaches to Governance in the European Union' (2002) 8(1) *European Law Journal* 1, 16. This article discusses the Commission's policy on OMC as an example of new governance.

[97] For discussion, see E Selinger and KP Whyte, 'Competence and Trust in Choice Architecture' (2010) 23 *Knowledge, Technology & Policy* 461, 463.

[98] E Shove, written evidence to Science and Technology Select Committee, *Behaviour Change* (n 60) 91.

becomes available and behaviourally-informed interventions are properly trialled. Concerns about the limited predictive capabilities of behavioural evidence may diminish as behavioural approaches develop and problems of over-extrapolation become less pressing. Even so, generating *more* behavioural data is no sure-fire way of producing *better* regulation, and there may be more persistent infrastructural and institutional reasons for being cautious in the face of increasing official enthusiasm for 'new' behavioural approaches.

More fundamental than information gaps is the issue of how behavioural evidence is translated into regulatory tools. By this, we mean the more intractable problems relating to the policy and institutional environments into which nudges are introduced. These draw attention to broader questions of the role of science (behavioural or otherwise) in regulatory decision-making. The EU is certainly no stranger to ideas and practices of science-intensive policy-making. Nor has the input of science and expertise into EU regulation escaped close and critical scrutiny. There is a sizeable literature on the 'regulatory turn' to science which cautions against placing unquestioning faith in singular and universal conceptions of 'sound science'.[99] Among other things it alerts us to the normative choices and assumptions involved in the construction of scientific facts, as well as claims to authority and impartiality. Regulatory science needs to be understood as being shaped by normative commitments, institutional cultures, and existing mechanisms of translating scientific understanding into policy action. The treatment of behavioural science in regulatory policy-making must be equally sensitive to context and the non-neutral assumptions and interwoven expectations of science in regulation. Yet, the policy discourse (at EU level and in individual Member States) tends to adopt a rather less critical attitude towards behavioural approaches to regulation. Our argument is that the turn to more behavioural science for greater effectiveness and legitimation brings its own set of ambiguities, which need to be properly addressed, not glossed over.

It may also be the case, except in certain narrowly defined circumstances, that elements of the EU regulatory context pose particular challenges to distilling lessons from behavioural science. For instance, nudging may exacerbate tensions between efforts to improve the visibility of EU regulation (through measures such as impact assessment) and the reliance of (many) nudge techniques on the non-transparent manipulation of choice environments. If nudge initiatives escape the full force of existing evaluation procedures (as we suggested they might), they could serve to deepen—not resolve—the legitimacy crisis within the EU. Moreover, there are unanswered questions about whether and to what extent behavioural approaches would be expected to achieve any degree of policy harmonisation

---

[99] For illuminating discussion, see eg B Wynne, 'Reflexing Complexity Post-genomic Knowledge and Reductionist Returns in Public Science' (2005) 22(5) *Theory, Culture & Society* 67; S Jasanoff, 'The Practices of Objectivity in Regulatory Science' in C Camic, N Gross and M Lamont (eds), *Social Knowledge in the Making* (Chicago, University of Chicago Press, 2011); B Wynne, 'Essay Review: Carving Out Science (and Politics) in the Regulatory Jungle' (1992) 22(4) *Social Studies of Science* 745.

between Member States. This is made all the more complicated by the problems of heterogeneity and 'semantic variance' that exists between them. Member State heterogeneity is an inevitable feature of EU regulation, but it becomes exaggerated when the 'units' of regulation are not states, but individuals, as is the case with regulatory nudging.

Oullier has recently declared that 'if a governing body such as the European Commission—infamous for its bureaucracy and resistance to change—can see the benefits of behavioural insights and alter its way of informing policy, then every government should follow its lead'.[100] The arguments in this chapter suggest that while we have reason to be optimistic about behavioural approaches to policy-making, we also have good reason to be cautious about their use in the hands of government and bureaucrats, including the European Union.

---

[100] O Oullier, 'Behavioural Insights are Vital to Policy-Making' (2013) 501 *Nature* 463.

4

Judge the Nudge: In Search of the Legal Limits of Paternalistic Nudging in the EU

ANNE VAN AAKEN*

I. INTRODUCTION

Nudging is gaining ground everywhere—in the US, the UK and the European Union: regulation-by-nudging has become fashionable. The concept of nudging can be defined as 'an aspect of choice architecture that alters people's behaviour in a predictable way without forbidding any options or significantly changing their economic incentives'.[1] Nudges can be paternalistic or not; the main point of nudging is that a policy or practice is only supposed to count as a nudge if it leaves the choice set essentially unchanged, that is without any non-trivial cost to freedom of choice. Nudges include those with a paternalistic purpose (paternalistic nudges, which are the focus of this chapter).[2] Is this a threat to liberal thinking, liberal states[3] and the rule of law? The discussion on regulation-by-nudging is

---

* This article draws on two of my German articles: 'Begrenzte Rationalität und Paternalismusgefahr. Das Prinzip des schonendsten Paternalismus' in M Anderheiden and others (eds), *Paternalismus und Recht* (Tübingen, Mohr Siebeck, 2006) and A van Aaken, 'Das deliberative Element juristischer Verfahren als Instrument zur Überwindung nachteiliger Verhaltensanomalien. Ein Plädoyer für die Einbeziehung diskursiver Elemente in die Verhaltensökonomik des Rechts' in C Engel and others (eds), *Recht und Verhalten Beiträge zu Behavioral Law and Economics* (Tübingen, Siebeck/Mohr, 2007).

[1] See RH Thaler and CR Sunstein, *Nudge: Improving Decisions about Health, Wealth, and Happiness* (New Haven, Yale University Press, 2008) 6. For more on paternalistic nudges, see C Sunstein, *Why Nudge? The Politics of Libertarian Paternalism* (New Haven, Yale University Press, 2014). For a critique of the notion, see DM Hausman and B Welch, 'To Nudge or Not to Nudge' (2010) 18 *Journal of Political Philosophy* 123.

[2] Nudging usually defines a very specific purpose of the measure (eg targeting obesity). Regulation-by-nudging is a means. But for a legal analysis it is important to distinguish the broader purpose of regulation-by-nudging. A nudge that has as its stated purpose the well-being of the person targeted by the nudge regulation is called a paternalistic nudge. Nudges that target externalities or the public good are referred to as such. Since paternalism poses special legal problems in liberal states, paternalistic nudges are the focus of this chapter.

[3] I use 'liberal', in the European, rather philosophical sense, not in the sense of political parties as in the US.

surprisingly devoid of the legal limits of nudging.[4] Although the property rights of firms potentially infringed by nudging measures are dealt with in more detail in the literature as well as by national and international courts and tribunals,[5] the potential infringement of the rights of those being nudged is neglected in legal analysis. Behavioural science (including cognitive psychology and behavioural law and economics)[6] and the legal or constitutional limits of paternalism[7] have long been unrelated research domains, particularly in European countries. But judges may at one point be confronted with a behaviourally informed regulation challenged by the individuals being nudged; and even before reaching a court, the

---

[4] For an exception, see A Alemanno and A Spina, 'Nudging Legally—On the Checks and Balances of Behavioural Regulation' (2014) 12 *International Journal of Constitutional Law* 2. For a very short treatment of the duty of neutrality of the state vis-à-vis choices of individuals in, eg voting or religious freedom (as a constitutional right), see Thaler and Sunstein, *Nudge* (n 1) 246f who state that outside of constitutional rights, only the effect of a nudge counts—whether nudges help or hurt people. This is a too narrow understanding of the scope of constitutional rights vis-à-vis state measures, at least in the EU.

[5] For an overview on tobacco regulation, see V Vadi, 'Tobacco Wars: Tobacco Control-related Investment Disputes in a Comparative Public Law Perspective' (2012) 9 *Transnational Dispute Management* (online journal). For Mayor Bloomberg's attempt to prohibit the sale of large sodas, see Supreme Court of the State of New York, Decision of 11 March 2013, available at: www.online.wsj.com/public/resources/documents/sodaruling0311.pdf.

[6] For an overview of the literature in behavioural law and economics, including the standard criticism, see J Arlen, 'Comment: The Future of Behavioral Economic Analysis of Law' (1998) 51 *Vanderbilt Law Review* 1765; S Issacharoff, 'Can there be a Behavioral Law and Economics?' (1998) 51 *Vanderbilt Law Review* 1729; C Jolls, CR Sunstein and RH Thaler, 'A Behavioral Approach to Law and Economics' (1998) 50 *Stanford Law Review* 1471; M Kelman, 'Behavioral Economics as Part of a Rhetorical Duet: A Response to Jolls, Sunstein, and Thaler' (1998) 50 *Stanford Law Review* 1577; RB Korobkin and TS Ulen, 'Law and Behavioral Science: Removing the Rationality Assumption from Law and Economics' (2000) 88 *California Law Review* 1051; CR Sunstein (ed), *Behavioral Law and Economics* (Cambridge, Cambridge University Press, 2000). For more fundamental information with regard to government regulation, see BD Bernheim and A Rangel, 'Behavioral Public Economics: Welfare and Policy Analysis with Non-Standard Decision Makers' (2005) NBER Working Paper No W11518; C Jolls and CR Sunstein, 'Debiasing through Law' (2006) 35 *Journal of Legal Studies* 199. In Germany, the discussion started late; see A van Aaken, *Rational Choice in der Rechtswissenschaft* (Baden-Baden, Nomos, 2003) 82–108 and C Engel and others (eds), *Recht und Verhalten. Beiträge zu Behavioral Law and Economics* (Tübingen, Siebeck/Mohr, 2007).

[7] For the US literature on behavioural economics and paternalism in the law, see C Camerer and others, 'Regulation for Conservatives: Behavioral Economics and the Case for "Asymmetric Paternalism"' (2003) 151 *University of Pennsylvania Law Review* 1211; EL Glaeser, T O'Donoghue and M Rabin, 'Studying Optimal Paternalism, Illustrated by a Model of Sin Taxes' (2003) 93 *American Economic Review* 186; JJ Rachlinski, 'The Uncertain Psychological Case for Paternalism' (2003) 97 *Northwestern University Law Review* 1165; C Sunstein and R Thaler, 'Libertarian Paternalism is not an Oxymoron' (2003) 70 *University of Chicago Law Review* 1159, 1202; R West, 'Comment: Rationality, Hedonism, and the Case for Paternalistic Intervention' (1997) 3 *Legal Theory* 125, 132 and latest Sunstein, *Why Nudge?* (n 1). For a critical view of the better knowledge of the government on individuals' welfare regarding paternalistic measures by the government, see EL Glaeser, 'Paternalism and Psychology' (2006) 73 *University of Chicago Law Review* 133 and very critical from an ethical perspective MD White, *The Manipulation of Choice. Ethics and Libertarian Paternalism* (New York, Palgrave Macmillan, 2013). See for Germany, van Aaken, 'Begrenzte Rationalität und Paternalismusgefahr' (n*) and B Fateh-Moghadam, S Sellmaier and W Vossenkuhl (eds), *Grenzen des Paternalismus* (Stuttgart, W Kohlhammer, 2010); R Neumann, *Libertärer Paternalismus* (Tübingen, Siebeck/Mohr, 2012).

legality of nudging should be scrutinised by legislators. This chapter concentrates solely on paternalistic nudges, but the main structure of the argument can be extended to all sorts of nudges, including those that target third party externalities or other general interest aims.

At issue is the question of how much paternalistic nudging the fundamental rights protection of the EU permits. There is a broad consensus regarding the admissibility of paternalistic measures[8] targeting mentally ill persons and adolescents, as these individuals are assumed not to possess full autonomous and rational decision-making powers. However, open questions arise for mentally healthy adults, since experiments conducted by behavioural economists and cognitive psychologists have called into question the rationality of fully capable and self-responsible adults. Individuals display systematic deviations from the classical rational choice assumption in several areas of life. People lack a clear, stable[9] and well-ordered set of preferences. Even if they possess such preferences, they might not be able to rationally pursue them because they are cognitively unable to do so. The definition of biases and heuristics need not be repeated here; suffice it to say that we can distinguish cognitive biases,[10] bounded willpower (especially important for paternalism)[11] and fairness preferences, all of which constitute a deviation from the assumption of the rational choice expected utility model,[12] which has long underlain most economics and regulatory policies.

Adequate assumptions about the behaviour of individuals are of eminent importance, especially for legal policy. Psychological insights may thus also challenge notions underlying the law. This fact gives rise to the question of the relation between the 'is' (positive analysis) and the 'ought' (normative analysis) in

---

[8] Paternalistic measures encompass paternalistic nudges. Whereas nudging describes certain means of inducing behavioural change, measures also include prohibiting choice or decisively changing the economic incentives. See the definition of nudges in Thaler and Sunstein (n 1). Sunstein writes that incentives are *not* nudges, C Sunstein, *Simpler: The Future of Government* (New York, Simon & Schuster, 2013) 39.

[9] Stable preferences are perhaps not even desirable throughout a person's life. Preferences might change—and justifiably so. Time is an important factor in the discussion on paternalism but is usually neglected.

[10] For details, see Sunstein (ed), *Behavioral Law and Economics* (n 6); Jolls and Sunstein, 'Debiasing through Law' (n 5); Thaler and Sunstein (n 1); A Tversky and D Kahneman, 'The Framing of Decisions and the Psychology of Choice' (1981) 211 *Science* 453A; A Tversky and D Kahneman, 'Judgment under Uncertainty: Heuristics and Biases' (1974) 185 *Science* 1124; A Tversky and D Kahneman, 'Loss Aversion in Riskless Choice: A Reference-Dependant Model' (1991) 107 *Quarterly Journal of Economics* 1039; D Kahneman, 'New Challenges to the Rationality Assumption' (1997) 3 *Legal Theory* 105; D Kahneman, 'A Perspective on Judgment and Choice. Mapping Bounded Rationality' (2003) 58 *American Psychologist* 697; D Kahneman and A Tversky, 'Prospect Theory: An Analysis of Decisions under Risk' (1979) 47 *Econometrica* 312; D Kahneman, *Thinking, Fast and Slow* (New York, Farrar, Straus and Giroux, 2011).

[11] For a definition, see n 20.

[12] *cf* GS Becker, *The Economic Approach to Human Behavior* (Chicago, University of Chicago Press, 1976); GS Becker, *Accounting for Tastes* (Cambridge, Harvard University Press, 1996). In the expected utility theory, the expected utility of option X is comprised of the sum of all outcomes x weighted by their probability p. The expected utility hypothesis is first and foremost a normative model. However, economists often use it as an assumption in descriptive models.

discussions about paternalism.[13] On the one hand, behavioural science, including behavioural economics, is a descriptive theory about the real behaviour of individuals. On the other hand, the entire theory of rationality and autonomy is of a heuristic and normative nature even if used as an 'as if' assumption in law, economics or legal policy. Also, the idea of 'a good life' towards which one can be nudged is a normative philosophical question.[14] Nevertheless, the positive and normative perspectives are connected within the legal system: (normative) regulatory aims and regulatory reasoning need grounding in positive theories and factual evidence in order to be effective. But there is also a risk of misuse of biases as an *ad hoc* justification of paternalistic (or other) state intervention.[15] Therefore, they should be treated with caution. Although behavioural economics is used to justify nudging, at this point the finding that an average man's rationality is subject to a de facto limitation does not support any state intervention per se;[16] the 'ought' cannot be derived from the 'is' (Hume's law). Rather, one must consider whether the purpose of the nudge is legitimate and whether the concrete measure taken is appropriate to reach the stated aim. The dangers and risks of remedying a bias also need to be taken into account.

Any legal system that protects liberties, like the EU's, is bound by law to use its 'correcting power' only proportionally and as prescribed by law—as stated in Article 52(1) of the European Charter of Fundamental Freedoms (CFR).[17] In liberal legal systems, measures that limit freedom need to be justified, and when in doubt, one should choose the *mildest* possible intervention. This requires a comparative analysis of different possible measures under the principle of proportionality. Although the new forms of paternalistic measures might be choice-preserving at first sight, they pose problems of paternalism not only from a philosophical but also from a legal perspective. The philosophical discussion about paternalism needs to be taken into account when the legal assessment is explored: it provides

---

[13] For details concerning the implication of bounded rationality on (normative) welfare economics, see Bernheim and Rangel, 'Behavioral Public Economics' (n 6).

[14] For an extensive discussion of this normative 'counterfactual', see ch 12 of this book, P Cserne, 'Making Sense of Nudge-Scepticism: Three Challenges to EU Law's Learning from Behavioural Science'.

[15] On the misuse argument, see also C Sunstein, 'The Storrs Lectures: Behavioral Economics and Paternalism' (2013) 122 *Yale Law Journal* 1826, 1871: 'It should not be necessary to emphasize that public officials have their own biases and their own motivations. With respect to efforts to defend paternalism, this point raises two separate problems. The first involves public choice theory: official judgments about welfare may be influenced by the interests of powerful private groups'. For an extensive study, see R Bubb and RH Pildes, 'How Behavioral Economics Trims Its Sails and Why' (2014) 127 *Harvard Law Review* 1593. Here Bubb and Pildes illustrate how nudging can go wrong although they do not use public choice analysis.

[16] G Gigerenzer and PM Todd, *Simple Heuristics that Make Us Smart* (Oxford, Oxford University Press, 1999); G Gigerenzer and DG Goldstein, 'Reasoning the Fast and Frugal Way: Models of Bounded Rationality' (1996) 103 *Psychological Review* 650; G Gigerenzer and R Selten (eds), *Bounded Rationality: The Adaptive Toolbox* (Cambridge, MIT Press, 2002). G Gigerenzer, 'On the Supposed Evidence for Libertarian Paternalism' (2015) *Review of Philosophy and Psychology* (Online Journal): http://link.springer.com/article/10.1007/s13164-015-0248-1/fulltext.html.

[17] European Union, Charter of Fundamental Rights of the European Union, 26 October 2012 [2012] OJ C326/2.

the background picture. The legal concern is triggered by two problems: first, the legality of paternalistic state action as such and, second, the changing nature of the means used.[18] Whereas coercive or mandated action can be legally challenged, persuasive or invisible measures are much harder to contest legally although they may have the same effect. Soft means (social norms, 'naming and shaming', etc) are not always softer, but they are more difficult to control legally than hard paternalistic measures, such as prohibitions, which can always be legally challenged.

In the following, the different aims of nudges will be distinguished (Part II). These are highly relevant to the legal assessment. A classification of paternalistic measures into three categories follows: prohibition of individual choice, isolated choice facilitation and communicative choice facilitation. A softer form of paternalism, namely de-biasing through procedures, is then introduced (Part III). This is followed by a proportionality analysis that is necessary to 'judge the nudge' in the European Union (Part IV). I conclude the discussion in Part V.

II. THE AIM OF NUDGES

In the current 'nudge' debate, there are two major themes requiring clarification. First, what exactly are the aims of nudges? Is the nudged individual to be protected against herself, are third party externalities to be reduced or is the public interest to be safeguarded? These questions are examined in Section A. Usually, nudges address rationality failures on the part of individuals. Thus, rationality is normally the cornerstone against which the effectiveness of a nudge is measured. But is this the correct cornerstone or should it rather be autonomy? Given the liberal underpinnings of the individual rights protected within the EU, this issue deserves legal scrutiny (Section B).

A. Separating Paternalistic Nudges from Nudges Benefitting Third Parties

Researching the term 'paternalism' in lexica yields very different definitions.[19] According to the *Stanford Encyclopedia of Philosophy*, paternalism is 'the interference of a State or an individual with another person, against their will, and defended or motivated by a claim that the person interfered with will be better off or protected from harm'.[20] This view encompasses only a limited number of measures,

---

[18] On this problem see the extensive discussion in Alemanno and Spina (n 4).
[19] For a summary discussion of the term 'paternalism' and its various forms in the philosophical literature, see K Möller, *Paternalismus und Persönlichkeitsrecht* (Berlin, Duncker & Humblot, 2005) 15–18.
[20] G Dworkin, 'Paternalism' in EN Zalta (ed), *The Stanford Encyclopedia of Philosophy* (online publication 2005), www.plato.stanford.edu/archives/win2005/entries/paternalism.

namely, bans and coercion. There has been a consensus that hard paternalistic measures for healthy adults are either unconstitutional or carry a heavy burden of justification in a liberal society. The focus has shifted to other, possibly milder, policy instruments and soft/libertarian paternalism.[21] An expansion of the notion of paternalism follows from the extension of paternalistic policy instruments such as nudges. This variety of paternalistic measures also provides assistance for a discussion of the principle of proportionality since milder policy instruments need to be taken into account (milder instruments trumping harder ones).

In attempts to assess the legitimate aim of a nudge targeting the well-being of an individual, the first problem is to distinguish this type of nudge clearly from a nudge targeting third party externalities.[22] If the only intent of the measure is to reduce third party externalities, protect the public or promote public welfare, paternalism is not involved. In principle, there is no problem with nudging if third parties or public goods are affected, and no special justification is necessary to delineate the rights of one person from those of others (together with the provision of public goods, making such allocative choices constitutes a core prerogative of states).[23] Thus, for example, the prohibition of smoking in public places in order to reduce third party externalities is permitted. Although many of the nudges were and still are discussed under the heading of paternalism, they do not all fall into this category.[24] Energy-saving nudges, for example, are not primarily paternalistic nudges since they ultimately target energy saving and the environment, and their primary aim is neither to protect the consumer's purse nor to induce savings behaviour.[25] Like any public intervention, non-paternalistic measures are subject

---

[21] See ibid for the terms 'soft paternalism' and 'strong paternalism': 'A weak paternalist believes that it is legitimate to interfere with the means that agents choose to achieve their ends, if those means are likely to defeat those ends. So if a person really prefers safety to convenience then it is legitimate to force them to wear seatbelts. A strong paternalist believes that people may be mistaken or confused about their ends and it is legitimate to interfere to prevent them from achieving those ends'. Sunstein (n 1) 58 defines soft paternalism as referring to 'actions of government that attempt to improve people's welfare by influencing their choices without imposing material costs on those choices'.

[22] Dworkin (n 20) states that conceptually three conditions are necessary: 'X *acts paternalistically towards* Y *by doing (omitting)* Z: Z (or its omission) interferes with the liberty or autonomy of Y. X does so without the consent of Y. X does so just because Z will improve the welfare of Y (where this includes preventing his welfare from diminishing), or in some way promote the interests, values, or good of Y'. For a discussion of the definition, see also Sunstein (n 1) 57ff.

[23] For an early study see, JS Mill, *On Liberty* (Kitchener, Batoche Books, 1859/2001) 13: 'That principle is, that the sole end for which mankind are warranted, individually or collectively, in interfering with the liberty of action of any of their number, is self-protection. That the only purpose for which power can be rightfully exercised over any member of a civilized community, against his will, is to prevent harm to others. His own good, either physical or moral, is not a sufficient warrant. He cannot rightfully be compelled to do or forbear because it will be better for him to do so, because it will make him happier, because, in the opinions of others, to do so would be wise, or even right ... The only part of the conduct of any one, for which he is amenable to society, is that which concerns others. In the part which merely concerns himself, his independence is, of right, absolute. Over himself, over his own body and mind, the individual is sovereign'.

[24] *cf* K Yeung, 'Nudge as Fudge' (2012) 75 *MLR* 122, 147.

[25] For details on energy nudges, see F Di Porto and N Rangone, 'Behavioural Sciences in Practice: Lessons for EU Rulemakers', see ch 2 in this book.

to the proportionality rule: even if the aim is legitimate, the means may not be proportionate—for example, if the measures are invisible or use shaming. However, the burden of justifying the measure under proportionality is lower in comparison to paternalistic nudges (see Part III below).

In liberal states, it is much more difficult to justify restrictions on individuals' choices for their own sake. A total prohibition of smoking would therefore be highly problematic from a legal perspective. Furthermore, nudges that target only the consumer of tobacco who is not causing externalities (eg by smoking in public places) also deserve special scrutiny.[26] It is therefore tempting for regulators to posit as the aim of the nudge some externalities or public goods. However, the pure specification of the aim of the measure by the regulator cannot be decisive; it needs to be scrutinised. For example, the aim of protecting the (prospective) community of insurance holders with healthy eating nudges (eg nudges aiming to reduce obesity) is a very slippery slope, since the protection of the insured against the depletion of insurance funds is only a secondary aim. A stated aim, such as protecting general welfare, can easily serve as a justification for what are in fact paternalistic measures and therefore needs special scrutiny by the courts.

B. The Aim of Paternalism: Rationality or Autonomy?

The nudging literature is unclear about what the ultimate aim of paternalistic nudging is. According to Thaler and Sunstein, nudges are a set of techniques by which the regulator aims 'to influence choices in a way that will make choosers better off, *as judged by themselves*' (emphasis added).[27] Unfortunately, this phrase is not further elucidated. Regulators often presume certain preferences and nudge accordingly—assuming their choice reflects the true preference of the nudgees. The use of revealed preferences as an analytical tool to evaluate individual welfare is considered by economists to be less susceptible to misuse than a projection of that individual's welfare by third parties, such as state regulators. Nevertheless, this process has its problems too: preferences are inferred from the actions of individuals ('people want what they choose'). Whether such acts reflect people's 'true' preferences is not part of the analysis; the rational hypothesis is used as an 'as if' assumption.[28] People show (at least) two different types of (possibly

---

[26] Nudging concerning alcohol is therefore much easier to justify since alcohol consumption per se tends to produce third party externalities such as traffic accidents and domestic violence. In systems where medical costs are largely mutualised, is it not the case that smoking—even smoking in private spaces or in isolation only—also produces third party externalities (cost of treating smoking-related diseases)? Of course, this externality is partly offset in the long run because smokers die younger, thereby saving other costs associated to pensions and age-related diseases). [just a remark]

[27] Thaler and Sunstein (n 1) 5.

[28] *cf* D McFadden, 'The New Science of Pleasure. Consumer Behavior and the Measurement of Well-Being' (2005) www.emlabberkeleyedu/users/webfac/dromer/e237_f05/mcfaddenpdf.

inconsistent) preferences: short-term and long-term.[29] Short-term preferences can be inconsistent with long-term preferences.[30] In theory, long-term perspectives can be valued as a preference to increase welfare, whereas short-term perspectives are a 'false' choice. This differentiation, however, is problematic for several reasons. First, the utility derived from the autonomous choice is ignored.[31] Second, people constantly weigh short-term pleasure against long-term potential utility losses (eg when eating chocolate, hang-gliding, drinking too much beer while watching the World Cup at the risk of getting too little sleep and suffering from a hangover). Inhibiting these activities would restrict the lifestyle choices of individuals. Third, the idea of a 'good life' is presumed by somebody else even though the state might not know an individual's preferences.

Individual autonomy is defined as

> an idea that is generally understood to refer to the capacity to be one's own person, to live one's life according to reasons and motives that are taken as one's own and not the product of manipulative or distorting external forces.[32]

Autonomy is a normative construct which not only reserves a free space for the individual but also determines who is responsible for certain actions. It underlies much of the legal order, including not only constitutional law and criminal law but also contract law.[33] Liberal notions of autonomy are non-instrumental. In other words, individuals do not need to use their autonomy to pursue objective welfare interests, they are not trustees for the public welfare, and they do not need to ensure their own welfare (eg a healthy body). Autonomy is neutral vis-à-vis any specific idea of life; it protects the formation of a person's own idea of a 'good life' and guarantees individuals room for their own choices. The liberal thinker Wilhelm von Humboldt viewed the legal system as an instrument for supporting people in making informed, autonomous and deliberate judgements, leaving the final decision to the individual. Support for making a decision rather than the restriction,

---

[29] Individuals would like to see themselves acting according to their long-term preferences. See for more details TC Schelling, 'Coping Rationally with Lapses from Rationality' (1996) 22 *Eastern Economic Journal* 251, 269 and RH Thaler, *Quasi Rational Economics* (New York, Russell Sage Foundation, 1991) Pt II. AK Sen, 'Maximization and the Act of Choice' (1977) 65 *Econometrica* 745, 779, speaks of entire hierarchies in the preference order and so-called meta-preferences that give the preference order a moral hierarchy. For example, an individual is capable of having a preference over her preferences: she can reflect upon her own preferences.

[30] The seminal work on the problem of self-constraint and the contradiction between short- and long-term preferences is J Elster, *Ulysses and the Sirens. Studies in Rationality and Irrationality* (Cambridge, Cambridge University Press, 1984). See also on this subject TC Schelling, *Choice and Consequences* (Cambridge, Harvard University Press, 1984) 83–112.

[31] If individual welfare is denoted as β, from a long-term perspective β would equal 1 and from a short-term perspective would be smaller than one ($\beta < 1$), both staying consistent with the intended welfare criteria and assuming some kind of meta-preferences that do not change during a lifetime. It is problematic that only welfare utility is considered. Any utility from an autonomous decision as such is disregarded. For more details, see Bernheim and Rangel (n 6) 4.

[32] J Christman, 'Autonomy in Moral and Political Philosophy' (2009) *Stanford Encyclopedia of Philosophy* www.plato.stanford.edu/entries/autonomy-moral/.

[33] See also Cserne (n 14).

manipulation or suppression of choice was Humboldt's policy instrument.[34] John Stuart Mill and Wilhelm von Humboldt[35] state three reasons for this view, which recur in the current discussion: 1) each individual knows best what is best for her, while the state has limited information about preferences; 2) not allowing free choice or preventing mistakes leads to infantilisation, and learning effects are an important means of progress (individually as well as for societies); and 3) individual originality is important for a healthy society because it promotes creativity and innovation (this is a consequentialist, welfarist argument).[36]

It is only at first glance that scholars of behavioural law and economics, such as Sunstein and Thaler, have a similar position: they define a policy as paternalistic 'if it attempts to influence the choices of affected parties in a way that will make choosers better off'.[37] This means that they implicitly assume that an objective state of well-being ('better off') exists for each individual which should be optimised (or which at least should not be diminished).[38] This does not restrict paternalistic measures. Quite the contrary: if, for example, a certain amount of health is deemed to be the minimum prerequisite for a 'good life', any behaviour potentially diminishing health, such as eating to the point of obesity, practicing dangerous sports or taking drugs ought to be restricted (by nudges). These restrictions might lead to a spartan lifestyle that is not consciously self-chosen.

Although nudges aim at a certain behaviour (oriented to outcome), such as saving for retirement or eating healthy food (as an objective state of affairs), not analysing the underlying baseline of the intervention would lead to a truncated analysis. A comprehensive analysis is especially necessary in liberal states relying on autonomous and responsible individuals. Often the aim of nudges is the de-biasing of a boundedly rational individual and/or the formation of a preference. But is the baseline then a fully rational decision (leading to a presupposed outcome, eg not eating the chocolate) or an autonomous decision? The blind spot of liberal paternalism is the notion of autonomy.[39] Indeed, paternalism is

---

[34] W von Humboldt, *The Sphere and Duty of Government (Ideen zu einem Versuch, die Grenzen der Wirksamkeit des Staats zu bestimmen)* (London, John Chapman, 1854 (first published in German 1792)) 24; Mill (n 23) 113f also only grants society the right to impose education on children in order to prepare them for autonomous life.

[35] Humboldt, *The Sphere and Duty of Government* (n 34) ch 3; Mill (n 23) ch 3.

[36] T Gutmann, 'Paternalismus und Kosequentialismus' (2011) *Preprints of the Centre for Advanced Study in Bioethics Münster*, available at: www.uni-muenster.de/imperia/md/content/kfg-normenbegruendung/intern/publikationen/gutmann/17_gutmann_-_paternalismus_und_konsequentialismus.pdf, 8ff. Gutmann criticises the fact that utilitarianism (of which Mill (n 23) was a representative) cannot safeguard against paternalism since its benchmark is aggregate welfare (not individual autonomy as a deontological value).

[37] Sunstein and Thaler, 'Libertarian Paternalism is not an Oxymoron' (n 7) 1162.

[38] ibid, 1163: 'The claim ... that almost all people, almost all of the time, make choices that are in their best interest or at the very least are better, by their own lights, than the choices that would be made by third parties ... is testable and false, indeed obviously false'.

[39] See also, B Fateh-Moghadam, 'Grenzen des weichen Paternalismus—Blinde Flecken der liberalen Paternalismuskritik' in B Fateh-Moghadam, S Sellmaier and W Vossenkuhl (eds), *Grenzen des Paternalismus* (Stuttgart, W Kohlhammer, 2010) 21–47.

the counterpoint of autonomy.[40] The implicit transition from autonomy to full rationality as a standard against which paternalistic intervention is permissible is problematic from a legal perspective. I submit that autonomy is the default standard against which any public intervention should be assessed. Nudge advocates fail to recognise this by assessing de-biasing against a full rationality standard: the human being who has a preference for a presupposed 'good life' is enabled to pursue it rationally.[41] But it cannot be the aim of state measures to achieve fully rational individuals; in liberal societies, I submit, it must be the enablement of autonomy. Even if behavioural research shows that people are only boundedly rational, it cannot discard the normative concept of autonomy, especially if the research is used for policy measures. Above a threshold of minimal conditions of rationality, autonomy and the principle of proportionality secure the liberty to pursue decisions that are not fully rational and that can even be irrational or unreasonable.

From a legal point of view, two levels must be distinguished: the decision that is desired by the regulation-by-nudging (some other 'good' state of affairs, such as a healthy body as the immediate aim of the nudge) and the mental processes underlying the decision which are simultaneously targeted (the abstract aim of the nudge). On the latter level, then, the question is whether full rationality or autonomy is the underlying baseline to be achieved by paternalistic measures.

The difference between regulation targeting the formation of preferences and thus autonomy (preference paternalism or end paternalism) and regulation aimed at correcting cognitive errors in order to help people pursue their own preferences rationally (cognitive paternalism or means paternalism) is crucial.[42] Preference paternalism assumes that the preferences of people are not yet formed and tries to push them towards an idea of a 'good life'. Cognitive or means paternalism, by contrast, takes the preferences as given and helps individuals to pursue them rationally, assuming that individuals have (eg cognitive) difficulties in rationally pursuing their already autonomously formed preferences (even if these contradict a determined version of a 'good life'). Paternalism that targets preferences (autonomy) needs to be subjected to greater scrutiny than the latter type of paternalism, which targets only cognition (rationality) and respects preferences and autonomy. Furthermore, both forms of paternalism might need different methods to de-bias individuals—a question that I will now take up.

---

[40] Christman (n 32) writes, 'Autonomy is the aspect of persons that undue paternalism offends against'. For a recent critique of the neglect of autonomy in nudging, see Yeung (n 24).

[41] The nudging literature relies heavily on the research on cognitive biases by Kahneman and Tversky; see (n 11).

[42] Sunstein (n 1) 63ff calls this distinction end and means paternalism. Admittedly, the distinction is not always clear-cut.

III. THE TOOLBOX OF PATERNALISM

Paternalism can be put in place by several types of tools, the most common of which will be analysed below. Since the proportionality principle demands, in terms of suitability and especially the determination of the least intrusive means, a comparative analysis of measures, one must evaluate the different paternalistic tools and their impact on autonomy (preference or end paternalism) and/or rationality (cognitive or means paternalism) comparatively.

Nudging measures are based on the psychological research initiated by Kahneman and Tversky. Kahneman differentiates between a fast and a slow system of human decision-making.[43] The first system is intuition, and the second is reason or logical thinking (reasoning). Intuitive decisions occur quickly, automatically, simultaneously, and without effort; they are associative and emotional. This system is prone to cognitive errors. Reasoning, by contrast, is slow, controlled, rule-governed, flexible and non-emotional. It requires effort. Human beings switch between these two systems when they have reason to do so—for instance, when they become aware of earlier failures of their own doing.[44] Stop signs, in whatever form, can make human beings switch from the fast to the slow system, which is less prone to biases, especially cognitive errors.

The legal system has different instruments at its disposal to intervene: (1) it can manipulate choice invisibly (choice manipulation), (2) it can command or prohibit certain choices explicitly (prohibitions), or (3) it can support choice (choice support). Supportive instruments can take the form of either a measure providing facilitation for an isolated decision by an individual, or a communicative process. An isolated choice facilitation instrument is limited to slowing down the decision of an *isolated individual* during the decision-making process. It is a stop sign aiming at inducing auto-deliberation. However, individuals usually communicate before they take important decisions. To the best of my knowledge, communicative choice facilitation instruments have been completely ignored by legal scholars and behavioural economists addressing paternalism.[45] A communication-oriented regulation of biases establishes rules in support of rationality and autonomy, and improves the basis for individual choice through communication and deliberation.[46] This kind of regulation provides especially strong stop signs, capable of influencing preferences and cognition while guaranteeing autonomy.

---

[43] Kahneman, *Thinking Fast and Slow* (n 10).

[44] Kahneman, 'A Perspective on Judgment and Choice' (n 10) 698 and, extensively, Kahneman, *Thinking, Fast and Slow* (n 10).

[45] These instruments are now being discussed in Germany, see in eg Fateh-Moghadam, 'Grenzen des weichen Paternalismus' (n 39) drawing on my article A van Aaken, 'Begrenzte Rationalität und Paternalismusgefahr' (n *). Mediation, sometimes mandatory before legal proceedings can be instituted, is a prime example; see on this issue A van Aaken, 'Das deliberative Element juristischer Verfahren' (n *).

[46] See the extensive discussion in van Aaken, 'Das deliberative Element juristischer Verfahren' (n *) and ch 13, Y Feldman and O Lobel, 'Behavioral Trade-offs: Beyond the Land of Nudges Spans the World of Law and Psychology', in this book, IV.A.

A. Invisible Choice Manipulation

Often, nudges are invisible. In many instances, people are (made) aware neither of the cognitive bias nor of the nudge that seeks to address it and are thus ignorant of the manipulation of their choice. Invisible nudges operating on the fast, unreflective, emotional system of thinking 'entail a subtle form of manipulation by taking advantage of the human tendency to act unreflectively and, to that extent, are inconsistent with demonstrating respect for individual autonomy'.[47] They thus replace one evil with another: diminishing autonomy for achieving 'better' decisions (better in some sort of 'objective' sense, such as the presumed objectively good outcomes for an individual or for society). This is highly problematic and very different from the transparency requirements for state action.[48] It impacts the rule of law to a considerable degree since law, and the measures based thereon, must be public and accessible to those targeted or affected by the measure. This is a prerequisite for them to be challengeable in courts: if the individual does not know she is nudged, she cannot challenge the measure.

One well-studied instrument is the so-called 'default rule'. The status quo of the allocation of rights influences decisions, mainly because of the endowment effect, but possibly also because of inertia, decision costs, transaction costs and the 'status quo bias'.[49] These nudges may, but need not be, invisible to the individual, thereby impacting autonomy.[50] If, for example, individuals do not know whether their country has an opt-in or an opt-out system of organ donation, they are unaware

---

[47] Yeung (n 24) 136. See also Alemanno and Spina (n 4) 25: 'It is undisputed that government transparency—which results in the recognition of a right of citizens to have access to government information and documents—foresees, as a necessary corollary, a correspondent governmental duty to provide information to citizens which are complete, accurate and reliable. As a result, any attempt at using information tools in order to influence behaviour and citizens' choice, such as mandating pictorial warnings consisting in vivid images of disease on tobacco, alcohol or junk food, could hardly be regarded as something less objectionable than government propaganda' (footnotes omitted). Yet Alemanno and Spina also deem that pure information can impact invisibly on choices. This is correct, but if there is any opportunity to nudge transparently, it needs to be taken.

[48] The transparency of a public debate or deliberation on (invisible) nudges is a different matter. What I am addressing here is not the time a measure is taken by the public authorities, ie the time a law is made, but the time the addressee of the measure is confronted with it. So even if there is a public discussion on nudging concerning organ donation, this is no substitute for the visibility of the nudge at the time an individual gets nudged. Both instances require transparency. See for an extensive discussion, PG Hansen and AM Jespersen, 'Nudge and the Manipulation of Choice. A Framework for the Responsible Use of the Nudge Approach to Behaviour Change in Public Policy' (2013) 1 *European Journal of Risk Regulation* 1. See also in the same vein, Feldman and Lobel (n 46) IV.B.1: 'Under a nudge approach, the law operates behind the scenes, in the background of private decision-making, serving to facilitate individuals choices … the law operates under cover'.

[49] Inertia may have different causes, the status quo bias being just one of them. There can be rational reasons for staying with the status quo, eg transaction costs.

[50] Sunstein (n 1) 125, admits that default rules may impact on autonomy, even a thin version of it. Bubb and Pildes in 'How Behavioral Economics Trims Its Sails and Why' (2014) 1594, hold that 'Many of these seemingly choice-preserving tools are not nearly as light touch as advertised. The default rules so central to BLE are often better viewed as preserving the formality of choice while, for many individuals, functioning as effective mandates'.

of their choice. This should not be permissible; I will return to choice-supporting nudges below.

If a rational choice, while respecting the autonomy and preferences of the individual, is the aim of a nudge (cognitive paternalism), then giving people the opportunity to correct themselves requires the initiation of learning processes. These are required for rational, yet fully autonomous, choices, which in turn are essential for sustainable outcomes (eg in regard to health), since absent the nudge people would otherwise go back to the undesired behaviour.[51] Experience itself is a de-biasing instrument; decisionmakers with more experience are less prone to biases.[52] Furthermore, the sustainability of a nudge is impacted without learning effects. Thus, nudges without learning effects should be impermissible because they do not change people's intrinsic motivation and reflection: people remain biased and continuously succumb to errors unless the nudge is present. Nudges have only a one-off short-term effect.[53] From an autonomy point of view, enabling learning is crucial. It is hard to justify a state keeping its citizens in the 'fast thinking' mode in cases where a 'slow thinking' mode can be initiated. However, this is the opposite of what we observe (eg when food is offered in a certain way): too often, nudges do exactly that, namely, they keep citizens in the 'fast thinking' mode rather than helping them to think more slowly and enabling meta-cognition (ie the knowledge an individual has about her own cognitive performance). This is especially true of invisible nudges.

The same applies for nudges using social norms, such as energy bills with additional information on the average use of neighbours,[54] because they play on the emotions of social shaming. Bovens argues that a

> [n]udge poses a threat to liberty as autonomy. It aims to modify behaviour by appealing to a-rational processes. A person who is subject to such a-rational processes is not fully in control of her agency and hence does not act in a fully autonomous manner.[55]

Bovens thus criticises the loss of moral agency. Hausman and Welch argue that

> [t]he paternalistic policies espoused by Thaler, Sunstein, and others, which involve negligible interferences with freedom (in the sense of the range of alternatives that can

---

[51] In the same vein, Feldman and Lobel (n 46) IV.A.2: 'The notion of sustainability is a general weakness of much of the nudge approach'. Feldman and Lobel use the long-term commitment and sustainability of the 'good choices' to measure the effectiveness of the regulation.

[52] EM Hafner-Burton, DA Hughes and DG Victor, 'The Cognitive Revolution and the Political Psychology of Elite Decision Making' (2013) 11 *Perspectives on Politics* 368, 368.

[53] Some decisions are one-off decisions, such as organ donation and retirement plans. Here, learning effects are less important. Instead, since they involve very important issues, a well-informed deliberate decision should be made and enabled. See in the same vein Feldman and Lobel (n 46) IV.A.2. See also Cserne (n 14).

[54] The effects of this 'social norm' on adequate energy behaviour is very strong. See, for experiments in the UK, P Dolan and R Metcalfe, 'Neighbors, Knowledge, and Nuggets: Two Natural Field Experiments on the Role of Incentives on Energy Conservation' (2013) CEP Discussion Paper No 1222, available at eprints.lse.ac.uk/51563/. This energy-saving strategy is based on the book of RB Cialdini, *Influence: The Psychology of Persuasion*, 3rd edn (New York, Harper Business, 2006).

[55] L Bovens, 'Real Nudge' (2012) 3 *European Journal of Risk Regulation* 43, 44.

be chosen), may threaten the individual's control over her choosing. To the extent that they are attempts to undermine that individual's control over her own deliberation, as well as her ability to assess her alternatives, they are prima facie as threatening to liberty, broadly understood, as is overt coercion.[56]

To sum up: we need to distinguish on an abstract level whether a nudge targets preferences and thereby autonomy (end paternalism) or just cognition (means paternalism). I submit that whenever possible, a nudge needs to activate the reflective mode of thinking. If the autonomy of the nudged individual is the underlying aim, invisible choice manipulation is not a proportionate paternalistic measure. Invisible nudges stifle autonomy and agency; they thus provoke what they are meant to remedy. The same holds true, though to a lesser degree, of nudges targeting cognition; without reflection, they might have only one-off short-term effects.

B. Prohibition of Choice and Mandatory Choice

A prohibition of choice is the strongest explicit paternalist instrument and places the most severe restriction on civil rights and liberties. Should the individual nevertheless choose the prohibited alternative, she risks bearing substantial costs. Prohibitions are result-oriented. They neither promote rational decision-making nor autonomy. Prominent examples are the prohibition of drugs and the mandatory requirement to wear a helmet or fasten a seatbelt while driving. Similarly, a mandatory choice prescribing a desirable decision (eg a compulsory saving plan or mandatory social insurance schemes) also falls under this category because the individual is prohibited to opt out of the system. Prohibitions do not differentiate between forming preferences and correcting cognitive errors or weakness of will. They do not allow for deliberate learning processes (although these might promote the formation of habits, eg the wearing of seatbelts). They are thus a hard paternalistic measure that needs to be evaluated accordingly in the proportionality analysis. Nevertheless, they are visible and can be challenged as an infringement of a fundamental right.

C. Instruments Supporting Choice

Instruments supporting choice do not prescribe a predetermined choice to the individual; they preserve the choice to decide freely. They attempt to facilitate a reflected rational and informed choice by the individual. They do not necessarily aim at preference formation (end paternalism) but at realising a respected preference by correcting cognition (means paternalism) and sometimes emotions—although the latter is often done invisibly and would thus fall under manipulation. Still, support for choice has a paternalistic impetus in the sense

---

[56] Hausman and Welch (n 1) 130.

that the measures aim at an increase in the individual's welfare (as understood subjectively by the nudged individual, thus safeguarding autonomy). Support for choice can be subdivided into two types: the first is considered to be isolated support not based on communication and provided to balance the cognitive deficit. It is result-oriented. The direction of influence is unilateral from the norm/measure to the individual to be nudged. By contrast, communicative support offers only form, not content—that is to say, it can aim at both, rationality and autonomy via communication and interactivity.

i. Isolated Instruments Supporting Choice

The isolated instruments supporting choice can be put in place by different measures. An initial approach is to give individuals full, accessible information. Information deficits and information asymmetries are market failures that justify state intervention.[57] Information not only contributes to sound decision-making, but also serves the purpose of increasing awareness of bias. This is illustrated by several consumer protection measures, such as the obligation to inform contractual parties to a consumer credit agreement about real interest rates. In a similar way, information campaigns (such as warning signs on cigarette packages, breast cancer warnings or 'safer sex' campaigns) can be initiated by the state. The way information is presented also matters for decision-making.[58] In other words: information is never neutral. It is sometimes difficult to differentiate between warning and preference formation (due to a campaign's inherent educational aim). Pure preference education would be very hard to justify in a liberal state. Nevertheless, if there is informational content in the warning and it is not pure taste manipulation, it is permissible, though subject to scrutiny.

Second, states can offer incentives for self-engagement, e.g. by creating the possibility to sign self-exclusion contracts for casinos.[59] Due to weaknesses of will,

---

[57] There are also discussions of the duty to disclose information to counteract information deficits, as well as government measures to educate people. However, these discussions are not held under the banner of paternalism. For Mill (n 23) 113ff, it is nevertheless obvious that education should target minors only. Educational measures for adults are inadmissible.

[58] This is the impetus for plain packing of cigarettes as proposed by the World Health Organisation (WHO) Framework Convention on Tobacco Control (FCTC), WHA Res 56.1, World Health Assembly, Annex WHO Doc A56.VR/4, 21 May 2003, entered into force on 27 February 2005, 42 ILM (2003) 518 and Guidelines for Implementation of Article 11 of the WHO Framework Convention on Tobacco Control (Packaging and Labelling of Tobacco Products) in Third Session of the Conference of the Parties of the WHO Framework Convention on Tobacco Control, Durban, South Africa, 17–22 November 2008, available at www.who.int/fctc/guidelines/article_11.pdf. The WHO's recommendations have been implemented in ever more countries, recently by the EU: Directive 2014/40/EU of the European Parliament and of the Council on the approximation of the laws, regulations and administrative provisions of the Member States concerning the manufacture, presentation and sale of tobacco and related products and repealing Directive 2007/37/EU.

[59] Some states in the US give gamblers the possibility to ban themselves from casinos by signing an ex ante agreement. See Bernheim and Rangel (n 6) 48.

individuals will most likely not be able to remedy time-inconsistent behaviour, but they can develop self-binding mechanisms to compensate for their weaknesses of will.[60] Also, the legal system can offer instruments and incentives that compensate for these weaknesses, and it can also support people in their quest for self-constraint. Here the legal system can be imagined as offering the rope for Ulysses to tie himself to the mast.

Third, default rules do not need to be invisible. This has been empirically studied in the US, with a special focus on company pension schemes: a significantly higher number of employees join a company's pension scheme when it is presented as an 'opt-out' rather than an 'opt-in' system.[61] By the same token, to give an example of a non-paternalistic nudge, opt-in default rules for organ donors result in significantly less donors than opt-out rules.[62] Although invisible default rules are often seen as unavoidable, there is a third possibility. People can be asked to choose explicitly. In other words, it is mandated that individuals actively choose one option. This means that people must decide at some point of time (eg when turning 18, renewing passports, or applying for a driving license). The result of the decision itself is left completely open, although information can and should be given, though as neutrally as possible. This is crucial for very important decisions such as pension plans or organ donation.

A fourth type of instrument is the 'regret mechanism', which aims at making it possible for individuals to think their decision through and let them decide afterwards whether the decision was based on a 'bias' and was therefore wrong. This mechanism gives the individual the opportunity to reverse a decision without incurring costs. Examples of 'regret mechanisms' are the laws governing withdrawal from off-premises contracts[63] and pre-established waiting periods (eg divorce law). Nevertheless, moral hazard problems (assuming the rational self-interested behaviour of consumers) are real and it is essential for lawmakers to consider and take them into account as well.

ii. Communicative Instruments Supporting Choice

The legal instruments designed to counteract biases assume that the decisionmaker is an isolated Robinson Crusoe; they target isolated individual decision-making

---

[60] On this model of the *homo economicus*, which endogenises the preferences dependent on willpower, see RD Cooter, 'Models of Morality in Law and Economics: Self-Control and Self-Improvement for the "Bad Man" of Holmes' (1998) 78 *Boston University Law Review* 903.

[61] Reference in Sunstein and Thaler (n 8); Thaler and Sunstein (n 1) chs 7 and 9. According to *The Economist* 27 August 2005, 62, there are also pension plans in New Zealand and Great Britain which make use of these behavioural effects from the presented alternatives. For a critique of extending default rules too easily to other issue areas, see LE Willis, 'When Nudges Fail: Slippery Defaults' (2013) 80 *University of Chicago Law Review* 1155.

[62] EJ Johnson and D Goldstein, 'Do Defaults Save Lives?' (2003) 302 *Science*, available online at www.webs.wofford.edu/pechwj/Do%20Defaults%20Save%20Lives.pdf.

[63] See Directive of the European Parliament and of the Council 2011/83/EU of 25 October 2011 on consumer rights [2011] OJ L/304 (arts 7 and 9).

without using the instrument of communication. Softening biases through processes—especially by *autonomising* deliberative or communicative processes—has been neglected.[64] These instruments are especially useful for end paternalism. Communicative solutions focus on the activation of individual reflections before a decision (such as the legal obligation of banks to provide individual explanations when selling high-risk shares),[65] on communicative rationality,[66] or on deliberation.[67] Here, consultations are mandatory. A prominent example is approval commissions in hospitals, where the rationality and autonomy of a patient's decision to take part in a clinical trial or to donate an organ is subjected to review by an independent commission. Here informed consent is necessary; information provided by the doctor alone is deemed insufficient.[68] Communicative solutions are therefore always possible in interactive situations (such as contracts, interactions between government and citizens). The interaction derives partially from the nature of the situation (eg negotiations, collective decision processes and conflicts; 'natural interaction situations'). However, interaction can also emerge from legal rules ('created interaction situations').

In this scenario, there are three models: first, one that only reviews the information transmission without consulting targeted persons (transmitter-oriented). This is not a communicative instrument to support choice. It is similar to information campaigns, using speech instead of text or pictures, eg health warnings on cigarette

---

[64] For more details, see van Aaken, 'Das deliberative Element juristischer Verfahren' (n *). The approach rests on the fundamental communicative nature of human beings, see for philosophical details J Habermas, *Between Facts and Norms: Contributions to a Discourse Theory of Law and Democracy* (Cambridge, MIT Press, 1996). For a philosophical underpinning, see A van Aaken, 'Deliberative Institutional Economics, or Does Homo Oeconomicus Argue?' in A van Aaken, C List and C Lütge (eds), *Deliberation and Decision Economics, Constitutional Theory and Deliberative Democracy* (Aldershot, Ashgate, 2004). See also Feldman and Lobel (n 46).

[65] See, eg German Supreme Court decision BGHZ, XI ZR 172/95 of 11 June 1996—in: NJW 1996, 2511, regarding the conclusion of a forward transaction on a stock exchange, where an increased need for information depending on the individual circumstances of the investor or the peculiarities of the forward transaction on the stock exchange was observed. An additional (pre-)contractual duty to inform must be in place to satisfy this need for information. A failure to inform will result in damages upon conclusion of the contract.

[66] For Habermas, rationality consists not so much in the possession of particular knowledge, but rather in 'how speaking and acting subjects acquire and use knowledge'. J Habermas, *The Theory of Communicative Action*, vol I: Reason and the Rationalization of Society (T McCarthy tr, Boston, Beacon, 1985) 11. 'Communicative rationality is not a substantive conception of reason … Rationality refers primarily to the use of knowledge in language and action, rather than to a property of knowledge. One might say that it refers primarily to a mode of dealing with validity claims, and that it is in general not a property of these claims themselves'. See M Cooke, *Language and Reason: A Study in Habermas's Pragmatics* (Cambridge, MIT Press, 1994) 38.

[67] A process is understood as being deliberative when three conditions are fulfilled: all affected parties take part, the decision is based on arguments from and for participants and the decision is guided by impartiality as well as rationality. See J Elster, 'Introduction' in J Elster (ed), *Deliberative Democracy* (Cambridge, Cambridge University Press, 1998) 8.

[68] Similarly, a person may end her own life, provided that she is capable of freely reaching a decision on this question; see *Pretty v United Kingdom* App no 2346/02 (ECtHR 29 April 2002) ECHR 423, ECHR 2002-III, paras 61ff. In some countries, eg Germany, pregnancy counselling is mandatory before an abortion (although this is not a strictly paternalistic measure).

packaging. Second, the perception of information or possible failures in the decision—such as the voluntariness of the act or the stability of the decision—can be reviewed interactively (recipient-oriented), for example investment information in banks. Third, there can be situations that require a consultation in which the decision will be generated during (or after) the meeting, for example in clinical trials. In the last two cases, the mechanisms used aim at safeguarding the rationality and/or autonomy of the decision.[69] Since the last process is costly, it should be used only for very important decisions.

Communicative procedures can be understood, first, as a tool to help the formation of preferences and, second, as a de-biasing instrument (ie a tool that can remedy cognitive biases).[70] This interactive component can structure and transform the individuals' reflections and preferences. Thus, preference formation as well as cognitive errors can be targeted through communication. Whether positive or negative information is emphasised will influence the individual focus on the way the information is given. Experiments have revealed that individuals confronted with a 'frame' as well as a 'counter-frame' were less subjected to the framing effect.[71] Interpersonal communication can also reduce the 'framing effect' when individuals are exposed to other frames during discussions.[72] This suggests that deliberative processes can be an important instrument of bias reduction. Furthermore, they fundamentally rest upon the necessity of presenting arguments and can thus target the autonomous, deliberated choice of the individual. Interpersonal communication can make biases impressively apparent for the person succumbing to them. First, deliberations can render someone aware of a bias—as a necessary prerequisite for auto-correcting the bias. Second, they can generate information. Third, deliberations can balance the failures of perception via communicative processes, generating new perspectives and simultaneously inducing the individual to confront these perspectives. To sum up: deliberation establishes rules for thinking and can eliminate the possible failures of intuition. It can also enable learning processes, preference formation and enhance autonomous decision-making.

---

[69] See B Fateh-Moghadam, 'Leitlinien für die Arbeit der Lebendspendekommissionen? Zur Legitimation von Verfahren im Medizinrecht' in C Rittner and NW Paul (eds), *Ethik der Lebensorganspende* (Basel, Schwabe, 2005) 131 in detail on live organ transplants.

[70] van Aaken, 'Das deliberative Element juristischer Verfahren' (n *); RB Korobkin, 'Psychological Impediments to Mediation Success: Theory and Practice' (2006) 21 *Ohio State Journal on Dispute Resolution* 281.

[71] JN Druckmann, 'Political Preference Formation: Competition, Deliberation and the (Ir)relevance of Framing Effects' (2004) 98 *American Political Science Review* 671, 675.

[72] JD Morrow, *Game Theory for Political Scientists* (New Jersey, Princeton University Press, 1994) 48; JN Druckmann, 'Political Preference Formation: Competition, Deliberation and the (Ir)relevance of Framing Effects' (2004) *American Political Science Review* 671, 675.

IV. JUDGING THE NUDGE IN THE EUROPEAN UNION

Having described different alternatives of paternalistic measures, we can now judge them. First, the rights possibly infringed by nudging regulation will be presented. Second, the interference with a right through a nudge will be discussed. Third, possible nudges will be assessed under the proportionality principle.

A. Rights Possibly Infringed by Nudging: Scope of Protection

First we need to define the 'right' against which the measure is judged. If there is no right that may be infringed by nudging measures, then there is no legal control by individuals of the measures taken by the EU.[73] In the EU, fundamental rights are guaranteed by multi-level protections.[74] We find these rights in the Charter of Fundamental Rights (CFR),[75] the European Convention of Human Rights (ECHR),[76] and the general principles common to the constitutional traditions of the Member States.[77] Since the ECHR informs the interpretation of the CFR as a minimum standard,[78] we will deal with the ECHR first before turning to the CFR and then to the common constitutional traditions of Member States.

The ECHR does not contain a right of general freedom to pursue any lawful activity such as feeding pigeons,[79] or horse riding in the forest[80] (in contrast to Art 2(1) of the German Constitution, or Basic Law).[81] Such a right has a very broad scope of protection and is subsidiary to other, more specific rights, but it limits a possibly paternalistic state without legal gaps. Nevertheless, Article 8 ECHR, with its protection of privacy, secures a sphere within which the individual can

---

[73] I focus only on measures taken by the EU or by Member States based on EU laws. The CFR obliges the EU to act and legislate consistently with the Charter, and enables the EU's courts to strike down EU legislation that contravenes it. The Charter applies to EU Member States implementing EU law but does not extend the competences of the EU beyond those given to it in the treaties.

[74] For a short description, see G Di Frederico, 'Fundamental Rights in the EU: Legal Pluralism and Multi-Level Protection after the Lisbon Treaty' in G Di Frederico (ed), *The EU Charter of Fundamental Rights From Declaration to Binding Instrument* (Dordrecht, Springer, 2011) 15.

[75] Due to the status as primary law in art 6(1) TEU. As art 6(3) states: 'Fundamental rights, as guaranteed by the European Convention for the Protection of Human Rights and Fundamental Freedoms and as they result from the constitutional traditions common to the Member States, shall constitute general principles of the Union's law'. Art 6(2) foresees the accession to the ECHR.

[76] European Convention for the Protection of Human Rights and Fundamental Freedoms, 213 UNTS 222, entered into force 3 September 1953.

[77] Case 11/70 *Internationale Handelsgesellschaft mbH v Einfuhr- und Vorratsstelle für Getreide und Futtermittel* [1970] ECR 1125 and Case 4/73 *J. Nold, Kohlen- und Baustoffgroßhandlung of the European Communities* [1974] ECR 491.

[78] D Ehlers, '§ 14 General Principles' in D Ehlers (ed), *European Fundamental Rights and Freedoms* (Berlin, De Gruyter, 2007) 378, para 13 and art 52(3)(2) CFR.

[79] BVerfG, 23.05.1980—2 BvR 854/79, BVerfGE 54, 143, 146.

[80] BVerfG, 06.06.1989—1 BvR 921/85, 3.BVerfGE 80, 137, 152ff.

[81] 'Every person shall have the right to free development of his personality insofar as he does not violate the rights of others or offend against the constitutional order or the moral law'.

freely pursue the development and fulfilment of her personality and autonomy.[82] It protects 'the free development of the personality'.[83] As the European Court of Human Rights has held numerous times,

> [i]n the Convention system, rights must be broadly construed and exceptions or limitations interpreted narrowly. This is even more so for Article 8 where the Court has consistently held that the notion of private life is a broad concept.[84] It encompasses, for example, the right to establish and develop relationships with other human beings and the right to identity and personal development.[85]

The issue of autonomy and paternalism came up under the 'veil' of jurisprudence. As Judge Tulkens held in a dissenting opinion: '"Paternalism" … runs counter to the case-law of the Court, which has developed a real right to personal autonomy on the basis of Article 8'.[86] The Court has held that 'private life' includes 'the rights to personal autonomy, personal development'.[87] This reasoning seems to be in line with the principle of autonomy described above.

But the scope of protection is specific, not subsidiary or gap-filling.[88] The obligation to wear a seatbelt, for example, is not seen as falling under the scope of protection of Article 8.[89] Nevertheless, a general prohibition on smoking or drinking alcohol must be judged differently, as a relevant commentator, Jochen Frowein, held.[90] Although the Court often intermingles the scope of protection with the gravity of interference (eg in environmental protection cases),[91] for the

---

[82] See also Resolution 428 (1970) of the Consultative Assembly of the Council of Europe, stating that the right to privacy 'consists essentially in the right to live one's own life with a minimum of interference'.

[83] See cases *KA and AD v Belgium* App no 42758/98 (ECtHR, 17 February 2005) para 83 and *Bigaeva v Greece* App no 26713/05 (ECtHR, 28 May 2009) para 22; C Grabenwarter, *European Convention on Human Rights. Commentary* (München, CH Beck, 2014) art 8, para 6; D Richter, 'Lücken der EMRK und lückenloser Grunsrechtsschutz' in O Dörr, R Grote and T Marhauhn (eds), *EMRK/GG, Konkordanzkommentar*, vol I, 2nd edn (Tübingen, Mohr/Siebeck, 2013) para 82.

[84] See on hunting, *Friend and others v United Kingdom* App nos 16072/06, 27809/08 (ECtHR 24 November 2009) para 41; *EB v France* [GC] App no 43546/02 (ECtHR 22 January 2009) para 43 and references therein.

[85] *Friend and others v United Kingdom*, para 41; *Niemietz v Germany* App no 13710/88 (ECtHR 16 December 1992) 33, para 29; *Bensaid v United Kingdom* App no 44599/98 (ECtHR 6 May 2001) para 47.

[86] Case of *Leyla Sahin v Turkey* App no 44774/98 (ECtHR 10 November 2005) Dissenting Opinion para 12. See for further references *Keenan v United Kingdom* App no 27229/95 (ECtHR 3 April 2001) ECHR 2001-III, para 92; *Pretty v United Kingdom* (n 68) paras 65–67; *Christine Goodwin v United Kingdom* App no 28957/95 [GC] (ECtHR 11 July 2002) ECHR 2002-VI, para 90. This applies notwithstanding the final judgments, which held the prohibition of veils in public places for security reasons to be in conformity with the ECHR. See the most recent case of *SAS v France* App no 43835/11 (ECtHR 1 July 2014).

[87] Case of *Evans v United Kingdom* App no 6339/05 [GC] (ECtHR 10 April 2007) para 71.

[88] Grabenwarter, *European Convention of Human Rights* (2014) art 8, para 5.

[89] *X* App no 8707/79 (EComHR 13 December 1979) DR 18, 255. JA Frowein, 'Article 8' in JA Frowein and W Peukert (eds), *EMRK Kommentar*, 3rd edn (Kehl am Rhein, NP Engel, 2009) para 7.

[90] Frowein, 'Article 8' (2009) para 7; *De Klerck v Belgium* App no 8307/78 (EComHR 1981) DR 21, 124, para 116.

[91] *Dubetska and others v Ukraine* App no 30499/03 (ECtHR 2 May 2011) para 105: 'The Court refers to its well-established case-law that neither Article 8 nor any other provision of the Convention guarantees the right to preservation of the natural environment as such … Likewise, no issue will arise if

sake of clarity and legal security, these two steps in the legal scrutiny of a measure should be distinguished. Thus, a general freedom of action, such as smoking, is either within the scope of protection or it is not. As we have seen, the scope of protection is to be interpreted broadly if in doubt; thus we may argue that, in principle, paternalistic measures targeting autonomy are covered by the scope of protection offered private life under Article 8 ECHR.

Turning to the EU Treaties, Article 2 Treaty on European Union (TEU) names freedom as a right to be protected directly after human dignity and thereby stresses its importance. Freedom is interpreted as a political and historical notion, as a principle on which the unification of Europe rests. Freedom is understood, on the one hand, as the freedom from tyranny and, on the other hand, as the possibility of autonomy for the individual. It also follows that the individual has priority over the collective. This is the background against which the definition of a potential subsidiary right of personal freedom must be judged. One may argue that any infringement of autonomy is covered by the protection of human dignity under Article 1 CFR.[92] Using a historical approach to determine the scope of protection, the Convention did not accept a proposal which read, 'Everyone's dignity and freedom must be respected'.[93] This proposal was meant to protect against paternalistic encroachments on freedom, but the Convention thought that dignity needed to stand on its own, without being 'diluted' by other rights or principles.[94] Which other fundamental rights of the CFR might then be infringed by paternalistic measures?

There is almost total consensus that neither Article 6 (the right to liberty and security) nor Article 7 CFR (respect for private and family life) comprises a right to general freedom of action as it does in Germany (because both articles are interpreted in the light of the ECHR).[95] Article 7 CFR, although protecting autonomy in principle, covers autonomy only insofar as it is connected in a qualified way to the enumerated protections (private and family life, home and communications). It does not complement the *status negativus* of the other rights of the CFR.[96]

---

the detriment complained of is negligible in comparison to the environmental hazards inherent in life in every modern city. However, an arguable claim under Article 8 may arise where an environmental hazard attains a level of severity resulting in significant impairment of the applicant's ability to enjoy his home, private or family life. The assessment of that minimum level is relative and depends on all the circumstances of the case, such as the intensity and duration of the nuisance and its physical or mental effects on the individual's health or quality of life'.

[92] Although there was a discussion in the Convent, human dignity is more than just a non-legally binding programme. See, eg M Borowsky, 'Artikel 1' in J Meyer (ed), *Charter der Grundrechte der Europäischen Union, Nomos Kommentar*, 3rd edn (Baden-Baden, Nomos 2011) para 7; Richter, *Lücken der EMRK* (n 83) para 19.

[93] Document Charter 4370/00 Contrib 233 of 15 June 2000, 11.

[94] Borowsky (n 92) para 8.

[95] See N Bernsdorff, 'Artikel 7' in J Meyer (ed), *Charta der Grundrechte der Europäischen Union*, 3rd edn (Baden-Baden, Nomos, 2011) para 15, who argues that this was explicitly excluded by art 52(3) CFR. Similarly, HD Jarass, *Charta der Grundrechte der Europäischen Union, Kommentar*, 2nd edn (München, CH Beck, 2013) Einleitung para 35.

[96] Bernsdorff, 'Artikel 7', ibid, para 15.

Nevertheless, like Article 8 ECHR, it has the potential for evolution and may indeed eventually evolve[97] and adapt to new forms of regulation.[98]

The critique that the CFR contains no explicit guarantee of freedom of action and may thus lag behind the scope of protection offered by rights in some Member States[99] can be considered exaggerated since the ECJ has arguably constructed such a right through general principles common to the constitutional traditions of the Member States (Art 6(3) TEU and Art 52(4) CFR). These rights can surpass the scope of protection of the ECHR, thereby taking into account the higher level of integration between EU Member States.[100] The relevant question is whether there is such a common tradition of a general right of freedom of action. Whereas some commentators deny this,[101] others, including the ECJ, affirm the existence of these common traditions.[102] However, the ECJ did so only in passing: while confirming the existence of the right, it did not elaborate on the common traditions.[103]

Even if the existence of a right of general freedom to pursue any lawful activity is denied or if the scope of protection under the CFR and ECHR is restricted, any nudging measure must be prescribed by law and must be proportionate.[104] It is a general principle of EU law that interferences by public authorities in the private

---

[97] Arts 52(3)(1) CFR; P Szczekalla, 'Freiheit im Europäischen Verfassungsverbund. Allgemeine Rechtsgrundsätze zwischen Instrumentalisierung und Auflösung?' (2005) *Deutsche Verwaltungsblätter* 286; Richter (n 83) para 82.

[98] See M Burbergs, 'How the Respect for Private and Family Life, Home and Correspondence Became the Nursery in Which New Rights are Born: Art 8 ECHR' in E Brems and J Gerards (eds), *Shaping Rights in the ECHR. The Role of the European Court of Human Rights in Determining the Scope of Human Rights* (Cambridge, Cambridge University Press, 2013) 315, 316 on personal autonomy as a right developed under art 8 and as a 'right to be left alone' (324).

[99] JF Lindner, 'EG-Grundrechtscharta—weniger Rechte für den Bürger?' (2001) *Bayrische Verwaltungsblätter* 523, 524.

[100] Richter (n 83) para 20.

[101] C Calliess, 'Art 6 GRCh' in C Calliess and M Ruffert (eds), *EUV/AEUV. Das Verfassungsrecht der Europäischen Union mit Europäischer Grundrechtecharta, Kommentar* 4th edn (München, CH Beck, 2011) para 8; Jarrass, *Charta der Grundrechte der EU* (2013) para 35 is sceptical about this right.

[102] See Judgment of the Court of 21 May 1987, Joined Cases 133 to 136/85 *Walter Rau Lebensmittelwerke and others v Bundesanstalt für landwirtschaftliche Marktordnung* [1987] ECR 2289, paras 15, 19. However, the argumentation by the ECJ is rather thin. Paragraph 15: 'In its third question, the Verwaltungsgericht asks in substance whether Community measures which have the effect of improving the position of certain undertakings and thereby place their competitors at a disadvantage are contrary to the general principles of Community law, and in particular to the principle of freedom to pursue a trade or profession, *the principle of general freedom to pursue any lawful activity* and the principle of freedom of competition'. The ECJ confirms the right in para 19: 'Accordingly, the answer to the third question must be that a decision ... does not conflict with ... the principle of general freedom to pursue any lawful activity'.

[103] Joined Cases 133/85 to 136/85 *Rau* [1987] ECR 2289, paras 15ff; Joined Cases 46/87 & 227/88 *Hoechst* [1989] ECR 2859, para 19; Case 85/87 *Dow Benelux* [1989] ECR 3137, para 30.

[104] In *Hoechst* [1989] ECR 2859, para 19, the ECJ stated, 'None the less, in all the legal systems of the Member States, any intervention by the public authorities in the sphere of private activities of any person, whether natural or legal, must have a legal basis and be justified on the grounds laid down by law, and, consequently, those systems provide, albeit in different forms, protection against arbitrary or disproportionate intervention. The need for such protection must be recognized as a general principle of Community law'.

sphere must not be arbitrary, need to be prescribed by law, justified by a legitimate aim and be proportionate.[105] In *Rau*, the ECJ stated,

> [i]t is settled case-law that in order to establish whether a provision of Community law complies with the principle of proportionality, it must be ascertained whether the means which it employs are suitable for the purpose of achieving the desired objective and whether they do not go beyond what is necessary to achieve it.[106]

Articles 52(1), (3), and (4) CFR in conjunction with Article 6(3) TEU as well as the principle of protection of the private sphere under Article 8 ECHR, Article 7 CFR and the common traditions, interpreted in the light of freedom under Article 2 TEU, can be said to secure a comprehensive protection of individual rights. Therefore, we can judge regulation-by-nudging in light of the proportionality principle and the requirement that any infringement be prescribed by law.[107] Article 52(1) CFR can be considered as 'last resort' compensation for a missing explicit right of general freedom to pursue any lawful activity.[108] In conclusion, any paternalistic nudge can be legally scrutinised under the ECHR as well as the CFR.

B. Interference with a Right

In principle, nudges are characterised by the fact that they uphold the individual's right to choose since they do not prescribe or prohibit choice. Is there thus any room for interference with the rights to dignity, liberty and privacy? The ECJ applies a broad concept of 'interference', which may even include indirect, non-targeted effects on an individual's sphere of liberty emanating from governmental action.[109] If the measure is aimed at the sphere of liberty, for example decision-making in private matters, there is no doubt that it counts as an interference. Furthermore, there must be a sufficient link between the measure in question and the effects experienced.[110] This is the case with nudges, even if they are invisible, since choice is targeted and influenced. In principle, whenever a state or the EU targets the behaviour of the individual within the sphere of private life according to the meaning of Article 8 ECHR or Article 7 CFR, it interferes with the respect for private life (although this can be proportionate and thus justified).[111] Rights not

---

[105] Jarrass (n 95) para 35; Richter (n 83) para 20.
[106] Instead of many cases, see *Rau* [1987] ECR 2289, para 34 and Case C-280/93 *Bananas I* [1993] ECR I-4973, holding that any restrictions on rights is permitted only if they do not constitute, with regards to the aim pursued, disproportionate and unreasonable interference undermining the very substance of that right.
[107] Art 52(1) CFR. See only C Calliess, 'Art 2 TEU' (2011) para 18f and S Peers and S Prechal, 'Art 52—Scope and Interpretation of Rights and Principles' in S Peers and others, *The EU Charter of Fundamental Rights* (Oxford, Beck, Hart, Nomos, 2014) 1455.
[108] Richter (n 83) para 20.
[109] Case C-84/95 *Bosphorus* [1996] ECR I-3953, paras 22f.
[110] See for details, Ehlers, '§ 14 General Principles' (n 78) 391, para 42.
[111] See also Grabenwarter (n 83) art 8, 190.

only protect against visible command-and-control measures by the EU or states but also against the manipulation and targeted influence on choice. The European Court of Human Rights (ECtHR) has held that particularly strict standards must be met when the interferences concerned take place in secret (as is the case, for example, with phone interceptions), but this argument can be extended to invisible nudges. Because the affected persons do not have the possibility to challenge the measure, very strong safeguards against abuse are called for.[112]

C. Proportionality under Article 52(1) CFR

Let us first turn to the structure of the proportionality assessment.[113] Interpreting constitutional principles,[114] such as fundamental rights, is an optimisation problem when objectives of general interest or rights and freedoms of others are concerned.[115] Structurally, this is the same for paternalistic measures, although here the balancing must not be done between two competing rights or principles, but between the autonomy of the individual and some kind of 'objective' individual welfare (eg health). The scrutiny is embodied in the proportionality principle.[116] It comprises four substeps of scrutiny: the measure needs to pursue a legitimate aim and to be judged suitable, necessary and proportionate *stricto sensu*.

The suitability analysis covers the question of whether the measure or the law is in principle suitable for achieving its aim.[117] The principle of necessity covers

---

[112] See only *Weber and Saravia v Germany* App no 54934/00 (ECtHR 2006) para 94: 'since the implementation in practice of measures of secret surveillance of communications is not open to scrutiny by the individuals concerned or the public at large, it would be contrary to the rule of law for the legal discretion granted to the executive or to a judge to be expressed in terms of an unfettered power. Consequently, the law must indicate the scope of any such discretion conferred on the competent authorities and the manner of its exercise with sufficient clarity to give the individual adequate protection against arbitrary interference'.

[113] See the comprehensive discussion in A Barak, *Proportionality. Constitutional Rights and Their Limitations* (Cambridge, Cambridge University Press, 2012) and for the CFR, Peers and Prechal (n 107).

[114] For the difference between rules and principle as applied here, see R Alexy, 'Zum Begriff des Rechtsprinzips' in R Alexy (ed), *Recht, Vernunft, Diskurs: Studien zur Rechtsphilosophie* (Frankfurt aM, Suhrkamp, 1995) 177. Alexy also discusses Dworkin's understanding of this distinction. Rules are applicable or not, but principles have to be put into practice relative to real and legal constraints. They are thus applicable even if they are not 'fully' satisfied: they are norms that can be more or less implemented, eg the democratic principle or the right to freedom of opinion.

[115] Graphically, one may clarify this point by drawing a utility curve on a coordinate plane which allows the balancing of two constitutional principles. Proportionality *stricto sensu* would be allowed only in a range above a certain ordinal number (securing the core of the right, see van Aaken (n 6) 315ff. See also R Alexy, *Theorie der Grundrechte*, 3rd edn (Frankfurt aM, Suhrkamp, 1996) 147f.

[116] This is settled case law; see for details T Tridimas, *The General Principles of EU Law* (Oxford, Oxford University Press, 2006) 141f. For a critique of the doctrine of proportionality that is less refined than that under, eg German constitutional law, see Ehlers (n 78) 394, para 48.

[117] One may even consider that a total prohibition of alcohol for adults is unsuitable, since it usually does not achieve its aims.

the question of whether there are other, less intrusive means with regard to the constitutional principle in question which are equally able to achieve the stated aim. The second and third subprinciples lend themselves easily to consequentialist and instrumental reasoning, as they require a comparative analysis of measures regarding the impact on the constitutional principle or right in question. EU legislators need to show that measures are suitable and necessary,[118] although the Court of Justice of the European Union will give legislators some discretion regarding prognosis, requesting that the reasons adduced to justify it must be 'relevant and sufficient'.[119] In many cases, though, there is no thorough empirical evidence regarding the consequences of the measure and/or other available alternatives.[120] It is in this process of legal scrutiny that nudges need to show their effectiveness, based on sound empirical evidence. The fourth principle, proportionality *stricto sensu* (measures need to be adequate) is more open to value judgements and does not lend itself easily to social science approaches but rather to rational justification in the application of the law.[121] It is here that nudges may fail on the grounds that they infringe the autonomy protected by fundamental rights, even if they are effective and necessary.

i. Legitimate Aim of a Nudge

The first step in judging the proportionality of a nudge is to examine its legitimate aim. Article 52(1) CFR refers to two categories of legitimate aims: the 'objectives of general interest recognized by the Union' and the 'need to protect the rights and freedoms of others'. Interventions targeting the common interest or reducing third party externalities are in principle allowed, but if the objective is solely the protection of individuals, intervention is deemed legally problematic by most of the literature. While it is unclear whether this list in Article 52(1) is exhaustive, Peers and Prechal favour a narrow reading 'given the requirement to interpret exceptions from human rights rules narrowly'.[122] Hillgruber declares as

---

[118] It has been argued that the new Directive on tobacco products, eg the plain packing measure, is not suitable or necessary, since information campaigns could also be undertaken (see Committee of the Regions, 30 April 2013, NAT-V-026, 3, para 7). Empirical studies are sceptical that the measures taken are suitable. See for details, M Hilf, E Pache and M Richter, *Rechtsgutachten zum Kommissionsvorschlag einer neuen Tabakproduktrichtlinie* (Baden-Baden, Nomos, 2014) 47ff for warnings on cigarettes and 78ff for plain packing with further references to empirical studies.

[119] Case C-274/99P *Bernard Connolly v Commission* [2001] ECR I-1611, para 41. This calls for regulatory impact assessment as proposed by the Commission itself. See for details: www.ec.europa.eu/smart-regulation/index_en.htm.

[120] But if there is evidence (eg because an impact assessment was conducted), it can help courts to analyse proportionality. See A Alemanno, 'A Meeting of Minds in Impact Assessment: When Ex Ante Evaluation Meets Ex Post Judicial Control' (2011) 17 *European Public Law* 485.

[121] From a legal theoretical point of view, see R Alexy, 'Die Gewichtsformel' in J Jickeli, P Kreutz and D Reuter (eds), *Gedächtnisschrift Jürgen Sonnenschein* (Berlin, Verlag de Gruyter, 2003) 771. See also, PP Craig, *EU Administrative Law* (Oxford, Oxford University Press, 2006) 670–72. Craig suggests that this step is a mechanism for not putting a disproportionate burden on one party only.

[122] Peers and Prechal (n 107) 1475, para 52.47.

unconstitutional any prohibition that does not focus on underage individuals or individuals with mental disabilities. According to him, policymakers should exclusively focus on the welfare of the general public, in keeping with the principle that 'neither worthlessness nor harmfulness of a conduct justify per se that the State prohibits a certain behaviour'.[123] Based on this, Hillgruber considers justifications of restrictions on the free will of legally competent individuals as inconsistent with the aim of protecting individuals' fundamental rights.[124] I would follow this approach more cautiously, favouring not an absolute prohibition but submitting such measures to a proportionality analysis with a heavy burden of justification.

The analysis of the aim of a nudge, even if it targets a certain behavior, for example eating, would be truncated if one were not to include the underlying abstract aim (bounded rationality or some kind of alleged wrongly used autonomy). This can be rationality (cognitive paternalism) or autonomy (preference paternalism). If autonomy is targeted as opposed to rationality, other measures are required to pass the proportionality test, since the former impacts the fundamental rights more profoundly. For its legality much thus depends on the type of nudge chosen. Those nudges that activate autonomous choice and learning processes, for example information and deliberation, can be deemed permissible if the nudge is of the preference formation type.

It can be difficult to identify the aim of the measure. For example, the obligation to wear a helmet can serve to protect the motorbike rider (paternalistic aim) and at the same time constitute a mechanism to save costs that the general public would bear in case of an accident.[125] The German Federal Constitutional Court has always been evasive—invoking the common interest as the aim of the measure[126]—and

---

[123] C Hillgruber, *Der Schutz des Menschen vor sich selbst* (München, Vahlen, 1992) 119 (my translation).

[124] ibid, 175. With a similar conclusion Möller, *Paternalismus und Persönlichkeitsrecht*; K Fischer, *Die Zulässigkeit aufgedrängten staatlichen Schutzes vor Selbstschädigung* (Frankfurt aM, P Lang, 1997).

[125] However, it must be considered that welfare arguments are always easy to find, eg self-destructive behaviour, which harms society via the social welfare system. The latter externality can be eliminated if insurance does not cover damages when the duty to fasten a seatbelt is disregarded. Another question is whether the cost should rest on the individual. The same questions arise when one analyses extremely dangerous sports. For a more detailed description of the admissibility of the duty to fasten a seatbelt, see I von Münch, 'Grundrechtsschutz gegen sich selbst?' in R Stödter and W Thieme (eds), *Hamburg, Deutschland, Europa FS Hans Peter Ipsen zum siebzigsten Geburtstag* (Tübingen, Siebeck/Mohr, 1977) 113. The conclusion here is that the admissibility is predominantly denied.

[126] See German Federal Constitutional Court (GFCC) decision, BVerfGE 90, 145, 184—Cannabis: '*Das allgemeine Konzept des Gesetzgebers, den Umgang mit Cannabisprodukten … umfassend zu verbieten, verstößt für sich nicht gegen das Übermaßverbot. Es wird durch die erstrebten Zwecke gerechtfertigt, die Bevölkerung—zumal die Jugend—vor den von der Droge ausgehenden Gesundheitsgefahren sowie vor der Gefahr einer psychischen Abhängigkeit von der Droge zu schützen*' ['The general concept of the legislator to generally prohibit the use of use of Cannabis does not violate the proportionality test. It is justified due to aim to protect the population—and the youth—against the health dangers and the danger of psychological dependency of the drug'; my translation]. See also para 174 where the protection of the health of the individual as well as the general population is cited as the aim of the prohibition.

is less rigorous than the doctrine.[127] The problem of discerning the aim of the paternalistic measure (individual protection or protection of the general public) lies in the often ambiguous way in which legislators state the aim(s) of a measure. Also, if general welfare is only indirectly impacted, the judge should be cautious about accepting the aim as legitimate, especially if the autonomy of the nudged person is interfered with (this is different for cognitive paternalism). Stating as an aim some kind of general welfare and letting this pass without legal scrutiny can easily be abused by public policymakers. Economist distinguish between indirect and direct external effects. Indirect effects are those which are conveyed via the market and prices. Those do not count as market failures. The same argument applies here: using indirect effects on the community of the insured as an argument to turn a paternalistic nudge into a nudge protecting the general welfare opens legal flood gates. In summary, if the direct target is the individual, and if only the harm to the individual indirectly leads to costs for society, the legitimacy of the aim is highly questionable and needs more scrutiny.

ii. Suitability of a Nudge

Let us now turn to suitability. Invisible nudges are unsuitable for enhancing the autonomy and sustainability of the decision, since they are purely outcome-oriented in a single decision by a targeted individual; they do not enhance the long-term sustainability of the decision through deliberation.[128] However, they might be suitable for enhancing rationality since they can correct cognition errors invisibly (means paternalism). By contrast, if possible, neutral information publicised by the state or mandatory information requirements for economic operators is a suitable means.[129] It can be used as a stop sign to induce individuals to deliberate on their actions (slow thinking instead of fast thinking). The state may prompt individuals to reflect upon their preferences (but not prescribe preferences per se) by setting up stop signs and activating the reflective mode of thinking. It may also ensure that the decision taken has been deliberated upon and is fully informed.

iii. Necessity of a Nudge

The necessity test is the most important one for the legal assessment of paternalistic nudges since it compares different sort of nudges: only the least

---

[127] The GFCC observed in its decision BVerfGE 59, 275, 278, on the constitutional appeal by a motorcyclist only that the duty to wear a helmet was suitable and that other measures such as the provision of information to wear a helmet was not efficient. The GFCC did not address the question of the constitutionality of the aim. Furthermore, in its decision on the duty to fasten a seatbelt (in NJW 1987, 180) the GFCC merely referenced the reasons given in the helmet decision.
[128] See, in the same vein, Feldman and Lobel (n 46).
[129] Of course information can be ineffective depending on the way it is given. If this is the case, the information would be unsuitable.

intrusive means is permissible. First, it is undisputed that prohibitions of choice infringe on fundamental rights in the most severe manner. Even if suitable for achieving the desired aim, a prohibition must be tested against alternatives in order to assess whether there are less restrictive means available to achieve the same aim. Instruments that support choice (ie those in which freedom of choice is not overruled) are a significantly softer tool compared to prohibitions of choice or mandatory choice.[130] Second, invisible nudges (manipulation) are not choice-enhancing but restrict choice invisibly: when compared to choice-enhancing nudges susceptible of achieving the same aim, invisible nudges would fail the necessity test. This poses a problem for default rules that are not openly communicated.

Instruments that support choice can provide incentive to refrain from self-damaging behaviour but they must be transparent. This kind of choice support comes in two forms. For cognitive errors, a pure stop sign might be enough. If preferences are undetermined (as in patient decisions), communicative choice support is an additional method. Communication processes lead to self-reflection and thus to autonomous decisions. They are instruments that support decisions by fostering rationality as well as autonomy. In some situations, the 'framing effect' could be better dealt with through deliberations as opposed to information statements, for example by presenting counter-frames. Moreover, communicative instruments supporting choice can focus on the construction and transformation of preferences in order to create a sustainable form of self-help. The individual is given the opportunity to reflect on her preferences, which ought to result in a reduction of failures caused by cognitive weaknesses. Autonomy is thereby enhanced. The same holds for mandatory active choosing in comparison to the default rules currently proposed in the nudging literature.

However, mandated communication, such as patient hearings, also entails freedom costs that need to be taken into account in the necessity analysis: processes can impose significant costs on individuals as the result of undesirable, time-consuming reflection. They should only be used for important decisions. They may also aggravate biases. Therefore, attention ought to be paid to framing the communication as neutrally as possible, including the presentation of counter-frames. These communicative instruments supporting choice may be a milder instrument than *de lege lata* prohibitions. For example, even though pregnancy counselling is not a problem of paternalism in the strict sense, the idea that a communicative instrument supporting choice may be preferable to a prohibition of abortion can be retained (at least in those cases in which an information

---

[130] The enhanced provision of information by the government is in principle not an infringement of basic rights. When the duty to inform is assigned to third parties—for example, in private legal matters—an infringement of their basic rights is possible. Even though such considerations need to be included in policy-making decisions, they will not be further addressed here; see van Aaken, 'Das deliberative Element' (n *).

brochure is considered to be insufficient). Similarly, instead of prohibiting drugs, one could consider an obligation to deliberate. Deliberation would be a requirement to receive new doses of (replacement) drugs (such as methadone for heroin addicts).[131] The deliberation would comprise an analysis regarding the preference for the consumption of the drug in question as well as a test of weaknesses of will and cognition.[132] Communicative instruments supporting choice are also present in private legal matters. Such is the case in situations related to the obligation to individual consultations and explanations when high-risk stocks are purchased. Insurance policies with deductibles in relation to the duty to wear a helmet, use seatbelts or not to engage in dangerous sports are further cases in point; here mandated communication with the insurance provider can be an option.

iv. Proportionality Stricto Sensu

Proportionality *stricto sensu* must also take into account a potential disproportionate burden on already autonomous and rational individuals. Nudges can be over-inclusive. For individuals who behave rationally (spontaneously), paternalistic measures cause costs in terms of autonomy restrictions without compensating through welfare enhancement (as understood by the nudger) since these rational individuals act single-handedly in their best interest.[133] Thus, a measure targeting a small minority while imposing costs on autonomy for the majority should be deemed disproportionate.

Furthermore, once it is ensured that the individual has an informed preference, a measure targeting preferences (autonomy) will inevitably fail the proportionality test *stricto sensu* since the decision is an informed, reflected, deliberate act. This autonomy must be respected even if the individual engages in self-damaging behaviour. Indeed, the choice as to whether a short-term preference or a long-term preference is to prevail in a given moment needs to be respected as well if the decision is deliberate and informed (eg information about the health consequences of tobacco use). Paternalistic nudges not respecting informed autonomous choice are disproportionate in liberal states.

---

[131] Although deliberation might (indeed) be difficult in the acute stages of addiction (or rather 'in the presence of withdrawal symptoms'), methadone strategies have worked on the premise that people deliberate and make an active choice for the replacement drug. This can be coupled with other support strategies to overcome addiction.

[132] For a comprehensive treatment of empirical results, neurological findings and legal implications, though without a discussion of communicative instruments supporting choice, see Bernheim and Rangel (n 6) 45ff.

[133] Similarly, T O'Donoghue and M Rabin, 'Doing It Now or Later' (1999) 89 *American Economic Review* 103; O'Donoghue and Rabin (n 7); Camerer and others (n 7) 1254.

V. CONCLUSION

The liberal tradition underpinning the current rule of law assumes that individuals have stable preferences and behave rationally. Accordingly, consumers and citizens can form sound preferences, adequately process information and make informed decisions about their own welfare. The research in cognitive psychology and behavioural economics has prompted a discussion on paternalism without testing the legal limits of paternalistic nudges. European lawmakers have the duty to respect the fundamental freedoms guaranteed in the EU. Under European law all nudges need to be legally assessed in terms of their permissibility, especially with regard to the proportionality principle under Article 52(1) CFR. Addressing nudging through the lens of proportionality not only increases the transparency of paternalistic instruments; it also refines and expands the choice of instruments. This is particularly relevant to communicative instruments supporting choice, because the communicative rationality has thus far not featured in any discussion on paternalism, despite its eminent role in forming individual preferences and preventing cognitive mistakes, and despite its potential for enabling learning. Deliberative processes are no panacea, but they could represent, under certain circumstances, a milder form of paternalism. Fostering individual autonomy (not necessarily full rationality) to pursue preferences is a traditional concern for liberal states and constitutional lawyers. Law can and should be used as a prominent instrument to do just this, but it must be subject to the legal limits of state action. It is an adequate means when careful consideration is given to whether an intervention is necessary and whether the mildest instrument has been chosen. We should be careful with a 'Brave New World of Nudging'.

Part II

De-Biasing Through EU Law and Beyond

5

Can Experts be Trusted and what can be done about it? Insights from the Biases and Heuristics Literature

OREN PEREZ*

EXPERTS PLAY AN important role in the European Union regulatory apparatus. They assist the EU Commission in multiple functions ranging from designing policies to the implementation of regulatory schemes (eg by giving advice on applications for various permits). Critiques have focused in this context on the problem of experts' conflict of interests (COI) which, due to misaligned incentives, can generate opinions that do not serve the public interest. In this chapter I want to focus on a different type of epistemic failure that could hinder the work of experts: their susceptibility to cognitive biases. This cognitive fallibility can generate mistaken policy advice even when incentives are not misaligned. The work of experts in the EU is channelled through two institutional venues: expert groups and regulatory agencies. The EU policy formation process is based to a large extent on the work of manifold expert groups. The Commission is advised by about 1,000 expert groups, which assemble more than 30,000 experts.[1] Expert groups are created by the Commission in one of two ways: (1) by a Commission Decision or other legal act, or (2) by a Commission service with the agreement of the Secretariat General.[2] Experts groups are comprised of government officials, civic players (associated with either private corporations or non-governmental organisations) and scientists.[3] Experts groups advise the Commission on a variety

---

* I would like to thank Atalya Shitrit and Einav Tamir for excellent research assistance and the editors for their good comments.
[1] See, Å Gornitzka and U Sverdrup, 'Access of Experts: Information and EU Decision-making' (2011) 34 *West European Politics* 48; J Metz, 'Expert Groups in the European Union: A *sui generis* Phenomenon?' (2013) 32 *Policy and Society* 267, 268. Current data about the number and composition of expert groups can be extracted from the Register of Expert Groups and Other Similar Entities, at ec.europa.eu/transparency/regexpert/index.cfm.
[2] Gornitzka and Sverdrup, ibid, 50. The establishment and work of expert groups is governed by the 'Framework for Commission Expert Groups: Horizontal Rules and Public Register' Brussels, 10 November 2010, SEC (2010) 1360 final.
[3] Gornitzka and Sverdrup found that scientists comprise a third of the experts' groups body; Gornitzka and Sverdrup, ibid, 54.

of issues ranging from policy needs on crime statistics, aggressive tax planning and double taxation to the conservation of large carnivores.[4] The other institutional venue in which experts play an important role is regulatory agencies such as the European Food Safety Authority (EFSA), the European Securities and Markets Authority (ESMA) or the European Integrated Pollution Prevention and Control (IPPC) Bureau (EIPPCB).[5] Thus, for example, EFSA is responsible for assessment of all risks associated with the food chain (including in sensitive issues such as Genetically Modified Foods (GM foods)). The risk assessment process is carried out by scientific experts in the context of issue-specific working groups.[6] The EIPPCB organises and coordinates the exchange of information between Member States and the industries concerned on best available techniques (BAT), which leads to the drawing up and review of BAT reference documents. These documents play a crucial role in the regulation of large industrial plants under the Industrial Emissions Directive (IED, 2010/75/EU).[7] The dependency of the regulatory system on experts reflects a broad phenomenon that is not unique to the EU.[8] This dependency persists despite all the effort that has been made by liberal politicians, civic groups and academic scholars to develop participatory mechanisms which could expand the knowledge base on which regulatory decision-making draws.[9]

---

[4] ALTER-EU, 'A Year of Broken Promises: Big Business Still Put in Charge of Experts Groups, Despite Commitment to Reform' (November 2013) 8 (providing details on all new Expert Groups created between 20 September 2012 and 20 September 2013 (www.alter-eu.org/documents/2013/11/a-year-of-broken-promises).

[5] See, respectively, the European Food Safety Authority (www.efsa.europa.eu/en); the European Securities and Marker Authority (www.esma.europa.eu); and the European IPPC Bureau (eippcb.jrc.ec.europa.eu/).

[6] For a detailed exposition of this process, see www.efsa.europa.eu/en/workflow/assessment.htm, and M Dreyer and O Renn, 'EFSA's Involvement Policy Moving towards an Analytic-deliberative Process in EU Food Safety Governance?' in C Holst (ed), *Expertise and Democracy* (ARENA Report No 1/14, 2013) 323.

[7] The EIPPCB is not strictly speaking an EU agency; however it was formed as a response to requirements set out in Art 13(1) of the Industrial Emissions Directive (IED, 2010/75/EU) OJ L 334/17.

[8] S Brint, *In an Age of Experts: The Changing Role of Professionals in Politics and Public Life* (Princeton, Princeton University Press, 1994); AN Kingiri, 'Experts to the Rescue? An Analysis of the Role of Experts in Biotechnology Regulation in Kenya' (2010) 22 *Journal of International Development* 325; A Rip, 'Experts in Public Arenas in H Otway' in M Peltu (ed), *Regulating Industrial Risks: Science, Hazards and Public Protection* (London, Butterworths, 1985) 94; G Majone, 'From the Positive to the Regulatory State: Causes and Consequences of Changes in the Mode of Governance' [1997] *Journal of Public Policy* 139; K Bäckstrand, 'Civic Science for Sustainability: Reframing the Role of Experts, Policy-makers and Citizens in Environmental Governance' (2003) 3 *Global Environmental Politics* 24.

[9] O Perez, 'Open Government, Technological Innovation and the Politics of Democratic Disillusionment: (E-)Democracy from Socrates to Obama' (2013) 9 I/S *A Journal of Law and Policy for The Information Society* 61; M Lee and C Abbot, 'The Usual Suspects? Public Participation under the Aarhus Convention' (2003) 66 *MLR* 80; AN Glucker et al, 'Public Participation in Environmental Impact Assessment: Why, Who and How?' (2013) 43 *Environmental Impact Assessment Review* 104; LF Odparlik and J Köppel, 'Access to Information and the Role of Environmental Assessment Registries for Public Participation' (2013) 31 *Impact Assessment and Project Appraisal* 324; J D'Silva and G Van Calster, 'For Me to Know and You to Find Out? Participatory Mechanisms, the Aarhus Convention and New Technologies' (2010) 4 *Studies in Ethics, Law, and Technology*.

The influence of experts on regulatory output creates a dilemma: how far can experts be trusted and what kind of mechanisms can be used to improve the epistemic credibility of their advice? Experts' judgement can fall prey to two types of distortive mechanisms: misaligned incentives due to external economic pressures and economically-independent cognitive failures. Misaligned incentives can distort the opinion of experts through both conscious and subconscious cognitive processes.[10] Two features of expert judgement makes this kind of judgement failure particularly problematic. First, the information provided by experts in regulatory contexts is mostly unverifiable. If an expert working for EFSA expresses the view that a certain GMO material is as safe as its conventional counterpart (or not) there is almost no way to verify whether he really believes that, or is conveying it because of a certain relationship he has with industry.[11] COI induced intellectual dishonesty is therefore difficult to supervise ex post. Second, because experts enjoy broad discretion in forming their opinions (reflecting the lack of clear standards for correctness and the lack of scientific consensus), experts are able to rationalise their views without damaging their intellectual self-image. Other types of dishonesty, such as stealing or cheating in exams, involve much bolder breaches of moral conventions and thus make such self-serving rationalisations more difficult to maintain.[12] Indeed, as Moore et al note, one of 'the most notable feature of the psychological processes at work in conflicts of interest is that they can occur without any conscious intention to indulge in corruption'.[13] These two features explain why the most efficient policy against the perverse effects of COI is to simply avoid it.[14]

The second category of judgement failure reflects either the lack of epistemic competency or the influence of various cognitive biases. The key distinction between the two categories of judgement failure is that the latter can occur even in

---

[10] TB Hugh and SW Dekker, 'Hindsight Bias and Outcome Bias in the Social Construction of Medical Negligence: A Review' (2009) 16 *Journal of Law and Medicine* 846 and MH Bazerman, G Loewenstein, and DA Moore, 'Why Good Accountants do Bad Audits' (2002) 80(11) *Harvard Business Review* 96.

[11] See, eg scientific opinion on application (EFSA-GMO-BE-2011-101) for the placing on the market of herbicide-tolerant genetically modified oilseed rape MON 88302 for food and feed uses, import and processing under Regulation (EC) No 1829/2003 from Monsanto, www.efsa.europa.eu/en/efsajournal/pub/3701.htm and G Loewenstein, CR Sunstein, and R Golman, 'Disclosure: Psychology Changes Everything' (2014) *Annual Review of Economics* (forthcoming).

[12] In a 2008 paper Amir and Ariely note the importance of standards as an antidote for cheating. When people operate in an environment of clear moral standards (ie standards that are less malleable to self-serving interpretations) and are mindful of them, dishonesty, they argue, is likely to decrease as people strive to maintain their self-image. N Mazar, O Amir, and D Ariely, 'The Dishonesty of Honest People: A Theory of Self-concept Maintenance' (2008) 45(6) *Journal of Marketing Research* 633. See further, FC Fang and Casadevall, 'Why We Cheat' (2013) 24(2) *Scientific American Mind* 30.

[13] DA Moore et al, 'Conflicts of Interest and the Case of Auditor Independence: Moral Seduction and Strategic Issue Cycling' (2006) 31(1) *Academy of Management Review* 10, 16.

[14] As Loewenstein et al argue, other policies, such as disclosure could actually generate counterproductive results due to various psychological effects such as moral licensing (reflecting experts' tendency to feel freer to pursue their own interests following disclosure). See also S Sah and G Loewenstein, 'Nothing to Declare Mandatory and Voluntary Disclosure Leads Advisors to Avoid Conflicts of Interest' (2014) 25(2) *Psychological Science* 575.

the absence of COI.[15] Another important distinction between these two categories is that COI induced biases usually lie within the control of the agent, whereas cognitive failures tend to reflect subconscious processes. While it is true that experts may refuse to admit that their judgement has been distorted due to COI (through processes of self-deception and self-serving rationalisation), the choice of whether to get entangled in a situation of COI is clearly within their control.[16]

Most of the literature (and regulatory effort) that explored the problem of monitoring experts' work has focused, as noted above, on the adverse effects of COI and measures that respond to this problem. Thus, for example, a paper by Robinson et al criticises EFSA for its failure to properly regulate COI in its risk assessment process, focusing on the example of GMO food.[17] A report by the Alliance for Lobbying Transparency and Ethics Regulation (ALTER-EU), which looked at all the expert groups established between 20 September 2012 and 20 September 2013, criticised the Commission for failing to meet its commitment to reform the experts consultation process, noting that 'Across all newly created Expert Groups, there are more corporate representatives than all other stakeholders combined'.[18]

This critique has driven the Commission to undertake several steps to improve the situation. It created a Register of Expert Groups and Other Similar Entities, which greatly improved the transparency of the expert consultation process and adopted an informal framework that governs the working of expert groups. Similarly, several EU regulatory agencies have developed specific procedures for managing COI. However, while these steps constitute a move forward they still fall short from providing a complete response to the critique against the EU expert system.[19] On May 2014, in a reflection of this dissatisfaction, the European Ombudsman, Emily O'Reilly, opened an investigation into the composition and transparency of the Commission's expert groups. As a first step, she asked interested persons and organisations for feedback on how balanced the representation of relevant areas of expertise and interest is in different groups, how transparent the groups are and how well the application procedures work.[20]

---

[15] I define COI as situations in which there is a gap between the experts' economic interests (eg due to links with industry) and the public interest.

[16] The affiliation of experts with industrial firms can also induce subconscious distortive processes, stemming from feelings of identification and desire to please which are not fully intentional. However, even in such cases the mere existence of the COI situation would usually be self-evident.

[17] See, C Robinson et al, 'Conflicts of Interest at the European Food Safety Authority Erode Public Confidence' (2013) 67 *Journal of Epidemiology and Community Health* 717 (focusing on the links of some of the experts involved in the assessment of GMO foods with the industry-funded International Life Sciences Institute (ILSI)).

[18] ALTER-EU (n 4) 3; and the European Court of Auditors, 'Management of Conflict of Interest in Selected EU Agencies' Special Report No 15 (European Union, Luxembourg, 2012) (www.eca.europa.eu/Lists/ECADocuments/SR12_15/SR12_15_EN.PDF).

[19] See Robinson et al (n 17), ALTER-EU (n 4) and the European Court of Auditors Report, ibid.

[20] European Ombudsman, 'Ombudsman Opens Investigation into Commission's Expert Groups', EO/14/12, 14/05/2014 (europa.eu/rapid/press-release_EO-14-12_en.htm).

In this chapter I want to focus on experts' susceptibility to cognitive biases.

The literature on cognitive biases suggests that the current regulatory focus on the question of COI, and its relative indifference to the problem of cognitive biases is a cause for concern. There is broad evidence demonstrating that expert judgement is subject to various biases, such as the hindsight bias, confirmation bias or quantification bias. In contrast to popular belief, experts are not immune to these biases.[21] The differences between experts and lay citizens in that regard are smaller than what is commonly assumed because they originate in a fundamental human tendency to couple type one intuitive processing and type two analytical processing in their reasoning. Further, experts, like lay citizens, tend to draw on various heuristics—even when such usage does not fit context.[22]

In this chapter I explore the implications of this phenomenon to the regulatory project. I start by examining those cognitive biases which are more critical to the work of experts in the regulatory context. I then examine the question of de-biasing. Are there institutional mechanisms that can be used in order to de-bias experts' judgement? This question is particularly important because conventional control mechanisms such as judicial review or tort liability have generally failed to fulfil this task. Courts have been reluctant to interfere in experts' reasoning through their administrative review powers, adopting in general a deferential approach.[23] Courts are generally not well equipped to deal with the task of reviewing the potential (cognitive) bias of experts' testimony. Judges already find it difficult to review experts' opinion on the merit. Asking them to take into account these additional sources of epistemic blunder seems to be asking too much.[24]

I examine to what extent the psychological literature on de-biasing could provide insights to the regulatory context, noting the linkages between potential de-biasing mechanisms and the current regulatory framework governing experts' behaviour.[25] I conclude with a reflection on the challenges and prospects of the de-biasing project. I argue in this context that some of the policy tools which were developed to deal with the problem of COI can also play a useful role in the effort to counter these alternative sources of judgement failure. There are therefore some interesting synergies between the regulatory responses to these dual policy challenges. The de-biasing project faces, however, some deep challenges, which need

---

[21] J Groopman and M Prichard, *How Doctors Think* (Houghton Mifflin Co, 2007).

[22] A Feeney, 'Simple Heuristics: From one Infinite Regress to Another?' (2000) 23 *Behavioral and Brain Sciences* 749.

[23] B Millerand B Curry, 'Experts Judging Experts: The Role of Expertise in Reviewing Agency Decision Making' (2012) 38 *Law and Social Inquiry* 67. For a rare exception, see DJ Gerber, 'Courts as Economic Experts in European Merger Law' in B Hawk (ed), *International Antitrust Law and Policy* (Fordham Corporate Law Institute, 2004) 475. Available at SSRN: ssrn.com/abstract=1116750.

[24] See, P Croskerry, 'Perspectives on Diagnostic Failure and Patient Safety' (2012) 15 *Healthcare Quarterly* 50, 54; CT Robertson, 'Blind Expertise' (2010) 85 *New York University Law Review* 174, 242–43.

[25] SO Lilienfeld, R Ammirati, and K Landfield, 'Giving Debiasing Away: Can Psychological Research on Correcting Cognitive Errors Promote Human Welfare?' (2009) 4 *Perspectives on Psychological Science* 390; P Croskerry, G Singhal and S Mamede, 'Cognitive Debiasing 1: Origins of Bias and Theory of Debiasing' (2013) 22 *BMJ Quality and Safety* ii58–ii64.

to be taken into account as we delineate its objectives. These challenges reflect, primarily, the broad range of cognitive biases underlying human reasoning (which calls for a differential, context-dependent de-biasing strategy) and the intrinsic limitations of self-reflexive, introspective de-biasing strategies. The scale and scope of these challenges mean also that attaining a bias-free decision-making environment is not achievable and our expectations from the de-biasing project should be formed with this in mind.

I. EXPERTS, COGNITIVE BIASES AND THE OBJECTIVITY IDEAL

The notion of expertise carries with it a strong connotation of objectivity. This connotation has deep roots across both civil law and common law traditions. Expert witnesses are expected to act as carriers of objectivity that can assist the court in the pursuit of truth by providing 'objective unbiased opinion in relation to matters within [their] expertise'.[26] This expectation is even stronger in civil law jurisdictions which draw heavily on court appointed experts in the fact-finding process.[27] A useful account of this expectation can be found in a recent report of the UK Civil Justice Council which states that:[28]

> Experts should provide opinions which are independent, regardless of the pressures of litigation. In this context, a useful test of 'independence' is that the expert would express the same opinion if given the same instructions by an opposing party. Experts should not take it upon themselves to promote the point of view of the party instructing them or engage in the role of advocates.

This perception of the expert as an objective, trustworthy source of knowledge also underlies EU regulatory framework which draws on experts to provide the Commission with the information it needs to fulfil its tasks. To a large extent the instrumental view of scientific expertise, which sees it 'as a way of vocalising the cause-and-effect of complex issues, and providing information that helps to frame a problem, fostering a collective debate and search for scientifically based solutions to existing problems' dominates the approach of the Commission to the role of experts.[29] Due to the Commission's limited resources it is highly dependent on experts that are not part of its institutional apparatus.[30]

---

[26] *Meadow v General Medical Council* [2007] 1 All ER 1 [21] (Anthony Clarke J).
[27] See, D Sonenshein and C Fitzpatrick, 'The Problem of Partisan Experts and the Potential for Reform through Concurrent Evidence' (2013) 32 *Review of Litigation* 1, 36–45; R Verkerk, 'Comparative Aspects of Expert Evidence in Civil Litigation' (2009) 13 *International Journal of Evidence and Proof* 167.
[28] Civil Justice Council, 'Protocol for the Instruction of Experts to give Evidence in Civil Claims' 5, para 4.3 (London, 2005, amended October 2009) (www.justice.gov.uk/courts/procedure-rules/civil/contents/form_section_images/practice_directions/pd35_pdf_eps/pd35_prot.pdf).
[29] See, D Rimkutė and M Haverland, 'How Does the European Commission Use Scientific Expertise? Results from a Survey of Scientific Members of the Commission's Expert Committees' *Comparative European Politics* (forthcoming) 3.
[30] ibid, 4.

Recent studies of experts' behaviour question this idealised picture of expertise, raising doubts about the objectivity and the reliability of experts' opinions. While this chapter cannot provide a complete list of the various biases that may hinder experts' judgement, it attempts at identifying those biases that are more relevant to the regulatory context. As noted above, most of the literature on experts has focused on the way in which experts' judgement could be distorted by external economic pressures.[31] This problem is particularly salient in situations in which experts work alongside industry as is the case in EFSA, ESMA or the EIPPCB.[32] At the extreme this bias may reflect the complete subjugation of the expert to the interests of a third party.[33] While the regulatory concern over this type of judgement failure is well justified I want to focus on those cognitive biases which are not related to COI.

The most important type of cognitive failure in this category concerns the phenomenon of motivated reasoning. Motivated reasoning reflects the fact that the process of belief acquisition does not necessarily aim at truth, but rather takes the form of directional reasoning, which is dominated by an attempt (possibly subconscious and emotively charged) to vindicate one's prior opinions. It could be reflected either in confirmation bias, which refers to 'the seeking or interpreting of evidence in ways that are partial to existing beliefs, expectations, or a hypothesis in hand'[34] or in disconfirmation bias, which refers to the fact that people seem unable to ignore their prior beliefs when processing counter-arguments or counter-evidence.[35] The problem of motivated reasoning was demonstrated in the context of both laypeople and experts' reasoning.[36] Thus, for example, studies of diagnostic decision-making have demonstrated that doctors are subject to confirmation bias

---

[31] TB Hugh and SW Dekker (n 10) 851; Robinson et al (n 17); R Burgess et al, 'The Political Economy of Deforestation in the Tropics' (2012) 127 *Quarterly Journal of Economics* 1707; Q Wang and X Chen, 'Regulatory Failures for Nuclear Safety—the Bad Example of Japan—Implication for the Rest of the World' (2012) 16 *Renewable and Sustainable Energy Reviews* 2610; D Carpenter and DA Moss, *Preventing Regulatory Capture: Special Interest Influence and How to Limit It* (Cambridge, Cambridge University Press, 2013).

[32] H Schoenberger, 'Integrated Pollution Prevention and Control in Large Industrial Installations on the Basis of Best Available Techniques—the Sevilla Process' (2009) 17 *Journal of Cleaner Production* 1526; T Daddi et al, 'The Effects of Integrated Pollution Prevention and Control (IPPC) Regulation on Company Management and Competitiveness' in R Welford (ed), *Business Strategy and the Environment* (Publishes online, 2013).

[33] See, HD Sperling, 'Expert Evidence: The Problem of Bias and Other Things' (1999) 4 *Judicial Review* 429 (in the context of judicial proceedings), ALTER-EU (n 4) Introduction (in the regulatory context) and M Busuioc, 'Rule-Making by the European Financial Supervisory Authorities: Walking a Tight Rope' (2013) 19 *EL Rev* 111.

[34] RS Nickerson, 'Confirmation Bias: A Ubiquitous Phenomenon in Many Guises' (1998) 2 *Review of General Psychology* 175.

[35] CS Taber, D Cann, and S Kucsova, 'The Motivated Processing of Political Arguments' (2009) 31 *Political Behavior* 137.

[36] For an analysis of the confirmation bias in the work of forensic experts, see PC Giannelli, 'Confirmation Bias' (2007) 22 *Criminal Justice* 60; PC Giannelli, 'Independent Crime Laboratories: The Problem of Motivational and Cognitive Bias' (2010) *Utah Law Review* 247. For studies looking at lay citizens, see RS Nickerson, 'Confirmation Bias: A Ubiquitous Phenomenon in Many Guises' (1998) 2 *Review of General Psychology* 175.

when they interpret evidence (eg symptoms or lack of symptoms), potentially leading to wrong treatment.[37] Another example is the 'prosecutorial bias', which was documented in the work of forensic experts that work in laboratories located in law enforcement agencies or prosecutors' offices, and is reflected in a selective treatment of the evidence in ways that support the agenda of the institution in which the laboratory is situated.[38]

Another important type of cognitive failure in this category relates to the hindsight and outcome biases. Hindsight bias reflects the fact that finding out that an outcome has occurred increases its perceived likelihood.[39] Outcome bias refers to the influence of outcome knowledge upon evaluations of decision quality and the potential responsibility or culpability of the decisionmaker to the outcome.[40] The difference between the two biases lies therefore in the fact that hindsight bias relates to retrospective estimates of predictability of an event and not to judgement of responsibility. Both biases can undermine the epistemic robustness of experts' testimony. In the medical context, for example, hindsight bias can lead to overestimating the probability of reaching a correct diagnosis when the correct diagnosis is already known.[41] Outcome bias could distort physicians' judgement on the appropriateness of care when they assess the treatment ex post.[42] In the regulatory context these biases could play a particularly important role whenever experts are called to evaluate past behaviour. A good example is the attempt of experts to analyse, retrospectively, the failure of the British Government to deal with the BSE (bovine spongiform encephalopathy) saga.[43]

A third type of (COI independent) bias which could be particularly devastating, when combined with confirmation bias, is anchoring. Anchoring is the tendency to fixate on specific features of a problem too early in the reasoning process, and to base the likelihood of a particular event on information available at the outset. This may often be an effective strategy. However, this initial impression could exert a persisting cognitive effect and evidence suggests that many people fail to

---

[37] BH Bornstein and AC Emler, 'Rationality in Medical Decision Making: A Review of the Literature on Doctors Decision-making Biases' (2001) 7 *Journal of Evaluation in Clinical Practice* 97, 99.

[38] EJ Reese, 'Techniques for Mitigating Cognitive Biases in Fingerprint Identification' (2012) 59 *University of California at Los Angeles Law Review* 1252; E Barkow, 'Prosecutorial Administration: Prosecutor Bias and the Department of Justice' (2013) 99 *Virginia Law Review* 271, 299, 319; AS Burke, 'Improving Prosecutorial Decision Making: Some Lessons of Cognitive Science' (2005) 47 *William and Mary Law Review* 1587.

[39] B Fischhoff, 'Hindsight is Not Equal to Foresight: The Effect of Outcome Knowledge on Judgment under Uncertainty' (1975) *Journal of Experimental Psychology: Human Perception and Performance* 288.

[40] Hugh and Dekker (n 10) 849.

[41] K Henriksen and H Kaplan, 'Hindsight Bias, Outcome Knowledge and Adaptive Learning' (2003) 12 *Quality and Safety in Health Care* 46; Bornstein and Emler (n 37) 98.

[42] ibid.

[43] E Millstone and P van Zwanenberg, 'Politics of Expert Advice: Lessons from the Early History of the BSE Saga' (2001) 28 *Science and Public Policy* 99; M O'Brien, 'Have Lessons been Learned from the UK Bovine Spongiform Encephalopathy (BSE) Epidemic?' (2000) 29 *International Journal of Epidemiology* 730.

adjust their estimations sufficiently in light of later information.[44] A related bias is the availability bias, which designates people's tendency to judge things to be more frequent if they come readily to mind. Events which are easier to imagine are judged to be more likely simply because they are more cognitively accessible. This heuristic is driven by the (problematic) assumption that the evidence that is most available is the most relevant. One of the primary features of cognitive availability is the vividness of the data.[45] Finally, there is a large literature documenting biases in the people's probabilistic reasoning—especially deviations from the Bayes theorem.[46]

II. THE DE-BIASING PROJECT

The special role played by experts in contemporary regulatory processes coupled by the thin regulatory framework that governs their work turns the question of their susceptibility to cognitive biases into a significant regulatory dilemma. Unfortunately the psychological literature on de-biasing is still in its early days, despite the huge progress that has been achieved in identifying and analysing the varied cognitive biases that affect expert reasoning.[47] De-biasing constitutes a broader interventionist strategy than nudging. A nudge is 'any aspect in the framing of a decision problem that can affect people decisions without changing economic incentives'.[48] Nudging attempts to influence people's choices in a welfare-enhancing way by changing, for example, the way information is presented or by changing default rules. De-biasing, as a general endeavour, may go beyond these constraints, by changing the set of choices,[49] increasing the transaction costs associated with a certain

---

[44] P Croskerry, 'Achieving Quality in Clinical Decision Making: Cognitive Strategies and Detection of Bias' (2002) 9 *Academic Emergency Medicine* 1184; SD Campbell and SA Sharpe, 'Anchoring Bias in Consensus Forecasts and its Effect on Market Prices' (2009) 44 *Journal of Financial and Quantitative Analysis* 369; GB Chapman and BH Bornstein, 'The More You Ask For, the More You Get: Anchoring in Personal Injury Verdicts' (1996) 10 *Applied Cognitive Psychology* 519.

[45] Croskerry, ibid; R McDermott, 'The Psychological Ideas of Amos Tversky and their Relevance for Political Science' (2001) 13 *Journal of Theoretical Politics* 5.

[46] G Gigerenzer and U Hoffrage, 'How to Improve Bayesian Reasoning without Instruction: Frequency Formats' (1995) 102 *Psychological Review* 684; J Koehler, 'The Base Rate Fallacy Reconsidered: Descriptive, Normative, and Methodoligical Challenges' (1996) 19 *Behavioral and Brain Sciences* 1; WS Richardson, 'We Should Overcome the Barriers to Evidence-based Clinical Diagnosis!' (2007) 60 *Journal of Clinical Epidemiology* 217.

[47] Lilienfeld et al (n 25).

[48] R Croson and N Treich, 'Behavioral Environmental Economics: Promises and Challenges' (2014) 58 *Environmental and Resource Economics* 335, 337 and CR Sunstein, 'Nudges.gov: Behavioral Economics and Regulation' in E Zamir and D Teichman (eds), *Oxford Handbook of Behavioral Economics and the Law* (Oxford, Oxford University Press, forthcoming).

[49] Both restricting or enlarging the set of options were found to help consumers to make better choices in some contexts; Ratner et al, 'How Behavioral Decision Research can Enhance Consumer Welfare: From Freedom of Choice to Paternalistic Intervention' (2008) 19 *Marketing Letters* 383, 391–92.

decision,[50] or by requiring the development of new institutional structures. In the context of expert decision-making the literature on de-biasing has focused on ways to shift cognitive processing from a System 1 mode of thinking (automatic, heuristic) to a System 2 (controlled, rule-governed) mode of thinking. This shift may permit System 2 processing to 'override' more automatic cognitive processes.[51]

Generally the literature distinguished between three ways in which the shift from System 1 to System 2 could be achieved: (a) introspective, meta-cognitive techniques which encourage the decisionmaker to study the biases that may undermine his/her reasoning and through a process of (meta-order) self-reflection revise his opinion to the extent that it was inflicted by biases;[52] (b) cognitive-forcing techniques which seek to influence the decisionmaker indirectly by changing some features of the task or the decision-making environment;[53] (c) introducing deliberative elements into the decision-making process which can prompt decisionmakers to consider and cope with other points of view.[54] Unlike the first mechanism, which draws on the expert internal mind-set, the latter two mechanisms do not require the decisionmaker to be cognisant of his/her internal mental process.

Introspective, self-reflexive strategies include, for example, the promotion of general bias awareness through brief, non-technical, and intensive tutorials in which specific biases are demonstrated to decisionmakers.[55] Other strategies in this category include the 'consider-*the-opposite*' technique (also known as 'consider-an-alternative strategy', 'perspective-taking', 'enlisting the devil's advocate'), which requires the decisionmaker to consider other views as part of his reasoning process.[56] Further techniques seek to develop awareness to particular biases.[57] *Cognitive-forcing techniques* include *checklists* or *methodological guidelines*, which could help experts resist the biases and failed heuristics that lead to decision-making errors.[58] Other instruments in this category are process-conditioning rules. Process-conditioning rules function as critical elements in the execution of a process to ensure that a correct procedure is followed, or to prevent an untoward

---

[50] In some cases we may want to prevent agents from making rush decisions and give them sufficient time to make a well-informed decision. Increasing the transaction costs associated with certain types of decisions can facilitate that goal. See, eg M Armstrong, 'Economic Models of Consumer Protection Policies' (2011) MPRA Paper No 34773, 8–9 for a general discussion and K Darr, 'Physician-assisted Suicide: Legal and Ethical Considerations' (2007) 40 *Journal of Health Law* 29 for an extreme example (describing the procedures for physician-assisted suicide under Oregon law).

[51] Lilienfeld et al (n 25) 393.

[52] BE Kahn, MF Luce and SM Nowlis, 'Debiasing Insights from Process Tests' (2006) 33 *Journal of Consumer Research* 131, 131.

[53] ibid.

[54] I Yaniv and S Choshen-Hillel, 'When Guessing What Another Person Would Say is Better than Giving Your Own Opinion: Using Perspective-taking to Improve Advice-taking' (2012) 48 *Journal of Experimental Social Psychology* 1022.

[55] Reese (n 38); P Croskerry, 'Diagnostic Failure: A Cognitive and Affective Approach' in K Henriksen et al (eds), *Advances in Patient Safety: From Research to Implementation (Concepts and Methodology)* (Rockville, Agency for Healthcare Research and Quality, 2005) 241.

[56] CG Lord, ML Lepper and E Preston, 'Considering the Opposite: A Corrective Strategy for Social Judgment' (1984) 47 *Journal of Personality and Social Psychology* 1231 and Reese (n 38) 1282–86.

[57] Croskerry (n 24); Croskerry (n 44).

[58] JW Ely, ML Garber and P Croskerry, 'Checklists to Reduce Diagnostic Errors' (2011) 86 *Academic Medicine* 307, 308. A Gawande, *The Checklist Manifesto* (India, Penguin Books, 2010).

event. For example, a customer using an automatic teller machine (ATM) cannot withdraw cash until the card is removed. Thus, the error of leaving the card in the machine is avoided.[59] *Deliberative mechanisms* facilitate perspective-taking through dialogical procedures.[60] Both cognitive-forcing techniques and deliberative mechanisms may involve interventionist measures that go beyond the classic 'nudging' repertoire.

The following table further elaborates this typology drawing on the de-biasing literature. This depiction is of course incomplete—it primarily seeks to provide a better sense of the de-biasing landscape.

Table 2: The de-biasing landscape

Type of de-biasing strategy	Forms of Realisations	Contexts of application (tasks, institution, bias)
Introspective, self-reflexive strategies	Promoting general bias awareness.[61]	Fingerprint identification (police, courts, anchoring bias through exposure to domain-extraneous information).[62]
	'Consider-the-opposite' technique[63]	Fingerprint identification (police, courts, anchoring bias through exposure to domain-extraneous information)[64]
	Developing concrete awareness to particular biases[65]	Clinical decision making (focusing on anchoring bias, confirmation bias, judgemental diagnosis and negative stereotyping, hindsight bias)
Cognitive-forcing techniques	*Checklists*[66]	Clinical decision-making;[67] differential diagnosis checklists; cognitive forcing checklists for specific diseases;[68] surgical safety lists;[69] intensive care.[70] See Annex A for an example

(continued)

[59] K Curran and D King, 'Investigating the Human Computer Interaction Problems with Automated Teller Machine Navigation Menus' (2008) 5 *Interactive Technology and Smart Education* 59; N Davinson and E Sillence, 'Using the Health Belief Model to Explore Users' Perceptions of "Being Safe and Secure" in the World of Technology Mediated Financial Transactions' (2014) 72 *International Journal of Human-Computer Studies* 154; Ely et al (n 58).

[60] Yaniv and Choshen-Hillel (n 54).
[61] Reese (n 38); Croskerry (n 24).
[62] Reese, ibid.
[63] Lord et al (n 56).
[64] Reese (n 38).
[65] Croskerry et al (n 25); Croskerry (n 24).
[66] Ely et al (n 58) 308; Gawande (n 58).
[67] Ely et al ibid; BM Hales and PJ Pronovost, 'The Checklist—a Tool for Error Management and Performance Improvement' (2006) 21 *Journal of Critical Care* 231.
[68] Ely et al (n 58).
[69] AB Haynes et al, 'A Surgical Safety Checklist to Reduce Morbidity and Mortality in a Global Population' (2009) 360 *New England Journal of Medicine* 491; EN de Vries et al, 'Effect of a Comprehensive Surgical Safety System on Patient Outcomes' (2010) 363 *New England Journal of Medicine* 1928.
[70] Hales and Pronovost (n 67); J Laurance, 'Peter Pronovost: Champion of Checklists in Critical Care' (2009) 374 *The Lancet* 443; CL Bosk et al, 'Reality Check for Checklists' (2009) 374 *The Lancet* 444.

Table 2: (*Continued*)

Type of de-biasing strategy	Forms of Realisations	Contexts of application (tasks, institution, bias)
		Cockpit safety checklists;[71] see Annex B for an example
	Process-conditioning rules[72]	Designing automatic teller machine (ATM) in a way which avoids the error of leaving the card in the machine[73]
	Natural sampling format[74]	Medical decision-making—diagnostic— especially interpretation lab-results (mammography)[75]
	Methodological guidelines which guide experts in forming their opinion	The GRADE system—clinical decision-making[76]
Deliberative mechanisms	Deliberative mechanisms encouraging perspective taking by exposing decisionmakers to the views of others[77]	Diversity enforcing procedures in expert committees[78]
	Public deliberation[79]	Procedural instruments encouraging civic participation in regulatory decision-making[80]

---

[71] A Degani and EL Wiener, 'Cockpit Checklists: Concepts, Design, and Use' (1993) 35 *Human Factors: The Journal of the Human Factors and Ergonomics Society* 345; L Lingard et al, 'Getting Teams to Talk: Development and Pilot Implementation of a Checklist to Promote Interprofessional Communication in the OR' (2005) 14 *Quality and Safety in Health Care* 340. A Degani and EL Weiner, *Human Factors of Flight-deck Checklists: the Normal Checklist* (Ames Research Center, 1990) and http://freechecklists.net/; http://www.dauntless-soft.com.

[72] Ely et al (n 58) 310.

[73] K Curran and D King, 'Investigating the Human Computer Interaction Problems with Automated Teller Machine Navigation Menus' (2008) 5 *Interactive Technology and Smart Education* 59; N Davinson and E Sillence, 'Using the Health Belief Model to Explore Users' Perceptions of "being safe and secure" in the World of Technology Mediated Financial Transactions' (2014) 72 *International Journal of Human-Computer Studies* 154.

[74] Gigerenzer and Hoffrage (n 46).

[75] ibid, 687; G Gigerenzer et al, 'Helping Doctors and Patients Make Sense of Health Statistics' (2007) 8 *Psychological Science in the Public Interest* 53, 56.

[76] GH Guyatt et al, 'What is "quality of evidence" and why is it important to clinicians?' (2008) 336(7651) *British Medical Journal* 995, 998.

[77] Yaniv and Choshen-Hillel (n 54).

[78] ibid, 1027.

[79] Perez (n 9); H Mercier and H Landemore, 'Reasoning is for Arguing: Understanding the Successes and Failures of Deliberation' (2012) 33 *Political Psychology* 243.

[80] Perez, ibid; Mercier and Landemore, ibid.

III. THE ILLUSION OF COGNITIVE STERILITY: ON THE LIMITS OF DE-BIASING

The idea of de-biasing provides an appealing vision: if we just spend more time and energy on finding ways to deal with these epistemic pathogens, solution would not be out of reach. But, as I will argue in this section, the literature offers only an incomplete response to the de-biasing challenge. Cognitive biases—like the other maladies and dysfunctions that characterise human nature—have an inherent stickiness. This does not mean that no effort should be made toward developing de-biasing mechanisms in regulatory contexts and others, but only that our expectations should be calibrated appropriately. Understanding the limits of the de-biasing project requires us to take a closer look at each of the different de-biasing techniques discussed above.

Consider first meta-cognitive techniques that encourage the decisionmaker to revise his/her opinion through a process of (meta-order) self-reflection, which should uncover the extent to which the initial reasoning was affected by biases. This strategy seems to be based on dubious foundations: why should we expect an agent whose reasoning process suffers from some sort of bias to be able to pull himself—through his own mental effort—from this 'cognitive abyss'? This solution seems to fall prey to the Munchhausen fallacy (Baron Munchhausen has succeeded, so the legend goes, to pull himself out of a mire by his own hair). One way in which the problematic of the meta-cognitive approach can be illustrated is by providing a complete depiction of the cognitive process it entails. Consider an agent (expert) who in state one has four items in his mindscape (which may designate some reasoning process). Drawing on the introspective de-biasing technique, at state two he evaluates the cognitive 'purity' of state one, which may lead him to change some aspects of his reasoning process. The agent uses System 2 mode of thinking (logical) to check for any distortions due to System 1 mode of thinking (automatic, heuristic). However there is no reason why this introspective process of self-examination should stop at state two as the agent has no reason to believe that at state two he is less susceptible to cognitive biases (as System 1 continues to operate in the background). Indeed there is every possibility that his reasoning process at state two was subject to some cognitive bias (whether the original bias or other). A reasonable agent should thus subject his reasoning process at state two to similar self-critique (state three). This process is likely to lead to infinite regress with no clear convergence point. Reflecting on the cognitive 'purity' of one's first order beliefs is not enough, for this only creates the need for subjecting any revised second order beliefs to similar introspective scrutiny and so on. No amount of introspective self-examination is ever enough, for, no matter when the reasoning process ends, there is always the possibility that some potential bias has been missed tainting the whole reasoning process (reflecting the unavoidable coupling of the two modes of thinking).[81] The following is a formal representation of the above argument.

---

[81] For more detailed argument about the pitfalls of infinite regress, see H Kornblith, *On Reflection* (Oxford, Oxford University Press, 2012) 13; R Rucker, *Infinity and the Mind: The Science and Philosophy of the Infinite* (Boston, Birkhäuser, 1982) 44.

1. State 1: {A, B, C, D};
2. State 2: {Eva$_1${A, B, C, D}→ A, B, C, ~D};
3. State 3: {Eva$_2${Eva$_1${A, B, C, D}→ A, B, C, ~D}→A, B, ~C, D};

...

(n) State n: {Eva$_{n-1}${Eva$_{n-2}${ Eva$_{n-3}$ ...

The idea that we can deal with cognitive biases simply through awareness and introspection—as suggested for example by Pat Croskerry (a leading figure in the literature on decisions and biases in medicine)[82]—seems therefore rather naïve. This critique does not mean to completely discard the value of critical introspection. It could certainly have an impact in some contexts. However I am quite sceptical of its usefulness as a general de-biasing method.

Cognitive forcing techniques seem more promising in that they do not depend on the introspective capacity of the agent. However, cognitive-forcing techniques generate their own set of problems. The first problem concerns the highly context-dependent nature of these techniques. This context-dependency refers both to the nature of task (eg diagnostic analysis and the safe operation of cockpit differ markedly from the risk assessment of GMO food) and potentially also to the background and personality traits of the agent (from educational history to his level of extraversion and openness to experience).[83] The context-dependency of cognitive-forcing techniques calls therefore for a 'tailor made' approach;[84] general solutions will not do. But developing differential de-biasing strategies creates a difficult regulatory challenge because they require costly design and implementation.[85] In the EU regulatory context, for example, a different set of cognitive forcing techniques may have to be developed for each of the different agencies.

A second problem underlying the use of cognitive-forcing technique is that they may create new types of cognitive biases—becoming themselves a new source of cognitive risk. Consider the following examples. Most ATMs are designed in a way which prevents users from withdrawing cash until the card is removed. This task-flow design prevents users from committing the error of leaving the card once

---

[82] Croskerry (n 44); P Croskerry and G Tait, 'Clinical Decision Making: The Need for Meaningful Research' (2013) 88 *Academic Medicine* 149; P Croskerry, 'Cognitive Forcing Strategies in Clinical Decisionmaking' (2003) 41 *Annals of Emergency Medicine* 110.

[83] J Mondak and KD Halperin, 'A Framework for the Study of Personality and Political Behaviour' (2008) 38 *British Journal of Political Science* 335; RR McCrae, 'Creativity, Divergent Thinking, and Openness to Experience' (1987) 52 *Journal of Personality and Social Psychology* 1258; M Baas et al, 'Personality and Creativity: The Dual Pathway to Creativity Model and a Research Agenda' (2013) 7 *Social and Personality Psychology Compass* 732.

[84] For discussion of tailor-made regulation, see O Perez, 'Electronic Democracy as a Multi-dimensional Praxis' (2003) 4 *North Carolina Journal of Law and Technology* 275; A Porat and LJ Strahilevitz, 'Personalizing Default Rules and Disclosure with Big Data' (2014) 112 *Michigan Law Review* (forthcoming); C Daugbjergand and KM Søndersko, 'Environmental Policy Performance Revisited: Designing Effective Policies for Green Markets' (2012) 60 *Political Studies* 399.

[85] Y Feldman and O Perez, 'Motivating Environmental Action in a Pluralistic Regulatory Environment: An Experimental Study of Framing, Crowding Out, and Institutional Effects in the Context of Recycling Policies' (2012) 46 *Law and Society Review* 405; O Perez, 'Courage, Regulatory Responsibility, and the Challenge of Higher-order Reflexivity' (2013) 8 *Regulation and Governance* 203.

the cash is withdrawn. This design utilises the insight that users tend to perceive the task as done once they achieve their desired goal (cash). The drawback of this design is that it allows people to make the mistake of leaving their cash behind once they have taken the card. If you think this scenario is far-fetched then you are wrong. The Royal Bank of Scotland has estimated that between 2004 and 2011, 300,000 customers have left their money behind.[86] The advantage the policy—card then cash—over the alternative—cash then card—is that there is a relatively efficient technological fix to the error of leaving cash behind. This technological fix consists in programming the ATM so that notes are sucked back into the machine if they are not collected within 30 seconds. When this happens, banks can automatically return the credit to customers' accounts (customers still face the risk that their cash would be taken by a passer-by during this 30 seconds period).[87]

However some of the risks created by cognitive forcing techniques do not have such easy fixes. The use of checklists in the aviation industry is a case in point. Checklists have been used to fulfil several objectives: aid the pilot in recalling the process of configuring the plane; provide a standard foundation for verifying aircraft configuration that will defeat any reduction in the flight crew's psychological and physical condition; allow mutual supervision (cross-checking) among crew members; and serve as a quality control tool by flight management and government regulators over pilots in the process of configuring the plane for the flight.[88] However, as Degani and Weiner note in a report prepared for NASA in 1990, checklists can also pose a potential safety risk because of the way they are used by pilots. The misuse of a checklist was determined by the National Transportation Safety Board (NTSB) as one of the probable causes of flight accidents in several different incidents.[89] One way in which checklists become a source of safety hazard is when checklist procedures become an automatic routine—what pilots have termed as 'sing-song'. The pilot in such a case would run the checklist, but the reply would be done from memory and not based on the actual state of the checklist item (which represents some configuration or state of the airplane as represented in the cockpit's instruments).[90] Degani and Weiner argue that this type of error is a product of the brain's pattern analysing mechanism, which allows us to execute complex cognitive tasks without conscious perception and information processing.[91] Unlike the ATM case, in this case the error generated by the checklist could lead to massive loss of human life.

---

[86] A Oxlade, 'Forgotten ATM money: Will you get a refund?' *The Telegraph*, 27 December 2012 (www.telegraph.co.uk/finance/personalfinance/consumertips/9767421/Forgotten-ATM-money-Will-you-get-a-refund.html); D Hyde, 'HSBC will now refund customers who left money at the ATM after RBS agrees to pay customers back £10m' *DailyMail*, 26 December 2012 (www.dailymail.co.uk/news/article-2253389/HSBC-refund-customers-left-money-ATM-RBS-agrees-pay-customers-10m.html).

[87] See, Hyde, ibid. There has been a policy change in UK banks in that context in 2012. Until 2012 many banks have followed a policy of 'manual' reclaiming, which required customers to explicitly ask for a refund. It seems that many customers have failed to follow this procedure; Oxclade, ibid.

[88] Degani and Wiener (n 71) 7.
[89] ibid, 2.
[90] ibid, 38–39.
[91] ibid, 39.

Deliberative mechanisms could also generate unexpected epistemic risks. The value of deliberative mechanisms lies in their capacity to counter biases such as confirmation, anchoring or availability biases, by introducing alternative viewpoints and forcing the experts to cope with them. A recent development in this field has been the emergence of digital-mediated participatory mechanisms, such as the US online platform 'regulation.gov',[92] where comments on federal regulations can be posted or, in Scotland, by the possibility to petition the Scottish Parliament online.[93] However, these mechanisms also open the way for shallow epistemological practices which could have an adverse effect on the quality of the decision-making process. A case in point is the phenomenon of large-scale email campaigns, which is made possible by digital technology. Websites such as MoveOn.org enable NGOs to mobilise protest against particular governmental policies in the form of mass emails. Such emails tend to be either exact duplicates of a letter prepared by the NGO or constitute a variant of a small number of broad claims about the inadequacy of the proposed rule, and thus do not provide new information for the regulator to consider. Further, this practice also creates an administrative burden on the regulator who has to develop new mechanisms that would allow it to cope with this mass data.[94]

IV. FROM THEORY TO POLICY: A REALISTIC VISION OF THE DE-BIASING PROJECT

The foregoing critique does not mean that the attempt to develop de-biasing mechanisms should be abandoned. It means, rather, that our expectations from the de-biasing project should be calibrated appropriately. In the regulatory context the mechanisms that should receive the greatest attention are cognitive-forcing techniques and deliberative mechanisms encouraging perspective taking. I focus below on several regulatory measures that realise this line of thinking and discuss the various challenges underlying their implementation.

One example of a cognitive-forcing instrument that can be used to improve expert judgement is methodological guidelines. Several examples can illustrate the potential benefits of this instrument. Consider, first, the GRADE system, which was developed by clinical doctors over the last 10 years in order to improve the quality of medical decision-making. The GRADE system—grading of recommendations assessment, development, and evaluation—offers a transparent and structured process for developing and presenting summaries of evidence, including its quality, for systematic reviews and recommendations in health care. Thus, for example, in the GRADE approach, randomised controlled trials (RCTs) count as

---

[92] www.regulations.gov.
[93] www.scottish.parliament.uk/gettinginvolved/petitions/index.aspx. See also, www.whitehouse.gov/open and https://gds.blog.gov.uk.
[94] SW Shulman, 'The Case against Mass E-mails: Perverse Incentives and Low Quality Public Participation in US Federal Rulemaking' (2009) 1 *Policy and Internet* 25.

high-quality evidence and observational studies as low-quality evidence supporting estimates of intervention effects. Further, the system also provides a structured reasoning process that leads from evidence to recommendations regarding healthcare interventions based on the trade-offs between benefits, on the one hand, and risks, burden, and potential costs, on the other hand, considering also values and preferences.[95] Another example from the medical field is the American Medical Association's (AMA) Guides to the Evaluation of Permanent Impairment (Sixth Edition, 2007) which provides guidelines for impairment rating. This guide seeks to minimise mistakes and inconsistencies in medical evidence given in tort cases regarding impairment levels.[96]

Another example, taken from a different context, is the Intergovernmental Panel on Climate Change (IPCC) 2010 policy for ranking scientific confidence in scientific claims. The policy is based on two qualitative indicators: the strength of the evidence and the level of agreement.[97] The following figure depicts the IPCC view of the relationship between evidence, agreement, and confidence. Confidence increases toward the upper right corner, as suggested by the increased shading.[98]

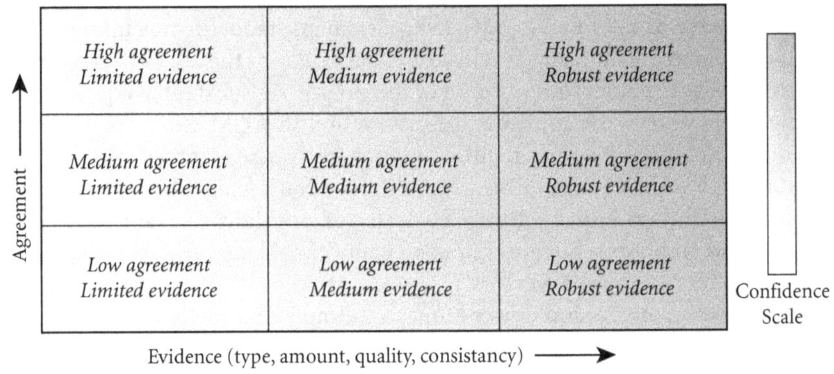

High agreement *Limited evidence*	*High agreement* *Medium evidence*	*High agreement* *Robust evidence*	
Medium agreement *Limited evidence*	*Medium agreement* *Medium evidence*	*Medium agreement* *Robust evidence*	
Low agreement *Limited evidence*	*Low agreement* *Medium evidence*	*Low agreement* *Robust evidence*	Confidence Scale

Agreement ⟶

Evidence (type, amount, quality, consistancy) ⟶

Figure 4: Courtesy of the Smithsonlan National Air and Space Museum Branch Library

---

[95] TJ Woodruff et al, 'An Evidence-Based Medicine Methodology to Bridge the Gap between Clinical and Environmental Health Sciences' (2011) 30 *Health Affairs* 931; G Guyatt et al, 'GRADE Guidelines: 1. Introduction—GRADE Evidence Profiles and Summary of Findings Tables' (2011) 64 *Journal of Clinical Epidemiology* 383.

[96] The AMA Guide was adopted by several US states. See, eg A Colledge et al, 'Impairment Rating Ambiguity in the United States: The Utah Impairment Guides for Calculating Workers' Compensation Impairments' (2009) 24 *Journal of Korean Medical Science* 232, 234.

[97] See, Intergovernmental Panel on Climate Change, 'Guidance Note for Lead Authors of the IPCC Fifth Assessment Report on Consistent Treatment of Uncertainties' (IPCC Cross-Working Group Meeting on Consistent Treatment of Uncertainties, Jasper Ridge, CA, USA, 6–7 July 2010), available at: wwsw.ipcc.ch/pdf/supporting-material/uncertainty-guidance-note.pdf. For further discussion, see G Yohe and M Oppenheimer, 'Evaluation, Characterization, and Communication of Uncertainty by the Intergovernmental Panel on Climate Change—an Introductory Essay' (2011) 8 *Climatic Change* 629.

[98] ibid, 3.

By forcing experts to use a detailed methodology these guidelines can prevent some cognitive errors and also facilitate critical appraisal of the ultimate opinion (which could expose ex facto the influence of hidden biases).

The development and implementation of methodological guidelines faces, however, several challenges. First, due to their highly context-dependent nature, their design and implementation is very costly. Second, and more importantly, the design of methodological standards is not a neutral process but in fact a highly value-laden process. For example, the IPCC's framework allows experts to take into account potentially devastating outcomes, even if they are not supported by strong evidence. The Guidance Note encourages author teams to provide information about the tails of distributions of key variables, stating that 'low-probability outcomes can have significant impacts, particularly when characterized by large magnitude, long persistence, broad prevalence, and/or irreversibility'.[99] This reflects a precautionary approach to the interpretation of scientific evidence. While the IPCC approach seems justified by the potential devastating effects of climate change, it is not 'objective'.

Methodological guidelines could also be subject to corporate influence. Such influence is deeply problematic because of the potential broad effect of such guidelines, ranging over an entire regulatory field. For example, Robinson et al argue that the design of the EFSA's GMO risk assessment standards was influenced by the bio-engineering industry, as reflected in particular by the use of the concept of comparative assessment (a rewording of the concept of 'substantial equivalence'). This concept adopts the controversial assumption that GM crops are equivalent to non-GM crops and do not require rigorous safety assessment.[100] Similarly, the authors of the AMA Guides have been criticised for having a bias toward lower impairment ratings and for being advocates of positions that are welcome to insurers and employers, but are chilling to plaintiff attorneys and those representing the interests of injured workers.[101]

The foregoing discussion does not mean to imply that methodological guidelines cannot be useful. However these challenges need to be taken into account in the drafting process. Below I sketch three regulatory elements that can contribute to the credibility of methodological guidelines.

1. Cross-institutional process: ensuring that the guidelines are created through a cross-institutional process could increase their credibility by allowing the voices of the whole scientific community to be reflected in the text. Further, such multi-focal processes can also minimise the risk of corporate capture. Thus, for example, the GRADE working group includes experts from various countries and institutions. The credibility of the GRADE approach stems, among other things, from the fact that it has been adopted by multiple organisations, from different countries.[102]

---

[99] ibid, 1.
[100] Robinson et al (n 17) 2.
[101] See Colledge et al (n 96) 236.
[102] See G Guyatt et al, 'An Emerging Consensus on Grading Recommendations?' (2006) 11 *Evidence Based Medicine* 2, 4.

2. Empirical validation: in many cases, even if substantial thought was invested in the design of such guidelines one cannot assume that they would fulfil their goal without rigorous empirical validation. Thus the development process must be supported by empirical work, which in most cases needs to be based on continuous research. Thus, for example, in the case of the AMA Guides, an important question is to what extent the Guides actually improve intra-raters consistency. This question can be examined by comparing ratings for particular injuries between different physicians. Because of the wide range of injuries covered by the Guides such empirical examination would be quite costly and indeed there is not enough evidence on that issue.[103] Another important empirical question concerns the association between impairment ratings and earnings losses. Because the AMA Guides were designed to measure the severity of impairment—the loss of function of a body part—and not the loss of ability to participate in major life activities, including the ability to work (which should determine the ultimate compensation level) it is important to assess the AMA Guides' ability to predict disability. To the extent that the AMA Guides fail to accurately predict future earning losses, for example, it is important to develop methodologies that would translate impairment ratings into levels of compensation.[104]

3. Reflexive process: no guidelines are going to be perfect. Thus the adoption of methodological guidelines must be supported by an institutionalised learning process which could facilitate learning from mistakes and continual improvement. There is a broad literature on experimental governance which could be drawn upon in that context.[105]

A second type of de-biasing mechanism consists of deliberative procedures encouraging perspective taking. One way in which perspective taking can be encouraged is by creating a pluralistic decision-making environment. I would like to consider two broad options in this context: the first focuses on the experts' selection process; the second focuses on public deliberation. Consider first the experts' selection problem: a good example for an attempt to extend the diversity of the experts' body is the IPCC new guidelines for the selection of lead authors and team members, and for handling conflicts of interest. These procedures reflect an attempt to enrich the epistemic horizon of the IPCC's working groups. According to the *Procedures for the Preparation, Review, Acceptance, Adoption, Approval and*

---

[103] See, eg Forst et al, *Journal of Occupational and Environmental Medicine* (2010). (Examining the consistency of the AMA Guides 6th edn for low back injuries).

[104] See, eg SA Seabury et al, 'American Medical Association Impairment Ratings and Earnings Losses Due to Disability', 10.1097/JOM.0b013e3182794417 (2013) 55, 286; J Bhattacharya et al, 'Evaluating Permanent Disability Ratings Using Empirical Data on Earnings Losses' (2010) 77 *Journal of Risk and Insurance* 231.

[105] O Perez, 'Courage, Regulatory Responsibility, and the Challenge of Higher-order Reflexivity' (2014) 8 *Regulation and Governance* 203; and C Overdevest and J Zeitlin, 'Assembling an Experimentalist Regime: Transnational Governance Interactions in the Forest Sector' (2014) 8 *Regulation and Governance* 22.

Publication of IPCC Reports, the composition of the group of Coordinating Lead Authors and Lead Authors shall aim to reflect the range of scientific views, geographical representation, mixtures of experts with and without previous experience in IPCC and gender balance.[106] The IPCC policy on conflict of interests (COI) reflects a similar sensitivity to the need to enrich the epistemic horizon of the IPCC output. According to the policy, bias represents the legitimate need to 'include individuals with different perspectives and affiliations', and can be managed by an 'author team composition that reflects a balance of expertise and perspectives'. COI is a state of affairs in which 'an individual could secure a direct and material gain through outcomes in an IPCC product', and contrary to bias, it should prevent a candidate from being nominated to IPCC teams. The COI policy of the IPCC clarifies that 'holding a view that one believes to be correct, but that one does not stand to gain from personally is not a conflict of interest'.[107] Whereas COI is conceived as a threat to the objectivity of the IPCC, 'bias' as defined in the IPCC COI policy (which does not reflect a cognitive bias but an epistemic standpoint), is conceived as a mechanism that can contribute to the deliberative strength of the IPCC.[108] Arguably the EU expert system enjoys a high degree of diversity given that many committees are made up of experts from various Member States. However, the critique of the EU experts selection process, by organisations such as ALTER-EU, which highlighted the deep influence of corporate representatives in the experts' committees, raises doubts on the credibility of the EU expert system despite of its projected diversity.[109]

An interesting mechanism that could be used to extend the diversity of the expert body as well as to counter potential corruptive pressures is blind selection or randomisation.[110] This mechanism could alleviate the problems associated with COI by severing the linkage between the expert and the agency that requires experts' services. It could also create a more diverse ideological membership. Such mechanism could be implemented by establishing an independent intermediary that would be responsible for allocating experts to agencies that require expert advice through either randomisation or blind selection.[111] A randomisation mechanism could be quite easily implemented in those fields (eg medicine, forensic science) in which the division between sub-disciplines is well developed and is embedded in a subspecialty-dominant practice environment.[112] It would be more

---

[106] Appendix A to the Principles Governing IPCC Work, para 4.3.2 (www.ipcc.ch/pdf/ipcc-principles/ipcc-principles-appendix-a-final.pdf).
[107] IPCC Conflict of Interest Policy (www.ipcc.ch/pdf/ipcc-principles/ipcc-conflict-of-interest.pdf).
[108] See O Edenhofer, 'Different Views Ensure IPCC Balance' (2011) 1 *Nature Climate Change* 229.
[109] ALTER-EU (n 4) 3 and the European Court of Auditors, 'Management of Conflict of Interest in Selected EU Agencies' (n 18).
[110] Such procedure is discussed in detail in Robertson (n 24) (in the judicial context).
[111] Robertson proposes the establishment of an intermediary agency that would function as a broker between sponsors of research (eg plaintiffs) and potential expert witnesses (eg doctors); Robertson, ibid, 206.
[112] DA Hirsh et al, '"Continuity" as an Organizing Principle for Clinical Education Reform' (2007) 356 *New England Journal of Medicine* 858, 863.

difficult to implement it in fields lacking clear subspecialty culture. In such fields the selection of experts would have to be made through a non-automated search process. It should be noted, however, that the proposal to limit the powers of EU regulatory agencies in the experts' selection process goes against well-established tradition that leaves the ultimate discretion for choosing the expert to the administrative agency in charge, and is thus likely to face strong opposition. The decision of the European Ombudsman on May 2014 to open an investigation into the composition and transparency of the Commission's expert groups provides an opportunity to reform the selection process.[113]

A second mechanism that can encourage perspective taking is public deliberative mechanisms, which facilitate external critique of the expert decision-making process. The challenge in this context is to develop participatory mechanisms than can actually challenge the insider expert view. Within the EU there is already a broad regulatory framework that seeks to facilitate public participation in regulatory decision-making. However, more effort is needed in order to incorporate public voices into the expert decision-making process. As Maria Lee notes in a recent paper, part of the difficulty lies in the preference of EU law for technical explanations of decision-making. The 'inscrutability of technical assessments' she notes 'may further increase the difficulties of looking behind technical advice, excluding contributions not defined in those technical terms'.[114] Expert advice remains extremely influential in the EU regulatory landscape.[115]

A good example of a participatory mechanism that seeks to go beyond a mere right-based approach to participation and attempts to create an institutional structure that would facilitate epistemologically meaningful civic participation is 'RegulationRoom'.[116] RegulationRoom is an experimental platform for public participation in government rule-making processes created by a cross-disciplinary group of Cornell researchers, the Cornell eRulemaking Initiative (CeRI). CeRI uses selected live rule-makings to experiment with human and computer support for public engagement and discussion. At the core of the project is an experimental online public learning and participation platform that facilitates broader, better public participation in federal rule-makings. RegulationRoom is an example of 'socially intelligent computing': by bringing together human, automated, and computer-assisted elements RegulationRoom supports knowledge acquisition and creation by users, individually and collectively.

---

[113] 'Ombudsman Opens Investigation into Commission's Expert Groups' (n 20).

[114] M Lee, 'The Legal Institutionalisation of Public Participation in the EU Governance of Technology' in R Brownsword, E Scotford and K Yeung (eds), *Oxford Handbook of Law and Regulation of Technology* (Oxford, Oxford University Press, forthcoming), draft presented at ECPR Regulatory Governance Conference, June 2014. Available at SSRN: ssrn.com/abstract=2461145, 10.

[115] Although the (political) institutions are expressly not bound by experts: ibid, 9. See also, A Inkinen, 'Public Participation in the Environmental Permit Processes at Regional Level' (2009) 39 *Finnish Enviroment* (helda.helsinki.fi/bitstream/handle/10138/38019/FE_39_2009.pdf?sequence=1).

[116] See, regulationroom.org/about/overview and CR Farina, M Newhart and J Heidt, 'Rulemaking vs Democracy: Judging and Nudging Public Participation that Counts' (2013) 2 *Michigan Journal of Environmental and Administrative Law* 124.

V. CONCLUSIONS

The regulatory initiatives described above offer only a partial response to the de-biasing challenge; more work should be done in order to examine how the insights of the psychological literature on de-biasing can be applied to the regulatory context. This work requires detailed institutional and doctrinal analysis of particular regulatory contexts backed by empirical analysis. The development and implementation of de-biasing mechanisms requires a delicate cost-benefit analysis which would involve balancing its projected epistemic benefits against the design costs as well as any projected adverse effects. Such balancing exercise would most likely have to be settled by intuitive (rather than analytical) judgement. But the search for de-biasing strategies should also take into account the intrinsic limitations of the de-biasing project as a whole. Ultimately the goal of the de-biasing project is not to create a 'sterile' epistemic arena (stripped of any 'biases' or somehow 'normalised'), in which competing epistemic claims can be resolved through objective, rational deliberation. Rather, the goal of developing such de-biasing mechanisms is to facilitate a more reflexive and epistemologically complex decision-making structure.

Annex A: Surgical safety checklist: www.who.int/patientsafety/safesurgery/en/

Annex B: Aviation-safety checklists (B-32 checklist, 1943)

B-32 CHECK LIST
Suitable For Use With 100 Octane Fuel Only

BEFORE ENTERING AIRPLANE

Visual Inspection of Airplane
Pitot Head Cover Removed
Tire and Oleo Inflation
Wheel Chocks in Place
Trim Tabs Neutral
Crew Inspection

Carburetor Air Filters—As REQUIRED
Carburetor Heat—OFF
Anti-Icers, Wings and Props—OFF
Electrical Hyd. Pump Switch—ON
Parking Brakes—ON
Hydraulic Brake Pressure—CHECK

BEFORE STARTING ENGINES

landing Gear Switch—NEUTRAL
Forms I and IA
Fuel and Oil
Loading. WITHIN C.G. LIMITS
Ignition OFF
Props PULL THROUGH 6 BLADES
Control Movement FREE
Altimeter—SET
Battery Switches—ON
A.P.U.—Start, Equalizer Switch OFF
Inverter Switch—MAIN ON
Prop. Feather Switches—NORMAL
Prop. Reverse Safety Switches—SAFE
Prop. Reverse Pitch Switch—NORMAL
Prop. Selector Switches—AUTOMATIC
Prop. Speed Control—2800
Prop. Master Motor Switch—ON
All Circuit Breakers—ON
Throttle—l000 R.P.M. Position
Turbo Boost Selector—0
Mixtures Controls—IDLE CUT-OFF
Intercooler Flaps—AUTOMATIC
Oil Cooler Flaps—AUTOMATIC

STARTING ENGINES

Fuel Selector Valves—TANK TO ENGINE
Booster Pumps—ON LOW
  (No Fuel Pressure Ind. until Mixture
  Conlrol is Moved)
Fire Guard and Call CLEAR
Master Ignition Swilch—ON
Ignition Switch—ON AFTER TWO
  PROP. REVOLUTIONS
Mixture—AUTO RICH AFTER
  ENGINE IS RUNNING

WARM UP

Fuel and Oil Pressures
Booster Pumps—OFF
Vacuum and Flight lndicator
Generators—ON, 28V
A.P.U. Equalizer Switch—ON
Inverter—CHECK
Wing Flaps—OPERATE
Prop. Control—CHECK R.P.M.
  CHANGE
Magneto—CHECK at 2000 R.P.M.

6

Overcoming Illusions of Control: How to Nudge and Teach Regulatory Humility

CLAIRE A DUNLOP AND CLAUDIO M RADAELLI[*]

I. INTRODUCTION

IN THIS CHAPTER we focus on how to use insights from behavioural theory in the process of impact assessment of policy proposals in the European Union (EU). At the outset, we reason that different types of bias exist in the process of policy-making, including biases in the minds of those who are carrying out an impact assessment of a given proposal. We then focus on the case of biases affecting the analysis of the non-intervention option. We argue that EU policymakers' biases can be reduced by modifying the cognitive architecture of the IA process and by using training in ways that encourage awareness and henceforth a culture of regulatory humility.

Over the last decade, the European Commission has developed an integrated approach to impact assessment of policy proposals—legislative or not. The impact assessment process is now a major step in the development of proposals by the European Commission. Recently, the European Parliament has invested in analytical capacity to work dialogically with the Commission and to carry out impact assessment studies of major amendments of the legislative drafts. Extant literature has established that the EU impact assessment system is, comparatively speaking (for example, in comparison to the systems of the 28 Member States and the United States), sufficiently robust and comprehensive in the coverage of different categories of costs and benefits.[1]

---

[*] Our chapter arises out of original research funded by the European Research Council (ERC) project *Analysis of Learning in Regulatory Governance (ALREG)*. A previous version was presented at the 'Nudging in Europe' workshop, University of Liège Law School, 12–13 December 2013. The authors would like to thank the workshop participants and, in particular, our editors Alberto Alemmano and Anne-Lise Sibony for their insightful comments. We also thank Christie Smith for all her help formatting the work.

[1] O Fritsch et al, 'Comparing the Content of Regulatory Impact Assessments in the UK and the EU' (2013) 33 *Public Money and Management* 445; A Renda, *Law and Economics in the RIA World*, Series in European Law and Economics (Amsterdam, Intersentia, 2011); CM Radaelli, 'Measuring Policy

In the debate of how to conduct impact assessment and train policymakers, there are calls for integrating the insights of behavioural science into policy-making and design regulatory options that take into account the various biases that affect citizens' responses.[2] But policymakers have a mind too, and therefore their own choices can be biased.[3] The starting point for this chapter is the potential impact of one overarching bias—the illusion of control.[4] The proposition is that this illusion—which leads humans to over-estimate their competence and ability to control outcomes—may be particularly damaging when the tendency to regulate is institutionalised. Specifically, while the EU impact assessment process obliges policymakers to consider the status quo option (non-intervention), this is rarely ever selected.

We should be clear: we do not claim that cognitive biases explain the preference for public intervention. There are different political and economic justifications for intervention. An organisation can also deliberatively decide to intervene because there is a regulatory obligation or a commitment made by elected politicians. Further, policymakers can manipulate IA procedures towards interventionist choices. If this is so, cognitive biases have no role to play since the organisation is not misdiagnosing the facts; rather it is manipulating them. Our angle is different: we are interested in increasing policy makers' awareness of 'regulatory humility'.[5] We believe this should be encouraged among policymakers, and specifically that the option of not using public intervention (so-called 'do nothing' option in IA) be given due consideration—whether it is rejected or not. The classic policy-making literature has always pointed toward the limits of policy-making and policymakers.[6] The increased complexity of the policy environment, the difficulty of getting evidence into policy, and greater clarity about human biases have all led to

---

Learning: Regulatory Impact Assessment in Europe' (2009) 16 *Journal of European Public Policy* 1145; JB Wiener and A Alemanno, 'Comparing Regulatory Oversight Bodies across the Atlantic: The Office of Information and Regulatory Affairs in the US and the Impact Assessment Board in the EU' in S Rose-Ackerman and P Lindseth (eds), *Comparative Administrative Law* (Cheltenham, Edward Elgar, 2010).

[2] A Alemanno and A Spina, 'Nudging Legally: On the Choices and Balances of Behavioral Regulation' (2013) 12 *International Journal of Constitutional Law* 429; P John, 'Policy Entrepreneurship in UK Central Government. The Behavioural Insights Team and the Use of RCTs' (2013) 29 *Public Policy and Administration* 257; P John et al, *Nudge Nudge, Think Think* (London, Bloomsbury, 2013); R Jones, J Pykett and M Whitehead, *Changing Behaviours: On the Rise of the Psychological State* (Cheltenham, Edward Elgar, 2013); CR Sunstein, 'Humanizing Cost-benefit Analysis' (2011) 2 *European Journal of Risk and Regulation* 3; R van Bavel et al, 'Applying Behavioural Science to EU Policy-Making' (2013) European Commission JRC Scientific and Policy Reports, available at: ec.europa.eu/dgs/health_consumer/information_sources/docs/30092013_jrc_scientific_policy_report_en.pdf; M Vandeberg, A Carrico and L Schultz, 'Regulation in the Behavioural Era' (2011) 95 *Minnesota Law Review* 715.

[3] See, eg H Montgomery, *The Financial Crisis—Lessons for Europe from Psychology* (Stockholm, Swedish Institute for European Policy Studies, 2011).

[4] EJ Langer, 'The Illusion of Control' (1975) 32 *Journal of Personality and Social Psychology* 311.

[5] CA Dunlop and CM Radaelli, 'Teaching Regulatory Humility: Experimenting with Practitioners' (2015) *Politics*.

[6] See especially BW Hogwood and L Gunn, *Policy Analysis for the Real World* (Oxford, Oxford University Press, 1984); HA Simon, 'Rational Choice and the Structure of the Environment' (1956) 63 *Psychological Review* 129; G Vickers, *The Art of Judgment* (London, Chapman and Hall, 1965) ch 8; A Wildavsky, *Speaking Truth to Power. The Art and Craft of Policy Analysis* (Boston, MA, Little and Brown, 1979) especially Pt 2.

a re-discovery of these limitations. The result has been a renewed call for regulatory humility and humble decision-making.[7] Essentially, we bring these insights about regulatory humility into the field of impact assessment, with the EU as our empirical reference, and develop our suggestions on how to de-bias policymakers.

The chapter is structured as follows. In section two, we set up the proposition that EU policymakers are especially susceptible to an illusion of control. Then we explore what can be done to mitigate a pre-eminent bias. We outline two categories of solutions. Section three looks at how the IA system in the EU can be implemented and amended in ways that 'go with the grain' of cognitive biases.[8] Here, we accept the reality of that policymakers often operate in 'fast' mode.[9] Rather than try to re-wire the policymaker's mind, we focus on re-wiring the context within which they work to ensure that what is automatic to them is also beneficial to policy-making. In short, how can we nudge EU policymakers to explore the 'do-nothing option', and indeed all policy options, with humility about the control they can exercise? Section four takes a slightly different tack. Here we focus on how policymakers can be exhorted to engage in more 'slow' thinking about the biases they carry. Such reflection—we argue—can be actively encouraged by appropriate training techniques and content. We explore the possible teaching tools that can be and are being used—including in-class behavioural experiments. The chapter concludes with a discussion of how some of these ideas can be taken forward by the Commission.

II. WHAT PREVENTS THE EU FROM 'DOING NOTHING'?

In his masterpiece on policy-making, *The Art of Judgment* (1965), Sir Geoffrey Vickers defines policy action as a product of policymakers' contextual reality judgements—their understanding of the institutional world in which they operate and rules and procedures that underpin that—and their judgements—the cognitive biases they hold: 'Facts are relevant only in relation to some judgments of value and judgments of value are operative only in relation to some configuration of fact'.[10] Thus, to understand policy-making, is to recognise how these two realities intertwine to produce action and practices. Consequently, we argue that the contextual and prevailing values of the EU may intertwine to produce a propensity toward taking policy action rather than selecting the 'do nothing' option. In short, it produces a situation in which regulatory humility may be in short supply.

What is the EU's contextual reality? What is the policy context in which 'doing nothing' is considered? What structural and institutional factors influence how IA is conducted? Deciding if, when and how to intervene are fundamental in all governance systems. The EU, however, poses some specific challenges. Control here

---

[7] Dunlop and Radaelli, 'Teaching Regulatory Humility' (n 5); A Etzioni, 'Humble Decision Making' (1989) 89 *Harvard Business Review* 122; E Etzioni, 'Humble Decision-Making Theory' (2014) 16 *Public Management Review* 611.
[8] P Dolan et al, *MINDSPACE Influencing Behaviour through Public Policy* (London, Cabinet Office, 2009) 7.
[9] D Kahneman, *Thinking, Fast and Slow* (New York, Penguin, 2011).
[10] Vickers, *The Art of Judgment* (n 6) 40.

is not simply a matter of whether policymakers should decide to 'do something' about a policy problem in analytical terms. There are of course legal principles at work, especially competence and subsidiarity, with their own relationship with IA.[11] Subsidiarity applies to determine whether the EU or the Member States are competent in the areas of 'shared competence'. Thus, the subsidiarity principle relates to WHO should act in relation to a given policy problem, whilst IA concerns WHAT should be done and only comes into play at the EU level if the EU is in principle competent. Logically, there could be policy domains where the EU is competent to act but the IA concludes that this is not the case, having considered the specific features of the policy problem. Equally, we could reason that the IA supports the non-intervention option even in domains of shared competence where the EU is competent by dint of subsidiarity. Although logically distinct, legal principles and IA analysis are related and in practice the views of the Commission on subsidiarity (eg think of a case where the Commission believes it should intervene because of subsidiarity arguments) constrain the usage of non-interventionist option in IA.

Some controversies confirm that IA analysis is blended with wider legal and political arguments—and not always with the best results. Some years ago the Commission looked at insurance premiums from the perspective of gender equality, and concluded, in the IA, that doing nothing would perpetuate imbalances. Frank Vibert criticised the Commission for having decided to intervene in a field where market forces 'correctly' appraise the different risk coefficient of men and women, and argued that there were no grounds to bring in a gender perspective on the economics of setting insurance premiums at work in the Member States. By opting to intervene, was the Commission making the wrong economic assessment, or was it pushing the boundaries of subsidiarity politically—or both?[12]

If there is a sort of in-built structural bias toward intervention, its roots are not in legal principles or IA standards. Regulatory theory argues that the Commission is a supra-national bureaucracy that has a structural preference for regulation, given the constraints it encounters in activating other policy instruments like taxation and expenditure.[13] In a sense, regulation is the essence of this bureaucracy.

To sum up, the overall mis-diagnosis of non-interventionist options may result from the application of legal principles, inaccuracies in economic analysis contained in IA, or the wider political roots of the EU regulatory state. We cannot deal with all three causes, especially because they differ markedly: some are structural, some are contingent. Given our focus on IA, it is better to focus on contingent causes—bearing in mind that the context is more complicated and has structural properties. Let us assume that policymakers involved in a given appraisal of policy options have already absorbed their fair load of bureaucratic culture (the Commission as regulatory bureaucracy as suggested by regulation theory) and legal views on competence and subsidiarity. We are left with more contingent or proximate

[11] For details, see ACM Meuwese, *Impact Assessment in EU Lawmaking* (The Hague, Kluwer Law International, 2008).
[12] F Vibert, *The EU's New System of Impact Assessment: A Scorecard* (London, European Policy Forum, 2004).
[13] GD Majone, *Regulating Europe* (London, Routledge, 1996).

causes involved in the biases affecting intervention and non-intervention. At this point, the question becomes: what of the values and cognitive biases that mediate how policymakers approach public policy choice?

The starting point is that as humans all policymakers, whether in the EU or elsewhere, they can suffer from over-confidence in their ability to control events.[14] Ellen Langer famously demonstrated this 'illusion of control' experimentally, confirming the central hypothesis that people struggle to distinguish between events determined by chance and those determined by skill.[15] This is true even in situations where exercising skill cannot affect the outcome. Second, people have genuine difficulty in distinguishing between skill- and chance-related situations. These are often closely related in people's experience. For example, there are elements of skill in chance situations such as dice games where participants can learn the odds.[16] And so, 'when a chance situation mimics a skill situation, people behave as if they have control over the uncontrollable event even when the fact that success or failure depends on chance is salient'.[17] The result is an illusion of control which hinders humans from understanding their limited impact on outcomes and conditioning influence of a wide range of specific biases.

Policymakers are required to understand that not all variables can be known nor their implications be understood; they work in a context where skill is mixed with chance. But, if they are biased by an illusion of control, they cannot fully appreciate the impact of chance and may struggle to identify the 'limits of the regulable'.[18]

This is the cognitive starting point for policy-making in the EU. The particular EU context (described above) combines with the illusion of control to create a policy-making environment in which cognitive biases may be masked and policy action favoured. Hinting at the socialisation effects of this context, Lord Cockfield was fond of saying that the attitude of the EU regulator was 'if it moves, harmonise it!'.[19] Indeed, even if we discount this political argument, the illusion of control on its own is sufficient to generate an under-estimation of the benefits of non-intervention. The question we address in the rest of the chapter is what can be done to address this potential blindness to bias.

The following two sections suggest some ways ahead. Inspired by Kahneman,[20] we explore two ways forward for EU policymakers—working with the biases to change behaviour fast and raising policymakers' awareness through reflection—changing their minds slowly.

---

[14] DA Armor and SE Taylor, 'When Predictions Fail: The Dilemma of Unrealistic Optimism' in T Gilovich, D Griffin, and D Kahneman (eds), *Heuristics and Biases: The Psychology of Intuitive Judgement* (New York, Cambridge University Press, 2002); S Taylor and J Brown, 'Positive Illusions and Well-being Revisited: Separating Fact from Fiction' (1994) 116 *Psychological Bulletin* 21; Langer, 'The Illusion of Control' (n 4).

[15] Langer (n 4).

[16] ibid, 324.

[17] ibid, 315–16.

[18] Vickers, *The Art of Judgment* (n 6) ch 8.

[19] Cited, amongst others, in A McGee and S Weatherhill, 'The Evolution of the Single Market—Harmonisation or Liberalisation' (1990) 53 *MLR* 578, 583; see also F Vibert, *The Itch to Regulate: Confirmation Bias and the European Commission's New System of Impact Assessment* (London, European Policy Forum, 2005).

[20] Kahneman, *Thinking, Fast and Slow* (n 9).

III. USING PROMPTS TO GUIDE POLICYMAKERS IN THE 'FAST' LANE

This section is dedicated to guiding policy-making in the cognitive fast lane. To work out how we might go with the grain of the illusion of control, we need to go back to why humans (and so policymakers) are motivated to control in the first place. The fact that 'most people hold overly positive views of themselves and their ability to effect change in the environment' is usually taken as indicative of psychological well-being.[21] Humans believe that control helps prove our competence.[22] As we take action, our perception of control increases as do our levels of psychological comfort.[23] The challenge in policy-making is to make the IA process in general, and consideration of the do nothing option in particular, activities which goes *with the grain of the strongest cognitive biases*. Indeed, as we shall see, that is the very logic behind the inclusion of the do nothing category in the first place; it exists to encourage policymakers to treat non-intervention as a positive choice. Yet, we know that IA in the EU could be more refined[24] and that the selection of the do nothing category rarely occurs.

The nudge proposition is that we can counteract this illusion of control and the risk of automaticity, by restructuring the policy-making environment. Behavioural theory reveals a huge array of biases supported by varying depths of evidence. The UK Cabinet Office captures nine biases with the 'most robust' effects in its influential 2009 report with the mnemonic title—*MINDSPACE*[25]—whose influence policymakers most need to understand. Here, we take each of these biases in turn to see how the IA system is designed to take account of them and might be amended further still. Essentially, we are concerned with the reforms that can be made to IA that restructure policymakers' cognitive architecture.

Table 3: MINDSPACE biases and policymakers[26]

Illusion of control	Policymakers …
Messenger	listen to experts and professional peers
Incentives	avoid losses and emphasise the baseline
Norms	observe professional socialisation
Defaults	overate precedence
Salience	attend selectively and confirm pre-existing beliefs
Priming	are susceptible to cues from the environment
Affect	make associations based on emotional responses
Commitments	seek to make and keep public promises
Ego	are motivated to act to feel good about themselves

---

[21] Taylor and Brown, 'Positive Illusions and Well-being Revisited' (n 14) 21.
[22] Langer, 'The Illusion of Control' (n 4) 323–24; RW White, 'Motivation Reconsidered: The Concept of Competence' (1959) 66 *Psychological Review* 297.
[23] Langer, 'The Illusion of Control' (n 4) 323.
[24] A Renda, 'Impact Assessment in the European Union' in CA Dunlop and CM Radaelli (eds), *International Handbook on Impact Assessment* (Cheltenham, Edward Elgar, 2015).
[25] Dolan et al, *MINDSPACE* (n 8) 7; see Table 3.
[26] Adapted from Dolan, ibid.

The first bias concerns the fact that ideas 'do not float freely';[27] rather, they are carried by messengers.[28] The identity and qualifications of the messenger informs our perception of the importance of what is said. Critically, we lend more weight to the advice of those who can lay claims to authoritative expertise on an issue or whose background resembles our own. Consider the power of an individual scientific adviser; her evidence is routinely given greater weight than that offered by the lay person.[29] That heavier weight emanates from the credibility she has been given by her peers—most commonly in the form of professional distinctions; research funding and career progression.[30] In IA, the power of external experts is usually harnessed in relation to evidencing individual aspects of policy options. This is necessary of course; policymakers need specialist inputs. However, where the opportunity to give evidence comes mid-way through the IA process—that is once the problem has been defined—policymakers' preferences may be set. To counter the illusion of control the decisional process would benefit from incorporating expert advice at a much earlier stage for example by inviting experts or 'critical friends', who have civil service background but have retired from the bureau, to comment 'upstream' in the IA process.[31] Highly regarded messengers should be invited to comment on how the questions are framed, not only on how they might be answered.

We can think about the messenger bias in relation to IA in a different way. Rather than taking advice from a small number of identifiable experts, policymakers can also draw upon the wisdom of anonymous crowds,[32] for example by using information markets that correct errors made by individual experts.[33] Surveying large groups of unnamed experts, stakeholders or citizens, offers one means to explore the unthinkable—rejecting policy action—in a way that carries minimal reputational damages for those involved should their advice later appear naïve or ill-considered. Such informational supply tools address the messenger bias, and reduce the possibility of groupthink,[34] while still going with the grain of control illusions. Policymakers still exercise choice but they do so with the knowledge that experts have been free to express their opinions about the merits and pitfalls of inaction as well as interventions.

---

[27] T Risse-Kappen, 'Ideas do Not Float Freely' (1994) 48 *International Organization* 185.
[28] RB Cialdini, *Influence: The Psychology of Persuasion* (New York, NY, Harper, 2007).
[29] B Wynne, 'May the Sheep Safely Graze? A Reflexive View of the Expert–Lay Knowledge Divide' in B Szerzynski and B Wynne (eds), *Risk, Environment and Modernity: Towards a New Ecology* (London, Sage, 1996); S Jasanoff, 'Technologies of Humility: Citizen Participation in Governing Science' (2003) 41 *Minerva* 233.
[30] D Allchin, 'Do We See through a Social Microscope? Credibility as a Vicarious Selector' (1999) 66 *Philosophy of Science (Proceedings)* S287.
[31] A Stirling, 'Opening Up or Closing Down?' M Leach, I Scoones and B Wynne (eds), *Science and Citizens: Globalization and the Challenge of Engagement* (London, Zed Books, 2005).
[32] J Surowiecki, *The Wisdom of Crowds: Why the Many are Smarter than the Few and How Collective Wisdom Shapes Business, Economies, Societies, and Nations* (New York, NY, Doubleday, 2004); C Sunstein, *Infotopia: How Many Minds Produce Knowledge* (Oxford, Oxford University Press, 2006).
[33] C Sunstein, 'Group Judgements: Statistical Means, Deliberation and Information Markets' (2005) June *New York University Law Review* 962.
[34] IL Janis, *Victims of Groupthink* (New York, Houghton Mifflin, 1972).

The next bias concerns how humans respond to incentives. It is known that we respond to incentives using mental shortcuts. One of the most powerful is the desire to avoid losses.[35] How does this interact with IA? Policymakers are incentivised to consider the do nothing option alongside all others. In many ways, the design of IA suits loss aversion bias. Cost-benefit analysis (CBA) may reinforce our tendency to fear loss more than we value gain. Since it is easier to calculate costs than it is benefits[36] and given that humans define losses and gains relative to a 'reference point',[37] if no such reference point exists for gains, or it is unclear or notional, the tendency to lend more weight to fully calculated losses may be stronger. We know, for example, that people are influenced more by nominal—that is numerical—values as opposed to notional or actual values.[38] We can hypothesise that where the numerical magnitude of a policy option can be calculated, loss aversion may be more evident.

Yet, the analytical context in the EU is not so straightforward. The following scenario is instructive. In his analysis of the first batch of EU IAs, Vibert notes that even where the net benefits (from an intervention) were left un-quantified—that is policymakers knew only the costs—the Commission never selected the do nothing option.[39] The issue here is that in order to perceive loss accurately (and so be averse to it), policymakers must be certain that they understand *both* the costs and benefits. Yet, the quantification of benefits is complex and lags behind the quantification of costs; in 2011 58.42 per cent of Commission IAs quantified benefits as compared with 88.12 per cent cost quantification.[40] In such circumstances, a clear calculation of loss cannot be made; this may push policymakers toward the default of taking action. In short, it is possible that the evidential base of IA in the EU (and indeed the UK)[41] frustrates the power of loss aversion and creates the conditions for the illusion of control to drive action.

Evidence from the United States (US) suggests that achieving parity in the calculation of benefits and costs is possible[42] and may go some way to harnessing the power of loss aversion. Of course, once we are able to calculate loss, the impact of loss aversion will be mediated by the size of the loss itself and in particular how

---

[35] D Kahneman and A Tversky, 'Choices, Values and Fames' (1984) 39 *American Psychologist* 341.

[36] W Harrington, L Heinzerling and RD Morgenstern (eds), *Reforming Regulatory Impact Analysis* (Washington DC, Resources for the Future, 2009).

[37] D Kahneman and A Tversky, 'Prospect Theory: An Analysis of Decision under Risk' (1979) 47 *Econometrica* 263; A Tversky and D Kahneman, 'Loss Aversion in Riskless Choice: A Reference-Dependent Model' (1991) 106 *Quarterly Journal of Economics* 1039.

[38] E Ert and I Erev, 'On the Descriptive Value of Loss Aversion in Decisions under Risk: Six Clarifications' (2013) 8 *Judgment and Decision Making* 214; P Raghubir and J Srivastava, 'Effect of Face Value on Product Valuation in Foreign Currencies' (2002) 29 *Journal of Consumer Research* 335.

[39] Vibert, *The EU's New System of Impact Assessment* (n 12) 9.

[40] CEPS (Centre for European Policy Studies) Impact Assessment Database—private communication with authors; Fritsch et al, 'Comparing the Content of Regulatory Impact Assessments' (n 1).

[41] In 2010, UK IAs quantifying costs and benefits were 80.4% and 57.1% respectively, see Fritsch et al, 'Comparing the Content of Regulatory Impact Assessments' (n 1) Table 2.

[42] C Cecot et al, 'An Evaluation of the Quality of Impact Assessment in the European Union with Lessons for the US and the EU' (2008) 2 *Regulation and Governance* 405.

this compares with the current situation. This emphasises the importance of how the baseline—which acts as the reference point—is framed and calculated in the IA process.

The third powerful bias explored concerns the power of social norms. In short, humans are influenced by the actions of others and 'herding' behaviour is common.[43] In a social setting this may take the form of people joining a queue even when they do not know what it is for. In the world of IA, we can think of policymakers conforming to professional norms of the bureau. These norms may be especially powerful because their observation is often materially rewarded in terms of career progression, salary, etc. The most famous bureaucratic norm is budget maximisation[44]—where intervention correlates positively with increased size and power of a department and with the individual prospects of civil servants. Again, this is one of the norms that IA processes and tools such as CBA are designed to counter. As has been noted already, without an accurate understanding of the costs and benefits of action, the biases toward intervention and control can go unchecked.

Moving beyond calculation, how might we go with the grain of social norms? What norms can be mobilised to counter the illusion of control in the IA process? New public management norms such as cutting 'red tape' can be mobilised to trigger reflection amongst policymakers. Given that norms become more powerful if they are personal, the IA process could usefully include prompts for policymakers to review what was saved by their department, or even their policy team, in previous years through regulatory compression.[45]

Linked to social norms, the human tendency to rely on defaults typifies Kahneman's fast thinking.[46] Where there are pre-set categories, we are more likely to select one of them than to question them or create our own. While perhaps the best-known tool is actually an ex post one—the sunset clause which creates legislation with an expiry date—the inclusion of a do nothing option in IA is designed to prevent policymakers from simply going with the flow. What more can be done to the policy-making flow that generates reflection on the limits of control and pitfalls of intervention ex ante? The IA process could be usefully augmented with questions relating to whether any horizon-scanning has been conducted that may suggest trade-offs from the decision or whether a post-decision evaluation has been considered and when this might take place. By asking such questions, policymakers may not ultimately reject the default option but it provides one way to structure the 'flow' of IA in a way that may stimulate reflection about the potential

---

[43] PW Schultz et al, 'The Constructive, Destructive, and Reconstructive Power of Social Norms' (2007) 18 *Psychological Science* 429.

[44] WA Niskanen, *Bureaucracy and Representative Government* (Edison, NJ, Transaction Publishers, 1971).

[45] BIS (UK Department of Business Innovation and Skills), *One-in, One-out: Fourth Statement of New Regulation* (London, HMSO, 2012).

[46] Kahneman, *Thinking, Fast and Slow* (n 9); see also CRM McKenzie, MJ Liersch and SR Finkelstein, 'Recommendations Implicit in Policy Defaults' (2006) 17 *Psychological Science* 414; Tversky and Kahneman, 'Loss Aversion in Riskless Choice' (n 37).

results of a policy decision (whether that is an intervention or not) a few years down the line.

In 2001, when he was Administrator of the US Office of Information and Regulatory Affairs (OIRA), academic risk analyst John D Graham pioneered the introduction of 'prompt letters'—a procedure whereby OIRA is able to propose that an agency consider a new regulation or reconsider an existing one. The impact of these in the US has been welcomed.[47] Such prompt letters offer one way for the fast thinking of the policymaker to be slowed down by the oversight body and to disrupt reliance on defaults. Until 2011, the European Commission's Impact Assessment Board (IAB) enjoyed the power to issue such prompts (art 6 of the former Rules of Procedure) but this power has been scrapped without explanation.[48]

Beyond defaults we have the matter of salience—our attention is drawn by what is relevant to us. Humans are vulnerable to 'cognitive dissonance' or confirmation bias—we process information selectively. We rationalise or ignore evidence which disconfirms what might prove us wrong.[49] This goes to the heart of the illusion of control—where we are over-confident about evidence that supports our pre-existing views because it is easier to encode. Going with the grain of this to counter the illusion of control requires that evidence which challenges assumptions is made easier to understand and harder to ignore. The IA evidence gathering process could be amended to require that the same evidence be framed in a variety of ways with the aim that it challenges the cognitive 'anchors' that guide policymakers.

A further dimension of salience concerns the disproportionate attention paid to unusual memorable events and images.[50] The tendency for policymakers to take 'knee jerk' action in the wake of trauma is well known in government and extensively theorised in political science.[51] The resulting legislation is often poorly considered[52] and difficult to reform. Given that traumatic events inject urgency into policy-making, because they are usually unexpected and tragic, going with the grain of this bias is both difficult and potentially undesirable. We should steer clear of artificially conjuring-up an attention grabbing event.[53] Rather, one possible solution is to understand that the salience of an event will diminish over

---

[47] JD Graham, 'Saving Lives through Administrative Law and Economics' (2008) 157 *University of Pennsylvania Law Review* 460.

[48] A Alemanno and ACM Meuwese, 'Impact Assessment of EU Non-Legislative Rulemaking: The Missing Link in "New Comitology"' (2013) 19 *European Law Journal* 76.

[49] L Festinger, HW Riecken and S Schachter, *When Prophecy Fails: A Social and Psychological Study of a Modern Group that Predicted the Destruction of the World* (Minneapolis, University of Minnesota Press, 1956).

[50] D Kahneman et al, 'When More Pain is Preferred to Less: Adding a Better End' (1993) 4 *Psychological Science* 401.

[51] Better Regulation Commission, *Risk, Responsibility, and Regulation: Whose Risk is it Anyway?* (London, Cabinet Office Publications, 2006); BD Jones and F Baumgartner, *The Politics of Attention* (Chicago, IL, The University of Chicago Press, 2005).

[52] Most famously, see R Baldwin, C Hood and H Rothstein, 'Assessing the Dangerous Dogs Act: When does a Regulatory Law Fail?' [2000] *PL* 282, on the UK's 1991 Dangerous Dogs Act.

[53] Dolan et al, *MINDSPACE* (n 8).

time as it becomes less easily to recall in the policymaker's (and citizen's) mind. Requiring that policymakers consider the inclusion of post-decision evaluation in policy options (including doing nothing) offers one way to harness the perspective brought by the passage of time.

Humans can be subconsciously primed to act in particular ways.[54] We each encounter priming most frequently in everyday life through the words, smells and visual stimuli used in marketing. In public policy, similar processes are at work. For example, we can think about the influence of stakeholders and key interest groups in policy-making—how they frame and present their arguments may have a powerful influence in determining the 'boundaries of the possible' in minds of policymakers.[55] Hindmoor provides an insightful example in his case study on the policy response to the 2001 foot and mouth (FAM) disease in sheep and cattle outbreak in the UK.[56] Here, the National Farmers' Union's (NFU) early and close access to government officials enabled them to successfully persuade against the use of emergency cattle vaccination.

Working with the priming bias requires that more messages get through to the bureau from the external policy environment early on (see the earlier discussion on messengers). Here, humble policy-making means that a single group or idea is not allowed to dominate without challenge. Again, IA encompasses a tool that can enable that: consultation. Yet, we know that consultation exercises can become dominated by a small group of actors who are often the best resourced,[57] hence we need to open up consultation processes and encourage pluralism.

Digging further into human subconscious, behavioural theory illustrates the role of affect and emotions on actions.[58] For example, the fear of regret is one of the most powerful drivers of human action. To avoid the negative emotions that accompany making a 'wrong' decision, humans tend to rely on precedents—what was successful/not unsuccessful last time? In organisational decision-making, this is the essence of what Simon famously called 'satisficing';[59] policymakers aim for decisions that are 'good enough'. The emotional rewards of incremental policy-making also bring rewards in policy terms—most obviously relative stability for those stakeholders who 'shape' policy and citizens who 'take' it.[60] Yet, fear of going beyond the status quo also carries its own risks—where the desire to control and produce predictable results may mean missing a potentially innovative solution.

---

[54] DE Meyer and RW Schvaneveldt, 'Facilitation in Recognizing Pairs of Words: Evidence of a Dependence between Retrieval Operations' (1971) 90 *Journal of Experimental Psychology* 227.

[55] Majone, *Regulating Europe* (n 13).

[56] A Hindmoor, 'Explaining Networks through Mechanisms: Vaccination, Priming and the 2001 Foot and Mouth Disease Crisis' (2009) 57 *Political Studies* 75.

[57] CA Dunlop et al, 'The Many Uses of Regulatory Impact Assessment: A Meta-Analysis of EU and UK Cases' (2012) 6 *Regulation and Governance* 23.

[58] For a summary, see ML Finucane et al, 'The Affect Heuristic in Judgment of Risks and Benefits' (2000) 13 *Journal of Behavioral Decision Making* 1.

[59] Simon, 'Rational Choice and the Structure of the Environment' (n 6).

[60] CE Lindblom, *The Intelligence of Democracy* (New York, NY, The Free Press, 1965).

The logic of IA works against emotion in general, and fear in particular. Lerner and Tetlock report results of an experiment and find that where participants are required to justify their decisions—for example in using tools such as IAs—they are rewarded with positive emotions for rigorous policy appraisal.[61] Where it is implemented fully and overseen vigilantly, IA processes may act as accountability tools which may counter the most negative consequences of affect.

Behavioural theory has established another cognitive bias concerning the importance of honouring public commitments.[62] We are loathed to break promises. Indeed, we make them with the deliberate intention of binding ourselves to a particular course of action. The desire among policymakers—as individuals and collectively—to be consistent with their commitments is strong. A recent example of this phenomenon is the UK implementation of EU-set targets on first generation biofuels. Even though the government accepted an emerging scientific consensus that the production of food crops into biofuel increased CO_2 emissions, its public commitment to the target and promises made to the nascent UK biofuel industry led to the implementation of the Renewable Transport Fuel Obligation (RTFO). Though institutional forces made policy reversal difficult, the psychological dimension was central to the Department for Transport's (DfT) decision to stick with the planned course of action.[63]

Much of this desire to be consistent is driven by the need for credibility and accountability—backing down on commitments results in a very public loss of both. This desire to stay true to one's word can be used to policymakers' advantage if part of the contract they make involves remaining open to future review and evaluation. Post-decision evaluation in the case of biofuels did not result in policy reversal but rather a reduction of targets. Though the policymakers in this case anticipated that this would be the course of action, the absence of any commitment to remain open to new knowledge at the time of the IA made the DfT appear inconsistent and focussed on controlling policy failure.

The final bias considered by *MINDSPACE*[64] concerns ego—we act and think about ourselves in ways that make us feel good. In policy-making, this bias is perhaps exemplified by credit-seeking and blame-avoidance.[65] Where a decision has resulted in policy success, departments and policymakers seek credit and, where things do not go according to plan, external forces or other actors are held responsible.[66] Such tendencies are also institutionalised in the complex and

---

[61] JS Lerner and PE Tetlock, 'Accounting for the Effects of Accountability' (1999) 125 *Psychological Bulletin* 255.

[62] eg H Staats, P Harland and HAM Wilke, 'Effecting Durable Change. A Team Approach to Improve Environmental Behavior in the Household' (2004) 36 *Environment and Behaviour* 341.

[63] CA Dunlop, 'The Temporal Dimension of Knowledge and the Limits of Policy Appraisal: Biofuels Policy in the UK' (2010) 43 *Policy Sciences* 343.

[64] Dolan et al, *MINDSPACE* (n 8).

[65] C Hood, *The Blame Game: Spin, Bureaucracy and Self-Preservation in Government* (Princeton, Princeton University Press, 2010).

[66] DT Miller and M Ross, 'Self-serving Biases in the Attribution of Causality: Fact or Fiction?' (1975) 82 *Psychological Bulletin* 213.

multi-layered structures of governments—none more so than the EU, where there is no shortage of actors who can be implicated in success and failure. This might be written into the DNA of government, but the misinterpretation of outcomes and events that ego encourages frustrates policy learning. For sure, policy-making is usually too complex to be able to identify a single hero or villain. But achieving a broad understanding of what parts of the policy-making system have and have not worked as expected is possible and important if successes are to be replicated and mistakes avoided in the future.

Again, ex post policy evaluation offers a way ahead. Dunlop et al have shown that even in the absence of a post-implementation evaluation, we can still identify sets of conditions that contribute to certain types of IA—political, instrumental, symbolic, dialogic.[67] By pairing an IA with its policy evaluation partner, we can take this further and piece together the necessary and sufficient conditions—that is recipes—that lead us to more or less accurate policy-making. Such learning is 'double-loop'[68] in that it generates lessons that will not simply allow policymakers to better understand the policy options selected but will tell them something about the fundamental decision to intervene and the level of control they have exercised (through policy). The dividends for the human ego are obvious; the benefits for policy-making and society are even greater.

IV. CREATING REFLECTIVE AND MINDFUL POLICYMAKERS IN THE 'SLOW' LANE

Responding to the behavioural sciences is not simply a matter of accepting and working with policymakers' biases by amending the choice architecture. For good governance to become self-sustaining, we require 'mindful'[69] policymakers with the ability to and who are in the habit of reflecting on how their 'appreciative systems'[70] mediate professional practice. We must accept and embrace the fact that the policymaker is a sentient being not Pavlov's dog![71] Thus, we must also attend to the information that policymakers have about biases.

Behind every IA process are professional policy officers. While we know that, in 2009, 90 per cent of OECD countries reported that they provide some form of IA training.[72] Since 2006, the Secretariat General (SG) of the Commission has run a central training programme on IA. This has been supplemented by other DGs with their own courses (eg in DG Enterprise external consultants are used). Between 2007 and 2013, around 15 per cent of IA officers received this training.[73] Similarly,

---

[67] Dunlop et al, 'The Many Uses of Regulatory Impact Assessment' (n 57).
[68] C Argyris and DA Schön, *Organizational Learning: A Theory of Action Perspective* (Reading, MA, Addison-Wesley, 1978).
[69] EJ Langer, *Mindfulness* (New York, Merloyd Lawrence, 1989).
[70] Vickers, *The Art of Judgment* (n 6).
[71] IP Pavlov, *Conditional Reflexes* (New York, NY, Dover Publications, 1927/1960).
[72] OECD, *Indicators of Regulatory Management Systems* (Paris, OECD, 2009).
[73] Private communication with SG official, June 2014.

while they may be aware of the behavioural sciences agenda and some of the better known cognitive biases, EU policymakers have not yet received instruction on the role these may play in policy-making.[74] This state of affairs is understandable. IA has only been part of EU governance for the last decade, and behavioural science is even newer to the policy scene. Our interest here is in proposing examples of training that can be, and have been, incorporated into IA training courses and into practitioner-focussed Masters in Business (MBA) and Masters in Public Administration (MPA) programmes. Training courses that are designed to inform policymakers and change their thought processes—rather than simply restructure behaviour—offer a way to generate longer-term engagement with the regulatory humility agenda. This long-term promise is rooted in the potentially powerful professional socialisation effects that can be generated by training[75]—the herding effect of social norms at work!

Before outlining a variety of training options, we must first state their purpose. Essentially, training enables practitioners to access their 'slow' thinking capacity. Such capacity is especially important for policymakers. As Schön argued 30 years ago, becoming an effective professional requires more than technical rationality and the ability to react to the decision-making context;[76] professionals must be able engage in reflective thinking about their world and place therein. Reflection concerns the ways in which we subject our own thoughts and actions—possible and enacted—to consideration. We can go further than this; reflexivity takes us deeper into the self and addresses the emotional dimension of reflection that speaks to the very heart of human biases—what is it that public administrators as human beings with values, feelings and boundaries bring to decision-making?

Reflection takes us back to the fundamental principles of the *Art of Judgment*.[77] Reflection makes the appreciative system stronger—for Vickers, this system works via feedback, determining which facts are relevant, and how they fare in relation to our norms. Interestingly for our argument, Vickers observes that: 'Change both massive and unpredictable makes inconsistent demands for rigidity on the one hand and flexibility on the other and poses the most basic policy choice of all, the choice of what to regard as regulable'.[78]

How can we train civil servants and policymakers to engage in reflective thinking about their cognitive biases? We argue for two pedagogic mechanisms. Behavioural theory can simply be incorporated into training using classic methods of case studies and academic literature to initiate reflection. Such lectures and small group work encourage participants to reflect on what they have read, heard and discussed about the limits of control. Second, more innovative methods are beginning to

---

[74] R van Bavel et al, 'Applying Behavioural Science to EU Policy-Making' (2013) European Commission JRC Scientific and Policy Reports, available at: ec.europa.eu/dgs/health_consumer/information_sources/docs/30092013_jrc_scientific_policy_report_en.pdf.

[75] DL Kirkpatrick, 'Techniques for Evaluating Training Programs' (1959) 13 *Journal of American Society of Training Directors* 21.

[76] DA Schön, *The Reflective Practitioner How Professions Think in Action* (New York, NY, Basic Books, 1983).

[77] Vickers, *The Art of Judgment* (n 6).

[78] ibid, 99.

appear in MBA (Masters of Business Administration) and MPA (Masters of Public Administration) training—specifically involving the use of in-class experiments—that may enable reflexive engagement.[79] Kolb's seminal work on experiential learning suggests that by creating opportunities for students to *reflect by doing*, the learning process is individualised, and concepts move from the abstract to the concrete.[80] We now propose a variety of ways in which the nine *MINDSPACE* biases can be illuminated using traditional and experimental teaching tools.

Messenger bias is most commonly demonstrated using framing experiments. In their studies of issue framing, Kahneman and Tversky found that the manner in which the same information or outcome is represented impacts upon the decision that is made.[81] Small changes in this framing can produce different decisions about the issue. By presenting similar groups of policy practitioners with the same information communicated by different people—for example, an expert, a practitioner peer, an interest group representative—we can separate out the impact of who is communicating evidence from the evidence itself. This is relatively easy to resource and can be modelled on evidence submitted for a real IA.

The earlier discussion on human responses to incentives emphasised the importance of creating a level analytical playing field where loss could be nominally calculated—thus harnessing the power of loss aversion. But, we can also encourage policymakers to reflect on how cognitive shortcuts mediate their analysis of CBA. Our European policymakers should not consider costs and benefits as entirely objective categories. Rather, they could usefully be exposed to the wider literature that emphasises the subjectivity embedded in CBA analysis itself and its interpretation.[82] Ackerman and Heinzerling's retrospective application of CBA provides an especially powerful set of case studies where lead would not have been removed from gasoline in the 1970s, the Grand Canyon would have been damned for hydroelectric power and workplace exposure to vinyl chloride would not have been outlawed in 1974 had CBA been used in the original decisions.[83]

Turning to experiments, it may not always be appropriate or possible to conduct in-class experiments. Yet, the impact of cognitive biases can be explored by presenting classic cases to students. In a recent article, Rowe uses insights from Asch's classic experiments on group conformity to explore the behavioural dynamics of small group teaching.[84] The experiment provides an opportunity

---

[79] See MH Bazerman, *Judgment in Managerial Decision Making*, 6th edn (Hoboken, NJ, John Wiley, 2005) on managerial applications.
[80] DA Kolb, *Experiential Learning* (Englewood Cliffs, NJ, Jossey-Bass, 1984).
[81] Kahneman and Tversky, 'Prospect Theory: An Analysis of Decision under Risk' (n 37).
[82] Notably, F Ackerman and L Heinzerling, *Priceless: On Knowing the Price of Everything and the Value of Nothing* (New York, NY, New Press, 2004); DM Driesen, 'Is Cost-Benefit Analysis Neutral?' (2005) 77 *University of Colorado Law Review* 335; R Parker, 'Grading the Government' (2003) 70 *University of Chicago Law Review* 1345.
[83] Ackerman and Heinzerling, *Priceless*, ibid.
[84] M Rowe, 'Thinking about Behaviour and Conformity in Groups: Some Social Psychological Resources' (2013) 31(2) *Teaching Public Administration* 218; S Asch, 'Studies of Independence and Conformity: A Minority of One against a Unanimous Majority' (1956) 70(9) *Psychological Monographs* 1.

for the practitioners to reflect on the power of group norms. In that case, practitioners were invited to reflect—through individual learning logs—on how group dynamics influenced decision-making in the teaching group. However, the logic can easily be extended to policy-making situations where departments within an organisation develop particular ways of doing things.

The need to think beyond defaults is an enduring theme in public administration literature. One particularly useful model that can alert policymakers to the wider implications of going with the flow is that of risk trade-offs. Created by John D Graham and Jonathan B Wiener,[85] trade-off analysis requires policymakers to address the possibility of four countervailing risks being created by taking policy action:

1. Has the same risk *transferred* to new population?
2. Has the old problem been *substituted* by a new one affecting the same population?
3. Has the risk been *transformed* creating an entirely new problem for a new group of people?
4. Has the risk been *offset* to create a similar one for the same group?

Inviting practitioners to explore these questions in relation to their own experiences of policy-making offers one way to stimulate reflection and heighten awareness of bias.

Similar simple teaching methods can be used to highlight the salience of the new. Specifically, availability and recall biases[86] can be illustrated by introducing policymakers to basic probability calculation.

Practitioners can be exposed to the power of priming and affect using the types of framing experiments outlined earlier. For example, the same news story can be delivered to practitioners in different ways—one simply read by a newsreader and the other with the reading accompanied by dramatic background images. The expectation here is that the group primed with emotive images will assume a higher risk of the event happening again.[87]

One way to explore the power of commitments is to unpack why policymakers might make commitments to their publics. There are various arguments about why humans make promises that they know will tie their hands. For policymakers, such declarations act as accountability and transparency tools[88] and are central to the identity of a professional policymaker. However, policy-making also requires agility and the willingness to change course. Case studies that highlight the

---

[85] JD Graham and JB Wiener (eds), *Risk Versus Risk* (Cambridge, MA, Harvard University Press, 1995).
[86] A Tversky and D Kahneman, 'Availability: A Heuristic for Judging Frequency and Probability' (1973) 4 *Cognitive Psychology* 207.
[87] See Bazerman, *Judgment in Managerial Decision Making* (n 79).
[88] Lerner and Tetlock, 'Accounting for the Effects of Accountability' (n 61).

difficulty of terminating or reversing failing policies offer one way of highlighting the potential pathologies associated with commitment bias.

Finally comes ego—how can we teach policymakers that they behave in ways that make them feel better about themselves? This is a sensitive area where course instructors risk alienating their practitioner students! Yet, the role of ego gets to the heart of the wider illusion of control that threatens to undermine regulatory humility. Dunlop and Radaelli broach the subject with MPA participants using a mix of case study, conceptual teaching, and an in-class experiment.[89] They first generate awareness about the idea of regulatory humility using the case study of legal scholar and activist Larry Lessig. Lessig argues it is necessary to protect the world against unworkable legislation controlling the internet. Specifically, he is concerned that future regulatory interventions aimed at increasing transparency in and control over the online world may at best be futile, and at worst produce unanticipated harms.[90] Practitioners are taken through this case study and encouraged to discuss the idea of regulatory humility and its roots in the classic policy and administration literatures. Deeper reflection is then encouraged by conducting one of Langer's illusions of control experiments with the practitioners.[91] Based around a lottery, the experiment demonstrates that even though this is entirely a chance situation, those practitioners who selected their lottery number—that is had exercised a choice—were more confident they would win. Course evaluations and assignments suggest that this combination of teaching tools produced extensive reflection amongst practitioners[92] and provides a useful template.

V. CONCLUSION

The current discussion on the role of behavioural science in the EU, well represented by the 'Introduction' to our volume, revolves around the issue of integrating the insights of cognitive and behavioural economics into EU policy-making. In the field of impact assessment, this has spawned emerging concerns about whether benefits and costs are objective entities or are refracted by perceptions and heuristics of those most affected by them. At the same time, there is an ongoing debate on the alleged reluctance of regulators to take into serious consideration the option of non-intervening. This is not a new concern; since the early 2000s there have been critiques of the artificiality of some doing nothing analyses. In this chapter, we have argued that the various biases that underpin the illusion of control produce neglect of policy abstinence.

There is room for optimism however. The EU context may indeed be favourable to behaviourally-informed interventions. Despite the fact that the institutionalisation

---

[89] Dunlop and Radaelli, 'Teaching Regulatory Humility' (n 5).
[90] L Lessig, 'Internet is Freedom' (Speech to the Italian Parliament, 11 March, 2010) www.youtube.com/watch?v=fe2UsBXr-ls.
[91] Langer, 'The Illusion of Control' (n 4).
[92] See Dunlop and Radaelli, 'Teaching Regulatory Humility' (n 5).

of IA in the EU pre-dates the influence of behavioural theory in policy-making, there is much in the design of IA that goes with the grain of cognitive biases—notably the emphasis on calculating losses. The challenge is to ensure that analyses and processes are rigorously implemented. Amendments that re-structure some aspects of the IA choice architecture are also required. One recurring theme in this chapter has been the need to structure-in ex post policy evaluation.[93]

Policymakers should also be trained to think, in slow mode, about the potential impact of their cognitive biases. The ideas and examples suggested in this chapter are in many ways tentative but they do suggest options for the future. First, it would be interesting to extend the use of conceptual and experimental teaching to samples of policymakers from the Commission. If the Commission has a structural predisposition for regulatory intervention, this should show up in the behaviour of its officers.

Second, the Commission has called for evidence on how to re-formulate its guidance on impact assessment. This guidance (the impact assessment guidelines)[94] should certainly include information on how those who are regulated respond to policy interventions. To some extent, whole segments of the impact assessment procedure, such as problem definition, regulatory options, benefits and costs, and macro-economic estimations should be calibrated and modified by using the insights of the behavioural sciences.[95] The interest in behavioural science is key to the current efforts of the US and European governments to moderate 'irritating' burdens and 'perceptions of administrative obligations'. And yet, guidance should also be clear and informative about the various forms of bias that occur *at the level of the officers preparing the impact assessment*. Their minds may trick them in the same way they tricks the citizen. Guidance on impact assessment should tell the policy-maker how to recognise and test for bias, among other things, by mentioning the risk of illusion of control. By combining training and guidance, governments have a chance of pushing the agenda for regulatory humility beyond nudging.

Third, think of the implications for training the Commission's officers. There is a market for training regulators, with courses on specific topics, including modules on IA.[96] The Commission has its own training modules, with input from private consultants, officers from the Secretariat General, and the Joint Research Centre. These modules include law and economics, and elements of public policy analysis. They have case studies and testimonies from the Commission's officers

---

[93] Commission Communication, 'Strengthening the Foundations of Smart Regulation—Improving Evaluation' COM (2013) 686 final, Brussels; OECD, *Framework on Regulatory Policy Evaluation* (Paris, OECD, 2014).

[94] Commission, 'Guidelines on Impact Assessment': ec.europa.eu/smart-regulation/impact/commission_guidelines/commission_guidelines_en.htm (accessed 20 March 2014).

[95] Alemanno and Spina, 'Nudging Legally' (n 2); R van Bavel et al, 'Applying Behavioural Science to EU Policy-Making' (2013) European Commission JRC Scientific and Policy Reports, available at: ec.europa.eu/dgs/health_consumer/information_sources/docs/30092013_jrc_scientific_policy_report_en.pdf.

[96] L Allio, 'The Market for Impact Assessment' in CA Dunlop and CM Radaelli (eds), *Handbook of Regulatory Impact Assessment* (Cheltenham, Edward Elgar, 2015).

who developed impact assessments in the past and share their experience. Our approach suggests a new way to train on IA and policy formulation. Some fascinating insights on policy-making can be taught by using methods that involve the 'subjects' of the experiment in a reflection about their own illusions and biases.[97]

An important aim of our volume is to discuss the challenges of integrating the sciences of nudging into the legal system of the EU. The impact assessment process is at the core of this system because it is there that policy proposals are appraised and developed. Indeed the impact assessment document is published on the same day the Commission publishes the draft proposal (for legislation or for a White Paper or a Communication). It is challenging to think of integrating experiments in training modules for officers who develop EU legal acts and policy in general, but also exciting to think about the possibilities ahead.

---

[97] Dunlop and Radaelli, 'Teaching Regulatory Humility' (n 5).

Part III

The Impact of Behavioural Sciences on EU Policies

7

Behavioural Sciences and EU Data Protection Law: Challenges and Opportunities

EOIN CAROLAN* AND ALESSANDRO SPINA[∞]

I. INTRODUCTION

IT IS WELL-KNOWN that changes in technology challenge traditional notions of privacy. The era of ubiquitous computing, online sharing and instant communications means that our world is increasingly a globalised goldfish-bowl in which our everyday behaviour is recorded in a digital form that makes it potentially susceptible to external scrutiny and supervision. The phenomenon of being continuously connected to the internet and using an always-on, always-recording, always-transmitting smartphone will only increase in the near future as other items—a fridge, a fork, a television, a toothbrush—become connected to the internet by default.[1] This expansion in the data-generating devices we possess is set to lead to an exponential increase in data—what some have described as an approaching 'digital tsunami'.[2]

To acknowledge the scale and scope of data does not lead to the conclusion that there is no need to protect individual privacy. As recent developments at both national and EU level have illustrated, preserving privacy is a public policy objective that remains capable of attracting public support,[3]

---

* This chapter is based on research funded by the Irish Research Council.
[∞] The views expressed in this chapter are solely those of the authors and do not represent the views of any institution.
[1] THA Wisman, 'Purpose Creep by Design: Transforming the Face of Surveillance through the Internet of Things' (2013) 4(2) *European Journal of Law and Technology*.
[2] S Rodota, 'Some Remarks on Surveillance Today' (2013) 4(2) *European Journal of Law and Technology*.
[3] A UK Ipsos-Mori survey published in May 2014, for example, showed that 91% of respondents regarded the privacy of emails as important with 85% regarding the privacy of internet browsing records as important (available at www.ipsos-mori.com/researchpublications/researcharchive/3407/Privacy-and-personal-data.aspx). A Gallup poll in June 2013 found that 53% of American citizens disapproved of the National Security Agency's collection of telephone and internet records (available at www.gallup.com/poll/163043/americans-disapprove-government-surveillance-programs.aspx); the Report of the White House's Big Data and Privacy Working Group Review found that 75% of the more than 24,000 respondents were concerned with the storage and security of data, with 81% expressing concern over current legal standards and oversight. A number of other US opinion polls suggesting

political[4] or legislative attention,[5] and judicial protection.[6] It is arguable, however, that the law has been slow to appreciate the novelty of the risks and challenges raised by the emerging era of Big Data and always-on surveillance. We also believe that the law has lagged behind the need to take adequate account of how individuals engage with these technologies. It is not only the technology that is different: behavioural scientists have shown that users respond to, and are influenced by, these technologies in specific ways. Crucially, these behavioural insights do not always equate to what the law assumes about how individuals act online. Put simply, the behavioural science suggests that EU law may expect too much of individuals when making (or acquiescing in) choices about privacy in an online environment. The resulting conceptual disconnect between legal privacy as it was and technological and behavioural reality as it is raises the possibility of a legal privacy regime which is both over-broad and under-inclusive.

This chapter is composed of three parts. The first part (Section II) considers the theoretical basis of the right to privacy. Privacy is not a stand alone value but is a function of related socially-valued objectives, such as liberty, freedom of expression, democracy and, in particular, the right to personal self-determination. It is intrinsically and constitutively based on protecting the capacity of individuals to determine their own life. Crucially, however, this part contends that privacy and autonomy are outward-facing interests which are primarily concerned with social interaction rather than solitude. This social dimension means, in turn, that any legal privacy regime must be cognisant of how the law shapes or responds to individual or social intercourse. At a time where much of this interaction takes place online or in other digital forms, the law's approach to data protection has particular importance. Yet, as this chapter shows, the behavioural science research casts serious doubt on whether traditional legal techniques can effectively vindicate the sort of social conception of privacy and autonomy that is outlined in Section II.

Taking up this theme, the second part (Section III) critically reviews EU law's traditional approach to privacy and autonomy with a specific focus on

---

public concern for privacy are summarised in G Greenwald, 'Major opinion shifts, in the US and Congress, on NSA surveillance and privacy', *The Guardian*, 29 July 2013 (available at www.theguardian.com/commentisfree/2013/jul/29/poll-nsa-surveillance-privacy-pew).

[4] The Edward Snowden revelations about data collection and surveillance programs led the White House to commission the *Liberty and Security in a Changing World* report from the Review Group on Intelligence and Communications Technology, to commission a subsequent report from a Big Data and Privacy Working Group, and to announce various intended amendments to the privacy and surveillance policies of US government agencies.

[5] The European Commission's proposal for a general Data Protection Regulation on the protection of individuals with regard to the processing of personal data and on the free movement of such data was passed by the European Parliament in March 2014 and awaits approval by the Council of Ministers under the co-decision procedure.

[6] Recent decisions which emphasise the importance of privacy as a protected value include the recognition by the Court of Justice of the European Union of a so-called 'right to be forgotten' (Case C-131/12 *Google Spain SL, Google Inc v Agencia Española de Protección de Datos, Mario Costeja González*, 13 May 2014); and the rulings prohibiting the warrantless searching of smartphones delivered by both the US Supreme Court (*Riley v California*, 573 US ____ (2014)) and the British Columbia Court of Appeal (*R v Mann* (2014) BCCA 231).

its data protection regime. The EU's system of data protection is informed by autonomy-oriented concepts such as personal consent, the right to object, and the obligation to provide information. This section relies on insights from the behavioural science literature to highlight the shortcomings of the current legal assumptions about the protection of individual decision-making through notices and consent forms.

The third part (Section IV) introduces and explores the emerging overlap between data protection and behavioural sciences in EU law. In particular, it highlights the extent to which—by contrast with the traditional approach described in Section III—behavioural findings may have informed the application and the development of EU data protection legislation. This Part considers whether this feature of proposed EU data protection laws may ultimately embody a more effective and behaviourally-informed regime for the protection of personal data.

II. PRIVACY AS SOCIAL INTEREST AND AUTONOMY OF INDIVIDUALS' BEHAVIOUR

Any discussion of how privacy might be protected must first address the more fundamental question of why it ought to be protected at all. The purpose of this part is to ground our discussion of how behavioural science suggests the necessity for reform of EU data protection laws by identifying what privacy is; why it is important; and why the law's defective assumptions about human behaviour mean that its traditional approach is ineffective.

It is well known that privacy itself is a contestable and much-contested notion. Robert Post has observed that: 'Privacy is a value so complex, so entangled in competing and contradictory dimensions, so engorged with various and distinct meanings, that I sometimes despair whether it can be usefully addressed at all'.[7]

This imprecision raises obvious difficulties in a legal context. Solove has pointed out how 'Abstract incantations of privacy' are not nuanced enough to capture the problems involved',[8] which inhibits the conduct of a proper balancing of interests by the relevant decisionmaker. Yet, for all the divisions in the academic and legal literature about the precise parameters of legal privacy rights, there is broad agreement amongst the majority of commentators that the protection of privacy is justified by a concern for the autonomy of the individual. Privacy-oriented ideas like refuge, freedom, creativity, and intimacy[9] are all either conditions for, or expressions of, the individual as an autonomous actor, engaged in the Kantian project of living life to the best of his or her abilities and on the basis of his or her own beliefs. In this way, privacy can be seen as a legal technique for protecting the deeper and

---

[7] R Post, 'Three Concepts of Privacy' (2001) *Georgia Law Journal* 2087.
[8] D Solove, 'A Taxonomy of Privacy' (2006) 154 *University of Pennsylvania Law Review* 477, 480.
[9] J Craig, 'Invasion of Privacy and Charter Values' (1997) 42 *McGill Law Journal* 355.

more foundational value of autonomy. Privacy is a prerequisite for, or antecedent to, individual autonomy. As Beate Rössler has explained:

> [T]he concept of privacy demarcates for the individual realms or dimensions that he needs in order to be able to enjoy the individual freedom exacted and legally safeguarded in modern societies ... such realms or dimensions of privacy substantialize the liberties that are secured because the mere securing of freedom ... does not in itself necessarily entail that the conditions are secured for us to be able to enjoy these liberties as we really want to.[10]

In general, this linkage between privacy and autonomy rests on a common behavioural observation at the heart of Bentham's famous *Panopticon*: that placing people under the inspection of someone that could *see without being seen*[11] would affect the attitudes and behaviour of those subject to it. The right to privacy resists this by creating the conditions for autonomous decision-making by individuals.

But what is autonomy? As with privacy, there can be a tendency in the political or popular discourse to associate it with the individual in isolation—to Warren and Brandeis' famous 'right to be let alone'.[12] This is often taken to justify what we call a 'negative autonomy' approach. The assumption here is that, provided that the law has prohibited interference in certain limited and protected areas, the individual has the privacy necessary to exercise their autonomy.

What we argue here is that this is an inadequate and unduly narrow conception of both privacy and autonomy. Our fundamental point is that the law, if it is to provide truly effective protection, must move beyond traditional negative techniques to instead take positive steps to create the conditions for the individual to act autonomously *within society*. Trust; authenticity; intimacy; friendship; social networks: these are all *in reality* empirical antecedents to genuine autonomy. The behavioural science literature establishes the necessity for the law to develop in this way; the pace of technological change makes this development urgent. We refer to this approach as 'positive autonomy'.

What then do we mean by autonomy? While the reasoning here is necessarily brief,[13] even a short description of how individuals *actually* behave shows the limitations of the law's negative approach to privacy protection. In principle, an autonomous individual is one who is capable of making his own choices. This logically means that the individual must therefore have his or her own will.

However, this process of self-reasoning also presupposes certain additional characteristics, many of which are rooted in the empirical reality of human behaviour. First of all, individuals must have a self-identity if they are to be able to further the project of living their *own* life in their *own* way. Secondly, the individual must have the capacity to question and evaluate that self-identity if it is to truly be said to be of their own design. Thirdly, the individual must have the ability and the opportunity to choose between courses of action which affect that self-identity. Finally,

---

[10] B Rössler, *The Value of Privacy* (Oxford, Polity, 2004) 72.
[11] J Bentham, *The Panopticon Writings* (London, Ed Verso, 1995).
[12] S Warren and L Brandeis, 'The Right to Privacy' (1890) 4 *Harvard Law Review* 193.
[13] For a fuller account of this argument, see E Carolan, 'The Right to Privacy' in E Carolan and H Delany, *The Right to Privacy: A Comparative and Doctrinal Analysis* (Dublin, Round Hall, 2007).

the individual must also have the ability to assess the consequences of the making of that choice for his self-identity. But this emphasis on the internal reasoning does not associate autonomy with introspection. To envisage the autonomous individual in such isolated terms would be contrary to both common sense and cognitive psychology. Individuals do not make decisions or seek self-definition in a vacuum. Our decision-making processes are influenced not only by our cultural context but also, more fundamentally, by our interactions with others. This means autonomy is about more than isolated introspection or abstract Kantian analysis. In fact, it is rarely about these things. Individuals most commonly exist and act in social settings—so understanding how people actually behave in these settings is an essential foundation for any legal efforts to support autonomy. As Charles Taylor put it, individual identity is the product of a dialogical process,[14] 'a conversational engagement with one's past and with others'.[15]

However, an analysis of human behaviour shows that this system of social self-examination is dependent upon a number of factual conditions. Trust and authenticity are core requirements. The individual who wishes to disclose aspects of their personality to others must be able to trust that others will not misuse that information and that their response to it is authentic—that it has not been polluted by other information of which the person disclosing information is unaware, or affected by other unknown considerations of context. If we are deceived in our social relations, we are deceived in ourselves. Our choices should not be distorted by the deliberate intervention of others (whether humans or algorithms), especially where that is something about which the individual could never have knowledge. Yet, when different users are shown different Google results, news stories, ads, Amazon recommendations and even prices without appreciating that these are individually-tailored rather than universal outcomes,[16] such distortion arguably already occurs.[17]

This is a point well illustrated by the recent controversy over an experiment run by Facebook's Data Science team. The team adjusted users' news feeds without their knowledge in an effort to assess whether showing more positive or negative posts would have an impact on user's own emotional state.[18] While some of the criticism of the experiment focused on its failure to obtain a specific consent, the

---

[14] C Taylor, *The Ethics of Authenticity* (Cambridge, MA, Harvard University Press, 1992).
[15] B Murchison, 'Revisiting the American Public Disclosure Tort' in AT Kenyon and M Richardson (eds), *New Dimensions in Privacy Law: International and Comparative Perspectives* (Cambridge, Cambridge University Press, 2006) 51.
[16] See C Sunstein, *Republic 2.0* (Princeton, Princeton University Press, 2009); RK Garrett, 'Echo Chambers Online?' (2009) 14 *Journal of Computer-Mediated Communication* 265; E Pariser, *The Filter Bubble* (London, Penguin, 2011).
[17] We refer here to thoughtful scholarship on the legal aspects of machine-learning algorithms, cf F Pasquale, *The Black Box Society. The Secret Algorithms that Control Money and Information* (Cambridge MA, Harvard University Press, 2015).
[18] The experiment found that emotions were transferred to users so that when positive expressions were reduced, people produced fewer positive posts and more negative posts; when negative expressions were reduced, the opposite pattern occurred. See A Kramera, JE Guillory and JT Hancockb, 'Experimental Evidence of Massive-scale Emotional Contagion through Social Networks' (2014) 111 *Proceedings of the National Academy of Sciences* 878.

adverse public reaction arguably has deeper roots in the sense of user responses and emotions being subject to deliberate manipulation about which the user could have had no knowledge. The affected users regarded what they were seeing on their news feeds as authentic[19] and responded to it in ways that would have felt authentic to them. Changing the context within which user engagement occurs, and changing it in a way likely to promote particular responses, taints the authenticity of the user response and has the potential to undermine both trust in, and the reliability of, the social responses that the user relies on in developing their social identity.

This has two major implications for our understanding of the relationship between autonomy and privacy. The first is that there is plainly a social dimension to autonomy as a value. Autonomy is both supported by, and to an extent defined through, forms of social interaction. This, in turn, supports the secondary conclusion that 'the most important aspects of privacy are those which facilitate constructive social action and intercourse'.[20] It is through the protection of privacy in this social sense that the conditions for the autonomous enjoyment of these freedoms are secured. Privacy thus 'derives its weight and importance from its capacity to foster the conditions for a wide range of other aspects of human flourishing'.[21]

What this means in the context of privacy regulation is that privacy (and its parent principle of autonomy) is not protected by a system based solely on keeping matters secret. It is the paradox of privacy that its value for the individual lies in the sharing that it permits—but that this moment of sharing is the very point at which the individual's privacy becomes exposed by the subsequent loss of control. We can see this difference when we try to conceptualise the difference between privacy and isolation.[22]

The argument being made here is twofold. First of all, privacy is not only a value in and of itself but rather facilitates a broader principle of autonomy. This should be borne in mind when considering how to calibrate the law's approach to privacy because it has implications for what the law should or should not protect. In particular, the critically important character of privacy's social dimensions means that the law must be concerned with more than mere secrecy.

The second point, which ensues from the first, is that the law should be concerned with broader processes of social sharing: what occurs prior to disclosure, what occurs at the moment of disclosure, but also what occurs after disclosure. This represents the 'choice architecture' in which individuals choose the degree of protection of their personal data. The fact that the moment of disclosure simultaneously

---

[19] Even though, the display of information in the individual user's newsfeed is not in abstract terms 'neutral' or objective but it depends always on the preference order operated by Facebook's proprietary algorithm.

[20] D Feldman, 'Privacy-related Rights: Their Social Value' in P Birks (ed), *Privacy and Loyalty* (London, Clarendon, 1997) 40.

[21] ibid, 21.

[22] A Roberts, 'Privacy and Political Theory' (2014) 690 Melbourne Legal Studies Research Paper 5.

presents privacy at its most valuable and most vulnerable underlines the necessity for an effective privacy and data protection regime to treat privacy as a dynamic and socially-situated concern. Social sharing *under certain conditions* is essential to genuine individual autonomy. This requires the law, if it is to be effective, to create or protect those conditions. This means that the law must take account of, and be sensitive to, the nature and integrity of the behavioural impulses that animate this social process. Put simply, the law cannot regulate social sharing if—as the next section argues—it does not understand how individuals behave.

III. THE CHALLENGES POSED BY BEHAVIOURAL SCIENCES TO THE TRADITIONAL APPROACH TO DATA PROTECTION

As observed at the outset, it is a commonplace of modern legal and academic commentary to bemoan how technological changes have adversely affected the privacy rights of individual citizens. Repetition should not, however, dull our appreciation of just how profound some of these changes have been, or may be in the future. While developments in technology have always required the re-consideration of certain legal or social norms, the changes that have occurred in the fields of surveillance, record-keeping and communications over the last two decades have been so significant in scale and in character that there is reason to believe that they involve a more fundamental shift in the relationship between citizen and state, between customers and corporations, and between corporate and government bodies. The ability of companies, service providers and public bodies to monitor and compile information about the behaviour and attitudes of consumers or citizens goes far beyond what could have been envisaged even two decades ago.[23]

The privacy implications of this mass data collection were highlighted by the Court of Justice of the European Union (CJEU) in the *Digital Rights Ireland* case:

> Those data, taken as a whole, may allow very precise conclusions to be drawn concerning the private lives of the persons whose data has been retained, such as the habits of everyday life, permanent or temporary places of residence, daily or other movements, the activities carried out, the social relationships of those persons and the social environments frequented by them.[24]

As the CJEU observed, the threat to privacy derives from an accumulation of technological characteristics which, once taken together, raise challenges that are very different from those with which the law was previously concerned. It is not only that technology today allows for the collection and accumulation of information on a larger scale—it is also that the information collected now includes a wide range of informal or low-level information or expression. Furthermore, data collection is no longer the sole or primary preserve of government bodies.

---

[23] *US v Jones*, 132 S Ct 945 (2012), per Alito J.
[24] Joined Cases C-293/12 and 594/12 *Digital Rights Ireland* [2015] QB 127, para 27.

The acquisition and compilation of information is now undertaken by our service providers, by our basic devices, and even by the friends or acquaintances who happily trade third parties' information for the prospect of some positive attention from peers.

A related change concerns the greater visibility of information or expression which, once again, would be unlikely to come to the attention of those outside the immediate zone of expression. The potential audience for individual expression has substantially increased, both because of the mechanisms chosen by many for communication and because of the ease with which third parties can draw attention to the actions or expression of others, regardless of their knowledge or content. With the advent of home automation, tracking sensors and other wearable devices, should the prudent now assume that any and all forms of conduct will be scrutinised, audited, assessed, and possibly transformed in reusable data?

This visibility is further enhanced by the technological developments which have made information more discoverable by others. Previously, even records which were formally public could, by virtue of the obstacles to identification and retrieval, acquire a certain level of 'practical obscurity'.[25] By contrast, the way that information is collected and recorded today means that it is easily stored, easily indexed, easily searchable, and thus difficult to obscure. This visibility refers not only to those services that allow individuals to find what they already know (or suspect) but also to the increasing development of services that push people in the direction of certain information. Service providers increasingly act as the editors or curators of popular attitudes and attention, with all of the influence over the visibility or presentation of an individual's profile which that entails.

Perhaps the most fundamental challenge to traditional privacy norms follows from the phenomenon of Big Data. The essential element of Big Data is the enhanced capacity to 'make use' of them through analytical tools such as digital algorithms.[26] Real-world examples abound of how apparently innocuous information can, when taken together with other items of information, provide substantial insights about matters which the individual may have thought to be private, or even secret. Studies have shown, for example, that private attributes such as sexual orientation can often be reliably established from a user's friends[27] or 'likes'[28] on Facebook. This potential intrusion is exacerbated by the increasing sophistication of data analytics. Gmail's reassurances that no one will ever read your emails provide little comfort when one considers that algorithms are likely to be much better than humans at interrogating the data to find out information about you—information even you may not have been aware of.

---

[25] *US Department of Justice v Reporters Committee*, 489 US 749 (1989).

[26] E Morozov, 'The rise of data and the death of politics', *The Observer*, 20 July 2014 available at: www.theguardian.com/technology/2014/jul/20/rise-of-data-death-of-politics-evgeny-morozov-algorithmic-regulation.

[27] C Jernigan and BFT Mistree, 'Facebook Friendships Expose Sexual Orientation' (2009) 14 (10) *First Monday* available at: firstmonday.org/ojs/index.php/fm/article/view/2611/2302.

[28] M Kosinski, D Stillwell and T Graepel, 'Private Traits and Attributes are Predictable from Digital Records of Human Behavior' (2013) *Proceedings of the National Academy of Sciences* 5802–05.

Individually, these characteristics differ substantially from those which would previously have been associated with the everyday forms of individual action or expression. Cumulatively, they create a radically altered environment for social interaction today. Against this backdrop, it appears particularly pertinent to consider whether the law as it stands is capable of confronting these new realities.

The law's traditional approach to privacy developed at a time when the acquisition of information was comparatively rudimentary and individual expression was more transient, less traceable, less permanent, and more limited in its potential audience and effect. The negative autonomy approach described in Part I was arguably adequate because of the de facto existence of the behavioural conditions for social sharing outside certain limited contexts (eg interaction with government agencies). Adapting these traditional doctrines may catch some of the harms that can occur today but it seems reasonable to assume that they may be oblivious to others. Indeed, it seems plausible that the application of traditional principles may result in the law over-reaching in some areas while overlooking others entirely. For example, the increased visibility of informal expression makes it likely that legal liability will attach to many types of informal expression which would formerly have avoided scrutiny. Conversely, the permanence and discoverability of information makes it more difficult for an individual or a court to accurately gauge whether, and to what extent, an actionable interference with privacy has occurred. Today's limited disclosure to some can easily—and unpredictably—become next year's information of interest to all.

Generally speaking, legal protection of privacy tends to be defined in terms of the preservation of a small number of principles that reflect a negative conception of autonomy. Privacy is roughly equated with the preservation of the individual's reasonable expectation, the provision of express consent, or a residual entitlement not to participate in the practice in question. In theory, each of these tests promotes an autonomy-oriented conception of privacy by preserving the individual's freedom of action. The law is satisfied on each of these tests by ensuring that the individual has, or has had, an opportunity to make other choices which might have led, or been expected to lead, to a different result.

There is a reasonable argument to be made, of course, that the preservation of individual freedom over privacy matters is all that the law can or should do. In a liberal democracy, there is an instinctive and well-founded opposition to the law seeking to protect persons from the consequences of their own choices—what Julin has criticised in the context of proposals for regulating tracking mechanisms online as 'implement[ing] paternalistic judgments that subjects of targeted marketing cannot make proper judgments for themselves'.[29]

On the other hand, however, there is an argument to be made that the current approach is not adequate to effectively protect the privacy of the individual when dealing with today's technologies. Given the changed characteristics and ubiquity

---

[29] TR Julin, 'Sorrell v IMS Health—May Doom Federal Do Not Track Acts' (2011) 10 *Privacy and Security Law Reporter* 1262.

of privacy-threatening technologies, the law's current approach fails to protect privacy because it fails to create the conditions for positive autonomy. It formalistically focuses on mechanistic indicia of individual choice while neglecting the social, cultural and technological context in which those 'choices' are made. In reality, what the behavioural science research shows quite clearly is that the simple making available of a choice is not enough to ensure that the individual actually understands, is aware of or has engaged with the issues involved—all of which would, for the reasons outlined in Part I, be necessary for the choice to be genuinely autonomous.

At EU level, the primary focus of this choice-oriented approach has been on the notion of consent. For example, Directive 2009/136/EC (the 'Cookies Directive')[30] introduces new rules for online service providers that require them to obtain visitors' 'consent' before serving cookies and similar tracking devices to users' computers. The Directive also specifies that this consent must be fully informed, a criterion which has been further fleshed out by an Opinion from the Article 29 Working Group which emphasises the necessity for any decision ostensibly providing consent to be, inter alia, specific, freely given, adequately signified, unambiguous and informed.

This reflects the Group's welcome recognition that:

> Consent is sometimes a weak basis for justifying the processing of personal data and it loses its value when it is stretched or curtailed to make it fit to situations that it was never intended to be used in. The use of consent 'in the right context' is crucial. If it is used in circumstances where it is not appropriate, because the elements that constitute valid consent are unlikely to be present, this would lead to great vulnerability and, in practice, this would weaken the position of data subjects in practice.

This scepticism about the efficacy and utility of online consent is supported by relevant behavioural sciences research. The law's assumptions that the provision by an individual of consent at a particular point of an ongoing legal relationship can be equated to the exercise by that individual of control, and that this can further be correlated with the autonomy interests of the consenting party, lack a firm empirical grounding. Research has demonstrated that the decision of an individual to disclose information can be influenced by a range of individual- or context-specific factors. Personality traits such as self-esteem have been shown to constitute one important factor in determining the likely level of disclosure by a given individual.[31] Yet, equally, the fact that that same individual may disclose

---

[30] By amending Art 5(3) of Directive 2002/58/EC (the e-Privacy Directive). Directive 2009/136/EC of the European Parliament and of the Council of 25 November 2009 amending Directive 2002/22/EC on universal service and users' rights relating to electronic communications networks and services, Directive 2002/58/EC concerning the processing of personal data and the protection of privacy in the electronic communications sector and Regulation (EC) No 2006/2004 on cooperation between national authorities responsible for the enforcement of consumer protection laws (OJ L 337 of 18.12.2009).

[31] R Chen, 'Living a Private Life in Public Social Networks: An Exploration of Member Self-disclosure' (2013) 53 *Decision Support Systems*, 661–68.

different content in different ways across different contexts indicates that personality traits are not themselves conclusive. Trust[32] and affect[33] have, for example, been shown to influence the individual's decision to disclose in particular contexts.

Notably, 'there is relatively little evidence that people's privacy concerns translate to privacy-enhancing behaviours while online'.[34] There may be various reasons for this. One is that there may simply be a divergence between the value people place on privacy in the abstract and that value they actually place on it in the context of a specific transaction. Yet, it may also be the case that this incongruity may be, in part, attributable not to a failure to value privacy but to a failure to value it correctly. Here, the heuristics, biases and cognitive limitations most famously identified by Tversky and Kahneman[35] may play their part. For example, the fact that few of us know or have experienced the direct consequences of privacy intrusion encourages availability and ambiguity biases in favour of further disclosure. The disparity of knowledge and expertise between the person whose data is collected—the 'data subject'—and the legal or natural persons that collect and use personal data (defined in EU law as 'data controllers') leads to incomplete or asymmetric information situations that may also favour disclosure. Issues of incommensurablity, hyperbolic discounting and loss aversion may arise when a concrete reward is offered in exchange for a form of information disclosure which, when considered out of context and without reference to distant potentially adverse events, appears innocuous. The widespread existence and popularity of online disclosure—especially when it is engaged in by our peers—anchors the value of privacy at very low levels, while also framing the choice to disclose as the positive, status quo position. In fact, it is increasingly common for some form of elevated disclosure to be provided as a basic prequisite to using the system or service itself.[36] In that scenario, how truly autonomous is the choice to consent?

Furthermore, the making of decisions in relation to information disclosure is perhaps a classic example of judging under uncertainty. It is not only that the

---

[32] DH McKnight, V Choudhury and C Kacmar, 'The Impact of Initial Consumer Trust on Intentions to Transact with a Website: A Trust Building Model' (2002) 11 *Journal of Strategic Information Systems* 297.

[33] H Li, R Sarathy and H Xu, 'The Role of Affect and Cognition on Online Consumers' Decision to Disclose Personal Information to Unfamiliar Online Vendors' (2011) 51 *Decision Support Systems* 434.

[34] A Joinson, AU Reips, T Buchanan and T and C Schofield, 'Privacy, Trust, and Self-disclosure Online' (2010) 25 *Human-Computer Interaction* 1.

[35] A Tversky and D Kahneman, 'Judgment under Uncertainty: Heuristics and Biases' (1974) 185 *Science* 1124. See also T Gilovich, *How We Know What Isn't So: The Fallibility of Human Reason in Everyday Life* (New York, Free Press, 1991); R Thaler and C Sunstein, *Nudge: Improving Decisions about Health, Wealth, and Happiness* (New Haven, CT, Yale University Press, 2008) 2; D Kahneman, *Thinking, Fast and Slow* (New York, Farrrar, 2011).

[36] In this context, the use of social networks such as Facebook or LinkedIn by public administrations is particularly challenging. On the one hand, there is an increasing demand for public institutions to use communication channels widely used in an effort to be more modern, open, and engaging; on the other hand, this means the indirect endorsement of social practices regarding personal information disclosure and privacy policies adopted by these social networks—which are managed by private commercial organisations. For a critical reflection on this paradox: A Spina, 'Open Government, Behavior Control and the Privacy Risk of Digital Government' in E Bohne, JD Graham and JCN Raasschelders (eds), *Public Administration and the Modern State* (London, Palgrave Macmillan, 2014).

individual in question may adopt various forms of poor privacy strategy—not reading the relevant terms and conditions; reading those terms but failing to understand them; inadequately valuing their personal information; valuing convenience in the short term over protection in the long term and so on. It is also that even the most perfectly rational and informed agent may not be able to accurately assess the costs and benefits of the proposed bargain. With digital disclosure, it is impossible for us to predict how the information may ultimately be used. In the same way that the development of information technology has allowed data which was effectively obscured when initially recorded in paper form to become widely available, future technologies may facilitate unanticipated uses by government or third parties of information provided now. That is, indeed, arguably currently the case with the increasing sophistication of data analytics. With the dawn of Big Data, it is possible to identify patterns of behaviour and personal characteristics which we would not even be aware of ourselves. How then can we be said to have given our informed consent to the disclosure of such data?

A similar concern exposing the limitation of individual consent may relate to the externalities of our choices with regard to the processing of personal data, in particular with regard to social networks of massive public datasets such as Google Maps. No individual choice in these contexts could be held to be neutral. The very fact that a person is not on Facebook could 'profile' the individual by singling out some possible characteristics such as shyness, social isolation, or a lack of technological competence. The same argument applies to the contested collection by Google of images of residential properties for processing in the Google Maps online database.[37]

These insights from the behavioural sciences clearly contradict the assumptions inherent in the negative autonomy approach. To expect—as the law does—an individual to make an informed decision about privacy when confronted with a complex, barely comprehensible choice architecture which requires a host of competing considerations to be weighed in a single moment of absolute consent is optimistic in the extreme. In light of the information asymmetries between data subjects and data controllers and the externalities that affect transactions of personal information, using privacy to preserve a theoretical freedom of action will not be enough to equip the individual to act in a genuinely autonomous way. Indeed, experimental data has suggested that efforts to enhance user control that simultaneously presume rational consent (like more salient privacy warnings) may be ineffective or even counter-productive.[38] Behavioural science shows that—if the objective is to foster positive autonomy in the online environment—EU law must go further to positively create the conditions that make that possible.

---

[37] Due to privacy concerns and litigation, Google Street View may blur the images of houses and other residential properties at the request of the person concerned. It is, however, argued that the very fact that someone has requested the blurring of the image of their property is in itself information which could be taken by third parties (such as potential burglars) to imply certain information, such as the wealth of residents.

[38] E Carolan and M Rosario Castillo-Mayen, 'Why More User Control Does Not Mean More User Privacy' (2015) 20 *Virginia Journal of Law and Technology* (forthcoming).

IV. AN INTEGRATED APPROACH TO BEHAVIOURALLY INFORMED DATA PROTECTION

As evidenced by some of the developments discussed in the previous section, awareness is growing of the cognitive limitations affecting individual decision-making, especially with regard to consent. Reflecting this, there are signs that data protection law is moving from a regime based on the presence—or often inference—of bare consent to one that facilitates the effective control of individuals over their private sphere of autonomy. This arguably indicates a growing appreciation of the behavioural limitations of a negative autonomy model. The Cookies Directive, the guidance issued by the Article 29 Working Group,[39] and the proposed General Data Protection Regulation can all broadly be regarded as positively empowering the individual to overcome the cognitive challenges or behavioural biases that inhibit the reflective choices about privacy and social sharing that are essential for autonomous action.

For example, the new Cookies Directive has—as the Article 29 Working Group makes clear—introduced a far more user-centered and behaviourally-sensitive concept of consent to EU data protection rules. Article 5(3) provides that:

> Member States shall ensure that the storing of information, or the gaining of access to information already stored, in the terminal equipment of a subscriber or user is only allowed on condition that the subscriber or user concerned has given his or her consent, having been provided with clear and comprehensive information, in accordance with Directive 95/46/EC, inter alia, about the purposes of the processing.

This more rigorous regime was justified on the basis that, while information might be stored for some valid purposes, it could also be used for other purposes involving 'unwarranted intrusion into the private sphere'. The Directive proclaimed that:

> It is therefore of paramount importance that users be provided with clear and comprehensive information when engaging in any activity which could result in such storage or gaining of access. The methods of providing information and offering the right to refuse should be as user-friendly as possible. (Recital 66)

The Article 29 Working Group has clarified that this means that consent, to be valid, must generally satisfy four distinct characteristics.

1. Specific information. To be valid, consent must be specific and based on appropriate information. In other words, blanket consent without specifying the exact purpose of the processing is not acceptable.
2. Timing. As a general rule, consent has to be given before the processing starts.
3. Active choice. Consent must be unambiguous. Therefore the procedure to seek and to give consent must leave no doubt as to the data subject's intention. There are in principle no limits as to the form consent can take. However, for consent to be valid it should be an active indication of the user's wishes. The minimum expression of

---

[39] See ch 8 by FZ Borgesius in this volume.

an indication could be any kind of signal, sufficiently clear to be capable of indicating a data subject's wishes, and to be understandable by the data controller (it could include a handwritten signature affixed at the bottom of a paper form, or an active behaviour from which consent can be reasonably concluded).
4. Freely given. Consent can only be valid if the data subject is able to exercise a real choice, and there is no risk of deception, intimidation, coercion or significant negative consequences if he/she does not consent.[40]

According to the Group, these guidelines will ensure that users are offered 'a real choice regarding tracking cookies'.[41] As pointed out in Part I, the existence of this kind of 'real choice' is a fundamental prerequisite for genuine user autonomy.

Another example can be found in the limitations that the European data protection supervisory authorities of the Article 29 Working Party have placed on consent as a valid legal basis for the processing of personal data by 'data controllers' in circumstances—such as employment[42]—where the data subject is presumed not to be in a position to express his will freely. The Article 29 Working Party has clarified that

> when consent is required from a worker, and there is a potential relevant prejudice that arises from not consenting, the consent is not valid in terms of satisfying either Article 7 or Article 8 as it is not freely given.

However, the Article 29 Working Party does not completely exclude the possibility of consent in the employment scenario but requires that any expression of consent should be analysed together with other contextual elements that can influence the decision of the data subject.[43] This acknowledges, for the reasons explained in Part I, that interference in the private sphere of autonomy can take the form of subtler limitations on the expression of a free choice.

The idea of facilitating genuine user choice also informs the approach espoused by the proposed new EU legislation on data protection or draft General Data Protection Regulation (GDPR). This is potentially important given that the traditional negative approach described in Part II was too often typified by a take-it-or-leave-it approach on the part of data processors. After all, an opt-out entitlement provides only an illusion of autonomous choice if the possibility of non-participation is purely speculative. In short, if all of the social activity a user cares about is happening on one website, the user is unlikely to regard abstention as a viable choice. Thus, the proposed requirements to provide users with a right to object to the processing of their data, or to subsequently seek to reclaim a degree of control over it, may facilitate more considered and continuous choices about the conditions in which they accept to allow data processing. The idea of 'data portability' by which users could move all personal data in switching to a different service provider of

---

[40] Working Document 02/2013, 'Providing Guidance on Obtaining Consent for Cookies' (2 October 2013) 3.
[41] ibid, 6.
[42] WP 48 on the 'Processing of Personal Data in the Employment Context'.
[43] Art 29 Working Party Opinion 15/2011 on the 'Definition of Consent', WP 148, 14.

a digital service such as social networks implies a more active and informed users' behaviour with regard to the processing of personal data.

Leaving aside the specific issue of consent, behavioural insights are increasingly evident in the recommendations and advisory opinions of the Article 29 Working Party. The Working Party's attitude to informing users shows, for example, a similar awareness of the kind of cognitive and decision-making limitations that support more interventionist regulatory policies in this area. For example, in a communication addressed to Google about its privacy policy,[44] the Article 29 Working Party has presented a list of compliance measures which specifically refers to detailed visualisation changes[45] or the use of a default rule for enabling a tracking code by passive users.[46]

Moreover, the CJEU seem ready to focus on the behavioural impact of the interferences into the private sphere of individuals caused by private and public actors. The 2014 judgments in the *Digital Rights Ireland*[47] and *Google Spain*[48] analyse data protection issues in a way that seem consistent with an understanding of EU law as committed to the promotion of positive autonomy. Indeed, this is arguably more consistent with a more European 'vision of governance' which, in contrast to the Anglo–American tradition of negative civil liberties, 'regards the state as the necessary player to frame the social community in which individuals develop' such that 'autonomy ... effectively depends on a backdrop of legal rights'.[49]

In *Digital Rights Ireland*, the court determined that the collection of a vast amount of apparently harmless communication information about calls, that is *metadata*, must be regarded as an interference into the private sphere of the

---

[44] 'Letter from the Article 29 Working Party on Google Privacy Policy', 23 September 2014, available at: ec.europa.eu/justice/data-protection/article-29/documentation/other-document/files/2014/20140923_letter_on_google_privacy_policy.pdf, and the Annex: 'List of Possible Compliance Measures': available at ec.europa.eu/justice/data-protection/article-29/documentation/other-document/files/2014/20140923_letter_on_google_privacy_policy_appendix.pdf.

[45] ibid, 1: 'Information: 1) The Privacy Policy must be immediately visible and accessible, for instance *visible without scrolling* and *accessible via one click*, from each service landing ... 3) Users *cannot be expected to read the Terms of Service update* to be made aware of important new purposes for the collection, processing sharing or any other use of their personal data. Such purposes must be presented in the Privacy Policy'(emphasis added).

[46] ibid, 2: 'Google could modify the JavaScript tag so it will inform users and ask for consent depending on the country. Google could also provide an option for users to disable Google analytics on a temporary or permanent site basis. Google could also set the default of the tracking code such that it disables for tracking for as long as consent has not been granted'.

[47] Judgment of the Court (Grand Chamber) of 8 April 2014 (requests for a preliminary ruling from the High Court of Ireland (Ireland) and the Verfassungsgerichtshof (Austria))—*Digital Rights Ireland Ltd* (C-293/12) *v Minister for Communications, Marine and Natural Resources, Minister for Justice, Equality and Law Reform, The Commissioner of the Garda Síochána, Ireland and the Attorney General, and Kärntner Landesregierung, Michael Seitlinger, Christof Tschohl and Others* (C-594/12) ECLI:EU:C:2014:238.

[48] Judgment of the Court (Grand Chamber) of 13 May 2014 *Google Spain SL and Google Inc v Agencia Española de Protección de Datos (AEPD) and Mario Costeja González* (Case C-131/12) ECLI:EU:C:2014:317.

[49] J Reidenberg, 'Resolving Conflicting International Data Privacy Rules in Cyberspace' (2000) 52 *Stanford Law Review* 1315, 1347.

individuals. This highlights the fact that all this information, at a face value meaningless, could be used to make inferences into the life of individuals as they could provide a quite detailed picture of the individual. Moreover, the court also considered that the possibility that this data could be used without the knowledge of the person concerned could generate in the minds of the person concerned 'the feeling that their private life is subject to constant surveillance'.[50] This echoes the idea, discussed in Part I, of trust and of control over information disclosure within social networks as necessary empirical conditions for individual autonomy. This confirms that the assessment of the interference into the private sphere has to be made on the basis of the potential impact on the behaviour of the individual.

Meanwhile in *Google Spain*, the court considered that the activity of a search engine in indexing information publicly available on the Internet according to the name of a person is a processing of personal data, and hence should be subject to all the requirements set in the data protection legislation. In essence, the court has given relevance to the fact that search engines have the capacity to structure information concerning a person and that this power could have important bearing with regard to the privacy of the person concerned. This is again related to the kind of empirical conditions of trust, control and authenticity that a positive account of autonomy requires, and that a legal right to privacy should aim to provide. While Google and others have highlighted that the personal information that is structured by the search engine is already publicly available, they underplay the aspect that has been made legally relevant by the court, that is that the 'visualisation' of information—the structured overview enabled by the assembling of different bits of personal information made by the search engine—is an interference into the private life of the person concerned[51] because it deprives him of the control over that information, of the ability to develop his social identity in particular ways, or of the trust in the authenticity of others' responses to him.

It is to be noted that a number of behaviourally-informed legal solutions are being discussed in the GDPR. These future legal solutions, which seem to respond to the cognitive problems of mandatory disclosure and the shortcomings of the consent model, might spearhead a development of EU law towards a more behaviorally-informed—and therefore potentially more effective—regime of protection of personal data. Although the final text of the GDPR might undergo substantial changes in the legislative process, the policies underpinning the draft legal provisions are noteworthy and indicative.[52]

For example, under article 85b, the Commission may lay down standard forms for 'obtaining verifiable consent'. In stressing the verifiable nature of the consent,

---

[50] *Digital Rights Ireland* (n 24) para 37, for a comment of the judgment, see A Spina, 'Risk Regulation of Big Data. Has the Time Arrived for a Paradigm Shift in EU Data Protection Law?' (2014) 2 *European Journal of Risk Regulation* 238.

[51] *Google Spain* (n 6) para 80.

[52] Please note that the references to specific articles and provisions of the draft GDPR in this paper relate to the text adopted with a very large majority by the European Parliament on 12 March 2014 and available at: www.europarl.europa.eu/sides/getDoc.do?pubRef=-//EP//TEXT+TA+P7-TA-2014-0212+0+DOC+XML+V0//EN.

the proposed standardisation requirement might address the problem that forms used to obtain data subjects' consent are drafted in a way to exploit the limited attention or biased assessments of probabilty on the part of the data subjects.[53] Similarly, article 13a and the Annex of the draft General Data Protection Regulation provide the obligation for data controllers to use standardised information notices which are visually presented as high-impact visual icons, with traffic-light symbols, directed at conveying a clear and concise message about the underlying data processing operations.[54]

Article 33 introduces the instrument of the Data Protection Impact Assessment. This is a new legal tool which should enable controllers of personal data to assess the concrete application of personal data processing[55]—and introduce the idea of risks in this domain—by paying attention, in particular, to the behavioural impact that data processing could have on data subjects. The idea of a Data Protection Impact Assessment to be performed by the controller before and especially during the intended processing suggests a more proactive, positive, and (hopefully) effective attitude to data protection obligations. Similarly, the legal recognition of concepts such as privacy 'by design' and 'by default' moves the compliance obligations for data controllers away from a negative observance of basic data protection principles towards a more interventionist regime for protecting personal data which takes seriously the behavioural limitations on the exercise by the data subject of his or her rights.[56]

Arguably the most important element demonstrating that the draft GDPR will be enriched with the insights coming from behavioural sciences is the legal relevance given to 'profiling'. This refers to the ability of the controller to analyse certain personal aspects or predict 'the natural person's performance at work, economic situation, health, personal preferences, reliability and behavior'.[57] Under the draft, profiling will trigger the obligation to adopt sound and fair data governance including respect for the rights of the concerned individual. This would seem to capture Big Data activities which focus on extracting value from data to produce predictive knowledge. As Big Data continues to develop, therefore, the draft GDPR would require a parallel development in data governance principles that keeps

---

[53] G Loewenstein, C Sunstein and R Golman, 'Disclosure: Psychology Changes Everything' (2014) *Annual Review of Economics* 391–419.

[54] For a review of private voluntary schemes using privacy icons and labelling to communicate complex and lengthy privacy policies to consumers, *cf* L Edwards and W Abel, 'The Use of Privacy Icons and Standard Contract Terms for Generating Consumer Trust and Confidence in Digital Services' (2014) CREATe Working paper, available at: zenodo.org/record/12506/files/CREATe-Working-Paper-2014-15.pdf.

[55] Interestingly, the data protection impact assessment should also contain 'an assessment of the context of the data processing': Art 33(3)(j) of the draft General Data Protection Regulation.

[56] Art 23(2) of the draft General Data Protection Regulation states that 'The Controller shall ensure that by default, only those personal data are processed which are necessary for each specific purpose of the processing … In particular, those mechanisms shall ensure that by default personal data are not made accessible to an indefinite number of individuals and that data *subjects are able to control the distribution of their personal data*' (emphasis added).

[57] Art 4(3a) of draft General Data Protection Regulation.

pace with the potential privacy intrusions of this evolving field of knowledge. Given that the basic benefit of Big Data is the identification of information about which subjects have—and could not have—any knowledge, an effective system of governance principles will require much more than the law's traditional protection of consent. A behaviourally-sensitive approach to data governance which allows for positive autonomy-preserving interventions seems the only way to promote effective privacy protection in the Big Data era.

V. CONCLUDING REMARKS

This chapter has discussed the transformative effects that a better understanding of human behaviour can bring to privacy and data protection law. At a conceptual level, it supports a move from a negative autonomy approach—epitomised by the right to be left alone—to a more positive account of informational self-determination. At a regulatory level, it highlights the empirical inefficacy of the law's traditional emphasis on formal consent. As the recent developments outlined in Part III show, taking account of behavioural insights can transform the interpretation of current EU data protection rules. More fundamentally, however, behavioural sciences can provide a robust methodological framework for the design and implementation of the proposed data protection reforms. EU data protection law is set to be shaped by behaviourally informed techniques directed at increasing the effectiveness of legal tools in influencing and changing behaviour. After two decades of lagging technological change, the law may—with the assistance of behavioural science—be coming closer to devising a sound, effective and context-adjusted privacy regime.

8

Behavioural Sciences and the Regulation of Privacy on the Internet

FREDERIK ZUIDERVEEN BORGESIUS

I. INTRODUCTION

THIS CHAPTER EXAMINES the policy implications of behavioural sciences insights for the regulation of privacy on the Internet, by focusing in particular on behavioural targeting.[1] This marketing technique involves tracking people's online behaviour to use the collected information to show people individually targeted advertisements.

This chapter distinguishes two ways in which policymakers can defend privacy in the area of behavioural targeting. Policymakers can aim to *empower*, or to *protect* the individual. First, policymakers can aim to empower people, and to put people in control over their personal information, for instance by enabling them to make choices in their own interests. The European legal regime regarding privacy in the area of behavioural targeting largely aims at individual empowerment. For example, the e-Privacy Directive requires firms to obtain the individual's consent for the use of tracking cookies for behavioural targeting.

Under the empowerment model, policymakers could also try to nudge Internet users towards disclosing less information. For instance, while marketers tend to argue that somebody gives implied consent if he or she does not opt out of behavioural targeting, policymakers could require firms to obtain the individual's opt-in consent. But behavioural sciences casts doubt on the potential of opt-in consent as a privacy protection measure. People tend to click OK to almost any request they see pop up on their screens. This is all the more true when firms make the use of a service conditional on the user's consent.

---

[1] The chapter builds on research of my PhD thesis (University of Amsterdam 2014): 'Improving Privacy Protection in the Area of Behavioural Targeting' (published by Kluwer Law International, 2015). A working paper that forms the basis for the chapter has been presented at the 6th Annual Privacy Law Scholars Conference (Berkeley, 7 June 2013), and the Nudging in Europe Conference (Liège, 12–13 December 2013). I am grateful for the comments received there. Furthermore, I thank Alberto Alemanno, Axel Arnbak, Bodó Balázs, Oren Bar-Gill, Christian Handke, Stefan Kulk, Florencia Marotta-Wurgler, Aleecia McDonald, Shara Monteleone, Alessio Pacces, Joost Poort, Anne-Lise Sibony, Omer Tene, Nico van Eijk, and Joris van Hoboken.

A second approach focuses on protection of the individual. This protective approach can also be recognised in current law regarding privacy. The Data Protection Directive has elements that aim to protect the individual. For example, even after a firm obtains an individual's consent, data protection law does not allow excessive personal data processing. And data protection law always requires firms to secure the data they process. But enforcing data protection law may not be enough to protect privacy in this area. I argue that, if society is better off when certain behavioural targeting practices do not happen, policymakers should consider banning them.

The chapter is structured as follows. Section II introduces the practice of behavioural targeting and related privacy problems. Section III discusses the current regulatory regime to protect privacy in this area, and shows informed consent plays a central role in the regime. Section IV analyses problems with informed consent through the lens of behavioural sciences. The section discusses information asymmetry, transaction costs, and biases that influence people's privacy decisions. Taking the behavioural insights into account, Section V discusses two ways to improve privacy protection in the area of behavioural targeting: empowerment and protection of the individual. Section VI concludes.

II. BEHAVIOURAL TARGETING AND PRIVACY

Much of the commercial data collection on the Internet is driven by behavioural targeting, a type of electronic direct marketing. Vast amounts of information about hundreds of millions of people is collected for behavioural targeting.

In a simplified example, behavioural targeting involves three parties: an Internet user, a website publisher, and an advertising network. Advertising networks are firms that serve ads on thousands of websites, and can recognise people when they browse the web. An ad network might infer that somebody who often visits websites about tennis is a tennis enthusiast. If that person visits a news website, the ad network might display advertising for tennis rackets. When simultaneously visiting that same website, somebody who visits many websites about economics might see ads for economics books.

A commonly used technology for behavioural targeting involves cookies. A cookie is a small text file that a website publisher stores on a user's computer to recognise that device during subsequent visits. Many websites use cookies, for example to remember the contents of a virtual shopping cart (first party cookies). Ad networks can place and read cookies as well (third party cookies). As a result, an ad network can follow an Internet user across all websites on which it serves ads. Third party tracking cookies are placed through virtually every popular website. A visit to one website often leads to receiving third party cookies from dozens of ad networks. In addition to cookies, firms use other tracking technologies for behavioural targeting, such as various kinds of super cookies, device fingerprinting, and deep packet inspection. Therefore, deleting cookies is not always enough to prevent being tracked.[2]

Behavioural targeting could benefit firms and consumers. Advertising funds an astonishing amount of Internet services. Without paying with money, people enjoy access to online translation tools, online newspapers, and email accounts, and can watch videos and listen to music. But behavioural targeting also raises privacy concerns.

Surveys show that most people do not want behaviourally targeted advertising, because they find it creepy or privacy-invasive. A small minority indicates it does not mind the data collection and prefers behaviourally targeted advertising because it can lead to more relevant ads.[3]

Three of the main privacy problems regarding behavioural targeting are: (i) chilling effects; (ii) a lack of control over personal information; and (iii) the risk of unfair discrimination and manipulation. First, chilling effects can occur because of the massive collection of information about people's online activities. Firms compile detailed profiles based on what Internet users read, what videos they watch, what they search for, etc. People may adapt their behaviour if they suspect their activities may be monitored.[4] For example, somebody who fears surveillance might hesitate to look for medical information on the web, or to read about politics. Regardless of how data are used at later stages, the mere collection of data can cause a chilling effect.

Second, people lack control over data concerning them. People do not know which information is collected, how it is used, and with whom it is shared (see Section IV, A). The feeling of lost control is a privacy problem. And large-scale personal data storage brings risks. For instance, a data breach could occur, or data could be used for unexpected purposes, such as identity fraud.[5]

Third, behavioural targeting enables social sorting and discriminatory practices: firms can classify people as 'targets' and 'waste', and treat them

---

[2] See generally on various tracking technologies: CJ Hoofnagle et al, 'Behavioral Advertising: The Offer You Cannot Refuse' (2012) 6(2) *Harvard Law & Policy Review* 273, 291; A Kuehn and M Mueller, 'Profiling the Profilers: Deep Packet Inspection and Behavioral Advertising in Europe and the United States' (1 September 2012) ssrn.com/abstract=2014181.

[3] See: J Turow et al, 'Americans Reject Tailored Advertising and Three Activities that Enable it' (29 September 2009) ssrn.com/abstract=1478214. In Europe, 7 out of 10 people are concerned that firms might use data for new purposes such as targeted advertising without informing them (European Commission, 'Special Eurobarometer 359: Attitudes on Data Protection and Electronic Identity in the European Union' (2011) cc.europa.eu/public_opinion/archives/ebs/ebs_359_en.pdf, 146. See for an overview of studies on people's attitudes towards behavioural targeting: my papers that are mentioned in n 1.

[4] See: M Foucault, *Discipline and Punish: The Birth of the Prison* (A, Sheridantr, New York, Random House LLC, 1977); NM Richards, 'Intellectual Privacy' (2008) 87 *Texas Law Review* 387.

[5] S Gürses, *Multilateral Privacy Requirements Analysis in Online Social Networks* (PhD thesis, University of Leuven) (KU Leuven (academic version), 2010) 87–91; MR Calo, 'The Boundaries of Privacy Harm' (2011) 86 *Indiana Law Journal* 1131.

accordingly.[6] And some fear that behavioural targeting could be used to manipulate people. Personalised advertising could become so effective that advertisers have an unfair advantage over consumers.[7] Calo warns for 'digital market manipulation' and 'mass production of bias'.[8] With modern personalised marketing techniques, 'companies will be in a position to figure out where and how consumers are irrational, and exploit that irrationality for gain'.[9]

Others worry that excessive personalisation can lead to an 'information cocoon',[10] or a 'filter bubble': 'a unique universe of information for each of us'.[11] This fear seems most relevant when firms personalise not only ads, but also other content and services. Briefly stated, the idea is that personalised advertising and other content could surreptitiously steer people's choices. For example, a search engine provider that personalises search results might provide links to conservative news to somebody who mainly visits conservative news sites. If users think they see a neutral picture, such personalisation might influence their worldview.

III. INFORMED CONSENT IN THE LAW

A. Data Protection Law

The right to privacy is a fundamental right in the European legal system, and is included in the European Convention on Human Rights (1950). The European Court of Human Rights interprets the Convention's privacy right generously, and holds that information derived from monitoring somebody's Internet usage is protected under the right to privacy.[12] The European Union Charter of Fundamental

---

[6] J Turow, *The Daily You: How the New Advertising Industry is Defining Your Identity and Your Worth* (New Haven, Yale University Press, 2011). In Lyon's words, social sorting involves 'obtain[ing] personal and group data in order to classify people and populations according to varying criteria, to determine who should be targeted for special treatment, suspicion, eligibility, inclusion, access, and so on' (D Lyon, 'Surveillance as Social Sorting: Computer Codes and Mobile Bodies' in D Lyon (ed), *Surveillance as Social Sorting: Privacy, Risk and Automated Discrimination* (London, Routledge, 2002) 20.

[7] See on unfair commercial practices and behavioural targeting: European Data Protection Supervisor, 'Privacy and Competitiveness in the Age of Big Data: The Interplay between Data Protection, Competition Law and Consumer Protection in the Digital Economy' (March 2014) secure.edps.europa.eu/EDPSWEB/webdav/site/mySite/shared/Documents/Consultation/Opinions/2014/14-03-26_competitition_law_big_data_EN.pdf.

[8] MR Calo, 'Digital Market Manipulation' (2013) University of Washington School of Law Research Paper No 2013-27, ssrn.com/abstract=2309703, 12.

[9] MR Calo, 'Why Opt Out of Tracking? Here's a Reason' (14 August 2013) cyberlaw.stanford.edu/blog/2013/08/why-opt-out-tracking-heres-reason.

[10] CR Sunstein, *Infotopia: How Many Minds Produce Knowledge* (Oxford, Oxford University Press, 2006) 9.

[11] E Pariser, *The Filter Bubble* (London, Penguin Viking, 2011) 9. Some authors are sceptical about the risks of filter bubbles. See, eg JVJ Van Hoboken, *Search Engine Freedom: On the Implications of the Right to Freedom of Expression for the Legal Governance of Search Engines* (PhD thesis, University of Amsterdam) (Information Law Series, Kluwer Law International, 2013) 286–287, 301.

[12] *Copland v United Kingdom* App no 62617/00 (ECtHR, 3 April 2007) paras 41–42.

Rights copies the Convention's right to privacy almost verbatim. In addition, the Charter grants individuals a separate right to the protection of personal data.[13]

To protect privacy in the area of behavioural targeting, the main legal instruments in Europe are the general Data Protection Directive (1995),[14] and the e-Privacy Directive's consent requirement for tracking technologies (2009).[15] Informed consent plays an important role in both Directives.

Data protection law is a legal tool that aims to ensure that the processing of personal data happens fairly and transparently.[16] Data protection law grants rights to people whose data are being processed (data subjects), and imposes obligations on parties that process personal data (data controllers, limited to and referred to as firms in this chapter).[17] Independent Data Protection Authorities (hereinafter DPAs) oversee compliance with the rules.[18] European DPAs cooperate in the Article 29 Working Party, an independent advisory body.[19] The Working Party publishes opinions on the interpretation of data protection law, which, although not legally binding, are influential. Judges and DPAs often follow the Working Party's interpretation.[20]

Since its inception in the early 1970s, data protection law has evolved into a complicated field of law. Borrowing from Bygrave, the core of data protection law can be summarised in nine data protection principles: the fair and lawful processing principle, the transparency principle, the data subject participation and control principle, the purpose limitation principle, the data minimisation principle, the information quality principle, the proportionality principle, the security principle, and the sensitivity principle.[21]

---

[13] Art 8 of the Charter of Fundamental Rights of the European Union: 'Protection of personal data' reads: '1. Everyone has the right to the protection of personal data concerning him or her. 2. Such data must be processed fairly for specified purposes and on the basis of the consent of the person concerned or some other legitimate basis laid down by law. Everyone has the right of access to data which has been collected concerning him or her, and the right to have it rectified. 3. Compliance with these rules shall be subject to control by an independent authority'.

[14] Directive 95/46/EC of the European Parliament and of the Council of 24 October 1995 on the protection of individuals with regard to the processing of personal data and on the free movement of such data [1995] OJ L281/31.

[15] Directive 2002/58/EC of the European Parliament and of the Council of 12 July 2002 concerning the processing of personal data and the protection of privacy in the electronic communications sector (Directive on privacy and electronic communications) [2002] OJ L201/37, as amended by Directive 2006/24/EC (the Data Retention Directive), and Directive 2009/136/EC (the Citizens' Rights Directive).

[16] See on data protection law as a 'transparency tool': P De Hert and S Gutwirth, 'Privacy, Data Protection and Law Enforcement. Opacity of the Individual and Transparency of Power' in E Claes, A Duff and S Gutwirth (eds), *Privacy and the Criminal Law* (Mortsel, Intersentia, 2006).

[17] Arts 2(a) and (h) of the Data Protection Directive.

[18] Art 8(3) of the European Union Charter of Fundamental Rights.

[19] The Article 29 Working Party is set up by Art 29 of the Data Protection Directive.

[20] See S Gutwirth and Y Poullet, 'The Contribution of the Article 29 Working Party to the Construction of a Harmonised European Data Protection System: An Illustration of "Reflexive Governance"?' in VP Asinari and P Palazzi (eds), *Défis du Droit à la Protection de la Vie Privée. (Challenges of Privacy and Data Protection Law)* (Bruxelles, Bruylant, 2008).

[21] LA Bygrave, *Data Privacy Law. An International Perspective* (Oxford, Oxford University Press, 2014) ch 5. Bygrave discusses eight principles, and sees the transparency principle as a part of the fair and lawful principle. I use a slightly different terminology than Bygrave.

Data protection law only applies when 'personal data' are processed: data that relate to an identifiable person.[22] Behavioural targeting often involves processing pseudonymous data: individual but nameless profiles. Many firms that use behavioural targeting claim they only process 'anonymous' data, and that data protection law does not apply to their activities.[23] But the Article 29 Working Party holds that behavioural targeting generally entails the processing of personal data, also if a firm cannot tie a name to the data it has on an individual. If a firm aims to use data to 'single out' a person, or to distinguish a person within a group, these data are personal data, according to the Working Party.[24]

In January 2012 the European Commission presented a proposal for a Data Protection Regulation,[25] which should replace the 1995 Data Protection Directive. At the time of writing, it is unclear whether the proposal will be adopted and the most optimistic view seems to be that the Regulation could be adopted in 2015.[26] While based on the same principles as the Directive, the proposal would bring significant changes. For instance, unlike a Directive, a Regulation has direct effect and does not have to be transposed in the national laws of the Member States. Under the proposal, DPAs could impose high fines. And the proposal always requires consent to be 'explicit'.[27] The proposal's Preamble emphasises the ideal of data subject control. 'Individuals should have control of their own personal data'.[28]

B. Informed Consent for Personal Data Processing

The current Data Protection Directive only allows firms to process personal data if they can base the processing on consent or on one of five other legal grounds. For the private sector, the most relevant legal grounds are: a contract, the balancing provision, and the data subject's consent.[29]

A firm can process personal data if the processing is necessary for the performance of a contract with the data subject.[30] For example, certain data have to

---

[22] Arts 2(a), (b), and 3(1) of the Data Protection Directive.
[23] See, eg the Interactive Advertising Bureau, 'Data About Your Browsing Activity is Collected and Analysed Anonymously' (Interactive Advertising Bureau Europe, 'Your Online Choices. A Guide to Online Behavioural Advertising', FAQ # 22. www.youronlinechoices.com/ma/faqs#22).
[24] Article 29 Working Party, 'Opinion 2/2010 on Online Behavioural Advertising' (WP 171) 22 June 2010, 9; Article 29 Working Party, 'Opinion 05/2014 on Anonymisation Techniques' (WP 216) 10 April 2014.
[25] European Commission, 'Proposal for a Regulation of the European Parliament and of the Council on the Protection of Individuals with Regard to the Processing of Personal Data and on the Free Movement of Such Data (General Data Protection Regulation)', COM (2012) 11 final, 2012/0011 (COD), 25 January 2012.
[26] See European Council, 'Conclusions of the European Council 26/27 June 2014' www.consilium.europa.eu/uedocs/cms_Data/docs/pressdata/en/ec/143478.pdf.
[27] See on consent: Art 4(8) and Art 7; on fines: Arts 78–79 of the European Commission proposal for a Data Protection Regulation (2012).
[28] Recital 6 of the European Commission proposal for a Data Protection Regulation (2012).
[29] The legal grounds are listed in Art 7 of the Data Protection Directive.
[30] Art 7(b) of the Data Protection Directive.

be processed for a credit card payment, or for a newspaper subscription. The 'necessary' requirement sets a higher threshold than 'useful' or 'profitable'.[31] Some Internet firms suggest a user enters a contract by using their services, and that it is necessary for this contract to track the user for behavioural targeting.[32] However, according to the Working Party, a firm can only rely on this legal ground if the processing is genuinely necessary for the provision of the service. The Working Party says that a contract is not a suitable legal ground for the processing of personal data for behavioural targeting.[33] In any case, the practical problems with informed consent to behavioural targeting which are discussed below would be largely the same if firms could base the processing for behavioural targeting on a contract.

The balancing provision allows certain data processing activities on an opt-out basis, without the data subject's prior consent. The balancing provision allows processing when it is necessary for the firm's legitimate interests, except where such interests are overridden by the data subject's interests or fundamental rights.[34] The balancing provision is the appropriate legal ground for innocuous standard business practices. For example, a firm can generally rely on the balancing provision for postal direct marketing of its own products to current or past customers. If a firm relies on the balancing provision for direct marketing, data protection law grants the data subject the right to stop the processing, by opting out.[35] The Data Protection Directive does not say explicitly whether behavioural targeting can be based on the balancing provision. But the most convincing view is that firms cannot base personal data processing for behavioural targeting on the balancing provision, in particular when it involves tracking somebody over multiple websites.[36] The data subject's interests must generally prevail over the firm's business interests, as behavioural targeting involves collecting and processing information about personal matters such as people's browsing behaviour. The Working Party confirms that firms can almost never rely on the balancing provision to process personal data for behavioural targeting.[37]

If firms want to process personal data, and cannot base the processing on the balancing provision or another legal ground, they must ask the data subject for

---

[31] See: ECtHR, *Silver and Others v United Kingdom* App no 5947/72 (1983) 5 EHRR 347, para 97: 'The adjective "necessary" is not synonymous with "indispensable", neither has it the flexibility of such expressions as "admissible", "ordinary", "useful", "reasonable" or "desirable"'.

[32] See, eg College Bescherming Persoonsgegevens, 'Investigation into the Combining of Personal Data by Google, Report of Definitive Findings' (z2013-00194) (November 2013, with correction 25 November 2013) www.dutchdpa.nl/downloads_overig/en_rap_2013-google-privacypolicy.pdf, 11.

[33] Article 29 Working Party, 'Opinion 06/2014 on the Notion of Legitimate Interests of the Data Controller under aArticle 7 of Directive 95/46/EC' (WP 217) 9 April 2014, 16–17.

[34] Art 7(f) of the Data Protection Directive.

[35] ibid, Art 14(b).

[36] See, eg P Traung, 'EU Law on Spyware, Web Bugs, Cookies, etc Revisited: Article 5 of the Directive on Privacy and Electronic Communications' (2010) 31 *Business Law Review* 216; B Van Der Sloot, 'Het plaatsen van cookies ten behoeve van behavioural targeting vanuit privacyperspectief (The placing of cookies for behavioural targeting from a privacy perspective)' (2011)(2) *Privacy & Informatie* 62.

[37] Article 29 Working Party, 'Opinion 06/2014 on the Notion of Legitimate Interests of the Data Controller under Art 7 of Directive 95/46/EC' (WP 217) 9 April 2014, 45.

consent.[38] The Working Party says consent is generally the required legal ground for personal data processing for behavioural targeting.[39] It follows from the Data Protection Directive's consent definition that consent requires a free, specific, and informed indication of wishes.[40] People can express their will in any form, but mere silence or inactivity is not an expression of will. This is also the predominant view in general contract law.[41] During the drafting of the Directive in the early 1990s, firms claimed the law should allow them to obtain 'implied' consent by offering people the chance to object, with an opt-out system.[42] Presumably firms assumed it would be easier to obtain consent through opt-out systems than through opt-in systems. But the European policymaker rejected the idea that a person expresses his or her will to consent to processing, merely because the person fails to object.[43]

In line with the transparency principle, consent has to be specific and informed. Consent cannot be valid if a consent request does not include a specified processing purpose and other information that is necessary to guarantee fair processing.

Furthermore, consent must be 'freely given'. For instance, if an employer asks an employee for consent, the consent might not be sufficiently voluntary, because of the imbalance of power. The employee might fear adverse consequences if he or she does not consent.[44] Negative pressure would make consent invalid, but positive pressure is generally allowed.[45] In many circumstances, current data protection law probably allows firms to offer take-it-or-leave-it choices. One data protection handbook contends:

> If, for instance, not consenting to having a supermarket's customer card results only in not receiving deductions from prices of certain goods, consent is still a valid legal basis for processing personal data of those customers who consented to having such a card.[46]

In sum, behavioural targeting generally entails the processing of personal data, also if firms do not tie a name to the data they have on individuals. The law usually requires firms to obtain the data subject's informed consent for personal data processing for behavioural targeting.

---

[38] Art 7(a) of the Data Protection Directive.
[39] Article 29 Working Party (n 37) 45.
[40] Art 2(h) of the Data Protection Directive.
[41] 'A statement made by or other conduct of the offeree indicating assent to an offer is an acceptance. Silence or inactivity does not in itself amount to acceptance', says Art 18(1) of the Vienna Convention on International Sale of Goods for instance. The Court of Justice of the European Union affirms that consent cannot be inferred from inactivity. See for instance: CJEU, Cases C-92/09 and C-93/09 *Schecke and Eifert* [2010] ECR 1-11063, para 63.
[42] See, eg International Chamber of Commerce, 'Protection of Personal Data: An International Business View' (1992) 8 *Computer Law and Security Report* 259, 262.
[43] E Kosta, *Consent in European Data Protection Law* (PhD thesis, University of Leuven) (Leiden, Martinus Nijhoff Publishers, 2013) 83–108.
[44] Article 29 Working Party, 'Opinion 15/2011 on the Definition of Consent' (WP 187) 13 July 2011, 13–14.
[45] Kosta, *Consent in European Data Protection Law* (n 43) 256.
[46] European Agency for Fundamental Rights, *Handbook on European Data Protection Law* (Publications Office of the European Union, 2014) 59.

C. Informed Consent for Tracking Technologies

European legal discussions on behavioural targeting often focus on the e-Privacy Directive's consent requirement for tracking technologies, rather than on the general data protection rules. The e-Privacy Directive complements the general data protection regime with more specific privacy rules for the electronic communications sector.[47]

In early proposals for the 2002 version of the e-Privacy Directive, article 5(3) required firms to ask consent before they placed certain kinds of cookies. After fierce lobbying by the marketing industry, the final version used ambiguous wording about a 'right to refuse'. The 2002 version of article 5(3) is usually interpreted as an opt-out system: websites had to offer people the possibility to object to tracking cookies.[48]

The e-Privacy Directive was updated in 2009. Since 2009, article 5(3) requires any party that stores or accesses information on a user's device to obtain the user's informed consent. For the definition of consent, the e-Privacy Directive refers to the Data Protection Directive, which requires a free, specific, and informed expression of will.[49] There are exceptions to the consent requirement, for example for cookies that are strictly necessary for a service requested by the user, and for cookies that are necessary for the transmission of communication. Hence, no prior consent is needed for cookies that are used for a digital shopping cart, or for log-in procedures. Article 5(3) applies regardless of whether personal data are processed. For ease of reading this chapter speaks of consent for 'cookies' or for 'tracking technologies', but article 5(3) applies to any information that can be stored or accessed on a user's device.

As many Member States missed the 2011 implementation deadline of the e-Privacy Directive, most national implementation laws are rather new. Member States vary in their approaches. For example, the Netherlands requires, in short, opt-in consent for tracking cookies.[50] In contrast, the United Kingdom appears to allow firms to use opt-out systems to obtain 'implied' consent.[51] However, the Working Party insists that the data subject's inactivity does not signify consent.[52]

---

[47] The e-Privacy Directive 2002/58 was updated by Directive 2009/136. This chapter refers to the consolidated version from 2009.

[48] S Kierkegaard, 'How the Cookies (Almost) Crumbled: Privacy & Lobbyism' (2005) 21(4) *Computer Law & Security Review* 310.

[49] Art 2(f) and Recital 17 of the e-Privacy Directive.

[50] The Dutch situation is a bit more complicated: see: FJ Zuiderveen Borgesius, 'Behavioral Targeting. Legal Developments in Europe and the Netherlands' (position paper for W3C Workshop: Do Not Track and Beyond, 2012), www.w3.org/2012/dnt-ws/position-papers/24.pdf.

[51] Information Commissioner's Office, 'Changes to Cookies on Our Website', 31 January 2013, www.ico.org.uk/news/current_topics/changes-to-cookies-on-our-website.

[52] Article 29 Working Party, 'Working Document 02/2013 Providing Guidance on Obtaining Consent for Cookies' (WP 208) 2 October 2013.

In conclusion, the European legal regime regarding privacy in the area of behavioural targeting focuses heavily on empowering individuals to make choices in their own best interests. Data protection law is deeply influenced by the idea of privacy as control over personal information. This privacy concept is prevalent since 1967, when Westin defined privacy as 'the claim of individuals, groups or institutions to determine when, how and to what extent information about them is communicated to others'.[53] Proposals to reform European data protection law also emphasise giving people control over personal information concerning them.

IV. INFORMED CONSENT IN PRACTICE

People's choices regarding privacy can be analysed using economic theory. Acquisti, one of the leading scholars on the economics of privacy, explains: 'privacy economics deals with informational trade-offs: it tries to understand, and sometimes quantify, the costs and benefits that data subjects (as well as potential data holders) bear or enjoy when their personal information is either protected or shared'.[54] Through an economic lens, consent to behavioural targeting can be seen as a transaction between a person and a firm. The user discloses personal information, in exchange for the use of a so-called 'free' service. But this 'transaction' is plagued by market failures. This chapter focuses on the market failure of information asymmetry.[55] Apart from standard market failures, section E below shows that there are 'behavioural market failures' regarding online privacy.[56]

A. Information Asymmetries

Information asymmetry 'means that a party in an interaction may know more about the activity that it is engaged in than does the other party'.[57] Since the 1970s, economists devote much attention to markets with asymmetric information, for example where consumers have difficulties evaluating the quality of products or services. Akerlof used the market for used cars as an example.[58] Suppose sellers

---

[53] AF Westin, *Privacy and Freedom* (London, The Bodley Head, 1970 (1967)) 7. See for alternative privacy concepts: S Gürses, *Multilateral Privacy Requirements Analysis in Online Social Networks* (PhD thesis, University of Leuven) (KU Leuven (academic version), 2010).

[54] A Acquisti, 'Nudging Privacy. The Behavioral Economics of Personal Information' (2009) 7(6) *IEEE Security & Privacy* 82, 72.

[55] Other market failures are also relevant for behavioural targeting, such as market power and externalities. See my papers that are mentioned in n 1.

[56] The phrase 'behavioural market failures' was introduced by O Bar-Gill, *Seduction by Contract: Law, Economics, and Psychology in Consumer Markets* (Oxford, Oxford University Press 2012).

[57] HJ Chang, *Economics: The User's Guide* (London, Penguin, 2014) 391.

[58] GA Akerlof, 'The Market for "Lemons": Quality Uncertainty and the Market Mechanism' (1970) 84(3) *Quarterly Journal of Economics* 488.

offer good cars and bad cars ('lemons'). Sellers know whether they have a good car or a lemon for sale, but buyers cannot detect hidden defects. A rational buyer will offer the price corresponding to the average quality of all used cars on the market. But this means that sellers of good cars are offered a price that is too low. Hence, owners of good cars will not offer their cars for sale. The result is that the average quality of used cars on the market decreases. Buyers will therefore offer lower prices, and fewer people will offer their cars for sale. The average quality of cars on the market will drop. Sellers thus do not compete on quality in a market characterised by asymmetric information about quality. Such a lemons situation can lead to products or services of low quality: a race to the bottom.

Information asymmetry is a type of market failure, which, from an economic perspective, justifies regulatory intervention, provided that legal intervention does not bring too much costs or economic distortions.[59] Following this line of reasoning, the main reason for responding to information asymmetry is protecting a well-functioning market, rather than paternalistic motives towards the consumer.

The current state of affairs regarding behavioural targeting is characterised by large information asymmetries. To make an informed choice, people must realise they make a choice. But research shows that most people are only vaguely aware that data are collected for behavioural targeting. For example, Ur et al found in interviews that participants were 'surprised to learn that browsing history is currently used to tailor advertisements'.[60] In a survey by Cranor and McDonald, only 40 per cent of respondents thought that providers of email services scan the contents of messages to serve targeted advertising. Twenty-nine per cent thought this would never happen, either because the law prohibits it, or because the consumer backlash would be too great. Cranor and McDonald conclude that people generally lack the knowledge needed to make meaningful decisions about privacy in the behavioural targeting area.[61] In addition, people who have learned how to defend themselves against tracking must update their knowledge constantly. For example, many firms have used flash cookies to respawn (re-install) cookies that people deleted. Hoofnagle et al summarise: 'advertisers are making it impossible to avoid online tracking'.[62]

---

[59] This chapter speaks of economics for ease of reading, but it would be more correct to speak of 'neoclassical economics', as there are also other schools of economic thought. See Chang, *Economics* (n 57) 109–69.

[60] B Ur et al, 'Smart, Useful, Scary, Creepy: Perceptions of Online Behavioral Advertising' (Proceedings of the Eighth Symposium on Usable Privacy and Security ACM, 2012) 4, 4. The interviews were conducted in the US. There is little evidence that in Europe in 2015 people have a better understanding of behavioural targeting.

[61] LF Cranor and AM McDonald, 'Beliefs and Behaviors: Internet Users' Understanding of Behavioral Advertising' (38th Research Conference on Communication, Information and Internet Policy (Telecommunications Policy Research Conference), 2 October 2010) ssrn.com/abstract=1989092. The research was conducted in the US.

[62] CJ Hoofnagle et al, 'Behavioral Advertising: The Offer You Cannot Refuse' (2012) 6(2) *Harvard Law & Policy Review* 273.

As Acquisti notes, if firms did ask consent for behavioural targeting, information asymmetry would still be a problem.[63] First, there are many firms involved in serving behaviourally targeted ads, and the underlying data flows are complicated. In addition, people do not know what will happen with their data. Will their name be tied to the profile of their surfing behaviour? Will their data be shared with other firms? If a firm goes bankrupt, will its database be sold to the highest bidder? Second, even if people knew what firms did with their data, it would be hard to predict the consequences. If a firm shares data with another firm, will the data be used for price discrimination? Will visits to a website with medical information lead to higher health insurance costs? If there is a data breach at a firm, will this lead to identity fraud?

If the privacy-friendliness of websites is seen as a product feature, the web has characteristics of a lemons market, say Vila et al.[64] It is hard for people to determine how much of their personal information is captured during a website visit, and how the information will be used. Some firms try to compete on privacy. To illustrate, a couple of search engine providers advertise they do not collect user data.[65] But website publishers rarely use privacy as a competitive advantage. Virtually every popular website allows third parties to track its visitors.[66] 'This situation looks like the classic market for lemons problem', says Strandburg. 'Consumers cannot recognize quality (here, absence of data collection for advertising) and hence will not pay for it. As a result, the market spirals downward'.[67] After interviewing people in the online marketing business, Turow concludes that competition pushes firms towards privacy invasive marketing practices, which confirms the lemons situation.[68] There also seems to be a lemons problem in the market for smartphone applications and social network sites.[69]

B. Transaction Costs

Data protection law aims to reduce the information asymmetry by requiring firms to disclose certain information to data subjects. The Data Protection Directive

---

[63] See A Acquisti and J Grossklags, 'What Can Behavioral Economics Teach Us About Privacy?' in A Acquisti et al (eds), *Digital Privacy: Theory, Technologies and Practices* (London, Auerbach Publications, Taylor and Francis Group, 2007).

[64] T Vila, R Greenstadt, and D Molnar, 'Why We Can't be Bothered to Read Privacy Policies. Models of Privacy Economics as a Lemons Market' in LJ Camp and S Lewis (eds), *Economics of Information Security* (Heidelberg, Springer, 2004).

[65] Two examples are: www.duckduckgo.com and my own favourite: www.startpage.com.

[66] CJ Hoofnagle and N Good, 'The Web Privacy Census' (October 2012) law.berkeley.edu/privacycensus.htm.

[67] KJ Strandburg, 'Free Fall: The Online Market's Consumer Preference Disconnect' (2013) *University of Chicago Legal Forum* 95, 156.

[68] J Turow, *The Daily You: How the New Advertising Industry is Defining Your Identity and Your Worth* (New Haven, Yale University Press, 2011) 199.

[69] See on social network sites and information asymmetry: J Bonneau and S Preibusch, 'The Privacy Jungle: On the Market for Data Protection in Social Networks' in T Moore, DJ Pym and C Loannidis (eds), *Economics of Information Security and Privacy* (Heidelberg, Springer, 2010).

obliges firms to provide the data subject information about their identity and the processing purpose, and all other information that is necessary to guarantee fair processing.[70] Website publishers can use a privacy policy to comply with data protection law's transparency requirements. These requirements also apply if a firm does not seek the data subject's consent, but relies on another legal ground for data processing.

But almost nobody reads privacy policies or consent requests. To illustrate, an English computer game store obtained the soul of 7,500 people. According to the website's terms and conditions, customers granted 'a non transferable option to claim, for now and for ever more, your immortal soul', unless they opted out. By opting out, people could save their soul, and could receive a £5 voucher. But few people opted out. The firm later said it would not exercise its rights.[71]

Marotta-Wurgler did research on the readership of end-user license agreements (EULAs) of software products. She analysed the click streams of almost 50,000 households, and finds an 'average rate of readership of EULAs … on the order of 0.1 percent to 1 percent'. On average, those readers did not look long enough at the EULA to read them.[72] 'The general conclusion is clear: no matter how prominently EULAs are disclosed, they are almost always ignored'.[73] There is little reason to assume the readership of privacy policies is much higher.

It is not surprising that privacy policies are hardly read: the transaction costs are too high.[74] Reading privacy policies would cost too much time, as they are often long, difficult to read, and vague. Cranor and McDonald calculate that it would cost someone several weeks per year to read the privacy policies of the websites he or she visits. The opportunity costs to citizens to inform themselves exceeded the revenues from the ad industry they might try to protect themselves from.[75] Furthermore, the language in privacy policies is too difficult for many. (I often have trouble deducing from a privacy policy what a firm plans to do with personal data). A quarter of Europeans say privacy policies are too difficult.[76] In one study,

---

[70] Arts 10 and 11 of the Data Protection Directive.
[71] Fox News, '7,500 Online Shoppers Unknowingly Sold Their Souls' (15 April 2010) www.foxnews.com/tech/2010/04/15/online-shoppers-unknowingly-sold-souls/.
[72] F Marotta-Wurgler, 'Will Increased Disclosure Help? Evaluating the Recommendations of the ALI's Principles of the Law of Software Contracts' (2011) 78(1) *The University of Chicago Law Review* 165, 168.
[73] ibid, 182.
[74] Transaction costs are 'any costs connected with the creation of transactions themselves, apart from the price of the good that is the object of the transaction' (HA Luth, *Behavioural Economics in Consumer Policy: The Economic Analysis of Standard Terms in Consumer Contracts Revisited* (PhD thesis University of Rotterdam) (Mortsel, Intersentia, 2010) 19). See also RH Coase, 'The Problem of Social Cost' (1960) 3 *Journal of Law and Economics* 1.
[75] Expressed in dollars, the opportunity cost of reading would be around $781 billion. All online advertising income in the US was estimated to be $21 billion in 2007. AM McDonald and LF Cranor, 'The Cost of Reading Privacy Policies' (2008) 4(3) *I/S: A Journal of Law and Policy for the Information Society* 540.
[76] European Commission, 'Special Eurobarometer 359: Attitudes on Data Protection and Electronic Identity in the European Union' (2011) ec.europa.eu/public_opinion/archives/ebs/ebs_359_en.pdf, 112–14.

more than half of the examined privacy policies were too difficult for a majority of American Internet users.[77]

If somebody read and understood a privacy policy, transaction costs could still be a problem. Moving to another service often involves transaction costs for the user, and 'when the costs of switching from one brand of technology to another are substantial, users face *lock-in*'.[78] For instance, transferring emails and contacts to another email provider costs time. If iTunes changes its privacy policy, many people might just accept. And when all of one's friends are on Facebook, it makes little sense to join another social network site. Firms can also use transaction costs strategically, for example to discourage people from opting out of tracking. To illustrate, refusing Google's advertising cookies takes five mouse clicks from the Google search page.[79]

Furthermore, it is often questionable whether people have a real choice regarding tracking. For instance, an Internet firm might have a dominant position or a monopoly.[80] Moreover, even if the market structure is competitive (in other words: when no firm has a monopoly or a similar position), there might not be any privacy-friendly competitors. After all, in a market with information asymmetry firms will generally not compete on quality or, in this case, on privacy-friendliness. Besides, somebody who wants to visit website X, may not see website Y as a valid alternative. As Helberger puts it, 'media is speech, and when consuming media content it does matter who the speaker is'.[81]

Privacy policies thus fail to inform people that use computers. It is even harder to inform people who use mobile devices with smaller screens. In sum, data protection law does not solve the information asymmetry problem.

C. Status Quo Bias

A hypothetical fully rational person would know how to deal with information asymmetry and uncertainty. For instance, a rational person could base his or her decision on what happens to people's personal data on average, and would not

---

[77] C Jensen and C Potts, 'Privacy Policies as Decision-making Tools: An Evaluation of Online Privacy Notices' (2004) Proceedings of the SIGCHI Conference on Human Factors in Computing Systems 471.

[78] C Shapiro and HR Varian, *Information Rules. A Strategic Guide to the Network Economy* (Cambridge, Harvard Business School Press, 1999) 104.

[79] See: College bescherming persoonsgegevens (Dutch DPA), 'Investigation into the Combining of Personal Data by Google, Report of Definitive Findings' (z2013-00194) www.dutchdpa.nl/downloads_overig/en_rap_2013-google-privacypolicy.pdf, 82. See generally on tactics that a firm can use to keep people in the default position that it prefers: LE Willis, 'Why Not Privacy by Default?' (2013) 29 *Berkeley Technology Law Journal* 61.

[80] See on competition law and personal data: European Data Protection Supervisor, 'Privacy and Competitiveness in the Age of Big Data: The Interplay between Data Protection, Competition Law and Consumer Protection in the Digital Economy' (March 2014) secure.edps.europa.eu/EDPSWEB/webdav/site/mySite/shared/Documents/Consultation/Opinions/2014/14-03-26_competitition_law_big_data_EN.pdf.

[81] See N Helberger, 'Freedom of Expression and the Dutch Cookie-Wall' (2013) Institute for Information Law, www.ivir.nl/publications/helberger/Paper_Freedom_of_expression.pdf, 12.

be optimistic about quality in a market with information asymmetry. But behavioural sciences insights suggest that people do not tend to deal with information asymmetry in a 'rational' way. Rather, they often rely on rules of thumb, or heuristics. Usually such mental shortcuts work fine, but they can also lead to behaviour that is not in people's self-interest. Privacy choices are influenced by several biases, such as the status quo bias and myopia.

The status quo bias, or inertia, refers to the power of the default.[82] Most people do not change the default option. This means that the default setting will have a big impact on the dynamics between the firm and the users. A famous example of the status quo bias concerns the percentage of organ donors. Countries that use an opt-out system (people donate their organs unless they express that they do not want to donate) have many donors, while countries that use an opt-in system have few donors.[83]

Marketers can leverage the status quo bias. Free trial periods of newspapers can lead to subscriptions for years, because—in line with the status quo bias—people do not get around to cancelling. 'Buy this pack of shampoo, and get a 2 euro refund', relies on transaction costs and the status quo bias. With such mail-in-rebates, many people fail to send in the coupon. As an aside, customers would also provide the firm with personal data, such as their name and bank account number, if they sent in the coupon.

Insights into the status quo bias help to understand the discussion about opt-in versus opt-out systems for behavioural targeting and other types of direct marketing. This opt-in/opt-out discussion basically concerns the question of who benefits from the status quo bias: the firm or the individual? As Sunstein puts it, 'true, we might opt out of a website policy that authorizes a lot of tracking (perhaps with a simple click)—but because of the power of inertia, many of us are not likely to do so'.[84] Marketers tend to argue they can obtain 'implied' consent with opt-out systems. Privacy advocates tend to prefer opt-in systems for privacy-intrusive practices.

The opt-in versus opt-out discussion has been going on for decades. When the European Commission presented a proposal for a Data Protection Directive in 1990, heated discussions ensued about the proposal's rules on direct marketing. Business organisations, including the European Direct Marketing Association, started lobbying intensely.[85] Marketers feared that direct mail marketing would only be allowed with the data subject's prior consent. The lobbying paid off. In 1992 the Commission presented an amended proposal, and said that firms can

---

[82] W Samuelson and R Zeckhauser, 'Status Quo Bias in Decision Making' (1988) 1(1) *Journal of Risk and Uncertainty* 7.

[83] EJ Johnson and D Goldstein, 'Do Defaults Save Lives?' (2003) 302(5649) *Science* 1338. For a discussion of nudging in this context, see in this volume chs 3 and 10.

[84] CR Sunstein, 'The Storrs Lectures: Behavioral Economics and Paternalism' (2013) 122(7) *Yale Law Journal* 1826, 1893.

[85] PM Regan, 'The Globalization of Privacy: Implications of Recent Changes in Europe' (1993) 52(3) *American Journal of Economics and Sociology* 257, 266–67; D Heisenberg, *Negotiating Privacy: The European Union, the United States, and Personal Data Protection* (Boulder, Lynne Rienner Publishers, 2005) 62.

rely on the balancing provision for direct mail marketing, which implies an opt-out system.[86]

When the 2009 e-Privacy Directive required informed consent for tracking cookies, again an opt-in/opt-out discussion followed. Recital 66 of the 2009 Directive that amended the e-Privacy Directive has caused much confusion:

[I]n accordance with the relevant provisions of [the Data Protection Directive], the user's consent to processing may be expressed by using the appropriate settings of a browser or other application.[87]

Many marketers suggest that people that do not block tracking cookies in their browser give implied consent to behavioural targeting. For instance, the Interactive Advertising Bureau, a marketing trade organisation, says '*default* web browser settings can amount to "consent"'.[88] However, the Working Party insists that the mere fact that somebody leaves the settings of his or her browser untouched does not mean that the person expresses the will to accept tracking cookies.[89]

A number of larger behavioural targeting firms offer people the chance to opt out of targeted advertising on a centralised website: youronlinechoices.com. However, participating firms merely promise to stop showing targeted ads, so they may continue to track people who have opted out.[90] In short, the website offers the equivalent of 'do not target', rather than 'do not collect'.[91] But even if the firms stopped collecting data after somebody opts out, they could not use the website's opt-out system to obtain valid consent, says the Working Party.[92] Valid consent requires an expression of will, which generally calls for an opt-in procedure.

The 2012 proposal for a Data Protection Regulation reaffirms that consent must be expressed 'either by a statement or by a clear affirmative action'.[93] History repeated itself: many firms lobbied to soften the requirements for consent. Those firms prefer a regime that allows them to collect personal data, unless people opt

---

[86] European Commission, 'Amended proposal for a Council Directive on the Protection of Individuals with Regard to the Processing of Personal Data and on the Free Movement of Such Data', COM (92) 422 final—SYN 287, 15 October 1992 [1992] OJ C311/30 (27.11.1992), 15.

[87] Directive 2009/136, Recital 66.

[88] Interactive Advertising Bureau United Kingdom, 'Department for Business, Innovation & Skills Consultation on Implementing the Revised EU Electronic Communications Framework, IAB UK Response' (1 December 2012) www.iabuk.net/sites/default/files/IABUKresponsetoBISconsultationonimplementingtherevisedEUElectronicCommunicationsFramework_7427_0.pdf, 2.

[89] Article 29 Working Party, 'Opinion 2/2010 on Online Behavioural Advertising' (WP 171) 22 June 2010.

[90] The opt-out page says: 'Declining behavioural advertising only means that you will not receive more display advertising customised in this way' (Youronlinechoices, FAQ# 21 www.youronlinechoices.com/ma/faqs#21).

[91] See on this difference: M Schunter and P Swire, 'Explanatory Memorandum for Working Group Decision on "What Base Text to Use for the Do Not Track Compliance Specification"' (16 July 2013) www.w3.org/2011/tracking-protection/2013-july-explanatory-memo/.

[92] Article 29 Working Party, 'Opinion 16/2011 on EASA/IAB Best Practice Recommendation on Online Behavioural Advertising' (WP 188) 8 December 2011.

[93] Art 4(8) of the European Commission proposal for a Data Protection Regulation (2012); see section IIIA of this chapter.

out.⁹⁴ In part, the lobbying succeeded. The European Parliament amended the proposal for the Regulation. The amended proposal allows firms, under certain conditions, to use behavioural targeting without the data subject's consent, on an opt-out basis (based on the balancing provision), as long as they do not tie a name to the data they process about individuals.⁹⁵

D. Myopia and Other Biases

More biases influence people's decisions regarding behavioural targeting. For instance, myopia, or present bias, refers to the effect that people tend to focus more on the present than on the future. People often choose for immediate gratification, thereby ignoring future costs. For example, myopia helps to explain why many people find it hard to save money for their retirement.

Because of myopia, people might choose immediate access to a service, also if this means they have to consent to behavioural targeting, contrary to their earlier plans. Suppose Alice reads about behavioural targeting, and decides not to accept any more tracking cookies. That night, she wants to read an online newspaper, and wants to watch the news online. Both websites deny entry to visitors that do not accept the tracking cookies of third parties.⁹⁶ While she was planning not to accept any more tracking cookies, Alice clicks 'yes' on both websites.⁹⁷

As noted, under the Data Protection Directive, consent must be 'freely given' to be valid.⁹⁸ But in most circumstances data protection law probably allows firms to offer take-it-or-leave-it choices. In principle, firms are allowed to offer people that consent something in return, such as a discount. This suggests that firms can make the use of a service dependent on consent to behavioural targeting. Hence, in principle current law seems to allow website publishers to install 'tracking walls', barriers that website visitors can only pass if they consent to being tracked.⁹⁹

---

⁹⁴ See, eg Facebook, 'Facebook recommendations on the Internal Market and Consumer Affairs draft opinion on the European Commission's proposal for a General Data Protection Regulation "on the protection of individuals with regard to the processing of personal data and on the free movement of such data"' github.com/lobbyplag/lobbyplag-data/raw/master/raw/lobby-documents/Facebook.pdf.

⁹⁵ See Art 2(a), Art 6(f), and Recitals 38 and 58a of the proposal for a Data Protection Regulation, consolidated version after LIBE Committee vote, 22 October 2013, www.janalbrecht.eu/fileadmin/material/Dokumente/DPR-Regulation-inofficial-consolidated-LIBE.pdf.

⁹⁶ Early 2013 this was the case in the Netherlands. The National Public Broadcasting Organisation and one of the larger newspapers (Volkskrant) both installed a tracking wall (www.publiekeomroep.nl and www.volkskrant.nl).

⁹⁷ In one Dutch survey, 30% does not want tracking cookies at all, and 41% only wants tracking cookies from some sites. However, 50% say they usually click 'OK' to consent requests for cookies (Consumentenbond, 'Cookiewet heeft bar weinig opgeleverd (Cookie law didn't help much)' (2014) www.consumentenbond.nl/test/elektronica-communicatie/veilig-online/privacy-op-internet/extra/cookiewet-heeft-weinig-opgeleverd/).

⁹⁸ Art 2(h) of the Data Protection Directive.

⁹⁹ See: N Helberger, 'Freedom of Expression and the Dutch Cookie-Wall' (2013) Institute for Information Law, www.ivir.nl/publications/helberger/Paper_Freedom_of_expression.pdf.

However, a tracking wall could make consent involuntary if people must use a website. For instance, say people are required to file their taxes online. If the tax website had a tracking wall that imposed third party tracking, people's consent to tracking would not be voluntary. According to the Dutch DPA, the national public broadcasting organisation is not allowed to use a tracking wall, because the only way to access certain information online is through the broadcaster's website.[100] The Working Party emphasises that consent should be free, but does not say that current data protection law prohibits tracking walls in all circumstances.[101]

Overconfidence and optimism biases are related to myopia. People tend to underestimate the risk of accidents and diseases, and overestimate the chances of a long and healthy life or winning the lottery. The success of 'buy now, pay later' deals can be partly explained by myopia and optimism bias.[102] Research suggests people also tend to underestimate the risks of identity fraud and of re-identification of anonymised data.[103]

The way information is presented can also influence decisions: the framing effect. For example, many people see a link to a privacy policy as a quality seal. Forty-one per cent of Europeans do not read privacy policies, because they think it is enough to check whether a website has one.[104] In a California survey the majority thought that the mere fact that a website had a privacy policy meant that their privacy was protected by law.[105] Turow at al argue that the phrase 'privacy policy' is misleading.[106] Facebook speaks of a 'data use policy', which seems a more apt name.[107]

Research suggests that privacy policies with vague language give people the impression that a service is more privacy-friendly than privacy policies that give more details.[108] Another study concludes that 'any official-looking graphic' can lead people to believe that a website is trustworthy.[109] Böhme and Köpsell find

---

[100] College bescherming persoonsgegevens 2013, 'Brief aan de staatssecretaris van Onderwijs, Cultuur en Wetenschap, over beantwoording Kamervragen i.v.m. cookiebeleid' (Letter to the State Secretary of Education, Culture and Science, on answers to parliamentary questions about cookie policy) (31 January 2013) www.cbpweb.nl/downloads_med/med_20130205-cookies-npo.pdf.
[101] Article 29 Working Party 2013, 'Working Document 02/2013 Providing Guidance on Obtaining Consent for Cookies' (WP 208) 2 October 2013.
[102] CR Sunstein and RH Thaler, *Nudge: Improving Decisions about Health, Wealth, and Happiness* (New Haven, Yale University Press 2008) 31–35.
[103] A Acquisti and J Grossklags, 'Privacy and Rationality in Individual Decision Making' (2005) 3(1) *IEEE Security & Privacy* 26.
[104] European Commission, 'Special Eurobarometer 359: Attitudes on Data Protection and Electronic Identity in the European Union' (2011) ec.europa.eu/public_opinion/archives/ebs/ebs_359_en.pdf> accessed 30 June 2014, 118–20.
[105] CJ Hoofnagle and J King, 'What Californians Understand about Privacy Online (UC Berkeley)' (3 September 2008) ssrn.com/abstract=1262130.
[106] J Turow et al, 'The Federal Trade Commission and Consumer Privacy in the Coming Decade' (2007) 3(3) *I/S: A Journal of Law & Policy for the Information Society* 723.
[107] Facebook, 'Data Use Policy' (15 November 2013) www.facebook.com/about/privacy.
[108] N Good et al, 'User Choices and Regret: Understanding Users' Decision Process about Consensually Acquired Spyware' (2006) 2(2) *Journal of Law & Policy for the Information Society* 283, 323.
[109] T Moores, 'Do Consumers Understand the Role of Privacy Seals in e-Commerce?' (2005) 48(3) *Communications of the ACM* 86, 89–90.

that people are more likely to consent if a pop-up looks more like an end-user license agreement (EULA). The researchers varied the design of consent dialog boxes and tested the effect by analysing the clicks of more than 80,000 people. They concluded that people are conditioned to click 'agree' to a consent request if it resembles a EULA.

> [U]biquitous EULAs have trained even privacy-concerned users to click on 'accept' whenever they face an interception that reminds them of a EULA. This behaviour thwarts the very intention of informed consent. So we are facing the dilemma that the long-term effect of well-meant measures goes in the opposite direction: rather than attention and choice, users exhibit ignorance.[110]

Furthermore, Acquisti et al discuss a control paradox. People share more information if they *feel* they have more control over how they share personal information. The researchers conclude that control over personal information is a normative definition of privacy: control *should* ensure privacy. But in practice, 'more' control can sometimes lead to 'less' privacy in the sense of higher objective 'risks associated with the disclosure of personal information'.[111]

E. Behavioural Market Failures

Behavioural sciences insights can help to explain the alleged privacy paradox: people say in surveys they care about privacy, but often divulge personal data in exchange for minimal benefits. Part of this is conditioning: many people click 'yes' to any statement that is presented to them. It is only a slight exaggeration to say: people do not read privacy policies; if they were to read, they would not understand; if they understood, they would not act.

Because privacy choices are context-dependent, caution is needed when drawing conclusions about the effect of biases. One bias might influence a privacy decision in one direction, while another bias might influence the decision in another direction.[112] Still, it would be naïve to ignore behavioural sciences when making laws that rely, in part, on the decisions of people whose privacy the law aims to protect.

Biases can lead to behavioural market failures. These are 'market failures that complement the standard economic account and that stem from the human propensity to err'.[113] Apart from questions of fairness, such behavioural market failures decrease social welfare, in the same way as conventional market failures. 'Free markets', explains Sunstein, 'may well reward sellers who attempt to exploit human

---

[110] R Böhme and S Köpsell, 'Trained to Accept? A Field Experiment on Consent Dialogs' (2010) Proceedings of the SIGCHI Conference on Human Factors in Computing Systems 2403, 2406.

[111] A Acquisti, L Brandimarte and G Loewenstein, 'Misplaced Confidences: Privacy and the Control Paradox' (2012) *Social Psychological and Personality Science* 1, 6.

[112] A Acquisti and J Grossklags, 'What Can Behavioral Economics Teach Us about Privacy?' in A Acquisti et al (eds), *Digital Privacy: Theory, Technologies and Practices* (London, Auerbach Publications, Taylor and Francis Group, 2007) eds.

[113] CR Sunstein, *Why Nudge? The Politics of Libertarian Paternalism* (New Haven, Yale University Press, 2014) 16.

errors. In identifiable cases, those who do *not* exploit human errors will be seriously punished by market forces, simply because their competitors are profiting from doing so'.[114] Several authors conclude there is a behavioural market failure regarding online privacy. Firms would not stay in business if they did not exploit people's biases. As Strandburg puts it, 'The behavioral advertising business model seems almost designed to take advantage of … bounded rationality'.[115]

V. HOW TO IMPROVE PRIVACY PROTECTION?

Considering the limited potential of informed consent as a privacy protection measure, I argue that policymakers should use a combined approach of empowering and protecting the individual. Compared to the current approach, policymakers should focus more on protection.

This chapter distinguishes empowerment and protection rules to structure the discussion, but the distinction is not a formal legal distinction. The chapter uses rules that aim for *data subject control* and rules that aim for *empowerment* roughly interchangeably. Examples of empowerment rules are default rules that give the data subject the choice to allow data processing or not, such as informed consent requirements.[116] Other empowerment rules aim to make data processing transparent for the data subject, or grant data subjects rights, for instance to access and correct their data.[117]

Protection rules are generally mandatory. They always apply, irrespective of whether the data subject has consented to processing. For instance, under data protection law firms must always secure the data they process.[118] Another example of data protection law's aim to protect people is the existence of independent Data Protection Authorities that oversee compliance with the rules, as required by the Charter of Fundamental Rights of the European Union.

A. Individual Empowerment

How could the law improve empowerment of the individual? To reduce the information asymmetry in the area of behavioural targeting, data protection law's transparency principle should be enforced more strictly. The Working

---

[114] ibid, 11.
[115] KJ Strandburg, 'Free Fall: The Online Market's Consumer Preference Disconnect' (2013) University of Chicago Legal Forum 95, 149. See also A Acquisti, 'The Economics of Personal Data and the Economics of Privacy' (background paper conference: The Economics of Personal Data and Privacy: 30 Years after the OECD Privacy Guidelines, 2010) www.oecd.org/internet/ieconomy/46968784.pdf, 6.
[116] See on the distinction between default and mandatory rules: I Ayres, 'Regulating Opt Out: An Economic Theory of Altering Rules' (2012) *Yale Law Journal* 2032.
[117] See Arts 10 and 11 (transparency) and Art 12 (access and correction) of the Data Protection Directive.
[118] Arts 17 (and 16).

Party says privacy policies and consent requests must be phrased in a clear and comprehensible manner.[119] The European Commission proposal for a Data Protection Regulation codifies this requirement.[120] Such a rule could discourage firms from using legalese in privacy policies, and would make it easier for DPAs to intervene when a firm uses a privacy policy or a consent request that is too vague. Given the fact that people currently would need several weeks per year to read privacy policies, such a rule would not be enough to ensure actual transparency. Still, the rule could help to lower the costs of reading privacy policies. And apart from data subjects, the press can also read privacy policies. A change in a firm's privacy policy could lead to media attention, and sometimes firms react to that.[121]

In view of the limited effect that privacy policies have in informing people, interdisciplinary research is needed to develop tools to make data processing transparent in a meaningful way. Calo argues that we should not forget about transparency and informed consent, before better ways of presenting information have been tried.[122] Indeed, the current 'failure of mandated disclosure' does not prove that legal transparency requirements will always fail.[123] For instance, perhaps icons could be useful to communicate the data processing practices of firms. The European Commission encourages the use of icons,[124] and the European Parliament has proposed to require firms to use icons to inform people about data processing practices.[125]

i. Consent for Tracking Technologies

Human attention is scarce, and too many consent requests can overwhelm people. Therefore, the scope of article 5(3) of the e-Privacy Directive is too broad. Article 5(3) requires consent for storing or accessing information on a user's device. This means the provision also requires consent for some cookies that are not used to collect detailed information about individuals. But there is little

---

[119] See Article 29 Working Party, 'Opinion 10/2004 on More Harmonised Information Provisions' (WP 100) 25 November 2004.

[120] Art 11 of the European Commission proposal for a Data Protection Regulation (2012); see on the proposed Regulation section III.A. of this chapter.

[121] eg after attention in the press, Facebook offered people a way to opt out of their 'Beacon' service (B Debatin et al, 'Facebook and Online Privacy: Attitudes, Behaviors, and Unintended Consequences' (2009) 15(1) *Journal of Computer-Mediated Communication* 83).

[122] MR Calo, 'Against Notice Skepticism in Privacy (and Elsewhere)' (2011) 87(3) *Notre Dame Law Review* 1027.

[123] The phrase 'failure of mandated disclosure' is from: O Ben-Shahar and C Schneider, 'The Failure of Mandated Disclosure' (2011) 159 *University of Pennsylvania Law Review* 647, 650.

[124] European Commission, 'Communication from the Commission to the European Parliament and the Council on Promoting Data Protection by Privacy Enhancing Technologies (PETs)', COM (2007) 228 final, Brussels, 2 May 2007, para 4.3.2.

[125] See Art 13(a), and the Annex, of the proposal for a Data Protection Regulation, consolidated version after LIBE Committee vote, 22 October 2013, www.janalbrecht.eu/fileadmin/material/ Dokumente/DPR-Regulation-inofficial-consolidated-LIBE.pdf. To me, the proposed six icons do not seem very clear. But it is possible that after a while, people would start to recognise the icons.

reason to ask consent for innocuous practices. For instance, perhaps certain types of cookies that are used for website analytics could be exempted from the consent requirement, provided they do not threaten privacy and are not used to construct profiles of people.[126]

It would probably be better if the consent requirement for tracking were phrased in a more technology neutral way. The law could require consent for the collection and further processing of personal data, including pseudonymous data, for behavioural targeting and similar purposes—regardless of the technology that is used. Phrasing the rule in a more technology neutral way could also mitigate another problem. In some ways the scope of article 5(3) may be too narrow. For instance, it is unclear to what extent article 5(3) applies if firms use device fingerprinting for behavioural targeting.[127]

ii. Privacy Nudges

Scholars have started to explore the possibilities for privacy nudges.[128] For example, Wang et al examine whether it is possible to help users of social network sites to avoid posting messages that they later regret.[129] A pop-up could warn people who post a status update on Facebook about how many people will be able to see that message. Such a warning can be made more forceful, for instance by including pictures of people who can see the post. Perhaps people would not post that 'drunk' picture if a pop-up reminded them that their bosses could see the picture too. The researchers conclude 'that privacy nudges can potentially be a powerful mechanism to help some people avoid unintended disclosures'.[130] Balebako et al have explored 'nudging users towards privacy on mobile devices', to help people with decisions regarding the sharing of location data.[131] There is also research on nudging people to avoid installing privacy-invasive smart phone apps.[132]

Setting defaults is a classic example of nudging. The status quo bias suggests that requiring opt-in consent for tracking could nudge people towards disclosing fewer

---

[126] The Data Protection Directive has the balancing provision for such innocuous practices (Art 7(f)). The Working Party argues for the introduction of an exception in Art 5(3) for certain types of innocuous analytics cookies (Article 29 Working Party, 'Opinion 04/2012 on Cookie Consent Exemption' (WP 194) 7 June 2012).

[127] See on device fingerprinting: G Acar et al, 'The Web Never Forgets: Persistent Tracking Mechanisms in the Wild' (Draft, 10 August 2014) securehomes.esat.kuleuven.be/~gacar/persistent/the_web_ never_forgets.pdf.

[128] A Acquisti, 'Nudging Privacy. The Behavioral Economics of Personal Information' (2009) 7(6) *IEEE Security & Privacy* 82.

[129] Y Wang et al, 'The Second Wave of Global Privacy Protection: From Facebook Regrets to Facebook Privacy Nudges' (2013) 74 *Ohio State Law Journal* 1307, 1307.

[130] ibid, 1334.

[131] R Balebako et al, 'Nudging Users towards Privacy on Mobile Devices' CHI 2011 workshop article www.andrew.cmu.edu/user/pgl/paper6.pdf.

[132] EK Choe et al, 'Nudging People away from Privacy-invasive Mobile Apps through Visual Framing' in, *Human-Computer Interaction–INTERACT 2013* (Heidelberg, Springer, 2013).

data.[133] Hence, if the goal is protecting privacy, behavioural sciences insights suggest that the law should require opt-in systems for valid consent. This implies that the existing rules regarding consent should be enforced. As noted, the European Commission proposal for a Data Protection Regulation tightens the requirements for consent.[134] The proposal also codifies the Working Party's view that a consent request may not be hidden in a privacy policy or in terms and conditions.[135]

iii. Tracking Walls

There is a problem when policymakers prescribe default settings to make behavioural targeting firms nudge people towards disclosing less data. Such firms may have an incentive to collect as much information as possible. As Willis notes, firms have many ways to persuade people to agree to tracking.[136] It is hard for policymakers to make firms use behaviourally informed instruments, if firms do not want to nudge people in the same direction as the policymaker. Sunstein puts it as follows:

> [I]f regulated institutions are strongly opposed to a default rule and have easy access to their customers, they may well be able to use a variety of strategies, including behavioral ones, to encourage people to move in the direction the institutions prefer.[137]

For instance, firms can offer take-it-or-leave-it choices, such as tracking walls on websites. Hence, even if firms offered transparency and asked prior consent for behavioural targeting, people might still feel they must consent.

Should the law do anything about take-it-or-leave-it choices regarding the enjoyment of privacy when using websites and other Internet services? Some have suggested that tracking walls and similar take-it-or-leave-it-choices should be prohibited.[138] Another option would be to ban such take-it-or-leave-it choices in certain contexts. (The next section returns to the topic of context-specific rules).

It has also been suggested that the law should require firms to offer a tracking-free version of their services, which has to be paid for with money.[139] Such a rule would enable people to compare the prices of websites. Now the 'price' of a website is usually hidden because people do not know which information about them is

---

[133] See CR Sunstein, 'Deciding By Default' (2013) 162(1) *University of Pennsylvania Law Review* 1.
[134] Art 4(8) of the European Commission proposal for a Data Protection Regulation (2012). See section III, A of this chapter.
[135] Article 29 Working Party, 'Opinion 15/2011 on the Definition of Consent' (WP 187) 13 July 2011, 33–35.
[136] LE Willis, 'Why Not Privacy by Default?' (2013) 29 *Berkeley Technology Law Journal* 61.
[137] CR Sunstein, *Simpler: The Future of Government* (New York, Simon and Schuster, 2013) 119.
[138] See, eg: K Irion and G Luchetta, 'Online Personal Data Processing and EU Data Protection Reform' (CEPS Task Force Report of the CEPS Digital Forum, 2013) www.ivir.nl/publications/irion/TFR_Data_Protection.pdf, 78.
[139] P Traung, 'The Proposed New EU General Data Protection Regulation: Further Opportunities' (2012) 2 *Computer Law Review International* 33, 42; Irion and Luchetta, 'Online Personal Data Processing and EU Data Protection Reform' (n 138) 38.

captured, nor how it will be used.[140] A requirement for firms to offer a tracking-free but paid-for version of their service would be less protective of privacy than a ban on tracking walls. Myopia might lead most people to choose the so-called free version, because they focus on the short-term loss of paying for a service, also if this means they have to consent to behavioural targeting, contrary to earlier plans.[141] Furthermore, many say it is 'extortion' if they have to pay for privacy.[142]

iv. Why Still Aim for Empowerment?

The behavioural sciences analysis suggests that the practical problems with informed consent are immense. So why still aim for empowerment? First, it seems unlikely that Europe would ever adopt a data protection regime without any role for informed consent, if only because the European Union Charter of Fundamental Rights lists consent as one of the possible legal grounds for personal data processing.[143] In addition, people's tastes differ. Some people would approve of a certain behavioural targeting practice, while others would not. Regulation with an informed consent provision has the advantage of respecting people's individual preferences. Taking away *all* privacy choices from the individual would probably make the law unduly paternalistic. Furthermore, it does not seem feasible to define all beneficial or all harmful data processing activities in advance. Indeed, several scholars that are extremely sceptical of informed consent as a privacy protection measure still conclude that a legal privacy regime without any role for informed consent is neither feasible nor desirable.[144]

Relying on informed consent, in combination with data protection law's other safeguards, will probably remain the appropriate approach in many circumstances. For those cases, transparency and consent should be taken seriously. Fostering individual control over personal information alone will not suffice to protect privacy in the area of behavioural targeting. But some improvement must be possible, compared to the current situation of almost complete lack of individual control over personal information.

---

[140] N Helberger, 'Freedom of Expression and the Dutch Cookie-Wall' (2013) Institute for Information Law, www.ivir.nl/publications/helberger/Paper_Freedom_of_expression.pdf, 19.

[141] See on the attraction of 'free' offers: D Ariely, *Predictably Irrational* (New York, Harper, 2008) ch 3; CJ Hoofnagle and JM Whittington, 'The Price of "Free": Accounting for the Cost of the Internet's Most Popular Price' (2014) 61 (3) *UCLA Law Review* (forthcoming) ssrn.com/abstract=2235962.

[142] LF Cranor and AM McDonald, 'Beliefs and Behaviors: Internet Users' Understanding of Behavioral Advertising' (38th Research Conference on Communication, Information and Internet Policy (Telecommunications Policy Research Conference), 2 October 2010) ssrn.com/abstract=1989092.

[143] See Art 8(2) of the European Union Charter of Fundamental Rights.

[144] See, eg S Barocas and H Nissenbaum, 'On Notice: The Trouble with Notice and Consent' (Proceedings of the Engaging Data Forum: The First International Forum on the Application and Management of Personal Electronic Information, October 2009) www.nyu.edu/pages/projects/nissenbaum/papers/ED_SII_On_Notice.pdf; DJ Solove, 'Privacy Self-Management and the Consent Dilemma' (2013) 126 *Harvard Law Review* 1879.

In conclusion, regarding the requirements for valid consent, the formal legal framework is in line with behavioural sciences insights. Firms are not allowed to infer consent from mere silence—and should not be allowed to do so. But even if firms offered transparency and asked for opt-in consent for tracking, the issue of take-it-or-leave-it choices and tracking walls would remain. As long as the law allows take-it-or-leave-it choices, opt-in systems will not be effective privacy nudges.

B. Individual Protection

A second legal approach to improve privacy protection in the area of behavioural targeting involves *protecting*, rather than empowering, people. If fully complied with, the data protection principles could give reasonable privacy protection in the area of behavioural targeting, even if people agreed to consent requests.

Of course, the Data Protection Directive is only relevant if the practice of behavioural targeting is found to come within the Directive's scope. This will be the case if pseudonymous data, such as the data that are used for behavioural targeting, are seen as personal data. Hence, from a normative perspective, data protection law should apply to behavioural targeting, including when firms use pseudonymous data. Apart from that, a sensible interpretation of data protection law implies that data that are used to 'single out' a person should be seen as personal data.[145]

While consent plays an important role in data protection law, its role is also limited. Consent can provide a legal ground for personal data processing. However, if a firm has a legal ground for processing, the other data protection provisions still apply.[146] Those provisions are mandatory. The data subject cannot waive the safeguards or deviate from the rules by contractual agreement. For example, even after a firm obtains an individual's consent, data protection law does not allow excessive personal data processing. And it follows from the purpose limitation principle that personal data must be collected for specified purposes, and may not be used for unexpected purposes.[147] Hence, a contract between a firm and a data subject would not be enforceable if it stipulated that the firm does not have to secure the personal data, or can use the data for new purposes at will.

The data minimisation principle, if effectively enforced, is an example of a data protection principle that could protect privacy, also after people consent to behavioural targeting. The Data Protection Directive says data processing must be 'not excessive' in relation to the processing purpose, and it follows from the Directive's

---

[145] See section III, A of this chapter, and in detail on the material scope of data protection law: ch 5 of my PhD thesis (see n 1 of this chapter).
[146] See CJEU, Case C-131/12 *Google Spain SL and Google Inc v Agencia Española de Protección de Datos and Mario Costeja González*, nyr, para 71.
[147] Art 6(1)(c), not excessive; and Art 6(1)(b), purpose limitation, of the Data Protection Directive.

structure that this requirement also applies if the processing is based on the data subject's consent.[148] The vast scale of data processing for behavioural targeting aggravates the chilling effects, and the lack of individual control over personal information. And large-scale data storage brings risks, such as data breaches. Compliance with the data minimisation principle could mitigate such privacy problems. Policymakers should explicitly codify that the data subject's consent does not legitimise disproportionate data processing. Such a rule could remind firms that consent does not give them carte blanche to collect personal information at will, and that a DPA could intervene if they did.

Perhaps the law could prohibit storing data for behavioural targeting longer than a set period of, to give an example, two days. Such a hard and fast rule would provide more legal certainty than the general data minimisation principle. Compared to estimating when the data minimisation principle requires deletion, complying with a maximum retention period of two days is easy for firms. As an aside, it is unclear whether storing tracking data for longer than a few days helps much to improve the click-through rate on ads.[149]

Data protection law's transparency principle can be interpreted as a prohibition of surreptitious data processing. Hence, while the last section discussed the transparency principle as a means to empower the individual, the principle could also be seen as more prohibitive. With some behavioural targeting practices, it would be hard for a website publisher to comply with data protection law's transparency requirements, even if it tried its best. For example, some ad networks allow other ad networks to buy access to individuals (identified through cookies or other identifiers) by bidding on an automated auction.[150] In such situations, the website publisher does not know in advance which ad networks will display ads on its site, and which ad networks will track its website visitors. In data protection parlance: the publisher does not know who the joint data controllers are.[151] Neither does the publisher know for which purposes the ad networks will use the data they collect. As noted, the Directive obliges data controllers to provide a data subject information about their identity, the processing purpose, and all other information that is necessary to guarantee fair processing.[152] Therefore, it is hard to see how the publisher could comply with the law's transparency requirements. If a publisher cannot give data subjects the information that is required by the Data Protection Directive, the processing is not allowed—and should not be allowed. Policymakers

---

[148] ibid, Art 6(1)(c) and Arts 6(1)and (e). In data protection literature, authors tend to speak of data minimisation. One could also speak of proportionality.

[149] See KJ Strandburg, 'Free Fall: The Online Market's Consumer Preference Disconnect' (2013) University of Chicago Legal Forum 95, 104–05.

[150] C Castelluccia, L Olejnik and T Minh-Dung, 'Selling Off Privacy at Auction' (2013) *Inria*, www.inrialpes.fr/planete/people/lukasz/rtbdesc.html.

[151] The Working Party says ad networks and website publishers are often joint data controllers, as they jointly determine the purposes and means of the processing. See: Article 29 Working Party, 'Opinion 2/2010 on Online Behavioural Advertising' (WP 171) 22 June 2010, 11.

[152] Arts 10 and 11 of the Data Protection Directive (see section IV, B of this chapter). See also: art 5(3) of the e-Privacy Directive.

should make more explicit that processing is prohibited, unless firms can comply with the transparency principle.

Data protection law has a stricter regime for 'special categories of data', such as data revealing race, political opinions, health, or sex life. The use of special categories of data for behavioural targeting and other types of direct marketing is prohibited, or, depending on the national implementation law, only allowed after the data subject's 'explicit' consent.[153] Strictly enforcing the existing rules on special categories of data could reduce privacy problems such as chilling effects. Let us take health data as an example. People might be hesitant to look for medical information on the web if they fear leaking information about their medical condition. The rules on special categories of data could be interpreted in such a way that the collection context is taken into account. For instance, arguably tracking people's visits to websites with medical information should be seen as the processing of special categories of data, as firms could infer data regarding health from such tracking information.[154] Furthermore, policymakers should consider banning the use of any health related data for behavioural targeting. The privacy risks involved in using health data for behavioural targeting outweigh the possible societal benefits from such practices.

The law could also prohibit take-it-or-leave-it choices in some circumstances or contexts.[155] For instance, public service broadcasters often receive public funding, and they have a special role in informing people. But if people fear their behaviour is being monitored, they might forego the use of public service media.[156] To reduce such chilling effects, policymakers should prohibit public service broadcasters to use tracking walls or similar take-it-or-leave-it choices. Policymakers could also go one step further, and prohibit all third party tracking for behavioural targeting on public service media. More generally it does not seem appropriate for public sector websites to allow third party tracking for behavioural targeting—even when people consent. It is not evident why the public sector should facilitate tracking people's behaviour for commercial purposes. Therefore, policymakers should consider prohibiting all tracking for behavioural targeting on public sector websites.

i. Using Transaction Costs Strategically

Policymakers could also use an intermediate option between default rules that aim to empower people and mandatory protective rules. Policymakers could use

---

[153] Art 8 of the Data Protection Directive.
[154] See CJEU, Case C-101/01 *Lindqvist* [2003] ECR I-12971, para 50: 'the expression "data concerning health" ... must be given a wide interpretation'.
[155] See on the importance of context for privacy: H Nissenbaum, *Privacy in Context: Technology, Policy, and the Integrity of Social Life* (Redwood City, Stanford Law Books, 2010).
[156] See N Helberger, 'Freedom of Expression and the Dutch Cookie-Wall' (2013) Institute for Information Law, www.ivir.nl/publications/helberger/Paper_Freedom_of_expression.pdf.

transaction costs strategically.[157] As noted, marketers understand the importance of transaction costs—and sometimes use them strategically. Opting out of behavioural targeting often takes more effort than opting in. On the website Youronlinechoices, managed by the Interactive Advertising Bureau, it takes three clicks and a waiting period to opt out of receiving behaviourally targeted ads.[158] In principle, policymakers could do something similar.

For example, policymakers could strengthen a nudge that consists of setting a default by adding transaction costs, thereby making the default stickier.[159] Perhaps one mouse click could be required to give consent to relatively innocuous kinds of tracking. Three mouse clicks could be required for more worrying practices. 'Sticky defaults', says Ayres, 'should be thought of as an intermediate category falling between ordinary defaults and traditional mandatory rules'.[160] Transaction costs could come in different shades, to introduce different degrees of stickiness for the default. In theory the law could require a 30 second waiting period, a phone call, or a letter by registered mail to opt in to certain practices.[161]

But caution is needed if policymakers consider adding friction to consent procedures in the area of behavioural targeting. A legal regime that adds transaction costs and allows firms to offer take-it-or-leave-it choices could lead to an unpleasant situation. Website publishers could use tracking walls, including if the lawmaker required three mouse clicks for consent. People would not enjoy clicking three times 'I agree' if they want to visit a website, and accept they have to agree to tracking. With that caveat, the conclusion still stands: the distinction between mandatory rules and opt-in systems (default rules) is not a black and white issue. In principle policymakers have a range of options.

In conclusion, enforcing and tightening the data protection principles could help to protect privacy in the area of behavioural targeting. An important topic that falls outside this chapter's scope is how enforcement of European data protection law could be improved, in particular when firms are based outside Europe.[162] Anyhow, enforcing data protection law may not be enough to protect privacy in the area of behavioural targeting. If society is better off when certain behavioural

---

[157] Thanks to Oren Bar-Gill for introducing me to this idea.

[158] In a non-scientific test, I had to wait 45 seconds. First I had to choose a country (click 1), then I had to click on 'your ad choices' (click 2). Next I had to wait until the website contacted the participating ad networks. Then I could opt out of receiving targeted advertising (click 3). For several ad networks the website gave an error message (Youronlinechoices www.youronlinechoices.com).

[159] If a nudge is made stronger by using transaction costs strategically, it might not count as a 'nudge' anymore, since it is not 'easy and cheap to avoid' (CR Sunstein and RH Thaler, *Nudge: Improving Decisions about Health, Wealth, and Happiness* (New Haven, Yale University Press, 2008) 6). I will leave this complication aside.

[160] I Ayres, 'Regulating Opt Out: An Economic Theory of Altering Rules' (2012) 121 *Yale Law Journal* 2032, 2087.

[161] See for a discussion: LE Willis, 'Why Not Privacy by Default?' (2013) 29 *Berkeley Technology Law Journal* 61, 121–28.

[162] See European Agency for Fundamental Rights, 'Data Protection in the European Union: The Role of National Data Protection Authorities' (2010) fra.europa.eu/sites/default/files/fra_uploads/815-Data-protection_en.pdf.

targeting practices do not happen, policymakers should consider banning them. Agreeing on prohibitions would be hard. But that should not be a reason to ignore this legal tool.

VI. CONCLUSION

To protect privacy in the area of behavioural targeting, the European Union mainly relies on the consent requirement for the use of tracking technologies in the e-Privacy Directive, and on general data protection law. With informed consent requirements, the law aims to empower people to make choices in their best interests. But behavioural studies cast doubt on the effectiveness of such an approach.

There is no silver bullet to improve privacy protection in this area. While current regulation emphasises empowerment and informed consent, without much reflection on practical issues, I argue for a combined approach of protecting and empowering people. To improve individual empowerment, the data protection rules should be tightened, and should be enforced more strictly. For example, long unreadable privacy policies should not be accepted. Aiming for empowerment will not suffice to protect privacy. Nevertheless, some improvement must be possible, as today personal data are generally captured and used without meaningful transparency or consent.

Policymakers could also try to nudge Internet users towards disclosing less data. For instance, policymakers could require firms to obtain the individual's opt-in consent for tracking. The discussion about privacy defaults has been going on for the past 25 years in Europe. Marketers have argued that they should be allowed to use opt-out systems to obtain 'implied' consent for direct marketing, and, more recently, for tracking cookies. In line with legal doctrine, European Data Protection Authorities say consent requires an expression of will, which generally calls for opt-in procedures. The debate essentially concerns the direction of a nudge: who benefits from the status quo bias, the firm or the data subject? However, such privacy nudges run into problems. As long as the law allows firms to offer take-it-or-leave-it choices, firms can easily persuade people to agree to tracking.

I argue that policymakers should focus more on protecting people. While the role of informed consent in data protection law is important, that role is limited at the same time. People cannot waive data the safeguards of protection law, or contract around the rules. The protective data protection principles should be enforced more strictly. For example, even after consent, excessive data processing is not allowed—and should not be allowed. But enforcing data protection law will not be enough to protect privacy. In addition to data protection law, more specific rules regarding behavioural targeting are needed. And if society is better off if certain behavioural targeting practices do not happen, policymakers should consider banning them. After all, the European Court of Human Rights requires privacy protection that is 'practical and effective, not theoretical and illusory'.[163]

---

[163] ECtHR *Christine Goodwin v UK* App no 28957/95 (2002) 35 EHRR 18, para 74.

9

EU Consumer Protection and Behavioural Sciences: Revolution or Reform?

ANNE-LISE SIBONY AND GENEVIÈVE HELLERINGER[*]

I. INTRODUCTION

CONSUMER LAW IS one of the first areas where lawyers have become aware of the relevance of behavioural insights.[1] One reason is that this relevance is striking: it does not take an expert in psychology to notice that many of the existing rules in the field of consumer protection are written with a fictional consumer in mind, one who reads labels, takes the time to scrutinise contracts and check the terms and conditions.

---

[*] The authors would like to thank Iris Demoulin and Audrey Zians for excellent research assistance.
[1] C Camerer et al, 'Regulation for Conservatives: Behavioral Economics and the Case for "Asymmetric Paternalism"' (2003) 151 *University of Pennsylvania Law Review* 1211; SI Becher, 'Behavioral Science and Consumer Standard Form Contracts' (2007) 68 *Louisiana Law Review* 117; R Incardona and C Poncibo, 'The Average Consumer, the Unfair Commercial Practices Directive, and the Cognitive Revolution' (2007) 30 *Journal of Consumer Policy* 21; F Rischkowsky and T Döring, 'Consumer Policy in a Market Economy: Considerations from the Perspective of the Economics of Information, the New Institutional Economics as well as Behavioural Economics' (2008) 31 *Journal of Consumer Policy* 285; E Avgoulea, 'The Global Financial Crisis and the Disclosure Paradigm in European Financial Regulation: The Case for Reform' (2009) 6 *European Company and Financial Law Review* 440; O Ben-Shahar, 'The Myth of the "Opportunity to Read" in Contract Law' (2009) 1 *European Review of Contract Law* 1; O Bar-Gill and F Ferrari, 'Informing Consumers about Themselves' (2010) 3 *Erasmus Law Review* 93; SI Becher and E Unger-Aviram, 'The Law of Standard Form Contracts: Misguided Intuitions and Suggestions for Reconstruction' (2010) 8 *DePaul Business & Commercial Law Journal* 199; O Ben-Shahar and CE Schneider, 'The Failure of Mandated Disclosure' (2010) 159 *University of Pennsylvania Law Review* 647; G Low, 'The (Ir)Relevance of Harmonization and Legal Diversity to European Contract Law: A Perspective from Psychology' (2010) 2 *European Review of Private Law* 285; H Luth, *Behavioural Economics in Consumer Policy: The Economic Analysis of Standard Terms in Consumer Contracts Revisited* (Antwerp, Intersentia, 2010); M Faure and H Luth, 'Behavioural Economics in Unfair Contract Terms: Cautions and Considerations' (2011) 34 *Journal of Consumer Policy* 337; S Issacharoff, 'Disclosure, Agents, and Consumer Protection' (2011) 167 *Journal of Institutional and Theoretical Economics* 56; V Mak, 'Standards of Protection: In Search of the "Average Consumer" of EU Law in the Proposal for a Consumer Rights Directive' (2011) 19 *European Review of Private Law* 25; HW Micklitz, LA Reisch and K Hagen, 'An Introduction to the Special Issue on "Behavioural Economics, Consumer Policy, and Consumer Law"' (2011) 34 *Journal of Consumer Policy* 271;

Behavioural sciences bring a language that is apt to describe what is wrong with the law. The language of science allows human foibles that everyone has experienced to become part of the serious discussion about the law. This is particularly true in consumer law for two reasons. First, consumer law focuses on individual behaviour (rather than corporate behaviour), which makes cognitive psychology directly relevant to the law.[2] Second, consumer law is intrinsically paternalistic in

---

G Spindler, 'Behavioural Finance and Investor Protection Regulations' (2011) 34 *Journal of Consumer Policy* 315; J Trzaskowski, 'Behavioural Economics, Neuroscience, and the Unfair Commercial Practises Directive' (2011) 34 *Journal of Consumer Policy* 377; WH van Boom, 'Price Intransparency, Consumer Decision Making and European Consumer Law' (2011) 34 *Journal of Consumer Policy* 359; O Bar-Gill, *Seduction by Contract: Law, Economics and Psychology in Consumer Markets* (Oxford, Oxford University Press, 2012); N Eyal, 'Informed Consent' in EN Zalta (ed), *Stanford Encyclopedia of Philosophy* (Stanford, Stanford University, Fall 2012); V Mak and J Braspenning, '*Errare humanum est*: Financial Literacy in European Consumer Credit Law' (2012) 35 *Journal of Consumer Policy* 307; C Ryan, 'Against Notice Skepticism in Privacy (and Elsewhere)' (2012) 87 *Notre Dame Law Review* 1027; A Salazar, 'Libertarian Paternalism and the Danger of Nudging Consumers' (2012) 23 *King's Law Journal* 51; A Scholes, 'Behavioural Economics and the Autonomous Consumer' (2012) 14 *Cambridge Yearbook of European Legal Studies* 297; N Helberger, *Forms Matter: Informing Consumers Effectively*, study commissioned by BEUC (European Consumer Organisation, 2013); J Malbon, 'Consumer Strategies for Avoiding Negative Online Purchasing Experiences: A Qualitative Study' (2013) 20 *Competition & Consumer Law Journal* 249; A Tor, 'Some Challenges Facing a Behaviorally-Informed Approach to the Directive on Unfair Commercial Practices' in T Tóth (ed), *Unfair Commercial Practices: The Long Road to Harmonized Law Enforcement* (Budapest, Pázmány Press, 2013) 9–18; O Bar-Gill and O Ben-Shahar, 'Regulatory Techniques in Consumer Protection: A Critique of European Consumer Contract Law' (2013) 50 *CML Rev* 109; H Beale, 'What Do Consumers Need Protection From?' (The Image(s) of the 'Consumer' in EU Law: Legislation, Free Movement and Competition Law conference in Oxford, UK, 27–28 March 2014); J Luzak, 'To Withdraw or Not to Withdraw? Evaluation of the Mandatory Right of Withdrawal in Consumer Distance Selling Contracts Taking Into Account Its Behavioural Effects on Consumers' (2014) 37 *Journal of Consumer Policy* 91; J Luzak, 'Passive Consumers vs the New Online Disclosure Rules of the Consumer Rights Directive' (2014) working paper, ssrn.com/abstract=2553877, forthcoming as a chapter in M Loos and I Samoy (eds), *Ius Commune: European and Comparative Law series* (Cambridge, Intersentia); K Purnhagen and E Van Herpen, 'Can Bonus Packs Mislead Consumers? An Empirical Assessment of the ECJ's Mars Judgment and its Potential Impact on EU Marketing Regulation' (2014) Wageningen Working Papers Series in Law and Governance 2014/07, papers.ssrn.com/sol3/papers.cfm?abstract_id=2503342; A Pape, 'Miscounselling in the German Insurance Market: Utility-Orientated Implications for the Meaning of Miscounselling' (2014) 37 *Journal of Consumer Policy* 561; O Ben-Shahar and CE Schneider, *More than You Wanted to Know: The Failure of Mandated Disclosure* (Princeton, Princeton University Press, 2014); AL Sibony, 'Can EU Consumer Law Benefit from Behavioural Insights? An Analysis of the Unfair Practices Directive' (2014) 6 *European Review of Private Law* 901; E Tscherner, 'Can Behavioral Research Advance Mandatory Law, Information Duties, Standard Terms and Withdrawal Rights?' (2014) 1 *Austrian Law Journal* 144; A Schwartz 'Regulating for Rationality' (2014) working paper, papers.ssrn.com/sol3/papers.cfm?abstract_id=2520017, forthcoming in *Stanford Law Review*; M Engel and J Stark, 'Buttons, Boxes, Ticks, and Trust: On the Narrow Limits of Consumer Choice' in K Mathis (ed), *European Perspectives on Behavioural Law and Economics, Economic Analysis of Law in European Legal Scholarship*, vol 2 (Dordrecht, Springer, 2015) 107; G Helleringer, 'Retail Investors and Disclosures Requirements' in K Mathis (ed), *European Perspectives on Behavioural Law and Economics*, vol 2 (Dordrecht, Springer, 2015) 193; I Ayres and A Schwartz, 'The No-Reading Problem in Consumer Contract Law' (2015) 66 *Stanford Law Review* 545.

[2] This is not to say that psychology is not relevant to analyse corporate behaviour, as, for example in the field of antitrust. The point is only that the relationship between cognitive and emotional traits of managers and corporate decision is more complex than in the case of a decision made by an individual consumer because other factors come into play (eg, the collective nature of decision-making, rules and norms of the organisation). 'Can behavioral antitrust explain the behaviour of

that it seeks to protect consumers from making decisions deemed bad for them and offers remedy when they do.[3]

The relevance of behavioural insights to consumer protection is universal and has already been largely pointed out in US academic literature. However, EU consumer law presents a number of specific features that shape the debate on whether and how legal rules could incorporate more behavioural wisdom.[4] A first difference with the US debates is that, when it comes to consumer protection, paternalism is not a hot issue. In Europe, very few authors feel the need to criticise or, as the case may be, justify paternalism.[5] In consumer law particularly, paternalism goes back such a long way in the national traditions of some of the founding Member States that it is hardly questioned. Therefore, the debate is not whether behavioural sciences provide evidence that is robust and general enough to justify paternalistic interventions but rather, given an avowedly paternalistic but arguably ineffective system of consumer protection, how a more behavioural approach could make EU law more relevant and European consumers better off. The second singularly European element has to do with the reasons why EU consumer law has evolved to an apparent anti-model of behavioural regulation, featuring a much-criticised 'cornucopia of mandatory information requirements'.[6] These differences require serious consideration because they relate to the very *raison d'être* of EU law, namely, the realisation of an internal market. The objective of building an internal market is not a relic that is worshiped as an act of devotion to the founding fathers of the Union. It is still very much on the agenda, as evidenced by the fact that the 'Digital Single Market' is a priority for the new Commission.[7]

---

firms?' is one of the unanswered questions identified by Reeves, see AP Reeves, 'Behavioral Antitrust: Unanswered Questions on the Horizon' (2010) June *The Antitrust Source* 1; M Amstrong and S Huck, 'Behavioral Economics as Applied to Firms: A Primer' (2010) 6 *Competition Policy International* 3. More generally, on behavioural antitrust, see AP Reeves and ME Stucke, 'Behavioral Antitrust' (2010) 86 *Indiana Law Journal* 1527; JC Cooper and WE Kovacic, 'Behavioral Economics and its Meaning for Antitrust Agency Decision Making' (2012) 8 *Journal of Law, Economics & Policy* 779; A Tor, 'Understanding Behavioral Antitrust' (2013) 92 *Texas Law Review* 573 and, from a European perspective, A Heinemann, 'Behavioural Antitrust: A "More Realistic Approach" to Competition Law' in K Mathis (ed), *European Perspectives on Behavioural Law and Economics*, vol 2 (Dordrecht, Springer, 2015) 211.

[3] We agree with Kerber that the normative issue of paternalism ought to be distinguished from the technical contribution of behavioural insights to better rule design, which can exist irrespective of the degree of paternalism of public intervention. W Kerber, 'Soft Paternalismus und Verbraucherpolitik' (2014) 40 *List Forum für Wirtschafts- und Finanzpolitik* 274. Nonetheless, in the debate to date, the association of behavioural insights with paternalism has been a strong one and this helps explain the focus on consumer law in the law and behavioural sciences literature.

[4] On the specificity of EU law vis-à-vis US law, see JQ Whitman, 'Consumerism Versus Producerism: A Study in Comparative Law' (2007) 117 *Yale Law Journal* 407 and HW Micklitz, 'The Politics of Behavioural Economics', 31 January 2015 (unpublished manuscript on file with the authors).

[5] This is not specific to consumer law. See more generally ch 14 in this volume by Alemanno and Sibony.

[6] Bar-Gill and Ben-Shahar (n 1) 113.

[7] J-C Juncker, 'A New Start for Europe: My Agenda for Jobs, Growth, Fairness and Democratic Change—Political Guidelines for the next European Commission', 15 July 2014, ec.europa.eu/priorities/docs/pg_en.pdf, 5.

This European imperative creates a specific set of constraints. Any reflection on a behavioural turn of EU consumer protection must therefore engage with the issue of free movement.

In this chapter, we do not review once more what behavioural insights are relevant to consumer law or why. Many articles have done this very well both in general[8] and with respect to specific issues.[9] It is now familiar to lawyers that consumers, as any ordinary mortals, use mental shortcuts to make decisions, rely on intuition (System 1) rather than deliberation (System 2), and are subject to inertia and hyperbolic discounting of future costs.[10] Our focus is on how behavioural insights are actually being incorporated and could be incorporated in existing or new rules.[11] Behavioural scholars sometimes present EU consumer law as archaic and counter-productive,[12] which spreads the view that a behavioural turn would constitute a revolution for EU consumer law. We do not subscribe to this view. We agree with the critics that behavioural insights helpfully shed a crude light on EU consumer law as it stands and assist in understanding why the law does not offer effective protection. However, our claim is that integration of behavioural insights will not constitute a revolution because existing EU law already contains the seeds of a behaviourally sound approach. Behavioural insights are not altogether ignored in the law as it stands, but they are often not well implemented. Reform rather than revolution can be contemplated. The issue with viewing the behavioural turn as a revolution is that, as well as having an unpleasant ring to most lawyers, a revolution is also unlikely, certainly in the EU context. This is due to the EU having a long tradition of *petits pas*,[13] and its legislative processes necessitating a high degree of consensus among institutions and Member States.

---

[8] Luth (2010) (n 1) 48–55 on information overload, risk perception, self-serving biases, status quo biases, framing, anchoring, and bounded willpower; Tscherner (n 1).

[9] See Becher (n 1) on cognitive dissonance, confirmation bias and low ball; Faure and Luth (n 1) on information overload, dread factor, availability heuristics, endowment effect, and overconfidence; Luzak, 'To Withdraw Or Not To Withdraw?' (n 1) on how status quo bias, endowment effect, loss aversion, regret avoidance, and the sunk cost fallacy could explain why consumers do not make use of their withdrawal rights.

[10] For a non-technical presentation: D Kahneman, *Thinking, Fast and Slow* (London, Allen Lane, 2011).

[11] The instruments we review in this article are: Council Directive 93/13/EEC of 5 April 1993 on unfair terms in consumer contracts [1993] OJ L95/29 (UCTD); Directive 2000/31/EC of 8 June 2000 on certain legal aspects of information society services, in particular electronic commerce, in the internal market [2000] OJ L178/1 (E-Commerce Directive); Directive 2005/29/EC of 11 May 2005 concerning unfair business-to-consumer commercial practices in the internal market [2005] OJ L149/22 (UCPD); Directive 2008/48/EC of 23 April 2008 on credit agreements for consumers [2008] OJ L133/66 (Credit Directive); Directive 2011/83/EU on consumer rights [2011] OJ L304/64 (CRD); and Regulation 531/2012 of 13 June 2012 on roaming on public mobile communications networks within the Union (recast) [2012] OJ L172/10 (Telecom Regulation). We will also refer to the now abandoned (at least in this form) proposed Regulation on a Common European Sales Law, COM/2011/0635 final (CESL).

[12] Bar-Gill and Ben-Shahar (n 1).

[13] Small steps. This phrase is often used to describe the method pragmatically advocated by Jean Monnet, one of the founding fathers of European integration.

The reflexion on law reform is timely as the Commission puts forward a legislative agenda of simplification[14] and seems keen to rely more on behavioural intelligence both in general and in the field of consumer law in particular.[15] In addition, the withdrawal of the project on European Consumer Sales Law (CESL) for revision,[16] while not linked to the behavioural critique the project received,[17] does open a new space for better behaviourally informed rule-making in relation to consumer protection. This could, in particular, concern cross-border online transactions, a priority for the new Commission in the framework of the Digital Single Market.[18]

In discussing these matters we begin, in section II, by laying the ground for the discussion by putting the current legitimacy crisis of EU consumer law in perspective. Specifically, we explain why EU law evolved to be an apparent anti-model of behavioural regulation and discuss whether the internal market constraints that still exist prevent a behavioural turn. We conclude that they do not. Building on this, section III deals with disclosure mandates and what to do next. The central feature of disclosure mandates in EU consumer law has been severely criticised in the light of behavioural findings and within this section we agree that they are over-used. We find that disclosure mandates, as a technique, can still serve a useful purpose and suggest how their use can be streamlined. We also point out that recent developments tend to make disclosures smarter and point to directions to pursue this evolution. Section IV deals with the core message of behavioural insights to policy makers: 'make it simple'. We find evidence of an intention to simplify which predates the current commitment of the Commission to make simplification a priority, but highlight that efforts to simplify have led to half-baked solutions that are not simple enough. EU attempts at simplifying various

---

[14] Commission Work Programme 2015, COM (2014) 910 final, 4.

[15] This commitment to behavioural policy-making is expressed in 'Legacy Document Consumer Policy 2010-2014' (Commissioner Mimica), ec.europa.eu/archives/commission_2010-2014/mimica/docs/legacy_consumer_report_2010-2014.pdf, 7. On the new behavioural intelligence unit (serving the Commission in general), see in this volume ch 14 by A Alemanno and AL Sibony. Regarding consumer policy in particular, the former Directorate General for Health and Consumer Protection (DG Sanco) has been a for-runner in conducting behavioural studies to prepare policy initiative and fostering behavioural literacy within the EU institutions. The transfer of consumer policy to DG Justice has not affected the practice of commissioning behavioural studies. Available studies can be found at: ec.europa.eu/consumers/consumer_evidence/index_en.htm. See also: 'Study on the Effects on Consumer Behaviour of Online Sustainability Information Displays' (2014): ec.europa.eu/digital-agenda/en/news/study-effects-consumer-behaviour-online-sustainability-information-displays-final-report-and; C Codagnone et al, 'Study on Online Gambling and Adequate Measures for the Protection of Consumers of Gambling Services' (2014): ec.europa.eu/internal_market/gambling/docs/initiatives/140714-study-on-online-gambling-final-report_en.pdf.

[16] Commission work programme for 2015, 'A New Start' Annex 2: List of withdrawals or modifications of pending proposals, COM (2014) 910 final, 12. The reason given for the revising the project is to 'fully unleash the potential of e-commerce in the Digital Single Market'.

[17] Several Member States were opposed to it on other grounds and it was not possible to find a majority in the Council. For a broad analysis of constitutionally grounded criticism of the European private law harmonisation project, see L Niglia, *The Struggle for European Private Law: A Critique of Codification* (Oxford, Hart Publishing, 2015).

[18] See n 7 and ec.europa.eu/digital-agenda/en/digital-single-market.

aspects of consumer life represents a behaviourally sound intuition but appears badly implemented notably because the wrong targets have been chosen for simplification. In this regard, we identify the main issue to be the reluctance on the part of the EU legislator to let go of the autonomous choice ideal regarding issues most consumers do not care about, such as the law applicable to the contract. We conclude that the heavy choice protection machinery should only be deployed for choices that do matter to consumers.

II. RECONCILING INTERNAL MARKET AND BEHAVIOURAL LEGITIMACY

The behavioural critique strikes EU consumer law at its heart by questioning its privileged regulatory approach: 'the information paradigm'.[19] More precisely, two canonical expressions of this paradigm have been the object of an unforgiving confrontation with psychological insights. First the 'average consumer' standard is shown to be inconsistent with the findings of behavioural research.[20] Second, critics ridicule information disclosure requirements,[21] which have constituted the tool of choice in EU consumer policy since its incipiency. We will only briefly recall the argument on the first point and focus on disclosures.

The average consumer standard paints a picture of the consumer that is largely at odds with empirical evidence.[22] He[23] is deemed to have enough slack in his mental bandwidth[24] to be 'reasonably well-informed and reasonably observant and circumspect'.[25] This wise shopper is not seriously affected by the no-reading tendency;[26] he will go online to check what is behind the small prints in an alluring advertisement[27] and read food labels.[28] He does not trust appearances and is not easily

---

[19] The 'information paradigm' characterises EU consumer law since it came into existence. In 1975, the first work programme on consumer policy was entitled 'First Programme for a Consumer Protection and Information Policy'. See N Reich and HW Micklitz, 'Economic Law, Consumer Interests and EU Integration' in N Reich et al (eds), *European Consumer Law* (Cambridge, Intersentia, 2014) 1, 21; S Weatherill, *EU Consumer Law and Policy* (Cheltenham, Edward Elgar, 2013) ch 4.

[20] Incardona and Poncibo (n 1), Mak (n 1), Helberger (n 1) 7 et seq.

[21] Bar-Gill and Ben-Shahar (n 1).

[22] Purnhagen and Van Herpen (n 1).

[23] The European Court of Justice uses 'he' as a generic. We will maintain this convention throughout the chapter.

[24] We use here the terminology of S Mullainathan and E Shafir, *Scarcity: Why Having Too Little Means So Much* (New York, Times Book, 2013).

[25] Established case law since Case C-210/96 *Gut Springenheide*, EU:C:1998:369, para 31.

[26] Ayres and Schwartz (n 1).

[27] Case C-122/10 *Ving Sverige*, EU:C:2011:299, interpreting the Unfair Commercial Practices Directive in a sense that would lead the national court seized of the matter to hold that an advertisement published in a newspaper by a travel agency reading 'New York from 7 820 crowns' was not misleading. See especially paras 66 and 71 inviting the national court to take into account elements published by the trader outside of the advertisement itself, for example on its website.

[28] Case C-51/94 *Commission v Germany*, EU:C:1995:352, para 34, holding that consumers who care about ingredients (contained in a sauce) read labels.

fooled by colours[29] or size of promotional markings on a package.[30] We know from behavioural studies that there is a large discrepancy between this idealised average EU consumer and the actual behaviour adopted by the average EU consumers.[31]

Certainly, when exploring disclosure mandates, it is undeniable that EU legislation, as it stands, is a textbook example of a system of consumer protection relying fundamentally on provision of information. Numerous mandatory disclosures illustrate an apparent act of faith that EU consumers are capable of making informed decisions so long as the relevant—if abundant—information is presented to them in 'a comprehensible manner'.[32] EU law embraces the 'opportunity to read' doctrine fully and, as such, disregards the no-reading problems.[33]

Just like laws of other jurisdictions, EU consumer protection law predates the behavioural awareness that characterises our time. There is therefore an obvious chronological explanation to why EU law is not more behaviourally savvy. But chronology is not the whole story. The recent 2011 Directive on consumer rights lists no less than 20 items of information, which have to be provided to the consumer before an online contract is concluded.[34] Disclosure mandates endure because they have always had a particular appeal in the European context.

First, information requirements appeared historically as a legitimate tool and, in some situations, the only tool available to EU institutions to pursue market integration. Consumer protection laws were initially national and, because they differed across Member States, they created obstacles to free movement. An early illustration may be found in *Rau*.[35] Belgian regulation mandated that margarine

---

[29] In Case C–51/94, ibid, the Court decided that the artificial yellow colour of a sauce sold as 'Béarnaise sauce' would not induce consumers to think the sauce was prepared according to the traditional recipe, with eggs and butter, and that, consequently, it would be enough to mention the ingredients on the label. The German regulation mandating a salient mention of non-traditional ingredients was thus declared incompatible with the internal market (failing the necessity test).

[30] In Case C-470/93 *Mars*, EU:C:1995:224, the Court held that 'Reasonably circumspect consumers may be deemed to know that there is not necessarily a link between the size of publicity markings relating to an increase in a product's quantity and the size of that increase'. For an empirical and legal critical analysis of this holding, see Purnhagen and Van Herpen (n 1). In many cases, the Court left it to the national courts to decide whether there was a genuine risk of confusion on the part of the relevant consumers and therefore a need for protection. See, eg Case C-220/98 *Estée Lauder*, EU:C:2000:8, where the Court held that EU law does not preclude the application of national legislation which prohibits the importation and marketing of a cosmetic product whose name incorporates the term 'lifting' in cases where the average consumer, reasonably well informed and reasonably observant and circumspect, is misled by that name, believing it to imply that the product possesses characteristics which it does not have (para 32). In all this line of cases, the Court instructs the national court to take into account the expectations of the average consumer. See, eg Case C-465/98 *Darbo*, EU:C:2000:184, para 20 and case law cited.

[31] Incardona and Poncibo (n 1); Mak (n 1).

[32] See Arts 5, 6 and 10 of Electronic Commerce Directive, Arts 7 and 17 of UCPD, Arts 4, 5, 6, and 21 of Directive on credit agreements for consumers; Art 9 of the project for a CESL; Arts 4, 14, and 15 of the Telecom Regulation; Arts 5 and 6 of the CRD. All Directives cited n 11.

[33] In addition to Ayres and Schwartz (n 1), see Becher and Unger-Aviram (n 1) and Y Bakos et al, 'Does Anyone Read the Fine Print? Consumer Attention to Standard Form Contracts' (2014) 43 *Journal of Legal Studies* 1, 1–35.

[34] Art 6 CRD (n 11).

[35] Case 261/81 *Rau v De Smedt*, EU:C:1982:382.

be sold in cubic packaging in order to avoid consumers confusing it with butter, which was sold in rectangular packaging. The rule created an obstacle to the marketing, in Belgium, of German margarine packaged in plastic tubs having the shape of a truncated cone. Because of the obstacle it caused, the Belgian regulation on margarine was found to violate the Treaty provisions on free movement of goods. According to the Belgian Government, the regulation at issue sought to prevent confusion and help consumers distinguish with ease between butter and margarine when shopping. Consumer protection was in principle a valid justification,[36] but Belgium could not establish the proportionality of the measure. The Court held that it would have been possible to achieve the legitimate aim of protecting consumers by providing them with the right information through labelling requirements. This option would have been less restrictive of trade because traders could have complied at a lesser cost by affixing a label on German margarine without changing the packaging.

This example illustrates a general virtue of information requirements in the perspective of achieving an internal market. For the Commission and for the Court, finding that consumers would be sufficiently protected by appropriate labelling had the advantage of helping market integration. At a time when empirical analysis was not around, Member States did not contest this approach by trying to show that information requirement were less effective than other measures. It is conceivable—though we confess lacking any relevant evidence backing this supposition—that, when consumers are used to receiving product information through the shape of a package, they expect information to come though the channels of vision and touch rather than in written form.[37] It is possible that consumers in this situation would make errors, at least temporarily, if, contrary to their expectations, the shape of packaging stopped being informative about the nature of the product and they had to read the label to find out what the product was. Evidence on the likelihood of such errors and learning time would have been relevant in *Rau*. Similarly, in other cases, empirical evidence, which was unavailable at the time, could very well have made a difference.[38] Had Member States been able

---

[36] Case 120/78 *Rewe-Zentral (Cassis de Dijon)*, EU:C:1979:42, para 8.

[37] The issue of whether packaging can indicate the nature of the product has been considered in cases about tri-dimensional trademarks. The shape of packaging has been held as capable of being indicative of the characteristics of the product. See Case C–218/01 *Henkel*, EU:C:2004:88, para 42, stating that it is for the fact-finder to 'the relationship between the packaging and the nature of the goods' (para 43). The presumption seems to be that shape of packaging is generally less distinctive than a sign. See to this effect Joined Cases C–456/01 P and C–457/01 P *Henkel*, para 46; Cases C–468/01 P to C–472/01 P, *Procter and Gamble v OHIM*, EU:C:2004:259, paras 56–57 where the Court added that regard must be had to 'the presumed *expectations* of an average consumer who is reasonably well-informed and reasonably observant and circumspect' (emphasis added). On the need to rely on '*specific and reliable data*', see Case C–299/99 *Philips*, EU:C:2002:377, para 65 (our emphasis).

[38] For a retrospective enquiry, see Purnhagen and Van Herpen (n 1). The authors replicated experimentally the problem which was at issue in *Mars* (n 30): did a marking '10% free' which occupied more than 10% of the surface of the packaging mislead consumers? Under German law, this was found misleading and prohibited, thus hampering the import in Germany of Mars bars manufactured in France, but the Court found that 'Reasonably circumspect consumers may be deemed to know

and willing to rely on behavioural studies at the time when all sorts of national consumer protection laws were litigated before the Court of Justice, the face of EU law might have been different. But history did not go that way. Based on precious little evidence that they would be effective enough to protect consumers, information requirements became the argument of choice to achieve negative integration.

The second reason consumer information became the tool of choice for positive integration is institutional in nature. Since the Community initially lacked any consumer policy competence, the first generation of consumer legislation was adopted using a legal basis for market integration which, until the Single European Act (1986), required unanimity in the Council. Under this framework, it was difficult to justify measures more intrusive than information regulation because Member States would object that the Community was acting *ultra vires*.[39] By the time the EU was later empowered to legislate in the field of consumer protection,[40] information requirements had become strongly embedded in the European consumer law culture. Disclosure mandates also had the advantage of not being disruptive of a national private law system, an important consideration since Member States have not welcomed EU involvement in the field of contract law. Until relatively recently, there were few reasons—besides common sense or disappointing results—to call information requirements into question. If anything, the preference for this regulatory technique was probably reinforced by the fact that economics had developed a language which provided theoretical justification for information requirements. If the 'market failure' consisted in 'asymmetries of information', the law could restore symmetry—and thereby well-functioning markets—by mandating that the better informed party (the trader) provides the less informed party (the consumer) with the relevant information. A scientific discourse gave legitimacy to a technique that primarily served market integration.[41]

This scientific legitimation of information regulation is now displaced by behavioural sciences. 'Regulating for information' is *passé* and the new challenge is to 'regulate for rationality'[42] or, put more simply, to help consumers overcome cognitive biases that may be exploited by traders. EU consumer law is going through a legitimacy crisis because it appears at odds with the newest science or, rather, with the science that has newly reached the circles where opinions on legitimacy of the law form. When the knowledge spreads that there is a science that has a *prima facie* claim to explain the phenomena that the law seeks to regulate, as is now the case

---

that there is not necessarily a link between the size of publicity markings relating to an increase in a product's quantity and the size of that increase' (para 24).

[39] European Commission, 'Consumer Policy in the European Community: An Overview' (1992): europa.eu/rapid/press-release_MEMO-92-68_en.htm.

[40] A specific legal basis for consumer protection was first introduced in the Maastricht Treaty in 1992 (Art 129A).

[41] For an analysis of how EU consumer law tracks the teachings of information economics, see Luth (n 1) 231 et seq.

[42] A Schwartz, 'Regulating for Rationality' (2014) Yale Law and Economics Research Paper No 517, papers.ssrn.com/sol3/papers.cfm?abstract_id=2520017, forthcoming in *Stanford Law Review*.

with behavioural sciences and consumer law, it becomes necessary for the law to acknowledge the relevance of scientific discourse. An analogy may help illustrate this point. Nowadays, it would be unacceptable for antitrust to ignore economics because it is commonly accepted that, however imperfect the science of economics, it does help explain competition.[43] Similarly, though with a time lag, there is a growing awareness that consumer law should not ignore psychology and behavioural economics, because they provide valuable insights on consumer behaviour.

European consumer law has exactly reached the stage when key institutional actors[44] and legal scholars active in the field of consumer law have become aware of the vast body of science pertaining to decision-making in general and to consumer decisions in particular. Even those commentators who are acquainted with this wealth of empirical studies through the condensed accounts offered in pop science books only, realise that EU law is, by and large, out of line with behavioural analysis.

There are normative implications to the introduction of behavioural insights into the legal discourse. These implications are indirect but real. They are indirect because behavioural sciences, unlike economics, are not associated with any particular normative agenda.[45] There are two reasons why behavioural accounts of consumer behaviour acquire a normative dimension. First, naming facts and pointing out their relevance for the law almost immediately translates as a prescription addressed to lawyers: if these facts are indeed relevant for the effectiveness of existing laws, the legal discourse *should* take them into account. This prescription is very difficult for lawyers to discard because doing so would amount to admitting that they do not care about the effects of rules. No policymaker and very few legal scholars—even in continental Europe—would subscribe to this view. The second reason why behavioural insights carry normative implications is because they redefine normality. Implicitly, the information paradigm defines what is expected of a 'good' average consumer. It is one who avails himself of the opportunity to read contract terms or, when he does not, accepts that it is fair that he should be bound by the small print he has not read. Psychology paints a very different picture of reality and, therefore, of normality. It is expected that consumers do not read contracts. This behaviour is not only predictable; it is also rational.[46] Here, psychology and economics converge to make us feel better about

---

[43] On the roots of the imperfect nature of economics, see D Hausman, *The Inexact and Separate Science of Economics* (Cambridge, Cambridge University Press, 1992).

[44] Regarding the Commission, see above n 15. On the consumers' side, the Bureau Européen des Unions de Consommateurs (BEUC), which as the European Federation of Consumer Associations is showing a growing interest in behavioural arguments. It has commissioned a study: N Helberger, 'Forms Matter: Informing Consumers Effectively' (2013), www.beuc.org/publication/reports (last visited 10 November 2014).

[45] Economic analysis presupposes that efficient allocation of resources/wealth maximisation is the goal. Some authors disagree with the view that behavioural sciences are normatively neutral. See HW Micklitz, 'The Politics of Behavioural Economics', 31 January 2015 (on file with the editors) and C McCrudden, 'Nudging and Human Dignity', VerfBlog, 6 January 2015, available at www.verfassungsblog.de/nudging-human-dignity/.

[46] About rational apathy, see Ben-Shahar, 'The Myth of the "Opportunity to Read"' (n 1).

reality and worse about the law that seems to ignore reality. The malaise has found its most vivid expression regarding disclosure requirements.

III. DISCLOSURE REQUIREMENTS: WHAT TO DO WITH THE CORNUCOPIA

In this section, our starting point is the critique of the EU cornucopia of mandatory disclosure requirements.[47] We agree with Bar-Gill and Ben-Shahar that information requirements, as they now exist in EU law, are largely ineffective. In the absence of available data, we are uncertain if they are as harmful as the two authors claim,[48] but we recognise that this is an empirical issue and we will leave it aside. Rather, we want to deal with the next issue: what to do now.[49] We tackle this question from a European perspective, which is somewhat different from the American context[50] when it comes to disclosure mandates.

Taking into account the current state of the internal market, we argue that throwing out the 'disclosure baby' with the bathwater would not be a good idea. Abandoning the favourite technique of EU law altogether is not only politically unrealistic, but would also be misconceived as some information requirements *are* helpful (A). What is required however is a shift of focus (B).

A. Information Disclosure as a Technique Should not be Abandoned

The first and strongest argument against disclosure mandates is that consumers do not read the information that is made available to them. Empirical evidence on the no-reading problem has been accumulating and has been much discussed.[51] It is not entirely one-sided. In Europe, the available data suggests that the non-reading phenomenon is extensive but not extreme, at least for contract terms.[52]

---

[47] Bar-Gill and Ben-Shahar (n 1).

[48] We do not dispute that compliance costs are passed on to consumers but wonder whether these costs are very large, notably because it is cheap to provide information online and there is quite a lot of guidance available for businesses on how to do so in order to comply with EU law. See Commission Guidance document (June 2014) ec.europa.eu/justice/consumer-marketing/files/crd_guidance_en.pdf and ECC-Sweden Guide (Nov 2014): www.konsumenteuropa.se/en/news-and-press-releases/pressmeddelanden/press-releases-2014/ecc-net-launches-a-guide-on-consumer-rights-for-online-traders/. Free advice is also available from EEC-Net (European network of consumer centre services).

[49] For a similar focus on positive proposals from a behavioural perspective, see Tscherner (n 1) 146.

[50] See chs 1 and 14 by A Alemanno and AL Sibony in this volume.

[51] Ben-Shahar and Schneider (2014) (n 1); Ayres and Schwartz (n 1); see also references cited by Luzak (2014) (n 1) 14, fn 62; F Marotta-Wurgler, 'Does Contract Disclosure Matter?' (2012) 168 *Journal of Institutional and Theoretical Economics* 94.

[52] We found no recent data on reading habits of labels. A Weser, 'Die informative Warenkennzeichnung: Eine Übersicht über den Stand der Praxis und der Literatur' (1977) 1(1) *Zeitschrift für Verbraucherpolitik*, 1977 80–89 at 85 mentions a Swedish study (in Swedish) going back to the 1970's. At the time, Sweden introduced one of the very early forms of information by labelling, the so-called

A 2010 Eurobarometer survey among consumers shopping online indicated that only 60 per cent of consumers do not read the terms and conditions.[53] In addition, it has been suggested (though not in a European context) that consumers are ready to read when they care.[54] This seems to leave a place for disclosure mandates on issues of special concern to consumers. In this regard there may be European specificities.

On many EU e-commerce websites there is important information missing, such as information about which country the site ships to. The information is crucial for a European e-shopper but its disclosure is not mandatory. As a result, it is often brought to the knowledge of the consumer only at the end of the purchase process in the frustrating form that the delivery address is rejected. Evidently, it is at the beginning of the process that the information should be given. If a website does not deliver goods in Belgium, a Belgium-based consumer has no interest in carefully selecting an item he cannot order. Here, the reader might think that this may be tough luck for consumers based in small countries but not a reason for more disclosure mandates. After all, if the consumers in question represent a sufficient buying power, the market should take care of their problem. The reality is that the market does not. This is precisely why the Commission is working on ways to overcome the 'home bias'.[55]

Our point is that, in the European context, mandatory disclosure is not always hypocritical. New mandates might even be useful. As the above example suggests, requiring e-commerce websites to make information about countries of delivery easily accessible from the very beginning of the navigation would make sense. The same goes for information about shipping cost for each country and accepted means of payments. Note that, unlike existing mandates, this would not be a pre-contractual requirement concerning information to be given to an individual consumer, but regulation of how and when commercial information must be made

---

'Möbel-Fakta', a mandatory labelling scheme for furniture. In a field study, it was found that only 30% of the shoppers noticed the labels at all, 20% could remember after the purchase that they had seen them, and only 3% reported that they had assessed the quality of the furniture with the help of the labels. Weser also cites another study on nutritional information in which 26.3% of the subjects paid attention to the label, 15.6% understood them, and 9.2% took them into account in their purchase decision. JR Lenahan et al, 'Consumer Reaction to Nutritional Labels on Food Products' (1973) *Journal of Consumer Affairs* 1–12. We would like to thank Philipp Hacker for bringing this survey and these studies to our attention.

[53] Special Eurobarometer No 342, 'Consumer Empowerment' (2011) ec.europa.eu/public_opinion/archives/ebs/ebs_342_en.pdf, pp 122-125. 27% declared that they did not read the terms and conditions of their contract and 30% that they did not read them carefully and completely. Allen and Overy, Online consumer research, 2011 found that 52% of the consumers in the six largest EU Member States never (5%) or only occasionally (47%) read the terms and conditions when purchasing online. Study cited by the Commission in the terms of reference for contract JUST/2011/JCIV/FW/0135/A4 (Testing of a Standardised Information Notice for Consumers on CESL, on file with authors).

[54] Becher and Unger-Aviram (n 1).

[55] The proportion of online shopping in Europe that is cross-border was only 12% in 2013, Digital Agenda Scoreboard 2014, ec.europa.eu/digital-agenda/en/news/scoreboard-2014-progress-report-digital-agenda-targets-2014, 3.

available to the public. More generally, the focus of disclosure mandates should not be restricted to content (eg list of countries). More attention should be given to context.

B. Shift of Focus

i. From Content to Context

Context matters.[56] This key lesson from behavioural sciences is not well reflected in EU consumer law as it stands. At present, the numerous provisions of EU law which mandate disclosure of information focus mainly on content (what must be disclosed) and language ('clear and comprehensible').[57]

Context is not completely ignored. For example, the extent of information that the trader must disclose varies in consideration of the medium used.[58] In particular, it is recognised that the same amount of information cannot be placed on a computer screen and on a telephone screen. For distance contracts (in practice B2C e-commerce), express consent of consumers is—happily—not necessary for paperless communication.[59] However, acknowledging that physical or digital reality creates constraints on communication constitutes a very minimal recognition of the importance of context. To be sure, law cannot take into account context of consumer decisions with the same level of granularity that psychology suggests is relevant. For example, it is not conceivable to have some legal rules for sunny days and others for rainy days, although it is established that weather influences purchasing behaviour.[60] But, between a recognition of the importance of context so limited that information overload is overlooked and an opening to context so wide that rules would dissolve, there is a middle ground that the EU legislator could realistically invest.[61]

Taking context into account in a meaningful manner may sometimes require empirical studies to inform the law, but not always. Presumptions based on common sense go some way as can be illustrated from the case law of EU courts. In trade mark cases for instance, the courts often need to assess whether the average consumer will find a sign distinctive. In this context, the General Court relies on (common sense) presumptions regarding the level of attention that a typical

---

[56] Helberger (n 1).
[57] See n 32.
[58] Arts 5(a) and 6(a) of CRD. The same is true in the context of appraising whether information is misleading under Art 7 UCPD (n 11).
[59] CRD (n 11) rt 8 and Commission Guidance document (June 2014) (n 48) 70 et seq.
[60] KB Murray et al, 'The Effect of Weather on Consumer Spending' (2010) 17 *Journal of Retailing and Consumer Services* 512.
[61] On information overload, see: G Miller, 'The Magical Number Seven, Plus or Minus Two: Some Limits on Our Capacity for Processing Information' (1956) 63 *Psychological Review* 81. See also G Howells, 'The Potential and Limits of Consumer Empowerment by Information' (2005) 32 *Journal of Law and Society* 349. For a discussion in the context of EU consumer law, see Tscherner (n 1) 148.

consumer will commit to a certain type of transaction. For example, regarding dishwasher tablets, the Court did not deem it necessary to request field data before it upheld the finding that 'the level of attention given by the average consumer to the shape and colours of washing machine and dishwasher tablets, being everyday goods, is not high'.[62] Similarly, EU legislation, despite its shortcomings, does not assume a constant level of attention of consumers. This is the rationale for requesting from traders that some items of information be made salient.[63]

EU disclosure mandates also accommodate some measure of adaptation to context based on presumptions, though occasionally not very convincing ones. An illustration can be found in the Consumer Rights Directive. The Directive requires Member States to make it mandatory for traders to provide 20 items of information to the consumer 'on paper or, if the consumer agrees, on another durable medium'.[64] As mentioned, this is certainly far too much information for the average consumers and it includes items consumers almost certainly do not care about, such as the geographical address at which the trader is established.[65] The point of interest for the present discussion is that, irrespective of its substantive requirements being behaviourally unwise, the Directive does take into account the fact that these requirements may not be practical in some contexts, for example, in the case of emergency plumbing services. This can be seen in the provision for a waiver of the mandatory disclosure requirement for 'off-premises contracts where the consumer has explicitly requested the services of the trader for the purpose of carrying out repairs or maintenance'. However, the Directive assumes too much when it provides that the waiver is only available for contracts of less than €200 (an optimistic estimate in the case of emergency plumbing services). It also creates a complex system as the waiver remains optional for Member States.[66] Member States can only opt in and adopt the waiver or opt out and have plumbers and other service providers carry boilerplate in their toolbox. There is an element of adaptation to context but in the form of a complex waiver from an ill-conceived substantive rule. A better course of action would be to take context into account at the stage of designing the disclosure mandate and keep implementation simple.

Timing is a dimension of context that is relatively neglected in existing legislation. When a piece of information is received, it is at least as important as

---

[62] Case T-337/99 *Henkel v OHIM*, EU:T:2001:221, para 48; Case C-342/97 *Lloyd Schuhfabrik Meyer*, EU:C:1999:323, para 26; Case T-30/00 *Henkel*, EU:T:2001:223, para 53 ; Case T-129/00 *Procter & Gamble*, EU:T:2001:231, para 59.

[63] CRD (n 11) art 8(2). The four items that have to be prominent are: i) the main characteristics of the goods or services; ii) the total price or monthly cost and additional charges or the way in which they will be calculated; iii) the duration of the contract or, if the contract is of indeterminate duration or is to be extended automatically, the conditions for terminating the contract; and iv) where applicable, the minimum duration of the consumer's obligations under the contract.

[64] CRD (n 11) art 7(4).

[65] CRD (n 11) art 6(1)(c). The consumer does care about the address where to send back items if he is not satisfied but that may be different from the address of the corporate seat of the seller, as is acknowledged by the CRD (art 6(1)(d) CRD).

[66] CRD (n 11) art 7(4).

whether it is received. Again, the time dimension is not completely ignored. This is obvious from the fact that many existing disclosure mandates are pre-contractual in nature. EU legislation states explicitly that information must be provided *before* the purchase[67] or, in the case of credit 'in good time before the consumer is bound by any credit agreement'.[68] Such focus on the pre-contractual stage is characteristic of the information paradigm: all information is given at the outset so as to allow the consumer to form an informed consent. Because consumers do not read the fine print, this is insufficient.

As discussed above, information about countries where goods are shipped should be given not just before the contract is concluded but be made easily accessible *earlier*, when a consumer starts browsing on an e-commerce website. The same goes for accepted means of payment.[69] Conversely, some information should be given to consumers *later*. It is much more useful to find the information necessary to return a good in the box rather than in a confirmation email received at the time the order was placed. As these examples illustrate, taking timing of information into account could be achieved relatively easily based on common sense observations and without much need for empirical evidence. It only takes a shift of focus on the part of the EU legislator.

In truth, this shift is already visible in some pieces of legislation. The Telecom Regulation, for example, recognises the importance of timing of information when it requires operators to send information on roaming charges by text message *every time* roaming services are used.[70] This is certainly justified because roaming rates are still relatively high in Europe and consumers tend to underestimate the cost of using the service. On the other hand, this example also illustrates the difficulty of getting context right in a legal rule when consumers form a heterogeneous group. In the case of roaming fees, frequent travellers presumably do not need the information and may be annoyed by text messages every time they cross an intra-EU border while infrequent travellers probably benefit from the reminder about roaming charges. However, the first category is certainly a minority so that the information on roaming charges is statistically important.[71] In addition, the cost imposed on more mobile consumers by annoying text messages does not seem great. The disclosure mandate therefore seems justified as it appears to be asymmetrically paternalistic.[72] Nonetheless, there is room for improvement. So long as

---

[67] Art 10 of E-Commerce Directive (n 11) arts 5 and 6 as well as Recital 34 of CRD (n 11) art 13 of CESL.

[68] Arts 5 and 6 of the Credit Directive (n 11).

[69] Commission Communication, 'Single Market Act II Together for New Growth' COM (2012) 573 final, 13.

[70] Art 15(2)(2). Telecoms Regulation (n 11) provides that 'roaming providers should provide their roaming customers, free of charge, with personalized tariff information on the charges applicable to those customers for data roaming services every time they initiate a data roaming service on entering another country'.

[71] O Bar-Gill, *Seduction by Contract* (Oxford, Oxford University Press, 2012) 37.

[72] Camerer et al (n 1).

roaming charges exist,[73] information on cost of use would be more meaningful to consumers than unit price, especially if given *in real time*.[74] Receiving a text giving the price of a cross-border call just *after* the call would make the consumer more aware of the cost of roaming than a per minute price given ex ante when they crossed the border. The same goes *a fortiori* for data roaming as price per megabyte are meaningless to all but the most IT savvy consumers.

In addition to taking better account of context in general, and timing in particular, EU disclosure mandates should also focus on what really matters.

ii. Focus on what Matters

An important idea emerging from behavioural sciences is that consumers cannot and do not want to make informed choice on everything.[75] We all have a limited bandwidth and save our precious mental resources for issues that matter to us. Ideal disclosures, therefore, are those that pertain to what consumers care about and only to that. It is not easy to translate this simple idea into legal design because rules are general while individuals differ as to what they care about. In this regard, it has been suggested that the power of big data could be harnessed to design personalised disclosures.[76] Selective and targeted information could be displayed and specific risks could be highlighted for each consumer, on the basis of his personal characteristics: regular user of certain services, above a certain age, etc. In the EU context, such personalised disclosure will raise thorny issues of data protection since explicit consent to the use of personal data is the basic principle.[77] How to regulate disclosure algorithms has not yet reached the legislative agenda.

A much simpler problem, where the solution is well within reach, is to identify items that all or most consumers in a given context (eg buying online) need protection from and will probably care about. As discussed above, examples of information which matter to a shopper include whether a website delivers where the consumer resides and whether he can pay with his credit card. For such items of probable interest to all, mandated disclosure seems reasonable. The issue is to take into account that consumers will not read much. In this regard, labelling of information makes sense.[78] The idea is to present information in a standardised manner making it easy for consumers to select those few items that are relevant to them.[79] Such a strategy can already be observed in the guidance document on the

---

[73] It is the intention of the Commission to ban them. 'Roaming charges in Europe have to disappear and they will disappear' writes Juncker in his political guidelines for the new Commission (n 7) 18.

[74] Bar-Gill makes the same suggestion in the US context. Bar-Gill (n 71) 245.

[75] CR Sunstein, *Choosing not to Choose: Understanding the Value of Choice* (Oxford, Oxford University Press, 2015).

[76] A Porat and L Starhilevitz, 'Personalizing Default Rules and Disclosures with Big Data' (2014) 112 *Michigan Law Review* 1417. C Sunstein, ibid, (n 75) Ch 6.

[77] Beale (n 1); FJ Zuiderveen Borgesius, 'Improving Privacy Protection in the Area of Behavioural Targeting' (PhD thesis, University of Amsterdam, 2014) and, by the same author, ch 8 in this volume.

[78] Ben-Shahar (n 1).

[79] ibid, 13.

Consumer Rights Directive where the Commission recommends a set of icons to signpost the various items of mandatory information.[80]

Further developments will need to consider the proposition that losses matter to consumers (more than gains). In this regard, it has been suggested that traders highlight potentially harmful terms and stress any departures from what consumers expect.[81] In addition, to counter over-optimism bias, traders should be required to put particular emphasis on what will happen if something occurs that the consumer will probably have over-discounted.[82] This could, for instance, take the form of a score calculated by reference to legally provided default rules: additional points would be credited for terms that are more pro-consumer than the default and points would be deducted for terms that are less protective than the default.[83] These recommendation seem to reflect the findings relating to loss aversion,[84] that a consumer will suffer more from giving up what he believes to be a standard right (if he has sufficiently well-formed expectations with regard to what his rights should be) than he would benefit from acquiring the limited right offered by the trader. There are two problems with this suggestion. The first is to ascertain consumers' expectations. The second is that it is not in the interest of traders to highlight losses. Recommendations therefore would probably be ineffective and the issue is whether the law should mandate that traders make consumers aware of the losses that the contract inflicts upon them. It may seem commendable in the perspective of protecting autonomy and informed consent but the case is less clear if we admit that consent is not informed and consumers do not want to give much attention to contract terms. We know that people are loss averse. We also know that people do not want to give attention to contract terms. What we do not know is which trade-off between information and tranquillity is preferable.[85] On this point, empirical studies would be very informative.

Mandating disclosure of information is certainly not a panacea, but it is not outright absurd. Consumers do need and do use information. To make good disclosure rules, there are three difficulties. The first is to avoid mandating information overload. The second is to take account of the context in which information will be used. The third is to address heterogeneous specific interests of consumers in particular pieces of information. EU law does not do a great job at tackling any

---

[80] Commission Guidance document on Consumers Rights Directive, ec.europa.eu/justice/consumer-marketing/files/crd_guidance_en.pdf, 70 et seq.

[81] Beale (n 1) 15.

[82] ibid.

[83] A similar algorithm was designed by F Marotta-Wurgler to rate the terms and conditions of software licences in F Marotta-Wurgler, 'Are "Pay Now, Terms Later" Contracts Worse for Buyers? Evidence from Software License Agreements' 38 *Journal of Legal Studies* 309, ssrn.com/abstract=799282.

[84] See R Korobkin, 'Wrestling with the Endowment Effect, or How to Do Law and Economics without the Coase Theorem' in E Zamir and D Teichman (eds), *The Oxford Handbook of Behavioral Economics and the Law* (Oxford, Oxford University Press, 2014) s 2.2.

[85] On behavioural trade-offs more generally, see ch 13 by Feldman and Lobel in this volume. This is an instance where, as Schwartz (n 1) points out, the regulator today needs new types of evidence, and when evidence is lacking, new default normative premises in order to intervene effectively in markets in which some consumers are making cognitive mistakes while others are not.

of these challenges but we have tried to show that it contains the seeds of its own improvements at least with respect to the first two. In particular, the EU legislator is now aware of the need to simplify access to information for consumers, streamlining and simplifying matters well beyond the issue of disclosures. 'Simplify!' is one of the central messages addressed by behavioural sciences to policymakers. In the next section, we look beyond information requirements and analyse attempts at simplification in EU consumer law in general.

IV. THE POTENTIAL FOR SIMPLIFICATION IN EU CONSUMER LAW

Simplification aims to increase navigability by shaping the choices consumers make or the actions they take. Simplification is not unknown to EU law. The EU has put a lot of effort into a simplification venture called harmonisation. This makes the internal market more navigable for businesses by sparing them the need to adapt their products, services and labels (among others) to different regulatory environments. This sort of simplification is mainly relevant for businesses, but it can also impact consumer decisions by making competing offers easier to compare. The single currency (Euro) or harmonised labelling requirements illustrate this point. The EU has also put in place other simplification mechanisms that help both consumers and businesses[86] or consumers specifically[87] to deal with the complexity of a multi-layer and multi-lingual market environment. Yet, by and large, the simplification effort has focused on businesses more than consumers. It is only recently that behavioural insights have been increasingly integrated in preparatory phases of legislation drafting from a consumer standpoint. The Commission has organised a framework contract so that behavioural studies can easily be commissioned from a handful of research consultancies.[88] The Commission now recognises that a simplified environment is conducive to more satisfactory outcomes[89] and seems to embrace the idea that if it wants people to do something, it should make it automatic, intuitive and meaningful:[90] in other words, as undemanding as possible on System 2.[91]

---

[86] SOLVIT is a network of national points of contact that help solve issues related with free movement by contacting the relevant authorities in any Member State and organising administrative cooperation: www.ec.europa.eu/solvit/index.
[87] EEC-Network is a network of national points. Of course the mere existence of several different networks makes things a little complex. The Commission announces efforts to streamline internal market help mechanisms. See Commission Communication, 'A Vision for the Internal Market for Industrial Products', COM (2014) 25 final, 11.
[88] For an example of such study, relating to retail investment decisions: based on empirical surveys as well as experimental, it shows that simplifying and standardising product information can slightly improve investment decisions. Study available at: ec.europa.eu/consumers/archive/strategy/docs/final_report_en.pdf. This 2010 study has been followed by the proposal for a Regulation on key information document for investment products (COM (2012) 352) that is in line with the main findings.
[89] See n 14.
[90] CR Sunstein, *Simpler. The Future of Government* (New York, Simon & Schuster, 2013) 210.
[91] ibid, 216: 'encourage the people who write the rule to step back and reduce the strain on the System 2 of people who are required to understand the rules'.

In our view, harmonisation of EU law has so far not dramatically simplified or improved the situation for consumers in Europe. Despite a broad commitment to simplification, which is in itself in line with behavioural insights, the strategic choices made in the details of the rules almost systematically display misconceptions about behavioural realities of decision-making. This can be seen at two different levels: first, the wrong targets for simplification have been picked (A) and second, the methods relied upon for the implementation of simplification impairs its effectiveness (B).

A. Wrong Targets

The attempt to encourage cross-border trade by adopting a common cross-border EU sales law, constitutes an illustration of the law-centred and myopic approach to simplification. The fact that consumers are interested in the products or services and not in the contract that comes with them has been largely disregarded.

The Draft Common European Sales Law (CESL)[92] was recently withdrawn from the legislative agenda for revision.[93] Its aims were to encourage intra-EU trade by making it simple for businesses to sell and for consumers to shop across borders. In the EU context, this strategy is sensible and, on its face, compatible with behavioural insights. In its details, the now to be revised CESL seems to have missed the actual concerns of consumers which are mundane and practical.

The starting point is not disputed: cross-border consumer transactions within the EU are rather limited and require parties to find their way in a challenging environment. Only 15 per cent of the European consumers have purchased at least once from a provider or a seller based in another EU country in 2012.[94] When approaching the issue, the Commission has focused on the fact that cross-border transactions in the EU are currently governed by national contract laws. The absence of a unified legal framework, so goes the thinking behind CESL, impedes transactions because of the complexity it creates. This would be true not only for professionals, who also have to face differences in tax law and administrative requirements, but also for consumers who are confronted with different foreign sales laws and therefore uncertain about their rights.[95] When asked, 44 per cent of European consumers responded that uncertainty about their consumer

---

[92] Regulation of the European Parliament and of the Council on a Common European Sales Law, Annex I: Common European Sales Law (hereinafter we refer to Annex I as 'CESL' and to the entire Regulation as 'Regulation').

[93] See n 16.

[94] Though the figure has nearly tripled between 2006 and 2012. See Flash Eurobarometer survey, 'Cross-border Trade and Consumer Protection', carried out in September 2012, 5. Reports can be found at ec.europa.eu/consumers/strategy/facts_eurobar_en.htm.

[95] See 'Impact Assessment of the Proposal for a Regulation of the European Parliament and of the Council on a Common European Sales Law', SEC(2011) 1165 final, 2.

rights discouraged them from purchasing from other EU countries.[96] In addition, 59 per cent of EU consumers feel confident about purchasing online from a retailer located in their own country, but only 36 per cent do about ordering online from a seller located in another EU country.[97] On this basis EU consumer law was set to redress a situation of low consumer confidence in cross-border shopping that the Commission analysed to be a consequence of a fragmented legal framework and the uncertainties it engenders.[98]

Having regard to insights from psychology about trust, one may however doubt if contract law really is the right tool for the problem at hand. Trust is a very complex phenomenon and operates at an emotional level that is not at all addressed by any simplification of contract law. The trust deficit may be accounted for by a much more general phenomenon than fear of a different contract law, namely a lack of trust towards 'strangers' from other Member States. Such fear from the unknown and interpersonal mistrust towards 'outsider' is well documented in social psychology.[99] Research also shows that there are effective ways to counteract the fear of what is foreign. Contacts, especially meaningful ones involving a common purpose, have the power to improve trust.[100] From a policy perspective, information campaigns developing familiarity with the cultures of other Member States would seem to be an apt translation for this insight. At policy level, meaningful contacts can be encouraged by actions such as twinning between cities, schools and university exchanges, and other initiatives with a cooperative purpose. Further inspiration could be drawn from private initiatives, such as the West-Eastern Divan Orchestra, founded by Daniel Barenboim and Edward Said, that brings together musicians from Spain and various Middle-East countries. Generally speaking, policy has only an indirect hand on this via the promotion of cultural interpenetration.

Contract law may not be the right tool to address the trust deficit but it is a tool in the hands of rule-makers and its use is still being considered. It is therefore appropriate to ask how it could and should take behavioural insights into account

---

[96] ibid. We cannot help but wonder whether such a high proportion would have been obtained if the survey had been run with open questions instead of multiple choice.

[97] ibid, 5. However, 32% affirm that they know where to get information and advice about cross-border shopping in the EU and 26% are interested in making a cross-border purchase within the EU during the next 12 months. See also European Commission, 'Strengthening the Consumer Evidence-base of EU Policies', Legacy Document Consumer Policy (2010–14) 6: 'Over 50% of consumers say that the internet is the retail channel in which they are most likely to come across misleading/deceptive or fraudulent advertising. In addition, consumers remain far less confident about buying online from sellers in other EU countries as opposed to domestically'.

[98] A different issue of trust, which CESL missed, is the lack of trust *of businesses* in cross-border trade (which increases the risk of credit card fraud significantly).

[99] For an overview of intergroup phenomena and their psychological explanations, see R Spears and N Tausch, 'Prejudice and Intergroup Relations' in M Hewstone, W Stroebe and K Jonas (eds), *An Introduction to Social Psychology*, 5th edn (Oxford, Blackwell/Wiley, 2012) 450.

[100] For an overview on current research on intergroup contact, see N Tausch and M Hewstone, 'Intergroup Contact' in JF Dovidio et al (eds), *Handbook of Prejudice, Stereotyping and Discrimination* (Thousand Oaks, Sage, 2010) 544.

in order to pursue effectively the aim of increasing cross-border trade while maintaining a high level of consumer protection. In this perspective, the EU legislator has not chosen suitable methods so far.

B. Inappropriate Methods

Behavioural literature highlights the importance of choice architecture such as opt-in, opt-out or required choice. It is relevant to EU law because EU regulates the choice architecture businesses can present to consumers. So far, the EU legislator has made questionable use of behavioural regulation tools. It has missed opportunities to simplify by preferring opt-in to opt-out (i) and by preferring grey lists to black lists (ii) both times under pressure from Member States.

i. Simplification by Opt-Out

The example of CESL is again interesting to consider. CESL was structured around an opt-in architecture. However, making the new regime the default option, subject to opt-out right, would have been the only path consistent with proclaimed goals of simplification of cross-border transactions. As structured, CESL was to be a new regime in addition to the 28 national contract law regimes. The idea was to give consumers the possibility of buying products across Member States on the basis of a single set of contract law rules. Consumers ordering online would have had the option of clicking on a 'blue button'. If selecting the blue button they would have selected as governing law the specially designed European sales regime over a national contract law. Typically a consumer in Vienna would have been able to order wine on a French e-commerce website and could have been offered the choice between French contract law and no delivery in Austria or the blue button contract with EU-wide delivery. In the Commission's analysis, the additional blue button regime offered a unified regime and had therefore the potential to increase navigability of the choice environment for parties to cross-border trade. Technology was to be an adjuvant of simplicity:[101] CESL would have offered a one-click choice of law. In itself, one-click is simple and that is a good thing, but, one-click or not, opt-in requires an active choice and, before opting for CESL, consumers were (seriously) expected to read and understand what that choice was about.

Behavioural insights provided useful guidance to design the one-click environment but have only been marginally taken into account as mere correctors of an otherwise behaviourally ill-fitting mandated-choice design. Typically, common sense suggests and empirical observations confirm the reluctance of consumers to read. Instead of acknowledging documented facts, the Commission tried to fight

---

[101] Stressing how technology can help design solutions that do not involve System 2, see CR Sunstein (n 90) passim.

this natural tendency to rational ignorance. It maintained that 'the use of CESL should be an informed choice'[102] and insisted that 'consumers must be aware of the fact that they are agreeing to the use of rules which are different from those of their pre-existing national law'.[103] Bar-Gill and Ben-Shahar commented that CESL had embarked on a 'formidable mission'.[104] The mission was pursued for some time with care and attention to details.[105] An empirical study was commissioned to determine how best to design and draft a two-page information notice which would have to inform consumers that, by pressing the blue button, they were about to leave the territory of their national law and enter that of the European Common Sales Law.[106] The Commission wanted to 'identify the most appropriate content of the standardised information notice on a Common European Sales Law by means of practical testing'.[107] It sought empirical input at the micro level when the problem arguably lay at the macro level. The elephant in the room was the very design put forward by CESL, which required informed consent to a choice of law clause. Unsurprisingly, the study found that changing the wording or layout of the notice has little impact[108] because consumers did not typically read the notice in detail.[109] It is not difficult to figure out why: choice of law does not matter to consumers. Applicable law is one of these clauses in a contract a consumer is never going to do anything about even if he does not like it, so it is entirely rational to ignore it.[110] This makes applicable law a feature consumers would choose not to choose.[111] Consumers are likely to prefer a default rule to be chosen and the democratic political structure enable them to entrust public authorities to make such choice. It is therefore futile to insist that consumers should make an active and informed choice about applicable law.

Our view is that if a European Sales Law is ever to help consumers and businesses, it should be the default solution. Opt-out rather than opt-in should be the rule. We write this in full knowledge of the fact that, in the current European

---

[102] CESL (n 11) Recital 23.
[103] ibid, Recital 22.
[104] Bar-Gill and Ben-Shahar (n 1) 117.
[105] A video explaining to businesses how CESL would work is available on DG Justice website: ec.europa.eu/justice/contract/CESL-demo/CESL1-Oct1-2.htm.
[106] Gallup Europe et al, 'Testing of a Standardised Information Notice for Consumers on the Common European Sales Law' (2013), ec.europa.eu/justice/contract/files/common_sales_law/cesl_gallup_consortium_final_report_en.pdf.
[107] Terms of references for tender JUST/2011/JCIV/FW/0135/A4 (framework service contract EAHC/2011/CP/01).
[108] The study (n 106) showed that most variations in the notice did not change attitudes to reading. Only a catchier title and a clearer introduction were retained as superior.
[109] Gallup study (n 106) 44. The authors explain that 'Half of consumers spend less than 7 seconds reading the Draft Notice and fewer than 15% view the Notice more than once. Only 32% of consumers scroll all the way to the end of the Draft Notice. Fewer than one in five respondents claim to have read the Draft Notice in full'.
[110] Ben-Shahar (n 1) 4 stressing that 'Choosing not to read is a more meaningful surrender to the unread terms when there is an option to read than when the option does not exist'.
[111] Sunstein (n 75).

context, what makes sense for consumers or businesses is not the real issue. Member States rather than the Commission insist on active choice because they want to protect the use of national contract laws. The practical solution may then be to keep the sub-optimal opt-in model, hypocritically request 'choice' in favour of CESL (or whatever the replacement legislative proposal will be called) and focus on alternative ways to nudge consumers by making the choice easy and attractive rather than informed.[112]

Though the Commission affirmed its willingness to simplify the choice for shoppers across borders, its preconceptions, as well as political pressures, have curtailed its actual use of behavioural recommendations. Similar circumstances have also hindered optimal use of another behaviourally fit tool: blacklists.

ii. Simplification by Blacklists

Resorting to a mandatory option is a policy choice that can sometimes be justified for behavioural reasons. This may sound counterintuitive at first because behavioural regulation is often associated with soft paternalism and non-compulsory instruments.[113] In reality, mandates can neutralise inertia as well as anchoring effects that weigh heavy on consumers' choices. Mandates can therefore be behaviourally justified. In this perspective, EU regulation of unfair contract terms could benefit from a higher degree of constraint imposed on traders.

The battle against unfair contract terms has long been an important target of EU consumer law. Warranting consumers that they will not be exposed to unfair terms when they enter standard contracts would create a safer environment for them and decrease the risk of entering into poor deals. From a behavioural standpoint, the issue is whether consumers actually resort to this protection. Beyond the well documented fact that only few consumers have sufficient incentives to challenge unfair terms, consumers are likely to be side-tracked by a framing effect and then locked by inertia. They will assume that a unilateral termination right benefiting the seller, or another abusive term, is part of the contract and necessarily binding. Therefore, they will not try and reverse the situation and challenge the term. Traders strategically use invalid terms, knowing that consumers are likely to follow the contract as written under the influence of a perception bias and a status quo effect. A blacklist of unfair terms would be easier than standards to refer to for consumers, for private enforcers (consumer associations) and also for public enforcers (ombudsmen, administrations, and courts). However, such a list would require maximal harmonisation and Member States have been reluctant to go along this path. The Unfair Contract Terms Directive (UCTD) as it stands does

---

[112] This probably will not make much difference to consumers. The Gallup study (n 106) found that 'Asking for explicit separate consent for the application of the CESL rather than implicit consent as part of agreeing to make the purchase does not have a significant impact on the average reading time of the Notice' (62).

[113] See Kerber (n 3).

not provide for a blacklist of terms automatically deemed unfair. The annexed list merely contains a non-exhaustive list of terms that are presumptively unfair (grey list). The proposed CESL did contain a blacklist of prohibited clauses,[114] but, as mentioned above, this instrument is now under revision. It is to be hoped that a blacklist will be kept in the revamped version.

A further step would be to organise preventive controls on standardised contracts.[115] The idea of sector specific authorised standard terms had been examined a few years ago but has not been followed.[116] The CESL showed traces of this idea and imposed a large number of boilerplate clauses.

On the progressive side, and in contrast to non-EU consumer law texts,[117] numerous pro-consumer provisions in CESL could not be contracted out.[118] More than 30 times, CESL stressed that 'The parties may not, to the detriment of the consumer, exclude the application of this Article [or Section, or Chapter] or derogate from or vary its effects'.[119] These mandatory provisions included withdrawal rights, disclosure rules, interpretation rules, restitution rules, risk of loss provisions, some of the implied and express warranties, rules relating to notices and communications, interest for late payments, grace periods, and prescription rules.[120] They trump the behavioural issues that more traditional grey lists create. To promote a simpler and more effectively protective environment for EU consumers, mandates should be encouraged in the revised version of CESL, along with a bolder use of opt-out options.

EU law is not blind to the relevance of a simple shopping environment to help consumers make good choices and ensure that they fully benefit from the protections that are available. Steps in that direction have been made before behavioural insights were on the table. Since the beginning of the internal market, harmonisation has contributed to increase navigability for consumers. The Commission is now openly committed to simplification and to the use of relevant behavioural lessons. It has, however, repeatedly made choices in the details of the rules that display misconceptions about the realities of decision-making. This is particularly apparent in connection with the targets that have been picked for simplification. They give away a law-centred approach that suffers from the limitations inherent

---

[114] See CESL, art 84(d).

[115] Luth (n 1).

[116] S Whittaker, 'On the Development of European Standard Contract Terms' (2006) 2 *European Review of Contract Law* 51.

[117] See, eg US, Universal Commercial Code (UCC) § 1-302: the default rule is that, but for a list of exceptions including the principles of good faith, diligence, reasonableness and care, provisions of the UCC may be varied by agreement..

[118] Bar-Gill and Ben-Shahar (n 1) 1 enumerated 81 of them.

[119] CESL arts 2, 10, 22, 27, 28, 29, 47, 64, 69, 70, 71, 72, 74, 75, 77, 81, 92, 99, 101, 102, 105, 108, 135, 142, 148, 150, 158, 167, 171, 177, and 186. In some of the articles, the sentence quoted in the text appears with slight variations. In a handful of articles, the phrase 'to the detriment of the consumer' does not appear.

[120] CESL arts 2, 10, para 3-4; ch 2, s 1 (10 articles); ch 2, s 3 (4 articles); arts 28, 29; ch 4 (8 articles); arts 64, 69, 70, 71, 72, 74, 75(2), 77; ch 8 (8 articles); arts 92(2), 99(3), 101, 102, 105; ch 11 (17 articles); arts 135, 142, 148(2), 150(2), 158, 167; ch 16, s 3 (4 articles); ch 17 (6 articles); art 186.

to contract law when it comes to addressing the consumers' trust deficit. The implementation of simplification has also relied on methods that were not necessarily the most appropriate from a behavioural standpoint. Opt-out options and blacklists change quite dramatically from the traditional harmonisation path and may be unwelcome for political reasons, despite their behavioural suitability. As a consequence, harmonisation of EU law has not so far considerably simplified or improved the situation of consumers in Europe.

V. CONCLUSION

At first glance, EU consumer law seems to be behaviourally ill-informed. Its numerous mandatory information requirements seem indicative of a pre-nudge state.[121] In this chapter, we have, however, argued that this point of view is partially inaccurate and, as a result, that EU consumer law does not need a revolution but a continued reform. EU consumer law has evolved and still does in a context where the internal market imperative was paramount. This context explains some of its seemingly behaviourally un-savvy features of EU regulation, in particular with relation to disclosure mandates.

A closer look at both EU legislation and case law shows that the seeds for behaviourally sound developments are sewn. Arguably, there have been youthful indiscretions and behavioural insights that have shed a rather unforgiving light on some EU regulatory attempts such as CESL. But the learning process has begun and the commitment of the Commission to take behavioural insight and empirical data into account in the preparation of consumer legislation is very encouraging for future developments.

---

[121] See ch 1 by AL Sibony and A Alemanno in this volume.

10

What can EU Health Law Learn from Behavioural Sciences? The Case of EU Lifestyle Regulation

ALBERTO ALEMANNO

I. INTRODUCTION

AT A TIME when behavioural sciences are gaining increasing attention for the design of population-wide health interventions,[1] this chapter discusses their potential contribution to EU health law and policy.[2] It does so by exploring in particular the role that behavioural insights might play in the framework of one of the most developed and rapidly-evolving areas of EU health intervention: the regulation of lifestyle-related risk factors.[3]

Despite its limited formal competences, the EU has become increasingly involved over the years in the field of health.[4] Besides its involvement in the recognition of a right to receive health care services across national borders,[5] the EU has also been regulating workplace hazards, clinical research, the placing into the market of pharmaceuticals, data protection of patients, as well as the qualifications of health professionals.[6] Most importantly, the EU has also progressively acted

---

[1] See, eg *World Development Report 2015: Mind, Society, and Behavior* (Washington DC, 2014); S Holland, 'Libertarian Paternalist and Public Health Nudges' in M Freeman et al, *Law and Global Health, Current Legal Issues*, vol 16 (Oxford, Oxford University Press, 2014) 331; T Marteau et al, 'Judging Nudging: Can Nudging Improve Population Health?' (2011) 342 *British Medical Journal* 263; K Glanz, BK Rimer and K Viswanath, *Health Behaviour and Health Education. Theory, Research and Practice*, 4th edn (San Francisco, Jossey-Bass, 2008); G Hastings, 'Making Use of Theory' in G Hastings (ed), *Social Marketing: Why Should the Devil Have all the Best Tunes ?* (Oxford, Butterworth, 2007) 17; RC Lefebvre, 'Theories and Models in Social Marketing' in PN Bloom and GT Gundlach (eds), *Handbook of Marketing and Society* (Thousand Oaks, CA, Sage, 2000) eds.

[2] For a systematic introduction to the field, see TK Hervey and JV McHale, *Health Law and the European Union* (Cambridge, Cambridge University Press, 2004).

[3] For an introduction, see A Alemanno and A Garde, 'The Emergence of an EU Lifestyle Policy: The Case of Alcohol, Tobacco and Unhealthy Diets' (2013) 50 *CML Rev* 6.

[4] See, eg Directive 2011/24/EU of the European Parliament and of the Council of 9 March 2011 on the application of patients' rights in cross-border healthcare [2011] OJ L88/45.

[5] Art 35 of the EU Charter of Fundamental Rights.

[6] See, eg E Randall, *The European Union and Health Policy* (Basingtoke, Palgrave, 2000); T Hervey, 'Mapping the Contours of European Union Health Law and Policy' (2002) 8 *European Public Law* 69.

to promote public health. In line with the World Health Organisation (WHO)'s recommendations,[7] the EU has adopted several strategies aimed at reducing the impact of the four major lifestyle risk factors responsible for non-communicable Diseases (NCDs):[8] smoking, harmful use of alcohol, unhealthy diets, and lack of physical activity.[9] As NCDs account for nearly 86 per cent of deaths and 77 per cent of the disease burden in the WHO European Region,[10] these alarming rates have led to a mounting agreement in the EU that a comprehensive policy 'to promote healthy lifestyle behaviours is needed'.[11]

Given the largely preventable nature of NCDs, both the WHO[12] and the EU[13] have recently recognised the role that regulation might play in inducing behavioural change.[14] By highlighting the importance of social and physical environments in shaping our conduct, behavioural sciences promise to help policymakers better understand human decision-making.[15] In particular, this discipline is expected to offer an innovative approach to the promotion of behaviour change leading to healthier lives.[16]

Behaviourally savvy interventions differ from the typical approaches used to induce behavioural change, such as rational persuasion, coercion, adjusting financial incentives, and bans.[17] Inspired by 'libertarian paternalism',[18] they suggest that policymakers, by exploiting some patterns of irrationality, often called 'cognitive biases', may steer citizens towards making positive decisions as individuals and for society while preserving individual choice.[19] Acting as 'choice architects',

---

[7] Political Declaration of the UN High Level Meeting on the Prevention and Control of NCDs (20 September 2011, Doc A/66/L 1).

[8] NCDs include cardiovascular diseases, cancers, chronic respiratory diseases, and diabetes type two.

[9] See, eg the EU Alcohol Strategy (2006) COM (2006) 625 final, the Obesity Prevention White Paper (2007) COM (2007) 279 final, and a Council Recommendation on smoke-free environments [2009] OJ C296/4.

[10] This includes, but is not limited to, the European Union countries and includes also Russia and many other neighbouring countries to the EU.

[11] European Commission, White paper, 'Together for Health: Strategic Approach for the EU 2008–13', 14689/07, COM (2007) 630 final.

[12] See the Political Declaration (n 7) which the UN General Assembly adopted unanimously on 19–20 September 2011: www.un.org/ga/search/view_doc.asp?symbol=A/66/L.1.

[13] Council of the European Union, Council Conclusions, 'Closing Health Gaps within the EU through Concerted Action to Promote Healthy Lifestyle Behaviours' (1 and 2 December 2011).

[14] On the role of law in health promotion see, eg B Thomas and L Gostin, 'Tackling the Global NCD Crisis: Innovations in Law and Governance' (2013) *Journal of Law, Medicine & Ethics* 16.

[15] J Wise, 'Nudge or Fudge? Doctors Debate Best Approach to Improve Public Health' (2011) *British Medical Journal* 342:d580; G Rayner and T Lang, 'Is Nudge an Effective Public Health Strategy to Tackle Obesity?' (2011) *British Medical Journal* 342:d2177.

[16] See, eg JE Painter et al, 'The Use of Theory in Health Behaviour Research from 2000 to 2005: A Systematic Review' (2008) 35 *Annals of Behavioral Medicine* 358.

[17] For an insightful critique of the use and design of incentives, see R Grant, *Strings Attached—Untangling the Ethics of Incentives* (Princeton, Princeton University Press, 2012).

[18] C Sunstein and R Thaler, 'Libertarian Paternalism is Not an Oxymoron' (2003) 70 *University of Chicago Law Review* 1159.

[19] See, eg J Baron, *Thinking and Deciding* (Cambridge, Cambridge University Press, 2007); D Ariely, *Predictably Irrational: The Hidden Forces that Shape Our Decisions* (New York, HarperCollins, 2008).

policymakers organise the context, process, and environment in which individuals make decisions affecting their health, and more specifically, their consumption.[20] Thus, given the potential significance of framing effects, policymakers are becoming increasingly aware that the way in which any information is conveyed must respect specific standards of appearance, ranging from the design, use of colours, and location on the relevant product. Analogously, default rules offer a promising way of easing people's choices and are as a result used across policy sectors by both public and private institutions. Likewise, defaults often have a large effect on social outcome as people tend—due to inertia and procrastination—not to make affirmative choices. Given their huge potential in affecting individual choices, sensible defaults can complement or provide an alternative to more traditional regulatory options such as restrictions or bans.[21] In the light of the above, default rules carry huge potential in health promotion, an area where the principle of autonomy severely constrains the legitimacy of regulatory action.[22] Thus, for instance, given the preponderant role played by accessibility in rising obesity rates, defaults can be used to promote access to healthy products and discourage accessibility to unhealthy foods.[23] There do not seem to exist more powerful defaults in obesity prevention than portion sizes or the dimension of plates.[24] However, when the target group is too diverse or the domain is familiar (eg organ donations), active choices (ie asking individuals to make their choice) might be a more sensible choice than default rules.[25] Also, simplification may potentially promote regulatory goals by easing participation and providing clearer messages to targeted groups about what they are expected to do.[26] This is because complexity may produce serious unintended consequences and undermine regulatory goals. An interesting example of attempted simplification in NCD prevention is the removal of information regarding tar, nicotine, and carbon monoxide yields (commonly referred to as TNCO).[27] By prohibiting the indication of TNCO information, the idea is to lead smokers towards believing that all cigarettes are equally dangerous. Because smokers (be they current or future) would no longer find any information about TNCO yields on their packs, they might consider all tobacco products similarly threatening.[28]

---

[20] ibid.
[21] See, eg E Johnson et al, 'Framing, Probability Distortions, and Insurance Decisions' (1993) 7(1) *Journal of Risk and Uncertainty* 35.
[22] See conclusive chapter of this volume by A Alemanno and AL Sibony.
[23] See, eg P Rozin et al, 'Nudge to Nobesity I: Minor Changes in Accessibility Decrease Food Intake' (2011) 6 *Judgment & Decision Making* 323.
[24] See, eg B Wansink, *Mindless Eating: Why We Eat More Than We Think* (London, Bantam, 2006) 10.
[25] G Carroll et al, 'Optimal Defaults and Active Decisions' (2005) NBER Working Paper No w11074.
[26] See, eg S Mullainathan, WJ Congdon and JR Kling, *Policy and Choice: Public Finance through the Lens of Behavioural Economics* (Washington, DC, Brookings Institution Press, 2011).
[27] WHO Framework Convention on Tobacco Control Working Group (hereinafter FCTC).
[28] Yet, the ensuing no-information policy sits uneasily with another well-established tobacco control policy aimed at establishing maximum content levels of tar, nicotine and carbon monoxide. See G Howells, *The Tobacco Challenge—Legal Policy and Consumer Protection* (Surrey, Ashgate, 2011) 7; A Alemanno, 'Nudging Smokers—The Behavioural Turn of Tobacco Risk Regulation' (2012) 3 *European Journal of Risk Regulation* 1.

Default, active choice, and simplification all influence choices without motivating people to consider their options consciously. They do not include openly persuasive interventions such as media or educational campaigns. Moreover, reliance on these tools is often provided through regulatory means and thus—as it will be illustrated below—do not necessarily constitute an alternative to regulation.[29] Yet while only a combination of policy instruments, such as legislation, regulation, and even financial and fiscal incentives, may induce behaviour change on the scale required to reduce the burden of chronic disease at the population level, a behaviourally informed approach may valuably complement the current 'regulatory mix'.[30] The inherent complexity of this emerging policy is epitomised by the multifactorial character of its underlying risk factors. Moreover the very nature of the EU itself gives rise to additional complex issues around roles, obligations and rights. In particular, the constitutional structure of the EU as a union of Member States with a diverse mix of cultural, social, political, economic, and welfare structures presents both challenges and opportunities for the development of an EU-wide 'lifestyle' policy. As will be illustrated, despite its promises in promoting healthier lifestyles, behavioural sciences might also contribute to augment rather than defuse this underlying complexity.

This chapter proceeds as follows. Section II sets the scene by providing a brief introduction to EU health law, in particular to the emerging EU lifestyle policy. Section III discusses the role that behavioural sciences might play in injecting a new, more realistic understanding of human decision-making into the preparation of health interventions. In turn, Section IV—after presenting the key regulatory tools capable of operationalising behavioural insights into policy-making—discusses how behavioural sciences might inform the NCD agenda. Section V focuses more specifically on what the EU lifestyle policy could learn from behavioural sciences while designing health interventions. A few concluding remarks (Section VI) identify the need to develop a framework capable of ensuring that behavioural consideration may inform and complement the EU health prevention action, and in particular, the NCD agenda through continuous experimentation.

---

[29] See introductory chapter in this volume by AL Sibony and A Alemanno. On the relationship between behavioural intervention and regulation see, eg L Bovens, 'The Ethics of Nudge' in T Grüne-Yanoff and S Ove Hansson, *Preference Change: Approaches from Philosophy, Economics and Psychology* (Berlin and New York, Springer, 2008); Marteau et al (n 1); C Sunstein, 'Empirically Informed Regulation' (2011) 78 *University of Chicago Law Review* 1362.

[30] A Alemanno, 'A Behavioural Approach to Health Promotion: Informing the Global NCD Agenda with Behavioural Insights' in A Alemanno and A Garde (eds), *Regulating Lifestyle—Europe, Alcohol, Tobacco and Unhealthy Diets* (Cambridge, Cambridge University Press, 2015).

II. AN INTRODUCTION TO EU HEALTH LAW AND THE EMERGENCE OF A EU LIFESTYLE POLICY

One of the constitutional principles governing EU legislative action is the principle of conferred or enumerated powers.[31] Under this principle, as enshrined in Article 5(2) of the Treaty on European Union (TEU),

> the Union shall act only within the limits of the competences conferred upon it by the Member States in the Treaties to attain the objectives set out therein.

This implies that, outside those limits, the Member States retain competence to act within the limits of the EU action. Today virtually all EU legislation pursuing a public health objective, such as product regulation—be they pharmaceutical, medical devices or food products—, has been based on the internal market legal basis provided by Article 114 Treaty on the Functioning of the European Union (TFEU). This is the most important Treaty provision relating to harmonisation: it empowers the EU to replace, by a qualified majority vote, divergent national legislations with a common rule applicable across the whole territory.[32] Yet since the objective pursued by lifestyle policies, such as labelling, advertising and product regulation restrictions, is generally to reduce the consumption rather than to promote the free movement and promotion of tobacco, alcohol or food products, reliance on this legal basis may appear, at least prima facie, somehow paradoxical.[33] The reason behind such a choice lies in the limited competences enjoyed by the EU in the area of public health. Although the protection of public health is one of the basic requirements that the EU has to take into account in the enactment of any of its policies or activities,[34] Member States remain generally competent to adopt public health measures. This is largely due to Article 168 TFEU, the EU public health legal basis. Like its predecessor Article 152 Treaty on the European Community (TEC), this provision explicitly excludes the possibility that the EU could harmonise the laws and regulations of the Member States in the pursuit of public health objectives.

Yet, despite its limited competence in public health, the European Union has progressively recognised the impact of health on the EU's economy, the well-being of—as well as inequalities among—its citizens.[35]

---

[31] See Art 8 TEU. See, eg K Lenaerts, 'The Rule of Law and the Coherence of the Judicial System of the European Union' (2007) 44 *CML Rev* 1625; A Pliakos and G Anagnostaras, 'Who is the Ultimate Arbiter?: The Battle over Judicial Supremacy in EU Law' (2011) 36 *EL Rev* 109.

[32] N de Sadeleer, 'Procedures for Derogations from the Principle of Approximation of Laws under Article 95 EC' (2003) 40 *CML Rev* 889.

[33] In the absence of sufficiently strong minimum standards at EU level, the Member States may be tempted, acting individually, to impose restrictions on public health considerations that could lead to a fragmentation of the internal market.

[34] See Art 9 TFEU and Art 35 of the Charter.

[35] eg in 2002, the difference in male life expectancy at age 20 years between the 15 countries that had been Members before 2004 (the EU15) and the Baltic States (Estonia, Latvia, and Lithuania) was 9.8 years.

As a result, the EU conducts today an active, yet largely inadequate, policy vis-à-vis the various health determinants. Some measures were adopted in the early days of the European Community, before the Member States explicitly granted some competence to the EU in the field of public health.[36] In particular, the first food labelling laws adopted at EU level pursued not only an internal market objective but also a public health objective. Thus, the Food Labelling Directive of 1979[37] and the Nutrition Labelling Directive of 1990[38] required that ingredients of foodstuffs be listed on most pre-packaged foodstuffs and regulated how nutritional information should appear on food labels. Following the introduction of a chapter on public health in the EU Treaties,[39] the EU has been under a legal obligation to ensure a high level of public health in all policy areas. Article 168 TFEU introduces a 'mainstream' duty that applies to both the EU and its Member States. Such a duty to mainstream health in all policies was further reinforced with the introduction, by the Lisbon Treaty, of Article 9 TFEU which confirms that

> in defining and implementing its policies and activities, the Union shall take into account requirements linked to the promotion of a high level of employment, the guarantee of adequate social protection, the fight against social exclusion, and a high level of education, training and protection of human health.[40]

The introduction of EU powers in the field of public health has led to the adoption of two health programmes, the first for the period of 2003–08[41] and the second for 2008–13.[42] These programmes aimed 'to promote health and prevent disease through addressing health determinants across all policies and activities',[43] not least 'by preparing and implementing strategies and measures, including those related to public awareness, on lifestyle related health determinants, such as nutrition, physical activity, tobacco, alcohol, drugs and other substances and on mental health'[44] and 'by tackling health determinants ... creating supportive environments for healthy lifestyles and preventing disease'.[45] Following the calls of the Council of the European Union for EU action on NCDs,[46] the EU adopted not only a

---

[36] Art 168 TFEU.
[37] Directive 79/112 [1979] OJ L33/1.
[38] Directive 90/496 [1990] OJ L276/40.
[39] Since the entry into force of the Maastricht Treaty in 1993, the EU Treaties have contained a specific chapter on public health that is now to be found in Art 168 TFEU. The first paragraph of this provision has imposed an obligation on the EU to ensure a high level of public health in all its policy areas. It is precisely with a view to implementing the Union's mainstreaming obligation that the Council emphasised, in its Conclusions of 8 June 1999, the necessity to integrate health protection requirements in all EU policies.
[40] See also Art 35 of the Charter.
[41] Decision 1786/2002 of the European Parliament and the Council [2002] OJ L271/1.
[42] Decision 1350/2007 of the European Parliament and the Council [2007] OJ L301/3.
[43] Art2(2)(c) of Decision 1786/2002 (n 41).
[44] ibid, Annex, para 3(1).
[45] Art 2(2) and point 2.2 of the Annex to Decision 1350/2007 (n 42). See also the White Paper, 'Together for Health' (n 11).
[46] Some of these calls have focused specifically on one specific risk factor, whilst others have tended to be more horizontal in nature targeting all risk factors. Examples of the latter type include: the

range of specific measures intended to curb the consumption of tobacco,[47] but it also adopted three strategies intended to tackle the major NCD risk factors more comprehensively and support its citizens in improving their lifestyles. These are the EU Alcohol Strategy (2006),[48] the Obesity Prevention White Paper (2007),[49] and a Council Recommendation on smoke-free environments (2009).[50] The latter complemented the adoption of the 2001 Tobacco Products Directive[51] and the 2003 Tobacco Advertising Directive.[52]

Following the entry into force of the Lisbon Treaty in December 2009, the public health legal basis adds two kinds of measures to the list of actions which could already be adopted in the past by the EU:

11. Paragraph 4(c): 'measures setting high standards of quality and safety for medicinal products and devices for medical use';
12. Paragraph 5: 'incentive measures designed to protect and improve human health and in particular to combat the major cross-border health scourges, measures concerning monitoring, early warning of and *combating serious cross-border threats to health*, and *measures which have as their direct objective the protection of public health regarding tobacco* and the abuse of alcohol, excluding any harmonisation of the laws and regulations of the Member States.

While this is the first expressed reference to tobacco and alcohol abuse control measures that has ever appeared in the Treaty, it is unlikely to provide a new legal basis for the adoption of EU-wide legally mandated measures such as plain packaging. This is because, despite the implicit recognition of tobacco as a key determinant of human health, the same provision expressly excludes the adoption of harmonised rules aimed at combating tobacco consumption. However, even though the scope of EU regulatory action remains considerably limited in the post-Lisbon era,[53] the role played by the EU in health matters should not be underestimated.[54] Thus, for instance, the current wording of Article 168 TFEU itself suggests that the scope of EU public health intervention, although limited to non-harmonisation action, should not only cover the prevention of diseases, but

---

Council Conclusions of December 2003 on Healthy Lifestyles; the Council Conclusions of June 2004 on Promoting Heart Health; the Council Conclusions of June 2006 on the Promotion of Healthy Lifestyles and the Prevention of Type II Diabetes.

[47] See in particular, Directive 2001/37 on tobacco products [2001] OJ L194/26, and Directive 2003/33 on tobacco advertising and sponsorship [2003] OJ L152/16.

[48] COM (2006) 625 final.

[49] COM (2007) 279 final. For an assessment of the EU's obesity prevention strategy, see A Garde, *EU Law and Obesity Prevention* (Alphen aan de Rijn, Kluwer Law International, 2010).

[50] [2009] OJ C296/4.

[51] Directive 2001/37 (n 47).

[52] Directive 2003/33 (n 47).

[53] See, eg P Craig, *The Lisbon Treaty—Law, Politics and Treaty Reform* (Oxford, Oxford University Press, 2010) 325; JC Piris, *The Lisbon Treaty—A Legal and Political Analysis* (Cambridge, Cambridge University Press, 2010) 320.

[54] Garde (n 49) 65.

also promote good health by 'obviating sources of danger to physical and mental health'.[55] Moreover, despite the limited competences enjoyed by the EU on public health matters, the nature and extension of those competences have progressively been enriched by the generous interpretation provided by the Court of Justice when called upon to judge the legality of harmonised measures grounded on the internal market legal basis, Article 114 TFEU.[56]

Overall, the constraints presented above curtail the ability of the EU to adopt a fully-fledged EU health policy. In particular, they render problematic the adoption of a comprehensive set of measures required to promote healthier lifestyles. However, given the significant population differences in life expectancy,[57] premature mortality, morbidity and disability between and within Member States,[58] the EU has recently found the resulting health conditions to be inconsistent with some of its core values, including solidarity, equity and universality.[59] In the light of these findings, it eventually expressed its commitment to 'accelerate progress on combating unhealthy lifestyle behaviours'.[60] This commitment seems to have been partly operationalised by the recently adopted third EU public health programme.[61] The programme, which will run from 2014 to 2020, builds upon the achievements of the previous public health programmes.[62] In particular, its third objective is to identify, disseminate and promote the uptake of validated best practices for cost-effective prevention measures by addressing the key risk factors, namely smoking, abuse of alcohol and obesity, as well as HIV/AIDS, with a focus on the cross-border dimension, in order to prevent diseases and promote good health.[63] Thus, the programme

> will support European cooperation and networking on preventing chronic diseases, including guidelines on quality cancer screening. Actions under this objective will also support measures which have as their direct objective the protection of public health

---

[55] See Art 168(1) TFEU.

[56] See, eg Case C-491/01 *British American Tobacco* [2002] ECR I-11453, paras 72–74; Case C-217/04 *United Kingdom v Parliament and Council* [2006] ECR I-3771, para 43 ('by using the expression "measures for the approximation" in Article 95 EC [now 114 TFEU] the authors of the Treaty intended to confer on the Community legislature a discretion, depending on the general context and the specific circumstances of the matter to be harmonised, as regards the method of approximation most appropriate for achieving the desired result, in particular in fields with complex technical features'). See also Case C-301/06 *Ireland v European Parliament* [2009] ECR I-593, paras 62–72.

[57] eg in 2002, the difference in male life expectancy at age 20 years between the 15 countries that had been Members before 2004 (the EU15) and the Baltic States (Estonia, Latvia and Lithuania) was 9.8 years.

[58] WHO Regional Office for Europe, 'Action Plan for Implementation of the European Strategy for the Prevention and Control of Non-communicable Diseases 2012–16', available at: www.euro.who.int/__data/assets/pdf_file/0019/170155/e96638.pdf >.

[59] European Commission, White paper, 'Together for Health' (n 11).

[60] Council of the European Union, Council Conclusions, 'Closing Health Gaps' (n 13).

[61] Regulation (EU) No 282/2014 of the European Parliament and of the Council of 11 March 2014 on the establishment of a third Programme for the Union's action in the field of health (2014–20) [2014] OJ L86/1.

[62] COM (2011) 709 final.

[63] Recital 14 of Regulation (EU) No 282/2014 (n 61) states: 'Chronic diseases are responsible for over 80% of premature mortality in the Union. The Programme should identify, disseminate and

regarding tobacco products and advertisement required by or contributing to the objectives of EU legislation in this field[64] and 'will focus on promoting good health and preventing diseases at EU level by helping and complementing Member States' efforts to increase their citizens' number of healthy life years'.[65] Finally, the proposed programme recognises that promoting good health at EU level is an integral part of the Europe 2020 Strategy for smart, sustainable and inclusive growth,[66] thus reinforcing the economic and social case for an EU intervention to prevent and control NCDs across the Member States.

As a result of this dynamics, the EU lifestyle policy emerges today as the result of a combination of both regulatory and self-regulatory measures adopted at either EU or national levels.[67] In particular, there appears to be a gradation in EU involvement, with a stronger intervention in relation to tobacco control, a lesser intervention in relation to alcohol control, with the EU nutrition and obesity prevention policy somewhere between the two.

Given the urgency of developing effective, population-based interventions aimed at tackling NCDs, the next section explores the extent to which, and how, EU health law, and in particular its emerging lifestyle policy, may learn from behavioural sciences.

III. THE PROMISES AND PITFALLS OF BEHAVIOURAL SCIENCES IN LIFESTYLE POLICY-MAKING

Although most individuals tend to value their health as priceless, they often engage in behaviours, typically characterised as self-destructive, that undermine it. If analysed through the lenses of behavioural sciences, this gap between values and actual conduct can be understood by using the dual 'cognitive system model' of human behaviour, which is central to behavioural sciences.[68] According to this increasingly popular understanding, while System 1 operates automatically and quickly, with little cognitive efforts and no sense of voluntary control, System 2 functions slowly as it deliberates, ponders and calculates various courses of action. As a result, while System 1 is driven by immediate feelings, intuitions and habits,

---

promote the uptake of evidence-based and good practices for cost-effective health promotion and disease prevention measures focused in particular on the key risk factors, such as tobacco use, drug use, harmful use of alcohol and unhealthy dietary habits, obesity and physical inactivity, as well as on HIV/AIDS, tuberculosis and hepatitis. Effective prevention would contribute to increasing the financial sustainability of healthcare systems'.

[64] Point 2.3 of the Explanatory Memorandum.
[65] ibid, Point 3.2.
[66] Communication from the Commission, COM (2010) 2020 final.
[67] See A Alemanno and A Garde (eds), *Regulating Lifestyle Risks—Europe, Alcohol, Tobacco and Unhealthy Diets* (Cambridge, Cambridge University Press, 2015).
[68] D Kahneman, *Thinking, Fast and Slow* (New York, Farrar, Straus and Giroux, 2011).

System 2 is driven by deliberation, calculus and intentions. As stated by Kahneman, 'although System 2 believes itself to be where the action is, the automatic System 1 is the hero' in our lives.[69] This system explains why people who wish to lose weight, for example, still buy the chocolate biscuits displayed at the counter. Or why people still have sex without protecting themselves while knowing about the existence of numerous sexually transmissible diseases.

Although today it clearly appears erroneous and short-sighted, most policy efforts in health treatment and promotion have historically targeted System 2 and disregarded System 1.[70] This has been the case for health interventions directed at preventing both communicable diseases (CDs) and non-communicable diseases (NCDs). Indeed, regulatory action aimed at health protection typically relies on 'command-and-control' mechanisms, such as coercion (eg using sanctions to ensure compliance) and bans (eg prohibiting smoking in restaurants or trans-fats in food) as well as market-based mechanisms, such as financial incentives (eg raising prices on alcoholic and unhealthy products or decreasing them for condoms).[71] Today, the most common regulatory interventions intended to attain health promotion objectives consist of disclosure requirements and information schemes, marketing restrictions, measures affecting product availability, as well as fiscal measures. Despite their different levels of social acceptability and degree of effectiveness in attaining health promotion goals, what all these mechanisms have in common is their reliance on a shared understanding of human decision-making. This posits that people are invariably rational, driven by self-interest and motivated by tangible incentives.[72] Thus, for instance, when introducing a nutritional labelling scheme to address information asymmetries typical of credence goods, policymakers tend to assume that: (i) the label will be read; (ii) the label will be understood; (iii) the label will inform the individual's purchase; and (iv) the label will determine the overall individual's consumption pattern vis-à-vis a given set of nutrients.[73] After decades of experimental research,[74] behavioural sciences have empirically proven these assumptions wrong, by showing instead that individuals deviate in predictable ways from neoclassical assumptions of rationality.[75] After documenting systematic errors in thinking in lay people (cognitive biases) and

---

[69] ibid, 21; D Ariely (n 19).

[70] One may think about standard patient consent forms.

[71] For an overview of regulatory techniques: R Baldwin, M Cave and M Lodge, *Understanding Regulation. Theory, Strategy, Practice* (Oxford, Oxford University Press, 2011); C Hood, H Rothstein and R Baldwin, *The Government of Risk: Understanding Risk Regulation Regimes* (Oxford, Oxford University Press, 2001).

[72] For an exhaustive introduction to rational choice theory, see RB Korobkin and TS Ulen, 'Law and Behavioural Science: Removing the Rationality Assumption from Law and Economics' (2000) 88 *California Law Review* 1051, 1060–66.

[73] For a broader critique of mandatory disclosure, see O Ben Shahar and CE Schneider, *More than You Wanted to Know: The Failure of Mandated Disclosure* (Princeton, Princeton University Press, 2014).

[74] See, eg the seminal article by D Kahneman and A Twersky, 'Judgment under Uncertainty: Heuristics and Biases' (1974) 185 *Science* 1124.

[75] For a popular treatment see, eg Kahneman (n 68); Ariely (n 19).

tracing those errors to the 'design of the machinery of cognition',[76] behavioural research tells us that individual choices are conditioned by, inter alia, context (eg the shelf where the product is placed), social influence (eg the eating and drinking habits of the people you hang out with), and framing (eg how the nutritional information is conveyed). In particular, evidence suggests that salient, vivid and colourful indications are more effective than statistical and abstract information sets.[77] To stay with our food label example, the recent attempts to turn nutritional information into 'traffic-light' systems build on such insights and aim to better convey its underlying health-related message.[78]

It has been demonstrated that health promotion policies, by not engaging with System 1, have 'often failed to have the desired effect in terms of reducing disease incidence and burden' and, as a consequence, have produced limited results in terms of health behavioural change.[79]

Private economic operators seem instead to have successfully integrated the idea that environmental and social factors lead to behavioural change into their sophisticated consumer and marketing campaigns over the years.[80] Empirical evidence suggests that ready availability of tobacco, processed foods and alcoholic beverages that are packaged, marketed, and engineered to stimulate our automatic, affective system has led us to increase our consumption of those products.[81] This alone seems to suggest that 'nudging' works in influencing consumption behaviour. This, however, seems to have been proven only when its objective is to worsen your health. But, what about using the same techniques in order to promote health and in particular healthier behaviours?

The next two sections will address this question by discussing what behavioural sciences, and in particular nudge-type intervention, have to offer to public health in general and to the EU lifestyle policy in particular.

IV. NUDGE AND NCD PREVENTION

Given the largely preventable nature of NCDs,[82] current efforts to promote healthier lifestyle predominantly aim at changing individual behaviour so as to

---

[76] See D Kahneman and A Twersky, 'Prospect Theory: An Analysis of the Decision under Risk' (1979) 47 *Econometrica* 263.

[77] For a complete and detailed analysis of the several findings of behavioural sciences relevant for regulatory policy see, eg Sunstein (n 29).

[78] See, eg M Friant-Perrot and A Garde, 'From BSE to Obesity—EFSA's Growing Role in the EU's Nutrition Policy' in A Alemanno and S Gabbi (eds), *Foundations of EU Food Law and Policy—Ten Years of European Food Safety Authority* (London, Ashgate, 2013).

[79] WHO Regional Committee for Europe, 'Behaviour Change Strategies and Health: The Role of Health Systems' (WHO, 2008).

[80] See, eg J Blythman, *Shopped: The Shocking Power of British Supermarkets* (London, Fourth Estate, 2014).

[81] See, eg T Lobstein, 'Tackling Childhood Obesity in an Era of Trade Liberalisation' in C Hawkes et al (eds), *Trade, Food, Diet and Health: Perspectives and Policy Options* (New York, Wiley Blackwell, 2010).

[82] WHO, *Global Status Report on Non-Communicable Diseases* (Geneva, WHO, 2011).

reduce overall consumption of tobacco, alcohol, and unhealthy diets, including excessive salt, fat, and sugar intake.[83] In other words, if people did not smoke, drank less, ate healthier diets, and were more physically active, the growing burden of NCDs, would be less alarming today. Therefore, one of the main challenges facing any form of lifestyle intervention, including the WHO's definition of the correct 'regulatory mix', is how to generate individual and population-wide behavioural change vis-à-vis these main lifestyle risk factors. While there is convincing evidence that healthy behaviours including smoking abstinence, weight management, blood pressure control and regular exercise are associated with longer life span and better quality of life,[84] the question remains how to induce individuals to embrace these practices.[85]

Given its inherent behavioural-change vocation, the legal system appears—at least on paper—well-suited to effectively take on such a role. Yet, any regulatory intervention aimed at promoting healthier lifestyles is highly contested. This is predominantly due to the multifactorial nature of NCDs (eg a multitude of factors is responsible for obesity) and their associated lifestyle risk factors as well as their important social gradients (socio-economics matter in the distribution of the burden of disease).[86] Challenges pertain to the legality of behavioural intervention (is it legal to induce behaviour?),[87] its design (how to motivate behavioural change?), legitimacy (should we motivate behavioural change?),[88] as well as the effectiveness of policy intervention (will it actually induce behavioural change?).[89] To date, few behaviourally informed interventions have been evaluated for their effectiveness in changing behaviour at the population level and virtually none has been evaluated for its ability to achieve sustained change of the kind needed to lead to health gains in the long term.[90] Critics to the behavioural paradigm argue that

---

[83] WHO Regional Office for Europe, 'Action Plan' (n 58) 1.
[84] See, eg WHO Regional Committee for Europe, 'Behaviour Change Strategies' (n 79) 1.
[85] Garde (n 49); R Magnusson and D Patterson, 'Role of Law in Global Response to Non-communicable Diseases' (2011) 378(9794) *The Lancet* 859; G Lien and K Deland, 'Translating the WHO Framework Convention on Tobacco Control (FCTC): Can We Use Tobacco Control as a Model for Other Non-communicable Disease Control?' (2011) *Public Health* 847; G Alleyne et al, 'Embedding Non-communicable Diseases in the Post-2015 Development Agenda' (2013) *The Lancet* 566; A Alemanno and A Garde, 'The Prevention of Non-Communicable Diseases in the European Union' in T Voon, A Mitchell and J Liberman (eds), *Regulating Tobacco, Alcohol and Unhealthy Foods: The Legal Issues* (London, Routledge, 2014).
[86] R Wilkinson and M Marmot (eds), *The Solid Facts: Social Determinants of Health*, 2nd edn (WHO, 2003).
[87] A Alemanno and A Spina, 'Nudging Legally: On the Checks and Balances of Behavioural Regulation' (2014) 12(2) *International Journal of Constitutional Law* 429.
[88] See, eg S Conly, *Against Autonomy—Justifying Coercive Paternalism* (Cambridge, Cambridge University Press, 2013); R Rebonato, *Taking Liberties—A Critical Examination of Libertarian Paternalism* (New York, Palgrave Macmillian, 2012); C Sunstein, 'The Storrs Lectures: Behavioural Economics and Paternalism' (2013) 122 *Yale Law Journal* 1826; P Guldborg Hansen and AM Jespersen, 'Nudge and the Manipulation of Choice: A Framework for the Responsible Use of the Nudge Approach to Behaviour Change in Public Policy' (2013) 4(1) *European Journal of Risk Regulation* 3; E Selinger and K Whyte, 'Is There a Right Way to Nudge? The Practice and Ethics of Choice Architecture' (2011) 5(10) *Sociology Compass* 923; L Bovens, 'Real Nudge' (2012) 3(1) *European Journal of Risk Regulation* 43.
[89] See conclusive chapter of this volume by A Alemanno and AL Sibony.
[90] Marteau et al (n 1); Holland (n 1).

both cognitive studies and behavioural insights can show why people might make certain decisions, but they are not robust enough to warrant reliable predictions about how people will behave in non-laboratory environments where variable perceptions of meaning exist.[91] It is indeed undisputable that an understanding of availability heuristics, social influences and status quo bias—to mention a few relevant behavioural traits—does not always lead to the same conclusions. It may well be that some of these biases work simultaneously in some parts of the populations, thus questioning their individual predictive power.[92] As a result, the diverse findings of behavioural research may point to different directions, even within the same subpopulation facing the same problem.[93] In sum, most behavioural insights relate to 'mechanisms rather than law-like generalizations'.[94] For purposes of policy, it would therefore be valuable to gain a better understanding of how the major findings of behavioural research apply within heterogeneous groups. Unfortunately, due to methodological and empirical complexity, current research has not been able to address the heterogeneity challenge

This is not, however, to suggest that the current health interventions, in particular within the framework of the NCD agenda, are totally indifferent to the findings of behavioural research. Today an increasing number of NCD prevention policies is—at least partly—inspired by, and often strives to integrate, behavioural insights. The most obvious illustrations include the use of graphic warnings on unhealthy products. While these warnings originated in tobacco control policy, they are gradually extending to alcohol and food products, notably the food high in fat, salt and sugar (HFSS).[95] These are either mandated by governments or provided voluntarily by the relevant producers in a number of countries and tend to take the form of reminders about general health risks associated with the consumption

---

[91] See also G Gigerenzer and R Selten, *Bounded Rationality* (Cambridge, MA, MIT Press, 2001) 10; E Selinger and K Powys Whyte, 'Competence and Trust in Choice Architecture' (2010) 23 *Knowledge, Technology & Policy* 461; A Burgess, 'Nudging Healthy Lifestyles: The UK Experiments with the Behavioural Alternative to Regulation and the Market' (2011) 3(1) *European Journal of Risk Regulation* 3; K Powys Whyte et al, 'Nudge, Nudge or Shove, Shove—the Right Way for Nudges to Increase the Supply of Donated Cadaver Organs' (2012) 12 *American Journal of Bioethics* 32; E Selinger and K Whyte, 'Is There a Right Way to Nudge? The Practice and Ethics of Choice Architecture' (2011) 5 *Sociology Compass* 923.
[92] A Schwartz, 'Regulating for Rationality' *Stanford Law Review* (forthcoming).
[93] See the chapter by O Lobel and Y Feldman in this volume.
[94] Sunstein (n 29).
[95] Graphic warnings are recommend by the Framework Convention on Tobacco control and are progressively extending to other unhealthy products, such as alcohol and food products high in fat, salt, and sugar (HFSS). In the alcohol sector, see 'Thailand—Health Warnings for Alcoholic Beverages'— G/TBT/N/THA/332 and Add.1—concern of US—11. In the food sector, Chile recently proposed an amendment to its Food Health Regulation which would place 'skull-and-bones-style' labels on the front-pack of any products considered as high in sugar, salt, calories, and saturated fat. The Draft Amendment and other implementing measures are due to come into force within a year from the adoption of the Law, ie in less than six months from now. The text of the Draft Amendment is available at: www.minsal.gob.cl/portal/url/page/minsalcl/g_proteccion/g_alimentos/prot_ alim_y_nutr.html (accessed 26 May 2015). To know more, see A Alemanno and A Garde, *Regulating Lifestyle Risks in Europe*, Swedish Institute for European Policy Studies (Stockholm, 2013).

of those products. Other illustrations include visual display bans at points of sale, visual prompts, portion sizes, and social norm feedback.[96]

Moreover, in recent times, major policy actions, such as the Global Strategy on Diet, Physical Activity and Health,[97] the NCD Political Declaration[98] as well as the 2013 NCD Action Plan,[99] have recognised—either expressly or implicitly—a role for behavioural insights in the formulation of new policies. Thus, the WHO Global Strategy on Diets, Physical Activity and Health clearly states that: 'Governments have a central role, in cooperation with other stakeholders, *to create an environment that empowers and encourages behaviour changes* by individuals, families and communities, to make positive, life-enhancing decisions on healthy diets and patterns of physical activity'.[100] To achieve this result, the WHO calls on the international community to promote 'applied research (e.g., into the reasons for physical inactivity and poor diet, and on key determinants of effective intervention programmes), combined with *the increased involvement of behavioural scientists*' (emphasis added).[101]

In turn, the 2011 Political Declaration on NCDs calls for the promotion and creation of 'an *enabling environment for healthy behaviours* among workers, including by establishing tobacco-free workplaces and safe and healthy working environments through occupational safety and health measures, including, where appropriate, through good corporate practices, workplace wellness programmes and health insurance plans' (emphasis added).[102] Similarly, yet more broadly, the 2013 NCD Action Plan recommends 'strengthening the capacity of individuals and populations to make healthier choices and follow lifestyle patterns that foster good health' through '*enabling environments*' (emphasis added).[103]

This brief analysis demonstrates that the WHO seems increasingly aware of the importance of both the social and economic environments to attain both individual and collective behavioural change. Yet, it does not expressly enlist 'behavioural informed' tools within the NCD 'regulatory mix', which, being formulated in broader terms, rather consists of 'the implementation of relevant international agreements and strategies, and education, legislative, regulatory and fiscal measures'.[104] Given

---

[96] This implies the provision of information on the healthy behaviour of others and is applied particularly in the context of alcohol consumption among students.
[97] www.who.int/dietphysicalactivity/en/.
[98] See the Political Declaration (n 7).
[99] www.who.int/nmh/events/2013/revised_draft_ncd_action_plan.pdf.
[100] WHO Global Strategy on Diets, Physical Activity and Health, para 11.
[101] ibid.
[102] NCD Political Declaration, para 43(a).
[103] 2013 NCD Action Plan, para 33.
[104] NCD Political Declaration, para 43 recommends to: 'Advance the implementation of multisectoral, cost-effective, population-wide interventions in order to reduce the impact of the common non-communicable disease risk factors, namely tobacco use, unhealthy diet, physical inactivity and harmful use of alcohol, through the implementation of relevant international agreements and strategies, and education, legislative, regulatory and fiscal measures, without prejudice to the right of sovereign nations to determine and establish their taxation policies and other policies, where appropriate, by involving all relevant sectors, civil society and communities, as appropriate'.

the open-textured language used in these documents and their wide understanding of regulatory action and best practices, a behavioural informed approach to NCD prevention does not appear excluded. Rather, the above-mentioned indications as well as the language used in these documents seem to encourage the international health community, including the EU, in the adoption of a behaviourally informed approach. Despite the existence of some insightful literature on these individual behavioural change interventions,[105] there has been little effort to articulate a framework capable of incorporating them into the regulatory process.

V. TOWARDS AN EU BEHAVIOURALLY-INFORMED LIFESTYLE POLICY?

By definition, lifestyle-related risks are extremely dependent on behaviour. Therefore, behavioural informed intervention in relation to these risks has the potential to make a real difference if well designed. For this reason, most of experimentation of behavioural policy-making thus far focused on them.[106] It is therefore no surprise that the EU has also been adopting some behaviourally inspired policy actions in recent years. The most notable example is offered by tobacco control. Article 10(1)(c) of the newly-adopted Tobacco Products Directive requires that each unit packet and any outside packaging of tobacco products shall carry combined health warnings covering 65 per cent of both the external front and back surface of the unit packet, and any outside packaging.[107] The choice of this new mandatory, combined warning scheme has been the subject of randomised control trials aimed at determining the most effective imagery and text in reducing the attractiveness of the packaging.

But behavioural sciences also informed other health-related policy areas, such as nutrition. Thus, for instance, the Commission, as part of its proposed Food Information Regulation, originally proposed that the 'front-of-pack' labelling of packaged food should become mandatory in order to facilitate healthier choices 'at a glance', that is without requiring that consumers engage in a thorough reading

---

[105] For a literature review, see European Center for Disease Prevention and Control, 'Systematic Literature Review to Examine the Evidence for the Effectiveness of Interventions that Use Theories and Models of Behaviour Change: Towards the Prevention and Control of Communicable Diseases' (Stockholm, 2013).

[106] In the UK the initial projects focused on smoking, organ donation, teenage pregnancy, alcohol, diet and weight, diabetes, food hygiene, physical exercise, and social care. See Cabinet Office Behavioural Insights Team, 'Applying Behavioural Insight to Health' (London, 2010) available at www.cabinetoffice.gov.uk/resource-library/applying-behavioural-insight-health.

[107] Directive 2014/40/EU on the approximation of the laws of Member States concerning the manufacture, presentation and sale of tobacco and related products [2014] OJ L127/1. In particular, this scheme combines a textual warning with a corresponding coloured photograph, thus making pictorial warnings on tobacco products compulsory (as opposed to optional as they have been since 2001) and the health message conveyed to consumers more effective.

of the nutrition table on the back of the pack.¹⁰⁸ However, this proposal did not make its way through the legislative process, and the Food Information Regulation as adopted in 2011 merely allows Member States to recommend a front-of-pack labelling scheme on a voluntary basis. This is what the UK has recently done with the agreement struck between the public health ministry and major retailers that food labels should combine traffic-light labels with reference intakes.¹⁰⁹ The idea behind the use of red, amber and green—which has been tested through a series of behavioural studies—is 'to guide the traffic' towards healthier choices and increase accessibility to nutritional information of a wide range of consumers, and assist them in making healthier food choices 'at a glance'. Moreover, it is believed that traffic-light labels may provide an incentive for manufacturers to develop healthier products—by reformulating their composition—thus avoiding the stigma that may be associated with having four prominent red lights on the front of their packaging. Eventually, the new Food Information Regulation requires that mandatory food information be 'marked in a conspicuous place in such a way as to be easily visible, clearly legible'.¹¹⁰ While falling short of requiring a 'front-of-the-pack' display, the Food Information Regulation also requires that the information be legible and presented per 100ml or per 100g.¹¹¹ These changes are intended to ensure that the information provided to consumers is both sufficient and clearly presented and therefore better able to facilitate—through a behaviourally-informed information scheme—healthier lifestyles.¹¹²

These illustrations suggest that the EU is progressively becoming aware of the potential of behavioural insights to induce behavioural changes and sometimes strives to incorporate them into its health interventions. Yet this limited set of interventions, being largely based on information schemes, seem to fall short of being part of a broader trend towards the systematic integration of behavioural sciences in EU (public health) policy-making. Moreover, the sudden success of behaviourally-savvy interventions seems to have more to do with the political acceptability of this underlying regulatory approach (information schemes rather than more coercive measures) than to their proven empirical effectiveness. Indeed, the major reasons for the lifestyle-focus of the first behaviourally informed measures is their potential to address the liberal reservations typically associated with

---

¹⁰⁸ See, eg WHO, Codex Committee on Food Labelling, 'What is "Front-of-Pack" Labelling?' (2012) available at www.who.int/nutrition/events/2013_FAO_WHO_workshop_frontofpack_nutritionlabelling_presentation_L'Abbe.pdf.

¹⁰⁹ On the UK scheme, see www.nhs.uk/Livewell/Goodfood/Pages/food-labelling.aspx. On 19 June 2013, the Department of Public Health published guidance on front-of-pack labelling: www.gov.uk/government/publications/front-of-pack-nutrition-labelling-guidance.

¹¹⁰ Art 13(1) of Regulation 1169/2011 on the provision of food information to consumers [2011] OJ L304/18.

¹¹¹ Arts 9(1)(l) and 29–35.

¹¹² Similarly, beverages containing more than 1.2% by volume of alcohol must clearly state their alcohol content: see Ar 9(1)(k) of Regulation 1169/2011(n 110) which repeals Commission Directive 87/250 [1987] OJ L113/57. As far as tobacco products are concerned, they must indicate the tar, nicotine and carbon monoxide yields on their labels: see Art 5(1) of Directive 2001/37 (n 47).

regulatory action vis-à-vis voluntary action. Indeed, unlike paternalists, who ban some things and mandate others, behaviourally informed intervention aims only to skew individual decisions without infringing greatly on freedom of choice.[113] Yet, this feature—as highlighted along this volume—represents at the same time the main virtue and weakness of behavioural informed policy-making.

Despite these limitations, our previous analysis made a case for more experimentation in behaviourally informed regulation in the EU lifestyle policy. This seems particularly true when examined in light of the limited results attained by self-regulatory schemes led by the food, alcohol, and tobacco industries.[114] While the evidence of what works in terms of behaviour change strategies is limited and too often anecdotal, several success factors have progressively been identified in policy-making. Today the first evaluation of the pioneering implementation of nudging in the UK suggests that behavioural change interventions focusing predominantly on lifestyle risks (eg tobacco, alcohol, unhealthy diets, and lack of physical activity) appear to work best when they are part of a package of regulation and fiscal measures.[115] As the UK Science and Technology Select Committee concluded, 'there is a marked lack of information about what works to change behaviour at policy level'.[116] Yet, given the potential for behavioural change of this innovative approach, choice architects must engage in the speculative and experimental process of designing the right interventions (eg display of choices, built-in environment, defaults, technologies, etc) that are adjusted for the biases and improve undesirable behaviours on average. Work on addressing clusters of behaviours, rather than single strands, and on understanding the behaviour of the most vulnerable and socially deprived members of society would also seem to be priority areas for investigation.

The NCD agenda established by the WHO does not seem to reject, but rather endorse, this experimental approach towards behavioural change. In these circumstances, there is an obvious need to evaluate the relative impact of the different policy instruments used and to monitor their impacts over time.

VI. CONCLUSIONS

Despite some resistance and significant methodological challenges towards the emergence of behaviourally informed regulation, there seems to be an incipient consensus around the idea that health policies, in particular lifestyle risk prevention interventions, cannot work effectively or efficiently if regulators do not consider how targeted people respond. In particular, an analysis of both the WHO

---

[113] 'Soft Paternalism: The State is Looking After You', *The Economist*, 6 April 2006.
[114] See, eg LL Sharma, SP Teret, and KD Brownell, 'The Food Industry and Self-regulation: Standards to Promote Success and to Avoid Public Health Failures' (2010) 100 *American Journal of Public Health* 240.
[115] Science and Technology Select Committee, *Report on Behaviour Change* (HL 2011).
[116] Science and Technology Select Committee, *Behaviour Change* (HL 2010–12) 18–19.

NCD Action Plan and of the EU lifestyle policy suggests an increased awareness of the roles played by environmental and social factors on behaviour change. Although the language employed falls short of operationalising the major behavioural insights into the NCD agenda, it clearly highlights that their integration into the current regulatory mix appears fundamental today for the design of any lifestyle policy intervention. The EU seems to have become progressively aware of the need to tap into the potential offered by behavioural sciences in the design of health intervention aimed at behavioural change. One may therefore reasonably expect the EU policymakers to engage more often with behavioural research in the development of their future health interventions, both when defining the policy problem and policy options available.

Yet, behavioural informed interventions are seldom sufficient to induce change from unhealthy to healthy behaviours for the good of the individual and of society as a whole.[117] In particular, it is submitted that without incorporating behavioural insights into more traditional forms of intervention it might be difficult to offset—what we have defined 'counter nudges'[118]—the potent effects of unhealthy nudges in existing environments shaped largely by industry. There is indeed a serious risk that, due to the high political acceptability of behaviourally inspired measures, notably of information schemes, policymakers may hesitate to adopt more stringent health measures, even when those are required by the gravity of the health issue at stake. In particular, by focusing on the 'choice architecture' alone, a behavioural approach to lifestyle intervention might fail to address the leading background incentives in consumer choice: the price, as influenced both by taxation and subsidies.[119] Likewise, the current empirical limitations in measuring the effectiveness of behaviourally informed policies in the design of population-wide health interventions may represent a major obstacle to their successful implementation.

However, although the first evaluation of the experimental application of nudges revealed mixed results,[120] it also illustrates that behavioural intervention, which is in its infancy, already offers additional models of public action.[121]

It is in the light of the above that this chapter demonstrates that while increased awareness, knowledge, and a better understanding of changed attitudes are necessary to behaviour change, only a combination of policy instruments, for example, legislation, regulation, individual economic incentives, such as minimum pricing and subsidies, as well as fiscal measures, may attain policy objectives. Seen from this perspective, a behavioural informed approach may complement the emerging regulatory mix of health prevention, especially within the NCD agenda. The challenge is to operationalise a behaviourally informed approach capable of

---

[117] See, eg WA Bogart, *Regulating Obesity?* (Oxford, Oxford University Press, 2013); *World Development Report* (n 1).
[118] See introductory chapter of this volume.
[119] See, on this point, Wise (n 15).
[120] 'Report on Behaviour Change' (n 115).
[121] 'Behaviour Change' (n 116) 18–19.

inducing behaviour change of the scale required to reduce the burden of chronic disease at the population level. This seems to present an additional challenge for the EU insofar as its action in health, and notably its role in promoting healthier lifestyle, is subject to the condition that it produces a 'Union Added Value'.[122] It remains therefore to be seen whether the gradual consideration of behavioural sciences into policy-making could contribute to tilt the balance towards EU—or Member States—action when examining the boundaries of EU health policy.

As behavioural change has recently become the focus of health promotion efforts, the most immediate lesson learned for EU health policy is that there is more to behaviour change than merely empowering the targeted individuals, communities and populations with the necessary information. It is about time to make that information smart within the framework of a more behavioural-aware lifestyle policy.

---

[122] See Art 1 of Regulation (EU) 282/2014 of the European Parliament and of the Council of 11 March 2014 on the establishment of a third Programme for the Union's action in the field of health (2014–20) [2014] OJ L86/1.

11

Conduct of Business Rules in EU Financial Services Regulation: Behavioural Rules Devoid of Behavioural Analysis?

PIETER VAN CLEYNENBREUGEL

I. INTRODUCTION

THE DEVELOPMENT OF a single rule book for financial services within the European Union has become the centrepiece of EU financial market regulation. A clear behavioural focus underlies the rule book, most directly manifested throughout the adoption of mandatory conduct of business rules. Despite such focus however, behavioural sciences' insights have only played a disparate and marginal role in the single rule book's set-up. Such insights have additionally almost completely been ignored in the development of EU and national enforcement structures, which continue to operate on the basis of neoclassical deterrence and rationality assumptions. As a result, the institutional and regulatory set-up of the EU financial services regulatory regime somehow constrains behaviourally inspired policy intentions.

This chapter identifies first the mismatch between behavioural intentions of the reform and the realities of EU financial services rule-making and enforcement. Secondly it explores whether such disconnect should be maintained. After providing a succinct overview of the development and scope of the EU single rule book enterprise and the role of mandatory rules therein (Section II), it submits that the structural features of EU financial market regulation generally leave little room for behavioural sciences' insights to be voiced in both the rule-making and enforcement stages (Section III). Arguing that the adoption of mandatory behavioural rules at the very least implies an EU legislative acknowledgement that neoclassical economic insights are no longer exclusively valid, the chapter subsequently conceptualises the extent to which behavioural sciences' insights could better be accommodated for within the present regulatory framework. Building upon the behavioural rules momentum presently prevailing in the field and taking the realities of the single rule book project into account, it proposes a gradual and modest incorporation of behaviourally inspired guideline standards complementing the EU's rule book project (Section IV).

II. THE DEVELOPMENT OF EU BEHAVIOURAL RULES FOR FINANCIAL SERVICES

The regulation of financial services has always been a part of the EU's market integration project.[1] Early regulatory initiatives sought to enable cross-border *market access* for financial services providers across different Member States.[2] The regulation of such access only *marginally* focused on directly regulating financial services providers' market behaviour within newly accessible markets. In light of the establishment of a single currency zone and accompanying monetary union however, an incomplete financial services regulatory framework became politically undesirable.[3] In the late 1990s, the European Commission therefore developed a Financial Services Action Plan (FSAP). The Action Plan envisaged 42 regulatory measures focusing on both wholesale and retail markets.[4] In addition, the Plan envisaged the creation of a 'single rule book' for financial services applicable across the European Union. The single rule book was to offer a uniform regulatory framework governing how the financial services transactions were to be conducted and enforced.[5]

FSAP proposals subsequently materialised into EU financial market legislation on four different levels of regulatory intervention.[6] Level one laid down general principles in EU Regulations and Directives.[7] Level two intended to implement

---

[1] A first reference in that respect has been the Segré Report in 1966, see, 'The Development of a European Capital Market. Report by a Group of Experts appointed EEC Commission', available at ec.europa.eu/economy_finance/emu_history/documentation/chapter1/19661130en382develeurocapi tm_a.pdf (last consulted 29 March 2014). More information on that report can also be found in I H-Y Chiu, *Regulatory Convergence in EU Securities Regulation* (London, Kluwer Law International, 2008) 1–2.

[2] F Woolridge, 'Some Recent Community Legislation in the Field of Securities Law' (1985) 10 *EL Rev* 6; G Ferrarini, 'Securities Regulation and the Rise of Pan-European Securities Markets: An Overview' in G Ferrarini, K Hopt and E Wymeersch (eds), *Capital Markets in the Age of the Euro. Cross-border Transactions, Listed Companies and Regulation* (London, Kluwer Law International, 2002) 282.

[3] 'Implementing the Framework for Financial Markets: Action Plan', ec.europa.eu/internal_market/ finances/actionplan/index_en.htm (FSAP), 5.

[4] ibid, 3.

[5] See, for an overview of regulatory activities directly flowing from the FSAP, ec.europa.eu/ internal_market/finances/docs/actionplan/index/100825-transposition_en.pdf. For an overview of national implementing rules, see ec.europa.eu/internal_market/finances/actionplan/transposition/ index_en.htm.

[6] 'Final Report of the Committee of Wise Men on the Regulation of European Securities Markets', available at ec.europa.eu/internal_market/securities/docs/lamfalussy/wisemen/final-report-wise-men_en.pdf (Final Report). E Ferran, *Building an EU Securities Market* (Cambridge, Cambridge University Press, 2004) 61.

[7] Final Report, 22–23. See also J Andersson, 'The Regulatory Technique of EU Securities Law—A Few Remarks' (2002) *European Business Law Review* 313.

those principles at the EU level through technical and detailed implementing legislation, be it through Regulations or Directives.[8] Level three foresaw the issuance of non-binding guidelines and recommendations on the transposition and interpretation of levels one and two Regulations and Directives. Those guidelines were to be adopted by newly established networks of national supervisory authorities, the so-called Committee of European Securities Regulators (CESR), the Committee of European Banking Supervisors (CEBS), and the Committee of European Insurance and Occupational Pension Supervisors (CEIOPS).[9] Level four focused on enhanced enforcement by the European Commission through the infringement procedure in Article 258 TFEU.[10]

The multi-level approach to EU financial regulation remains in place today. In the wake of the 2008 global financial crisis however, level three networks have been replaced by fully-fledged European Supervisory Authorities comprising the cornerstone of an enhanced European System of Financial Supervision.[11] The crisis also particularly prompted the adoption of additional legislative initiatives directly addressing financial products, financial services and financial markets.[12]

The extensive layers of regulation that have gradually come to be developed at the supranational level basically pursue two main objectives. First, EU rules continue to promote cross-border market access for both providers and recipients of financial services. Secondly, and more importantly, those rules also seek to contribute to a more *fair* market environment in which financial market operators— including consumers of financial services—are effectively protected.[13] Those protective rules first and foremost address the structure and soundness—as well as the liquidity and solvency—of financial market operators and could therefore

---

[8] Final Report, 28. On the differences between Levels 1 and 2, see Y Avgerinos, 'Essential and Non-essential Measures: Delegation of Powers in EU Securities Regulation' (2002) 8 *European Law Journal* 269.

[9] For CESR, see Commission Decision 2001/527/EC [2001] OJ L191/44, replaced by Commission Decision 2009/77/EC [2009] OJ L25/18. For CEBS, Commission Decision 2004/5/EC [2004] OJ L3/28, replaced by Commission Decision 2009/78/EC [2009] OJ L25/23. For CEIOPS, Commission Decision 2004/6/EC [2004] OJ L3/30, replaced by Commission Decision 2009/79/EC [2009] OJ L25/28.

[10] Final Report, 40.

[11] Regulation 1093/2010 of the European Parliament and of the Council of 24 November 2010 establishing a European Supervisory Authority (European Banking Authority) amending Decision 716/2009/EC and repealing Commission Decision 2009/78/EC [2010] OJ L331/12; Regulation 1094/2010 of the European Parliament and of the Council of 24 November 2010 establishing a European Supervisory Authority (European Insurance and Occupational Pensions Authority) amending Decision 716/2009/EC and repealing Commission Decision 2009/79/EC [2010] OJ L331/48; Regulation 1095/2010 of the European Parliament and of the Council of 24 November 2010 establishing a European Supervisory Authority (European Securities and Markets Authority) amending Decision 716/2009/EC and repealing Commission Decision 2009/77/EC [2010] OJ L331/84. The three Regulations essentially follow the same structure and will collectively be referred to as the ESA Regulations.

[12] For that distinction, see I H-Y Chiu (n 1) 13.

[13] See the overview in V Colaert and T Van Dyck, 'Financial Services' in H Micklitz, J Stuyck and E Terryn (eds), *Consumer Law—Ius Commune Casebooks for the Common Law of* Europe (Oxford, Hart Publishing, 2010).

be considered mainly *prudential* in nature.[14] In addition however, EU financial market rules to a large extent dictate provisions that directly regulate or confine the market *behaviour* of individuals and financial services providers. In so doing, the conduct of financial services' business has gradually been subject to more EU regulatory control, resulting in a bundle of *conduct rules* confining financial services providers' market behaviour for the benefit of more vulnerable or less informed services recipients.

Conduct of business rules simultaneously appear in two formats throughout the current EU regulatory framework. On the one hand, some rules directly prohibit financial services providers from engaging in particular actions. On the other, some other rules directly impose obligations on financial services providers in particular circumstances. Those obligations either include a general obligation to make the market more transparent (for example disclosing important or relevant information) or a particular obligation to take special circumstances into account (for example classifying clients in accordance with a particular investor profile). Both types of obligations essentially provide rights to investors or financial consumers that can be invoked and enforced against a financial services provider.

Prohibitions appear throughout the EU regulatory framework. The Market Abuse Directive imposes a prohibition on insider trading and includes presumptions in that regard.[15] The 2012 Short Selling Regulation explicitly prohibits particular short selling transactions.[16] In the wake of crisis, credit rating agencies have been regulated, resulting in those entities being prohibited from engaging in particular transactions.[17] Other prohibitions relate to the activities of undertakings for the collective investment in securities (UCITS),[18] to hedge funds (or 'alternative investment funds') investment decisions,[19] and to activities conducted on particular trading platforms.[20]

---

[14] On the concept of prudential regulation, see FS Mishkin, 'Prudential Supervision: What Works and What Doesn't?' in FS Mishkin (ed), *Prudential Supervision: What Works and What Doesn't?* (Chicago, University of Chicago Press, 2001) 1.

[15] Art 2 Directive 2003/6/EC on insider dealing and market manipulation (market abuse), as regards the implementing powers conferred on the Commission [2008] OJ L81/42 (Market Abuse Directive).

[16] Art 12–14 Regulation 236/2012 of the European Parliament and of the Council of 14 March 2012 on short selling and certain aspects of credit default swaps [2012] OJ L86/1 (Short Selling Regulation). The Regulation additionally provides for a disclosure regime.

[17] See Annex A of Regulation 1060/2009 of the European Parliament and of the Council of 16 September 2009 on credit rating agencies [2009] OJ L302/1 (CRA Regulation).

[18] Art 50(2) Directive 2009/65/EC of the European Parliament and of the Council of 13 July 2009 on the coordination of laws, regulations and administrative provisions relating to undertakings for collective investment in transferable securities (UCITS) [2009] OJ L302/32.

[19] See Directive 2011/61/EU of the European Parliament and of the Council of 8 June 2011 on Alternative Investment Fund Managers and amending Directives 2003/41/EC and 2009/65/EC and Regulations (EC) No 1060/2009 and (EU) 1095/2010 [2011] OJ L174/1 (AIFM Directive).

[20] See Regulation 648/2012 of the European Parliament and of the Council of 4 July 2012 on OTC derivatives, central counterparties and trade repositories [2012] OJ L201/1.

EU-imposed direct prohibitions are complemented by general disclosure obligations on financial services providers. Those obligations seek to protect investors by offering them all necessary information that allows for informed decision-making. The Prospectus and Transparency Directives both contain extended disclosure obligations,[21] as do the Market Abuse Directive,[22] the AIFM Directive[23] and the Short Selling Regulation.[24] General information obligations do not differentiate between the recipients of information. Whether or not an investor is familiar with investment products and decisions, general disclosure obligations assume that every investor will be able to make an informed decision on the basis of the disclosed information.

In addition to general disclosure obligations, EU regulatory instruments contain particular obligations aimed at protecting less informed financial services recipients. In those situations, EU law provides for additional mandatory rules to avoid the adoption of irrational investment decisions. The Markets in Financial Services Directive (MiFID) exemplifies such particular obligation-structured set of conduct rules.[25] Article 19 of that Directive imposed a rather vague standard on Member States to ensure that investment firms under their supervision act fairly, honestly and professionally and in the best interest of their clients. That obligation was subsequently followed up by the introduction of a set of regulatory standards those firms have to take into account as a matter of EU law.[26] Investment firms were asked to classify their clients in particular categories, determining the extent of legal protection offered by harmonised EU rules when engaging upon financial transactions covered by MiFID.[27] Whereas those rules were originally rather vague in scope and nature, a subsequent implementing Directive crystallised all particular standards mentioned in the basic regulatory framework into more detailed EU rules that were equally to be implemented at the national levels. Those additional rules set out in even greater detail the obligations imposed on investment firms.[28] In practice, those rules require investment firms to develop individualised client profiles, in accordance with which protective rules will apply

---

[21] Directive 2003/71/EC on the prospectus to be published when securities are offered to the public or admitted to trading, as regards the implementing powers conferred to the Commission [2008] OJ L76/37; and Directive 2004/109/EC on the harmonisation of transparency requirements in relation to information about issuers whose securities are admitted to trading on a regulated market, as regards the implementing powers conferred on the Commission [2008] OJ L76/50.
[22] Art 6 Market Abuse Directive.
[23] Art 26–27 AIFM Directive.
[24] Art 5–7 Short Selling Regulation.
[25] Directive 2004/39/EC on markets in financial instruments, as regards the implementing powers conferred on the Commission [2008] OJ L76/33 (MiFID).
[26] See Art 19(2)–(10) MiFID.
[27] See V Colaert, 'Welke bescherming voor welke belegger? Cliëntenclassificatie pre en post MiFID' (2007) *Forum Financier* 396.
[28] Commission Directive 2006/73/EC of 10 August 2006 implementing Directive 2004/39/EC of the European Parliament and of the Council as regards organisational requirements and operating conditions for investment firms and defined terms for the purposes of that Directive [2006] OJ L241/26.

with different intensity.²⁹ Clients classified as retail investors benefit from more extensive mandatory legal protection, including a right to more extensive and comprehensible investment information provided by the financial institution.³⁰ A similar investor protection focus can be detected in the key investor information document (KIID) investors are entitled to prior to transacting with a UCITS. Rather than merely disclosing all relevant information (as a prospectus would do), the KIID requires the provision of the most relevant information for aspiring investors to be disclosed in accessible terms.³¹ Key information documents oblige financial institutions to outline—in a simplified form—the key features and pitfalls of particular investments. A proposal for a Key Information Document (KID) in relation to packaged retail investment products (PRIPS) is presently also under consideration.³²

III. BEHAVIOURAL RULES DEVOID OF BEHAVIOURAL ANALYSIS?

Despite a significant increase in behaviourally informed rules in the EU financial regulatory framework, behavioural sciences' insights have only received marginal attention in the EU's single rule book built-up. This section outlines the limited attention for behaviourally inspired regulatory techniques (A) and provides an explanation as to why behavioural sciences' insights had an only limited function in the rule-making (B), and enforcement (C) stages of EU financial services regulation.

A. Limited Attention for Behaviourally Inspired Regulatory Techniques

The post-FSAP regulatory framework has been hailed as an effective and appropriate *'new governance'* toolkit to establish, maintain and update supranational financial regulation.³³ The design of EU financial services regulation exemplifies attention for and reliance on new governance techniques. EU financial rule-making

---

²⁹ This system is referred to as the 'know your customer' regime, for a schematic overview of client categorisation, see the European Securities and Markets Authority's guidance document, available at www.esma.europa.eu/system/files/08-003.pdf.

³⁰ Art 19(4)–(5) MiFID.

³¹ See Commission Regulation 583/2010 of 1 July 2010 implementing Directive 2009/65/EC of the European Parliament and of the Council as regards key investor information and conditions which must be met when providing key investor information or the prospectus in a durable medium other than paper or by means of a website [2010] OJ L176/1.

³² See the proposal for a regulation for a new Key Information Document (KID), available at ec.europa.eu/internal_market/finservices-retail/investment_products/index_en.htm.

³³ See for that perspective, W Van Gerven, 'Bringing (Private) Laws Closer to Each Other at the European Level' in F Caffagi (ed), *The Institutional Framework of European Private Law* (Oxford, Oxford University Press, 2006) 57–60.

processes start from the laudable assumption that participative governance results in more effective regulatory solutions. Attention to transparency,[34] stakeholders' participation,[35] and the accountability of expert decision-making[36] is firmly embedded in the regulatory framework. In the wake of crisis, a belief in self-regulated financial markets has given way for a publicly regulated and functionally differentiated sphere of regulation.[37] Administrative regulation—preferably adopted in a command-and-control mode[38]—thus serves to develop a particular rule-oriented framework of governance. Alternative techniques of governance, including soft law guidelines or recommendations[39] and administrative enforcement cooperation mechanisms[40] play a mere subordinate role in the EU's rule-making process. As such, new governance is entirely complementary and contributing to the development of an ever-thicker set of binding, applicable and supposedly enforceable EU rules.[41]

The EU's increasing attention to developing behavioural rules directly addressing the conduct of financial services providers implies that the neoclassical frameworks of rational market investors do not appear sufficient from an EU policymakers' point of view. Specific insights and techniques from the behavioural sciences would therefore appear more easily to gain room within this framework. The client classification, KIID and KID proposals clearly depart from the assumption that all investors make predictably rational investment decision. By imposing additional legal obligations and by entitling investors to additional information, the EU clearly chose to rely on 'mandatory rules' that oblige financial institutions to simplify and communicate particular investment risks. The application of those rules is only mandatory, however, if an investor belongs to a particular predetermined group of non-professional investors or when (s)he is taking an investment decision falling within the ambit of the KIID and KID proposals.

More recent post-crisis ex post regulatory intervention tools equally allow for behaviourally inspired considerations to be taken into account. The 2012 Short Selling Regulation provides a good example in that regard. According to the Regulation, national authorities and the European Securities and Markets Authority (ESMA) can take action to address short positions and their detrimental effect on the markets. In addition to imposing the disclosure of short positions

---

[34] Recital 55 ESA Regulations.
[35] ibid, Art 37.
[36] ibid, Art 3.
[37] See J Black, 'Restructuring Global and EU Financial Regulation: Character, Capacities, and Learning' in Wymeersch, Hopt and Ferrarini (n 2) 36, referring to a set of centralised legal powers is (mis)matched by very little operational or regulatory capacity to effect change at the supranational level.
[38] R Baldwin, M Cave and M Lodge, *Understanding Regulation. Theory, Strategy, Practice*, 2nd edn (Oxford, Oxford University Press, 2011) 105–09.
[39] See Art 16 ESA Regulations.
[40] ibid, Art 19.
[41] G Ferrarini, 'Contract Standards and the Markets in Financial Instruments Directive: An Assessment of the "Lamfalussy" Regulatory Architecture' (2005) *European Review of Contract Law* 29.

and a prohibition on trading,[42] the Regulation also allows ESMA temporarily to prohibit or impose conditions on the trade in 'shorted' instruments.[43] The Regulation does not specify the scope and nature of the conditions ESMA could impose in that respect.[44] ESMA itself also did not provide any additional guidance as to the scope and format of conditions it would impose in those circumstances. Whereas the mere possibility of imposing conditions limiting the scope and scale of short selling transactions would in theory allow for behavioural enforcement techniques to take shape—nudging natural or legal persons away from particular financial transactions—the current legal framework does neither outline nor structure or restrain the types and kinds of conditions that could be imposed. As a result, room for behaviourally inspired enforcement techniques can be said to exist. In practice however, the room thus created has not been used so far to develop a behaviourally inspired enforcement framework.

Within the EU financial services regulatory framework, behaviourally-inspired techniques are generally limited to the above-mentioned client classification structured mandatory rules and potential conditional ex post intervention examples. The limited scope of behaviourally inspired rule-making techniques can directly be related to the design and enforcement structures underlying EU financial services regulation. First, behavioural EU financial regulatory rules emerge from a decision-making process in which only detailed rules rather than vague standards can be adopted. In addition, the same group of experts remains involved at all stages of the process, which creates a risk of 'self-capture' in that potentially impedes behaviourally informed techniques and approaches to further take shape. Secondly, EU conduct rules are generally enforced throughout national jurisdictions as specific applications of national rules or principles on non-contractual liability law. National judges generally include conduct of business analysis into existing public and private law categories. In doing so, they indirectly promote rather than replace the rationalising legal standards generally underlying those national law frameworks. Both specific design elements institutionalise particular biases that impede a more structured attention to behavioural sciences' insights from taking shape in the context of EU financial services regulation.

B. Status Quo Bias and Group Thinking at Work in the Regulatory Design Process

The EU financial services rule-making process promotes the development of an expert-based rule-structured framework that promotes and sustains a rule

---

[42] Arts 5–8 Short Selling Regulation.
[43] ibid, Art 28(1)(b).
[44] Art 12 Short Selling Regulation nevertheless provides for some conditions under which trade could be continued.; the situation referred to in Art28 relates to ESMA's interventions in exceptional circumstances.

book status quo bias (i) and group thinking dynamics (ii). Both features result in behaviourally inspired techniques being granted a mere complementary role in the present regulatory design framework.

i. Rule Book Status Quo Bias

Although the development of *behavioural* rules remains high on the EU financial services policy agenda, more attention is devoted to the development of *rules* than to the behavioural techniques aimed at making those rules work. The Preambles to the post-crisis ESA Regulations clearly highlight this when they state that

> [t]here is a need to introduce an effective instrument to establish *harmonised regulatory technical standards* in financial services to ensure, also through *a single rulebook*, a *level playing field* and adequate protection of depositors, investors and consumers across the Union.[45]

The essentially rule-making nature of this project also serves as an explanation for the limited scope for additional experiments in new governance in this realm. The rule book thinking attitude prevailing throughout the FSAP-inspired rulemaking process fundamentally defines the scope and outlook of that process. The development of a single rule book in that understanding becomes a desirable status quo, in accordance with which all regulatory design elements should be structured. As such, rule book thinking status quo bias emerges.

Rule book thinking creates a situation in which the development of regulatory targets reflective of behavioural sciences insights appears to be downplayed. Rules in that understanding exclusively or at least mainly contribute to the coherence and completeness of a rule book as such. Whilst behavioural sciences insights could be incorporated in such an understanding, this will only be the case if and to the extent that their inclusion fits the rule book. Behavioural sciences insights are therefore not deliberately taken into account when designing those rule book rules, but only when they would fit the overall rule book development project.

The development of the client classification system in MiFID and the contrasting design of the market abuse prohibition exemplify this rule book thinking bias. MiFID obliges investment firms to classify their clients and to develop an investor profile on an individualised basis[46] to determine whether or not less protective conduct of business rules will apply. As such, EU law provides default rules to investors that deserve more protection, nudging investment firms to provide such protection.[47] Rule-making efforts have not however focused on developing

---

[45] Recital 22 Regulation 1093/2010.
[46] See Art 19(5) MiFID.
[47] On default rules, see A Alemanno and A Spina, 'Nudging Legally. On the Checks and Balances of Behavioural Regulation, papers.ssrn.com/sol3/papers.cfm?abstract_id=2337459, 11; and C Sunstein, 'Impersonal Default Rules vs Active Choices vs Personalized Default Rules: A Triptych', available at ssrn.com/abstract=2171343.

the conditions within which individual investors really deserve protection. They rather focused on outlining in more detail the particular 'default' obligations rather than addressing individual cases. As such, behavioural concerns became a focal point for a new rationalising reality in which the 'average financial services consumer' replaces the rational market investor and receives default protection. The development of a rule book—whilst being the main focus here—only indirectly, coincidentally and without serious behavioural consideration put into it, contributes to a specific behaviourally guided rather than truly behaviourally informed governance framework. Within that framework, the prevention of irrational investor behaviour is considered to be an important policy consideration, without however directly being informed and guided by behavioural sciences' insights.

The seemingly coincidental nature of the EU's reliance on behavioural techniques becomes even clearer when comparing the *MiFID* approach to other EU regulatory frameworks, such as the market abuse and short selling prohibitions. The Market Abuse Directive contains a general definition of what market abuse amounts to and establishes presumptions of market abuse when engaging in particular suspicious market transactions.[48] The same goes for the general prohibition on short selling. In the latter two instances—and contrary to the investment profile situation—EU law rather seems to be operating from a rational market participant perspective. Presumptions and prohibitions are meant to address presupposed rational behaviour, without however truly addressing to what extent seemingly irrational actions could be explained or addressed through the legal system.[49]

This example confirms that behaviourally informed concerns do play some role, without however fundamentally guiding the design of the EU single rule book in financial services. Although investor or consumer protection comprise fundamental policy objectives in the EU rule book's design, the development of a clear set of behaviourally inspired nudging techniques cannot be detected throughout the field. Rather disparate and self-standing attempts to nudge market operators are completely supplementary to the felt necessity of creating a rule book for financial services, which takes centre-stage across all three levels of rule-making. Behavioural sciences insights that have found their way into the new regulatory framework happen to reflect a coincidental technique if and to the extent that it fits the aims envisaged by creating a single rule book.

---

[48] Art 2 Market Abuse Directive. The adoption of a new Market Abuse Regulation is presently being considered, see ec.europa.eu/internal_market/securities/abuse/ for background. See on that issue also M Böse, 'Case Note Case C-45/08, *Spector Photo Group NV, Chris Van Raemdonck v Commissie voor het Bank-, Financie- en Assurantiewezen*, Judgment of the European Court of Justice of 23 December 2009, nyr' (2011) 48 *CML Rev* 199.

[49] Art 2(1)(b) Short Selling Regulation. See for background and on more detailed implementation initiatives, ec.europa.eu/internal_market/securities/short_selling/index_en.htm.

ii. Group Thinking: Self-captured Rule-making Processes

The institutional system in place at present further intensifies such bias by developing an essentially *self-captured* rule-making framework.[50] As EU financial services regulation is considered a highly specialised field of law, experts and stakeholders' input play an invaluable role in the rule-making process.[51] The very same stakeholders with the very same vested interests and institutional capabilities nevertheless consistently re-appear throughout the regulatory process.[52] The newly established European Supervisory Authorities (ESAs) are composed of representatives of national supervisory authorities within a Board of Supervisors. That Board of Supervisors is ultimately responsible for the proposition of draft technical standards and for the development of more detailed guidelines, recommendations and other reports. At the same time, those national representatives are also consulted or delegated to represent their government when discussions on the scope of Level 1 measures take place. Whereas this system ensures continuity and aims to bring more consistency throughout the rule-making process, it also threatens to create a tunnel view towards developing regulatory proposals. If and to the extent that such tunnel view is limited to developing a single rule book at all costs, institutional attention to the use, scope and necessity of particular behavioural sciences' insights threatens to be sacrificed in favour of developing and refining that rule book. As the same actors are involved throughout the process and the development of a single rule book seems to be an essential feature, ESA Boards of Supervisors are likely to be captured by such tunnel view.

The foregoing institutional limits do not however imply that behavioural sciences insights cannot find room in the EU financial regulation framework. Rather, behavioural insights have been taken into account in disparate fields of EU financial regulation—such as MiFID client classification—without however giving much consideration to which of those insights and regulatory techniques might work best in this field of law. Incremental attention paid to behavioural rules nevertheless highlights that at least behavioural sciences' insights could rather easily be incorporated in the regulatory framework and that overly attention to developing a single rule book actually amounts to *self-capture*, that is Boards of Supervisors being biased towards the single rule book project and such bias being

---

[50] On the effects of institutional frameworks on substantive law developments, see C Scott, 'The Governance of the European Union: The Potential for Multi-Level Control' (2002) 8 *European Law Journal* 65. On the role of law as a variable for institutional developments, see G Morgan and S Quack, 'Law as a Governing Institution' in G Morgan et al (eds), *The Oxford Handbook of Comparative Institutional Analysis* (Oxford, Oxford University Press, 2010) 275–308.

[51] See Art 37 ESA Regulations for details regarding the creation of specialised stakeholders groups. For background, see also M Everson, 'A Technology of Expertise: EU Financial Services Agencies' *LSE 'Europe in Question'* Discussion Paper Series, June 2012, available at www.lse.ac.uk/europeanInstitute/LEQS/LEQSPaper49.pdf.

[52] See L Hancher and M Moran, 'Organizing Regulatory Space' in L Hancher and M Moran (eds), *Capitalism, Culture and Economic Regulation* (Oxford, Oxford University Press, 1989) 271–301; C Scott, 'Analysing Regulatory Space: Fragmented Resources and Institutional Design' [2001] *PL* 329.

enlarged by their multifocal institutional roles within that framework. As such, the institutional structure of EU financial services rule-making creates a dynamic yet seemingly closed group environment in which the rule book project takes shape. Compliance with group dynamics and group thinking will in that regard eventually determine the format, scope and scale of the EU single rule book, as well as the room created for behaviourally-inspired regulatory techniques therein.

C. Rationality through the Back Door of EU Law Enforcement

The scarce attention granted to behavioural sciences' insights in the EU rule-making process does not even find its match at the enforcement level. At this stage, despite their promises, behavioural sciences' insights are completely absent from EU enforcement initiatives. Virtually no behaviourally inspired enforcement techniques are relied upon in either the public or private enforcement of EU financial regulation. The absence of behaviourally structured elements also results in significant uncertainty as to which actors (financial institutions, supervisory authorities, judges) should be incentivised to engage in behaviourally inspired enforcement tailored to the particular needs of a specific transaction context. Traditional command and control techniques as well as reliance on rational presumptions under national private law reintroduce 'rationalised' assumptions about human behaviour. Both public and private enforcement structures contribute to the limited appearance of behaviourally inspired insights in the field of EU financial services regulation.

i. Public Enforcement of EU Financial Regulation

Public enforcement of EU financial regulation generally relies on classical command-and-control techniques of law enforcement. Two dimensions need to be distinguished in that regard. First, the European Commission retains command and control powers under its infringement procedure in Article 258 TFEU to supervise and fine Member States that fail properly to implement EU financial regulation.[53] In doing so, the Commission does not directly intervene in financial services providers' behaviour, but rather controls Member States' behaviour. Such enforcement strategies do not directly concern financial services providers and will not further be discussed here.

Secondly, EU law also directly requires Member States' authorities to impose effective sanctions on breaches of EU-determined financial regulation. Whereas EU legislation does only on some occasions mandate direct sanctions—such as the

---

[53] See also E Wymeersch, 'The European Financial Supervisory Authorities or ESAs' in Wymeersch, Hopt and Ferrarini (n 2) 256.

revocation of a financial firm's authorisation[54]—Member States generally remain at liberty to develop an effective sanctioning mechanism. In the wake of the crisis, a Commission Communication on reinforcing sanctioning regimes in the financial services sector[55] made clear that the divergence across Member States' regulatory regimes had to disappear. The Commission stated that 'further convergence and reinforcement of sanctioning regimes is necessary to prevent risk of improper functioning of financial markets and will provide important benefits'.[56] To attain this objective, it introduced a plan for the approximation of national sanctioning regimes, centred around six key components: (1) introducing one or more types of administrative sanctions that must be available in all Member States in cases of violations of key EU provisions; (2) the obligation for all national authorities to publish and disclose the sanctions they imposed; (3) a sufficiently high level of administrative fines at threshold level to ensure deterrence is sufficiently guaranteed; (4) the availability of sanctions for both individuals and financial services firms; (5) particular circumstances that always need to be taken into account (such as the financial benefits gained by the infringer, the financial strength of the latter, the duration of the violation, etc), potentially also including and advocating criminal sanctions in this field;[57] and (6) appropriate mechanisms to ensure the effective application of sanctions in coordination with actions by other national authorities.[58] In outlining this approach, the Commission clearly favoured a direct and effective sanctioning approach to maintain the effective enforcement of EU financial regulation. The Communication did not at all mention alternative enforcement techniques, but rather sought to reinforce an effective 'hard law' sanctioning apparatus.[59]

The same approach prevails in the newly established enforcement system—in which the new European Supervisory Authorities play an important role—that presently supplements national enforcement structures. The ESAs have been provided with supplementary enforcement powers that can effectively address financial market participants. The authorities can adopt binding individual decisions addressed to national supervisory authorities and/or individual financial institutions in cases of breach of substantive EU financial regulation,[60] 'emergency

---

[54] See Art 18 Directive 2013/36/EU of the European Parliament and of the Council of 26 June 2013 on access to the activity of credit institutions and the prudential supervision of credit institutions and investment firms, amending Directive 2002/87/EC and repealing Directives 2006/48/EC and 2006/49/EC [2013] OJ L176/338.

[55] Commission Communication, 'Reinforcing Sanctioning Regimes in the Financial Services Sector', eur-lex.europa.eu/LexUriServ/LexUriServ.do?uri=COM:2010:0716:FIN:EN:PDF.

[56] ibid, 10.

[57] On the limited opportunities for EU action in that regard, see ibid, 11 and 14.

[58] ibid, 12–15.

[59] Contrast, inter alia, M Barr, S Mullainathan and E Shafir, 'Behaviorally Informed Regulation' in E Shafir (ed), *Behavioral Foundations of Public Policy* (Princeton, Princeton University Press, 2012) 440–64.

[60] Art 17 ESA Regulations.

situations'[61] and towards the settlement of disagreements between competent national authorities in cross-border situations.[62] An ESA body cannot adopt a binding individual decision without first reminding a national authority of its obligations, addressing guidelines or recommendations and allowing the Commission to address a non-binding advice to the Member State concerned.[63] In addition, the competent ESA can only adopt a decision addressed to individual market participants or financial institutions where the relevant requirements of the EU's substantive financial law framework are directly applicable to financial institutions and where national supervisory authorities did not take appropriate action. Binding individual decisions therefore remain an *ultimum remedium*. These decisions are always supposedly addressed to individual supervisors or market participants and are not general in nature. They nevertheless allow direct intervention in the financial markets. Binding decisions are also additionally subject to review by a newly established Board of Appeal.[64] Although the ESAs cannot generally impose fines, their decisions are binding in the national legal orders and will have to be directly enforced by national authorities. ESA decisions are thus meant to give additional force and focus to weak(er) national authorities.

More recent EU legal instruments have further extended this approach thus effectively transforming ESAs into fine-imposing sanctioning bodies or in bodies that can directly prohibit particular transactions. First, Regulation 513/2011 of 11 May 2011 designated ESMA as the responsible authority for the registration[65] and on-going supervision of credit rating agencies established in the European Union.[66] ESMA would also prepare draft regulatory technical standards concerning the information to be provided by a credit rating agency.[67] Most importantly however, it would directly enforce potential infringements of EU law. In so doing, the EU legislator believes that credit rating agencies can be induced into compliance with the EU regulatory framework. Secondly, individuals or legal persons engaging upon or intending to engage upon short sale transactions should *notify—disclose*—the relevant national competent authority if they retain a significant

---

[61] ibid, Art 18.
[62] ibid, Art 19.
[63] The so-called 'Giegold Report on the Proposal for a Regulation of the European Parliament and of the Council Establishing a European Securities and Markets Authority (COM(2009)0503—C7-0167/2009—2009/0144(COD)), available at www.europarl.europa.eu, makes this especially clear. National judges will have to apply and enforce regulatory and implementing technical standards. It could even be argued that national judges might be called upon to enforce guidelines and recommendations with which national supervisory authorities agreed to comply. Binding decisions should be considered as EU law in the national legal orders and are deemed to provide the effects generally attributed to directly applicable EU standards, see proposed—but later discarded—Recital 19 ESA Regulations explicitly confirming this position in the Giegold Report, 16.
[64] Art 60 ESA Regulations.
[65] Art 15 CRA Regulation.
[66] But not for the oversight of the users of credit ratings, Recital 9 Regulation 513/2011 of the European Parliament and of the Council of 11 May 2011 amending Regulation 1060/2009 on credit rating agencies [2011] OJ L145/30. CRAs should rely on a back-testing model, see Art 8(3) CRA Regulation.
[67] Recital 11 Regulation 513/2011.

short position.⁶⁸ As mentioned above, ESMA retains discretion whether or not to intervene in the markets and to impose additional conditions on particular transactions. Whilst incorporating the potential for a behaviourally attuned enforcement approach and for the imposition of incentives to financial institutions to adapt their buying and selling practices, the scope of such conditional ESMA intervention has not been considered as a tool for fine-tuned or alternative public enforcement schemes that would also involve financial institutions as publicly nudged actors in ensuring compliance with conduct of business rules.

Public enforcement approaches to EU financial regulation are remarkably cloaked in a 'rational market operator' image. Such image presupposes that effective sanctioning tools will create a sufficient amount of deterrence that will refrain financial market operators from engaging in market-adverse behaviour. In so doing, EU financial regulation did not truly address the underlying causes of the crisis, but rather sought to avoid them by imposing harder and more effective sanctions in a post-crisis world. Any behavioural concerns whatsoever do not appear to have been voiced in the recently extended supranational enforcement framework.

ii. Rationalising Private Enforcement in EU Financial Regulation

Contrary to the public enforcement frameworks in EU and national administrative law, the private enforcement of financial regulation takes place in accordance with national private law frameworks and is generally overseen by national judges. Private enforcement relates to situations where an individual claims that a financial institution did not comply with its obligations under EU law, for example with developing an appropriate investor profile or with faithfully executing the investment order made by a client.⁶⁹ In those situations, disputes generally arise under national contract law or national rules on non-contractual liability. National judges generally only rely on EU rules to operationalise and refine generally accepted rules and standards governing contract performance or 'duties of care' triggering non-contractual liability.

Given that private enforcement claims are directly related to a particular dispute, it could have been expected that a judge would like to take note of individual situations, motives and background reasons that guided the behaviour of both investor and financial services firm.⁷⁰ Reality does not however meet those expectations, as national judges tend to rely on existing doctrines in national private law. Those

⁶⁸ Art 5 Short Selling Regulation.
⁶⁹ See for a Belgian perspective, M Kruithof, 'Privaatrechtelijke remedies tegen inbreuken op reglementaire gedragsregels inzake beleggingsdiensten: zorgplicht, know your customer en best execution' in H Daems et al, *Bescherming van de consument in het financieel recht—La protection du consommateur en droit financier* (Antwerp, Intersentia, 2012).
⁷⁰ On the need for a more situational assessment in this field, see already J Hanson and D Kysar, 'Taking Behavioralism Seriously: The Problem of Market Manipulation' (1999) 74 *New York University Law Review* 632.

doctrines—that often require the court to ask what a reasonable financial market investor or investment firm would have done in the circumstances of a particular case—essentially rationalise the assessment framework within which individual investment decisions are to be judged. Rather than adopting a behavioural sciences' perspective, national judges re-introduce rational market actor models that implicitly still underlie national private law and that have already partially been addressed throughout EU financial regulation.[71] Private enforcement cannot therefore be considered an alternative to bring about more behavioural sciences' insights into this field of law. On the contrary, it tends to maintain and reverse any behavioural tendencies that would already have been going on at the EU level.

Investment services' conduct of business rules exemplify this approach. EU obligations to faithfully execute investment transactions and to develop appropriate client classification profiles have consistently been relied upon as starting points for a private law-oriented analysis on the basis of which national private law doctrines could be applied. Those doctrines essentially only resulted in well-known 'rationality-oriented' legal frameworks being applied and in behavioural considerations being downplayed. Enforcement standards such as the *bonus pater familias* or *reasonable duty of care* requirements do not generally focus on the particular and potentially irrational behavioural treads underlying a particular private law dispute.[72] From that point of view, the very structure and features of private enforcement are even less prone to behavioural sciences' insights than public enforcement proves to be.

IV. COMPLETING THE RULE BOOK: THE NEED FOR A *COMPLEMENTARY* BEHAVIOURAL APPROACH

The increasing importance of behavioural rules shows that neoclassical assumptions about rational investors are no longer considered guiding across this policy domain. As a result, policy room emerges for behavioural sciences' insights to be taken seriously at both the rule-making and the enforcement stages in EU financial regulation. At the same time however, EU financial services regulation is still a rather narrow-minded governance project, with regulatory initiatives being adopted or fine-tuned in the service of developing the single rule book.

The work-in-progress nature of the EU single rule book creates significant opportunities to better integrate behaviourally inspired regulatory techniques within the framework, if and to the extent that reliance on such techniques contributes to the aims set by the EU legislator. Whilst rule book thinking bias and

---

[71] Kruithof (n 69) offers illustrations.
[72] eg D Busch, 'Why MiFID Matters to Private Law—the Example of MiFID's Impact on an Asset Manager's Civil Liability' (2012) 7 *Capital Markets Law Journal* 386.

self-capture in rule-making and the deterrence through sanctions and 'national private law' centeredness frames in enforcement somehow limit the promotion of behavioural sciences' insights, small adaptations could be proposed to tailor the incorporation of behaviourally inspired regulatory techniques with the EU rule-making project. This section therefore proposes a modest strategy forward to at least consider the inclusion of behavioural sciences' insights more prominently within the minds of EU financial regulators. To that extent, it advocates the development of a *proportional impact assessment* test adopted by the experts developing those rules. This test would exemplify and operationalise calls for a more integrated approach towards behaviourally informed regulation in the European Union.[73]

In accordance with the test, the introduction of behaviourally-inspired regulatory techniques in both the rule-making and enforcement stages should be limited to, and premised on, a preliminary assessment as to the desirability, necessity and format of such intervention. In all those stages, policymakers would be invited to reflect more intensively upon the need for and scope of behaviourally inspired regulatory techniques so as to be included in the single rule book's design and to support its implementation and enforcement. As the adoption of behavioural rules provides an important step towards creating an EU financial services legal regime in its own right, it can be expected that behaviourally inspired techniques will predominantly serve as tools to refine, tailor or re-organise existing behavioural rules to the necessities of vulnerable consumers or investors the rules seek to protect. Prior to incorporating behaviourally inspired techniques in the regulatory framework, it therefore needs to be assessed whether, and to what extent, more attention to behavioural sciences' insights is truly necessary at this stage. In order to assess and improve the regulatory process, all stages of the test should be conducted in as public a setting as feasible.

The proportional impact assessment test would require policymakers—when designing rule book elements or enforcement structures and methods accompanying it—to critically reflect upon the actual aims of the behavioural rules they seek to develop, refine or implement at that stage. Only when the specific aims of particular envisaged rules are made clear, can it be determined whether and to what extent behavioural sciences' insights can offer a specific and more desirable technique to regulate particular strands of behaviour. Whilst such desirability assessment is at times already discussed upon and considered,[74] this stage of the test would invite policymakers to render the actual protective aims clearer and to

---

[73] See, for a proposal to integrate behaviourally inspired insights into the administrative law-making process, Alemanno and Spina (n 47) 10.
[74] The Key Information Document (KID) in the proposed PRIPS Regulation is an example in that regard.

consider what kind of behavioural sciences' insights need to be translated into EU law. In the particular context of EU conduct of business regulation, attention should be paid as to whether the development of more mandatory rules and client categorisation mechanisms should be envisaged. Additionally, the development of more protective 'default rules' rather than mandatory rules for particular types of clients could be envisaged, as well as the 'framing' of particular important investment information offered. In so doing, the format and shape of conduct of business rules could directly be influenced or fine-tuned on the basis of behaviourally inspired insights.

Once the desirability of behaviourally-inspired rules or techniques has been established, the need for particular rules or standards accommodating deviations from rational behaviour will have to be considered. As in the client classification of KID situations outlined above, policymakers would have to decide upon whether particular obligations and instruments are necessary to allow such deviations to be countered by more or less intrusive regulation. Only when such interventions are deemed necessary in light of the aims the rules seek to bring about could their inclusion be considered.

To that extent that behaviourally-inspired regulatory intervention is considered necessary, the format of such intervention should become the next focal point of discussion. Policymakers will have to determine whether a blanket prohibition, a case-by-case assessment or an alternative to a prohibition could be considered or whether alternative methods or formats of regulation should be applied. So far, such assessments have merely focused on tailored and simplified disclosure obligations, yet alternative techniques of regulatory intervention could equally be considered if deemed necessary for the purposes of the rules to be created. In making that assessment, attention necessarily has to be paid to the distributive effects of behaviourally framed conduct of business rules. As has convincingly been argued, interventions that restrict freedom of choice impose a cost on rational citizens who do not err.[75] Prior to considering whether or not behavioural mandatory or default rules will have to be adopted, the costs imposed on investors not in need of additional protection will have to be considered and preferably balanced.[76]

The test outlined above can be operationalised in a set of guideline standards that provide 'impact assessment' benchmarks in accordance with which EU behavioural rules can be refined in accordance with behavioural sciences' insights. In that understanding, the existing rules are not necessarily bad or useless, but less prone to incorporate behavioural sciences' insights if they remain unsupported by guidelines on how to effectively design behaviourally informed financial regulation.[77] Guideline standards would ensure that awareness for behavioural sciences'

---

[75] J Rachlinski, 'Cognitive Errors, Individual Differences, and Paternalism' (2006) 73 *University of Chicago Law Review* 224.
[76] A Tor, 'The Methodology of the Behavioral Analysis of Law' (2008) 4 *Haifa Law Review* 321.
[77] C Sunstein, 'Empirically Informed Regulation' (2011) 78 *University of Chicago Law Review* 1349.

insights will be increased throughout and better integrated within the single rule book process currently taking shape in the European Union. It is well-known that guideline standards differ from binding rule-making rules by virtue of being more vague, open-ended and prone to different interpretations in different settings.[78] The proposals advocated here argue in favour of designing standards that incorporate behavioural sciences-proof approaches to rule-making and enforcement. Those guideline standards would serve as policy guidelines. They would not replace the rule book and enforcement structures in place, but would rather guide the development of those structures into behaviourally informed regulatory strategies. Two different sets of guideline standards can be proposed in that regard.

First, a set of rule-making guideline standards could address what types of behaviourally informed regulation could take shape. In the particular EU context, those standards should seek to address at what level behaviourally informed regulatory techniques and principles could best be fitted within the EU rule book project. Three basic premises can be considered particularly guiding in that regard. First, the framing, presentation and scope of disclosed information should be at the centre of behaviourally tailored EU financial regulation. Irrational investment decisions should be avoided as far as possible, which can be done by strategically influencing the framing of disclosed information. Second, in order to avoid biases against otherwise rational investors, framing measures should be developed as much as possible on an individualised basis. The present client classification systems to some extent take such individual differences into consideration. EU rules will have to enable an individualised approach, without however frustrating entitlements to legality, legal certainty and predictability that financial institutions and investors are entitled to. Third, a sufficient amount of flexibility and opportunities to deviate from default, or even mandatory rules, should be envisaged. As learning effects may result in investors taking better informed investment decisions, such effects should be accounted for throughout the regulatory process.

Secondly, in the realm of enforcement, additional guideline standards could be proposed as well. Given that national administrations and judges rely on particular sanctioning tools and frameworks enabling such tools, behaviourally inspired sanctioning techniques and alternative sanctioning modes could be proposed as standards to take into account by national and supranational enforcement bodies. Such standards would better allow different enforcement bodies to decide upon the most appropriate sanctioning approach within a particular case and would structure different authorities' discretion towards finding the most appropriate enforcement solution applicable to this case. Guidance standards could at a later stage comprise the basis for a harmonised approach towards EU financial law enforcement. As vague guidelines structuring enforcement strategies, they would effectively allow enforcement authorities to choose the most appropriate enforcement strategy; this nevertheless requires such strategies to be common across, and

---

[78] L Kaplow, 'Rules versus Standards. An Economic Analysis' (1992) 42 *Duke Law Journal* 580.

known among, the different enforcement bodies. Educational initiatives to introduce those alternative strategies would therefore present a necessary accompaniment of enforcement guidance standards in this respect. Enforcement guidelines would particularly address to what extent regulators should or could intervene on a case-by-case basis. Those guidelines would particularly address the need for adopting specific framing conditions (such as approving or imposing a template of KID documents for each particular financial institution), the scope and legal limits of nudging supervisory authorities can engage in[79] and the freedom of choice that should be left to financial institutions to frame and present particular mandated information.

Developing a regulatory process in which behaviourally inspired insights are more openly and structurally taken into account provides a first step in further refining the regulatory framework and the single rule book structure into an adapted and behaviourally inspired regulatory framework ever more in the service of the vulnerable investor operating within and benefiting from the internal market in financial services.

V. CONCLUSION

EU financial services regulation has gradually, but firmly, developed into a thickly regulated field of EU internal market law. Supranational behavioural rules have consistently been developed within a multi-layered framework of regulatory governance.

Whereas the development of behavioural rules demonstrates that EU regulators feel a need to protect financial services recipients—and thus hint at the need to correct the rational market investor image pervading neoclassical economic thought—the EU's regulatory approach allows for little, or at least limited, efforts at integrating 'behavioural sciences' insights into both rule-making and enforcement processes. At the rule-making stage, the multi-layered regulatory framework invites a rule book thinking biased and 'self-captured' group thinking process of regulatory decision-making focused on either overly vague or overly detailed rules. Those rules impede behaviourally guided regulatory techniques from gaining a rightful place in the EU financial services regulation framework. At the same time, however, the introduction of rules and the accompanying need for compliance programmes, incentives and other elements result in behavioural sciences

---

[79] See on those limits, Alemanno and Spina (n 47) 16–25.

insights to be potential candidates for inclusion at this stage. The obligation for investment firms to develop individualised investor profiles provides a good illustration in that regard, which is nevertheless somehow frustrated or limited by its inclusion in an ever thicker set of rules. At the rule-enforcement stage, the application of EU rules by national judges and within national private law frameworks results in rationalising—quasi-neoclassical—legal standards and presumptions framing the behavioural intentions of EU financial services regulation in classical legal doctrines. Behavioural intentions at the supranational level, if already timidly available, are thus thwarted within the rational confines of classical private law doctrines.

Recognising behavioural sciences' complementary potential at the rule-making stage and seeking to address the rationalising shortcomings at the enforcement stage, this chapter proposed the development of an additional behaviourally inspired impact assessment manual containing rule-making and enforcement guidance standards. Those standards would leave the accountability and legitimacy mechanisms of multi-layered rule-making and national enforcement mechanisms in place, but would also promote attention towards behavioural techniques to remedy rationalising tendencies that underlie both rule-making and enforcement frameworks. As such a balance could be struck between the necessities of a developing single rule book and the subsidiary need for a more structured response to behavioural sciences' inspired policy concerns.

Part IV

Problems with Behaviourally Informed Regulation

12

Making Sense of Nudge-Scepticism: Three Challenges to EU Law's Learning from Behavioural Sciences

PÉTER CSERNE

I. INTRODUCTION

IN THE LAST decades, empirical research on human behaviour has become increasingly relevant in both public policy debates and legal reforms. Regulatory impact assessment is a routine requirement or recommended complement of new legislative proposals, while interdisciplinary approaches such as empirical legal studies and behavioural law and economics have a growing impact on legal research. The rise of behaviourally informed regulation is arguably a new wave in this trend.

This 'behavioural turn' is welcomed in both policy-making and academic circles.[1] In the epistemic community of EU lawyers, there is much discussion about, and high expectations from, empirically informed regulation.[2] It promises a fact-based solid ground for effective, smart, responsible regulation, cutting through endless ideological debates. Interestingly, behavioural studies are sometimes expected to provide scientific backing for lawyers' ideas and intuitions about how 'real people' behave, as opposed for example to the rational self-interested

---

[1] Note that this increased interest is mutual: policymakers and legal scholars provide a market for behavioural economists whose research on human cognition and decision-making has the potential of becoming relevant for regulatory reform projects aiming at changing laws and policies. For instance, Daniel Kahneman made this telling remark: 'Actually, I think behavioral economics is the only hope for having psychology gain influence on policy. It is perhaps different in Europe, but in the United States, the gatekeepers who control academic input into policy are economists and lawyers. You can't do anything except through economists and lawyers'. M Zeelenberg, 'Psychologists Can Influence Society Only by Influencing Economists. Interview with Daniel Kahneman' (2008) 5 *Tilburg Research* 3, 12–13. It seems that by 'doing something', Kahneman means for his profession, psychology, to have an impact on policy-making.

[2] See, eg J-U Franck, 'Vom Wert ökonomischer Argumente bei Gesetzgebung und Rechtsfindung für den Binnenmarkt' in K Riesenhuber (ed), *Europäische Methodenlehre. Handbuch für Ausbildung und Praxis*, 2nd edn (Berlin, Walter de Gruyter, 2010) 160, 165. Many chapters in this volume, including the Introduction illustrate and document this growing interest.

agents in standard economic models, thus turning critics of orthodox economic analysis into enthusiasts of behavioural economics.[3]

In the old days legal philosophers used to start their treatises on law with metaphysics and philosophical anthropology. Their arguments about the nature of law were built upon a view about human nature. Nowadays, such an endeavour would look obscure and out of date to many lawyers. After all, we have science, that is empirical behavioural and social science to tell us how people behave, and the law at its best seems to be nothing more and nothing less than a sophisticated technique of governance, or to use a somewhat old-fashioned term, social engineering.[4] Yet, when we look at actual law-making processes and their outcomes: legal rules and decisions, in EU law and elsewhere, they seem to resist an easy import of empirical insights.

If we look more closely at modern law, and EU law is no exception in this regard, we shall find a tension between these 'old' and 'new' understandings of the nature of law. On the one hand, law seems to be committed to an idea of human agency. It provides normative guidance to reasonable agents. On the other hand, it is a regulatory technique in the service of policy goals. As long as there is tension between these two normative understandings of law, the general character of EU law as *law* is contested. This tension will be one of the determinants as to whether EU law is receptive to behavioural insights. While there are obstacles to the incorporation of behavioural insights even under the social engineering view, the view of law as normative guidance raises a specific kind of concern—or so I shall argue in this chapter.

In philosophical terms, my argument is based on considerations about the epistemology of law, that is the law's distinct way of knowing and thinking about the world.[5] How is law's *episteme* related to philosophical, scientific and everyday knowledge and why does this matter? Law is a relatively autonomous social practice, with its own internal rationality.[6] In terms of systems theory, one could roughly say that the law constructs a specific perspective for itself so that it can

---

[3] To be sure, behavioural studies are better seen as a way to test intuitions rather than systematically provide backing for them, and evidence is often counter-intuitive. Yet one of the reasons for the warm reception of (popularised versions of) behavioural economics among lawyers is arguably the concordance of many findings with common sense ideas of bounded rationality, bounded willpower, etc.

[4] For a classic statement of this view, see R Pound, 'The Lawyer as a Social Engineer' (1954) 3 *Journal of Public Law* 292.

[5] See, eg P Legendre, *L'amour du censeur. Essai sur l'ordre dogmatique* (Paris, Editions du Seuil, 1974); WT Murphy, *The Oldest Social Science? Configurations of Law and Modernity* (Oxford, Oxford University Press, 1997); A Rabagny, *L'image juridique du monde* (Paris, PUF, 2003); A Supiot, *Homo juridicus. On the Anthropological Function of the Law* (London, Verso, 2007); G Samuel, 'Interdisciplinarity and the Authority Paradigm: Should Law be Taken Seriously by Scientists and Social Scientists?' (2009) 36 *Journal of Law and Society* 431. I have discussed these issues in more detail in P Cserne 'Objectivity and the Law's Assumptions about Human Behaviour' in J Husa and M van Hoecke (eds), *Objectivity in Law and Legal Reasoning* (Oxford, Hart Publishing, 2013) 171–93.

[6] For an accessible overview, see S Taekema, 'Relative Autonomy: A Characterisation of the Discipline of Law' in B van Klink and S Taekema, *Law and Method* (Tübingen, Mohr Siebeck, 2011) 33.

observe its environment as distinct from itself.[7] In some sense, this distinctness of law's *episteme* is commonplace, in line with widely shared professional experience of lawyers. In legal procedures, at least the official participants approach reality through a certain 'filter'.[8] They are supposed to take on a 'legal worldview' and argue as if law's assignment of rights and duties, roles and responsibilities truly assigns people those things. Legal procedures follow elaborate rules on the burden of proof, the admissibility of various kinds of evidence, etc. These rules determine what can and should be taken as established fact *for the purposes of* a certain procedure or, metaphorically, in the eyes of the law. These determinations may differ from what counts as proven for scientific purposes or what is plausible in everyday interactions. This relationship between legal and scientific 'truth' has been and continues to be a topic of academic interest, doctrinal concern and policy challenge.[9] While aspects of this topic will reappear in this chapter, I am concerned less with the establishment of facts in legal procedures and more with the 'legal construction of reality' that operates at the level of law-making.

The chapter presents the argument in two parts. The first part distinguishes three kinds of challenges to the integration of empirical knowledge about human behaviour into (EU) law: epistemic (related to how policy-relevant empirical knowledge is generated), institutional (how this knowledge is channelled and transferred into legislation and other legal procedures) and normative (related to law's commitment to counterfactual models of human behaviour and non-instrumental goals).

While outlining these challenges is meant to make zealous advocates of the import of behavioural insights into EU law more cautious, they do *not* justify, let alone require, abandoning the project of behavioural law and economics or behaviourally informed regulation or anything similarly radical.[10] My typology of challenges is meant to contribute to a better understanding of what is at stake in the debate about EU law's learning from behavioural sciences, and how this learning process may go astray. Many of those who criticise or resist behavioural (law and) economics ('nudge-sceptics') tend to lump these three reasons together, thus

---

[7] N Luhmann, *A Sociological Theory of Law* (London, Routledge & Kegan Paul, 1985); G Teubner, 'How the Law Thinks. Toward a Constructivist Epistemology of Law' (1989) 23 *Law and Society Review* 727.

[8] See, eg C Engel, '[Book review of] Sunstein (ed) *Behavioral Law and Economics*' (2003) 67 *Rabels Zeitschrift* 406.

[9] For an accessible entry point into this somewhat obscure field, see D Nelken, 'Can Law Learn from Social Sciences?' (2001) 35 *Israel Law Review* 205. See also SS Silbey (ed), *Law and Science vol I Epistemological, Evidentiary and Relational Engagement* (Aldershot, Ashgate, 2008); J Yovel and E Mertz, 'The Role of Social Science in Legal Decisions' in A Sarat (ed), *The Blackwell Companion to Law and Society* (London, Blackwell, 2004) 410.

[10] For such radical criticisms see, eg MD White, 'Behavioral Law and Economics: The Assault on Consent, Will, and Dignity' in G Gaus, C Favor and J Lamont (eds), *New Essays on Philosophy, Politics and Economics: Integration and Common Research Projects* (Stanford, Stanford University Press, 2010) 201; MD White, *The Manipulation of Choice. Ethics and Libertarian Paternalism* (New York, Palgrave Macmillan, 2013).

adding further confusion to a discussion which is already quite complex. The goal of the first part is to disentangle these reasons and also to distinguish them from other types of nudge-sceptical arguments which are relevant but unconvincing or domain-specific.[11] Distinguishing reasons for 'nudge-scepticism' is not an exercise in academic pedantry; it is practical and useful because the (absolute and relative) weight of the reasons for scepticism varies across legal areas and policy problems. This typology is meant to bring some structure and nuance to the debate.

The second part of the chapter will elaborate on the third challenge, called normative, by explaining some less obvious and implicit features of the law's assumptions about human agency. It matters both academically and practically whether and how policymakers' awareness of and enrichment by behavioural research translates into changes in the doctrinal scaffolding of legal systems. Yet, until recently, little attention has been paid to the specific implications of behavioural insights for legal doctrine and for wider normative aspects of the law.[12] In particular, there is little discussion on whether and how this incorporation challenges the law's assumptions about human agency, embedded in fundamental legal concepts and doctrines such as consent and responsibility. I shall identify a certain ideal of law embedded in legal doctrines which is in tension with behavioural decision theory, insofar as the latter is based on a naturalistic view of human behaviour, that is a view that human behaviour can be fully understood in terms of the natural sciences. While I identify the normative challenge this tension generates, at the end the question about the compatibility of behaviourally informed regulation and (EU) law turns out to be a practical, not a theoretical one: the adequacy of

---

[11] A recurrent theme and concern in discussions about behavioural research and nudging relates to whether they justify a kind of 'new paternalism'. The concern of this chapter is a different one. Here it is *not* suggested that policymakers and legislators should resist behavioural insights *because* relying on them would end up justifying paternalistic regulations (and possibly, thereby putting societies on a slippery slope where individual freedom gets more and more limited and citizens end up at the mercy of supposed experts imposing their own preferences on them). Whether the latter argument (with or without the slippery slope part) is plausible or not, has little to do directly with the nature of law as normative guidance and its underlying assumptions. Although paternalism is morally problematic and paternalism by the government raises additional moral (and in liberal democracies, also legal) concerns, these concerns are sufficiently distinct from and hence not directly relevant for the issue of tension or compatibility between behavioural insights and (EU) law I am concerned with here. In my view, it is an open question whether behavioural findings indeed justify more or less paternalistic regulation than we currently have. I take *this* to be the relevant comparison, not the one between hard paternalism and a hypothetical libertarian 'regulatory' regime. On whether behavioural economics brings new arguments to the philosophical and policy discussion on paternalism, see P Cserne, *Freedom of Contract and Paternalism. Prospects and Limits of an Economic Approach* (New York, Palgrave Macmillan, 2012) 43–50, 137–39. On paternalistic nudges see, A van Aaken, 'Judge the Nudge: In Search of the Legal Limits of Paternalistic Nudging in the EU', in this volume.

[12] A Alemanno and A Spina, 'Nudging Legally: On the Checks and Balances of Behavioural Regulation' (2014) 12 *International Journal of Constitutional Law* 429, and van Aaken, 'Judge the Nudge' (n 11), are two recent exceptions. These analyses of nudging in law are similar but not identical to the present one. Their main arguments are based on specific substantive legal principles (rule of law, legality, etc) or moral premises (non-perfectionist liberalism), rather than on the epistemic character of legal doctrine.

the law's model of human behaviour depends on what we can and want to achieve through law as a specific regulatory technique.

II. THREE REASONS FOR NUDGE-SCEPTICISM

A. The Prima Facie Case for Import

Although the idea that regulation and policy reforms should be 'scientifically founded' is hardly a new one, arguably a new phase began when regulatory ideas such as libertarian paternalism and nudging have become widely known among policymakers and the informed public. As we know more about how people behave, including how they respond to regulation of their behaviour, it stands to reason to take this knowledge into account in regulatory design. It seems highly relevant, if not indispensable, for a responsible policymaker to know whether a certain regulation is compatible with these empirical insights.

This prima facie case for integrating the insights of behavioural research into regulatory policies is apparently even stronger with respect to EU law. After all the entire project of the EU may be conceived, to a large extent, as a teleological one aiming at wide-ranging political, economic and social goals, including market integration, balanced and sustainable growth, etc, and law has been identified as a key instrument to achieve these goals.[13] The stereotypical features of EU law reinforce this impression: goal-oriented and principle-based legal instruments, and purposive, consequence-based (*effet utile* style) legal reasoning are not only compatible with but almost compellingly calling for a non-formalistic, empirically-driven approach to law.[14]

In brief, it almost comes naturally to look at EU law as a policy instrument for social engineering, and to require policymakers to draw on empirically based knowledge about goals and means, benchmarks and impact, and the like. Almost. Yet the enthusiastic reception of behavioural insights in (EU) legal scholarship is sometimes just as superficial as the arguments of nudge-sceptics.

---

[13] This was the key overarching idea of the 'integration through law' project of the 1980s, see M Cappelletti, M Seccombe and JH Weiler, *Integration through Law: European and American Experiences* (Berlin, Walter Gruyter, 1986). See also D Augenstein, *Integration through Law Revisited. The Making of the European Polity* (Farnham, Ashgate, 2012).

[14] See, eg P Westerman 'Breaking the Circle: Goal-legislation and the Need for Empirical Research' (2013) 1 *Theory and Practice of Legislation* 395. Westerman argues that 'Goal-regulation increases the need for a more empirical orientation because (i) lawmaking is increasingly outsourced to non-legal experts and its concepts are often derived from non-legal discourse. (ii) Many rules are drafted on the basis of an empirical assessment of the level of performance that can reasonably be expected. (iii) Rules are primarily drafted in view of the achievement of policy-goals which invites to a constant monitoring of the ways in which these rules effectively contribute to the achievement of goals', ibid, 395. She characterises goal-regulation thus: 'In goal-legislation the central legislator no longer issues detailed rules that tell people how they should act; what they should do or refrain from doing. Rather, in goal-legislation the central legislator confines itself to stating broad policy goals, and leaves it to other parties to make sure that these goals are furthered and/or achieved. A good example of goal-legislation is the framework-directives that are formulated by the EU', ibid, 397.

B. The Epistemic Challenge

In the past decades psychological and neuro-scientific research has produced, extensively tested and documented a vast body of empirical knowledge on human decision-making, both in general and in economic and legal contexts. To simplify, the gist of the results is that, compared to the rational utility-maximiser of orthodox economic models, individuals are boundedly rational and boundedly selfish. People exhibit limited cognitive abilities and attention, and incomplete self-control. Human behaviour is often characterised by loss aversion, the endowment effect and framing effects. By using mental shortcuts or heuristics, individuals cope with complex decision-making situations reasonably well, while optimisation, in the sense of rational choice theory, would require an amount of information and a capacity of information processing that are well beyond the reach of human agents. This is, of course, a very condensed and simplified version of what has become an immense body of empirical knowledge on human judgement and decision-making, in part systematised, in part theorised, under various, partially overlapping headings such as behavioural decision theory, cognitive psychology, theories of bounded rationality, behavioural economics, adaptive rationality, etc.

This body of empirical research on human judgement and decision-making has been produced with or without possible policy impact in the researchers' mind but the findings are available to policymakers and legal decision-makers. I shall argue that the use of these insights in a legal context faces three kinds of difficulty. The first one is an epistemic challenge and concerns how policy-relevant empirical knowledge is generated.[15] Like any result of empirical research, the body of behavioural findings is fragmented, potentially unreliable and theoretically indeterminate.

Empirical research is often narrow in scope and its findings cannot be formulated at a high level of generality. While research shows how particular behavioural mechanisms work in certain contexts, it can provide empirical support for at most middle-range theories. Thus, the first epistemic limit of using empirical insights in policy design concerns its scope: an instrumental approach based on these empirical findings should have a rather narrow focus or alternatively, the question whether and what kind of generalisation is acceptable should be addressed.[16]

Those who raise this concern about the relatively low *level of abstraction* of behavioural findings in a critical tone, often also suggest that there is a need for broad general theories both in theoretical model-building[17] and in practical policy

---

[15] Although if we think of the fast-spreading culture of experimentation in governments, the above assumptions about the practice of policy-making is too simplifying, it still seems plausible that lawmakers take empirical findings as given in the sense that they can do little about empirical knowledge production. At any rate, these epistemic matters raise challenges which are distinct from the two other challenges I discuss below.

[16] I thank Anne-Lise Sibony for the pertinent and precise formulation of this point.

[17] This argument is raised in economics with reference to the internal criteria of scientific discourse. One of the key topics is the methodological status of the rationality assumption in economics, apparently

design and decision-making. They compare rational choice theory as a general theory of human behaviour (or its economic specifications such as the model of a profit-maximising firm) to the findings of empirical research in behavioural economics. They claim that a patchwork of findings about biases, even if each is sound and reliable in its narrow context, cannot form the basis of responsible regulation or, for example, economic assessments in competition law cases.[18]

Behavioural decision-making research is mostly conducted in experimental settings where the *internal and external validity* of findings is always of concern.[19] Although policymakers are often not aware of how scientific knowledge is generated and published, even a quick glance at the sociology of science may make one disillusioned about some of the results. The various, in part perverse, incentives of publishing in modern academia raise potential concerns within the scientific community. There are concerns about possible biases towards 'surprising results' in publication (more precisely the tendency to publish moderately surprising, ie non-trivial yet not altogether outlandish results in order to get attention and citation), about the representativeness of the published results relative to the entire body of findings, the unduly concentrated attention to certain popular or trendy research subjects, and similar features of research practice.[20] What is worrisome here is that policymakers and legal scholars grab at empirical findings without being able to assess their reliability.

A further epistemic concern for channelling behavioural economics or, for that matter, any empirical research into policy design is *theoretical indeterminacy*. Simply put, as theories are always revisable, at the time of a practical decision, even the most qualified policymakers and experts do not and cannot know which theoretical hypothesis, if any, is true. While uncertainty is a general feature of human practice, experience has shown various pragmatic ways out. Practice suggests and usually adopts one of the following strategies: relying on the overlapping consensus among scientists in a limited domain of cases where there is such consensus; using rules of thumb to pick one theory; or simply conducting more empirical (so-called case or event) studies to gather data, instead of testing an underlying theoretical model. For instance, while many behavioural economists and most behaviourally informed legal scholars work comfortably and often unreflectively within the conceptual framework of dual-system theory (distinguishing between

---

challenged by behavioural findings. See, eg VL Smith, *Rationality in Economics. Constructivist and Ecological Forms* (Cambridge, Cambridge University Press, 2008); RB MacKenzie, *Predictably Rational: In Search of Defenses for Rational Behavior in Economics* (Berlin, Springer, 2010); Y Foka-Kavalieraki and AN Hatzis, 'Rational after All: Towards an Improved Theory of Rationality in Economics' (2011) 12 *Revue de Philosophie Economique* 3.

[18] We have heard such arguments at the conference in Liege, especially in the competition law panel, represented by Alexander Winterstein's practical viewpoint.

[19] For this and other epistemic issues on empirically informed policy-making, see N Cartwright and J Hardie, *Evidence-Based Policy: A Practical Guide to Doing It Better* (Oxford, Oxford University Press, 2012).

[20] For a brief overview and some examples, see Trautmann 'Empirical Knowledge in Legislation and Regulation: A Decision Making Perspective' (2013) 1 *Theory and Practice of Legislation* 533.

an intuitive System 1 and a reflective System 2), this theory is disputed on conceptual, methodological and empirical grounds within philosophy, psychology, and neuroscience.[21] This issue of theoretical indeterminacy raises an epistemic challenge as to how regulators should handle policy-relevant (dual-system) theory-laden psychological findings in normative contexts and requires further arguments about second-best policy-making.

With respect to each kind of epistemic limit in empirical research, there are various proposals to reduce such effects and in general to make the research process transparent. Still, the lack of robustness remains. Most empirical findings are not robust enough to allow for confident policy conclusions.[22] The epistemic challenge can make one sceptical about proposals for nudging, almost suggesting that it is futile for policymakers to expect solid empirical finding coming from behavioural sciences. More optimistically, what can convince nudge-sceptics of the usefulness of behavioural insights *in this epistemic respect* is that (or when) the findings of behavioural sciences can be shown to be transparent, relevant and robust. Policy-making takes place unavoidably under the circumstances of uncertainty and on the basis of revisable theories. Empirical findings will never provide definitive results but incomplete evidence is arguably better than no evidence. When we consider alternatives from the perspective of the policymaker, one question to ask is whether nudge-sceptics have arguments to say that empirically-driven errors in policy-making, for example decisions based on unfounded generalisations, should be minimised even if it means continuing with a potentially high level of errors based on wrong intuitions or on normative premises?[23] To answer this kind of questions, complex epistemic meta-rules would be needed.[24]

---

[21] See, eg G Keren and Y Schul, 'Two Is Not Always Better Than One: A Critical Evaluation of Two-System Theories' (2009) 4 *Perspectives on Psychological Science* 533. As a matter of sociology of science it is interesting to observe how this theory, also known as System 1—System 2 or dual processing theory, eg as popularised in D Kahneman, *Thinking Fast and Slow* (London, Penguin, 2012), has framed policy-relevant research in behavioural economics. Eg Feldman and Lobel, 'Behavioral Trade-Offs', in this volume, IV.A.i seem to accept this theory without question. See also the quote from Kahneman in (n 1) above.

[22] This point is well explained and illustrated in Trautmann (n 20).

[23] I thank Anne-Lise Sibony for the pertinent and precise formulation of this question.

[24] See O Perez, 'Courage, Regulatory Responsibility, and the Challenge of Higher-Order Reflexivity' (2013) 8 *Regulation & Governance* 203–21. Y Feldman and O Lobel, 'Behavioral Trade-Offs', in this volume, draw attention to the selective reception of psychological insights into policy. Without discussing the epistemic or other reasons for this selectivity, they suggest 'to expand the interface between psychology and law'. By doing this they explicitly argue from the standpoint of behavioural scientists. Even though they acknowledge 'costs and benefits' of the integration of behavioural insights, they are ultimately imperialistic about psychology telling policymakers what they should do, thus they implicitly assume that all trade-offs are 'behavioural': if policymakers considered more relevant research, they would design better policies. See the chapter by Dunlop and Radaelli, in this volume, on humility in the integration of knowledge into policy-making. See also Section IV of this chapter on the unavoidable normative premises.

C. The Institutional Challenge

Modern law in general, and EU law-making, administration, and adjudication in particular, rely on a number mechanisms to channel empirical knowledge into law, including regulatory impact assessment, forensic expertise, or consequence-based judicial reasoning.[25] These mechanisms evidence both the perceived relevance of such empirical research in practical regulatory contexts and the institutional constraints that limit its use. Institutional challenges are related to the actors and channels of the 'knowledge transfer' from empirical research to policy-making; they concern the capacities and constraints of the various mechanisms that channel empirical research into political decision-making, and more specifically into legislation, administration, or adjudication. There is likely to be a significant loss and distortion of information on the way from research labs and journal articles to policymakers and legislators, judges, and bureaucrats.[26]

Such institutional limits are not specific to behavioural insights or, for that matter, to EU law. All political and legal procedures are characterised by more or less severe limitations, including time constraints, limited expertise, and the potential for capture by private interests. Obviously, there are huge differences across jurisdictions, institutions and possible legal domains as well. The main reason for nudge-scepticism in this regard is that law as an institutional mechanism is less receptive to empirical insights than interested and motivated private parties, for example businesses that want to harness behavioural biases of actual and potential customers. Perhaps the legal system is also less receptive than non-legal regulatory mechanisms—a point I discuss below.

Law as a practical enterprise of social control appears resistant to the integration of systematic empirical science of any kind.[27] This resistance is often due to how legal institutions evolved (or were designed) to deal with facts in general and empirical evidence in particular. For instance, as investigations are costly in terms of time, information-processing capacity or other resources, when facts need to be established in legal procedures, procedural law (or the law of evidence in English terms) requires different levels of confirmation in different contexts.[28] Even in

---

[25] See C Radelli and CA Dunlop, 'Learning in the European Union: Theoretical Lenses and Meta-Theory' (2013) 20 *Journal of European Public Policy* 923, and their chapter in this volume.

[26] CR Sunstein, 'The Storrs Lectures: Behavioral Economics and Paternalism' (2013) 112 *Yale Law Journal* 1826, and *Why Nudge? The Politics of Libertarian Paternalism* (New Haven, Yale University Press, 2014) ch 5, discuss some of these challenges, in terms of the government's 'knowledge problem' and 'public choice problem'.

[27] C Engel, 'The Difficult Reception of Rigorous Descriptive Social Science in the Law' in N Stehr and B Weiler (eds), *Who Owns Knowledge? Knowledge and the Law* (New Brunswick, Transaction Publishers, 2008) 169, also as Max Planck Institute for Research on Collective Goods, Working Paper No 2006/1, www.coll.mpg.de/pdf_dat/2006_01online.pdf (accessed 8 September 2014).

[28] To be sure, this is not the only reason for using different standards of proof, eg in criminal and civil cases.

law-making it would be overly ambitious to expect every piece of legislation to be systematically 'evidence-based'. Modern regulatory theories and practice suggest and use various techniques to respond to uncertainty, complexity, and lack of information. One of them is small-scale experimental legislation.[29] These may significantly improve the information base of behavioural regulation but, as we have seen in the previous section, there is often too little reliable and robust information available even for a benevolent and unbiased policymaker. And in many cases, benevolence and lack of biases are hollow aspirations.

Another kind of institutional challenge presents itself in modern complex legal systems which have developed highly sophisticated doctrinal structures. The adaptation of concepts and doctrines of a systematised body of law to empirically founded policy objectives generate systemic tensions. This challenge is similar to the one identified in comparative law scholarship regarding legal transplants. For instance, in the EU, each national system of private law reacts differently to the tensions generated by what are claimed to be empirically informed consumer protection Directives.[30] Comparative experience suggests that cross-jurisdictional differences in receptivity to behavioural insights may be due to differences in the institutionalisation and systematisation of law and in lawyers' professional self-understanding in that particular system, rather than to differences in policy preferences.[31] Intra-systemic tensions are not equally strong everywhere: their importance is contingent and domain-specific. As far as it can be judged in general, such doctrinal tensions are less prominent in EU law, where an instrumental and purposeful understanding of law dominates over formalism,[32] than, for example, in the laws of those EU Member States where formalism plays a larger role.

Intuition suggests a further reason why EU law might have an advantage over Member State laws in terms of this institutional challenge. This has to do with the motivation of lawmakers. To the extent that EU level law-making is either better isolated from or more costly to be influenced by special interest groups than legislations at a national or sub-national level, it is more likely that non-partisan empirical information will be available and used in law-making. Although I am not aware of solid evidence in this respect and such findings are difficult to appreciate generally, other chapters in this volume raise plausible doubts about the readiness of regulators to rely on empirical evidence, at least in specific contexts.[33]

---

[29] See, eg S Ranchordás, 'The Whys and Woes of Empirical Legislation' (2013) 1 *Theory and Practice of Legislation* 415.

[30] See the chapter on consumer law by Anne-Lise Sibony and Geneviève Helleringer, chapter 9 in this volume.

[31] The conflict between democratic principles and the authority of experts adds another set of considerations that limits any kind of empirically founded policy design. This issue will not be addressed in this chapter.

[32] See n 14 and accompanying text.

[33] See especially chapter 11 in this volume, where Pieter Van Cleynenbreugel suggests three reasons why in financial regulation there is less reliance on behavioural insights than would be necessary: 'rule book thinking bias', 'regulatory self-capture', and 'ex post national private law rationalisation'.

Behavioural decision-making research in fact helps us to better understand the nature of the institutional limits to the practical uses of behavioural research itself, thus providing an interesting recursive loop. Burgeoning research under the label of 'behavioural political economy'[34] suggests that one should not be overoptimistic[35] about how the information generated in empirical research is used by legal officials or more broadly in political and legal institutional mechanisms. What seems plausible is that in order to make nudging feasible, serious limitations of information, time and human resources as well as potential cognitive and motivational biases of policymakers need to be overcome.

D. The Unavoidability of Normative Premises and the Scope for 'False' Assumptions

Were it not for limited empirical evidence, regulatory capture, time pressure, or lack of motivation, could then law in general and EU law in particular be made genuinely scientific? Surely, this would mean translating empirical knowledge into good law by finding the best legal techniques to serve the public interest. This would come close to what was suggested in the introduction as the view of law as social engineering or evidence-based governance.

One may ask, however, whether law in general or EU law in particular is best viewed as such an instrument or technique of social engineering. For, even if we attribute important social functions or purposes to law in terms of changing incentives, it might fulfil those functions and serve those purposes in a manner that makes law distinct from the micro-management of human behaviour, 'governance by standards and indicators'[36] or techno-regulation.[37] This question needs to be addressed, I submit, if one comes to ponder the relevance of behavioural insights for EU law.

Is this a serious challenge to nudging by law? At first sight, the challenge refers to the idea that the standards for policy-making and legal design are not merely matters of empirical knowledge. There is a clash between two discourses here, empirical and normative, that cannot be easily overcome.[38] Even by taking the instrumental view of law under ideal epistemic and institutional conditions, it is not possible to justify any policy or legal reform with reference to empirical findings *only*, that is without normative arguments. In other words, even if law is

---

[34] For an explanation of the term see, eg N Berggren, 'Time for Behavioral Political Economy? An Analysis of Articles in Behavioral Economics' (2012) 25 *Review of Austrian Economics* 199.
[35] Pun intended.
[36] See, eg B Frydman and A Van Waeyenberge (eds), *Gouverner par les standards et les indicateurs: de Hume aux rankings* (Brussels, Bruylant, 2013).
[37] For an explanation of the term see, eg K De Vries and N van Dijk, 'A Bump in the Road: Ruling out Law from Technology' in M Hildebrandt and J Gaakeer (eds), *Human Law and Computer Law: Comparative Perspectives* (Berlin, Springer, 2013) 89.
[38] There are many ways of understanding this clash. See in general Nelken (n 9).

seen as a policy instrument, empirical findings of behavioural research *alone* do not determine how the law should 'model' its subjects and regulate their behaviour.

This consideration seems trivial but is worth emphasising because behaviourally based regulatory ideas, such as libertarian paternalism or nudge, are sometimes believed or at least claimed and advertised to be able to answer all regulatory questions empirically. They promise, first, to surpass long-standing normative controversies about individual autonomy and the limits of governmental action (they claim to be libertarian and paternalist at the same time), and second, to be inevitable (by necessity, it is claimed, there is always a default option, therefore, the question is not whether choice architecture is necessary but what kind of choice architecture 'we want'—a clearly normative question). Both of these general claims have been heavily disputed in the literature; it seems that they are largely false and even contradict each other.[39]

Normative questions are in fact at the core of behavioural economics, in the following sense. When researchers discover and conceptualise a so-called behavioural bias, it is not always easy to tell which features belong to the autonomous or rational self and what counts as a bias, that is an anomaly that potentially requires or justifies regulatory correction. Talking about biases or errors assumes a benchmark. We can only tell if a certain behavioural pattern is biased if we have a baseline. Whether short-term or long-term preferences should be respected, or how much risk-averseness is considered a bias requires a baseline. But what should that be? In some cases it is taken to be rational choice but in other cases, rational choice theory is indeterminate.[40] For instance, when conceptualising dynamic inconsistency or self-control problems, behavioural economics implicitly assumes that such biases occur against the background of something real and unbiased that can be described in terms of a well-defined baseline such as a rational decision-making self. Any such baseline, however, is both controversial and normatively loaded. There is no normatively neutral way to define a baseline for biases. While empirical findings may provide relevant arguments in philosophical debates about the self and autonomy, empirical research is not self-standing: it cannot clarify such conceptual issues on its own or without evaluative choices. This lack of conceptual clarity surrounding biases or human errors has important consequences, both practical and theoretical. Behavioural research cannot explicate what counts as a bias without normatively loaded conceptual choices and cannot contribute to policy-making without taking sides in normative debates.

Should the risk-attitudes or the inter-temporal preferences be respected as reflecting individual values and choices or should they be considered as biases

---

[39] For a succinct refutation of these claims see, eg O Amir and O Lobel, 'Stumble, Predict, Nudge: How Behavioral Economics Informs Law and Policy' (2008) 108 *Columbia Law Review* 2098; L Bovens, 'Real Nudge' (2012) 3 *European Journal of Risk Regulation* 43. For book-length critical assessments of libertarian paternalism and nudge, see R Rebonato, *Taking Liberties: A Critical Examination of Libertarian Paternalism* (New York, Palgrave Macmillan, 2012) and White, *The Manipulation of Choice* (n 10).

[40] LA Fennell, 'Willpower and Legal Policy' (2009) 5 *Annual Review of Law and Social Science* 91.

in need of correction? Should 'revealed' or 'laundered'[41] preferences matter for policymakers? Should short-term or long-term interests matter? Questions like these indicate that the conceptual groundwork of behavioural research unavoidably relies on normative assumptions about the nature of human well-being (welfare, interests, happiness, etc), whether these assumptions are implicit or explicit.

Another point to notice is that when it comes to policy-making, there is scope for 'false' assumptions about human behaviour. What these assumptions should be depends on both empirical and non-empirical considerations. As an example, consider the common assumption in mainstream economic theory that consumers and firms are 'self-interested'. This is sometimes interpreted as an empirical generalisation which in certain contexts approximates descriptive accuracy. For instance, strangers in a non-repeated interaction are assumed to behave in a more or less narrowly self-interested way. Behavioural decision-making research has been concerned with the descriptive accuracy of this assumption for a long time and also contributed to a better understanding of the normative consequences of the empirical findings on non-selfish behaviour in various contexts. Bounded self-interest counts among the key generalisations of behavioural findings, supposedly contradicting mainstream economic theory.[42]

From the practical perspective of policy design, however, the assumption of self-interestedness may have an altogether different role than a generalisation for description or explanation.[43] It can be conceived of as a counterfactual assumption made with a practical goal in mind, viz of designing an institutional order which is workable even if a significant proportion of the population does not support it voluntarily. In a scenario of institutional design where regulators want to prevent that a non-cooperative selfish minority exploit the (perhaps virtuous or otherwise internally motivated) majority who cooperate voluntarily, the argument for assuming selfishness is not a theoretical (or factual) but a prudential (counterfactual) one: incentive compatibility.[44] Roughly, it can be understood in this way: in order to be stable and effective, an institutional mechanism or policy should not go systematically against the self-interest of those subject to the institutional rules or policy nor should it generally require supererogatory individual actions that would rely on the exercise of moral virtues.

---

[41] For this term, see R Goodin, 'Laundering Preferences' in J Elster and A Hylland (eds), *Foundations of Social Choice Theory* (Cambridge, Cambridge University Press, 1986) 73.

[42] There is a large body of evidence on non-selfish behaviour, including 'altruistic punishment' (E Fehr and S Gächter, 'Altruistic Punishment in Humans' (2002) 415 *Nature* 137–40 (10 January 2002) and 'genuine' altruism, see E Fehr and KM Schmidt, 'The Economics of Fairness, Reciprocity and Altruism. Experimental Evidence and New Theories' in S-C Kolm and JM Ythier (eds), *Handbook of the Economics of Giving, Altruism and Reciprocity*, vol 1 (Amsterdam, Elsevier, 2006) 615.

[43] And economics may be understood as ultimately a policy science. See HR Varian, 'What Use is Economic Theory?' (1989) unpublished working paper, online: people.ischool.berkeley.edu/~hal/Papers/theory.pdf.

[44] See JO Ledyard, 'Incentive Compatibility' in SN Durlauf and LE Blume (eds), *The New Palgrave Dictionary of Economics*, 2nd edn (London, Palgrave, 2008), accessible online: www.dictionaryofeconomics.com/article?id=pde2008_I000027.

To illustrate both general points about the complex interaction of empirical findings and normative claims, consider another example, the design of consumer protection policy. Suppose that policymakers have solid empirical evidence to suggest that in certain types of transactions consumers generally fall prey to certain behavioural 'biases'. Should regulation aiming at consumer protection 'map' these biases into the law and thereby stabilise them? Or should it rather 'overshoot' with its assumptions of consumer rationality in order to let consumers develop through autonomous, although less than fully rational choice? If one takes a static view of consumer welfare, the fist alternative may seem preferable: boundedly rational or less than autonomous consumers should be protected against decisions that reduce their welfare. Dynamic considerations concerning learning effects, however, may suggest overestimating agents' autonomy or rationality in order to allow for the development of a capacity of rational and more fully autonomous choice through learning from (objectively or subjectively) wrong decisions. This would mean that the rules should be counterfactually modelled on rational or autonomous consumers. There are, of course, many other considerations that are relevant for the choice between these regulatory strategies. For instance, the regulator would need to know whether the transactions are one-off or recurrent, the biases are transient or persistent, responsive to additional information or time, etc. In other words, the lesson seems to be that policymakers should 'get the facts right' first. But once the factual baseline is there, one also needs a normative benchmark to start thinking about under- or overshooting with assumptions about 'rationality', 'selfishness' or other features of human decision-making in institutional or policy design.

This example suggests a more general claim. Empirical research is important for reasonable regulatory design but it is just one ingredient. Empirical knowledge is not decisive on the normative question whether institutional designers or policymakers and those responsible for legal design at various levels of decision-making should base their models, recommendations and regulatory instruments on 'true' assumptions about human behaviour or rather on 'false', that is counterfactual assumptions. From the perspective of institutional design or policy-making, empirical findings (psychological insights) are indeed crucial but institutional design also requires non-empirical criteria to determine the 'model' of human behaviour underlying (supporting) various policies. In this respect, the entire exercise is inevitably, though not exclusively, value-driven.

III. THE NORMATIVE CHALLENGE

This second part of the paper goes further and argues that the compatibility of behavioural research with the law depends crucially on their respective assumptions about human agency. Law as normative guidance (ideally) functions differently from a simple instrumental technique of social engineering and serves its purposes in a manner that make it distinct from other governance mechanisms. This poses a normative challenge to behaviourally informed legislation, based on arguments about the nature of law.

In a sense, this normative challenge can be read as a special aspect of the problem of institutional design, mentioned above. To the extent that policy instruments take a legal form, policy design cannot ignore the question as to how these driving values behind policies are brought in accord with the normative assumptions embedded in fundamental legal rules and doctrines. The question can be put like this: what happens when policy ideas are being transformed into legal rules and doctrines which are initially and often implicitly based on assumptions about human agency? In what follows, I shall argue that these assumptions of the law set normative limits to the import of behavioural insights into law.

A. Law as Normative Guidance: 'A Distinct Form of Social Control'

The laws of a well-functioning modern political community rely, at least to some extent, on assumptions about the moral agency and personhood of its members. These assumptions are related to a certain ideal of law as normative guidance, according to which the law gives reasons for action to its addressees who should be able to either obey or disobey the law.[45]

What I have in mind here is a rather simple idea about the epistemology of law in general, that is not specific to but also applicable to EU law. Lawyers look at human behaviour differently than natural scientists or psychiatrists. In law, we attribute motives and reasons to people and much of the law is about persuading people (or, more generally, giving them reasons) to act upon, refrain from acting upon, or sometimes to change their motives and reasons.

At the same time, some regulatory techniques, old and new, behaviourally informed or not, seem to disregard agency. Road-bumps would be a good example. When the regulation/governance/management of people operates through physical or technological restriction of their action space or manipulates their behaviour in such a way that they are forced or tricked into choosing or doing what the regulator wanted, without necessarily being conscious of being so treated, we are dealing with an instance of governance or social engineering which runs counter to the ideal of law as normative guidance. These interventions, whether based on behavioural insights or not, physically (or in the online world, virtually) constrain the action space of agents. Sometimes they are referred to as techno-regulation;[46] in effect, they represent a special kind of choice architecture.

Such (techno-)regulation is not wrong per se. Sometimes this is an acceptable or even commendable way of managing the behaviour of people. In other contexts, less so. For instance, it would seem a crazy idea to use techno-regulation only for preventing murder or treason. When techno-regulation is supported by

---

[45] See, eg LL Fuller, *The Morality of Law*, 2nd edn (New Haven, Yale University Press, 1969).
[46] For a definition of the term techno-regulation and an informative discussion, see reference in n 37, and RE Leenes, 'Framing Techno-Regulation: An Exploration of State and Non-State Regulation by Technology' (2011) 5 *Legisprudence* 143.

solid empirical findings of behavioural research, it may be an effective, (prudentially or all-things-considered) desirable and even justifiable course of action. In some cases it seems desirable that a smart physical or virtual choice architecture prompts people to choose in certain ways, without directly communicating the purpose of the choice architecture in place. For instance, it might be a good idea to send energy and tax bills along with carefully formulated information about peer behaviour, in order to trigger and harness social norms. Informing customers about the purpose of this exercise may make it counter-productive.

My argument is that by running counter the ideal of law as normative guidance, techno-regulation is in tension with a certain normative ideal embodied in law, including EU law. Obviously, this argument is only relevant to the extent that EU law, or more precisely the political community of which EU law is the law, is or should be committed to such an ideal. There seem to be some evidence for such a commitment, in part direct and explicit in form of a commitment to the protection of basic constitutional rights,[47] in part implicit, as inferred from rules and doctrines either in EU law or in principles common to the laws of the Member States.[48] In what follows, the distinctness of a legal, as opposed to a behavioural or social engineering perspective on human behaviour will be highlighted by spelling out what certain legal doctrines often implicitly assume about human agency. In the next section I discuss the law's assumptions about agency implicit in doctrines of legal responsibility as an example.

If we look at law as a normative framework for mainly voluntary interaction ('law as a guide'), we assume individuals as responsive to reasons.[49] This 'legal individualism' means that the law 'operates with a category which for it is irreducible'.[50] If, in contrast, we look at law as a governance mechanism, which is distinguished

---

[47] On constitutional rights as limits to nudging, see chapter 4 in this volume by A van Aaken (n 11).

[48] Sometimes the law makes its assumptions explicit, eg when a written constitution explicitly discusses certain features of human nature as a basis for human rights or when the official legislative reasons for certain consumer protection rules refer to consumers' (lack of) capacity to take well-considered economic decisions. Not independently of their supra-national nature, EU policies are, on the one hand, often very explicit about the policy problems they are addressing, while, on the other hand, they are sometimes notoriously and deliberately vague in terms of the goals to be achieved. There is a lot of interpretative work to be done and probably some non-trivial normative assumptions to be made, if one attempts to justify this view fully and to specify the scope and strength of such a commitment. For a more detailed analysis of the law's assumptions on human agency, see P Cserne, 'Between "Metaphysics of the Stone Age" and the "Brave New World": HLA Hart on the Law's Assumptions about Human Nature' in M Jovanović and B Spaić (eds), *Jurisprudence and Political Philosophy in the 21st Century: Reassessing Legacies* (Frankfurt, Peter Lang, 2012) 71.

[49] HLA Hart, *Punishment and Responsibility. Essays in the Philosophy of Law* (Oxford, Oxford University Press, 1968) 44.

[50] Murphy, *The Oldest Social Science?* (n 5) 197. With its focus on individual reasons for action, law is a unique and in some sense outdated regulatory system. As Murphy, ibid, 195–96, argues, 'In terms of the epistemic capacities and capabilities of modern societies, legal systems have … at once a primitive and a sophisticated understanding of those subjected to them through legal processes … Yet if the sophistication resides in scepticism and the primitiveness in what can perhaps be only called obscurantism and naivety, the question is why law continues to seem so important in our age. To some degree … law and the legal process have become a way of compensating for our sense of the inadequacy of the world we have created. In the drama of the courtroom in particular, we re-enact the idea that the individual matters and is a proper focus of attention. In this dramatic setting, the language of responsibility seems appropriate; here, mechanisms of blame and of hierarchy come naturally'.

by its reliance on coercion as the ultimate enforcement mechanism ('law as goad'), then the term 'law' becomes a catch-all category which includes all kinds of regulation that are capable of serving policy goals determined by a legally authorised regulator. In the latter case, there is no principled limit to rely on insights from behavioural economics, psychology, neuroscience, or any other empirical finding and to include them in the toolkit of what could be called manipulation.[51]

While law is typically backed by coercion, at least in some core areas such as contract, tort or criminal law, it works well when it is more than a goad, that is when it makes an appeal to human agents for how to behave and leaves it to them to decide to obey or disobey. This ideal of law as normative guidance, a specific way of social control, can be contrasted with 'conditioning' or 'manipulation'.[52]

Behind these alternatives, there are different views of human nature. Insofar as modern legal systems follow the ideal of law as normative guidance, there is a potential systematic discrepancy between the 'legal worldview' (law's interpretative scheme of society) and empirical knowledge. The epistemology of law suggests that some of the assumptions about human agency and personhood that are embedded in legal doctrines are potentially in conflict with naturalistic theories about human behaviour.

B. An Example: Responsibility

Legal doctrines on responsibility provide the prime example. HLA Hart's analysis of legal responsibility suggests that an entire set of doctrines related to legal responsibility are based on a certain view of personhood which in turn derives from our everyday notions and intuitions about human agency, as reflected in ordinary language. If, however, we look at these doctrines in a reductionist way, for example only in light of the goal of minimising social costs, it becomes unclear whether and how the law is distinct from and preferable to what could be a more effective way of cost minimisation. For instance, supporters of an economic theory of tort law could ask:

> Why should a legal system bent on minimizing the harm arising from human conduct by its regulation of that conduct pay attention to our ordinary concepts of action? Why should it attend to the way in which we identify separate actions, and so the limits of action?[53]

---

[51] Such reliance on empirical research is not necessary, of course. Law as goad is fully compatible with evidence-free regulation.

[52] 'It is thinkable that legal control of conduct might take the form of Brave New World conditioning, so that people were never tempted to disobey the law, or of preventive or incapacitating measures, so that people were unable to disobey. In contrast with such forms of control the law of crime and tort, quite apart from sanctions, makes its primary appeal to individuals as intelligent beings who are assumed to have the capacity to control their conduct, and invites them to do so. It defers coercion and punitive measures until it is shown that this primary appeal has broken down, viz. until a crime has been committed or some harm has been done'. HLA Hart and AM Honoré, *Causation in the Law*, 2nd edn (Oxford, Clarendon Press, 1985) lxxix.

[53] ibid, lxxix.

In other words, why should legal doctrine reflect our common sense understanding of human agency and personhood? Does regulatory design need to take these legal doctrinal constructs into account at all?

In response to such questions, some legal scholars refer to 'the virtues of the distinctive form which the legal control of conduct takes'.[54] For instance, Hart and Honoré argue that our moral intuitions about human agency provide a reason for maintaining the legal doctrine of responsibility.[55] This distinctively legal way of controlling human conduct seems to have, if not an essence, at least a distinctive form. In a way, this form is also related to empirical facts about human behaviour or our ordinary views of these facts. Certain features of the law seem to be required by empirical facts about the human predicament. While not conceptually or logically necessary, these features of human nature are 'practically necessary'. In 'our world' as we know it, that is in the phenomenological world, people individuate actions and think of each other as responsible for their doings, at least in central cases.

This is in accord with some deeply ingrained moral intuitions which we use in everyday interactions and communication.[56] The common sense idea of personal responsibility assumes that there are persons who consider themselves and each other as authors of their doings. When dealing with each other as fellow persons, that is not as patients or experimental subjects, persons care about intentions and faults of their own and of others. They take on this 'humane' perspective, instead of that of a psychiatrist or neuroscientist.[57]

It should have become clear by now why this ideal of law as normative guidance is in tension with behavioural economics and nudging. Whether formally legitimised by a legal regulatory framework or not,[58] some regulatory techniques associated with nudging, as far as their operative mechanism is concerned, seem

---

[54] ibid.

[55] ibid, lxxx–lxxxi: 'the idea that individuals are primarily responsible for the harm which their actions are sufficient to produce without the intervention of others or of extraordinary natural events is important, not merely to law and morality, but to the preservation of something else of great moment in human life. This is the individual's sense of himself as a separate person whose character is manifested in such actions ... This sense of *respect for ourselves and others as distinct persons* would be much weakened, if not dissolved, if we could not think of ourselves as separate authors of the changes we make in the world'. Hart made a similar argument in an earlier essay: 'Human society is a society of persons; and persons do not view themselves or each other merely as so many bodies moving in ways which are sometimes harmful and have to be prevented or altered. Instead persons interpret each other's movements as manifestations of intentions and choices, and these subjective factors are often more important to their social relations than the movements by which they are manifested or their effects ... This is how human nature in human society actually is and as yet we have no power to alter it. The bearing of this fundamental fact on the law is this. If ... it is important for the law to reflect common judgments of morality, it is surely even more important that it should in general reflect in its judgments on human conduct distinctions which not only underlie morality, but pervade the whole of our social life'. Hart, *Punishment and Responsibility* (n 49) 182–83.

[56] They can be suspended in certain other, eg psychiatric contexts.

[57] PF Strawson, 'Freedom and Resentment' (1962) 48 *Proceedings of the British Academy* 1.

[58] To be sure, this is an important issue in itself, and is discussed, eg by Alemanno and Spina, 'Nudging Legally' (n 12) and van Aaken, 'Judge the Nudge' (n 11).

to disregard agency. They provide choice architecture in a broad sense of the term but cannot be seen as normative guidance. They manipulate the physical or virtual action space of (potential) agents in a way that is either non-transparent or does not allow realistic options to choose (disobey). For instance, information provision about peer behaviour where transparency would make the intervention futile can be seen as a regulatory tool, which manipulates the behaviour of subjects in a non-conscious or at least non-rational way, that is without being recognised or recognisable by the subjects of manipulation. Such interventions may be more or less effective and more or less supported by findings of behavioural research. What is of concern here is that, to the extent they run counter the ideal of law as normative guidance, these interventions are in tension with law as normative guidance. The normative challenge from agency lies not in how a certain behaviourally informed regulatory intervention was designed (this is a matter for the epistemic and institutional challenges) but how it operates.

It is also important to stress that while some behaviourally informed regulatory interventions, such as mandated information disclosure, are easily compatible with agency, other instances of choice architecture are less so. Compatibility is a matter of degree. Cases such as sticky default rules where transparency and/or easy opt-out are doubtful are best seen as intermediate cases. To the extent they are transparent and grant realistic options to choose, they are instances of normative guidance.

The previous discussion assumes that the term 'law', in its central meaning, refers to a regulatory mechanism, which operates through normative guidance. It presupposes human agents who are capable of following reasons. This is qualitatively distinct from manipulation or mere coercion that governs or manages behaviour, for example by altering the action space of the agents when they cannot do otherwise than obey. Whether inspired by behavioural insights or not, these techniques use law as goad, not as guide.

Yet, if we think about how our action space is constrained in everyday life in the regulatory state by physical barriers (by speed bumps, at airports, in public transport, etc), encryption technologies (in our dealings with online or digital products) or nudges (a default option has been chosen for us or information and advice is provided to us in a certain format), the tension between law as normative guidance and behaviourally informed governance mechanisms seems omnipresent, even if its strength varies through time and across domains of social interaction. Does the normative challenge provide a decisive argument against reliance on behavioural insights in EU law?

C. Law vs Governance? Law as Governance?

The previous section advanced the following claim. In order to operate as normative guidance, the law should take certain 'fundamental facts' about human agency into account. But what sort of *should* exactly is this? Where does the law end? How much 'cure, manipulation, conditioning, and propaganda'[59] are allowed within law in general and EU law in particular?

The question is ambiguous. In one sense, it concerns a semantic problem of what would disqualify certain techniques of regulation or 'governance' from the semantic field of law, requiring those techniques of social control to be called non-legal. Alternatively, the question can be understood conceptually. In this view, law is conceptually linked to a certain ideal (law as normative guidance) and we are asking for a point where too much use of techno-regulation or manipulative practices would turn a legal system into a regulatory regime that is 'less than legal'. Regulatory techniques that do not take human agency into account would be seen as non-legal in a substantive sense or as perversion of the law, even if formally valid or authorised. In other words, there seems to be a point where formally valid law becomes something fundamentally different from a mechanism of social control of and for reasonable individuals.

This conception of law as normative guidance of individual actions may have consequences for the import of psychological or neuro-scientific insights into the law. But in the first instance it suggests that not all government action follows the pattern of normative guidance. It may operate in a different, governance mode as well.

Interestingly, legal history suggests that this tension between law and governance has been with us for many centuries. With reference to both historical and contemporary sources, the Dutch legal theorist Bas Schotel evidences a separation, throughout the last few centuries of Western law, between what he calls 'juridical law' on the one hand and governance or legally unlimited policy-making on the other and argues for the autonomy of law and legal knowledge.[60] Juridical law or *iurisdictio* in Bracton's terminology,[61] is a domain where lawyers as a professional group have developed a body of doctrinal knowledge and expertise, in the name of which they attenuate and moderate factual and normative information and claims, deciding on their legal relevance, that is impact on the outcome of juridical processes. Governance or *gubernaculum*, in contrast, is characteristic for areas of policy where goals are set by political rulers (democratically elected or not) and imposed on human practice more or less directly, without lawyerly intervention. Schotel's (historical) examples of governance include foreign policy and taxation. One of his modern examples is (EU) migration policy, which explicitly defines its goal as 'the efficient management of migration flows'[62]—a policy purpose clearly at odds with the idea of law as normative guidance.

---

[59] See the quote in n 52 above.

[60] B Schotel, 'Legislation, Empirical Research and Juridical Law' (2013) 1 *Theory and Practice of Legislation* 501.

[61] For the distinction, see CH McIlwain, *Constitutionalism. Ancient and Modern* (Ithaca, Cornell University Press, 1947).

[62] As has been made explicit recently with respect to the 'Asylum, Migration and Integration Fund', see eg ec.europa.eu/dgs/home-affairs/financing/fundings/migration-asylum-borders/index_en.htm.

This suggests that in some domains of social interaction, the perceived need for legal doctrinal knowledge is stronger than in others, and the role of the governance mode of official conduct explicitly or implicitly overrides the normative guidance or juridical mode. But it also raises a further question as to whether and why legislation should respect or maintain a relatively autonomous sphere of doctrinal legal knowledge or juridical expertise, with its own rationality. In this sense, the role of behavioural findings in EU law turns out to be a matter of normative, possibly moral, debate not about the limits of the influx of empirical knowledge in legislation but the scope of normative guidance and juridical law within the set of instruments of social control.

IV. CONCLUSION

Behavioural research in psychology and economics has produced a fascinating and growing body of empirical knowledge on human decision-making and judgement. Being informed about these findings is crucial for responsible policy-making and legislation. Still, the compatibility of behavioural insights with (EU) law is a relevant and contested issue. This chapter aimed at advancing this discussion by systematising the difficulties of incorporating behavioural economics into law into three kinds of challenges: epistemic, institutional, and normative, and explicating one of the normative challenges coming from law's assumptions on human agency.

I have also argued that libertarian paternalism and nudge are oversold by claiming that they can obviate political and ideological disagreements. As an empirical project, behavioural decision-making research is not determinative on whether any regulation is desirable. All it can show is whether a certain intervention is effective, relative to the goals a regulator wants to achieve. To be more, behavioural economics relies on normative assumptions even in its conceptual groundwork.

While an instrumental view of the law seems to make the integration of empirical knowledge into legal policy necessary, both institutional and normative features of the law set limits to this integration. This resistance, to be sure, is not complete, rather selective and partial. An important but underestimated reason for resistance lies in the nature of law as normative guidance. Law is more than a simple technique of command and control; legal doctrines are interwoven with common sense moral intuitions about human agency, some of which are themselves supported by rational arguments. Apart from practical and epistemic reasons, this raises moral concerns about the project of making law genuinely scientific.

13

Behavioural Trade-Offs: Beyond the Land of Nudges Spans the World of Law and Psychology

YUVAL FELDMAN AND ORLY LOBEL

I. INTRODUCTION

THE MOST DRAMATIC developments in twenty-first-century policy come from neither the field of economics nor from law, but from psychology. In July 2013, the United States Government announced plans to form a 'Behavioral Insights Team'. A similar behavioural insights team has operated in the United Kingdom since 2010, and other initiatives are quickly forming across Europe and elsewhere around the world. The hope is that government in all its regulatory and policy arms will learn how to subtly shape people's behaviour and choices. In the United States, new initiatives in both state and federal departments have already adopted insights from the behavioural field, attempting to make public policy more effective and, at the same time, less disruptive and coercive.[1] The contemporary regulatory state aims to use psychology to make people pay their taxes on time, eat healthier, save more, waste less, work harder, study longer, and be more philanthropic. In the broadest and most ambitious terms, law will draw on psychology to improve society as a whole.

Behavioural engineering has been most recently popularised by the idea of *nudges*, associated with the book by that name by Cass Sunstein and Richard Thaler.[2] Nudges, referring to small cognitive bias driven adjustments to the decision-making process, represent, however, only a sliver of the insights revealed in the fascinating new body of interdisciplinary studies in law, economics, and psychology. In fact, the wealth of studies in the past few decades is so mind boggling that it is easy to see why it seems simpler to avoid the breadth and complexities of

---

[1] 'Behavioral Insights Team' Documentary, Fox News, available at: www.foxnews.com/politics/interactive/2013/07/30/behavioral-insights-team-document.

[2] R Thaler and C Sunstein, *Nudge: Improving Decisions about Health, Wealth and Happiness* (New Haven, CT, Yale University Press, 2008).

psychological knowledge and focus merely on a relatively narrow set of lessons. And yet, like everything in life, without considering the complexities, initiatives become flat and often fail.

The purpose of this chapter is to present areas of behaviourally informed legal policy in which the fuller picture of psychology is overlooked and to suggest ways to move toward a more meaningful integration between the various behavioural–legal trends that have been extremely popular in recent years. The lack of coherence between the different sub-literatures is pervasive and related to the fact that each one strand of research was developed separately. Most importantly, the lack of awareness of insights developed in areas of behavioural research, which are less known to legal scholars, leads to very limited and sometimes inadvertent policy recommendations based on a partial view of the scope and potential of the various branches of psychology.

In earlier years, when law and policy were based on a traditional view of rational choice, which assumes that people make deliberative choices to maximise their interests, there was no room for an understanding of behavioural trade-offs. By contrast, in recent years, as policymakers have become increasingly committed to incorporating the science of human behaviour into law, we can no longer legitimately (nor effectively) consider only a handful of aspects of human behaviour. Naturally, for any given policy initiative, there will be limited resources and knowledge which will require some simplification and certain trade-offs between conflicting behavioural insights. But, these trade-offs need to be generated through awareness and reflection. We hope that by recognising the breadth and depth of the psychological literature it will be possible to create a behavioural policy which will address the full meaning and potential of behavioural law and policy.

The chapter proceeds as follows. Section II briefly introduces recent policy initiatives in both Europe and the United States to demonstrate the breadth and scope of the behavioural brush over policy. Section III analyses some of the earlier critiques of the adoption of behavioural research into policy, which focus on the validity, generalisability and translatability of the behavioural insights into policy in action, and the legitimacy of the policy initiatives from a normative perspective. Section IV then shifts the focus to the narrowness of the literature that has been adopted by government and offers a fuller picture of the fields of behavioural research that must shape the policymaker's toolbox. Once the enriched vision of behavioural law is introduced, Section V proposes a framework for better-informed and sustainable policy. We offer a new taxonomy of the trade-offs that are pervasively present in the adoption of regulatory solutions to social challenges.

II. SIMPLY SIMPLE: RECENT BEHAVIOURAL INITIATIVES

The range of initiatives that build on behavioural research is impressive. Insights into behavioural sciences, and how these insights can be used to affect people's choices, have recently become a priority for governments around the world. In

2010, the UK Government set up the Behavioural Insights Team, often called the 'Nudge Unit', to apply these visions to public policy.[3] In July 2013, news sources began to report that the White House was planning to assemble a similar team in the United States. According to a government document, the team would aim to 'scale behavioural interventions that have been rigorously evaluated, using, where possible, randomised controlled trials'.[4] The document also laid out several policy initiatives that had already benefited, according to the White House, from implementation of these behavioural insights: increasing college enrolment and retention, getting people back to work, improving academic performance, increasing retirement savings, increasing adoption of energy efficient measures, and increasing tax compliance.[5] The announcement of the creation of a behavioural policy team received criticism from those concerned about 'big brother' and 'nanny state' policies. And yet, the great interest in employing behavioural insights to law all across the world indicates a growing consensus among regulators about the validity and effectiveness of bringing behavioural economics into law. Leading behavioural economist and advisor to the UK's Behavioural Insights Team, Richard Thaler, sums up his advice for policymakers into two succinct points. First, if you want to encourage some activity, you need to make it easy; second, you cannot create evidence-based policies without evidence.[6] The initiatives adopted into policies vary considerably. Mostly the initiatives focus on setting consumer defaults and understanding choice architecture. Such initiatives consider ways in which immediate decision-making can be improved by packaging information and choices differently, for example, by changing the set default to an opt-out rather than opt-in. In Sunstein's new book, *Simpler*, the reader gets a 'brief guided tour' of such default manipulation and opt-in/opt-out structures.[7] The examples provided in *Simpler* include the area of savings in which a change in the default of enrolment to an opt-out produces significant results on the participation rates of employees in pension plans. Similarly, with regard to health insurance, Sunstein reminds us that whether or not enrolment in a health care programme is mandated, changing the default from having to be enrolled (whether or not it is required by law) to automatic enrolment makes a great difference in operationalising the programme. A classic third example of the impact of choice architecture in the welfare area is enabling a greater number of low-income families to take advantage of their right to free school lunches through automatic enrolment.[8]

---

[3] Cabinet Office, *Behavioural Insights Team*, available at: www.gov.uk/government/organisations/behavioural-insights-team; the Behavioural Insights Team has been privatised in February 2014 (www.behaviouralinsights.co.uk). For a more modest discussion in the European context, please see R van Bavel et al, 'Applying Behavioural Science to EU Policy-Making' (2013) European Commission JRC Scientific and Policy Reports, available at: ec.europa.eu/dgs/health_consumer/information_sources/docs/30092013_jrc_scientific_policy_report_en.pdf.

[4] Above n 1.

[5] ibid.

[6] R Thaler, 'Watching Behavior before Writing the Rules', *The New York Times*, New York, 8 July 2012.

[7] C Sunstein, *Simpler: The Future of Government* (New York, Simon and Schuster, 2013).

[8] ibid, 107.

In the context of environmental policy, with the goal of reducing paper and saving more trees, creating a default presumption that most of us want to be paperless in payroll notifications and other bills will be more effective than having to fill out some paperwork to get the paperless process going.

Modern developments in the field of behavioural economics reveal the many ways in which human rationality is bounded. People take patterned shortcuts in their decision-making, which often veers the individual off the path of the typical rational and self-interested actor. An understanding of bounded rationality is important because lawmakers can create policies that improve efficiency by helping actors make more rational decisions that maximise their utility.[9] A prime example of bounded rationality arises in the context of public health, particularly with governments becoming increasingly concerned about overweight populations and obesity. For many years, the American Federal Government has attempted various campaigns aimed at improving public health (and of course, the benefits associated with that improved health such as lower healthcare costs). Basic rationality predicts that people who choose to eat healthy and exercise see the benefit of long-term health as more important than the benefit of the short-term happiness they might feel from unhealthy lifestyle habits. However, the research on bounded rationality reveals how aspects such as accessibility, willpower, presentation of the risks, and even surrounding factors such as the type of music being played in the background at the gym or cafeteria may affect people's eating and exercising habits.[10] Bounded rationality explains that the choices people make do not necessarily reflect their preferences. People may value long-term health as important and have a general desire to lose weight, but that does not necessarily translate into 'successive action' because eating healthier and exercising are extremely difficult to sustain.[11] Other factors, such as the human predisposition to prefer high-fat, high-calorie foods, a culture that promotes unhealthy eating and a sedentary lifestyle, as well as the perceived or actual higher cost of healthy foods, also negatively impact the actor who wants to lose weight.[12] Taking all of the behavioural research into account, lawmakers can enact policies that more accurately reflect the longer-term stated individual choices of living a healthy life. The cafeteria policy[13] has served as a prime example of nudge-style policy. Shifting the order of choices available to kids in a cafeteria, presenting the healthier choices first creates the desirable effect of more kids choosing those fruits and veggies and filling up their tray with healthier choices before arriving at the fat loaded options.[14]

---

[9] R Korobkin and T Ulen, 'Law and Behavioral Science: Removing the Rationality Assumption from Law and Economics' (2000) 88 *California Law Review* 1051, 1075.

[10] K Garcia, 'The Fat Fight: The Risks and Consequences of the Federal Government's Failing Public Health Campaign' (2007) 112 *Pennsylvania State Law Review* 529, 542.

[11] ibid, 543.

[12] See ch 10, 'What Can EU Health Law Learn from Behavioural Sciences'.

[13] Thaler and Sunstein explaining about Nudges: 'A school cafeteria might try to nudge kids toward good diets by putting the healthiest foods at front'. See Thaler and Sunstein, *Nudge* (n 2).

[14] Thaler and Sunstein, *Nudge* (n 2).

A recent study, conducted through combined efforts of experts in the fields of law and psychology about consumer fraud prevention, helps provide another example of how irrationalities can be tackled by policy. The study analysed the factors that affect consumers' vulnerability to fraud, examining consumer susceptibility to deception where an unusual contract clause is detected but the consumer is then persuaded to proceed with the deal.[15] The researchers hypothesised that customers would be vulnerable to the deception of the opposite party through reassurances or explanations, even if those proffered explanations did not make sense.[16] The study revealed that of those participants who detected the inappropriate contract clause, 80 per cent went on to sign the contract after a senseless explanation.[17] The study's findings lend themselves to immediate policy suggestions for consumer fraud laws: for example, restricting the informal stages where companies may interact with consumers in order to convince them to overlook an inappropriate contract clause and deeming contracts 'unfair' even when the consumer proceeded to sign it in cases where an explanation was meaningless but impactful.[18] Beyond fraud, studies on consumer behaviours lend themselves to insights about why so many consumers tend to spend beyond their means often leading to paralysing debt.

III. CONTEMPORARY CRITIQUES OF BEHAVIOURAL LAW AND ECONOMICS

The common theme that threads across the contemporary initiatives is that people cannot be trusted to have the time, the energy, or good judgement to make the right decisions all the time. Therefore, they should be helped by designing the decision-making environment such that it prevents the poor decisions from happening. This approach has been criticised in the past on various grounds, mostly from perspectives on individual autonomy and paternalism.[19] With traditional regulatory approaches, there has been more controversy concerning the fields of regulation, for example, of personal well-being, healthy eating, savings and consumer financial choices. The psychology underlying the nudge approach has provided the policymaker with unconventional tools that enable intervention with presumably less controlling power. While nudges have been marketed as powerful triggers but non-interventionist, the assertion that policy based upon behavioural economics is simultaneously more effective and less interventionist

---

[15] J Choplin, D Pogrund Stark, and J Ahmad, 'A Psychological Investigation of Consumer Vulnerability to Fraud: Legal and Policy Implications' (2011) 35 *Law and Psychology Review* 61.
[16] ibid, 62.
[17] ibid, 81.
[18] ibid, 95–101.
[19] For a recent discussion of the problems associated with this, please see R Rebonato, *Taking Liberties: A Critical Examination of Libertarian Paternalism* (Basingstoke, Palgrave Macmillan, 2012).

than traditional command-and-control approaches is not without critique. A lively ongoing debate cautions against some of the main assumptions of the nudge approach. Most of the criticism about the contemporary behavioural policy base is philosophical in nature and asks about the implications of using insights from psychology to individual autonomy and choice. For example, Gregory Mitchell has argued that nudge approaches misuse the concept of libertarianism, subjugating 'the liberty of irrational individuals to a central planner's paternalistic welfare judgments'. Mitchell warns that nudges are in fact designed to capitalise on the irrational tendencies of private citizens to enable the paternalistic planner to direct their lives.[20]

The very term 'libertarian paternalism' may have distorted much of the message about the significance and meaning of behavioural policy.[21] The term attempts to suggest that, compared to traditional modes of command and control, using behavioural insights is less interventionist on the one hand and more individualistic and self-regarding on the other. Liberal democracies regulate behaviour in a very large range of fields and in the sense of translating research into public policy, nearly any regulatory approach could be deemed as taking some responsibility from the individual's need to gain information on his own. However, this perspective obscures the ways in which welfare and well-being are part of a social collective project. Indeed, many interventions that draw on behavioural insights are concerned with third-party externalities and the need for central coordination.[22] For example, risk taking, whether financial or physical, affects society as a whole and entails high costs if left to market regulation alone, as we have certainly seen in several cycles of recent economic crises.[23] Employing behavioural insights also inevitably includes redistributive effects, that Colin Camerer and others have termed 'asymmetric paternalism', benefiting those who err more frequently in their judgement.[24]

Amir and Lobel have argued that in the political attempt to reach bipartisan commitment for policy, nudge neglected to fully account for the range of regulatory solutions that must be employed given the insights of behavioural economics.[25] Instead, policymakers and thought leaders tend to narrow the regulatory tools to a small set of iconic choice architecture modules. Amir and Lobel argue that a better approach is to understand behavioural economics as aiding the regulator to expand the regulatory toolbox, drawing on the broad spectrum

---

[20] G Mitchell, 'Libertarian Paternalism is an Oxymoron' (2005) 99 *Northwestern Law Review* 1033.
[21] O Amir and O Lobel, 'Stumble, Predict, Nudge: How Behavioral Economics Informs Law and Policy' (2008) 118 *Columbia Law Review* 2098.
[22] O Amir and O Lobel, 'Liberalism and Lifestyle: Informing Regulatory Governance with Behavioural Research' (2012) *European Journal of Risk Regulation* 17; See also Amir and Lobel, 'Stumble, Predict, Nudge' (n 21).
[23] ibid.
[24] C Camerer and others, 'Regulation for Conservatives: Behavioral Economics and the Case for "Asymmetric Paternalism"' (2003) 151 *University of Pennsylvania Law Review* 1211, 1211–12.
[25] Amir and Lobel, 'Liberalism and Lifestyle' (n 22). See also Amir and Lobel, 'Stumble, Predict, Nudge' (n 21).

from command-and-control through collaborative regulation to self-regulation that is offered by the new governance school of thought.[26] More recently, Bubb and Pildes have characterised this problem of nudge-style prescriptions being too narrowly focused on choice-architecture as a 'trimming of their sails', in which behavioural law and economics cuts off a range of options because of ideological preference for seemingly non-interventionist proposals. Bubb and Pildes, continuing the critique of the non-interventionist theme that pervades behavioural law and economics, similarly argue that it is the combination of the 'two seductive dimensions of [behavioural law and economics]—its appeal as social science and as politics' that are in tension, because the insights that come out of the behavioural social science in fact often require much more forceful regulatory solutions than the behavioural law and economics school of thought has been willing to advocate.[27] Moreover, the nudge-style tools employed by policymakers are in fact stronger than behavioural law, and economics scholars are willing to admit.[28] As will become clear in the next sections, we largely agree with this critique and expand it. We argue that it is in fact the breadth of behavioural insights and the depth of the field itself that present tensions in how to operationalise its insights. Next generation behavioural policies must decouple from an attachment to a particular set of solutions. It is clear that lessons from psychology can and should inform law and policy. However, as Amir and Lobel argue, 'if policymakers are to become consumers of the discipline of judgment and decision-making, they must be wise consumers'.[29]

Policymakers should take into account the wealth of knowledge developed in the social sciences as well as be attuned to differences between policy domains. Take for example the recent dietary related suggestions regarding NYC former mayor—Michael Bloomberg's intervention in the size of soda cups, barring supersized cups,[30] or changing the defaults in consumer credit card contracts by setting a lower sum of money as the default credit that a consumer will have to pay at the end of each month. In such context, we are dealing with domains in which commercial firms have already created a nudge to consume more soda by playing with the sizes of the cups or by placing a really low sum of money of $10 or $15 in the credit bill one receives. In such situations,[31] when corporate competitors market similar options to consumers that have little choice or input on the available sets

---

[26] On new governance, see generally, O Lobel, 'The Renew Deal: The Fall of Regulation and the Rise of Governance in Contemporary Legal Thought' (2004) 89 *Minnesota Law Review* 342.
[27] R Bubb and RH Pildes, 'How Behavioral Economics Trims Its Sails and Why' (2014) 127 *Harvard Law Review* 1593.
[28] ibid, 1606: 'Moreover, somewhat ironically, the nudges recommended by BLE scholars are often not as light-touch as advertised … Work in BLE has generally not subjected these tools to sufficient analysis to evaluate their effects'.
[29] Amir and Lobel, 'Stumble, Predict, Nudge' (n 21).
[30] This ban on the maximal size of cups, was struck down by the New York State Court of Appeals on 26 June 2014. M Grynbaum, 'New York's Ban on Big Sodas is Rejected by Final Court', *The New York Times*, New York, 26 June 2014.
[31] Compare with the concept of 'counter-nudging' discussed in the Introduction to this book.

of choices, the criticism about paternalism proves rather weak. In such contexts, providing more choices and designing the decision-making environment seems indeed less interventionist than more direct forms of regulation, for example, in the case of soda bans, completely forbidding the sale of larger cups instead of requiring a delay on the decision of whether to upgrade the cup size, and still receive the discount derived from the previous purchase of soda.

IV. SHIFTING THE DEBATE: EXPANDING THE BEHAVIOURAL WORLD

While the earlier critiques of behavioural engineering are highly important and need to be continuously deliberated, our approach here pushes forward the debates about the adequacies of behavioural law and economics in several new grounds.[32] We take an insider's stance, as researchers immersed in behavioural research. Our concern is primarily with the question of sustainability and commitment to the integration of behavioural sciences into law and policy. Our goal is first to expand the interface between psychology and law. Then, once the footprint of behavioural studies that contribute to policy is expanded, our second goal is to illuminate the trade-offs between different types of solutions and to account for the relative costs and benefits of behavioural approaches in any given situation. We argue that to take psychology into consideration, a more informed analysis is required.

The need for an expanded and integrated approach to behavioural policy stems from the independent developments in each strand of the behavioural sciences, each of which have immense potential in contributing to better policy and many of which are absent for the most part from policy analysis. Most importantly, a narrow view of the world of law and psychology can lead to very limited and sometimes inadvertent policy recommendations. More often than not, contemporary behavioural policy approaches appear to be based on the partial view by legal scholars of the scope and potential of the various branches of psychology.[33] There are no doubt important exceptions. In recent years, there are indications of expansion of the behaviourist lens as policymakers build on theories related to behavioural ethics, social norms, and social proof. Still, the expansion is slow and scattered, lacking a consistent discussion or systematic cohesive framework.

In what follows, we demonstrate our argument through some of the most basic behavioural trade-offs, which we expose in the current behavioural analysis of legal literature. We show how, *when push comes to nudge*, some of the most celebrated recent behavioural policy suggestions can be in tension with central

---

[32] For an alternative view of these trade-offs please see the discussion of 'second order gap' in A Tor, 'The Methodology of the Behavioral Analysis of Law' (2008) 4 *Haifa Law Review* 237.

[33] eg calling for limiting the freedom of contract due the various cognitive biases, ignoring the psychological advantages of giving people the freedom to choose. For an elaboration of that point, see Y Feldman, 'Control or Security: A Therapeutic Approach to the Freedom of Contract' (2002) 18 *Touro Law Review* 503.

law and social science insights. We focus on an initial list of policy trade-offs that exemplify how the balance between the competing theoretical literatures is offset by the over emphasis of one angle of the pendulum. The typology of four trade-offs includes:

1. Outcome vs process.
2. Invisible vs expressive law.
3. Voluntary compliance vs monitoring.
4. Universal vs targeted nudging.

A. Outcome vs Process: Toward the Integration of Sustainable Deliberative Processes

i. Dual Reasoning and Deliberation-Free Nudges

The concept of two systems of reasoning has gained popular recognition in Kahneman's book, *Thinking Fast and Slow* and it lies at the core of much of the research on behavioural law and economics.[34] The general concept differentiates between an automatic, intuitive, and mostly unconscious process (labelled System 1) and a controlled and deliberative process (labelled System 2).[35] An impressive body of research has been conducted in an attempt to compare the two types of decision-making systems in terms of the way they operate and in their efficacy. This line of research has shown in recent years that for certain tasks, such as visual tasks, System 1 leads to better performance relative to System 2 while in other tasks, such as those requiring greater analytics, System 2 outperforms System 1.[36] For the most part, behavioural law and economics takes a more critical approach of the functioning of System 2 and is relatively inclined to use biases associated with System 1 as a way to improve people's lives, for example, in the defaults set in 'save more tomorrow' type plans or changing the default rules in credit card bills. While some of these reforms are effective and important, this regulatory lens of shifting decision-making from System 2 to System 1 has flattened the discussion without rigorous analysis of the costs and benefits of these shifts.

---

[34] D Kahneman, *Thinking, Fast and Slow* (New York, Farrar, Straus and Giroux, 2011).

[35] O Amir et al, 'Deciding without Resources: Psychological Depletion and Choice in Context' [2009] *Journal of Marketing Research* 46; K Stanovich and RF West, 'Individual Differences in Reasoning: Implications for the Rationality Debate?' (2000) 23 *Behavioral and Brain Sciences* 645; J St BT Evans, 'In Two Minds: Dual-Process Accounts of Reasoning' (2003) 7 *Trends in Cognitive Sciences* 454; AP Dijksterhuis et al, 'On Making the Right Choice: The Deliberation without Attention Effect' (2006) 311 *Science* 1005; Amir and Lobel, 'Stumble, Predict, Nudge' (n 21); AP Dijksterhuis and LF Nordgren, 'A Theory of Unconscious Thought' (2006) 1 *Perspectives on Psychological Science* 95; D Kahneman, 'A Perspective on Judgment and Choice: Mapping Bounded Rationality' (2003) 58 *American Psychologist* 697; TD Wilson and JW Schooler, 'Thinking Too Much: Introspection Can Reduce the Quality of Preferences and Decisions' (1991) 60 *Journal of Personality and Social Psychology* 181.

[36] See, eg Z Rusou, D Zakay, and M Usher, 'Pitting Intuitive and Analytical Thinking against Each Other: The Case of Transitivity' (2013) 20 *Psychonomic Bulletin & Review* 608.

These shifts become salient when observing the impact that heuristics and biases research has had on policy and when considering the interplay between Systems 1 and 2. The imbalance is most striking when considering the neglected role of deliberation in contemporary policy approaches. On an individual level, nudge approaches largely assume that the desired outcomes in our daily decisions can be directed without deliberation through default design. On the public level, the role of law in influencing public understandings of the social and the moral meaning of behaviours—good and bad—is sidestepped in favour of a view of the law as a useful tool in simplifying decision-making processes. Little attention is given for the interactive and dynamic understandings and identification with the law that follow from people's interactions with law and policy.

ii. Deliberations and Decisions

The current behavioural regime focuses on getting people to the correct result with little need for deliberation.[37] The focus is on default rules, opt-outs, and designing simpler paths to a direct single 'right choice'. Naturally, the process through which people get to the desired decision—be it to save more money or to donate more organs—becomes secondary to the actual optimal choice. The rationale behind this approach is clear: with growing knowledge of the fact that people are bad decisionmakers, who lack either the motivation or the cognitive abilities for making the right choices, less attention should be given to tools such as increased access to information and more effort should be made to ensure that consumers arrive at the 'right' decisions concerning financial and health practices.[38] This approach is problematic, however, because it overlooks important ways in which deliberation positively affects choices and commitment. The choice architecture approach neglects the behavioural implications for long-term perceptions and sustainability of policy.

In the following paragraphs, we will review some of the theories that emphasise the importance of deliberation in ensuring such sustainability. The lack of sustainability is a general weakness of much of the nudge approach. This is particularly surprising given the important research conducted by scholars such as Tyler and Darley[39] on commitment and compliance. In practice, the knowledge about the effectiveness of the nudging theory in the long term is relatively limited.[40] Moreover, many of the lab studies presently being used as a basis for

---

[37] It should be noted that we are focusing here on individual deliberation, which should not be confused with the discussion on the role of public deliberation regarding the usage of nudges, which we discuss in the latter stages of the chapter.

[38] O Ben-Shahar and CE Schnider, 'The Failure Mandated Disclosure' (2011) 159 *University of Pennsylvania Law Review* 647.

[39] TR Tyler and JM Darley, 'Building a Law-Abiding Society: Taking Public Views about Morality and the Legitimacy of Legal Authorities into Account when Formulating Substantive Law' (1999) 28 *Hofstra Law Review* 707.

[40] TM Marteau et al, 'Judging Nudging: Can Nudging Improve Population Health?' (2011) 342 *British Medical Journal* 263.

the nudge approach demonstrate one-shot short-term effects. For the most part, behavioural economics research consists of lab experiments which lack the rich social and organisational context of real market interactions and much of the effects being cited as the basis of changes in decision-making are measured within minutes or even seconds from the time participants were exposed to the stimuli.[41]

An impressive and yet rather neglected body of psychology literature pertains to the importance of active participation of people in making decisions and the importance of voice and participation in shaping people's behaviour in ways that are publicly desirable. Civic participation enhances and empowers citizens' feelings of efficacy and belief in their ability to be part of the democratic process.[42] Public policy that undermines the focus on awareness and deliberation and focuses more on supplementing personal judgement and active involvement may undermine these positive processes from happening.[43] Deliberation and awareness carry unique procedural benefits from an outcome perspective that takes into account aspects such as sustainability and long-term commitment by people.

A related aspect of sustainability could be learned from the discussion on operational empowerment devices.[44] For example, field experiments show that people's decision whether to climb the stairs or use the escalator can be changed more effectively by colouring stairs in interesting ways compared with dissemination of information about the importance of exercising.[45] And yet, such an insight is rather hard to scale. First, the idea that stairs in all buildings should look like pianos or be otherwise artfully painted is unrealistic. Second, even if such an initiative would be pursued, it would likely be self-defeating, as the very results showing people's interest in walking up colourful stairs stem from their currently exotic nature. Hence, since it is seems fair to estimate that there is a limit to the number of stairs that can be coloured with piano painting, and there is a reason to believe that scarcity drives the interest, there is greater room for combining such nudges with deliberation that could enhance learning, internalisation, and consequently sustainability.

Beyond making each individual decision and ensuring the sustainability of optimal choices, it is worth considering another behavioural aspect associated with the optimal level of deliberation: regret aversion. A famous paper on the ability of parents to deal with dire consequences of their choices demonstrates the cost of deliberation and autonomy.[46] The study was done in a unique context—parents who needed to make abortion decisions regarding foetuses with minor

---

[41] Amir and Lobel, 'Stumble, Predict, Nudge' (n 21).
[42] RJ Dalton, 'Citizenship Norms and the Expansion of Political Participation' (2008) 56 *Political Studies* 76.
[43] EL Deciand RM Ryan, 'Self-Determination Theory: When Mind Mediates Behavior' (1980) 1 *Journal of Mind & Behavior* 33; MI Friedman and GH Lackey Jnr, *The Psychology of Human Control: A General Theory of Purposeful Behavior* (Santa Barbara, CA, Praeger, 1991).
[44] Discussed in ch 2 'Behavioural Sciences in Practice: Lessons for EU Rulemakers'.
[45] ibid.
[46] S Botti, K Orfali, and SS Iyengar, 'Tragic Choices: Autonomy and Emotional Responses to Medical Decisions' (2009) 36 *Journal of Consumer Research* 337.

medical issues. It was shown using a mix of qualitative and quantitative methods that the French parents had less autonomy and firmer doctor advice, relative to American parents who faced a similar dilemma, but with less authoritative advice from doctors. While the context of the described study is particular, it suggests an additional consideration—the post-decision-making feeling of responsibility by American parents, which is affected by their great level of discretion and amount of deliberation that were put into the decision, relative to the French parents.

Relatedly, self-determination theories show that people are more satisfied when they have independent personal choices.[47] Lack of control in one's environment induces desperation and other unpleasant feelings.[48] For instance, elderly residents in nursing homes that were given control over routine choices lived longer and reported higher rates of well-being than residents that did not have control over the set of choices.[49] Additionally, another study hypothesised that in social settings one's control over her own decisions could change her interpretation and, consequently, her preferences of the situation.[50] The theory about the relationship between control and well-being seems to be straightforward.[51] Thompson summarises this relationship in the following way, 'we feel better about ourselves, we are physically healthier, perform better under adversity, and are better able to make desired behavioural changes if we have a sense of behavioural control'.[52] The improvement in personal well-being through increased self-direction in our everyday activity aimed at achieving future goals (referred to as 'the implicit agency of daily life') is demonstrated in a myriad of contexts.

The literature on procedural justice describes the importance of the perception of fairness of policy for the parties' ability to accept the policy's outcomes.[53] The implications of procedural justice have been considered in the context of a range

---

[47] EL Deci and RM Ryan, *Intrinsic Motivation and Self-Determination in Human Behavior* (Heidelberg, Springer, 1985).

[48] M Seligman, *Helplessness: On Depression, Development, and Death* (New York, WH Freeman, 1975).

[49] E Langer and J Rodin, 'The Effects of Choice and Enhanced Personal Responsibility for the Aged: A Field Experiment in an Institutional Setting' (1976) 34 *Journal of Personality and Social Psychology* 191; J Rodin and EJ Langer, 'Long-term Effects of a Control-relevant Intervention with the Institutionalized Aged (1977) 35 *Journal of Personality and Social Psychology* 897.

[50] S Choshen-Hillel and I Yaniv, 'Agency and the Construction of Social Preference: Between Inequality Aversion and Prosocial Behavior' (2011) 101 *Journal of Personality and Social Psychology* 1253.

[51] KD Markman et al, 'The Impact of Perceived Control on the Impregnation of Better and Worse Possible Worlds' (1995) 21 *Personality and Social Psychology Bulletin* 588. See also JM Burger, 'Negative Reactions to Increases in Perceived Personal Control' (1989) 56 *Journal of Personality and Social Psychology* 246; SM Miller, 'Why Having Control Reduces Stress: If I Can Stop the Roller Coaster, I Don't Want to Get Off' in J Garber and M Seligman (eds), *Human Helplessness: Theory and Applications* (Michigan, Academic Press, 1980).

[52] S Thompson, 'Naturally Occurring Perception of Control: A Model of Bounded Flexibility' in G Weary, F Gleicher and KL Marsh (eds), *Control Motivation and Social Cognition* (Heidelberg, Springer, 1993).

[53] M Erez and R Arad, 'Participative Goal Setting: Social, Motivational and Cognitive Factor' (1986) 71 *Journal of Applied Psychology* 59.

of legal fields.[54] The literature suggests two key factors may increase one's sense of procedural justice: having a voice and having perceived control over the process.[55] Both types of processes require some level of awareness and deliberation by the individual prior to making their decisions. Of course, not all forms of participation are equal, and important frontiers in the literature examine differences between mere technical participation and participation based on deliberative processes and cognitive effort. For example, Perez states that, from current studies, it seems unclear to what extent people's participation in online government projects has been able to produce deliberative processes.[56]

Given the importance of both process and outcome—achieving outcomes and deepening the involvement of people in a deliberative process—the next step is to realise that different social challenges will point to the varying ways to draw the balance between considerations that sometimes conflict. Here, we merely argue for a more prudent and nuanced approach to using behavioural sciences. Such an approach asks to what extent overcoming processes and obtaining desired outcomes is more important than triggering active individual involvement in making the decision in a particular policy context. There may be situations when a one-shot decision sustains a long-term outcome. For example, in decisions like saving for pension or organ donations, once the decision is made, the default becomes sticky enough to sustain a lifetime result. In those cases, we may conclude that a commitment mechanism driven by deliberative processes is of lesser importance. In contrast, in contexts such as consumerism, fiduciary duties, contract performance, health and dietary decisions, in which commitment is needed, the role of participation and deliberation should be given more weight due to its effect on commitment to the decision over time.[57]

---

[54] For a general overview of the relationship between procedural and distributive justice see, eg T Tyler, *Why People Obey The Law* (New Haven, Yale University Press, 1990); J Thibaut and L Walker, *Procedural Justice: A Psychological Analysis* (Hillsdale, Lawrence Erlbaum Associates, 1975). For a thorough description of the important role of participation and procedural justice among the various justice theories, see J Greenberg, *The Quest for Justice on the Job: Essays and Experiments* (Beverly Hills, Sage, 1995) 23; T Tyler and K McGraw, 'Ideology and the Interpretation of Personal Experience, Procedural Justice, and Political Quiescence' (1986) 42 *Journal of Social Issues* 115.

[55] For research on the relevancy of control over a process of increasing the sense of procedural fairness associated with it see, eg K Leung and Wai-Kwan Li, 'Psychological Mechanism of Process Control Effects' (1990) 75 *Journal of Applied Psychology* 613; J Greenberg and R Folger. *Procedural justice, participation, and the fair process effect in groups and organizations* (New York, Springer, 1983) 235–56.

[56] O Perez, 'Open Government, Technological Innovation and the Politics of Democratic Disillusionment:(E-) Democracy from Socrates to Obama' (2012) Bar-Ilan University Public Law and Legal Theory Working Paper: papers.ssrn.com/sol3/papers.cfm?abstract_id=2078741.

[57] In that context, compare the work of Eigen on form contracts, where he has demonstrated in a field research that the more involvement of people in the contracting process they are more likely to be committed to its performance. Z Eigen, 'When and Why Individuals Obey Contracts: Experimental Evidence of Consent, Compliance, Promise, and Performance' (2012) 41 *Journal of Legal Studies* 67. Recently Cass Sunstein explicitly recognised that greater involvement in the process of making decisions is likely to increase one's identification with her decision. 'In addition, passive choice will, almost by definition, decrease choosers' feelings of identification with the outcome. In part for that reason, any kind of default rule, including a highly personalized one, may not create the kinds of motivation that can come from active choosing' C Sunstein, 'Deciding By Default' (2013) 162 *University of Pennsylvania Law Review* 1, 51.

Several new additions to nudge campaigns seem to adopt an understanding of the significance of process by focusing on community-based identity and encouraging citizens' participation. For example, while most nudges in the context of smoking and drinking attempt to reduce awareness—hiding them from the public sphere, or requiring the invisibility of alcohol in public sphere by requiring a brown bag masking of the bottle, other approaches in the UK attempt to increase awareness of how much other people really drink, because people generally overestimate how much others drink.[58] In other contexts, people are provided with various ways to communicate to others the problems they see both in the consumer and government platforms. Very recently, Tyler and others have suggested using procedural justice to improve people's following of medical recommendations.[59]

B. Invisible Nudges vs Expressive Law: Life is Not a Cafeteria

i. Law's Meaning

Related to the trade-off between the process and the outcome is the dual role of law—as directing behaviour and serving an expressive function. The central point of tension between expressive law and the nudge approach concerns the visibility of law. Under expressive law theory, law should be made public thereby triggering various expressive mechanisms to reflect, as well as to change, the norms and values of the particular society. Under a nudge approach, the law operates behind the scenes, in the background of private decision-making, serving to facilitate individual choices. These two approaches can conflict—in the first, law is front and centre as the driving force behind the social change, while in the second, the law operates under cover. From a psychological standpoint, there are key differences between such deliveries of the law. Under one approach, the law is majestic, authoritative, and engaging. Under the other, the law is hidden and coy. Law's global message of authority is vastly different under each approach.[60]

The literature on expressive law and on social meaning views law's language and its visibility to the public as one of its most important tools.[61] Making something into a law, by using certain words and contexts, can shape the meaning of

---

[58] Compare with R Cooter, M Feldman and Y Feldman, 'The Misperception of Norms: The Psychology of Bias and the Economics of Equilibrium' (2009) 4 *Review of Law & Economics* 889, making the general argument regarding people over-estimation of unethicality and constrains on changing that view.

[59] T Tyler, A Mentovich and S Satyavada, 'What Motivates Adherence to Medical Recommendations? The Procedural Justice Approach to Gaining Deference in the Medical Arena' (2013) *Regulation and Governance*, DOI: 10.1111/rego.12043.

[60] Compare with the recent paper by Alemanno and Spina on that point. See A Alemanno and A Spina, 'Nudging Legally—On the Checks and Balances of Behavioural Regulation' (2014) 12 *International Journal of Constitutional Law* 429.

[61] Almost two decades ago, Sunstein wrote about the expressive function of law and defined the expressive function of the law as follows: 'At least for purposes of law, any support for a statement should be rooted not simply in the intrinsic value of the statement, but also in plausible judgment

important concepts such as parenthood, safe driving, and good citizenship. The expressive function of the law can help people determine what the prevailing social norm is,[62] how your behaviour will be viewed by others if you violate the law,[63] what is the best course of action when one needs to coordinate her behaviours with others,[64] and what are the reputation costs at risk for engaging in certain behaviours.[65]

The research on law and social science highlights the symbolic effects of law in society and on the role of legality in social change. Legality, wherever it is found, shapes cultural changes in society.[66] Scholars such as Anderson and Pildes,[67] and Adler[68] also focus on language, recognising the declarative and constitutive cultural powers of law. Within this tradition, legal scholars have suggested that

---

about *its effect on social norms*' (emphasis added): C Sunstein, 'On the Expressive Function of the Law' (1996) 144 *University of Pennsylvania Law Review* 2021, 2045. It should be recognised that there are scholars who take on the language-based approach to what expressive function of the law means. MD Adler, 'Expressive Theories of Law: A Skeptical Overview' (2000) 148 *University of Pennsylvania Law Review* 1363 (making a thorough discussion of the expressive function of the language of the law). In a comprehensive attempt to define the expressive function of the law, Anderson and Pildes propose the following: 'Expression refers to the ways that an action or a statement (or any other vehicle of expression) manifest a state of mind'. See ES Anderson and RH Pildes, 'Expressive Theories of Law: A General Restatement' (2000) 148 *University of Pennsylvania Law Review* 1503, 1506.

[62] RH McAdams, 'An Attitudinal Theory of Expressive Law (New and Critical Approaches to Law and Economics)' (2000) 79 *Oregon Law Review* 339; see also D Dharmapala and RH McAdams, 'The Condorcet Jury Theorem and the Expressive Function of Law: A Theory of Informative Law' (2003) 5 *American Law & Economic Review* 1.

[63] The assumption being that in a democratic state, laws represent the preferences of people regarding what is a desirable behaviour. This assumption is often challenged in reality as, eg while most countries have a tax code, there is a huge variation in the perceived normative desirability of those people who evade taxes across different countries.

[64] R McAdams, 'A Focal Point Theory of Expressive Law' (2001) 86 *Virginia Law Review* 1649, 1650–63. For empirical evidence, see RH McAdams and J Nadler, 'Testing the Focal Point Theory of Legal Compliance: Expressive Influence in an Experimental Hawk/Dove Game' (2005) 2 *Journal of Empirical Legal Studies* 87, 87–96.

[65] A typical example of the cost-related account of social norms can be found in Cooter's analysis: 'With group pressures, an increase in an act's popularity lowers its cost. Imposing a non-legal sanction on someone often involves a risk of retaliation, which decreases as more people obey the norm. The risk of a non-legal sanction often increases as more people obey the norm, thus *lowering the relative costs of conforming to the norm*' (emphasis added). See R Cooter, 'Do Good Laws Make Good Citizens? An Economic Analysis of Internalized Norms' (2000) 86 *Virginia Law Review* 1577, 1585. See also DM Kahan, 'Social Influence, Social Meaning, and Deterrence' (1997) 83 *Virginia Law Review* 349, 352–61.

[66] O Lobel, 'Paradox of Extralegal Consciousness' (2007) 120 *Harvard Law Review* 937. These studies consider the role of law in social change, symbolic politics, evolution of social values and the notion of 'legal consciousness'.

[67] In a comprehensive attempt to define the expressive function of the law, Anderson and Pildes propose that: 'Expression refers to the ways that an action or a statement (or any other vehicle of expression) manifest a state of mind'. See ES Anderson and RH Pildes, 'Expressive Theories of Law: A General Restatement' (2000) 148 *University of Pennsylvania Law Review* 1503, 1506.

[68] MD Adler, 'Expressive Theories of Law: A Skeptical Overview' (2000) 148 *University of Pennsylvania Law Review* 1363, provides a thorough discussion of the expressive function of the language of the law. Adler thinks that the work of LEN scholars on norms cannot be defined as expressive, since they do not focus on the language of the law.

when examining the effects of law, one should focus not only on its operational functions but also on its declarative purpose and responsibilities.[69] Laws influence people both by making authoritative statements and by reproaching them using the language of the law.[70] In other words, we use laws to affect social norms and to change judgements and behaviour.[71] Language has an essential and creative role in social change.[72]

In contrast, the nudge approach tends to push for focusing on simplicity and flattening of policy messages. The law needs to be almost unnoticed. People do not even need to know that a given action is unlawful or undesirable since, under the nudge approach, the role of law is not to shape people's values, but to create a choice architecture. Choice architecture will lead people to make the right choices with as limited as possible deliberation and awareness to the fact that they are making a choice as well as to the fact that the law is behind these initiatives.

The original idea of the expressive concept of law was to lead people to internalise social norms, to recognise the wishes of the legislator, to understand what social practices should be abandoned, and to identify certain practices as shameful. Following some of the writing on form contracts and snap legal decisions, it seems that the outcome of this line of research is to minimise unnecessary words and require as little attention as possible to what the law asks them to do. Hence, the simpler nudge approach not only limits the participation process of people in determining the decisions they take, as the previous argument has suggested, it also changes the function of law from shaping the social meaning of people's behaviour to simply altering their decision, without the target of regulation knowing that the law is even operating in the background. Publicising that the law is behind the choice architecture, especially in areas such as health, transactions, and

---

[69] This approach has been used in a wide variety of legal doctrines. Anderson and Pildes (n 67) 1532, hold its most practical relevance is in the contexts of employment and constitutional law where courts strike down laws that express unconstitutional purposes or attitudes. Other notable areas in which the expressive functions of the law have been taken into account include voting rights: R Pildes and R Niemi, 'Expressive Harms, "Bizarre Districts", and Voting Rights: Evaluating Election-District Appearances after *Shaw v Reno*' (1993) 92 *MichiganLaw Review* 483; laws regarding homosexuality, (W Van Der Burg, 'The Expressive and Communicative Functions of Law' (2001) 20 *Law & Philosophy* 31) especially with regard to signalling moral standing of the state through existing, though not enforced, laws and anti-discrimination laws. Another interesting and important area in which expressive theories of law have been featured is criminal punishment. Significant in this field is the work of DM Kahan, 'Social Influence, Social Meaning, and Deterrence' (1997) 83 *Virginia Law Review* 349, 352–61, regarding the expressive meaning of criminal sanctions (for an historic perspective, see J Feinberg, 'The Expressive Function of Punishment' (1965) 49 *The Monist* 397). This forms the foundation of his theory highlighting the importance of shaming in criminal punishment. According to the shaming theory, fines and community service are problematic as criminal punishments because they carry no shaming factors.

[70] D Fox and CL Griffin Jnr, 'Disability-Selective Abortion and the Americans with Disabilities Act' (2009) *Utah Law Review* 845.

[71] C Sunstein, 'On the Expressive Function of the Law' (1996) 144 *University of Pennsylvania Law Review* 2021, 2025.

[72] E Mertz, 'Legal Language: Pragmatics, Poetics, and Social Power' (1994) 23 *Annual Review of Anthropology* 435.

'consumer affairs' may even impede a person's ability to make mindless choices. Perhaps most globally, the idea of default design downplays our notions of law. It attempts to present itself as something different, not exactly law in an authoritative way, not exactly regulation, but rather a design mechanism, a rule structure, a choice architecture. Psychologically, this masking of law has a cost, which the rich literature on expressive law discussed below, has documented.

ii. Expressive Nudges

As suggested above, while legal scholarship is rich with understandings of the expressive function of the law giving it innovative mechanisms,[73] the nudge approach seems to abandon this important literature. While we recognise the advantages of invisible law and choice architecture, it is our belief that even with greater focus on unaware decisions associated with this approach, making the law more visible to the public should not be downplayed without careful discussion.

Naturally, the focus on snap decisions has led to an abandonment of discussion on the expressive function of the law and social meaning which seems to be associated with public deliberation. However, what we try to suggest is that the focus on snap decisions might highlight a different view of what expressive law should mean behaviourally. Various lines of research in cognitive psychology show that choice of words can completely alter the meaning people assign to a situation, especially with limited awareness.[74] Shifting the focus of expressive law to research on framing effects can enrich and add important layers of sophistication for behaviourally based legal policy.[75]

C. Trust vs Voluntary Compliance

The next trade-off embedded in the new behavioural based legal policy relates to levels of trust in people's good nature. One of the most important deviations from rational choice models was related to the recognition of people's ability to cooperate voluntarily.[76] Research done by legal scholars like Lynn Stout[77] and

---

[73] See Y Feldman, 'The Expressive Function of Trade Secrets Law' (2009) 6 *Journal of Empirical Legal Studies* 177, for a review of many of the competing behavioural mechanisms to the expressive function of law.
[74] EF Loftus and JC Palmer, 'Reconstruction of Automobile Destruction: An Example of the Interaction between Language and Memory' (1974) 13 *Journal of Verbal Learning and Verbal Behavior* 585.
[75] See, eg TE Nelson, ZM Oxley and RA Clawson, 'Toward a Psychology of Framing Effects' (1997) 19 *Political Behavior* 221. A popular usage of framing is the context of taxation see, eg EJ McCaffery and J Baron, 'Framing and Taxation: Evaluation of Tax Policies Involving Household Composition' (2004) 25(6) *Journal of Economic Psychology* 679.
[76] eg A Sen, *Rationality and Freedom* (Cambridge, MA, Harvard University Press, 2004); JC Cox, 'How to Identify Trust and Reciprocity' (2004) 46 *Games and Economic Behavior* 260.
[77] L Stout, *Cultivating Conscience: How Good Laws Make Good People* (Princeton, Princeton University Press, 2010).

Yochai Benkler[78] calls for more sophisticated ways to enhance people's cooperation and contribution to public goods, suggesting that people will cooperate if you trust them to be cooperative and will become less cooperative if you treat them as self-interested individuals.[79] This notion of people's good nature is partly challenged by emerging research by scholars like Bazerman, Banaji, Ariely, and Shalvi,[80] which suggests that good people do bad things.[81] The emerging picture of the human character is a far more complex one in which people mostly seek to promote their own self-interest as long as they can feel good about themselves. According to this theory, by giving people the ability to choose how to behave, many good people might engage in self-deception mechanisms such as moral disengagement or elastic justification and exploit that trust to shirk, engage in dishonest behaviour, or violate the law.

Elsewhere Feldman discussed the effects of legal ambiguity on the likelihood that people will behave in a desirable way.[82] For example, Haisley and Weber[83] find that people prefer to take ambiguous risks when the ambiguity allows them to justify unfair behaviour. Dana and others[84] find that people are less generous in situations in which they can appeal to moral ambiguity in explaining their actions. Similarly, Hsee[85] found evidence that people make choices that satisfy their preferences, if they can exploit existing ambiguity about which decision may complete the assignment. Feldman and Teichman[86] find that under conditions of

---

[78] Y Benkler, *The Penguin and the Leviathan: How Cooperation Triumphs over Self-Interest* (Crown Business, 2011).

[79] EY Chou, N Halevy and JK Murnighan, 'The Relational Costs of Complete Contracts' (IACM 24th Annual Conference, Istanbul, July 2011).

[80] For a review, see Y Feldman, 'Behavioral Ethics Meets Behavioral Law and Economic' in E Zamir and D Teichman (eds), *Oxford Handbook of Behavioral Law and Economics* (Oxford, Oxford University Press, 2014 forthcoming).

[81] N Mazar, O Amir and D Ariely, 'The Dishonesty of Honest People: A Theory of Self-Concept Maintenance' (2008) 45 *Journal of Marketing Research* 633; MM Pillutla, 'When Good People Do Wrong: Morality, Social Identity, and Ethical Behavior' in D De Cremer, R van Dijk and JK Murnighan (eds), *Social Psychology and Organizations* (London, Taylor & Francis Group, 2011); J Hollis, *Why Good People Do Bad Things: Understanding Our Darker Selves* (New York, Penguin Group (US) Inc, 2008); MR Banaji and AG Greenwald, *Blindspot: Hidden Biases of Good People* (New York, Delacorte Press, 2013).

[82] Y Feldman and HE Smith, 'Behavioral Equity' (2014) 170 *Journal of Institutional and Theoretical Economics* 137.

[83] EC Haisely and RA Weber, 'Self-Serving Interpretations of Ambiguity in Other-Regarding Behavior' (2010) 68 *Games and Economic Behavior* 614.

[84] J Dana, DM Cain and RM Dawes, 'What You Don't Know Won't Hurt Me: Costly (but Quiet) Exit in a Dictator Games' (2006) 100 *Organizational Behavior and Human Decision Processes* 193.

[85] CK Hsee, 'Elastic Justification: How Tempting but Task-Irrelevant Factors Influence Decisions' (1995) 62 *Organizational Behavior and Human Decision Processes* 330.

[86] Y Feldman and D Teichman, 'Are All Legal Probabilities Created Equal?' (2009) 84 *New York University Law Review* 980. See also Y Feldman, 'The Complexity of Disentangling Intrinsic and Extrinsic Compliance Motivations: Theoretical and Empirical Insights from the Behavioral Analysis of Law' (2011) 35 *Washington University Journal of Law & Policy* 11; Y Feldman, 'Bounded Ethicality and the Law: A Proposed Framework for the Incorporation of Ethical Decision Making Research into Behavioral Law and Economics' in E Zamir and D Teichman (eds), *Oxford Handbook of Behavioral Law and Economics* (Oxford, Oxford University Press, 2014).

legal ambiguity people will formulate a minimal interpretation of what the law or contracts requires from them. With the greater recognition of the nudge approach, that people make decisions without full awareness to the consequences of their behaviour, more thought should be put into the question of people's nature and the effects of this low degree of awareness on their interactions with compliance and the law.

The following behaviourally-based dilemma further exemplifies this concern. On the one hand, researchers like Darley and Robinson[87] and Cooter[88] suggest that law should be aligned with people's moral norms to ensue voluntary compliance and support for government punishment. Governments need to maintain legitimacy by such alignment. At the same time, behavioural ethics teaches us about the dissonance between people's need to promote their self-interest and their need to maintain their self-perception.[89] The kinds of behaviours that people are publicly negatively judged for are the types of behaviours that most regulatory schemes attempt to regulate (eg explicit racist comments). However, according to the views of behavioural ethics, we should be more worried as a society about violations, which could be seen by ordinary people as justifiable (eg getting a non-monetary political support). The problem here is that from the classical law and norms literature (the first line of literature reviewed above) public support will be relatively minor for harsh enforcement especially against those violations.

Let's consider, for example, the area of conflict of interests. Taking the first approach would suggest that law should punish those who engage in a material conflict of interest, where it is possible to clearly show that money was the main reason for their violation. Such instances are much more likely to be seen as corrupt by the general public and hence focusing on them is likely to give the state the legitimacy it needs. Since most people would see such conflict of interest as violating moral norms, they would tend to support the public action. In contrast, according to the behavioural ethics approach, the greater risk to the public does not come from the most obvious and blunt conflict of interest (eg clear cut bribes), but rather from the more subtle ones,[90] where many otherwise normative people are likely to prefer their own self-interest, since they have more options to self-deceive themselves about the lack of wrong-doing in their own behaviours.[91]

---

[87] PH Robinson and J Darley, 'The Utility of Desert' (1997) 91 *Northwestern University Law Review* 453.
[88] R Cooter, 'Do Good Laws Make Good Citizens? An Economic Analysis of Internalized Norms' (2000) 86 *Virginia Law Review* 1577, 1585.
[89] N Mazar, O Amir and D Ariely, 'The Dishonesty of Honest People: A Theory of Self-Concept Maintenance' (2008) 45 *Journal of Marketing Research* 633.
[90] L Lessig, *Republic, Lost: How Money Corrupts Congress and a Plan to Stop It* (New York, Grand Central Publishing, 2011), arguing that the corruption of good people is much more likely to harm the public in contrast to those obvious cases of corruption, where people can easily recognise the wrong doing associated with such acts.
[91] M Bazerman and A Terbnussel, *Blind Spots: Why We Fail to Do What's Right and What to Do About it* (Princeton, Princeton University Press, 2011).

An additional example is related to the tension between voluntary and mandatory compliance, an important area within the psychological literature investigates the interplay between extrinsic and intrinsic motivation.[92] Intrinsic motivation is the sense of morality inherent within the individual while extrinsic motivation relies on incentives and rewards.[93] Most generally, the crowding out literature suggests that when people attribute their behaviour to external rewards, they discount any moral incentives for their behaviour, thereby lowering the perceived effect of intrinsic motivation. As applied to the regulatory incentives, crowding out theory predicts that external incentives that utilise monetary rewards or punishments may undermine intrinsic motivations.[94] For instance, paying people in return for their blood might lead donors to view the event as a transaction rather than a charitable act, thereby eroding altruistic blood donations.[95]

In a series of lab-based experiments, Deci found that tangible rewards undermine intrinsic motivation for a range of activities.[96] Many of the studies on the crowding out effect of incentives and on enforcement are summarised by Bowles.[97] Along those lines, Falk and Kosfeld[98] demonstrated this broader point using a principal-agent experiment in which participants could either let the agent decide the production amount or set a lower boundary. In settings in which a lower boundary was set, agents produced less than in those in which the principal

---

[92] J M Harackiewicz and C Sansone, 'Rewarding Competence: The Importance of Goals in the Study of Intrinsic Motivation' in C Sansone and JM Harakiewicz (eds), *Intrinsic and Extrinsic Motivation: The Search for Optimal Motivation and Performance* (Michigan, Academic Press, 2000); EL Deci and RM Ryan, 'The "What" and the "Why" of Goal Pursuits: Human Needs and the Self-Determination of Behavior' (2000) 11 *Psychology Inquiry* 227.

[93] EL Deci, R Koestner and RM Ryan, 'A Meta-Analytic Review of Experiments Examining the Effects of Extrinsic Rewards on Intrinsic Motivation' (1999) 125 *Psychological Bulletin* 627; T Kasser and RM Ryan, 'Further Examining the American Dream: Differential Correlates of Intrinsic and Extrinsic Goals' (1996) 22 *Personality and Social Psychology Bulletin* 280.

[94] E Fehr and S Gachter, 'Do Incentive Contracts Undermine Voluntary Cooperation?' (2002) University of Zurich Inst for Empirical Research in Econ Research Paper 34: papers.ssrn.com/sol3/papers.cfm?abstract_id=313028; E Fehr and A Falk, 'Psychological Foundations of Incentives' (2002) 46 *European Economic Review* 687, 724; E Fehr and B Rockenbach, 'Detrimental Effects of Sanctions on Human Altruism' (2003) 422 *Nature* 137. For a general review, see BS Frey, *Not Just for the Money: An Economic Theory of Personal Motivation* (Cheltenham, Edward Elgar, 1997); GA Akerlof, 'Labor Contracts as Partial Gift Exchange' (1982) 97 *Quarterly Journal of Economics* 543; BS Frey and R Jegen, 'Motivation Crowding Theory: A Survey of Empirical Evidence' (2000) Centre for Economic Studies and Information Institute for Economic Research, Research Paper 245: ssrn.com/abstract=203330.

[95] RM Titmus, *The Gift of Relationship: From Human Blood to Social Policy* (New York, News Press, 1971) arguing that monetary payments to givers of blood could diminish the amount of blood given voluntarily.

[96] EL Deci, R Koestner and RM Ryan, 'A Meta-Analytic Review of Experiments Examining the Effects of Extrinsic Rewards on Intrinsic Motivation' (1999) 125 *Psychological Bulletin* 627. U Gneezy and A Rustichini, 'Pay Enough or Don't Pay at All' (2000) 115 *Quarterly Journal of Economics* 791

[97] S Bowles, 'Policies Designed for Self-Interested Citizens May Undermine "The Moral Sentiments": Evidence from Economic Experiments' (2008) 320 *Science* 1605; see also Y Feldman, 'The Complexity of Disentangling Intrinsic and Extrinsic Compliance Motivations: Theoretical and Empirical Insights from the Behavioral Analysis of Law, (Symposium—For Love or Money)' (2011) 35 *Washington University Journal of Law and Policy* 11.

[98] A Falk and M Kosfeld, 'The Hidden Costs of Control' (2006) 96 *American Economic Review* 1611.

left the decision about the production amount entirely in the hands of the agents. In *post hoc* questioning, agents said that they regarded the lower boundary as a sign of distrust and were therefore less cooperative. Building on this rich literature, policymakers must consider inadvertent consequences of mandatory top-down compliance requirements on the intrinsic ethical motivations that individuals have to comply voluntarily. The next section continues this enquiry with regard to the variances different individuals exemplify in their intrinsic and extrinsic motivations to act.

D. Universal vs Targeted Nudges

The fourth trade-off concerns heterogeneity and the understanding that a one-choice-fits-all architecture will be off the mark for certain populations. When we focus on the lowest common denominator, we decrease uncertainty and ensure minimal compliance, but we also risk crowding out the motivation of those intrinsically motivated.

How much effort should one put on attempting to determine what is the true motivation or specific cognitive abilities of the regulated population? Should the variation in motivations lead to a focus on the motivation that works across the board or should targeted regulation apply, differentiating between diverse groups of people according to their levels of commitment and motivation to comply?

People often vary in their internal level of commitments to ethical behaviour.[99] Following the 'W effect' argument[100] with regard to magnitude, there is room to expect that with varying levels of intrinsic motivations among individuals, various sums of money will have a different effect on each subgroup. In a previous study, we demonstrated that those who were intrinsically motivated were not significantly affected by framing of incentives, while those who had less intrinsic motivation were more likely to be affected by extrinsic motivation.[101] A somewhat different finding regarding the differences in perception of incentives by those with high and low motivation comes from Perez and Feldman, demonstrating that those who were low on intrinsic motivation were more likely to prefer deposits to fines in recycling contexts, while the opposite was true for those who were high on intrinsic motivation.[102] These findings suggest that the people's level of intrinsic motivation significantly moderates the effect of extrinsic motivation

---

[99] Y Feldman and O Lobel, 'The Incentives Matrix: The Comparative Effectiveness of Rewards, Liabilities, Duties and Protections for Reporting Illegality' (2010) 88 *Texas Law Review* 1151.

[100] U Gneezy, 'The W effect of incentives' *University of Chicago Graduate School of Business* (2003). In this case, intrinsic motivation was measured on a scale of environmental commitment as well as sensitivity to the distance from one's home to a recycling bin.

[101] Feldman and Lobel (n 99).

[102] Y Feldman and O Perez, 'How Law Changes the Environmental Mind: An Experimental Study of the Effect of Legal Norms on Moral Perceptions and Civic Enforcement' (2009) 36 *Journal of Law and Society* 501.

on behaviour, raising the following question: should a policymaker collect these insights and target regulation differently with regard to those who are internally committed and those who are not?[103] A possible move in that direction could be seen in a work by Porat and Strahilevitz, who have argued for an even more radical approach: calling for the creation of personalised default rules which will be based on the Big Five personality scale, tailored to people's contractual preferences.[104]

The literature on cognitive depletion further gives us some clues as to how to understand the dilemma of targeted preferences. In a recent article, Amir and Lobel examine how different age groups process choices in relation to future risk planning in diverse decision-making environments. The article demonstrates across multiple experiments that when cognitive resources are available, older participants opt for more prudent financial and retirement choices, but that this pattern does not hold in situations when people's cognitive resources are depleted. The study finds an increased effect of resource depletion for older compared to younger participants. At a theoretical level, such findings suggest that some of the difference in risky financial choices between older and younger decisionmakers rests in the ability of each age group to override their intuitive and automatic responses to such decisions. At a policy trade-off level, the study demonstrates how some nudge solutions will work better for some populations and be ineffective or even counter-productive with others. In another study on whistleblowing, Feldman and Lobel find gender differences in people's ethical commitment to compliance and social enforcement. Most importantly, these differences actively interact with the institutional and legal background rules. The kinds of law and psychology studies point to the problematic notion that a policymaker can simply choose a point of intervention without a deeper understanding about the interplay between identity-based characteristics and the policy solution.

V. A SPOT ON THE SPECTRUM: TOWARD SCHEMATIC
SOLUTIONS OF BEHAVIOURAL TRADE-OFFS

The tensions within the psychology literature reveal the need for a more nuanced regulatory framework and the expansion of the behavioural regulatory toolbox. Future work will need to create a fuller taxonomy of the areas of law where shifting

---

[103] While preparing the revised version of this draft, we came across a working paper by some of the leading regulation scholars (Cunningham, Kagan and Thornton) who similarly suggest that, 'those who are differently motivated are likely to respond very differently to a deterrence strategy. While it may be effective when applied to the recalcitrant and perhaps to reluctant compliers it will be counter-productive as regards corporate leaders ... and irrelevant to the incompetent'. Nevertheless, they treat this challenge as too complex from a legal policy-making perspective: 'but inspectors are for the most part, incapable of knowing the motivation of those they are regulating, with the result that a "pure" deterrence strategy may achieve very mixed results'.

[104] A Porat and LJ Strahilevitz, 'Personalizing Default Rules and Disclosure with Big Data' (2014) 112 *Michigan Law Review* 1417.

the balance in one direction would be justified. As discussed above, different social challenges will point to different solutions on the spectrums of outcome/process; covert/expressive; mandatory/voluntary; targeted/universal. At times, the nature of the decision-making, whether it involves a one shot choice or repeat over time behaviour will help determine the spot on the spectrum. In contexts like a pension plan, in which once the decision has been made, people are less likely to reverse it, sustainability is less important and hence getting people to the right choice (outcome being the dominant focus) might be more important than in areas like health or nutrition, where choices need to be reaffirmed on a daily basis. Similarly, the dilemma about the expressive versus invisible law will also be dependent on context. In areas where the expertise of the state, its moral or consensual power, is highly relevant, using it might outweigh the costs of informing people that the choice architecture presented to them is based on law. In social issues in which preferences for process are strong and the solutions contested, more weight should be given to process. Focusing on trust may be more important in areas that are difficult to monitor while focusing on directed regulation is desirable. With regard to the question of universality, focusing on the common denominator might be more important in areas in which the costs of mistakes are disproportionately large relative to the benefits of performing intrinsically. Since variation in motivations is likely to increase the chance of making mistakes and mistakes are costly, a greater analysis should be made in each context about the level of desirable compliance and its counter-costs. For example, in the context of trade secrets, one egregious leak may be detrimental to a company,[105] while with many environmental protections, outcomes are important but they are mostly with regard to long-term and aggregate behaviours. While the ultimate goal may be to move as many people as possible to environmentally responsible behaviours, the costs of some private non-compliance are not very high. In other words, in this context making few mistakes in motivations is not as costly since the effort is to increase the average recycling.

VI. CONCLUSION

This chapter aims to demonstrate the importance of an enriched perspective of law and psychology research for next generation behavioural legal policies. We argue that often nudge style approaches over-emphasise certain behavioural insights while ignoring others. The result is that that many legal interventions advocated

---

[105] At the same time, here too an overly broad definition of trade secrets and misappropriation can have detrimental consequences to innovation. O Lobel, *Talent Wants to be Free* (New Haven, Yale University Press, 2013); Y Feldman, 'The Expressive Function of the Trade Secret Law: Legality, Cost, Intrinsic Motivation and Consensus' (2009) 6 *Journal of Empirical Legal Studies* 177.

by behavioural law and economics are based on a tunnel vision that obscure the wealth and complexities of contemporary behavioural research and may result in inadvertent effects. Even when accounting for all aspects of the behavioural landscape, an informed and integrative policymaker must take into account inherent trade-offs between these conflicting psychological effects. Such balancing should be based not only on theoretical understanding but also on a combination of empirical research and normative considerations, which will consider the context of the specific reform at hand. It is our belief that by working through these behavioural trade-offs, it is possible to generate a more sophisticated and enriched use of behavioural economics in legal policy.

14

Epilogue: The Legitimacy and Practicability of EU Behavioural Policy-Making

ALBERTO ALEMANNO AND ANNE-LISE SIBONY

*N*UDGE AND THE LAW took as a point of the departure the growing interest, in both policy and academic circles, towards the use of behavioural sciences in policy-making. Our goal was to explore the major implications of such use for the legal system, in particular that of the European Union.

In this conclusive chapter we do not intend to summarise each individual contribution; rather, we aim to draw lessons on what EU law can learn from behavioural sciences from the examples reviewed in this volume. These lessons can be organised in two major lines of enquiry, which characterise the incipient nudge debate generally. Section I explores when is it legitimate for public authorities to use psychology and other related behavioural sciences to inform policy. Section II examines how can, in practice, behavioural insights be incorporated into the decision-making processes. While not all individual contributors have expressly addressed these queries, they have—if implicitly—taken a stance on those issues, which are central to the emergence of behavioural informed intervention. In line with the declared objective of our editorial venture, in this conclusive chapter, we strive to unpack our contributors' major findings in order to provide a European perspective over both the issues of legitimacy and that of practicability of behavioural informed action. Where needed, we contrast it with the US dominated nudge debate. Finally, we offer some conclusive remarks aimed at sketching the future research agenda of European scholars interested in the integration of behavioural sciences into the law.

I. LEGITIMACY

Given the portrayal of behavioural regulation as an instrument of an emerging manipulative, nudging state, the legitimacy debate surrounds—and sometimes monopolises—the public discourse prompted by nudging. It is therefore no surprise that a great deal of academic attention has been paid to the philosophical, ethical and other abstract implications of such a prospect.[1] The major concerns involve autonomy,[2] dignity,[3] and moral development[4] as well as a less defined risk of manipulation. Several contributions to this volume build on this literature and add to the legitimacy debate by offering a European or, more specifically, an EU-oriented analysis.

In this section, we first build upon the reflexions gathered in this volume around the issue of legitimacy of behavioural intervention in an attempt to reformulate the legitimacy debate in light of the European perspective (A). In particular, we discuss the need to rethink the relationship between autonomy and deliberation in the light of the notion of 'choice architecture' and that of 'mental bandwidth'[5] (B). We claim that, given the inherent constraints to our own ability to choose, autonomy should be rethought. Several contributors to this volume share this conclusion and advance some recommendations to this purpose. We then highlight the importance of cultural differences in shaping the socio-legal context in which we discuss the legitimacy of behavioural interventions (C). Differences in administrative, legal, political and philosophical culture contribute to the formation of very different contexts, which in turn influence the legitimacy discourse on both sides of the Atlantic. We refer to this multifactorial and multifaceted phenomenon as cultural differences in regulatory philosophy. Finally, some concluding remarks highlight why and how the EU appears less likely to offer strong resistance to the use of behavioural insights in its own legal order based on legitimacy grounds.

A. Autonomy and the Inevitability of Choice Architecture

Autonomy is a central concern in any discussion on behavioural intervention. The classic ethical debate surrounding nudge starts with a principled defence of normative individualism, that is the ability to order our lives according to our

---

[1] See, eg S Conly, *Against Autonomy—Justifying Coercive Paternalism* (Cambridge, Cambridge University Press, 2013); R Rebonato, *Taking Liberties—A Critical Examination of Libertarian Paternalism* (New York, Palgrave Macmillian, 2012); MD White, *The Manipulation of Choice: Ethics and Libertarian Paternalism* (Palgrave MacMillan, 2013); CR Sunstein, 'The Storrs Lectures: Behavioral Economics and Paternalism' (2013) 122 *Yale Law Journal* 1826 et seq; PG Hansen and AM Jespaersen, 'Nudge and the Manipulation of Choice: A Framework for the Responsible Use of the Nudge Approach to Behaviour Change in Public Policy' (2013) 4(1) *European Journal of Risk Regulation* 3; E Selinger and K Whyte, 'Is There a Right Way to Nudge? The Practice and Ethics of Choice Architecture' (2011) 5(10) *Sociology Compass* 923; L Bovens, 'Real Nudge' (2012) 3(1) *European Journal of Risk Regulation* 43 and, lastly, CR Sunstein, 'The Ethics of Nudging' (2015, forthcoming).
[2] JD Wright and DH Ginsburg, 'Behavioral Law and Economics: Its Origins, Fatal Flaws, and Implications for Liberty' (2012) 106 *Northwestern University Law Review* 1033.
[3] J Waldron, 'It's All for Your Own Good' (2014) New York Review of Books; and C McCrudden, 'Nudging and Human Dignity', *VerfBlog*, 6 January 2015, available at www.verfassungsblog.de/nudging-human-dignity/.
[4] L Bovens, 'The Ethics of Nudge' in T Grüne-Yanoff and SO Hansson (eds), *Preference Change: Approaches from Philosophy, Economics and Psychology* (New York, Springer, 2008) 207–20.
[5] S Mullainathan and E Shafir, *Scarcity: Why Having Too Little Means So Much* (New York, Times Books, 2013).

decisions, which governs our modern constitutional states.⁶ Critics of behavioural policy-making argue that nudging constitutes an infringement on individual autonomy because, despite its choice-preserving promise, it inevitably involves an unacceptable substitution of individual preferences with government preferences.⁷ Such substitution—they claim—is only legitimate in a very limited set of circumstances.⁸ In the case of less visible behavioural interventions, this objection seems particularly strong.

According to this view, autonomy is reduced every time a policy intervention leverages an element of individual decision-making process other than deliberation.⁹ In particular, the claim is that autonomy is unacceptably reduced when a person could not uncover the manipulation even if she used her best effort to activate reflective thinking.¹⁰ In line with this argument, many object to any intervention aiming to change consumption patterns of energy, alcohol, or food by altering the defaults or providing information.¹¹

However, to fully address this critique of nudging it is necessary to unpack its premises, in particular the relationship it assumes between autonomy and deliberation. As highlighted by Baldwin, public nudging is not a monolith and must be broken down into at least three different categories depending on the impact of public intervention on individual autonomy. According to this perspective, first degree nudges consist of 'mere' provision of information (eg labelling), second degree nudges rely on biases and heuristics but can be detected (eg defaults), whereas third degree nudges shape decisions and preferences in a manner that is 'resistant to unpacking' (eg vivid warnings). If analysed against the autonomy critique, the first two categories of nudges appear less problematic than the third one. In general terms, this is the case because while the first two categories of nudges are predominantly directed to System 2, third degree nudges target instead System 1. The latter nudges being the most insidious, often acting at the visceral level,¹² emerge as one of the most Machiavellic forms of intervention.

In the case of defaults, the possibility of an opt-out seems apt to address the liberal reservations typically associated with regulatory limitation of autonomy.¹³

---

⁶ D von der Pfordten, 'Five Elements of Normative Ethics—A General Theory of Normative Individualism' (2012) *Ethic Theory Moral Practice* 449.

⁷ For a classic account see, eg EL Glaeser, 'Paternalism and Psychology' [1973] *University of Chicago Law Review* 133, 136–39. See also Rebonato (n 1).

⁸ In this volume, ch 4 by A van Aacken expresses this view. On the difficulties associated with identifying these circumstances, see Conly (n 1).

⁹ R Baldwin, 'From Regulation to Behaviour Change: Giving Nudge the Third Degree' (2014) 77 *MLR* 831.

¹⁰ See in this volume, ch 3 by M Quigley and E Stokes, and ch 10 by A Alemanno. See also B Bogart, *Regulating Obesity* (Oxford, Oxford University Press, 2013).

¹¹ For an illustration, see E Johnson et al, 'Defaults, Framing and Privacy: Why Opting In—Opting Out' (2002) 13 *Marketing Letters* 5.

¹² R Calo, 'Against Notice Skepticism in Privacy (and Elsewhere)' (2012) 87 *Notre Dame Law Review* 1027.

¹³ See, eg Rebonato (n 1); Whyte (n 1) ch 4.

By definition, a default rule—such as automatic enrolment in a pension scheme—enables the addressee to opt out and decide not to save. If the (formal) possibility to choose is the issue, surely that possibility still exists. Yet, according to some, this is insufficient to legitimise the underlying manipulation of a default change.[14] Individuals should still be allowed to exercise actual choice regardless of the context in which they are called upon to make that choice.

The classic counter-argument to this perspective is that choice architectures have to be determined one way or another since neutral default scenarios do not exist.[15] Thus, contrary to conventional wisdom, default rules such as automatic renewal for a magazine subscription, although typically disguised, do not fall from the sky but are the fruit of a deliberate choice of businesses.[16] Therefore, behaviourally informed intervention can be legitimised by the need to offset the negative consequences stemming from the established defaults that do not promote the greater good but only the interests of the relevant industries.[17] This is what underpins the regulatory strategy known as 'debiasing through law'. As Jolls and Sunstein point out, this strategy is legitimate to address clear cases of errors (eg perception of risk different from statistical risk).[18] Beyond this safe harbour—where behavioural intervention can hardly be criticised as a violation of autonomy[19]—the legitimacy debate needs to take place on all interventions that more broadly seek to rely on behavioural insights in the pursuit of objectives considered legitimate by the pubic authorities. The whole space of behavioural intervention open to debate—from straightforward debiasing cases to more complex cases for intervention—is what we call public nudging.[20] Public nudging is characterised by the intention to help people correct errors they may be subject to and avoid short sightedness in their choices. We find it helpful to have an additional, specific label for public interventions that respond to exploitative use of behavioural foibles by market forces. We call this 'counter-nudging'. This notion tries to capture our belief that, when discussing legitimacy concerns about behavioural public intervention, regulation of private influence ought to be distinguished from pure government influence on people. This is because, as argued in the introductory chapter, these two types of behavioural intervention raise different objections and call for different levels of scrutiny.[21]

---

[14] ibid.

[15] For the most recent formulation, see Sunstein, 'The Ethics of Nudging' (n 1).

[16] For a recent, powerful critique of marketing power and the need to 'fight back', see G Hastings, *The Marketing Matrix: How the Corporation Gets Its Power and How We Can Reclaim It* (London, Routledge, 2014).

[17] For a similar perspective, A Oliver, *Behavioural Public Policy* (Cambridge, Cambridge University Press, 2013) 13. For a more conceptual approach to behaviour, market and policy, MS Barr, 'Behaviourally Informed Regulation' in E Shafir (ed), *The Behavioral Foundations of Public Policy* (Princeton, Princeton University Press, 2012) 440–61.

[18] C Jolls and CR Sunstein, 'Debiasing through Law' (2006), 35 *Journal of Legal Studies* 199, 230.

[19] As illustrated in our introductory chapter, these are circumstances in which even libertarians may agree on state intervention insofar as this may promote—rather than threaten—individual freedom. See in this volume, ch 1 by A Alemanno and AL Sibony.

[20] See in this volume, ch 1 by A Alemanno and AL Sibony.

[21] ibid.

B. Autonomy and Individual Deliberation

In this volume, several contributions touch upon the relationship between autonomy, deliberation and legitimacy of public intervention. The classical autonomy arguments are presented by van Aaken. She argues that invisible nudges operating on the fast, unreflective, emotional system of thinking 'entail a subtle form of manipulation by taking advantage of the human tendency to act unreflectively and, to that extent, are inconsistent with demonstrating respect for individual autonomy'.[22] This argument assumes that conscious individual reflection is the touchstone of autonomy and asserts that, as a result, influencing individual decisions by targeting System 1 constitutes in itself an infringement on autonomy.

To see in what sense autonomy could be limited by behavioural intervention, one ought to consider not only the meaning of 'autonomy', but also that of 'restriction'. To use an analogy with competition law, a restriction of competition is appraised in the light of the competition that is reasonably possible on a given market. This entails taking into account the constraints resulting both from market characteristics and existing regulation. There is only a restriction of competition if undertakings distort through their behaviour whatever competition can reasonably be expected *in the context*.[23] Where no effective competition is possible, whatever undertakings do is not a restriction of competition. Similarly, a realistic appraisal of what counts as a restriction of individual autonomy on the part of public authorities should take into account what can reasonably be expected of humans making a decision in a given context. In other words, how much autonomy is likely to be exercised in a given context should matter when assessing whether and how much behavioural intervention restricts autonomy.

For instance, when purchasing a song online, extremely few people would deem it worth their time to read 68 pages of terms and conditions. In such a situation, it is entirely reasonable to assume that little attention will be expanded in making the decision to engage in the transaction. Behavioural consumer protection laws could prohibit lengthy text and mandate instead very short statements or icons. In a case such as this one, the objection to behavioural intervention in the name of autonomy seems entirely abstract and outright unconvincing. It is of course possible to argue that, by giving up on providing consumers with all the information needed to make a fully informed choice, behavioural consumer protection deprives individuals of an opportunity to exercise their autonomy. It is possible but lacks either common sense or good faith. The more reasonable view is that there is no restriction because consumers would in all likelihood not have availed themselves of the possibility of making a fully informed decision. Since life is too short to devote our time pondering upon every singly choice we face, our understanding of autonomy should be less idealised. Perhaps deliberation is not the only hallmark of autonomy.

---

[22] Chapter 4 in this volume by A van Aaken.
[23] See, eg Joined Cases 209–15 & 218/78 *van Landewyck a.o. v Commission*, EU:C:1980:248, para 153; Joined Cases 240, 241, 242, 261, 262, 268 & 269/82 *Stichting Sigarettenindustrie a.o. v Commission*, EU:C:1985:488, para 96.

We recognise of course that not all cases are as simple as the disproportionately lengthy terms and conditions. Where individual differences in behaviour are large or where their magnitude is unknown, it is difficult to assess what would 'in all likelihood' have happened. Only progress in empirical behavioural knowledge will bridge this analytical gap. Our point here is only to address what we feel is an overbroad use of the notion of 'restriction of autonomy'.

Equally, we do not want to suggest that mandatory simplified disclosure is a miracle cure.[24] People may of course still ignore information given to them in simplified, smarter form. Yet, if anything, such mandated simplification makes it more likely (not less) that the addressees—consumers in this case—will consciously take it into account and make a minimally but sufficiently informed decision. In this sense, harnessing the power of fast thinking—in our example by mandating more efficient communication of information—*increases* (from a very low baseline) the probability that autonomy is meaningfully (if not fully deliberatively) exercised.[25]

Holding, on the contrary, that 'autonomy' is *reduced* every time intervention targets System 1 amounts to the paradoxical view that individual decision-making deserves, in principle, the same degree of protection against interference by government, irrespective of whether deliberate reflective choice or automatic decision-making is at stake. To embrace this argument leads to severing the link between autonomy and deliberation. Autonomy, then, would be characterised by the freedom to determine one's goals—even mindlessly—and without distinction between immediate goals and possibly conflicting higher order or long-term goals. To us, this seems a singularly confusing and rather abstract notion of autonomy. Only individual choice fetishism can support such an overbroad understanding of the notion. Intuitively, some choices deserve more protection than others.

Behaviourally inspired interventions take it for granted that individual's choices often do not reveal stable preferences. They maintain well-being as the normative criterion but detach the definition of well-being from individual, autonomous choice. This disconnect causes unease but overstretching the concept of autonomy begs the question of its real boundaries. For this reason, defining autonomy in terms of an absolute right to set one's preferences over a range of outcomes is not very helpful. We propose instead to rethinking autonomy as a specific way of making decisions in a given context.

Under this view, a whole range of behavioural interventions would be neutral vis-à-vis the exercise of autonomy.[26] Such would be the case of intervention that aims to change the outcome of individual decisions (eg to foster enrollment in a pension plan or joining an organ donor register) but does not purport to change

---

[24] O Ben-Shahar and C Schneider, *More than You Wanted to Know: The Failure of Mandated Disclosure* (Princeton, Princeton University Press, 2014).

[25] For a broader claim that, if we allow public authorities to make (certain) decisions for us (eg by changing the defaults), we gain not only in personal welfare but also in autonomy see, eg Conly (n 1). See also on this point, Sunstein, 'The Ethics of Nudging' (n 1).

[26] This is however not necessarily true vis-à-vis other values, such as dignity. See McCrudden (n 3).

how the choice is actually made. Nudging people when they would not deliberate does not reduce autonomy. Behavioural interventions rather steer behaviour *within* the sphere that people navigate using System 1. Nudges improve navigability in life: they do not awaken rationality but do not *reduce* the sphere of deliberation either. This seems to be true for all three types of nudges identified by Baldwin. Yet, besides behavioural interventions targeting either System 1 (framing, vivid warnings) or 2 (provision of information), there seems to exist a fourth category that seeks to prompt a switch from System 1 to System 2. Examples include reminders, but also choice prompts aimed at triggering a deliberative, instead of an automatic, choice.[27] This last category of measures ('System 2 wake up!' measures) are more intrusive because by prompting active choosing they interfere with the process of decision-making.[28] It may of course be legitimate to awaken rationality. It enhances autonomy in the classical sense, because it seeks to extend the domain of deliberation, but it is nonetheless intrusive. This is because, unlike mere nudging, it interferes with a second order choice: the choice of a mental process (automatic vs deliberative). Given the limited number of decisions we can take fully deliberatively, we need to select the instances for which we keep our scarce deliberative resources. This second order 'choice' is often unconscious though it can be made conscious. The decision-making pattern of an individual is shaped by environment and by experience.[29] It may be viewed as more intimate and more identity-defining than preferences regarding outcomes (think for example about reading/not reading an instruction manual: mostly this is experienced as a personality trait with which interference is not welcome). Although this is an empirical question in need of investigation, individual attitudes towards alternative ways of making a decision may well prove more stable than preferences. If this is so, the question is whether a meaningful notion of autonomy should include the freedom for every individual to decide what decisions she wants to take reflectively and what decisions she is happy to take automatically. This would seem to be a stronger defence of autonomy and one that would apply beyond nudges to other forms of behaviourally oriented intervention.

In this line of thinking, interference with cognitive processes—and in particular with the balance an individual strikes between decisions driven by System 1 and those shaped by System 2—should raise more legitimacy concerns than interference with preferences regarding outcomes.[30] In line with a more orthodox view,

---

[27] Note this is not a new modus operandi for public intervention. Cooling off periods rely on the natural re-awakening offered by the granting of time ex post choice.

[28] One may observe that also defaults, depending on how they are framed, might induce the regulatee to come to realisation that she might opt out and therefore trigger a switch from System 1 to System 2 decision process.

[29] For an accessible account of such switches, see J Lehrer, *How We Decide* (New York, Houghton Mifflin, 2009).

[30] This is because preferences, unlike what is assumed in neoclassical economics, are not stable and do not characterise an individual. Decision-making patterns owe more to a person's personality and life history. They constitute individual characteristics in a much deeper sense than preferences, which can be transient and superficial. As such, they deserve to be interfered with only with caution.

van Aaken in her contribution expresses the opinion that 'It is hard to justify a state keeping its citizens in the "fast thinking" mode in cases where a "slow thinking" mode can be initiated'.[31] The difficulty with this argument is scarcity of attention.[32] We simply do not have the cognitive resources to take all the decisions slowly. Therefore, we—either individually or collectively—need to decide what set of decisions we take deliberatively and what set of decisions we take automatically.[33] If people constantly had to make choices deliberatively, their autonomy would in fact be reduced.[34] Therefore, respecting individual differences in the way people manage their limited 'mental bandwidth'—to use the terminology of Mullainathan and Shafir[35]—would seem a better, and more demanding agenda for those who wish to object to behavioural regulation on principled grounds. For our part, we think that interference with decision-making processes can be justified on policy grounds. Our point is that this kind of interference is the one that deserves more careful scrutiny than interference with so-called preferences, because 'preferences' are a construct that does not capture well what deserves protection from government interference both because those are often not deeply ingrained and because they are often the product of market forces.

As previously observed, and contrary to conventional wisdom, not all behavioural interventions target System 1 only. Many target both System 1 and System 2. Smart information disclosure requirements, for example, are specifically designed to ensure that choices are informed.[36] They rely in part on the functioning of System 1 to catch our attention but do seek to prompt reflection about our preferred course of action in a way that dull disclosures do not (because they are ignored). In a situation of lack of information, limited information or bias, such behavioural interventions do not infringe individual autonomy.[37] Under the classical view of autonomy (which is inherently related to deliberation), they rather make the decision *more* autonomous by rendering it more deliberative than the heteronomous decisions taken under the influence of choice architectures designed by corporations to serve private interests. Under the procedural view of autonomy just outlined, there is no reduction in autonomy when interventions seek to steer behaviour *within* the sphere that people navigate using System 2. Such is the case not only for the provision of information and defaults—which target System 2— but also for reminders and prompt choices—which although target System 1 aim at awakening System 2.

---

[31] For a similar argument, prioritising education over behavioural intervention, see G Gigerenzer, *Risk Savvy: How to Make Good Decisions* (New York, Penguin Group, 2014).

[32] Mullainathan and Shafir (n 5).

[33] In the absence of a collective decision, it is the market alone that is set to shape—through advertising and other marketing techniques—how individuals strike a balance between their deliberative and automatic selves.

[34] Sunstein, 'The Ethics of Nudging' (n 1).

[35] Mullainathan and Shafir (n 5).

[36] Sunstein, 'The Ethics of Nudging' (n 1).

[37] However, while a nudge might be justified when it helps counteracting a behavioural bias, such a bias is not a necessary justification for a nudge-type intervention. Sunstein, 'The Ethics of Nudging' (n 1).

This discussion shows that individual autonomy is in need of a rethink. Although autonomy is a fundamental value, its operationalisation in an age characterised by a rapid increase in cognitively-intensive tasks requires more nuanced views as to what individual decisions deserve protection from interference by government. As a matter of fact, not all decisions are equally deliberative. Normatively, it is not equally important that all individual decisions be taken more reflectively. This implies that prompting deliberation, while often viewed positively, does not always enjoy the same degree of legitimacy. Autonomy, if it is to remain a meaningful value, should not require conscious, active and deliberative choice all the time. The protection of autonomy, which ought to be provided by constitutional rules, needs to be devised in a flexible way so as to allow individuals, businesses, and public authorities to deal with bounded rationality in the pursuit of their respective legitimate goals.

In other words, those concerned with autonomy should not confine their argument to the abstract availability of choices; they should consider the distinct imperative to respect the balance between those decisions we want to take deliberately and those that we prefer to take automatically. It is for each individual to strike a balance between these modes of decision-making. Arguably, this is a dimension of individual autonomy that deserves closer consideration in the discussion on the legitimacy of public nudging and perhaps more generally. As we cannot realistically decide everything in life in a deliberative manner, deliberation cannot be the touchstone of what we value and protect in individual decisions under the name of autonomy. Instead, the focus should shift to when and how we accept to be assisted or influenced in our decision-making, either by private or public intervention. In this perspective, behaviourally informed intervention will appear problematic in far fewer circumstances than is generally thought because it generally improves navigability of choices. This revised perspective on autonomy does not however legitimise all behavioural interventions. If this were the case, the new perspective would be useless as it would amount to neutralising autonomy as a normative criterion to assess the legitimacy of public intervention. This is not what we have in mind. Rather, we invite lawyers and philosophers to look into what could be called a procedural conception of autonomy—where the term does not refer to legal procedures but to decision-making procedures. Future research should aim at identifying more precisely what restricts autonomy in a world in which autonomous decisions cannot realistically be equated with decisions taken in a fully deliberative manner.

C. Publicity and Collective Deliberation

A related but distinct element in the autonomy discourse is the level at which the relevant deliberation takes place. In the classical argument just discussed, the focus is on individual deliberation. Yet, one critical question for behaviour change strategies in any policy area is how targeted population groups are collectively involved in the decisions that are taken as well as in the associated development, implementation, monitoring, and evaluation of strategies. As noted by Jolls and Sunstein,

> there is no reason to think government would have to conceal or make ambiguous its efforts to correct people's errors. Citizens need not be disturbed to learn what government is doing, and there is no reason for regulators to keep their efforts secret.[38]

Over and beyond error-correcting intervention, a 'publicity principle' should apply to all choice architects, public and private alike.[39] Since lack of transparency is what renders an action 'manipulative', the publicity principle emerges as the most promising strategy to avoid behavioural interventions being dismissed as 'manipulations'.[40]

Several contributors to this volume highlight the importance of developing behavioural inspired approaches capable of enhancing people's capacity to deliberate and make conscious decisions.[41] Quigley and Stokes identify the most immediate consequences flowing from the adoption of a behavioural informed approach in EU law. They warn that turning to behavioural science for greater effectiveness and legitimation may bring its own set of ambiguities, which need to be properly addressed, not glossed over. In particular, they argue that nudging may exacerbate tensions between, on the one hand, efforts to improve the visibility and evidence base of EU action, through procedures such as regulatory impact analysis (RIAs) and, on the other hand, reliance on behaviourally savvy interventions based on non-transparent manipulation of choice environments. In our view, such conflicts between transparency and efficacy, when they arise, need to be dealt with in an open and transparent manner. It would be worth asking people in Europe (and perhaps elsewhere) if they would in principle, or in specific instances, consent to laws and regulation that take their fallibility into consideration. Our hunch is that they may very well do (we realise that this is a difficult claim to test as framing of the question would be crucial).[42] After all, most citizens—despite widespread present and optimism biases—do not think of themselves as super-cognisant *homini oeconomici*.

Feldman and Lobel offer an additional and converging argument in favour of openness and publicity. They base their claim in favour of designing more conscious behavioural interventions on grounds of procedural justice and on the expressive function of the law. In their view, when the law creates a choice

---

[38] Jolls and Sunstein (n 18) 231.

[39] R Thaler and CR Sunstein, *Nudge: Improving Decisions about Health, Wealth and Happiness* (New Haven, Yale University Press, 2008) 244.

[40] This is however not to deny that even with full transparency there is a risk of some degree of manipulation. Sunstein, 'The Ethics of Nudging' (n 1).

[41] See in this volume ch 2 by Di Porto and Rangone, ch 3 by Quigley and Stokes, ch 4 by van Aaken, as well as ch 13 by Feldman and Lobel.

[42] The European Commission Joint Research Center entrusted one of us (Alemanno) to run a mapping exercise aimed at gaining an understanding of the practice, perceptions and institutional designs of behavioural informed approaches across the EU. A report is expected to be published by the end of 2015.

architecture, there is a risk that its expressive function is de-activated. As a result, the law would shape behaviour but not its underlying values. This, they argue, does not only reduce deliberation; it may also change the function of the law.

While we are aware of the limits of current EU practice of RIAs, we believe nevertheless that a fully-fledged regulatory impact assessment, inclusive of RCTs, would constitute the privileged framework for incorporating behavioural considerations into EU policy-making. A revised framework for impact assessment should be equally open to the consideration of all regulatory tools, as traditional tools initially put in place with no particular regard for behavioural insights may very well prove behaviourally sound.[43] Within this process of regulatory analysis, behavioural considerations may not only allow policymakers to consider a broader set of regulatory options and test their effectiveness through RCTs, but also to empower citizens to have a say through the public consultation process accompanying IAs. This might increase the accountability of the regulatory outcome and most importantly address the 'manipulation' concern often raised vis-à-vis nudge-type interventions.

D. Cultural Differences in Regulatory Philosophy

At a very general level, the sentiment on the relationship between governmental action and autonomy, although largely underpinned by political philosophy considerations, is considerably shaped by culture. As Europe and the United States differ considerably in relation to their general perception of libertarian arguments, the legitimacy debate surrounding the behavioural intervention presents different contours. 'Many Americans abhor paternalism'.[44] This is why in the US it makes sense to brand nudging as 'libertarian paternalism': 'libertarian' makes paternalism more acceptable. In Europe, fewer are bothered by paternalism and tagging a policy proposal as libertarian is a lot less likely to constitute an effective marketing strategy. Indeed, such branding may well be counter-productive as, in many European countries 'libertarian' is considered extreme and even 'liberal' is loaded with antisocial connotations.[45] Libertarian and liberal are polarising rather than consensual terms in the public debate.

---

[43] See, eg in the US, Executive Order 12866 establishes a requirement of cost-benefit analysis. 3 CFR § 638 (1994); in the EU, European Commission, 'Impact Assessment Guidelines', SEC(2009) 92. For a timid attempt at integrating behavioural insights into EU policy-making, see Joint Research Centre, EU Commission, 'Applying Behavioural Sciences to EU Policy-making' (2013), available at ftp.jrc.es/EURdoc/JRC83284.pdf.

[44] CR Sunstein, 'It's For Your Own Good!' Book Review of Sarah Conly's *Against Autonomy*, The New York Review of Books (April 2013) 1.

[45] Libertarianism is a compartively extreme form of liberalism that emphasises the value of individual autonomy and liberty. See E Mack and GF Gaus, 'Classical Liberalism and Libertarianism: The Liberty Tradition' in GF Gaus and C Kukathas (eds), *Handbook of Political Theory* (London, Sage, 2004).

Europe does not only offer a specific institutional context, posing its own challenges for testing, implementing and embedding behaviourally informed policies. It is also a unique, composite polity, in which, as the above example suggests, words do not always carry the same connotations or even meaning than in the US.[46] Such differences in word use are not only of academic interest. They can have practical consequences, notably because what is politically realistic creates an often implicit filter through which even scholars view what lessons from behavioural sciences could profitably be put to use in the sphere of rule-making.[47] In the US, scholars who present their research as behavioural law and economics may have 'trimmed their sails' by discarding from their analysis insights from psychology that support policy intervention of a kind they are not keen to advocate or do not judge politically viable.[48] In Europe, where there is only a niche market—with less demand and as a result less supply—for non-paternalistic policies, the same filters are less likely to apply. The EU may well offer waters where it will be possible hoist the behavioural sails more fully. This is all the more so that legal culture in Europe[49] appears welcoming to behavioural insights. More specifically, as Cserne points out, one distinctive characteristic of EU law is its goal-oriented nature and broad reliance on purposive, consequence-based legal reasoning ('*effet utile*-style').[50] These traits are not only compatible with but compellingly calling for a non-formalistic, empirically-driven approach to law. In brief, it almost comes naturally, especially in the light of the objectives pursued by the Union,[51] to look at EU law as a policy instrument for the pursuit of a better life.

The technocratic character of EU law-making constitutes a further relevant characteristic to assess the porousness of EU legal system to behavioural insights. Behavioural informed intervention is inherently technocratic, and it does not require per se the participation of citizens. Yet given the dual democratic legitimacy of the EU—which lies in both representative and participative democracy[52]—this top-down, technocratic-like intervention might prompt resistance to nudging.

Therefore, the legitimacy of this particular form of behavioural informed intervention depends on citizens' acceptance of the technocratic and 'manipulative' nature of the policy as well as on citizens' trust in the 'choice architects'. In other words, the legitimacy critique boils down to the question of how comfortable citizens are with having experts and bureaucrats designing policies that reorient

---

[46] See also in this volume, ch 1 by A Alemanno and AL Sibony.
[47] See the discussion in ch 13 by Y Feldman and O Lobel.
[48] R Bubb and RH Pildes, 'How Behavioral Economics Trims Its Sails and Why' (2014) 127 *Harvard Law Review* 1593.
[49] Using the singular does not suggest that the legal culture is uniform across Europe. On diversity within European legal culture, see G Helleringer and K Purnhagen, *Towards a European Legal Culture* (Oxford, Hart Publishing, 2014).
[50] See in this volume, ch 12 by P Cserne.
[51] Art 3 TEU reads : 'The Union's aim is to promote peace, its values and the well-being of its people'.
[52] See Art 10 TEU. A von Bogdandy, 'Democratic Legitimacy of Public Authority beyond the State— Lessons from the EU for International Organizations' (2011) Jean Monnet Working Paper 01/11.

the exercise of their individual autonomy.[53] At this juncture, cultural differences between Europe and the US certainly play a role: while this deserves closer attention from political philosophers and political scientists and possibly a few qualifiers, Europeans appear on the whole more tolerant of paternalist bureaucrats than Americans.[54]

To sum up, while there is common ground between the EU and US when discussing the legitimacy dimension of behavioural intervention, the normative baselines for approaching it are clearly different. Given its socio-legal and political context, the EU is less likely to offer strong resistance to the use of behavioural insights in its own legal order. While institutional practice does not yet show widespread use of cognitive based regulatory intervention, the growing interest for behavioural studies at EU level—but also in a growing number of Member States[55]—does lend some support to our claim.

II. PRACTICABILITY

Once the legitimacy concerns have been overcome, the remaining questions pertain to how to effectively integrate behavioural sciences into policy-making. In other words, how can behavioural insights be used given the current state of science on the one hand and legal constraints on the other? That is what we mean for practicability of behavioural informed intervention.

While behavioural sciences demonstrate the limits of rational action and provide a better understanding of human behaviour, there is no ready-made framework for incorporating their insights into policy-making.[56] This represents a challenge for both legal scholars, whose job is to design bridges between behavioural insights and the law, and policymakers, whose mission is to walk those very same bridges when making laws. Policy-making is context dependent. Policymakers should have regard to the scientific validity underlying behavioural findings. Yet this aspiration to scientific rigour does not lead to a unique model of behavioural policy-making and the different cultural and social settings will play a role.[57] Operationalisation

---

[53] We have addressed this concern and attempted to offer a solution in the previous section, (C) 'Publicity and Collective Deliberation'.

[54] For a comparative analysis of US and European societies, see A Martinelli, *Transatlantic Divide* (Oxford, Oxford University Press, 2007). See also JQ Whitman, 'Consumerism Versus Producerism: A Study in Comparative Law' (2007) 117 *Yale Law Journal* 340.

[55] See in this volume, ch 1 by A Alemanno and AL Sibony.

[56] See, eg, Science and Technology Select Committee, *Report on Behaviour Change* (HL, July 2011); 'A Practitioner's Guide to Nudging' *Rotman Management Magazine*, available at www-2.rotman.utoronto.ca/facbios/file/GuidetoNudging-Rotman-Mar2013.ashx.pdf.

[57] According to Dunlop and Radaelli, however, they also exist as endogenous factors shaping the integration of behavioural insights into policy-making. This would be due to nine different biases that may affect the outcome of regulatory impact assessment and, in particular, play to the detriment of the 'do nothing' option. To correct this activism bias, they argue that it is important to include behavioural insights in training of the policymaker and make concrete proposals on how this can be done. See ch 6 by C Dunlop and C Radaelli.

of behavioural insights therefore calls for an analysis of two distinct dimensions: methodological challenges of behavioural policy-making and institutional requirements.

A. Methodological Challenges to Ensure Effectiveness

The promise of behavioural informed policy-making is to increase effectiveness of policies. However, critics put forward that one should not be too quick to infer improvement of policy outcome from the use of generalisations of existing empirical studies. In fact,—as demonstrated by Feldman and Lobel—science provides many more insights than just the few lawyers tend to focus on when they first discover a field such as behavioural studies.[58] The gist of the critique is common to any legal use of science; it consists in a sound questioning of the proper inferences that can be drawn from empirical studies to inform the law. Issues to consider pertain to relevance of empirical data for legal use,[59] internal and external validity of studies,[60] as well as robustness.[61] All of these issues deserve to be put in perspective. The history of using science in law tends to repeat itself and is made up of cycles of irrational hopes on the part of lawyers that science will help solve the problems they face, followed by disappointment when it becomes clear that science answers different questions.[62] To break this cycle, policymakers and lawyers need to adjust their expectations of what science can bring to their pursuits and recognise how much still needs to be decided without the support of science.

In relation to legal use of behavioural insights, five major difficulties arise. First, the ecological (or external) validity of experiments can be questioned: behavioural sciences are fundamentally empirical[63] and extant studies do not always analyse heuristics and biases in contexts that are relevant for regulation. For example, consumers in a supermarket do not necessarily behave like students who are required to perform tasks on a computer in a lab. As a result, it cannot be assumed that real life agents fall victims of the very same cognitive errors made by experimental subjects or that they do to the same extent. This limitation is difficult to overcome because we lack a theory of cognitive function that could help predict how real life decisions are taken.[64] Because rational consumers with certain specific preferences and irrational consumers can end up making the same choices (eg of credit

---

[58] See ch 13 by Y Feldman and O Lobel.
[59] See ch 3 by M Quigley and E Stokes.
[60] An experiment is said to have external validity when its outcome can be generalised to a real-world setting, outside the laboratory. It is said to have internal validity when the outcome of the experiment is not due to external factors that were not taken into account and measured in the experiment, ie when it reliably establishes a causal relationship between variables.
[61] Robustness describes the possibility to reproduce experimental results with different data sets.
[62] Feldman and Lobel, ch 13.
[63] eg A Tor, 'The Methodology of the Behavioral Analysis of Law' (2008) 4 *Haifa Law Review* 237.
[64] D Schwartz, 'Regulating for Rationality' *Stanford Law Review* (forthcoming).

card contract or phone plan), policymakers cannot know which fraction of the observed behaviour is the product of bias rather than rational choice.[65] A distinct but related concern about ecological validity is to do with the fact that relatively little is known about the sensitivity of the human cognitive and emotional foibles to cultural differences. This issue is particularly weighty in the European context, where the same legislation applies from Portugal to Poland. More studies will be needed to distinguish universal from culturally-sensitive biases before the results of studies conducted in one country can be extrapolated to others.

Second, the temporal dimension of influencing mechanisms is often overlooked. Many studies document immediate effect of context on decision but leave open the question of how lasting the effects measured are. This is exemplified by mandatory information schemes, such as pictorial warnings used in tobacco products. The effectiveness of warnings tends to decrease over time as the novelty effect wears off.[66] More critically, the specific effects of behavioural-change policies are difficult to discern from those stemming from the overall policy action, which may also include non-behavioural-informed action.

Third, studies that evidence the existence of a bias are rarely informed about how widespread that bias is in the population. This is generally referred to as the heterogeneity problem.[67] Citizens differ in the degree to which they display various biases, due to individual characteristics but also experience. Actual consumers are more experienced than experimental subjects insofar as the latter usually face the experimental task for the first time. Individuals also differ materially in their cognitive styles, some being more analytical and others more intuitive. In addition, the current behavioural studies commonly test for one bias at the time. However, given the possibility that several biases affect an agent's choice at the same time, policymakers should be aware of the 'many bias' problem.[68] Moreover, behavioural studies may not indicate how intense a distortion of decision patterns the bias causes. This raises the question of whether debiasing intervention is warranted where one lacks knowledge about the extent of the problem to be cured. From a policy standpoint, the issue is not only whether the benefits exceed costs. Distribution effects are also difficult to assess: if, for example, one seeks to protect consumers from making a certain type of mistake, the intervention will likely impose costs on regulatees and, ultimately, on the consumers who did not need the protection in the first place, because they might be capable of debiasing themselves.[69]

---

[65] Schwartz, ibid, names this problem 'observational equivalence': rational consumers and irrational consumers behave in ways that are 'observationally equivalent' from the point of view of the regulator.
[66] GT Fong, D Hammond and SC Hitchman, 'The Impact of Pictures on the Effectiveness of Tobacco Warnings' (2009) 87(8) *Bull World Health Organisation* 640.
[67] See, eg Schwartz (n 64).
[68] ibid.
[69] C Camerer et al, 'Regulation for Conservatives: Behavioral Economics and the Case for "Asymmetric Paternalism"' [2003] *University of Pennsylvania Law Review* 1211; and Schwartz (n 64).

Fourth, public authorities seem to lack a full picture of the fields of behavioural research that must shape the policymaker's toolbox.[70] This is largely due to a narrow reading—sometimes use[71]—of the relevant behavioural literature that has been studied by the proponents of behavioural informed policy-making and taken up by governments. As result of such a selective understanding of behavioural insights, policymakers may enact limited and sometimes inadvertent policy recommendations that are based on a partial view of the scope and potential of the various branches of psychology. Trade-offs between different types of solutions are pervasively present in the adoption of policies addressing social challenges. In order for policymakers to become wiser consumers of the discipline of judgement and decision-making,[72] they must be better trained to recognise these trade-offs.

The fifth challenge posed by legal use of behavioural insights is linked to what may be called the granularity gap. Legal rules are general. Psychologists focus instead on context-dependence: they study how various contextual parameters influence decisions. Yet, the law needs to be written to apply in a variety of contexts. Rules cannot distinguish beyond a certain level of detail and, due to the inherent coarseness of legal categories (eg professional seller and consumer), they cannot account for a myriad of circumstances, which may weigh on individual decisions (eg the colour of the background of an e-commerce website, the music in a restaurant). This implies that a wealth of behavioural knowledge might be too detailed to appear on the radar of lawyers, who observe the world through a low-resolution screen.

To address these concerns, it has been proposed that behaviourally informed interventions be tested prior to any large-scale and general implementation.[73] The aim of a behavioural study is to gain a better understanding of how people act and sometimes think and feel too. Several methodologies are currently used for putting policies to test. The most widely used method is surveys. They consist in questioning a large sample of individuals about their attitude, beliefs and expectations through a questionnaire. While the way in which the questionnaire is framed may greatly influence the outcome, surveys generally score high in terms of external validity as they capture what people 'out there' think. Yet, because stated preferences may not coincide with revealed preferences (the intention–action gap), surveys are not always the best instruments to predict how people will act in practice. Experiments constitute a second method, which partly addresses the major limitation of behavioural surveys. An experiment reconstructs in the controlled environment of a lab a decision context that bears some resemblance to a policy relevant situation. It is then designed to measure how subjects respond to a change

---

[70] See ch 13 by Feldman and Lobel.
[71] Bubb and Pildes (n 48).
[72] O Amir and O Lobel, 'Stumble, Predict, Nudge: How Behavioral Economics Informs Law and Policy' (2009) 108 *Columbia Law Review* 2098, 2122.
[73] The leading guidance is offered by the UK Behavioural Insights Team and is called EAST (Easy, Attractive, Social and Timely). See UK Cabinet Office/NESTA, 'EAST, Four Simple Ways to Apply Behavioural Insights' (2013).

in one element that mimics a policy choice. This enables us to draw conclusions on the effect of the manipulated element on participants' actual behaviour. By identifying cause-and-effect relationships, experiments may provide reliable results that are replicable in different places and at different times. Because laboratory experiments involve relatively small samples, it is crucial that they be designed so as to ensure their representativeness of the real world. However, ideally, behaviour should be observed in its real environment as opposed to laboratory settings.[74] The methodology enabling such an observation is generally referred to as randomised control trial (RCT).[75] In line with a feature of medicine established since the last century, this methodology is aimed at empirically testing different policy options, measure and compare outcomes. RCTs are specific experiments in which the efficacy of an intervention is studied by comparing the effects of the intervention on a population that is randomly divided into groups. The groups are exposed to a differential course of treatment: one of them—the control group—is not treated (or receives a 'placebo'), whilst the other group—the intervention group—is exposed to the 'treatment'. The impact of the intervention is then measured by comparing the results in both groups.

The rationale behind the extension of RCT from the pharmaceutical sector to that of public policy-making must be found in the promise of highly effective results of behavioural intervention at low cost. A behavioural intervention is said to 'work' when it is capable of producing the desired change in behaviour on the targeted population. It is against this backdrop that controlled experiments on new regulatory measures are set to become the new benchmark to assess the real impact of a proposed governmental intervention.[76] The emerging use of RCTs in policy-making is therefore perceived as an approach capable of assessing *in concreto* the impact of regulatory measures, in contrast to conventional regulatory impact analysis (RIAs). RIAs are traditionally performed on the basis of prospective, and therefore theoretical, calculations of costs and benefits.[77] It is, however, not always possible to run RCTs and therefore other methods, such as survey, experiments as well as qualitative research techniques,[78] can be used to appraise new behavioural policy proposals.

---

[74] See, eg M Abramowicz, I Ayres and Y Listokin, 'Randomizing Law' (2011) 159(4) *University of Pennsylvania Law Review* 929.
[75] For an introduction to RCTs in policy-making, see R Glennerster and K Takavarasha, *Running Randomized Evaluations: A Pratical Guide* (Princeton, Princeton University Press, 2014).
[76] See the document produced by the UK Government, *Test, Learn, Adapt Developing Public Policy with Randomised Controlled Trials* (2012) available at www.gov.uk/government/publications/test-learn-adapt-developing-public-policy-with-randomised-controlled-trials, as well as that elaborated by the Joint Research Centre of the EU Commission and edited by R van Bael, 'Applying Behavioural Sciences to EU Policy-Making' (2013), available at ftp.jrc.es/EURdoc/JRC83284.pdf.
[77] CR Sunstein, *Simpler. The Future of Government* (New York, Simon & Schuster, 2013) 187.
[78] These include several research methods, used in qualitative behavioural sciences, such as focus groups, semi-structured interviews and participant observation.

Although no specific methodology to assess behavioural informed interventions has imposed itself, the use of RCTs and other supporting evidence might contribute, by becoming easily reproducible in different jurisdictions, to render behavioural policy-making scalable in nature.[79] While the methodological difficulties that we have illustrated in this section seems to mitigate the universalistic narrative that is currently characterising the nudge discourse and facilitating its rapid diffusion, they also urge the scientific and policy community to embrace a culture of policy testing.

B. Institutional Design of Behavioural Policy-Making

The question of how to best organise the integration of behavioural policy-making within current governmental settings is also particularly relevant in today's cognitive based regulation debate. The UK, being the first mover, seems to have set up the golden standard for behavioural institutional design: a dedicated unit, the Behavioural Insights Team (BIT), initially placed within the Cabinet Office, and made of few experts, specialised in several behavioural disciplines, who work in direct contact with the different government departments. When advising public administrations or charities on the integration of behavioural insights, the BIT relies on a wide range of practical measures to change citizens' behaviour, spanning from re-wording the content of letters sent by public authorities to taxpayers[80] to using small 'thank you' gifts to reward charitable donations.[81] An institutional experience whose development appears almost antithetical to that of the UK can be observed in Denmark, where a bottom-up organisation, called iNudgeU, animated by academics, civic advocates and behavioural professionals, has created a self-proclaimed Danish Nudge Network.[82] Interestingly enough, while the BIT has acquired its autonomy from the Cabinet Office and been granted a private sector status,[83] the Danish Nudge Network has progressively been incorporated into the Danish Government. If they differ in the chronology and direction of change between public and private sector, both experiences however have in common that

---

[79] On RCTs as applied to policy-making, R Jones, J Pykett and M Whitehead, *Changing Behaviours—On the Rise of the Psychological State* (Cheltenham, Edward Elgar, 2013) 174.

[80] Paper of the Behavioural Insight Team, 'Applying Behavioural Insights to Reduce Fraud, Error and Debt' (2012) available at www.gov.uk/government/uploads/system/uploads/attachment_data/file/60539/BIT_FraudErrorDebt_accessible.pdf; in 2013, the British tax authority HMRC applied some of the insights presented in the paper to adopt a variation on the standard letter used to urge taxpayers to file their returns on time.

[81] *cf*: Paper of the Cabinet Office and Behavioural Insight Team, 'Applying Behavioural Insights to Charitable Givings' (2013) available at: www.gov.uk/government/uploads/system/uploads/attachment_data/file/203286/BIT_Charitable_Giving_Paper.pdf.

[82] A similar experience emerged in Norway where the Stordalen Foundation launched green nudges.

[83] The Unit still provides services to the UK Government but also to private sector entities and foreign governments. www.behaviouralinsights.co.uk/.

a dedicated unit has been created. An alternative or complementary model would be to educate policymakers in government departments on a wider scale.[84]

Across Europe, the level of nudge awareness is very diverse:[85] in many countries, the initial excitement about the novelty of behavioural sciences and its innovation potential has not yet reached the policy-making circles, let alone legal academia. We might call this the pre-nudge stage, meaning that the eponymous book has not yet been widely read. A second circle is made up of countries in incipient nudge stage, where awareness of behavioural regulation is present but restricted to very restricted circles. In this category, Germany[86] and France[87] have shown some sign of interest for behavioural policy-making, but, at the time of writing, it is not clear whether they will go as far as to set up dedicated units. In the Netherlands, the Scientific Council for Government Policy (WRR) recently published a report entitled *Policy-Making with Knowledge of Behaviour*.[88] The UK, and partly Denmark, represent a more mature nudge stage, where cognitive based interventions are tested, used and publicly debated. No country seems to have reached a post-nudge stage yet. Of course, these stages—and possibly others that would need to be added— form a continuum. In addition, there may be different styles of nudge maturity. In the European context, the development of Member State expertise about behavioural regulation progresses in parallel with developments at EU level. In time, this may raise questions regarding the federalism of behavioural regulation.[89] In particular, it will be interesting to observe whether and how behavioural arguments may be brought to bear on subsidiarity appraisal, for example, if Member States can establish that, in some policy areas, different behavioural patterns justify regulation at national rather than at EU level.

In the meantime, the European Union established a 'Foresight and Behavioural Insights Unit', which is located within the EU Commission Joint Research Centre. The unit's raison d'être is to centralise the efforts currently undertaken by some Directorates General of the EU Commission, such as DG Consumer Protection and Health (SANCO), to integrate behavioural insights into EU policy-making. By overcoming the current institutional fragmentation, the unit is expected to develop a robust methodology and to foster a behavioural mindset among the

---

[84] CR Sunstein, 'Nudging: A Very Short Guide' (2014) 37 *Journal of Consumer Policy* 583, 587.

[85] At the time of writing the European Commission is engaged in a mapping exercise aimed at collecting practices of behavioural policy-making across its Member States. Its outcome is expected to be published in the form of a report by the end of 2015.

[86] In Germany, the Government announced it was hiring psychologists, behavioural economists as well as anthropologists to test new methods of 'efficient government', P Plickert and H Beck, 'Kanzlerin Angela Merkel sucht Verhaltensforscher', FAZ, 26 August 2014, www.faz.net/aktuell/wirtschaft/wirtschaftspolitik/kanzlerin-angela-merkel-sucht-verhaltensforscher-13118345.html.

[87] www.modernisation.gouv.fr/les-services-publics-se-simplifient-et-innovent/par-des-services-numeriques-aux-usagers/le-nudge-au-service-de-laction-publique.

[88] Thanks to Frederik Borgesius for the translation and for bringing this to our knowledge. The report (in Dutch) is available on the WRR website: www.wrr.nl/publicaties/publicatie/article/met-kennis-van-gedrag-beleid-maken/.

[89] See ch 3 by M Quigley and E Stokes.

EU Commission civil servants. It remains to be seen what influence this institutional effort will have into the EU administrative culture and whether it will affect the national level. For the time being, the EU 'Nudge Unit' has not yet decided which of the various institutional design models to embrace—if any. Given the EU constitutional and institutional specificities, one cannot rule out that the EU will develop a new, autonomous model.

Also the OECD is showing some interest for behavioural approaches to regulation. After the publication of a report on *Behavioural Economics and Policymaking*,[90] the OECD is set to include 'behavioural economics' in its 2015 Regulatory Policy Outlook. One may therefore expect the OECD to recommend its members to tap into the potential of behavioural findings when conceiving their better regulation agenda. Given the OECD's success in promoting innovative regulatory approaches, its embrace of behavioural regulation could be instrumental to the diffusion of a behavioural orientation to governments of its member countries.

The benefit of behavioural insights is not reserved to rich countries. The World Bank placed behavioural approaches at the centre of its *World Development Report 2015*.[91] By integrating a behavioural perspective on development policy, this report provides a richer understanding of why people save, use preventive health care, work hard, learn, and conserve energy. It provides a basis for innovative and inexpensive interventions and highlights the following elements for policy attention: the role of choice architecture; the scope for social rewards; frames that influence whether or not a norm is activated; information in the form of rules of thumb; as well as opportunities for experiences that change mental models or social norms.

While it might be too early to salute the emergence of a global behavioural policy-making movement, there is clearly a common trend among this set of recent initiatives taking place at national, European and international level.[92]

III. CONCLUSIONS

Contributions to *Nudge and the Law* individually and collectively demonstrate that the dominant policy models in the EU are based on a rather naïve understanding of what drives behaviour. These models assume people tend to make insightful, well-planned and informed decisions guided by considerations of personal utility. This assumption seems shared across policy areas. Behaviourally informed policy-making is instead cognisant of the role played by framing and defaults, by the gap between intention and action as well as by the many other perceptions, impulses, judgements, and decision processes that characterise human decision-making. It

---

[90] P Lunn, *Regulatory Policy and Behavioural Economics* (Paris, OECD, 2014).
[91] World Bank Group, *World Development Report 2015: Mind, Society, and Behavior* (Washington, DC, World Bank) available at openknowledge.worldbank.org/handle/10986/20597.
[92] For an analysis of the political economy of nudging, see HW Micklitz, *The Politics of Behavioural Economics*, 31 January 2015 (on file with the editors).

is against this backdrop that behavioural insights, by providing a more nuanced, realistic account of how people make decisions, may offer European Union law a fertile ground upon which it can develop more effective, less costly policies making life easier for most citizens.

Yet the promises accompanying the emergence of behavioural policy-making must be analysed—in the European Union as elsewhere—in the light of the two most serious sources of reservations that this phenomenon has prompted thus far: its legitimacy and practicability.

The legitimacy challenge for behavioural regulation can be viewed through the prism of two trade-offs: first, between the desire to preserve autonomy and the inevitability of 'choice architecture' and, second, between the aspiration to reflective decision-making and the reality that 'mental bandwidth' is a scarce resource. The framework that is needed to approach these challenging trade-offs should include the need not only to respect individual deliberation but also openness and collective deliberation. This is where the practical challenges of behavioural policy-making, and more specifically, those of institutional design reside.

Although there is no single ready-made framework for incorporating behavioural insights into policy-making, several efforts have been undertaken to assist policymakers in determining whether and how to consider behaviour when legislating. On the one hand, policymakers are increasingly getting acquainted with several methods for conducting behavioural studies, such as experiments, survey, and RCTs. On the other hand, while no institutional framework emerges as preferable over the others, several options exist to design institutional settings capable of ensuring some behavioural consideration in policy-making. Policymakers can count on several institutional approaches when it comes to refine their understanding of human behaviour in the policy process, be it a dedicated unit within government or a looser network of experts providing on-demand advice to government.

The current approaches display shortcomings: the lack of a cognitive theory, the absence of a framework for deciding in face of heterogeneity at the population level and the difficulties to extrapolate from extant behavioural studies. They also share a positive common feature: they strive to inject a culture of testing and experimentation into policy-making. As such, they belong to a broader trend aimed at inserting evidence into policy-making in order to invest limited public funding into those policies that 'work'. This trend is effectively conveyed by the title of a recent book: *Show Me the Evidence*.[93] Rather than relying on anecdotal evidence or, what is worse, emotions, behaviourally informed regulation tends to emerge as more evidence-based than conventional regulation.[94] Importantly,

---

[93] R Haskins and G Margolis, *Show Me the Evidence—Obama's Fight for Rigor and Results in Social Policy* (Washington DC, Brookings Institution Press, 2014).

[94] Yet this is not to suggest that policymakers should automatically infer from behavioural studies that 'everyone is crazy or everyone is sane'. Policymakers must realise that in the absence of a cognitive theory they cannot sensibly make inferences from subjects' laboratory choices to real life context. Schwartz (n 64).

behavioural sciences broke the monopoly of economics as the only social science that is recognised as relevant and useful by policymakers.[95] That is where the major promise of behavioural regulation lies in today EU's policy-making: a more open and evidence-informed approach to policy development.

Several constitutional traits of the European Union suggest that its policy-making could not only accommodate but also benefit from the integration of new bodies of evidence, such as behavioural sciences. First, the goal-oriented drive behind EU policy-making seems particularly prone to empirically driven approaches to law. Second, the fact that EU legislation is initiated by the Commission, a technocratic, non-elected body endowed with sizeable resources and largely insulated from immediate political pressure, may be conducive to evidence-based experimentation. Third, the tension existing between the competence of the EU and that of its Member States, which is typical of any federal system, might find comfort in the integration of a body of knowledge capable of injecting fresh empirical guidance on how to draw, interpret and operationalise that demarcation line. The appeal of behavioural-informed approaches should not lead us to underestimate the significance of their effects on legal systems. While behavioural considerations may allow policymakers to consider a broader set of regulatory options and test their effectiveness through RCTs, their use should be subject to public as well as constitutional scrutiny so as to increase the accountability of the regulatory outcome.

Despite the potential role that behavioural insights might play in informing EU policy-making, research on the proper and appropriate use of behavioural insights in policy-making is still in its early days. In Europe, a lot of work remains to be done.[96] Without ruling out that they may be similarities with questions discussed in the US context, this volume demonstrates that the approach undertaken by the US-dominated scholarship on behaviourally informed intervention is not always best suited to address legal and policy issues in the EU. It is by keeping in mind this caveat that we hope to have made a case for more joint involvement of EU legal scholars and empirical researchers into this promising interdisciplinary field of study. Lawyers may indeed significantly contribute to development of behavioural policy-making. First, by complementing the role played by economists or other experimental researchers—in particular psychologists –, they can raise a set of legally relevant questions in the design of behavioural experiments. Second, lawyers may contribute to provide context to the conception and execution of those experiments thus contributing to render them less abstract and more policy-relevant. Third, lawyers as well as other actors involved in the legal

---

[95] D Kahneman, Foreword to E Shafir (ed), *The Behavioral Foundations of Public Policy* (Princeton, Princeton University Press, 2012) vii.

[96] We echo here the call of Tor for an increased breadth of behavioural law and economics (beyond the US and beyond the fields of law that have drawn most scholarly attention so far). A Tor, 'The Next Generation of Behavioural Law and Economics' in Klaus Mathis (ed), *European Perspectives on Behavioural Law and Economics* (Heidelberg, Springer, 2015) 17.

profession, such as judges and policymakers, may also offer a privileged yet largely unexploited sample for some behavioural testing.[97] They may contribute to encourage true cross-cultural behavioural studies by broadening the sample so as to render it more representative. To sum up, behavioural informed intervention needs lawyers as much as lawyers need behavioural considerations in their action.

It is in the light of the above that we hope that the chapters of this volume will be of use to future scholars. We view them as invitations to engage with the research agenda that we have strived to outline in this volume with the help of our contributors.

---

[97] Student bodies have come to be the predominant study population for many psychology and behavioural researchers. However, a recent survey of the psychology and behavioural economics literature suggests that American college students are outliers, quite atypical of the world population. See 'The University Student as a Model Organism' (2010) 13 *Nature Neuroscience* 521.

Index

abortion decisions 311–12
accountability 69, 150, 154, 261, 275, 335, 346
Ackerman, Frank 153
Acquisti, Alessandro 188, 190, 197
active choosing xi–xiii, xvi, xvii, 110, 237–8
Adler, Matthew D 315
administrative practices 19
adolescents, targeting 85
advertising 194, 239, 241 *see also* **behavioural targeting and regulation of privacy**
affect 144, 149–50, 154, 171
age groups 85, 108, 322
agency
  human agency, assumptions about 292–5, 299
  principal-agent experiments 320–1
Akerlof, George 188–9
alcohol 236, 241–7
  deliberations and decisions 314
  EU Alcohol Strategy 241
  evidence-based policy 64, 66
  financial incentives 244
  free movement 239
  manipulation 327
  private and family life, right to respect for 102
  self-regulation 251
  warnings 247
  WHO Global Strategy 248
Alemanno, Alberto 71
Alliance for Lobbying Transparency and Ethics Regulation (ALTER-EU) 118, 134
Alternative Investment Fund Managers (AIFM) Directive 259
ambiguity, effects of legal 318–19
American Medical Association's (AMA) Guides to Evaluation of Permanent Impairment 131–2
Amir, On 306–7, 322
anchoring 122–3, 125, 130, 148, 231
Anderson, Elizabeth S 315
anonymised data 196
anonymous crowds, wisdom of 145
Ariely, Dan 1, 318
The Art of Judgment. Vickers, Geoffrey 141, 152
Article 29 Working Group 173–5, 183–6, 194, 196, 198–9, 201
'as judged by themselves' standard viii–ix, 89
Asch, Solomon 153–4

ATM machines 129
attention
  average consumer standard 221–2
  defaults 15
  experiments 285
  limits vi, 4–5, 43, 177, 199–200, 284–5, 332
  media 199
  nudging xi, 10–11
  regulatory design vi
  salience 148
  service providers 168
  simplification 43
  terms and conditions 225
Australia (NSW), behavioural insights team in 62
autonomy xi–xii
  active choosing xi–xii
  behavioural bias xi
  choice architecture 326–8
  consumer law 225, 329
  data protection 163–7, 172–4, 178
  defaults xii, 94, 327–8, 332
  definition 164
  deliberations and decisions 313, 326, 329–33
  disclosure 225, 330
  freedom of choice, preservation of xii, 330–1
  fundamental rights 102–3, 107
  individual autonomy, definition of 90
  informed choices xi
  legitimacy 326–33, 345
  manipulation xiv–xv, xviii, 94–6, 327, 329
  negative autonomy 164, 169, 172–4, 178
  nudging viii, xi–xii, 19, 326–33
  paternalism xi, 86, 89–96, 99, 100, 108–10, 112
  positive autonomy 164, 170, 172, 175
  privacy 102, 163–7, 172–4, 178
  proportionality 92, 96, 106–9, 111
  rationality 91, 95, 331, 333
  self-identity 164–5
  social sharing 166–9
  toolboxes 12
  trade-offs 305–6
availability bias 123
availability heuristics 52, 123, 247
average consumer standard 214–15, 218, 221–3
aviation industry, checklists in the 129, 137
Ayres, Ian 206

Baldwin, Robert   12, 327, 331
Balebako, Rebecca   200
Banaji, Mahzarin R   318
bans   15, 51–2, 57, 88, 201–2, 205–7, 236–7, 244, 248
   choice architecture   xvii
   data protection   180, 205–7
   defaults   15, 237
   health data, tracking   205
   health law and lifestyle policy   236–7, 255, 308
   paternalism   88, 251
   take-it-or-leave-it choices   201
   tobacco, sale of   51–2, 57
   tracking walls   202
   visual display bans at points of sale   248
Bar-Gill, Oren   219, 230
Barenboim, Daniel   228
Bayes theorem   123
Bazerman, Max   1, 318
behavioural bias *see* biases
behavioural sciences, making use of   24, 29–59
   behavioural targeting   179–207
   choice amongst different regulatory options   54–9
   cognitive-based strategies   30, 36–48
   design of regulation   30
   empowerment   30, 36–7, 41–53
   lesson learning for rulemakers   53–9
   nudging strategies   30, 36–41, 49–52
   privacy   179–207
   regulatory process, cognitive-based approach to   30–6
   rulemaking   29–36
   strengths and weakness of cognitive-based regulatory tools   48–53
   unresponsive behaviours   29, 30, 31, 33, 53–4
Behavioural Studies for European Policies (BESTEP)   62
behavioural targeting and regulation of privacy   24, 179–207
   advertising networks   180
   behavioural targeting, definition of   179
   benefits of advertising   181
   biases   182
   chilling effects   181
   competitive advantage, privacy as a   190
   conditional on consent, services made   179
   consent   179–80
   control, lack of   181
   cookies   179, 180–1, 200
   data protection   180, 182–8
   deep packet inspection   181
   discrimination, risk of unfair   181–2
   empowerment   179, 188, 198–203, 207
   information asymmetries   188–90
   information cocoons   182
   informed consent   182–201, 203, 207
   manipulation   181–2
   nudging   179
   opt-in/opt-out consent   179
   private and family life, right to respect for   182–3
   protection of individuals   179, 180, 198
   targets, classifying people as   181–2
   waste, classifying people as   181–2
   worldview, influencing   182
behavioural trade-offs   301–24
   autonomy   305–6
   behavioural law and economics   301–8
   bounded rationality   304
   choice architecture   303, 306, 317, 321, 323
   command-and-control   306–7
   consumer law   225, 305
   defaults   147, 303–4, 309, 317, 322
   easy, making activities   303
   empowerment   52–3
   environmental policy   304, 323
   evidence-based policies   303
   expanding the behavioural world   308–22
   invisible nudges versus expressive law   309, 314–17
   legitimacy   345
   market failure   188
   new governance   307
   nudges   301–2, 305–17
   opt-in/opt-out systems   303
   outcome versus processes   309–14, 323
   over-simplification   25
   paternalism   305–6, 308
   practicability   340
   psychology   301–2, 305–11, 314, 317, 322–4
   rational choice theory   302
   recent behavioural initiatives   302–5
   redistributive effects   306
   regulatory toolboxes   306–7
   schematic solutions   322–3
   simplification   302
   social sciences   307
   third party externalities   306
   training   154
   trust versus voluntary compliance   309, 317–21, 323
   universal versus targeted nudging   309, 321–2, 323
Belgium   16, 215–17
Ben-Shahar, Omri   219, 230
Benkler, Yochai   318
Bentham, Jeremy   164
best available techniques (BAT)   116
better-off, state of being   91
biases *see also* **debiasing**
   affect   144, 149–50, 154
   availability bias   123
   baselines   290
   behavioural targeting   182, 192–8

case studies 154–5
choice architecture xvi–xvii
commitments 144, 150, 154–5
communication-oriented regulation 93
confirmation bias 119, 122–3
conflicts of interest 119
consider-the-opposite technique 124
costs 50
culture 339
data protection 171, 173, 194–5
defaults viii, 144, 147–8, 154, 193
disconfirmation bias 121
ego 144, 150–1
emotions 144, 149–50
empowerment 50, 58, 202
evidence-based policy 75–6, 144
experts 19, 115, 117, 119–37, 145
financial services regulation 262–6, 270–1
framing 153
freedom of choice, preservation of xvii
guidance, re-formulation of 146
health law and lifestyle policy 236, 244, 247
hindsight bias 119, 122
incentives, response to 144, 146–7, 153
information deficits and asymmetries 97
informed consent 177, 192–8
institutional challenges 287–8
judges 19
loss aversion bias 146–7, 153
many bias problem 339
market failure 197–8
messengers, bias as carried by 144, 145–51, 153
mistakes xvi–xvii
myopia/present bias 195–7, 202
new sources of bias 128–9
norms
   premises, unavoidability of
      normative 290–1
   social norms, power of 144, 147
nudging xvi–xviii, 18–19, 36, 42, 58, 123–5, 301, 327
objectivity ideal 120–3
officials xvi–xviii
optimism bias 46–7, 52, 196, 225, 334
outcome bias 122
overconfidence bias 46, 196
paternalism x–xi, 85–7, 93–6, 98–100, 110
practicability 339
precedents, reliance on 149
preservation 36
priming 144, 149
privacy 171, 173, 182
prosecutorial bias 122
public opinion xvi
public sector xvi–xviii, 18
publication 285
reflection 152–3
regret 98, 149

regulatory impact assessments 24, 139–51, 156
salience 144, 148–9
smart information nudging 39
status quo 10–11, 47, 192–5, 200–1, 207, 247, 262–4
System 1 mode of thinking 124, 127, 309–10
System 2 mode of thinking 124, 127, 309
training 152–5, 156–7
big brother policies 303
biofuel industry 150
blacklists 229, 230–3
blame-avoidance 150–1
Bloomberg, Michael 307
Böhme, Rainer 196–7
boomerang effect 40, 58
bounded rationality 198, 283, 292, 304, 333
Bovens, Luc 95
bovine spongiform encephalopathy (BSE) 122
Bowles, Samuel 320
Bracton, Henry 298
brain imaging 35
Brandeis, Louis 164
Bubb, Ryan 307
buy now, pay later deals 196
Bygrave, Lee Andrew 183

cafeteria policy xiv, 304
Calo, Ryan 12, 182, 199
Camerer, Colin 306
Cartwright, Nancy 74
case studies 151, 153–5
Charter of Fundamental Rights of the EU 103–5
   data protection 198, 202
   dignity 103
   explicit guarantees, lack of 104
   independent data protection authorities, requirement for 198
   informed consent and behavioural targeting 182–3, 198, 202
   nudging 101
   privacy 182–3
   proportionality 86, 106–11, 112
checklists 124, 129, 136–7
chilling effects 181, 204, 205
choice amongst different regulatory options 54–9
choice architecture
   autonomy xii
   active choosing xii
   alteration 7
   autonomy 326–8, 332, 345
   biases xvi–xvii
   consumer law, simplification of 229
   contract law vii

cultural differences 336–7
defaults xii
democracy v
forms vii
freedom of choice, preservation of vii
health law and lifestyle policy 236–7
human agency, assumptions about 293–4, 297
inevitability, of v, vii, 326–8, 345
legitimacy 326–8
navigability, increases in viii
neutrality vii
normative challenges 297
nudging xvii–xviii, 316–17
paternalism ix, 83
publicity 334–5
social sharing 166–7
trade-offs 303, 306, 317, 321, 323
universal versus targeted nudging 321
welfare ix, xviii, 303
cigarettes *see* smoking and tobacco
class actions 16, 49
clinical research 74, 99–100, 130–1, 235, 341–2, 345–6
Cockfield, Arthur (Lord Cockfield) 143
codes of commercial conduct 42
cognitive bias *see* biases
cognitive-forcing techniques 124–5, 128–30, 136
command-and-control
defaults 51
financial services regulation 261, 266
fundamental rights 106
health law and lifestyle policy 244
nudging 19, 299
smart disclosure requirements 17
trade-offs 306–7
Commission
Behavioural Studies for European Policies (BESTEP) 62
consumer law, simplification of 226–7, 232
data protection 176–7
DG SANCO 62, 343
Directorates-General 62, 151–2, 343
Digital Single Market 211, 213
do-nothing option 146
experts 115–20, 135
financial services regulation 256, 257, 266–7
Foresight and Behavioural Insights Unit (JRC) 343–4
home bias 220
I Will If You Will report 68
icons, use of 199
impact assessments, guidelines on 77–8
informed consent, standard forms for 176–7
initiation of legislation 346
insurance premiums 142
Joint Research Centre (JAC) 62, 74, 156, 343–4

lobbying 193–4
Policies to Encourage Sustainable Consumption report 68
prompt letters 148
randomised controlled trials (RCTs) 74
regulatory impact assessment 139–42
training 151–5, 156–7
White Paper on Governance 79–80
Committee of European Banking Supervisors (CEBS) 257
Committee of European Insurance and Occupational Pension Supervisors (CEIOPS) 257
Committee of European Securities Regulators (CESR) 257
common sense 23, 71, 221, 223, 229–30, 280, 295–6, 299
communicative instruments supporting choice 98–100
comparative law and legal transplants 288
comparisons
market failure 21–2
prices of websites 201–2
products or services, facilitating comparison of 47
websites 49
competition 49–50, 329
compound interest 44
conduct of business rules in financial services regulation 24, 255–75
accountability 261, 275
Alternative Investment Fund Managers (AIFM) Directive 259
behavioural analysis, rules as being devoid of 260–70
behavioural rules 255–75
bias 262–6, 270–1
command-and-control 261, 266
Commission 256, 257, 266–7
complementary behavioural approach, need for a 270–4
completing the rule book 270–4
defaults 264, 272–3
design of regulation 262–3, 265–6, 273
deterrence 267, 269, 271
disclosure 259
educational initiatives 274
enforcement 255, 257, 262, 266–75
European Securities and Markets Authority (ESMA) 261–3, 268–9
European Supervisory Authorities (ESAs)
Board of Supervisors 265
European System of Financial Supervision 257
experts 261–3, 265, 271
fair market environment 257
Financial Services Action Plan (FSAP) 256, 263

fines 267–8
format of rules 258
framing 273–4
general principles in Regulations and Directives 256–7
global financial crisis 257–8
governance 260–1, 270, 274
group thinking in regulatory design process 262–3, 265–6
guidelines 257, 272–5
harmonisation 267, 273
information 259
infringement procedure 257, 266
institutional limits 265–6
investment services 270, 275
Key Information Document (KID) 260, 261, 272, 274
key investor information document (KIDD) investors 260, 261
levels of intervention 256–7
limited attention for behaviourally inspired regulatory techniques 260–2
mandatory rules 255, 272
Market Abuse Directive 258, 259, 264
market integration 256
Markets in Financial Services Directive (MiFID) 259, 263–4
new governance toolkit 260–1
nudging 262, 263–4
obligations, imposition of 258–9
packaged retail investment products (PRIPS) 260
participation in rule-making 260–1
private enforcement, rationalising 269–70
prohibitions, imposition of 258–9
proportional impact assessments 271, 275
Prospectus Directive 259
public enforcement 266–9, 270
rationality 255, 264, 266–70, 272–5
retail market 256, 260
rule book status quo bias 262–4
rule-making 255, 260–6, 270–5
sanctions 266–9, 271, 273
self-capture 262, 265–6
self-regulation 261
Short Selling Regulation 258, 259, 261–2
soft law 261
status quo bias 262–4
technical and detailed implementing legislation 256–7
transparency 258, 259, 261
wholesale market 256
conferred or enumerated powers 239
confirmation bias 119, 122–3
conflicts of interest 115, 117–19, 121, 134, 319
conflicts of law 15
Conly, Sarah 5 n23, 7 n40, 327 n8, 330 n25, 335 n44

consent *see also* **informed consent and behavioural targeting; opt-in/opt-out systems**
conditional on consent, services made 179
cookies 170, 179–81, 199–200
data protection 170, 173, 176–8
manipulation xv
privacy 170, 173, 176–80, 199–201
consider-the-opposite technique 124
constitutional traditions 90, 101, 294
consumer law *see* **consumer law, disclosure requirements in; consumer law, simplification of**
consumer law, disclosure requirements in 219–26
autonomy 225
average consumer standard 221–3
behavioural sciences 214–15, 219–26, 233
Consumer Rights Directive 215, 222, 225
context, from content to 221–4
defaults 225
delivery, countries of 220–1
empirical evidence 221–3
home bias 220
informed consent 223, 225
internal market 219
mandatory disclosure 219–25
matters, focus on what 224–5
missing information on e-commerce websites 220–1
no-reading problem 219–20
opt-in/opt-out systems 222
over-optimism bias 225
paternalism 223
personalised disclosure 223
pre-contractual stage 223
recommendations 225
salience 222
shift of focus 221–6
specific risks 224
timing 222–4
trade-offs 225
waiver 222
consumer law, simplification of 226–33
behavioural sciences 213–14, 226–33
blacklists 229, 230–3
choice architecture 229
Commission 226–7, 232
contract law 227–9, 232–3
cross-border shopping, low confidence in 227–9
defaults 229–30
European Consumer Sales Law (CESL) project 227, 229–31
grey lists 229, 232
harmonisation 226–7, 232–3
inappropriate methods 227, 229–33
information campaigns on different cultures 228

internal market   226, 232
labelling   226
nudging   230
opt-in/opt-out systems   229–33
paternalism   231
single currency   226
trust   228–9, 233
unfair contract terms   231–2
wrong targets   227–9
consumer protection   24, 209–33 *see also* **consumer law, disclosure requirements in; consumer law, simplification of**
activism of consumers   42
anti-model of behavioural regulation   211
autonomy   329
average consumer standard   214–15, 218
behavioural sciences   24, 209–33
Consumer Rights Directive   215
defaults   15
deliberation   212
design of policies   292
disclosure   213–15, 217, 219–26, 232–3
empirical evidence   218
European Consumer Sales Law (CESL) project   213, 233
fraud   305
free movement   212, 215–17
hyperbolic discounting of future costs   212
inertia   212
information   214–16
institutions   217–18, 288
internal market   211–12, 213–19
intuition   212
mandatory information requirements   211, 233
market integration   217
mental shortcuts   212
no-reading problem   214–15, 219–20
opportunity to read doctrine   215
paternalism   210–11
reform not revolution, requirement for   212–13, 233
ultra vires   217
United States   211
context
autonomy   329
consumer law   221–4
data protection   174, 178
disclosure   221–4
experts   120, 125–6, 128, 136
health law and lifestyle policy   245
informed consent and behavioural targeting   197
institutions   336
labelling   6
learning   xvi
methodological guidelines   132

practicability   337, 339–40
rationality   18–20
regulation   17–19
regulatory impact assessment   141–3
social influences   4
contract law *see also* **terms and conditions**
autonomy   90
consumer law, simplification of   227–9, 232–3
defaults   15
off-premises contracts, withdrawal from   98
protection of individuals   203
social ordering   vii
standard forms   176–7, 231–2
unfair contract terms   231–2, 305
control *see also* **command-and-control**
behavioural targeting   181
control groups   73
data subject control   184
illusion of control   24, 140–1, 143–4, 147, 156
motivation   144
paradox   197
privacy   181
self-determination   312–13
skill and chance, distinguishing between   143
social control   287, 293–5, 298
cookies
behavioural targeting   179–81, 199–200
consent   170, 179–81, 200
Cookies Directive   170, 173–4
data protection   170, 173–4
default web browser settings as amounting to consent   194
definition   180
deletion   181
e-Privacy Directive   194
exemptions from consent requirements   200
first party   180
flash cookies   189
informed consent and behavioural targeting   187, 189, 199–200
myopia bias   195
opt-in/opt-out systems   187
refuse, right to   187
third party   180
website analytics   200
cooling off periods   48
Cooter, Robert   319
Cornell eRulemaking Initiative (CeRI)   135
costs benefit analysis   139, 146–7, 153, 155
counter-nudging   3, 11, 18–20, 252, 328
Cranor, Lorrie Faith   189, 191
credit rating agencies, regulation of   258, 268
credit seeking   150–1
Croskerry, Pat   128
crowding out   320
Cserne, Péter   336

culture
  biases   339
  changes   315
  differences   326, 335–7
  humility, culture of regulatory   139–41, 149, 155
  information campaigns   228
  legitimacy   326, 335–7
  paternalism   337
  technocratic character of EU law-making   336–7

Dana, Jason   318
dangerous sports   111
Darley, John   310, 319
Darwell, Stephen   xi
data minimisation principle   203–4
data protection and privacy   24, 161–78
  access and correct data, right to   198
  affect and emotion   171
  always-on surveillance   161–2
  analytical tools   168
  anonymised data, re-identification of   196
  Article 29 Working Party   183–6, 194, 196, 198–9, 201
  behavioural sciences to traditional data protection, challenge of   167–72
  behavioural targeting   182–8, 190–6, 198, 202–7
  biases   171, 173, 194–5
  Big Data   162, 167–8, 172, 177–8
  Charter of Fundamental Rights of the EU   198, 202
  citizen and state, relationship between   167
  Commission   176–7
  consent   170, 173, 176–8, 194–5
  context   174, 178
  Cookies Directive   170, 173–4
  customers and corporations, relationship between   167
  data analytics   168, 172
  data collection   167–8, 172
  data controllers   171, 174
  data governance principles   177–8
  data portability   174–5
  data protection authorities   198, 207
  Data Protection Directive   180, 184, 190–1, 195–6, 203–4
  data protection principles   203, 207
  Data Protection Regulation, proposal for   184, 188, 194–5, 199, 201
  data subject control   184, 198
  defaults   177, 198, 207
  design, privacy by   177
  disclosure   165–6, 169–72, 176
  discoverability of information   168–9
  employment   174
  empowerment   198–9, 207
  General Data Protection Regulation   173–7
  government and corporate bodies, relationship between   167
  health law and lifestyle policy   235
  impact assessment   177
  informed consent   170, 172, 176–7, 182–8, 190–6, 198, 202–7
  integrated approach to behaviourally informed data protection   173–8
  let alone, right to be   164
  manipulation   166
  mass data collection   167
  maximum retention period   204
  metadata   175–6
  opt-in/opt-out systems   195
  paternalism   169
  personalised disclosure   223
  personality traits   170–2
  popular attitudes and attention, service providers as editors or curators as   168
  privacy, definition of   163
  privacy policies   199
  private and family life, right to respect for   182–3
  protection of individuals   198, 203, 207
  pseudonymous data   203
  public policy   161–2
  public support   161–2
  regulation   161–7
  retention   204
  security of data   198
  social interest, privacy as a   163–7
  social sharing   166–71, 173
  special categories of data   205
  surreptitious data processing   204
  surveillance   176
  take-it-or-leave-it choices   195
  technological change   161–4, 167–70, 178
  tracking walls   195–6
  transaction costs   190–1
  transparency   191, 198–9
  trust   166, 171, 176
debiasing
  empowerment   36, 41–2
  errors of judgment   12
  experts   119–20, 123–37
  framing   44
  limits   127–30
  paternalism   87, 91, 95, 100
  practicability   339
  regulatory impact assessments   141
  self-reflexive, introspective debiasing strategy   120, 124–5, 127
  System 2 mode of thinking   viii
  toolboxes   12
Deci, Edward L   320
declarative purposes of law   316
defaults   14–16 *see also* **opt-in/opt-out systems**

Index

active choosing xii, xvii, 110
autonomy 94, 327–8, 332
biases viii, 144, 147–8, 154, 193
Big Five personality scale 322
choice architecture 98
class actions 49
command-and-control 51
consent, web browser settings as 194
consumer law 15, 225, 229–30
contract law 15
data protection 177, 198, 207
definition 37–8
delegation 16
deliberations and decisions 313
design 317
disclosure 225
empowerment 198, 207
environmental policy 304
financial services regulation 262–3, 265–6, 273
health law and lifestyle policy 237–8
health insurance, enrolment in 303
inertia and procrastination xii, 4, 14, 38
learning xvi
legal presumptions 15–16
mandated informed consent 15
manipulation 94–5, 98, 110, 303
neutrality ix
nudge, definition of vi
objections v–vi
organ donation, presumption of consent to 15
overdrafts, mandated default option for 15
positive silence rule 14
pre-ticked boxes on e-commerce websites 15
privacy 177, 200–1, 206
private international law 15
private sector 46
prohibitions 16
protection of individuals 205–6
regulation 49, 50–1, 57–8
simplification 229–30
sticky defaults 206
System 1 mode of thinking 147, 309
toolboxes 13, 14–16
tracking codes 175
trade-offs 303–4, 309, 317, 322
transparency 198
welfare 51
Degani, Asaf 129
deliberations *see also* **System 2 mode of thinking (slow, calculative, and deliberative)**
autonomy 326, 329–33
collective deliberation 333–5, 345
communicative instruments supporting choice 99, 112
consumer protection 212
decisions 93, 109, 310–14

experts 124, 130
individual deliberation 333–4
legitimacy 333–5, 345
level of deliberation 333–4
nudging 309–10
outcome versus processes 310–14
process-conditioning rules 125
public deliberation mechanisms 135
publicity 329–35, 345
RegulationRoom 135
System 1 and 2 modes of thinking 93, 109
sustainable processes 309–14
delegation 16, 265
democracy v, ix, 162, 169, 336
Denmark, iNudgeU in 342
depletion, literature on cognitive 322
deterrence 267, 269, 271
device fingerprinting 180, 200
diet and food 236–7, 246–8, 251
calorie labelling 66–7, 71, 73, 307–8
evidence-based policy 64, 66
labelling 14, 66–7, 71, 73, 214, 240, 245, 249–50
manipulation 327
obesity/weight vi, xiii, 91, 237, 241–3, 304
self-regulation 251
soda cups, size of 307–8
social norms ix
warnings 247
WHO Global Strategy 248
Digital Single Market 211, 213
dignity v–vi, ix, xii–xiii, xv, xviii, 103, 105
direct marketing 180, 193–4, 205, 207
disclosure
autonomy 330
codes of commercial conduct 42
consumer law 213–15, 217, 219–26, 232–3
data protection 165–6, 169–72, 176
financial services regulation 42, 259
framing 44
free market xvii
health law and lifestyle policy 244
mandates 68, 213, 215, 217, 232–3, 244
nudging 200
privacy 165–6, 169–72, 176
smart disclosure requirements 12–14, 17
smart information nudging 57
System 2 mode of thinking viii
unintended disclosures 200
discrimination vii, 181–2, 190
do-nothing option 12, 141–3, 144, 146–7, 155
dominant position 192
double loop learning 151
Downs, Julie S 73
drugs, prohibiting 110
dual reasoning *see* **System 1 mode of thinking; System 2 mode of thinking**
Dunlop, Claire A 151, 155

education and learning
 active choosing   xvi
 choice architecture   xvi
 communicative instruments supporting choice   100
 context   xvi
 defaults   xvi
 double loop learning   151
 financial services regulation   274
 health law and lifestyle policy   46, 238
 information, provision of   xvi
 manipulation   xiv
 nudge-scepticism   25
 prompted choice   xvi
 reminders   xvi
 rulemakers, lessons learned for   53–9
 targeting   36–7, 42, 46, 53, 57–8
 training   139–41, 151–5, 156–7
ego   144, 150–1, 155
elderly people   52, 85
electronic direct marketing   180
emergence of behavioural policy-making   1–25
emotions
 biases   144, 149–50
 cooling off periods   48
 data protection   171
 empowerment   30, 36, 41, 48
 intuition   93
 labelling   9–10
 nudging   30, 36, 39–41, 51, 57
 overcoming   30, 36, 48
 public interest   57
 regulation   9–10, 57, 144, 149–50
 timing off choice   48
 training   154
empowerment   41–53
 behavioural sciences   30, 36–7, 41–53
 behavioural targeting   179, 188, 198–203, 207
 biases   50, 58, 202
 big data philosophy   52–3
 codes of commercial conduct   42
 competition   49
 consumer activism   42
 debiasing techniques   36, 41–2
 drawbacks   52–3
 education to raise awareness   42
 emotional responses, overcoming   30, 36, 41, 48
 empirical evidence   41–2
 energy efficient purchasing behaviour   42
 examples   36–7
 financial incentives, lack of   36
 financial relationships and disclosure   42
 framing information   41, 44–6, 53
 freedom of choice, preservation of   36
 health law and lifestyle policy   36–7, 41–2, 46, 52

 informed consent   41–2, 188, 198–203, 207
 nudging   36–7, 39, 42
 operational devices   311
 privacy   179
 protection of individuals   198, 203
 public interest   50
 rational choice   42
 regulation   49–51, 58
 resources, demands on   52
 rulemaking   36–7, 41
 simplification   37, 43–5, 47–8, 52–3
 strategies   30, 41–8
 targeted education   36–7, 42, 46, 53
 trade-offs   52–3
end-user licence agreements (EULA), pop-ups resembling   191, 196–7
energy
 efficiency   38–9, 42, 44–5, 50, 69, 71, 88
 Energy Labelling Directive   45
 Green Behaviour report (Sustainable Consumption Round Table)   68
 inertia   43
 manipulation   327
 smart meters to measure household energy consumption   69
 social influence   38–40, 69, 95, 294
enforcement
 financial services regulation   255, 257, 262, 266–75
 private enforcement   269–70
 public enforcement   266–9, 270
 universal appeal of behaviourally informed intervention   2–3
 voluntary interaction   295
environmental policy
 'A' principles of sustainable consumption (affordability, availability, attractiveness and awareness)   68
 defaults   304
 European Integrated Pollution Prevention and Control (IPPC) Bureau (EIPPCB)   116, 121
 evidence-based policy   62–3, 67–71
 green consumerism   68–70
 I Will If You Will report (Commission)   68
 individual behaviour and personal responsibility   67–71
 Intergovernmental Panel on Climate Change (IPCC) policy   131–2, 133–4
 Policies to Encourage Sustainable Consumption report (Commission)   68
 private companies, role of   70
 Procedures for Preparation, Review, Acceptance, Adoption, Approval and Publication of IPCC Reports   133–4
 trade-offs   304, 323
 working groups   133–4
epistemology   136, 280, 284–6, 293, 295, 299

e-Privacy Directive   179, 183, 187, 194, 199–200, 207
error *see* **mistakes**
ethics
  agency   95–6, 293
  'as judged by themselves' standard   viii–ix
  autonomy   xi–xii, 326–7
  biased officials   xvi–xviii
  choice architecture   xvii–xviii
  concepts and definitions   vi–ix
  defaults to   v–vi, viii
  democracy   v
  dignity   v–vi, xii–xiii
  discrimination, promotion of   vii
  freedom of choice, preservation of   xviii
  gender   322
  illicit reasons   vi, ix, xvii
  intuition   296
  justification, burden of   v, viii
  learning   xvi
  manipulation   xiii–xv, xviii
  navigability, increases in   viii
  nudging   v–xviii
  paternalism   ix–xi, xii, xvii
  regulatory state   xvii
  self-government   v, ix, xviii
  transparency   xvii–xviii
  trust versus voluntary compliance   318–19
  unfair behaviour, justification of   318
  welfare, promotion of   v–vi, xviii
  whistleblowing   322
Europe 2020 Strategy   243
European Commission *see* **Commission**
European Consumer Sales Law (CESL) project   213, 227, 229–31, 233
European Convention on Human Rights (ECHR)   101–6
European Direct Marketing Association (EDMA)   193
European Food Safety Authority (EFSA)   116, 117, 121, 132
European Integrated Pollution Prevention and Control (IPPC) Bureau (EIPPCB)   116, 121
European Parliament (EP)   139, 199
European Securities and Markets Authority (ESMA)   116, 121, 261–3, 268–9
European Supervisory Authorities (ESAs)   265, 267–8
European System of Financial Supervision (ESFS)   257
evidence-based policy   61–82
  applied research at population level, lack of   72–3
  assumptions   71–6
  better regulation   62, 77
  biases   75–6
  causal connections, strength of   63
  credibility cycle   76
  efficiency standpoint   24
  environment policy   62–3, 67–71
  ex ante and ex post evaluation   79
  experimental legislation   288
  generalisability   74–5
  governance   79–80, 289
  harmonisation   77–80
  health policy   62–3, 64–7, 71, 73, 77
  heterogeneity   77–80
  impact assessment   77–9
  institutional challenges   288
  methodological guidelines   131–2
  methodological observations   71–6
  nudging   61–3, 71–3, 75–80
  organ donation   76
  potential problems with use of regulatory tools   63–76
  practicability   345–6
  principles, problem of   75–6
  randomised controlled trials   71, 72–5
  regulation   41–2, 77–80, 144
  reproducibility   74
  toolboxes   63
  trade-offs   303
  transferability   74–5
  United Kingdom   74
  whether policies will work   72–5
exercise   36–7, 66, 236, 246, 248, 251
experts   115–37
  biases   19, 115, 117, 119–37, 145
  blind selection or randomisation   134–5
  Civil Justice Council (UK)   120
  civil law traditions   120
  cognitive-forcing techniques   124–5, 128–30, 136
  cognitive sterility, illusion of   127–30
  Commission   115–20, 135
  common law traditions   120
  conflicts of interest   115, 117–19, 121, 134
  court-appointed experts   120
  creation of expert groups   115, 118
  debiasing project   119–20, 123–37
  deliberative mechanisms into decision-making process, introduction of   124, 130
  designing policies   115
  diversity of expert bodies   134–5
  epistemic failure   115, 117–18
  expert groups   115–18
  external economic pressures   117, 121
  financial services regulation   261–3, 265, 271
  heuristics   24, 119, 124
  implementation of regulatory schemes   115
  incentives   117
  introspection   120, 124–5, 127–8
  intuition   119, 136
  judgment failure   117–18
  mistaken policy   115
  nudging   123–5

objectivity ideal   120–3
public interest   115
Register of Expert groups and Other Similar Entities   118
regulation   115, 116–18, 123, 127, 136
reliability   121
selection process   134–5
transparency   118, 135
trust   24, 117, 120
experiments   340–2 *see also* **randomised controlled trials (RCTs)**
cause-and-effect relationships   340–1
evidence-based policy   59, 67, 288
framing   153
group conformity   153–4
principal-agent experiments   320–1
training   153–4, 156
unresponsive behaviours   53
experts   119–20, 123–37
biases   xvi
blind selection or randomisation   134–5
changing set of choices   123
cognitive-forcing techniques   124–5, 128–30, 133–7
cognitive sterility, illusion of   127–30
consider-the-opposite technique   124
consumer fraud   305
contexts of application   120, 125–6, 128, 136
debiasing   119–20, 123–37
deliberative mechanisms into decision-making process, introduction of   124, 130
differential, context-dependent strategy   120
epistemology   136
forensic expertise   287
forms of realisations   125–6
institutional structures, development of new   124
introspection   120, 124–5, 127–8
introspective, meta-cognitive techniques   124
intuition   136
limits of debiasing   127–30
meta-cognitive techniques   127
nudging   123–5
process-conditioning rules   124–5
public deliberation mechanisms   135
rationality   136
regulation   123, 127, 136
selection process   135
self-reflexive, introspective debiasing strategy   120, 124–5, 127
System 1 mode of thinking   124, 127
System 2 mode of thinking   124, 127
theory to policy, from   130–5
transaction costs   123–4
transparency   135
types of strategy   125–6
welfare   123

expressive law versus invisible nudges   309, 314–17
eye-tracking   35

Facebook   165–6, 172, 192, 196, 200
fair trial, right to a   103
Falk, Armin   320
false assumptions   289–92
Farley, Thomas   67
fascist governments   vii
fast decision-making *see* System 1 mode of thinking (fast, automatic, and intuitive)
Faure, Michael   209 n1, 212 n9
Feldman, Yuval   318–19, 321, 334–5, 338
filter bubbles   182
financial incentives, lack of   vi, 36
financial services *see* **conduct of business rules in financial services regulation**
fine print, reading the   214, 218, 223
fines   2, 267–8
food *see* **diet and food**
foot and mouth disease (FAM), policy response to   149
Foresight and Behavioural Insights Unit (Commission JRC)   343–4
formalism   288
framing   4–5
communicative instruments supporting choice   110
compound interest   44
counter-framing   100
debiasing   44
disclosure   44
empirical evidence   44
empowerment   41, 44–6, 51, 53
epistemic challenges   284
experiments   153
financial services regulation   273–4
health law and lifestyle policy   237, 245
household appliance labelling   44–6
myopia bias   196
nudging   18–19, 51, 317
smart information nudging   38
unfair contract terms   231
France   343
fraud   181, 196, 305
free movement   212, 215–17
free services   188
free trials   193
freedom costs   110
freedom of choice, preservation of
autonomy   xii, 330–1
biases   xvii
choice architecture   vii
empowerment   36
fundamental rights   112
nudging   vi, xviii, 19, 36

opt-in/opt-out systems 3
paternalism x–xi, 96–100
Frowein, Jochen 102
fundamental rights 101–6, 112 *see also*
Charter of Fundamental Rights of the EU
  autonomy 102–3, 107
  command-and-control 106
  constitutional traditions 101
  dignity 103, 105
  elderly persons 85
  European Convention on Human Rights 101–6
  fair trial, right to a 103
  freedom of choice, preservation of 112
  general principles of law 101, 104–5
  infringement 101–6
  manipulation 106
  mentally ill persons 85
  nudging 101–6, 112
  paternalism 85–6, 96, 101–6, 108, 112
  permissibility, assessment of 101
  private and family life, right to respect for 101–5
  prohibition of choice 96
  proportionality 86, 104–5, 107–8
  scope of protection 85, 101–6

gender 134, 142, 322
general principles of law 101, 104–5
Germany xii, 108–9, 343
Gigerenzer, Gerd 2 n3, 86 n16, 123 n46, 126 n74, 247 n91, 332 n31
global financial crisis 257–8
GM (genetically modified) food 116, 132
goad, law as 295
goal-oriented legal instruments 283, 336
good life, ideal of the 90, 92
Google
  cookies 192
  defaults 175
  Gmail 168
  Google Maps 172
  search engines, indexing by 176
  tracking code by passive users, default rule for enabling a 175
  visualisation changes 175, 176
governance
  Commission White Paper 79–80
  data governance principles 177–8
  evidence-based governance 289
  financial services 260–1, 270, 274
  new governance 260–1, 307
  normative challenges 297–9
  nudge-scepticism 297–9
  road-bumps 293
GPS analogy vi, viii, x, xiii
GRADE System 130–1, 132
Graham, John D 148, 154
granularity gap 340

grey lists 229, 232
group thinking 262–3, 265–6
guidelines
  administrative guidance 16–17
  experts 124, 130–4
  financial services regulation 257, 272–6
  methodological guidelines 124, 130–4
  moral agency 293
  normative guidance, law as 293–5
  regulatory impact assessment 156
  social control 293–5
  transposition and interpretation of legislation 257

Haisley, Emily 318
Hardie, Jeremy 74
harmonisation
  consumer law, simplification of 226–7, 232–3
  evidence-based policy 77–80
  financial services regulation 267, 273
  health law and lifestyle policy 239, 242
  labelling 226
  unfair contract terms 231
Hart, HLA 295–6
Haskins, Ron 345–6
Hausman, Daniel M 95–6
health and safety 153, 235, 248
health and health care *see also* **health law and lifestyle policy**
  clinical research 74, 99–100, 130–1, 235, 341–2, 345–6
  GRADE system 130–1
  medical data 205
  medical evidence in tort cases, minimising mistakes and inconsistencies in 131
  methodological guidelines 131–2
  Surgery Safety Checklist 136
health law and lifestyle policy 235–53
  see also **alcohol; diet and food; smoking and tobacco**
  across borders, right to receive services 235
  active choices 237–8
  advertising 239
  availability heuristics 247
  bans 236–7, 255, 308
  behavioural sciences 24, 235–53
  biases 121–2, 236, 244, 247
  choice architecture 236–7
  clinical research 235
  command-and-control mechanisms 244
  conferred or enumerated powers 239
  confirmation bias 121–2
  context 245
  cross-border health issues 241
  data protection 235
  defaults 237–8, 303
  diet 236, 237, 246, 247–8, 251

dignity xiii
disclosure and information schemes 244
education 46, 238
emergence of policy 239–43
empowerment 36–7, 41–2, 46, 52
evidence-based policy 62–3, 64–7, 71, 73, 77
exercise 36–7, 66, 236, 246, 248, 251
experiments 67
framing effects 237, 245
harmonisation 239, 242
health programmes, adoption of 240–2
hindsight bias 122
HIV/AIDS 242
inertia 237
information asymmetries 244
informed consent 41–2, 46
insurance, enrolment in 303
internal market 239–40, 242
intuition 243–4
irrationality 236
labelling 239–40, 244–5, 249–50
libertarian paternalism 236
mainstreaming duty 240
media campaigns 238
non-communicable diseases (NCDs) 236–53
nudging 36–7, 64–7, 245–9, 252, 314
obesity 237, 241–3, 304
outcome bias 122
paternalism 91, 251
pharmaceuticals on market, placing 235
policy actions 248, 252
Political Declaration on NCDs 248
procrastination 237
qualifications 235
rationality 236, 244–5, 304
recommendations 314
regulation 235–9, 243, 246, 248–9
self-regulation 243
simplification 237–8
social influences 245, 247, 252
social norms ix
status quo bias 247
System 1 243–5
System 2 243–4
tar, nicotine, and carbon dioxide yields (TNCO), information on 237
trade-offs 304
workplace hazards 235, 248
World Health Organization 236, 246, 248, 251–2
Heinzerling, Lisa 153
Helberger, Natali 192
helmets 108–9, 111
herding behaviour 147
heterogeneity 77–80, 321, 339, 345
heuristics
  availability heuristics 52, 123, 247

biases x
experiments 338
experts 24, 119, 124
information asymmetries 193
nudging 327
privacy 171
rationality 30, 86
regulation 36, 58, 155
salience 310
Hillgruber, Christian 107–8
Hindmoor, Andrew 149
hindsight bias 119, 122
HIV/AIDS 242
Honoré, Tony 296
Hoofnagle, Chris Jay 189
household appliance labelling 44–6
Hsee, Christopher K 318
human rights *see* **fundamental rights**
Humboldt, Wilhelm von 90–1
humiliation xii, xiii
humility, culture of regulatory 139–41, 149, 155

icons, use of 199
identity fraud 181, 196
immediate gratification 195–7
impact assessment *see* **regulatory impact assessment**
incentives
  biases 144, 146–7, 153
  experts 117
  financial incentives, lack of vi, 36
Industrial Emissions Directive 116
inertia
  blacklists 231
  consumer protection 212
  consumer switching 43–4
  defaults xii, 4, 14, 38
  definition 3–4
  do-nothing option 12, 141–3, 144, 146–7, 155
  health law and lifestyle policy 237
  nudging vi, 37, 57
  pre-ticked boxes 18
  products or services, facilitating comparison of 47
  simplification 144
  System 1 mode of thinking viii
infantilisation 81
information *see also* **disclosure**
  accessibility 52–3
  asymmetries 49, 97, 192–3, 198–9, 217, 223, 244
  cocoons 182
  competition 49
  consumer protection 211, 214–16, 233
  cultures 228
  deficits 97

discoverability 168–9
financial services regulation 259
learning xvi
market failure 217
missing information 220–1
neutral information 40–1, 97–8, 109–10
nudging 7, 327
paradigm 214, 218, 223
paternalism 100, 109, 112, 189
relative risk information xiv
simplification 43–5, 52–3
smart information nudging 38–40, 51–3, 57
Unfair Commercial Practices Directive 49
welfare, decisions on 112
informed consent *see also* **informed consent and behavioural targeting**
consumer law 223, 225
cookies 170
data protection 172
health care 41–2, 46
mandated informed consent 15
standard forms 176–7
informed consent and behavioural targeting 182–98
balancing provision 185–6
behavioural market failures 197–8
biases 192–7
bounded rationality 198
Charter of Fundamental Rights of the EU 182–3, 198, 202
competitive advantage, privacy as a 190
consent, definition of 187
context 197
cookies 187, 189, 192, 194–5, 199–200
data protection 182–8, 190–6, 198, 202–7
default web browser settings as amounting to consent 194
discrimination 190
dominant position 192
employers 186
empowerment 188, 198–203, 207
e-Privacy Directive 183, 187, 199–200, 207
European Data Protection Authorities 207
exceptions 187
explicit consent 184, 194–5, 205
free services 188
freely given, consent must be 186
implied consent 186, 187, 193, 207
improving privacy protection 198–207
Independent Data Protection Authorities (DPAs) 183–4
information asymmetries 188–90, 192–3, 198–9
myopia/present and other biases 195–7, 202
nudging 179, 200–1, 203, 206–7
opportunity costs 191
opt-in/opt-out systems 185–7, 193–4, 203, 207

price discrimination 190
privacy 182–201, 203, 207
privacy, definition of 188
privacy policies 196–7, 199, 201, 207
protection of individuals 198, 203–7
pseudonymous data 184, 200, 203
silence as consent 203
special categories of data 205
specific consent 186
status quo bias 192–5
trade-offs 188
transaction costs 190–2
transparency 186, 198–9, 202–5, 207
waiver 207
infringement procedure 257, 266
insider dealing 258
institutions
biases 287–9
challenges 281, 287–9, 299
consequence-based judicial reasoning 287
consumer protection 217–18
context 336
design 292–3, 342–4, 344
financial services regulation 257, 266
limits 257, 266
methodological guidelines 132
motivation of lawmakers 288
new structures, development of 124
nudge-scepticism 281, 287–9, 299
regulatory impact assessments 141–2, 155–6
insurance 111, 142
Interactive Advertising Bureau 194, 206
interest groups 149
interest payments 44
Intergovernmental Panel on Climate Change (IPCC) policy 131–2, 133–4
internal market 211–19, 226, 232, 239–40, 242
Internet *see also* **behavioural targeting and regulation of privacy**
continuous connection 161
data protection 176
elderly persons 52
humility in policy-making 155
social networks 164, 172, 175–6, 190, 192, 200
transparency 155
introspection 120, 124–5, 127–8
intuition *see also* **System 1 mode of thinking (fast, automatic, and intuitive)**
analytical processing 119
communicative instruments supporting choice 100
consumer protection 212
experts 119, 136
health law and lifestyle policy 243–4
human agency 295–6, 299
institutional challenges 288
moral intuitions 296

Index   363

investment services   270, 275
invisible nudges   94–6, 98, 109–10, 309, 314–17
irrationality *see* rationality
isolated choice facilitation   87
Issacharoff, Samuel (co-author of Camerer)   84 n6, 209 n1

Joint Research Centre (JAC) (Commission)   62, 74, 156, 343–4
Jolls, Christine   12, 328, 334
judgment failure   117–18

Kahneman, Daniel   9, 93, 147, 152, 171, 309
Kant, Immanuel   163, 165
Kerber, Wolfgang   211 n3, 231 n113
Key Information Document (KID)   260, 261, 272, 274
key investor information document (KIDD) investors   260, 261
knee jerk action   148
Köpsell, Stefan   196–7
Korobkin, Russell   39 n40, 48 n97, 49 n101, 50 n110, 84 n51, 100 n70, 225 n84, 244 n72, 304 n9
Kosfeld, Michael   320

labelling   5–10
  academic behaviours   8–10
  average consumer standard   214
  behavioural government action   6–8
  calories   66–7, 71, 73
  cognitive system, by passing the   6
  consumer law, simplification of   226
  definitional issues   6
  emotions and law   9–10
  Energy Labelling Directive   45
  food   14, 66–7, 71, 73, 214, 240, 245, 249–50
  free movement of goods   216
  front-of-pack labelling   249–50
  harmonisation   226
  health law and lifestyle policy   239–40, 244–5, 249–50
  household appliance labelling   44–6
  non-verbal communication   6
  nudge, use of word   5
  Nutrition Labelling Directive   240
  toolboxes   11–12
  traffic-light systems   245, 250
  transplants   6
  United States   6–7
Langer, Ellen   143
language   21, 191–2, 196, 199, 298, 315–16
Latour, Bruno   76
law and economics   323–4
  behavioural law and economics   8–9, 84, 91, 279, 281, 305–9, 324, 336
  Commission   156–7

counter-nudging   18
critiques of behavioural law and economics   305–9
paternalism   91
psychology   8–9, 336
rationality   75
regulation   279, 281
scepticism   22–3
System 2 mode of thinking   309
trade-offs   32
law, meaning of   314–17
learning *see* education and learning
Lee, Maria   135
legalease, use of   199
legitimacy of EU behavioural policy-making   325–37
  autonomy   326–33, 345
  choice architecture   326–8
  cultural differences   326, 335–7
  deliberation   329–35, 345
  internal market   213–19
  manipulation   326
  mental bandwidth   326
  nudging   18, 327–8
  paternalism   86
  practicability debate   24
  psychology   325
  public sector   11
  regulation   11
  trade-offs   345
  trust versus voluntary compliance   319
lemons problem in market   188–9, 190
Lerner, Jennifer S   150
Lessig, Larry   155
let alone, right to   164
liberal states   89–92, 97, 111–12
libertarian paternalism   ix–x, 236, 290, 299, 306, 335
lifestyle *see* health law and lifestyle policy
Lobel, Orly   306–7, 322, 334–5, 338
Loevinger, Lee   72
loss aversion bias   146–7, 153
lottery numbers, selection of own   155
Lowenstein, George   62, 67, 69, 72
lowest common denominator   321, 323
Lunn, Peter   2 n4, 8 n44, 44 n74, 52 n121, 344 n90
Luth, Hanneke   8 n44, 191 n74, 209 n1

McDonald, Aleecia M   189, 191
magazine/newspaper subscriptions   185, 193, 328
magnetic resonance imaging (MRI)   35
mail-in rebates   193
mainstreaming duty   240
Maniates, Michael   70
manipulation   xiii–xv, 23
  autonomy   xiv–xv, xviii, 94–6, 327, 329

behavioural targeting   181–2
consent   xv
cultural differences   336–7
data protection   166
defaults   94–5, 98, 110, 303
definition   xiii–xiv
dignity   xv, xviii
educative, nudges as being   xiv
empowerment   50
fundamental rights   106
governance   298
invisible choices   94–6, 98, 110
legitimacy   326
marketing   3
normative challenges   293, 295, 297
nudging   49, 94–6, 110
paternalism   93, 96
privacy   166, 179
publicity   334–5
relative risk information   xiv
System 1   xiv, xv, xviii
System 2   xv
taste   97
toolkits   295
transparency   xiv–xv, 94, 334
warnings   xiv, xv
Margolis, Greg   345–6
Market Abuse Directive   258, 259, 264
market failure   18, 21–2, 97, 188, 197–8
Markets in Financial Services Directive (MiFID)   259, 263–4
Marotta-Wurgler, Florencia   191
Masters in Business (MBAs)   152–3
Masters in Public Administration (MPAs)   152–3, 155
media   199, 205, 238
mental bandwidth   214, 326, 332, 345
mental disabilities, persons with   85, 108
mental shortcuts   146, 193, 212, 284
migration flows   298
Mill, John Stuart   91
mindfulness   151–5
MINDSPACE (UK Cabinet Office)   144–51
mistakes
behavioural limitations   29
biases   xvi–xvii
choice architecture   100, 110
do-nothing options   12
experts   115
facts, of   x
insulating strategies   12
judgment, of   12
market failure   197–8
medical evidence in tort cases, minimising mistakes and inconsistencies in   131
preferences   112
prescription errors in NHS   64

rationality   109
systematic mistakes   xi
Mitchell, Gregory   75, 306
mobile devices
apps   190
lemons problem in market   189O
nudging   200
privacy policies   192
small screens   192
Moore, Don A   117
morality *see* ethics
motivation   121, 144, 288, 320–3
Mullainathan, Sendhil   332
Mullane, Maggie   79
Munchausen fallacy   127
myopia/present bias   195–7, 202

nanny state policies   303
National Transportation Safety Board (NTSB)   129
naturalistic theories   295
necessity   106–7, 110
Netherlands   192, 196, 343
new governance   260–1, 307
new public management norms   147
newspaper subscriptions   185, 193, 328
no-reading problem
autonomy   329
consumer law   214–15, 219–20
empowerment   192
market failure   197
opportunity to read doctrine   215
privacy policies   191–2, 196, 207
small print, checking the   214, 218, 223
terms and conditions   172, 214–15, 219–20, 329
non-verbal communication   6
norms
challenges   292–9
empirical knowledge   289–90, 292, 294
guidance, law as normative   293–5
human agency, assumptions about   292–5, 299
individualism   326–7
manipulation   293, 295, 297
naturalistic theories about human behaviour   295
new public management norms   147
nudge-scepticism   292–9
premises, unavoidability of   281, 289–92
responsibility   295–7
social norms   ix, 144, 147, 167, 315–16
nudge-scepticism   279–99
behavioural economics   280, 284–5, 290, 295–6, 299
behavioural sciences   25, 279–99
command-and-control   299
contested, law as   280

empirical knowledge 279–81, 284, 287, 291–2, 296, 299
epistemic challenges 280, 284–6, 299
false assumptions 291–2
governance and law 297–9
import of behavioural insights 283, 293
institutional challenges 281, 287–9, 299
nature of law 280–1, 292
normative challenges 292–9
normative premises, unavoidability of 281, 289–92
policy-making 280–1
reasons for nudge-scepticism 281–99
responsibility 295–7
truth, relationship between legal and scientific 281
nudging 2–19 *see also* **defaults; nudge-scepticism; opt-in/opt-out systems; System 1 mode of thinking (fast, automatic, and intuitive); System 2 mode of thinking (slow, calculative, and deliberative); warnings**
administrative practices 19
'as judged by themselves' standard viii–ix
autonomy viii, xi–xii, 19, 326–33
awareness 343
behavioural targeting 179
biases xvi–xviii, 18–19, 36, 42, 58, 123–5, 301, 327
categories 36–41
choice architecture 316–17
cognitive-based strategy 37–41
consumer law, simplification of 230
counter-nudging 3, 11, 18–20, 252, 328
cultural differences 336
defaults vi, 37–8, 51, 200–1, 327
definition of a nudge vi
deliberation 309–10
drawbacks 51–2
emotional responses, exploiting/neutralising 30, 36, 39–41, 51, 57
empowerment 36–7, 39, 42, 200–1, 203, 207
environmental policy 67–71
ethics v–xviii
evidence-based policy 71–2, 75–80
examples 36–7
experts 123–5
expressive law 309, 314–17
financial incentives, lack of vi, 36
financial services regulation 262, 263–4
first degree nudges 327
framing 18–19, 51, 317
freedom of choice, preservation of vi, xviii, 19, 36
health law and lifestyle policy 36–7, 64–7, 245–9, 252
incipient nudge stage 343
inertia and procrastination vi, 37

information 7, 327
invisible nudges 94–6, 98, 109–10, 309, 314–17
judging the nudge 101–11, 112
last resort, as 58
law, meaning of 314–17
legitimacy 18, 327–8
libertarianism 306
manipulation 49, 94–6, 110
mature nudge stage 343
mobile devices 200
necessity 109–11
nudge, definition of vi
outcome versus processes 309–11
paternalism 49, 83–112, 306
pre-nudge stage 343
privacy 179, 200–1, 203, 206–7
private nudging, regulation of 18
public interest 50, 58
public nudging 18–20, 328, 333
publicity 334
rationality 306
regulation xvii, 49–51, 57–8, 61–3
reminders vi, xvi, xvii, ix, 4, 223, 247–8, 331–2
second degree 327
simplification 57
single nudge tools 51
smart information nudging 38–40, 51–3, 57
strategies 30, 36–41, 51–2, 54
suitability of a nudge 109
third degree 327
trade-offs 301–2, 305–17
universal versus targeted nudging 309, 321–2, 323
use of word 'nudge' 5
violence, private and public persons nudging people towards ix
welfare 18–19
Nutrition Labelling Directive 240

obesity/weight vi, xiii, 91, 237, 241–3, 304
objectivity 120–3, 134
O'Donoghue, Ted (co-author of Camerer) 84 n7, 111 n133
OECD Regulatory Policy 2015 344
off-premises contracts, withdrawal from 98
official-looking graphics, use of 196–7
one-click choice of law 229
online behaviour *see* **behavioural targeting and regulation of privacy**
open data initiatives 47–8
opportunity costs 191
opportunity to read doctrine 215
opt-in/opt-out systems 37–8, 51, 327–8
behavioural targeting 179, 185–7
class actions 49
consumer law 222, 229–33

cookies 187
data protection 193–5
disclosure 222
empowerment 193, 203, 207
e-Privacy Directive 194
freedom of choice, preservation of 3
informed consent 185–7, 193–4, 203, 207
organ donors 15, 17–18, 57–8, 64–5, 72, 76, 94–5, 98–9, 193
pension plans, participation in 303
privacy 179, 200–1, 207
simplification 229–33
status quo bias 193–4, 200–1
trade-offs 303
optimism bias 46–7, 52, 196, 225, 334
O'Reilly Commission 118, 135
organ donations, opt-in/opt-out systems for 15, 17–18
autonomy 99
barriers to donation 65
driving licence applications, signing up during 61, 64–6
evidence-based policy 76
goal, deciding on the 64–5
invisible choice manipulation 94–5
paternalism 98
prompted choice 61, 64–6, 72
reciprocity condition 64–5
status quo bias 193
successful transplants, number of 64–6
targeted education 57–8
Oullier, Olivier 82
outcome bias 122
outcome versus processes 309–14, 323
overconfidence bias 46, 196
overdrafts, default options for 15

packaged retail investment products (PRIPS) 260
packaging
cigarettes 39–41, 51–2, 57, 241
plain packaging 39–41, 51–2, 57, 241
warnings 51
Panopticon 164
participation 260–1, 312–14
paternalism ix–xi
asymmetric paternalism 306
autonomy xi, 86, 89–96, 99, 100, 108–10, 112
bans xvii
biases x–xi, 85–7, 93–6, 98–100, 110
choice architecture ix, 83, 96–100
consumer law 210–11, 223, 231
cultural differences 337
data protection 169
debiasing 87, 91, 95, 100
disclosure 223
empowerment 50, 202
end paternalism 96
excessive paternalism 57

freedom of choice, preservation of x–xi, 96–100
fundamental rights 85–6, 96, 101–6, 108, 112
hard paternalism 87
health law and lifestyle policy 91, 251
information 100, 109, 112, 189
libertarian paternalism ix–x, 236, 290, 299, 306, 335
mandates xvii
means paternalism x, 96, 109
mistakes about fact x
nudging ix–xi, xii, xvii, 49, 83–112
preferences 89–92, 96, 100, 108, 112
presumption against paternalism xi
privacy 169
proportionality 24, 87–8, 92–3, 96, 106–11, 112
regulation 57
respect for persons xi
simplification 231
soft paternalism x, 87
toolboxes 93–100
trade-offs 305–6, 308
warnings ix, x–xi, 108–9, 112
welfare, promotion of ix, x–xi
payment for tracking-free services 201–2
Peers, Steve 107
pension plans, participation in 61, 98, 303, 323
Perez, Oren 313, 321
personhood 295–6
pharmaceuticals on market, placing 235
physical activity 36–7, 66, 236, 246, 248, 251
Pildes, Richard H 307, 315
pollution *see* environmental policy
Porat, Ariel 322
positive silence rule 14
Posner, Richard 9
Post, Robert 163
practicability of EU behavioural policy-making 325, 337–45
context 337, 339–40
empirical evidence 338
granularity gap 340
institutional design 342–4, 345
legitimacy 24
methodological challenges to increase effectiveness 338–42
operationalisation of behavioural insights 337–8, 346
practicability, definition of 337
psychology 340
public authorities 340
rationality 337–8
temporal dimension 339
testing 340–1, 345–7
trade-offs 340

precautionary approach   132
precedents, reliance on   149
Prechal, Sacha   107
preferences   89–92, 96, 100, 108, 110–12, 332
pregnancy counselling   110–11
prescription errors in NHS   64
pre-ticked boxes   10–11, 15, 18
priming   144, 149, 154
principle-based legal instruments   283
privacy   101–5, 188 *see also* **behavioural targeting and regulation of privacy; data protection and privacy**
privacy policies
   consent requests, prohibition on hiding   201
   data use policy   196
   end-user licence agreements (EULA), pop-ups resembling   196–7
   language   191–2, 196, 199
   media attention after changes to policies   199
   misleading, phrase as being   196
   mobile devices   192
   no-reading problem   191–2, 196, 207
   official-looking graphics, use of   196–7
   quality seals, as   196
   small screens   192
   take-it-or-leave-it choices   201, 207
   transaction costs   199
   use of legalese in   199
   vague language, use of   196, 199
private international law   15
private sector
   attention   vi
   corporate bodies and government, relationship between   167
   defaults   46
   environmental policy   70
   methodological guidelines   132
   public interest   11
   regulation   vi, 11, 18–20
   steering behaviour   10–11
procedural justice   312–14. 334–5
processes
   outcome, versus   309–14, 323
   process-conditioning rules   124–5
procrastination   vi, 3, 14, 37, 237
professional socialisation   152
promise-disappointment cycles   76
prompts   61, 64–6, 72, 144–51, 332
proportionality
   autonomy   92, 96, 106–9, 111
   Charter of Fundamental Rights of the EU   86, 106–11, 112
   choice architecture   112
   common interests   107, 108–9
   dignity   xii
   empirical evidence   107
   free movement of goods   216
   fundamental rights   86, 104–5, 107–8

   impact assessments   271, 275
   invisible choice manipulation   96
   justification   108
   legitimate aim   105–9, 216
   liberal states   111
   mental disabilities, persons with   108
   necessity   106–7
   nudging   106–11, 112
   objective individual welfare   106
   paternalism   24, 87–8, 92–3, 96, 106–11, 112
   preferences   111
   private and family life, right to respect for   105
   protection of individuals   204
   rationality   92, 107, 111
   salience   148
   stricto sensu   107, 111
   suitability analysis   106–7
   third parties   107
   transparency   106–11, 112
   underage people   108
   welfare   111
prosecutorial bias   122
Prospectus Directive   259
protection of individuals from behavioural targeting
   Charter of Fundamental Rights of the EU   198
   chilling effects   204, 205
   contracts   203
   data minimisation principle   203–4
   data protection   198, 203–4, 207
   defaults   205–6
   empowerment distinguished   198, 203
   informed consent   198, 203–7
   mandatory rules   198, 203, 205–6
   privacy   179, 180, 198, 206
   security of data   198
pseudonymous data   203
psychology
   consumer fraud   304
   empirical psychology   9
   legitimacy   325
   practicability   340
   scarcity, of   10
   social psychology   8
   trade-offs   301–2, 305–11, 314, 317, 322–4
public health *see* **health law and lifestyle policy**
public interest   11, 18, 50, 57–8, 115, 289–90
public opinion   xvi, 161–2
public policy   149, 156–7, 161–2
public sector
   attention   vi
   biases   xvi–xviii, 18
   inertia   14
   legitimacy   11
   practicability   340
   public interest   11, 18

regulation 11
toolboxes 340
websites 205
publicity of deliberation 329–35, 345

qualifications of health professionals 235
Quigley, Muireann 334

Rabin, Matthew (co-author of Camerer)
  84 n7, 111 n133
Radaelli, Claudio M 155
randomised controlled trials (RCTs) 74,
  130–1, 341–2, 345–6
rationality
  autonomy 91, 95, 331, 333
  average consumer standard 218
  behavioural targeting 182
  bounded rationality 198, 283, 292, 304, 333
  choice architecture 112
  consumer protection policies, design of 292
  empowerment 42
  financial services regulation 255, 264,
    266–70, 272–5
  governance 299
  health law and lifestyle policy 236,
    244–5, 304
  information 4, 192–3
  mistake 109
  neoclassical assumptions 2, 244, 255, 261,
    270, 274–5
  nudging 306
  paternalism 85–100, 107–10, 112
  practicability 337–8
  preferences 112
  privacy 182
  prohibitions 96
  proportionality 92, 107, 111
  rational choice theory 42, 284–5, 302,
    317–18
reassurances and explanations 99, 111,
  168, 305
recommendations 225, 314
redistribution 306
reflection 151–5
regret aversion 98, 149, 311–12
regulation 7, 30–6 *see also* **regulatory impact assessment**
  agencies 115, 116–18
  anti-model of behavioural regulation 211
  baseline, analysis of the 32
  better regulation 62, 77
  boomerang effects 57
  choice amongst options 54–9
  combined strategies 57–9
  communication-oriented regulation 93
  context 17–19
  costs 48–9, 50
  data protection 161–7
  defaults 49, 50–1, 57–8

design vi, 30, 48–9, 262–3, 265–6, 273, 292
  effectiveness 31
  emotions 9–10, 57
  empowerment 49–51, 58
  evidence-based policy 77–80
  examples of design programmes vi
  experiments 59
  experts 115, 116–18, 123, 127, 136
  failure 41–2
  health law and lifestyle policy 235–9, 243,
    246, 248–9
  information, collection of 34–5
  justification 53
  legitimacy 11
  maintenance 35–6
  market failure 31
  mix 238, 246, 248, 252–3
  nudging xvii, 49–51, 57–8, 61–3
  paternalism 57
  policy impetus behind a policy 18
  potential impacts, evaluation of 33–4
  privacy 24, 161–7, 179–207
  private sector vi, 10–11
  public interest 31, 50
  public sector vi, 11, 18–20
  regulatory process 30–36
  self-regulation 78, 243, 251, 261, 306–7
  simplification 16
  single strategies, limits of 57
  smart and evidence-based regulation 21, 62
  strengths and weaknesses 48–53
  targeting 57–8
  techno-regulation 293–4, 298
  toolboxes 11–14, 306–7
  traditional regulation, combined with 50,
    55–9
  transparency 49–50
  unresponsive behaviours 53–4
  universal appeal of behaviourally informed
    intervention 2
Regulation Room 135
regulatory impact assessment 33, 139–57
  awareness 139–40
  behavioural theory in policy-making
    139–57
  biases 24, 139–51, 156
  Commission 77–8, 139–42
  context 141–3
  costs benefit analysis 139, 146–7, 153, 155
  data protection 177
  do-nothing option 141–3, 144, 146–7, 155
  double loop learning 151
  European Parliament 139
  evidence-based policy 77–9
  guidance, re-formulation of 156
  humility, culture of regulatory 139–41,
    149, 155
  illusion of control 140–1, 143
  institutional factors 141–2, 155–6, 287

integrated approach   139
legislative drafts, major amendments to   139
mindfulness   151–5
policy-making   139–57
professional policy officers   151–2
prompts to guide policymakers in the cognitive fast lane, using   144–51
proportional impact assessments   271, 275
publicity   334–5
reflection   151–5
shared competence   142
slow lane, creating reflective and mindful policymakers in   151–5
structural factors   141–2
subsidiarity   142
training   139–41, 151–5, 156–7
what should be done   142
who should act   142
reminders   vi, xvi, xvii, ix, 4, 223, 247–8, 331–2
Renewable Transport Fuel Obligation (RTFO) (UK), implementation of   150
resources, demands on   52
responsibility   295–7
road bumps   293
roaming charges   223–4
Robinson, Clare   118, 132
Robinson, Paul H   319
Rössler, Beate   164
Rowe, Dave   153–4

safe harbour   328
Said, Edward   228
salience   40, 144, 148–9, 222
sanctions   2, 266–9, 271, 273
satisficing   149
scarcity, psychology of   10
Schön, Donald   152
Schotel, Bas   298
science and technology studies (STS)   76
Scottish Parliament online   130
search engines, indexing by   176
seatbelts   102, 111
self-capture   262, 265–6, 271, 274
self-deception   118, 318–19
self-determination   162, 312–13
self-engagement, incentives for   97–8
self-government   v, ix, xviii
self-help   110
self-identity   164–5
self-interest/selfishness   33, 193, 244, 279–80, 284, 291–2, 304, 318–19
self-regulation   78, 243, 251, 261, 306–7
Selinger, Evan   80
semantics   80, 298
Shafir, Eldar   1, 332
Shalvi, Shaul   318
Sheffrin, Steven   79
Short Selling Regulation   258, 259, 261–2

Show Me the Evidence. **Haskins, Ron and Margolis, Greg**   345–6
Schwartz, Alan   210 n1, 214 n26, 215 n33, 217 n42, 219 n51, 225 n85, 247 n92
silence   14, 186, 203
Simon, Herbert   149
Simpler. **Sunstein, Cass R**   303
simplification
 administrative guidance   16–17
 behavioural intervention   16–17
 choices   44, 47–8
 cognitive and behavioural limitations, overcoming   43
 comparison amongst products or services, facilitating   47
 compliance and administrative costs   16
 consumer law   213–14, 226–33
 consumer switching   43–4
 consumers, information asked of   44
 consumer law   226–33
 cooling off periods   48
 design-driven solutions   16
 empowerment   37, 43–5, 47–8, 52–3
 energy use, information on   43
 health law and lifestyle policy   237–8
 information   39, 43–5
 low-level legal instruments   16
 nudging   57
 open data initiatives   47–8
 over-simplification   25
 regulation   16
 smart information nudging   39
 toolboxes   13, 16–17
 trade-offs   302
single currency   226
skill and chance, distinguishing between   143
slow decision-making *see* System 2 mode of thinking (slow, calculative, and deliberative)
small group think   152
small print, checking the   214, 218, 223
smart and evidence-based regulation   21, 62
smart disclosure requirements   12–14
smart information nudging   38–40, 51–3, 57
smoking and tobacco   236–7, 239–43, 245–51
 advertising   241
 deliberations and decisions   314
 dignity   xiii
 empowerment   52
 evidence-based policy   64, 66
 Framework Convention on Tobacco Control   40
 framing   46
 fundamental rights   102–3
 optimism bias   52
 paternalism   88–9
 plain packaging   39–41, 51–2, 57, 241
 smart disclosure requirements   14
 smoke-free environments   241, 248

standardised packaging 40
tar, nicotine, and carbon dioxide yields (TNCO), information on 237
third party externalities 88–9
warnings viii, xii–xiv, xv, 6, 39–40, 51, 247, 249, 339
welfare xiii
snap decisions 316–17
social approval/disapproval, indicating 40
social control 287, 293–5, 298
social engineering 280, 283, 289, 292–3
social influences 3, 4, 38–40, 69, 95, 245, 247, 252, 294
social networks 164, 172, 175–6, 190, 192, 200
  see also **Facebook**
social norms ix, 144, 147, 167, 315–16
social ordering vii
social shaming 95–6
social sharing 166–71, 173
social sorting 181–2
soft law 261
software products, end-user licence agreements (EULAs) for 191
Solove, Daniel J 163
Spina, Alessandro 71
standard forms 176–7, 231–2
status quo bias
  Data Protection Regulation, proposal for 194–5
  defaults 193
  financial services regulation 262–4
  health law and lifestyle policy 247
  opt-in/opt-out systems 193–4
  pre-ticked boxes 10–11
  privacy nudges 200–1, 207
  products or services, facilitating comparison of 47
  rule book 262–4
  trade-offs 188
  transaction costs 190–2
sterility, illusion of cognitive 127–30
Stokes, Elen 334
stop signs 93, 109–10
Stout, Lynn 317–18
Strahilevitz, Lior 322
Strandburg, Katherine Jo 190, 198
subsidiarity 142, 343
sunset clauses in legislation 147
Sunstein, Cass R 11, 12–13, 16, 89, 91, 95–6, 193, 197–8, 201, 301–3, 328, 334
Surgery Safety Checklist 136
surveillance 161–2, 176, 181
surveys 145, 340–1
switching 43–4
symbolic effect of law 315
System 1 mode of thinking (fast, automatic, and intuitive) vii–viii
  autonomy 329–32

biases 124, 127, 309–10
defaults 147, 309
dignity xii
epistemic challenges 285–6
ethics vii–viii
experts 124, 127
graphic warnings viii
health law and lifestyle policy 243–5
inertia viii
invisible choice manipulation 94–5
manipulation xiv, xv, xviii
outcome versus processes 309–10
paternalism 93, 109
prompts 144–51
System 2 mode of thinking 124, 309–10
System 2 mode of thinking (slow, calculative, and deliberative) vii–viii
  autonomy 331–2
  biases 124, 127, 309
  debiasing viii
  disclosure viii
  epistemic challenges 285–6
  ethics vii–viii
  experts 124, 127
  health law and lifestyle policy 243–4
  invisible choice manipulation 95
  manipulation xv
  outcome versus processes 309–10
  paternalism 93, 109
  precommitment strategies viii
  regulatory impact assessments 151–5
  System 1 mode of thinking 124, 309–10
  training 151–5

take-it-or-leave-it choices 195, 201, 205–7
targeting see also **behavioural targeting and regulation of privacy**
  education 57–8
  empowerment 36–7, 42, 46, 53
  universal versus targeted nudging 309, 321–3
tax 61, 196
taxonomies, production of 12–13
Taylor, Charles 165
technocratic character of EU law-making 336–7
technological change 161–4, 167–70, 178
techno-regulation 293–4, 298
Teichman, Doron 318–19
Telecom Regulation 223–4
terms and conditions see also **privacy policies**
  autonomy 329–30
  consent requests, prohibition on hiding 201
  good faith 329
  inappropriate clauses, persuasion to overlook 305
  no-reading problem 172, 214–15, 219–20, 329

small print, checking the 214, 218, 223
standard terms 231–2
unfair contract terms 305
Tetlock, Philip E 150
Thaler, Richard H 11, 16, 89, 91, 95–6, 301–3
Thinking Fast and Slow. Kahneman, Daniel 1, 309
third parties 88–9, 107, 306
Thompson, Suzanne C 312
time
  disclosure 222–4
  empowerment 52
  management xi
  practicability 339
  timing of choice rules 48
testing 340–1, 345–7
tobacco *see* **smoking and tobacco**
toolkits/boxes 11–17
  codes, distinguished from 12
  evidence-based policy 63
  manipulation 295
  multiple toolboxes 13
  notices, distinguished from 12
  paternalism 93–100
  public sector 340
  regulatory 306–7
  taxonomies, production of 12–13
  unresponsive behaviours 54
  what law can do with tools 13–17
Tor, Avishalom 5 n20, 9 n47, 17 n88, 210 n1, 211 n2, 272 n76, 308 n32, 338 n.3, 346 n96
tort
  economic theory 295
  mistakes and inconsistencies in medical evidence, minimising 131
tracking walls 195–6, 201–2, 206
trade-offs *see* **behavioural trade-offs**
trade secrets 323
traffic-light systems 245, 250
training 139–41, 151–5, 156–7
transaction costs 135, 193, 199, 205–7
translation of behavioural insights into policy-making 10–20
  private entities steering behaviour 10–11
  public entities steering behaviour in public interest 11
  regulatory contexts 17–19
  toolbox, drawers and tools 11–17
transparency
  autonomy ix
  choice architecture 97
  competition 49
  data protection 191, 198–9
  defaults 198
  dignity ix
  empowerment 49, 198–9, 202–3
  epistemic challenges 286

experts 118
financial services regulation 258, 259, 261
informed consent and behavioural targeting 186, 198–9, 202–5, 207
Internet 155
manipulation xiv–xv, 94, 334
normative challenges 297
nudging xvii–xviii
open data initiatives 47
proportionality 106–11, 112
protection of individuals 204–5
regulation 49–50
Transparency Directive 259
welfare ix
trust
  consumer law, simplification of 228–9, 233
  data protection 166, 171, 176
  experts 24, 117, 120
  privacy 166, 171, 176
  trade-offs 309, 317–21, 323
  voluntary compliance 309, 317–21, 323
truth, relationship between legal and scientific 281
Tulkens, Françoise 102
Turow, Joseph 190, 196
Tversky, Amos 93, 152, 171
Tyler, Tom R 310, 314

Ubel, Peter 62, 69, 72
UCITs (undertakings for the collective investment in securities) 258, 260
underage persons 108
Unfair Commercial Practices Directive 49
unfair contract terms 231–2, 305
United Kingdom
  biofuel industry 150
  Cabinet Office 61, 144, 342
  Civil Justice Council 120
  cookies 187
  Defra 67–8
  energy efficiency 69
  evidence-based policy 61–2, 72–4
  foot and mouth disease (FAM), policy response to 149
  Framework for Pro-Environmental Behaviours 68
  health law and lifestyle policy 64
  House of Lords' Science and Technology Committee 72
  Midata 47
  MINDSPACE (Cabinet Office) 144–51
  Nudge Unit 61–2, 64, 69, 72–3, 301, 302–3, 342–3
  Organ Donation Register 61
  psychology and law 8
  Renewable Transport Fuel Obligation (RTFO), implementation of 150

United States
American Medical Association (AMA) 131–2
Behavioural Insights Team 301, 303
big brother and nanny state policies 303
calorie labelling in New York 66–7
comparisons 21
consumer protection 211
Cornell eRulemaking Initiative (CeRI) 135
costs benefit analysis 146–7, 153
cultural differences 335–7
economic analysis of law 9
emotions 9–10
energy efficiency 38–40, 69
Grand Canyon for hydroelectric power, use of 153
labelling 6–7
law and behavioural economics 22–3
law and economics 22–3
libertarian paternalism 335
My Data 47
obesity 304
Office of Information and Regulatory Affairs (OIRA) 148
pension schemes, opt-in/opt-out systems of 98
psychology and law 8–9
randomised controlled trials (RCTs) 303
regulation.gov 130
soda cups, size of 307–8
trade-offs 303
warnings 6
welfare maximisation 23
universal versus targeted nudging 309, 321–3
unresponsive behaviours 29, 53–4
unusual memorable events and images, disproportionate attention paid to 148
Ur, Blasé 189

van Aaken, Anne 329, 332
Vibert, Frank 142, 146
Vickers, Geoffrey. *The Art of Judgment* 141, 152
Vila, Tony 190
vinyl chloride, workplace exposure to 153
violence, private and public persons nudging people towards ix
visibility of law 314, 316–17
voluntary compliance 2–3, 294–5, 309, 317–21, 323
vulnerable people 52–3, 85, 108, 251, 258, 271, 274

waiting periods 49, 98, 206
waiver 207, 222

Wallace, David Foster vii
Wang, Yang 200
warnings
'as judged by themselves' standard ix
cigarette packages viii, xii–xiv, xv, 6, 39–40, 51, 247, 249, 339
food 247
free market xvii
graphic viii, xii–xiv, xv, 6, 247
information deficits and asymmetries 97
legitimacy 327
manipulation xiv, xv
minority groups ix
notice, as 6
nudge, definition of vi
Warren, Earl 164
weaknesses of will 96–8, 110–11
Weber, Roberto 318
websites *see also* **cookies**
comparison websites 47, 49
default browser settings as amounting to consent 194
missing information 220–1
pre-ticked boxes 15
prices of websites, comparison of 201–2
public sector 205
publishers 180
Weiner, Earl M 129
Weiner, Jonathan B 154
Welch, Brynn 95–6
welfare
choice architecture ix, xviii, 97, 303
defaults 51
dignity xii–xiii
experts 123
long-term preferences 90
market failure 197–8
maximisation 23
nudging v–vi, xviii, 18–19
objective individual welfare 106
paternalism ix, x–xi, 108–9, 112
proportionality 111
West-Eastern Divan Orchestra 228
Westin, Alan F 188
whistleblowing 322
Whyte, Kyle 80
Wilkinson, T Martin xiii
Willis, Lauren E 201
Woolgar, Steve 76
workplace hazards 153, 235, 248
World Bank. *World Development Report* 344
World Health Organization (WHO) 236, 246, 248, 251–2

youronlinechoices.com 194, 206

www.ingramcontent.com/pod-product-compliance
Lightning Source LLC
Chambersburg PA
CBHW071238300426
44116CB00008B/1088